MEDIA AND CULTURE

An Introduction to

Mass Communication

Richard Campbell

Middle Tennessee State University

St. Martin's Press
New York

> "We are not alone."
>
> For my great family—Chris, Caitlin, and Dianna
> (who introduced me to *The X-Files* and
> occasionally like to watch a TV show
> without my critical interruptions)

Sponsoring editor: Suzanne Phelps Weir
Director of development: Marian Wassner
Managing editor: Patricia Mansfield Phelan
Senior project editor: Erica T. Appel
Senior production supervisor: Joe Ford
Senior marketing manager: John Britch
Art director: Lucy Krikorian
Publishing associate: Simon Glick
Text design: Robin Hessel Hoffmann
Graphics: Burmar
Photo research: Alice Lundoff
Cover design: Kay Petronio

Library of Congress Catalog Card Number: 95-73208

Copyright © 1998 by St. Martin's Press, Inc.

All rights reserved. No part of this book may be reproduced, stored in a retrieval system, or transmitted by any form or by any means, electronic, mechanical, photocopying, recording, or otherwise, except as may be expressly permitted by the applicable copyright statutes or in writing by the Publisher.

Manufactured in the United States of America.

3 2 1 0 9 8
f e d c b a

For information, write:
St. Martin's Press, Inc.
175 Fifth Avenue
New York, NY 10010

ISBN: 0-312-11961-5

Acknowledgments and copyrights appear on pages 489–490, which constitute an extension of the copyright page.

Brief CONTENTS

CONTENTS

chapter 2

information and new technology:
media at the crossroads 32

PART II SOUNDS AND IMAGES 56

chapter 3

sound recording and popular music 56

chapter 5
television and the power of
visual culture 118

The mass media play a role in all of our autobiographies. We watch television and go to movies to find stories that remind us of our own experience or transport us to remote times and places. We read books and magazines for clues to the past and help with the present. We scan newspapers and surf the Net for information and affirmation. We go to the mass media for stories about our neighbors and our world.

Media and Culture offers a personal and global journey through the media landscape. As a textbook for an introductory mass media course, it provides maps and tools for navigating the cultural terrain. It invites students to evaluate the mass media and shape their direction. As citizens and consumers, we have choices. We can watch the media as detached observers, praising the media when they perform well and blaming them for our social predicaments. Or we can become active players. We can analyze the stories that media industries tell and sell. We can even challenge our media to perform at high levels and encourage them to serve our democratic ideals.

The journey through the media landscape is different for each of us and for each generation. For my grandmother, who died in 1994 at age ninety-two, the mass media played an important role. Over the years, especially after she could no longer read the *Dayton Daily News*, she watched a lot of television. Her favorite shows included *Lawrence Welk*, soap operas, studio wrestling, *Dallas*, *60 Minutes*, and the national news. A fervent FDR Democrat, my grandmother was no couch potato. She talked politics with her TV set. She occasionally yelled at Ronald Reagan and Mike Wallace. Her own views on Serbian-Croatian conflicts were shaped not only by her childhood but by years of exposure to American media.

For my children's generation, the mass media play another role. They grew up watching *Mr. Rogers' Neighborhood* and *Sesame Street*. As they got older, they introduced their wary parents to MTV and *Beavis and Butt-head*. Over the years, we watched *The Simpsons*, *Northern Exposure*, *Seinfeld*, and the Chicago Bulls as a family. Eventually, my son began devoting more energy to music and his guitar—to blues, rock, and jazz—and less to television. My daughter, meanwhile, read hundreds of R. L. Stine books and at age ten fell in with the Mighty Morphin Power Rangers. At age twelve she outgrew them, discovering old horror movies and *The X-Files*, whose viewing became another family ritual.

The mass media are part of everyone's life story. But to understand our lives in the context of a larger world, we need some distance from personal history. We need to stand back from our experience and view the media's impact through a larger lens. And that is where this book comes in.

Media and Culture asks each of us to become critical consumers of the media and engaged citizens in the society that the media help shape. *Media and Culture* offers directions for surveying the cultural landscape and tools for critiquing the media's influences on democratic life and consumer culture. In probing historical events and contemporary trends in mass communication, the book asks students to become cultural activists—to investigate and challenge the power of the mass media in daily life.

Five key perspectives and themes guide *Media and Culture*.

A Critical Viewpoint

Media and Culture introduces students to four stages of the critical thinking and writing process: description, analysis, interpretation, and evaluation. The text uses these stages to examine the historical context and current processes that shape the mass media as part of American culture. This critical framework structures chapter content, and the Critical Process exercises at the end of each chapter provide opportunities for students to engage in critical inquiry.

Media Technology and Convergence

Media and Culture examines the key technological developments that have changed the world, from the printing press and telegraph (with its electronic dots and dashes) to television and the Internet (with its digital ones and zeroes). The text takes us on a journey from the Industrial Age to the Information Age, explaining the phenomenon of media convergence: the confluence of home, school, and business computers, TV sets, telephones, radio, CD players, VCRs, e-mail, video games, newspapers, fax machines, magazines, and communication satellites.

The organization of *Media and Culture* takes into account the dramatic influences of electronic and digital communication on the social world. Since converging forms of mass communication integrate aspects of print, electronic, and digital culture in daily life, the text begins with the stories of media convergence. Rather than starting chronologically with the oldest mass medium, the book, the industry chapters open with the media students know best: music, radio, television, cable, and film. Placing past and present communication developments within a contemporary perspective, *Media and Culture* then looks at older media within the context of the new forms that have reshaped print culture.

A Cultural Perspective

An understanding of culture is indispensable for understanding the contemporary mass media as well as their history. Culture provides the framework in which all media develop, and in turn people use media frames to give meaning to their lives. Using a narrative approach, *Media and Culture* investigates the media as part of the rituals of everyday culture. Most mass media, whether news, prime-time television, magazines, film, paperback novels, or advertising, use storytelling to tap into our shared beliefs and values, and so does *Media and Culture*. Each chapter presents the events and issues surrounding media culture as compelling stories that map the uneasy and parallel developments of consumer culture and democratic society.

Values and Ethics

To develop a critical perspective toward the mass media, students need to incorporate values and ethics into the way they experience the media in daily life. Media books often ghettoize the subject of ethics by treating it as a separate, isolated chapter near the end of the book. *Media and Culture*, however, weaves discussions about values into the larger story. The text looks at how values are depicted in mass communication and at ethical questions that challenge media practitioners.

Media Economics and Democracy

To become better citizens and discerning consumers, students must pay attention to the complex relationship between democracy and capitalism, between the marketplace of ideas and the global consumer market. To that end, *Media and Culture* addresses the significance of the dramatic rise in multinational media systems. It invites students to explore the implications of the 1996 Telecommunications Act and the tight control that a handful of mammoth international companies exercise over the production and distribution of commercial mass media. Ownership issues are therefore an integral part of the individual media chapters. In addition, Chapter 13 looks critically at the global picture and encourages students to participate in the debates over ownership. Each chapter ends with a discussion of the impact of various mass media on the nature of democratic life.

organization of the text

Media and Culture is divided into five parts. Part 1, "Mass Media and the Cultural Landscape," establishes the foundation for the book. Chapter 1 defines the text's key concepts and introduces critical processes for investigating media industries and issues. Chapter 2 introduces the newest mass medium, the Internet, and the concept of *media convergence*, the integration of print, electronic, and digital mass communication.

Part 2, "Sounds and Images," covers the media that students know well—music (Chapter 3), radio (Chapter 4), television (Chapter 5), cable (Chapter 6), and movies (Chapter 7). These media have had the most dramatic impact on the cultural landscape during the twentieth century. The chapters in Part 2 provide historical and industry overviews and examine each medium's social, economic, and cultural impact.

Part 3, "Words and Pictures," covers the first media—the print and early image industries that made mass communication possible. These mass media, which pioneered engraving, photography, and advertising, include newspapers (Chapter 8), magazines (Chapter 9), and books (Chapter 10). These media had their greatest impact during America's formative years, yet they endure and remain central to daily life. They have proven their adaptability in the face of the new media industries that emerged during the twentieth century.

Part 4, "The Business of Mass Media," examines advertising (Chapter 11) and public relations (Chapter 12), both thriving, independent industries that provide crucial support for the mass media. The chapters offer a historical overview of these professions, examining how they are organized and the social and ethical issues their practitioners face. In addition, a separate chapter on media economics and the cultural marketplace (Chapter 13) introduces economic analysis, critiques trends in media consolidation, and examines the ways that companies operate on a global level.

Part 5, "Democratic Expression and the Mass Media," takes up a range of key issues affecting media and culture: values, ethics, and journalism (Chapter 14); media effects and cultural approaches to research (Chapter 15); and legal controls and freedom of expression (Chapter 16). This concluding section addresses such important subjects as the public journalism movement, mainstream and alternative research strategies, and the impact of the First Amendment on the mass media.

chapter highlights

In *Media and Culture*, each chapter has a consistent structure and many special features:

- *Preview Stories*. Every chapter opens with a recent or historical media story that foreshadows issues and concepts raised in the chapter.

- *Case Studies*. Every chapter highlights an individual, industry, or issue that captures the spirit of a particular medium. Sample case studies feature Madonna, the Web, radio talk shows, Ted Turner, racism and movie theaters, Dorothy Day and I. F. Stone, the *Utne Reader*, comic books, women and advertising, television ratings, *60 Minutes*, and copyright violations and rap music.

- *Examining Ethics*. These dynamic, visual sections focus on ethical issues in the mass media, including such topics as teens and TV talk shows, television's impact on community values, Nike and sneaker commercials, PR and sweatshops, book censorship, and hidden TV news cameras.

- *Tracking Technology*. Old and new innovations in media technology are highlighted in these sections, which feature discussions of such topics as free expression in cyberspace, shortwave radio, communication satellites, movie delivery, alternative zines, and the Internet's Project Gutenberg.

- *The Global Village*. International developments in mass communication are another featured subject. Explorations of world music, the global digital revolution, and television in Brazil are among the topics covered.

- *Review Questions*. Summary questions at the end of each chapter help students reflect on the major concepts and issues examined in the text.

- *Questioning the Media*. A series of open-ended questions challenge students to think about issues beyond those examined in the chapter. Valuable in provoking class discussions, these questions ask students to think about the media's influence, both on their own lives and on the larger society.

- *The Critical Process*. Each chapter features an assignment or activity that challenges students to build on the critical approach outlined in Chapter 1. These projects include critiquing magazine advertising, examining newspapers' international coverage, studying an independent publisher or record label, and thinking about distinctions between high and low culture.

the *media and culture* program

Media and Culture is also available for purchase in combination with *What's Next in Mass Communication: Readings on Media and Culture* and/or *Media Career Guide*. Please use the correct ISBN for the combination selected when ordering through a campus bookstore.

> *Media and Culture*: 0-312-11961-5
> *Media and Culture/What's Next in Mass Communication*: 0-312-18246-5
> *Media and Culture/Media Career Guide*: 0-312-18280-5
> *Media and Culture/What's Next in Mass Communication/Media Career Guide*:
>   0-312-18282-1

To help students further expand their perspective on the role of the media in contemporary culture, the *Media and Culture* program offers the following additional resources.

www.mediaculture.com

By visiting *www.mediaculture.com*, students gain a further appreciation for the media's role in our consumer culture. The interactive study guide gives students the opportunity to critique the media and to examine the advantages and pitfalls of using the Web as a source for academic work, news, and entertainment. Students and professionals can take part in discussions on provocative media topics. Media critics examine the cultural implications of the latest-breaking changes in the media field. The Web site features our "Careers Workbench," which provides guidance on media careers today. Numerous links to hundreds of mass communication sites will give students further information about the world of advertising, newspapers, electronic media, public relations, and more.

Untangling the Web: *A Guide to Mass Communication on the* Web
by Deborah Greh, St. John's University

For instructors and students who are inexperienced online, *Untangling the Web* offers practical advice on accessing information through the Internet. It also provides ideas for incorporating the Web site exercises and resources for *Media and Culture* into the multimedia classroom.

What's Next in Mass Communication: Readings on Media and Culture
by Christopher Harper, Ithaca College

This collection of readings reflects the transformation of mass media today and important social issues of the digital age. As its title suggests, this anthology focuses on the future, asking students to question the roles of journalists, viewers, and readers as we move toward the new millenium and beyond. Covering both electronic and print media, the selections engage students in compelling debates on such hot topics as: the controversial "computer gaps" based on race, age, or income; the longevity of television and newspapers; the pros and cons of public journalism; online vs. printed magazines; trends for niche publications; advertising campaigns of the future; and privacy in cyberspace. Chapters open with overviews of the topics and close by asking students to consider and debate the issues raised by the selections.

Media Career Guide: Preparing for Jobs in the 21ˢᵗ Century
by James Seguin, Robert Morris College

Designed for students considering a major in communication studies and mass media, this practical and student-friendly guide includes a comprehensive directory of media jobs, practical tips, career guidance that encourages specialized reading, print and electronic research, guided self-assessments, and sample cover letters and resumes for communication/media jobs.

The St. Martin's Video Library
by Bettina Fabos, University of Iowa, Christopher Martin, University of Northern Iowa, and Richard Campbell

The St. Martin's Video Library consists of more than one hundred high-interest contemporary and historical media documentaries and media-related entertainment films, organized around compelling cultural, ethical, and economic issues explored in *Media and Culture*. Instructional resources are included in the *Instructor's Resource Manual* to help instructors make the most of the videos in the classroom. Upon adoption of *Media and Culture*, instructors are eligible to select video materials from the library, building their own library over time with continued purchase of new texts from St. Martin's.

Instructor's Resource Manual
by Bettina Fabos, University of Iowa, Christopher Martin, University of Northern Iowa, and Richard Campbell

The *Instructor's Resource Manual* is especially useful for schools offering multiple sections of introduction to mass communication. It includes course syllabi for a range of teaching approaches, suggestions for lesson plans, video tips and activities, and general guidelines and hints for novice teaching assistants. The manual features a comprehensive section for teaching assistants on leading discussion sections, filled with numerous small-group activities and discussion questions to complement the critical process sections found in the text. Instructors are encouraged to take advantage of the resources on the Web site and to contribute to the instructional materials available for *Media and Culture* by responding to the Web site questionnaire or to the form that concludes the *Instructor's Resource Manual*.

Testing Program

Media and Culture offers a complete testing program, available in print and for Windows and Macintosh environments. Each chapter includes multiple-choice, true-false, and fill-in-the-blank exercises, as well as short- and long-answer essay questions. Sample midterm and final examinations are also included in the testing program. Instructors are encouraged to mix and match, add and delete, and experiment with these innovative testing materials.

▮ acknowledgments

I want to thank the many fine and thoughtful reviewers who contributed ideas to *Media and Culture*: Paul Ashdown, University of Tennessee; Terry Bales, Rancho Santiago College; Russell Barclay, Southern Methodist University; Thomas Beell, Iowa State University; Fred Blevens, Southwest Texas State University; Stuart Bullion, University of Maine; William Covington, Bridgewater State University; Robert Daves, *Minneapolis Star Tribune*; Charles Davis, Georgia Southern University; Thomas Donahue, Virginia Commonwealth University; Ralph R. Donald, University of Tennessee at Martin; John P. Ferre, University of Louisville; Donald Fishman, Boston College; Elizabeth Atwood Gailey, University of Tennessee; Bob Gassaway, University of New Mexico; Anthony Giffard, University of Washington; Zhou He, San Jose State University; Barry Hollander, University of Georgia; Sharon Hollenbeck, Syracuse University; Anita Howard, Austin Community College; James Hoyt, University of Wisconsin at Madison; Joli Jensen, University of Tulsa; Frank Kaplan, University of Colorado; William Knowles, University of Montana; Michael Leslie, University of Florida; Janice Long, University of Cincinnati; Kathleen Matichek, Normandale Community College; Maclyn McClary, Humboldt State University; Robert McGaughey, Murray State University; Joseph McKerns, Ohio State University; Debra Merskin, University of Oregon; David Morrissey, Colorado State University; Michael Murray, University of Missouri at St. Louis; Susan Dawson O'Brien, Rose State College; Patricia Bowie Orman, University of Southern Colorado; Jim Patton, University of Arizona; John Pauly, St. Louis University; Ted Pease, Utah State University; Janice Peck, University of Colorado; Tina Pieraccini, SUNY–University of New Mexico; Peter Pringle, University of Tennessee; Sondra Rubenstein, Hofstra University; Jim St. Clair, Indiana University Southeast; Jim Sequin, Robert Morris College; Donald Shaw, University of North Carolina; Martin D. Sommernes, Northern Arizona State University; Linda Steiner, Rutgers University; Jill Dianne Swenson, Ithaca College; Sharon Taylor, Delaware State University; Hazel Warlaumont, California State University at Fullerton; Richard Whitaker, Buffalo State College; Lynn Zoch, University of South Carolina.

I would especially like to thank Anita Howard (Austin Community College), Sharon Hollenbeck (Syracuse University), Sondra Rubenstein (Hofstra University), Jim Sequin (Robert Morris College), and Linda Steiner (Rutgers University), who sat around a table with an early draft of this manuscript and pointed me in the right directions.

I am very grateful to everyone at St. Martin's Press who supported this project through its many stages. I wish that every textbook author could have the kind of experience I had with these people: Ed Stanford, Steve Debow, Alice Lundoff, Judy Voss, and Hanna Shin. I worked with a remarkable group of development editors: Bob Nirkind, Barbara Muller, and Joanne Tinsley. Thanks also to Simon Glick for his extraordinary work researching and improving the feature boxes. I particularly appreciate the tireless work of Marian Wassner, director of development; Erica Appel, senior project editor, who made sure I got the details right; and Joe Ford, senior production supervisor. I am especially grateful to my acquisitions editor, Suzanne Phelps Weir, who believed in this textbook from the beginning and respected my ideas and teaching goals throughout the project.

Many other people deserve thanks. When I left high school teaching for graduate work in media studies, I fell in with a number of fine teachers at both the University of Wisconsin at Milwaukee and Northwestern University who helped shape the way I think about many of the issues raised in this book. Thanks in particular to Earl Grow, George Bailey, Sharon Murphy, Jack Ellis, and Leah Vande Berg. I am especially grateful to David Eason and Douglas Gomery, who have kept in touch over the years and whose ideas will always influence how I think about media and culture.

I want to thank my former students at Marquette University, the University of Wisconsin at Milwaukee, Mount Mary College, and the University of Michigan. Some have contributed directly to this text, and thousands have endured my courses over the years—and made them better. Special thanks to Michael Epstein, Bettina Fabos, Rosanne Freed, David Freund, Ethel Goodstein, Deborah Locke, Chris Martin, Joe Moreau, Anny Rey, Mark Rogers, Joe Won, and Marilyn Yaquinto.

I am blessed with many supportive friends, family members, colleagues, and scholars who have made special contributions to this text in their own ways: Pat Aufderheide, Dick and Molly Campbell, Harry Campbell, Tom Campbell, Mary Sue Campbell, Chris Campbell, James Carey, Tom Connery, Robert Daves, Herb Eagle, Stuart Ewen, Jon Friendly, Ted Glasser, Herman Gray, Dennis Hartig, Peter Hayes, Mary Heller, June Howard, Mick Hurbis-Cherrier, Katherine Hurbis-Cherrier, Joli Jensen, Robin Kelley, Conrad Kottak, Marion Marzolf, Bob McChesney, Barbra Morris, Melissa Motschall, Hayg Oshagan, Dick Pack, Peter Parisi, John Pauly, Janice Peck, Jimmie Reeves, Jay Rosen, Terri Sarris, Leslie Savan, Michael Schudson, Norm Sims, Linda Steiner, David Thorburn, Mary Ann Watson, Kate West, and Jack Williamson.

I am especially thankful for the friendship of my writers' group—Randy Milgrom, Rob Pasick, Jim Tobin, and John Bacon—who read many of these chapters in early drafts and made great suggestions. Living for a time in a world outside academia, I am grateful to these guys for helping me keep my bearings. For that, I am also grateful to my Friday night group (they know who they are), among the most honest and courageous people I know, who helped keep me relatively sane throughout the last hectic year of this project.

I am most grateful, though, to the people I most love: my son, Chris, my resident expert on Robert Johnson, Stevie Ray Vaughan, and the blues; my daughter, Caitlin, my authority on the Nickelodeon channel and R. L. Stine; and, most of all, my wife, Dianna, whose expert editing, critical judgment, and daily support are constant resources and special gifts.

—Richard Campbell

Mass Communication
A Critical Approach

In April 1996, seven-year-old Jessica Dubroff died in a plane crash near Cheyenne, Wyoming, along with her father, Lloyd, and her flight instructor. Outfitted with extenders so that her feet could reach the pedals, Jessica was trying to become the youngest person to fly a plane across the North American continent. To hype the event, Jessica's father spent $1,300 on two hundred baseball caps proclaiming "Women Fly." He also supervised a letter Jessica wrote to the White House, inviting President Clinton for a ride. The president's staff declined the invitation.

Flying the small Cessna 117B, Jessica and her crew left Cheyenne carrying too much weight and facing stormy weather. That same morning, the severe weather convinced a Wyoming commercial pilot to stay on the ground. But a number of self-imposed pressures and commitments faced the adults on Jessica's flight. To officially break the record, they needed Jessica to perform the feat before her eighth birthday in May. They also faced media obligations—television crews and news reporters waited at stops along the way. One of the items recovered at the crash site, a smashed portable TV camera, belonged to ABC. Jessica's father had planned to use the camera to document the flight for the network.

In the wake of the crash, the media's role in the publicity stunt was criticized. Ted Koppel on ABC's *Nightline* implicated the news media. "We need to begin by acknowledging our own contribution," he said, referring to ABC, other major networks, and various magazines and newspapers that had publicized the events leading up to the failed flight. He also commented on the interdependent relationship between people's thirst for public validation and the media's hunger for dramatic events: "We feed off one another—those of you looking for publicity and those of us looking for stories."

J. Mac McClellan, editor of *Flying*, noted that his magazine refused to cover the flight or to promote dangerous aerial stunts. He cast the media as major villains, largely responsible for the tragic drama that ensued: "Jessica's flight is the kind of thing that, absent media coverage, would never have happened."[1] In the end, the fatal crash became the top story on network television and made the front page of most daily newspapers across the country. In 1997, a National Transportation Safety Board report concluded that the flight instructor in charge tried too hard to maintain a schedule driven by "media commitments."

Jessica's story attests to the powerful role mass media play in daily life. At their worst, the news media exploit tragedies for commercial gain. Reporters not only documented Jessica's odyssey but also capitalized on it, feeding the media's appetite for telling and selling stories. Negotiations for the rights to book and movie versions of the story followed quickly on the heels of the tragedy, demonstrating the media's influential role in promoting a celebrity culture, elevating both star media performers and ordinary people, like Jessica, who do extraordinary things.

The mass media's impact, however, goes beyond telling dramatic tales or maintaining a celebrity culture. Although the growth of specialized channels and products has fragmented media audiences, many people still share interests in movie characters, talk-show topics, and sports figures, as well as the big story on the evening news. At their best, the mass media reflect and sustain the values and traditions of American democracy, not only by engaging diverse audiences but by watching over society's institutions, making sense of its important events, and chronicling the changes in our daily lives.

The growth of media industries, commercial culture, and new technologies—cable, computers, televisions, satellites—offers a challenge to all of us. If we can learn to examine and critique the powerful dynamics of the media, we will be better able to manage the rapid changes going on around us. In the chapters that follow, we will investigate the history and structure of media's major institutions. In the process, we will develop an informed and critical view of their multiple impacts on community and global life. Our goal is to become not only more critical as consumers of mass media but also more engaged as citizens who accept responsibility for the shape and direction of media culture.

culture and the evolution of mass communication

One way to understand the role and impact of the media in our lives is to understand the cultural context in which the media operate. Often, culture is symbolically spelled with a capital "C" and is associated with *art*, the unique forms of expression that give pleasure and raise awareness about what is true, good, and beautiful. Culture, however, can also begin with a small "c." According to this view, culture is a broad category identifying the ways that people live at particular historical times. This idea of culture includes fashion, sports, architecture, education, religion, and science, as well as media products. Although we can study permanent cultural forms, such as novels or songs from various historical periods, culture is always changing. It encompasses a society's art, beliefs, customs, games, technologies, traditions, and institutions. It also encompasses a society's modes of **communication**: the process of creating symbol systems that convey information and meaning (for example, language, Morse code, film, or computer codes).

Culture is made up of both the *products* a society fashions and, even more important, the *processes* that forge those products and reflect a culture's diverse values. Thus, **culture** may be defined as the symbols of expression that individuals, groups, and societies use to make sense of daily life and to articulate their values. According to this definition, when we listen to music, read a book, or watch television, we are not asking "Is this art?" but are instead trying to identify or connect with something or someone. In other words, we are assigning meaning to the book or TV program. Thus, culture is a process that delivers the values of a society through products or other meaning-making forms. For instance, the American ideal of rugged individualism has been delivered for decades through a tradition of book, movie, and television westerns and detective stories.

Culture embodies a society's values, but the mass media distribute those values. We may say, then, that the **mass media** are the cultural industries—the channels of communication—that produce and distribute songs, novels, newspapers, movies, online computer services, and other cultural products to large numbers of people. The historical development of media and communication can be traced through several overlapping eras in which newer forms of technology and knowledge disrupted and modified older forms. These eras, which all still affect society, are *oral, written, print, electronic,* and *digital.* The first two eras refer to the primary communication of tribal or feudal communities and agricultural economies. The last three phases feature the development of **mass communication**: the process of designing and delivering cultural messages and stories to diverse audiences through media channels as old as the book and as new as the Internet. Hastened by the growth of industry and modern technology, mass communication accompanied the gradual shift of rural populations to urban settings and the rise of a consumer culture.

> "For the press, the real lesson may be that there's a big difference between covering Charles Lindbergh . . . and turning a 7-year-old into yet more fodder for the **American hype machine.** From now on, press releases touting child exploits that might be dangerous should be tossed where they belong—into the **circular file.**"
> — Jonathan Alter, *Newsweek,* April 1996

oral and written communication

In most early societies, information and knowledge first circulated slowly through oral traditions passed on by poets, teachers, and tribal storytellers. As alphabets and the written word developed, however, a manuscript culture began to complement and then overshadow oral communication. Documented and transcribed by philosophers, monks, and stenographers, a manuscript culture served the ruling classes. Working people were generally illiterate, and the gap between peasants and rulers was vast. These eras of oral and written communication occurred over many centuries. Although exact time frames are disputed, historians generally consider these eras part of civilization's premodern period, spanning 1000 B.C. to the mid-fifteenth century.

Early tensions between oral and written communication played out among ancient Greek philosophers and writers. Socrates (470–399 B.C.), for instance, made his arguments through public conversations and debates. This dialogue style of communication became known as the *Socratic method,* and it is still used in university law schools and college classrooms. Many philosophers who supported the superiority of oral tradition feared that the written word would threaten public discussion by offering fewer opportunities for the give and take of conversation. In fact, Socrates' most famous student, Plato (427–347 B.C.), sought to banish poets, whom he saw as purveyors of thoughts less rigorous than those of oral storytelling. These debates foreshadowed similar discussions in the twentieth century regarding the dangers of television and the Internet. Do contemporary technologies, such as TV talk shows and anonymous online chatrooms, cheapen public discussions and prevent us from forming face-to-face associations and talking more personally to one another?

printed communication

The invention of the printing press and moveable metallic type in the fifteenth century provided the industrial seed that spawned modern mass communication. From the time of Johannes Gutenberg's invention, it took about four hundred years for the print era to evolve and to eclipse oral and written traditions.

The printing press, among its many contributions, introduced a method for mass production. Presses and publications spread rapidly across Europe in the late 1400s and early 1500s. Many early books were large, elaborate, and expensive, taking months to illustrate and publish. They were usually purchased by wealthy aristocrats, royal families, church leaders, and prominent merchants and politicians. Gradually, however, printers reduced the size and cost of books, making them available to more people.

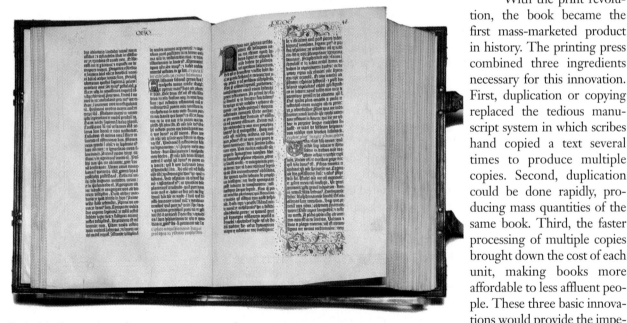

Probably the most revolutionary development in media history, the printing press and the mass production of books paved the way for both a consumer market and the democratic spread of knowledge. This Latin Bible was printed in Germany about 1455 by Johannes Gutenberg and Johann Fust.

With the print revolution, the book became the first mass-marketed product in history. The printing press combined three ingredients necessary for this innovation. First, duplication or copying replaced the tedious manuscript system in which scribes hand copied a text several times to produce multiple copies. Second, duplication could be done rapidly, producing mass quantities of the same book. Third, the faster processing of multiple copies brought down the cost of each unit, making books more affordable to less affluent people. These three basic innovations would provide the impetus behind the Industrial Revolution, assembly-line production, modern capitalism, and the rise of consumer culture in the twentieth century.

The printing press also paved the way for major social and cultural changes by transmitting knowledge across national boundaries. Mass-produced printed materials spread information faster and farther than ever before, extending communication outside the realm of isolated community life. Such widespread information ushered in the concept of nationalism, allowing people to think of themselves not merely as members of families or tribes but as part of a country with interests broader than local or regional concerns.

With the revolution in industry came the rise of the middle class and an elite business class of owners and managers who gained the kind of clout once held only by the nobility. Whereas oral and writing societies had decentralized and local governments, the print era marked the ascent of more centralized nation-states. As print media lessened the role of oral and manuscript communication, they became commercial and political leaders' key tools for distributing information and maintaining social order.

As with the Internet today, however, no single business leader or political party in democratic societies gained total control over books and technology. Instead, the mass publication of pamphlets, newspapers, magazines, and books helped to spread and democratize knowledge. Literacy rates rose among the working and middle classes as publications of all sorts became affordable. Industrialization required a more educated workforce, but printed literature and textbooks also encouraged compulsory education, thus extending learning beyond the world of wealthy upper-class citizens.

Just as the printing press fostered nationalism, it also nourished the competing ideal of individualism, which would become a fundamental value in American society in the nineteenth and twentieth centuries. With all sorts of ideas and treatises available, people came to rely less on their local community and their commercial, religious, and political leaders for guidance. By challenging tribal life, the printing press "fostered the modern idea of individuality," disrupting "the medieval sense of community and integration."[2] In urban and industrial environments, many individuals became severed from the traditions of rural life, which had encouraged community cooperation in premodern times.

By the mid-nineteenth century, the ideal of individualism permeated the rise of commerce and increased resistance to government interference in the affairs of self-reliant entrepreneurs. The democratic impulse of individualism also undermined religious authority. Printers and writers circulated views counter to traditional doctrine. Ultimately, the printing press and the wide distribution of knowledge facilitated large social movements, including the Protestant Reformation and the Industrial Revolution.

electronic and digital communication

In Europe and America, the impact of industry's rise was enormous: Factories replaced farms as the main centers of work and production. During the 1880s, roughly 80 percent of Americans lived on farms and in small towns; by the 1920s and 1930s, most of this population had shifted to urban areas that had new industries and economic opportunities. The city had overtaken the country as the focus of national life. A relatively stable rural existence gave way to urban and suburban lifestyles that were more unsettled, mobile, and diverse.

In America, the gradual transformation from an industrial, print-based society to an informational era began with the arrival of the telegraph in the 1840s. The telegraph made four key contributions to communication. First, it separated communication from transportation, making media messages instantaneous—unencumbered by stagecoaches, ships, or the pony express.[3] Second, the telegraph in combination with the rise of newspapers transformed "information into a commodity, a 'thing' that could be bought or sold irrespective of its uses or meaning."[4] By the Civil War, news had become a valuable product, foreshadowing its contemporary role as a phenomenon that is both enormously profitable and nearly unavoidable. Third, the telegraph made it easier for military, business, and political leaders to coordinate commercial and military operations, especially after the installation of the transatlantic cable in the late 1860s. Finally, the telegraph was an omen of future technological developments such as the fax machine and cellular phones. Although modern telegraphy marked the full-blown arrival of the print era, it also planted the earliest seeds for even faster forms of electronic and digital communication.

The rise of film at the turn of the century and the development of radio in the 1920s were early signposts, but the electronic phase of the Information Age really began in the 1950s and 1960s. The dramatic impact of television on daily life, beginning in the 1950s, marked the arrival of a new visual and electronic era. With the coming of the latest communication gadgetry—ever smaller personal computers, cable television, direct broadcast satellites, remote phones, beepers, faxes, and electronic mail (e-mail)—the Information Age passed into a digital phase. *Electronic* innovations, for instance, included hand-cranked and later rotary dial telephones, whereas *digital* innovations brought Touch-Tone technology. In digital communication, images, texts, and sounds are converted (encoded) into electronic signals (represented as varied combinations of binary numbers—ones and zeros), which are then reassembled (decoded) as a precise reproduction of a TV picture, a magazine article, or a telephone voice. On the Internet's various World Wide Web pages, image, text, and sound are all digitally reproduced and transmitted globally.

> "We are in great haste to construct a magnetic telegraph from Maine to Texas; but Maine and Texas, it may be, have nothing **important to communicate. . . .** We are eager to tunnel under the Atlantic and bring the old world some weeks nearer to the new; but perchance the first news that will leak through into the **broad flapping American ear** will be that Princess Adelaide has the whooping cough."
> —Henry David Thoreau, *Walden*, 1854

New electronic and digital technologies, particularly cable television and the Internet, have developed so quickly that traditional communication leaders have lost some of their control over information. For example, network news lost a portion of its influence and audience in the 1992 and 1996 presidential election to CNN's Larry King, the Comedy Channel, MTV, radio talk shows, and various Internet newsgroups and chat lines. The technology of e-mail, which has assumed some of the functions of the postal service, is outpacing attempts to control it within national borders. A professor sitting at her desk in Ann Arbor, Michigan, can instantly send a message to a research scientist in Warsaw, Poland, who can now respond without fear of government agents opening his mail. As recently as 1990, written letters between the two might have taken months to reach their destinations.

mass media and the process of communication

As far back as 1935, the Lindbergh baby kidnap-murder trial raised concerns about electronic news and the impact of the media. In the 1990s, the mass media reported the sordid sagas of the Menendez brothers, the British royal family, and the mysterious Unabomber. Of course, for impact, nothing approached the criminal trial of former football star O.J. Simpson. With its universal theme of the fallen hero, the case drew an enormous amount of media attention, including gavel-to-gavel coverage on CNN and Court TV.

Although often labeled and discussed disparagingly as "the media," these institutions are not a single entity. The mass media constitute a wide variety of industries and merchandise, from documentary news programs about tragic famines in Africa to infomercials about personal hygiene products. The word *media* is, after all, a Latin plural form for the singular noun *medium*. Although television, newspapers, music, movies, magazines, books, billboards, direct mail, broadcast satellites, and the information highway are all part of the media, these remain largely discrete segments, each quite capable of producing worthy products as well as pandering to society's worst desires, prejudices, and stereotypes.

The criminal and civil trials (1995–97) of O.J. Simpson spurred heated public debate on racial differences, spousal abuse, and legal reform. The trials, which educated the world about the U.S. justice system, were a media bonanza for lawyers, catapulting several to prominence and launching cable shows such as CNBC's *Rivera Live* and CNN's *Burden of Proof*.

Painting all media with the same broad brush is not only inaccurate—it also reflects the distrustful view that many people hold toward prominent social institutions, from local governments to daily newspapers. In this book, we will attempt to replace an often misdirected and cynical perception of the media with an attitude of genuine criticism.

a linear model of mass communication

To develop a critical perspective of the media, we need insight into how the mass communication process works. One of the most influential ideas about the media is the linear model of communication. In this model, mass communication is conceptualized as the process of producing and delivering messages to large audiences. According to the linear model, mass communication is a component system, made up of **senders**—the authors, producers, agencies, and organizations—who transmit **messages**—the programs, texts, images, sounds, and product advertisements. Through a mass media **channel**—newspapers, books, magazines, radio, television, or the Internet—senders pitch their messages to large groups of **receivers**—readers, viewers, citizens, and consumers. In the process, **gatekeepers**, such as editors, producers, and other media managers, function as message filters. Media gatekeepers make decisions about what types of messages actually get produced for particular audiences. The process occasionally allows **feedback**, in which citizens and consumers return messages to senders or gatekeepers through letters to the editor, phone calls, e-mail, or as audience members of talk shows.

Although the linear model explains certain aspects of the communication process, media messages usually do not flow smoothly from a sender at point A to a receiver at point Z. Like fish in turbulent water, words and images are in flux, spilling into each other and crisscrossing in the flow of daily use. Media messages are encoded and sent in written and visual forms, but senders often have very little control over how their messages are decoded, or whether the messages are ignored by readers and viewers.

▪an alternative approach to mass communication

Individuals and societies bring diverse meanings to cultural messages because of factors such as gender, age, educational level, ethnicity, and occupation. For instance, when rapper Ice-T's heavy metal group Body Count produced the song "Cop Killer" in the early 1990s, police organizations and urban teens interpreted the lyrics in dramatically different ways. Some police groups wanted to ban the song, arguing that it would lead to violence, while fans of the band asserted that the song correctly portrayed the power of police authority in urban America.

It is sometimes easy to assume that producers of media messages are the active creators of communication and that audiences are merely passive receptacles. This may describe some situations, but as the "Cop Killer" example illustrates, audiences also shape and bend media messages to fit their own values and viewpoints. This phenomenon is known as **selective exposure**: Audiences seek messages and produce meanings that correspond to their beliefs and values. Thus, in the process of mass communication, audiences are actively interpreting, refashioning, or rejecting messages that flow through various media channels.

At its most significant level, the mass communication process can alter a society's perception of events and attitudes. Throughout the twentieth century, for instance, courageous print journalists covered world wars and other armed conflicts, helping the public to comprehend the magnitude and tragedy of such events. In the 1950s and 1960s, television news reports on the civil rights movement led to crucial legislation that transformed the way many white people viewed the problems and aspirations of African Americans. In the early 1990s, the televised Clarence Thomas–Anita Hill Senate hearings placed the usually private issue of sexual harassment on the larger public agenda. In addition, the best media coverage in the aftermath of the first Simpson trial stirred public discussion regarding both legal reform and domestic abuse. In each of these instances, the mass media played a key role in changing awareness, attitudes, and even policy.

▪the role and impact of the mass media

Concerns about popular forms of culture have often upset the status quo and led to periodic public outcries. At the turn of the century, newly arrived immigrants who spoke little English gravitated to cultural events whose enjoyment did not depend solely on understanding the English language, such as boxing, vaudeville, and the new medium of silent film. Consequently, these popular events occasionally became a rallying cry for many groups, including the Daughters of the American Revolution, local politicians, religious leaders, and police vice squads, who not only resented the commercial success of immigrant culture, but feared these "low" cultural forms would undermine traditional American values.

Debates about culture and media are not new. The earliest discussions date from the ancient Greeks. Socrates, himself accused of corrupting youth, worried that children exposed to stories "without distinction" would "take into their souls teachings that are wholly opposite to those we wish them to be possessed of when they are grown up."[5] The playwright Euripides, on the other hand, believed that art should imitate life, that characters should be real, and that artistic works should reflect the actual world even when that reality was sordid.

In *The Republic*, Plato developed the classical view of art: It should aim to instruct and uplift. He worried that some staged performances glorified evil and that

In the 1950s, television images of early civil rights struggles, which visually documented the inequalities faced by black citizens, had a profound effect on the United States. In 1957, the governor of Arkansas refused to allow black students like Elizabeth Eckford (*left foreground*) to enter Little Rock's Central High School, even though segregation had been outlawed by the Supreme Court in 1954. In response, President Dwight Eisenhower sent in the army to integrate the school and control angry white mobs.

common folk watching might not be able to distinguish between art and reality. Aristotle, Plato's student, occupied a middle ground in these debates, arguing that art should provide insight into the human condition but should entertain as well.

Since the early Greeks, concerns about the impact of culture have continued. In the 1950s, the emergence of television and rock and roll generated countless points of contention. For instance, the phenomenal popularity of Elvis Presley set the stage for many of today's debates over rap lyrics and television's negative influences. In 1956 and 1957, Presley made three appearances on the *Ed Sullivan Show*. The public outcry against Presley's "lascivious" hip movements was so great that by the third show camera operators were instructed to shoot the singer from the waist up. Thousands of protective parents refused to allow their children to watch Presley's performances. In some communities, objections to Presley were motivated by class bias and racism. Many white adults believed that this "poor white trash" singer from Mississippi was spreading rhythm and blues, a "dangerous" form of black popular culture.

Today the stakes are even higher. Given the reach and spread of print, electronic, and digital communication, culture and its myriad mutations play an even more controversial role in society. People used to share their common interests in radio or TV characters and major news stories in backyard, barroom, and coffee-shop conversations, but the proliferation of specialized publications and personalized channels has fragmented the media audience. Many citizens have become critical of the lack of quality in so much contemporary culture and concerned about the overwhelming amounts of information now available. Even the computer, once heralded as the educational salvation for children, has created confusion. When kids announce they are "on the computer," parents may wonder whether they are writing a term paper, playing a video game, talking to a cyberspace pen pal, shopping for sneakers, or downloading pornography.

In recent years, it has become common for political candidates to question and attack various forms of the mass media for their negative impact. In 1992, for example, Vice President Dan Quayle denounced the "family values" portrayed on a *Murphy Brown* episode, which championed single motherhood. In 1995, presidential candidate Bob Dole condemned media conglomerate Time Warner for its partial ownership of a

11

controversial rap music label. Congress got into the act in 1996, an election year, by rewriting the nation's telecommunications laws. These laws will require all TV manufacturers, starting in 1999, to equip sets with the V-chip, a technology that lets adults block inappropriate TV programs from the view of children.

By the mid-1990s, the mass media had given the public much to be concerned about. Talk shows exploited personal problems for commercial gain (see "Examining Ethics: Teens and TV Talk Shows" on page 14). Television research once again documented the connection between aggression in children and violent entertainment programs. Children watched nearly forty thousand TV commercials each year. Debates also raged about curbing kids' exposure to pornography and adult subject matter on the Internet. Yet, although media depictions may worsen social problems, research has seldom demonstrated that they directly *cause* our society's major afflictions. For instance, when a young middle school student kills a fellow student over a pair of basketball shoes, should society blame the ads that glamorized the shoe and the network that carried the ad? Or are parents, teachers, and religious leaders failing to instill strong moral values? Or are economic and social issues involving gun legislation, consumerism, and income disparity at work here as well? While the shoe manufacturer bears responsibility as a corporate citizen, did the ad itself cause the tragedy, or is the ad symptomatic of larger problems?

With American mass media industries earning nearly $200 billion annually, the economic stakes are high. Large portions of media resources now go into studying audiences, capturing their attention, and taking their consumer dollars. This process involves trying to influence everything from how people vote to how they relax to how they shop. Like the air we breathe, the fallout from the mass media surrounds us. But to monitor the media's "air quality," a responsible citizenry must pay attention to diverse media messages that we too often take for granted.

> **"Skyscrapers were citadels** of the new power of finance capitalism. . . . Far above the thronging sidewalks, they elevated the men who controlled much of the capital that lubricated the workings of **organized cultural enterprises**— publishing companies, film studios, theatrical syndicates, symphony orchestras. Culture . . . was becoming increasingly organized during the twentieth century. And the model for that organization was the hierarchical, bureaucratic corporation."
>
> —Jackson Lears, historian

surveying the cultural landscape

Some cultural phenomena are popular, and others are not. Some appeal to certain age groups or social classes; some, such as rock and roll, jazz, and classical music, are popular worldwide. Other cultural forms, such as Tejano, salsa, or Cajun music, are popular only in certain regions or communities. Some aspects of culture are considered elite in one place (opera in the United States) and popular in another (opera in Italy). Most societies, however, arrange culture into hierarchical categories.

culture as a hierarchy

In twentieth-century America, critics and audiences have established a hierarchy of culture. At the top is what is frequently labeled **high culture**, such as ballet, the symphony, art museums, and classic literature. At the bottom of the ladder is popular or **low culture**, such as soap operas, rock and rap music, talk radio, comic books, and monster truck pulls (see Figure 1.1). High culture, standing for "good taste" and often supported by wealthy patrons and corporate donors, has become associated with "fine

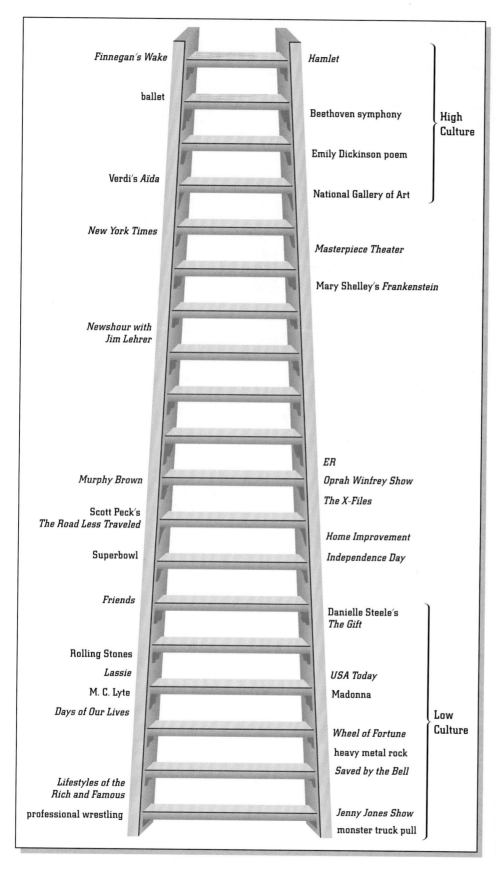

Finnegan's Wake

Hamlet

ballet

Beethoven symphony

} **High
Culture**

Emily Dickinson poem

Verdi's *Aïda*

National Gallery of Art

New York Times

Masterpiece Theater

Mary Shelley's *Frankenstein*

Newshour with
Jim Lehrer

ER
Oprah Winfrey Show
The X-Files

Murphy Brown

Scott Peck's
The Road Less Traveled

Home Improvement

Superbowl

Independence Day

Friends

Danielle Steele's
The Gift

Rolling Stones
Lassie
M. C. Lyte
Days of Our Lives

USA Today
Madonna

**Low
Culture**

Wheel of Fortune
heavy metal rock
Saved by the Bell

Lifestyles of the
Rich and Famous

professional wrestling

Jenny Jones Show
monster truck pull

Figure 1.1
Culture as a Hierarchy
Culture is diverse and difficult to categorize. Yet throughout the twentieth century we have tended to think of culture not as a social process but as a set of products sorted into high, low, or middle positions on a cultural ladder. Look at this highly arbitrary arrangement and see if you agree or disagree. Write in some of your own examples. Be ready to argue.

Why do so many people view culture this way? What are the strengths and limitations of thinking about culture in these terms?

DONNA   SCOTT   JOHN
DONNA'S SETTING UP HER FRIENDS SCOTT AND JOHN; SCOTT HAS A SECRET CRUSH ON JO

In March 1995, the *Jenny Jones Show* taped a program in Chicago about secret admirers. One participant, Scott Amedure, who identified himself as gay, revealed his affections for another guest, Jonathan Schmitz, a heterosexual. Humiliated by the revelation, Schmitz returned to Michigan, bought a shotgun, and three days later killed Amedure. Although the program never aired, the story intensified public concern over talk shows, already under attack for exploiting sexual topics and ambushing gullible guests.

As a result, some local TV stations dropped the most offensive programs, and large advertisers such as Philip Morris and Proctor & Gamble reduced their advertising support. Meanwhile, the *Jenny Jones Show* disavowed legal responsibility, claiming guests had been told their admirers might be of either sex. In 1996, after doctors and his family documented Schmitz's precarious psychological history, he was convicted of second-degree murder; Amedure's family immediately filed a $25 million civil suit against the *Jenny Jones Show*, arguing that the program's producers did a poor job of screening its guests.

Although this incident was tragic and atypical, such talk-show topics and tactics have become standard daytime fare. These practices raise serious ethical questions. Complicating any discussion of ethics, however, are the competing values that govern how talk shows handle topics and guests. Most media organizations have ethical codes that guide how professionals should behave in different situations. But beyond self-regulatory codes, how can consumers criticize and shape the ethics of media institutions?

Arriving at ethical decisions is a particular kind of criticism involving several steps. These include (1) laying out the case; (2) pinpointing the key issues; (3) identifying the parties involved, their intent, and their competing values; (4) studying ethical models and theories; (5) presenting strategies and options; and (6) formulating a decision or policy.[1] As a test case, we will look at the topic of teenagers, sex, and talk shows. Our goal will be to make some ethical decisions and to lay the groundwork for a policy that programs might implement regarding suitable subject matter and the treatment of guests. We will follow the six steps just mentioned. (See Ch. 14, p. 396, for details on solving ethical problems.)

Examining Ethics Activity: As a class or in smaller groups, design a policy to guide talk shows on topics involving teens and sex. Start by researching the topic; find as much information as possible. For instance, look at the ten-point talk show "bill of rights" that Geraldo Rivera's program developed in early 1996 as a response to criticism. Look at the guidelines from other talk shows.

Do they provide appropriate counseling for guests, and what form does the counseling take? Indicate whether the ethics policy should be government mandated or an industry-wide guideline. Finally, send the policy to various talk shows; ask for their evaluations and whether they would consider implementing it.

TALK TV'S TOP SHOWS

Oprah Winfrey (King World)
Montel Williams (Paramount)
Regis & Kathie Lee (Buena Vista TV)
Jenny Jones (Warner Bros.)
Sally Jessy Raphael (Multimedia)
Maury Povich (Paramount)
Ricki Lake (Columbia TriStar)
Jerry Springer (Multimedia)
Leeza (Paramount for NBC)

Source: Nielsen Syndication Service

Talk Show Titles

- Honey, I have a secret.
- Housewives vs. Strippers
- Should parents do time for their kid's crimes?
- Low-life Teenagers
- My teen can't go without sex.
- Irresponsible Teen Moms
- My daughter looks like a slut!
- My mom is a slut.
- Mother ran off with her daughter's fiancé.
- You're too old to be dating a teen.

The Foundation of "The Geraldo Rivera Show": The Bill of Rights and Responsibilities

1. Integrity and honesty
Guests will be fully informed well in advance that this is a forum where misrepresentation and exploitation have no place.

2. Solutions over shock
We will engage viewers without pandering to them. Shows should help our guests and our audience gain insight and resolve problems they face.

3. Respect for our guests
Guests should not be used for sport or spectacle. Civility must prevail.

4. No studio violence
Physical violence will not be tolerated. Any acts of studio violence will be edited out of the final product.

5. Professional responsibility
Counselors, therapists, trained professionals, and experts will be a prominent show component.

6. After-care
Professional help will continue to be made available in appropriate cases to guests in need.

7. Light over heat
We will continue to tackle tough social issues in a responsible, nonsensational, informational manner.

8. Children may be watching.
While producing for an adult audience, we will bear in mind that some children may be watching. Mature subject matter always will be placed in an acceptable context for daytime viewing.

9. Community outreach
We will link the home audience with resources in their communities, acting as a powerful clearinghouse that is not readily available elsewhere.

10. Accentuating the positive
While taking a hard look at hard topics, we will emphasize the positive aspects of our life and times, rather than dwell on the negative or the bizarre. We will emphasize solutions, values, and community spirit.

art," which is available primarily in libraries, theaters, or museums. In contrast, low or popular culture has become aligned with the questionable tastes of the "masses," who enjoy the commercial "junk" circulated by the mass media. Whether or not we agree with this cultural ladder, the high-low hierarchy has become entrenched, often determining or limiting the ways culture is discussed today.[6]

Some critics are concerned that popular culture in the form of contemporary movies, television, and rock music distracts students from serious literature and philosophy, thus ruining their imaginations and undermining their abilities to recognize good art.[7] Discounting a person's ability to value Aristotle and Aerosmith concurrently, this critical view pits popular culture against the more traditional forms of high art and culture. The assumption is that because popular forms of culture are made for profit, they cannot be experienced with the same personal intensity as more elite art forms.

Another concern is that popular culture exploits classic works of literature and art. The best example may be Mary Wollstonecraft Shelley's dark Gothic novel *Frankenstein*, written in 1818 and ultimately transformed into multiple popular forms. Today, the tale is best remembered by virtue of a 1931 film version starring Boris Karloff as the towering monster. In addition to the movies (twenty-seven different versions), television turned the tale into *The Munsters*, a mid-1960s situation comedy. Eventually, the monster was resurrected as sugar-coated Frankenberry cereal. In the recycled forms of the original story, Shelley's themes about abusing modern science and judging people based on appearances are often lost or trivialized.

Unlike an Italian opera or a Shakespearean tragedy, many elements of mass culture have short life spans. The average

Today, Mary Shelley, author of *Frankenstein*, might not recognize the popular culture's mutations of her Gothic classic. First published in 1818, the novel has inspired more than twenty-five film adaptations and sparked the creation of everything from the 1960s sitcom *The Munsters* to a sugar-coated cereal.

newspaper circulates for about twelve hours, then lands in a recycle bin or at the bottom of a bird cage; the average magazine circulates for about five to seven days; a Top-100 hit on the radio lasts about one month; and the average TV series less than ten weeks. Although endurance does not necessarily denote quality, in the view of many critics, better forms of culture have staying power. These critics argue that popular forms promote a culture that is unstable and fleeting, that they follow rather than lead public taste. In the television industry, this is known as "least objectionable programming" or LOP: Network gatekeepers pander to mediocrity by putting on bland, disposable programming that will not disturb or challenge a typical viewer.

A final concern of critics is that popular culture is not just undermining or exploiting high culture but that it has inundated the cultural environment, driving out higher forms of culture and cheapening public life.[8] This concern is supported by data showing that TV sets are in use in the average American home for more than seven hours a day, exposing adults and children each year to thousands of hours of TV commercials and popular culture. According to the critics, the prevalence of media products prevents the public from experiencing genuine art. Forty or more radio stations are available in most cities; cable systems with 60 to 120 channels are in place in more than 65 percent of all U.S. households; and CD players, computer online services, and VCRs are increasing in popularity. Thus, the chance of more refined culture transforming the media environment or even finding a substantial audience has become unlikely.

Accordingly, the concern is also that the impact of popular culture, especially its visual forms, has undermined democratic reasoning. According to this view, popular media may inhibit social progress by transforming audiences into cultural dupes, seduced by the promise of products. A few conglomerates, which make large profits from media products, may be distracting citizens from examining economic disparity and implementing change. Seductive advertising images contradict the actual lives of many people, who cannot afford the products offered in the marketplace. In this environment, art and commerce have become blurred, damaging the audience's power to make cultural distinctions. Sometimes called the "Big Mac" theory, this view suggests that people are so addicted to popular media fare that they have lost not only the will to challenge social inequities but also their discriminating taste for finer things.

"OH, WE NEVER WATCH TELEVISION, WE'RE PSEUDOINTELLECTUALS."

Copyright © Bob Schochet

culture as a map

To depict culture as an ongoing process and to account for individuality, it is helpful to imagine culture as a map. Maps represent large, unwieldy spaces that spread out in all directions. Maps highlight main highways and familiar urban centers, but they also include scores of side roads and small towns, diverting our focus to unexplored areas.

A map model of culture demonstrates that, on the one hand, cultural phenomena may seem conventional, recognizable, stable, and comforting. On the other hand, they may tend toward the innovative, unfamiliar, unstable, and challenging. Most forms of culture, however, demonstrate both of these tendencies. For example, we may buy the CD of a favorite artist for its innovation *and* familiarity. We may listen to a particular song to complement a mood, to distance ourselves from problems, or to reflect critically on the song's lyrics.

17

We know that people have complex cultural tastes, needs, and interests based on their particular backgrounds. It is not surprising then that our cultural forms—from blues music and opera to comic books and classic literature—contain a variety of messages. Just as Shakespeare's plays were packed with both obscure and popular references, TV episodes of *The Simpsons* today may include allusions to the Beatles, Kafka, the *Adventures of Ozzie & Harriet*, Tennessee Williams, talk shows, and *Citizen Kane*. In other words, cultural products and their meanings are "all over the map," suggesting that, in spite of many critics' tendencies to rank culture vertically, we should not think about our cultural environment merely as a product hierarchy.

Traveling Back to the Good Old Days. Some critics of popular culture assume that society was better off before the latest developments in mass media. They resist the idea of redrawing established cultural maps. The nostalgia for some imagined "better past" has always operated as a device for condemning new cultural phenomena. In the nineteenth century, in fact, a number of intellectuals and politicians worried that rising literacy rates among the working class might create havoc. How would the aristocracy maintain its authority and status if others could read? Throughout history, returning to familiar terrain, to "the good old days," has been a frequent response to new forms of popular culture, which over the years have included the waltz, silent movies, jazz, comic books, rock and roll, soap operas, rap music, and tabloid newspapers.

Familiar Landmarks and Unexplored Territory. The appeal of culture is often its ring of familiarity, pulling audiences toward the security of repetition and common landmarks. Consider, for instance, television's *Lassie* series. More than five hundred episodes now exist in syndication; many had a familiar and repetitive plot line: Timmy, who arguably possessed the poorest sense of direction and suffered more concussions than any TV character in history, gets lost or knocked unconscious. After finding Timmy and licking his face, Lassie goes for help and saves the day. Adult critics might mock this melodramatic formula, but many children find comfort in the predictability of the story. This quality is also illustrated when night after night children ask their parents to read Margaret Wise Brown's *Good Night, Moon*. Like children, adults also seek a kind of comfort, often returning to the same songs, the same plays, the same poems, and the same television programs.

On the other hand, we also seek the new—aspects of culture that demonstrate originality and complexity. For instance, James Joyce's *Finnegans Wake* (1939) created language anew and challenged readers, as the novel's poetic first sentence illustrates: "riverrun, past Eve and Adam's, from swerve of shore to bend of bay, brings us by commodius vicus of recirculation back to Howth Castle and Environs." A revolutionary work, crammed with historical names and topical references to events, myths, songs, jokes, and daily conversation, Joyce's novel remains a challenge to decode.

> "TV is a genre of reruns, a formulaic return to what we already know. Everything is familiar. Ads and old programs are constantly recycled. It's **like mythology, like the Homeric epics**, the oral tradition, in which the listener hears passages, formulae, and epithets repeated over and over again. There is a **joy in repetition**, as children know when they say, 'Mommy, tell me that story again.' "
>
> —Camille Paglia,
> *Harper's*,
> 1991

shifting values in modern culture

In contemporary life, cultural boundaries are being tested; the lines between information and entertainment have blurred. Consumers now read newspapers on their computer screens. Media corporations do business across vast geographic boundaries.

In the 1936 film *Modern Times*, director Charlie Chaplin satirized modern industry and confronted the dehumanizing aspects of a futuristic manufacturing plant. In the 1980s, IBM produced a television commercial using the character of Chaplin's Little Tramp to tout the intimacy of the company's latest line of personal computers.

We are witnessing *media convergence* wherein satellite dishes and computer modems easily access new and old forms of mass communication. For a fee, everything from magazines to movies is channeled into homes through computer modems and TV monitors. To place these shifts and convergences in historical context, scholars have traced the meandering route of cultural values through the *modern* period (from the full-blown arrival of the Industrial Revolution in the nineteenth century) to one that is frequently labeled *postmodern* or contemporary.

What it means to be *modern* is complicated. As we have seen, the process of modernization involved individuals and societies responding to changing economic circumstances. Captains of industry employed workforces and new technology, creating efficient manufacturing centers and inexpensive products aimed at making everyday life better and more profitable. Printing presses and assembly lines made major contributions in this transformation, and modern advertising spread the word about new gadgets to American consumers.

Cultural responses to modernization often manifest themselves in the mass media. For example, Aldous Huxley, in *Brave New World* (1932), created a fictional world cautioning readers that modern science and technology posed a threat to individual dignity. Charlie Chaplin's film *Modern Times* (1936), set in a futuristic manufacturing plant, also told the story of the dehumanizing impact of modernization and machinery. Writers and artists, in their criticisms of the modern world, often point to technology's ability to alienate us from one another, capitalism's tendency to foster greed and consumerism, and government's inclination toward creating bureaucracies that oppress rather than help people. Among the major values of the modern period, four have manifested themselves frequently in the cultural environment: *celebrating the individual, believing in rational order, working efficiently*, and *rejecting tradition*.

These values of the modern period were originally embodied in the printing press and later in newspapers and magazines. The print media encouraged the vision of individual writers, publishers, and readers who circulated new ideas. Whereas the premodern period was guided by strong beliefs in a natural or divine order, becoming modern meant elevating individual self-expression to a central position. Along with democratic breakthroughs, however, individualism and the Industrial Revolution triggered modern forms of hierarchy, in which certain individuals and groups achieved higher standing in the social order. For example, those who managed commercial enterprises gained more control over the economic ladder, but an intellectual class of experts, who mastered specialized realms of knowledge, gained increasing power over the nation's social, political, and cultural agendas.

To be modern meant to value the capacity of organized, scientific minds to solve problems. Progressive thinkers maintained that the printing press, the telegraph, and the railroad in combination with a scientific attitude would foster a new type of informed society. At the core of this society, the printed mass media, particularly newspapers, would educate the citizenry, helping to build and maintain an organized social framework.[9] Journalists strove for the modern ideal through a more objective approach to reporting. They discarded ornate or decorative writing and championed a lean and neutral look. The modern style of front-page news de-emphasized descriptive detail, humor, commentary, and historical context. The lead sentences that reported a presidential press conference began to look similar, whether on the front page in Atlanta, Georgia, or Zap, North Dakota. Just as modern architecture made many American skylines look alike, the front pages of newspapers began to resemble one another (see Figure 1.2).

Figure 1.2
Premodern vs. Modern News
These two stories, separated by 161 years, illustrate some differences between premodern and modern news. The 1834 story includes asides, humor, and opinion by the writer; the 1995 story seems objective, stripped of any direct evidence of the reporter's viewpoint. The 1834 story is more dramatic in its description of the crimes; the 1995 story focuses on facts—who, what, when, where—revealing that even specific ages and the exact address of the motel are important. The 1834 story treats the crime irreverently; the 1995 story treats the crime seriously. What are the pros and cons of each style? What attitudes toward the victims are represented by the different styles of reporting?

NEW YORK SUN

VOLUME II.   NEW YORK, JULY 4, 1834   NUMBER 23.

POLICE OFFICE

Patrick Ludwick was sent up by his wife, who testified that she had supported him for several years in idleness and drunkenness. Abandoning all hopes of a reformation in her husband, she bought him a suit of clothes a fortnight ago and told him to go about his business, for she would not live with him any longer. Last night he came home in a state of intoxication, broke into his wife's bedroom, pulled her out of bed, pulled her hair, and stamped on her. She called a watchman and sent him up. Pat exerted all his powers of eloquence in endeavoring to excite his wife's sympathy, but to no purpose. As every sensible woman ought to do who is cursed with a drunken husband, she refused to have anything to do with him hereafter—and he was sent to the penitentiary.

ANN ARBOR NEWS   # POLICE BEAT

November 19, 1995

Ann Arbor police expect to arraign on Monday an Allen Park man who is accused of assaulting his female companion in a local hotel room early Friday morning after she refused to have sex with him.

The 48-year-old man was arrested Saturday in Allen Park by police there, Ann Arbor police said Saturday. The 33-year-old woman, who lives in Wyandotte, told investigators that the man struck her in the head with a bottle and punched her when she would not consent to sex.

Employees at the Ramada Inn Ann Arbor, 3750 Washtenaw Ave., said the man and woman checked in around 2 a.m. Friday.

Finally, to be modern meant to throw off the past's rigid mores, to break with tradition. Modern journalism became captivated by timely and immediate events. As a result, the more standardized forms of front-page journalism, which championed facts and current events, often failed to analyze sufficiently the ideas underlying these events.

shifting values in postmodern culture

For many, the changes occurring in contemporary, or postmodern, society are identified only by a confusing array of examples: remote controls, Nike ads, shopping malls, fax machines, David Letterman, *Beavis and Butt-head*, *USA Today*, car phones, MTV, and Madonna (see "Case Study: The Material Girl as Postmodern Icon" on page 22). Some critics argue that postmodern culture represents a way of seeing—a condition (or malady) of the human spirit. Chiefly a response to the modern world, controversial postmodern values are playing increasingly pivotal roles in our daily lives. Four values, in particular, have surfaced in the so-called postmodern period: *opposing hierarchy*, *diversifying and recycling culture*, *questioning scientific reasoning*, and *embracing paradox* (see Table 1.1).

One of the main values of contemporary culture is an opposition to hierarchy. Many are challenging the sometimes arbitrary line between high and low culture, while others are blurring the distinctions between fact and fiction or art and commerce. For example, a new television vocabulary now includes *docudrama* (the daily reenactment of O.J. Simpson's civil trial on cable's E! channel), *infotainment* (*Entertainment Tonight*), and *infomercials* (Cher's talk show about her cosmetics line). In magazines, the often arresting Benetton clothing ads combine stark social com-

TABLE 1.1
Trends across Historical Periods*

	Premodern (before 1700s)	Modern (after 1800s)	Postmodern (since 1960s)
Range of work hierarchies	peasants/merchants rulers	factory workers/ managers/ national CEOs	temp workers/ managers/ global CEOs
Major work sites	field/farm	factory/office	office/home/"virtual" or mobile office
Communication reach	local	national	global
Communication transmission	oral/manuscript	print/electronic	electronic/digital
Communication channels	storytellers/ elders/town criers	books/newspapers/ magazines/radio/ television	television/cable/ Internet/multimedia
Communication at home	quill pen	typewriter/ computer	personal or laptop computer

* The examples in this table identify some of the significant trends in the premodern, modern, and postmodern periods of society.

Source: For a slightly different view, see Charles Jencks, "The Three Eras of Civilization," in *What Is Post-Modernism?* 3rd ed. (New York: St. Martin's Press, 1989), 47.

The Material Girl as Postmodern Icon

poseur?

feminist?

**savvy
business
woman?**

in control?

genius?

tasteless?

crass
self-promoter?

Born the daughter of devout Catholics in Bay City, Michigan, in 1958, Madonna Louise Ciccone has arguably commanded more international attention than any cultural figure since the Beatles. Since the Vatican condemned her 1991 *Blonde Ambition* world tour and a new release sold "only" two million copies, critics have been writing her obituary as a pop superstar. However, the parade of Letterman and Leno jokes, the number of academic treatises trying to uncover her meaning, and the publication of *The "I Hate Madonna" Handbook* suggest that she remains a controversial symbol for both positive and negative aspects of postmodern culture.

In 1989, Pepsi-Cola withdrew an expensive two-minute TV ad starring Madonna on the day after her controversial "Like a Prayer" music video premiered on MTV. Almost immediately after its release, Italy banned the video when a Catholic group threatened court action. The same song, used as background in the commercial, netted $5 million of

Pepsi's money for Madonna. The video tells a fairly conventional story of a woman who sees a white man commit a crime while an innocent black man takes the rap. As an eyewitness, Madonna's character comes forward to tell the truth. Beyond the basic plot, however, the video blurs the border between the sacred and the secular, between religious fervor and sexual energy. When various groups protested the video and its use of Christian symbols (burning crosses and Madonna kissing a black saintlike figure), Pepsi decided to withdraw the ad. Although the ad used none of the footage from the music video, Pepsi feared the negative publicity and potential boycotts.

Over the years, such boundary blurring has been Madonna's hallmark. She has been, in her words, "pushing buttons" to provoke cultural disputes since her 1984 single "Like a Virgin" became the year's biggest pop hit. In 1990, a sexually explicit video, "Justify My Love," was banned by MTV. The video tested the borders between heterosexuality and homosexuality and again mixed religious symbols with

sexual images. Later, Madonna appeared on *Nightline* to defend herself and to promote the independent release of the banned video. *Nightline* slyly decided to air the video and drew one of its largest audiences ever.

Although her personal conduct has been heavily criticized, Madonna's defenders argue that she has become one of the premier entrepreneurs in a media world where men have historically called the shots. She has also contributed to social causes, and she appeared in voter-education promotions for MTV in the early 1990s, which helped register millions of young voters (although Madonna herself was not registered).

Critics chide her for her imitativeness. Perhaps no one has been assailed more often than Madonna for not being original. One writer criticized her for continually imitating old movie icons, "inventing herself as a mutable being, a container for a multiplicity of images."[1]

Other critics argue that there's more than photocopying going on in Madonna's work. Although her music videos deliberately recall pop culture goddesses from Greta Garbo to Marilyn Monroe, Madonna reinvents them with a contemporary spin. Unlike the original icon, for instance, the Monroe of Madonna's 1985 "Material Girl" coquettishly rejects her wealthy suitors at will. On a *Saturday Night Live* appearance in 1993, Madonna appeared in a "Wayne's World" skit to make fun of her own music and image.

Madonna has continually split the feminist and critical community. Some assess her as a no-talent master of self-promotion, who perpetuates the stereotype of women as sex objects and "boy toys." Culture critic and Madonna fan Camille Paglia believes that many feminists are simply threatened by Madonna's overt celebration of eroticism: "Madonna is a true feminist.... [She] has taught young women to be fully female and sexual while still exercising total control of their lives."[2]

Another media critic, Michael McWilliams, makes a different case. He says that Madonna is despised because her fans are not the conventional adults and mainstream critics who condemn her: "What [the mainstream] never understood about Madonna was her thrill in role playing—changes in hair color, costumes, body tones, complete images—in much the same way that her greatest fans [gays, blacks, kids, and teens] have had to role play in order to survive."[3]

One of the strongest critiques of Madonna comes from African American scholar Bell Hooks, who has written about the postmodern paradox of the singer's cultural image in "Madonna: Plantation Mistress or Soul Sister?" Hooks admires Madonna for "creating a cultural space where she can invent and reinvent herself and receive public affirmation and material reward."[4] Yet Hooks notes that Madonna's many personas often subordinate the black and gay characters she uses in her white-girl-makes-good dramas, perpetuating conventional hierarchies. In *Truth or Dare*, the film documenting her 1990 concert tour, Madonna surrounds herself with what she describes as "emotional cripples" (mostly racial minorities, gay men, and other members of oppressed groups) so that she can fulfill her need "to be a mother." In the end, contradictions surround Madonna: her music seems to champion oppressed groups at the same time that it has made her wealthy and a global icon for consumer culture.

Career Achievements

1958: Born Madonna Louise Ciccone in Bay City, Michigan, August 16

1984: First hit single, "Holiday," peaked at No. 16

1984: First Top 10 hit, "Borderline," peaked at No. 10

1984: First No. 1 hit on the pop charts, "Like a Virgin"

1985: Feature-film acting debut in *Desperately Seeking Susan*

1987: Received People's Choice Award for Favorite Female Musical Performer

1988: Broadway acting debut in *Speed the Plow* by David Mamet

1992: Received Grammy for Best Music Video—Long Form for "Madonna: *Blonde Ambition World Tour Live*"

1992: Released the controversial book, *Sex*

1995: Eleventh No. 1 single, "Take a Bow," making her the female performer with the most No. 1 songs to date according to *Billboard*. Received MTV Video Music Award for Best Female Video for the Same Song

1997: Received Golden Globe Award for Best Actress in a Motion Picture for *Evita*

An example of postmodern style, television's *Northern Exposure* (1990–95) routinely criticized science, saluting instead the ability of nature to bewilder rational inquiry. In the series, Dr. Joel Fleischman, a Columbia-educated New Yorker, endured a wise tribal medicine man whose diagnosis of various ailments confounded the doctor's modern techniques.

mentaries with low-key sales pitches. At the movies, the fusion of comedy and tragedy in *Pulp Fiction* (1994) or *Fargo* (1996) is representative of postmodern style.

Another contemporary value (or vice) emphasizes diversity and fragmentation, including the wild juxtaposition of old and new cultural styles. In a suburban shopping mall, for instance, Doubleday books and Gap clothes border a Vietnamese, Italian, and Mexican food court, while a Muzak version of the Beatles' "Revolution" plays in the background. Part of this stylistic diversity involves borrowing and then transforming earlier ideas from the modern period. In music, rap deejays sample old R&B, soul, and rock classics to reinvent songs. Borrowing in rap is often so pronounced that the original artists and record companies have frequently filed for copyright infringement. Critics of postmodern style contend that it borrows too heavily and devalues originality, emphasizing surface over depth and recycled ideas over new ones. Throughout the twentieth century, for example, films have been adapted from books and short stories. Now, films often derive from popular TV series: *Addams Family Values*, *The Brady Bunch*, *The Fugitive*, *The Flintstones*, *Maverick*, and *Mission Impossible*, to name just a few. To capitalize on and keep pace with TV's large audience, other media often promote the copy over the original.

Another tendency of postmodern culture is to raise doubts about scientific reasoning. Rather than seeing science purely as enlightened thinking, postmodernists view it as laying the groundwork for modern bureaucratic problems. They reject rational thought as "the answer" to every social problem, instead lauding the premodern values of small communities. Internet users, for example, are seen as reclaiming in electronic form lost conversational skills and letter-writing habits. Even the current popularity of radio and TV talk shows, according to this view, is partly an attempt to recover lost aspects of oral traditions. Given the feelings of powerlessness and alienation in the contemporary age, one attraction of the talk-show format has been the way it encourages ordinary people to participate in discussions with celebrities and experts.

Although some forms of contemporary culture raise questions about rational science, other postmodern forms warmly embrace technology. Blockbuster films such

24

as *Jurassic Park* and *Independence Day* do both, doubting modern science but depending on technological wizardry for their execution. During the modern period, art and literature frequently criticized the potential dangers of machines. Postmodern style, however, does not seem as critical of new technologies. For example, MTV offers its popular *Unplugged* program, which not only spurns electronic sounds for rock music's acoustic heritage but also serves up high-tech wizardry in its music videos or in programs such as *Liquid Television*.

Many forms of contemporary culture generally accept technology. There is, however, a fundamental paradox in this uneasy postmodern alliance. As modern writers and artists have pointed out, new technologies often eliminate jobs and physically isolate us from one another. Conversely, new technologies can draw people together to discuss politics on radio talk shows, electronic town-hall meetings, or Internet newsgroups. Our lives today are full of such incongruities.

critiquing media and culture

Just as communication is not always reducible to the linear sender-message-receiver model, many forms of media and culture are not easily represented by the high-low metaphor. We should, perhaps, strip adjectives like *high*, *low*, *popular*, and *mass* from culture. These modifiers may artificially force media forms into predetermined categories. Instead of focusing on these labels, we should be looking at a wide range of issues generated by culture, from the role of storytelling in the mass media to the global influences of media industries on consumer culture. We should also be moving toward a critical perspective that takes into account the intricacies of the cultural landscape.

A fair critique of any cultural form requires a working knowledge of the particular book, poem, program, or music under scrutiny. For example, to understand W. E. B. Du Bois's essays, critics immerse themselves in his work and in the historical context in which he wrote. Similarly, if we want to develop a meaningful critique of *The Simpsons*, it is essential to understand the contemporary context in which that TV program is produced. The critical process helps us grasp why particular writers or programs have a distinctive influence on culture.

To begin this process of critical assessment, we must imagine culture as more complicated and richer than the high-low model allows. We must also assume a critical stance that enables us to get outside our own preferences. We may like or dislike Selena's Tejano ballads, KRS-One's political rap, or Pearl Jam's grunge rock, but if we want to criticize this music intelligently, we should understand what various types of music have to say and why their messages have appeal for particular audiences. The same approach applies to other cultural forms. If we critique a newspaper article, we must account for the language that is chosen and what it means; if we analyze a film or TV program, we need to slow down the images in order to understand what they mean.

steps in the critical process

It is easy to form a cynical view of the stream of advertising, talk shows, rock stars, and tabloids that flood the cultural landscape. But cynicism is no substitute for solid criticism. Our goal is to strike a balance between taking a *critical* position (developing knowledgeable interpretations and judgments) and becoming *tolerant* of diverse forms of expression (appreciating the distinctive variety of cultural products and processes).

A cynical view usually involves some form of intolerance and either too little or too much information. If, for example, we endured the glut of news coverage devoted to the O.J. Simpson trials from 1995 to 1997, we might easily have become cynical about our legal system. However, *information* in the form of news facts and *knowledge* about a complex social process such as a criminal trial are not necessarily the same thing. The critical process stresses the subtle distinctions between amassing information and becoming knowledgeable.

Developing a critical perspective involves mastering four overlapping stages, each building on the others:

- *Description*: paying close attention, taking notes, and researching the subject under scrutiny

- *Analysis*: discovering and focusing on significant patterns that emerge from the description stage

- *Interpretation*: asking and answering the "What does that mean?" and "So what?" questions about one's findings

- *Evaluation*: arriving at a judgment about whether something is good, bad, or mediocre, which involves subordinating one's personal taste to the critical assessment resulting from the first three stages

Let us look at each of these stages in more detail.

Description. If we decide to focus on how well the news media serve democracy, we might critique the fairness of several programs or stories from *60 Minutes* or the *New York Times*. We start by describing the programs or articles, accounting for their reporting strategies, and noting what persons are featured as interview subjects. We might further identify central characters, conflicts, topics, and themes. From the notes taken at this stage, we can begin comparing what we have found to other stories on similar topics. We can also document what we think is missing from these accounts— the questions, viewpoints, and persons that were not included—and other ways to tell the story.

Analysis. In the second stage of the critical process, we isolate *patterns* that call for closer attention. At this point, we decide how to focus the critique. Since *60 Minutes*

Calvin and Hobbes
by Bill Watterson

Reprinted with permission. All rights reserved.

© 1990 Universal Press Syndicate

has produced thousands of hours of programs, our critique might spotlight just a few key patterns. For example, many of the program's reports are organized like detective stories, reporters are almost always visually represented at a medium distance, and interview subjects are generally shot in tight close-ups. In studying the *New York Times*, on the other hand, we might limit our analysis to countries that get covered more regularly than others, recurring topics chosen for front-page treatment, or the number of quotes from the same set of experts.

Interpretation. In the interpretive stage, we try to determine the *meanings* of the patterns we have analyzed. The most difficult stage in criticism, interpretation demands an answer to the "So what?" question. For instance, the visual space granted *60 Minutes* reporters—compared to the close-up shots used for interview subjects—might mean that the reporters appear to have control. They are given more visual space in which to operate, while interview subjects have little room to maneuver within the visual frame. As a result, the subjects often look guilty, and the reporters look heroic—or at least in charge. If we look again at the *New York Times*, its attention to particular countries might mean that the paper tends to cover nations in which the United States has more vital economic interests, even though the *Times* claims to be neutral in its reporting of international news.

Evaluation. The fourth stage of the critical process focuses on making an informed judgment. Building on description, analysis, and interpretation, we are better able to evaluate the fairness of a group of *60 Minutes* or *New York Times* reports. At this stage, we can grasp the strengths and weaknesses of the news media under study and make critical judgments measured against our own frames of reference—what we like and dislike as well as what seems good or bad about the topics we analyzed.

This fourth stage differentiates the reviewer (or *previewer*) from the critic. Most newspaper reviews, for example, are dictated by daily time constraints and space limits. Although these reviews may give us important information about particular programs, they often begin and end with personal judgments— "This is a quality show," or "That was a piece of trash"—which should be the final stage in any substantial critical process. Regrettably, most reviews do not reflect such a process; they do not move much beyond the writer's own frame of reference.

> "A **cynic** is a man who, when he smells flowers, looks around for a coffin."
> —H. L. Mencken

benefits of a critical perspective

Developing an informed critical perspective allows us to participate in a debate about media culture as a force for *both* democracy and consumerism. On the one hand, the media can be an impetus for democratic tendencies. Consider the role of television in documenting racism and injustice in the 1960s; the use of video technology to reveal oppressive conditions in China and Eastern Europe or to document crimes by urban police departments; and the appearance of political rap music, as black-produced commerce, drawing attention to social injustice. The media have also helped to renew interest in diverse cultures (see "The Global Village: Bedouins, Camels, Transistors, and Coke" on page 28).

On the other hand, competing against these democratic tendencies is a powerful commercial culture that reinforces a world economic order controlled by fewer and fewer multinational corporations. For instance, when Poland threw off the shackles of the Soviet Union in the late 1980s, one of the first things its new leaders did was buy and dub the American soap operas *Santa Barbara* and *Dynasty*. For some Poles, these

Upon receiving the Philadelphia Liberty Medal in 1994, President Vaclav Havel of the Czech Republic described postmodernism as the fundamental condition of global culture, "when it seems that something is on the way out and something else is painfully being born." He described this "new world order" as a "multicultural era" or state in which consistent value systems break into mixed and blended cultures:

> For me, a symbol of that state is a Bedouin mounted on a camel and clad in traditional robes under which he is wearing jeans, with a transistor radio in his hands and an ad for Coca-Cola on the camel's back.... New meaning is gradually born from the...intersection of many different elements.[1]

Many critics, including Havel, think that there is a crucial tie between global politics and postmodern culture. They contend that the people who overthrew Yugoslavia and the Soviet Union were the same people who valued American popular culture—especially movies, rock music, and television—for its free expression and democratic possibilities.

As modern communist states were undermined by the growth and influence of transnational corporations, citizens in these nations capitalized on the developing global market, using portable video and audio technology to smuggle out tapes of atrocities perpetrated by totalitarian regimes. Thus it was difficult for political leaders to hide repressive acts from the rest of the world. In *Newsweek*, CBS news anchor Dan Rather wrote about the role of television in the 1989 student uprising in China:

Television brought Beijing's battle for democracy to Main Street. It made students who live on the other side of the planet just as human, just as vulnerable as the boy on the next block. The miracle of television is that the triumph and tragedy of Tiananmen Square would not have been any more vivid had it been Times Square.[2]

At the same time, we need to examine the impact on other nations of the influx of popular culture—the second biggest American export (after military and airplane equipment). Has access to an American consumer lifestyle fundamentally altered Havel's bedouin on the camel? What happens when CNN or MTV are transported to remote African villages that share a single community TV set? These questions still need answers. A global village, which through technology shares culture and communication, can also alter traditional rituals forever.

To try to grasp this phenomenon, we might imagine how we would feel if the culture from a country far away gradually eroded our established habits. This, in fact, is happening all over the world as American culture becomes the world's global currency. Although newer forms of communication such as e-mail have in some ways increased citizen participation in global life, in what ways have they muted the values of older cultures? Our current postmodern period is double-coded: It is an agent both for the renewed possibilities of democracy and for the worldwide spread of consumerism and American popular culture.

28

CNN's Larry King has made his mark on cable television, interviewing politicians and celebrities such as Elizabeth Taylor. But many journalists resented King's role in the 1992 elections. For example, Texas business tycoon Ross Perot used his appearances with King to bypass the conventional news media and successfully launch his third-party presidential candidacy.

shows were a relief from sober Soviet political propaganda, but other Poles worried that their country had inherited another kind of indoctrination, starring American consumer culture.

This example illustrates that contemporary culture cannot easily be characterized as one thing or another. Binary terms such as *liberal* and *conservative* or *high* and *low* have less meaning in an environment where so many boundaries have been blurred, so many media forms have converged, and so many diverse cultures exist. Modern distinctions between print and electronic culture have begun to break down chiefly due to the increasing numbers of individuals who have come of age in *both* a print *and* an electronic culture.[10] Either/or models of culture, such as the high-low view, are making room for more inclusive models, similar to the map metaphor for culture discussed earlier.

What are the social implications of the new, blended, and merging cultural phenomena? How do we deal with the fact that public debate and news about everyday life now seem as likely to come from Oprah, Larry King, or popular music, as from the *New York Times*, *Nightline*, or *Newsweek*?[11] Clearly, such changes challenge us to reassess and rebuild the standards by which we judge our culture. The search for answers lies in recognizing the significant links between cultural expression and daily life. The search also involves monitoring how well the mass media serve democratic practices and involve a rich variety of people as consumers and citizens.

Democracy requires the active participation of interested citizens. Part of this involvement means watching over the role and impact of the mass media, a job that belongs to each citizen, not just to paid media critics. In this textbook, we begin the job by examining the historical contexts and current processes that shape media products. By probing various media industries, we can then develop a framework for tracking the ways in which media industries perform. By becoming more critical consumers and engaged citizens, we will be in a better position to influence the relationships among mass media, democratic participation, and the cultural landscape.

REVIEW QUESTIONS

1. Define culture, mass communication, and mass media, and explain their interrelationships.

2. What does it mean to spell and define culture with a small "c" or with a capital "C"?

3. What are the key technological breakthroughs that accompanied the transition to the print and electronic eras? Why were these technologies significant?

4. Explain the linear model of mass communication and its limitations.

5. How does an alternative approach to mass communication differ from the linear model?

6. Describe the hierarchical model of culture. What are its strengths and limitations?

7. Describe the map model of culture. What are its strengths and limitations?

8. What are the chief differences between modern and so-called postmodern values?

9. What are the four steps in the critical process? Which of these is the most difficult and why?

10. What is the difference between cynicism and criticism?

11. Why is the critical process important?

QUESTIONING THE MEDIA

1. Using music or television as an example, identify a performer or program you once liked but then began to dislike as you got older. Your tastes changed. Why did this happen?

2. What evidence of demonizing the media have you seen in your own life? Draw on comments from parents, teachers, religious leaders, friends, news media, etc. Discuss whether these criticisms have been justified.

3. Pick an example of a popular media product that you think is harmful to children. How would you make your concerns known? Should the product be removed from circulation? Why or why not? If you think the product should be banned, how would you do it?

4. Make a critical case either defending or condemning MTV's controversial cartoon *Beavis and Butthead*, a TV talk show, professional wrestling, a rap group, or a soap opera. Use the four-step critical process to develop your case.

5. Try to develop your own model of culture that differs from the hierarchical and map models described in the chapter. How would your model help us to better understand the ways culture works?

6. Although in some ways postmodern forms of communication, such as e-mail, MTV, and CNN, have helped citizens participate in global life, in what ways might these forms harm more traditional native cultures?

In small groups, or as a class, write the headings *quality* and *trash* on the board or a sheet of paper. As a group, agree on one or two television shows that serve as examples of trashy programs and quality programs. In another column, if necessary, place any programs that are in dispute—those that may divide group opinion. (Films, books, magazines, and advertisements could be used here as well.) Your column headings should look like this:

Quality   *Trash*   *In Dispute*

1. For each set of programs, gather ammunition and evidence. On a separate piece of paper, *describe* the programs by listing their narrative features: basic plots, central conflicts or tensions, typical subject matter, major themes, main characters, and how tensions are resolved.

2. Now return to your listing of programs. Under each category, name and *analyze* the attributes that led your group to classify the programs as you did. Identify as many characteristics as you can and then summarize which virtues are necessary for a quality show, which vices make a show trashy, and which elements make a particular show hard to classify.

3. Examine the patterns among the characteristics you have chosen, and *interpret* what this means. Why did you pick the characteristics you did for each category? Why did you associate particular features with quality or with trash? What made your disputed programs a problem for different members of your group? Why do some viewers (or readers) gravitate to trashy shows? What might the programs mean to those audiences? For the programs you could not easily categorize, what led to their disputed standing?

4. *Evaluate* the programs from your lists. Assess whether these shows are good or bad for society. Should restrictions be placed on some programs even if this means testing the First Amendment protection of the press and free speech?

   Discuss the differences that were evident in your group between individual tastes and the critical standards used to make judgments. Are more categories needed to evaluate programs adequately? If so, what categories should be added?

   What standards did your group use to judge merit? Why is it important to make critical judgments of this sort?

In a remote Egyptian desert, many miles and many hours from Cairo, a Coptic monk surveys the barren landscape. A hermit, the monk lives in a nearby cave where he practices his Christian faith. Not far away, bedouin nomads living in makeshift thatched huts tend their camels, goats, and sheep. The time could be 350 A.D., but it's not. The monk uses a laptop computer. Online, he e-mails a group of middle-school students who are thousands of miles away in Zeeland, Michigan. He tells them about his life; the students respond with messages about their own culture. The year is 1997.

The monk's cave and the bedouin huts are near the excavation site of a fourth-century Coptic monastery. There, archaeologists are unearthing clues to the religious order's early history. The Copts, the first group to spread Christianity throughout Egypt in a time before the rise of Islam, also founded the Christian monastic movement. The discovery of their ancient monastery has become part of "Odyssey in Egypt," a ten-week online project that lets students work "virtually" alongside scientists as they dig up ancient pottery and other artifacts. The archaeologists update the bedouins on their findings and issue progress reports via e-mail. The Michigan students experience what it must be like to go on an archaeological dig and can ask questions and correspond with the project participants and the nearby residents.[1]

The students and the monk are pioneers, exploring the frontiers of the borderless place called *cyberspace*. This virtual space collapses not only the distance between geographic places, but the time between the past and the present as well, as "Odyssey in Egypt" attests. New technologies along the information highway have helped create cyberspace, establishing the intersection of personal computers and modems, high-speed telephone links, communication satellites, television screens, and other key developments. They allow a monk and a group of students—continents and cultures apart—to communicate, taking part in a vast, interconnected web that is full of possibility.

Frontier metaphors have often been used to explain the complexity and potential of the Information Age. In fact, new media observers Daniel Burstein and David Kline have argued that cyberspace is "like the Old West," nourishing "a culture of zealous individualism and entrepreneurialism. It has its gold rushes (Wall Street), its uncharted land (the Internet), its territories newly opened to farmers and homesteaders (the World Wide Web), a pony express (electronic mail), plenty of outlaws (hackers) but nary a sheriff (security), and its few settled towns (e.g., America Online and Prodigy) where decent folk can enjoy some of the comforts of civilization."[2] Of the "uncharted land" of that highway section called the **Internet**—the vast central network of high-speed telephone lines designed to link and carry computer information worldwide—Burstein and Kline write: "Simply put, the Internet is ungovernable . . . you can pretty much do what you want—and, for the most part, there's no sheriff or posse to stop you."

Although the Old West metaphor offers a way to view contemporary media development, the vocabulary of the new communication technology has fixed on the highway metaphor, which fits the map model of culture introduced in Chapter 1. Imagine the traditional media—books, newspapers, television, and radio—as an older interstate highway system now intersected by a sprawling poorly planned major freeway, much of it still under construction and fed by thousands of new capillary roads, some paved, some dirt, some extending into Egyptian deserts.

Unlike interstate highways built by federal and state governments, however, the information highway has been taken over and expanded by private enterprise, although it was initially established and subsidized by the government. What difference will this make? It may be too early to tell, but we do know that when private commercial managers took over radio broadcasting in the 1920s and 1930s, they helped build the United States into the world's foremost producer of communication technology and content. At the same time, though, they dramatically thwarted the growth of nonprofit and educational broadcasting.

Predictions about the cultural and social impact of the Information Age veer in many different directions. One view suggests that the information highway will lead to a utopian global village, shattering outdated geographical boundaries and building exciting communities linked by computers. Another prediction suggests that the information highway will lead to false communities, where people will remain isolated from each other and where growing reams of data will make it hard to distinguish information from misinformation. Not unlike the native cultures of the bedouins or the Old West, some people will be left out or left behind.

The full impact of the new information highway, like all emerging mass media, will evolve slowly. Cable TV, for example, which operated in only 13 percent of American households in 1975, took nearly twenty years to reach 60 percent of U.S. homes. Who gets left behind and who has access in the Information Age remain central concerns for citizens. Who manages the highway has immense implications for the future and for democracy. The task for critical media consumers is to sort through competing Internet and highway predictions, analyzing and determining how the "new and improved" Information Age can best serve the majority of citizens and communities.

origins of the information highway

Although many branches of the information highway still resemble dirt roads, the rapid technological advances that accompany the new routes pose a major challenge to cable TV and to the more traditional media. By the 1990s the information highway was increasingly **interactive**, allowing immediate two-way communication (like telephones) between senders and receivers of media messages. In addition, many side roads along the highway were virtually unregulated, open to all kinds of opportunities and mischief. The Internet alone comprises more than fifty thousand informal and global computer networks, connected by telephone lines. These networks can access books, newspapers, magazines, music, movies, interactive games, e-mail, thousands of information databases, and many other items. With its ability to transport both mass communication and personal conversation, the information highway has also begun to break down conventional distinctions among various media and between private and public modes of communication.

> "The medium, or process, of our time—electric technology—is reshaping and restructuring patterns of social interdependence and every aspect of our personal life."
> —Marshall McLuhan, 1967

the evolution of a new mass medium

The term *Industrial Age* usually refers to the period spanning the development of the steam engine in the 1760s to mass assembly-line production in the 1900s, an era that transformed manufacturing and consumer culture. By a similar measuring stick, the Information Age has barely begun. It has passed through an early phase marked by broadcasting to a phase that features the convergence of personal computers, telephone lines, electronic mail, cable television, and communication satellites.

Most mass media evolve through various stages, which are initiated not only by the diligence of great inventors, such as Thomas Edison, but by social, cultural, political, and economic circumstances. For instance, both telegraph and radio developed as new industrialized nations sought to expand their control over colonies and to transmit information more quickly. The phonograph, too, emerged because of the social and economic conditions of a growing middle class with more money and leisure time. Today, the information highway is a contemporary response to similar sets of concerns: transporting messages more rapidly while appealing to middle- and upper-middle-class consumers.

Within the appropriate conditions, media innovations emerge in three stages. First is the novelty or development stage, in which inventors and technicians try to solve a particular problem, such as making pictures move, transmitting voices through the air without wires, or sending mail electronically. Second is the entrepreneurial stage, in which inventors and investors determine a practical and marketable use for the new device. For example, early radio or wireless technology relayed messages to and from places where telegraph wires and cables could not go, such as military ships at sea. Part of the information highway also had its roots in the ideas of military leaders who devised a communication system—now known as the Internet—that could survive nuclear wars or natural disasters.

The third stage in a new medium's development involves a breakthrough to the status of *mass* medium. At this point, businesses figure out how to market the new device as an appealing product for home or office. Although the government and the navy played a central role in radio's early years, commercial entrepreneurs eventually took radio into its broadcasting phase in which it began reaching millions of people. In the same way, the Pentagon developed the prototype for the Internet, but commercial interests began taking over, extending its reach nationally and globally.

When entrepreneurs placed radio's technical parts inside a piece of living-room furniture and began marketing the "radio box" along with its programs, radio became a mass medium. Similarly, in the 1980s and 1990s, online computer services and the Internet began featuring mass communication services and marketing them through computers, modems, and phone lines. Following this innovation, the Internet grew rapidly, becoming "the most wide-ranging interactive mass medium in history."[3] By 1997, nearly fifty million people worldwide had regular access to the Internet.

the birth and growth of the internet

The real national highway system and the new information highway have similar military origins. During the Eisenhower administration in the 1950s, military and government leaders originally planned an interstate highway grid to make it easier to transport military vehicles across the country in the event of a national emergency. Begun in the late 1960s as a Defense Department communication system, the original Internet—called ARPAnet by the government and nicknamed "the Net"—allowed military and academic researchers to conduct sensitive government probes that would survive even in the event of a nuclear disaster. In developing the Net prototype for the military, the Rand Corporation, a Cold War think tank, conceptualized a communications network with no central authority. Ironically, one of the most hierarchically structured and centrally organized institutions in our culture, the national defense industry, created the Internet, possibly the least hierarchical and most decentralized social network ever conceived. Each computer hub in the Internet has similar status and power, so nobody can own the system outright and nobody has the power to kick others off the network. There isn't even a master power switch, so authority figures cannot shut off the Internet in an emergency. For one model of the Internet, see Figure 2.1.

The original military idea for the Internet called for a communications network with no central authority. In his book *Media Virus*, Douglas Rushkoff describes the concept: "Rather than establishing a potentially vulnerable central command post from which orders trickled out to other remote locations, each of thousands of locations in the system were capable of performing all the command functions. If messages from, say, Atlanta normally route through Dallas in order to reach Los Angeles, but the Dallas system were hit, the system would automatically reroute the message through other systems. Imagine a chain-link fence. Even if you punch out a big hunk of fence, the rest is still interconnected enough to conduct electricity."

During its developmental stage, the military computer network permitted different people in separate locations to communicate with one another. By simply leasing existing telephone lines, they used the system to send letters and memos electronically (e-mail) and to post information on computer *bulletin boards*, which are sites that list information about particular topics, such as health issues, computer programs, or employment services. At this stage, the Internet was mainly used by universities and government research labs, and later by corporations, especially companies involved in computer software and other high-tech products, to transmit and receive text information.

The Internet Is a Network of Networks

The Internet

ALT. XXXXX
REC. XXXXX
MISC. XXXX

©GAA GRAPHICS

Figure 2.1
The Structure of the Internet
Source: Eric Gagnon, *What's on the Internet*, Summer/Fall 1995 (Berkeley: Peachpit Press, 1995), 7.

Newsgroups are thousands of organized online conferences consisting of hundreds of individual messages, or **postings**, which are continuously broadcast over the Internet 24 hours a day. Newsgroups and their associated messages are organized according to a computer program called **Usenet**, which transmits newsgroups and their new messages to thousands of individual servers on the Internet.

Colleges and Universities were the first organizations to use the Internet for exchange of scientific research and for work by Computer Science departments. Many students who used the Internet in college now push their employers in private industry to link to the Net, fueling a rapid growth in its business use.

Electronic Mail is one of the Internet's major attractions. E-mail messages are flashed in seconds across the Net and end up on a single server where the recipient's Internet account resides (sort of like a home address).

The Internet consists of a central network, or **backbone**, of high-speed telephone lines designed specifically to carry an extremely high volume of computer data at an extremely high speed. It was created by the Department of Defense in the 1960s as a scientific research and military contractors' network. Universities, government agencies, and defense contractors were the first groups to connect to these high-speed computer links, but now commercial access providers can lease their own high-speed lines to get access to the Internet.

Servers are individual **host computers** owned and operated by corporations, universities, government agencies, and (sometimes) private individuals, all connected by special high-speed telephone lines to the Internet. You may connect to a server to download files, such as **FAQs** (using a process called **FTP**), or send mail messages to an individual whose Internet mail address resides there.

Commercial Internet Access Providers such as America Online, Compuserve, Delphi, Netcom, PSI, and others connect to the Internet via high-speed lines. Most people gain access to the Internet this way, since government and university funding and sponsorship of the Internet is rapidly giving way to ownership by many different telecommunications companies, both large and small.

Who's on the Net? Individuals who work for corporations, universities, or other organizations; students; and private individuals who purchase access from **commercial Internet public access** providers.

By 1982, the Net had hit its entrepreneurial stage: The National Science Foundation invested in a high-speed communication network designed to link computer centers around the country. This innovation permitted dramatically increased use of the Internet. Then, after the dissolution of the Soviet Union in the late 1980s, the ARPAnet military venture officially ended. By that time, however, a growing network of researchers, computer programmers, commercial interests, and amateur hackers had tapped into the Net, creating tens of thousands of decentralized intersections. As the military had predicted, the lack of central authority meant that the Net could not be knocked out. By 1993, the Net developed multimedia capability, allowing users to travel with pictures, sound, and video.

Just as most radio pioneers did not foresee the potential of radio, many pioneers of the Net did not predict how rapidly its mass appeal would spread beyond national and military interests. The Internet system comprises worldwide computer networks that communicate directly through Internet Protocol (IP), a computer language that allows any computer on any network to send data electronically to any other computer on an equal basis. The Internet today consists of fifty thousand regional computer networks called **servers**: individual "host" computer centers run (or hosted) by universities, corporations, and government agencies, all interconnected by special high-speed phone lines. In 1996, these networks served between twenty and forty million individual and institutional users per day.[4]

> "The Internet . . . works like a nonprofit food co-op; **it has no owner**, is managed by volunteers and derives operating costs from its members, who pay connection fees to large regional computer hubs that direct the system's traffic. . . ."
>
> —Steve Stecklow,
> *Wall Street Journal*,
> 1993

The Net allows users to find information on virtually any subject, to talk with computer pen pals all over the world, and to participate in discussions about favorite hobbies and social issues. Over the Net, users can also trade software, organize clubs, play games, arrange dates, find internships, and download articles, documents, and books. In the beginning, such connections took place in **newsgroups**, which now account for tens of thousands of loosely organized computer conferences consisting of bulletin boards and individual messages, or postings, which are circulated twenty-four hours a day.

Newsgroups come in two basic varieties: moderated and unmoderated. In a moderated group, a volunteer monitors the discussion topic by screening posted messages, deciding which are appropriate, and eliminating inappropriate "mail" for the whole group. Although some users complain that moderators exercise too much authority, this editorial control feature attempts to raise the quality of newsgroup content by eliminating clutter. By the mid-1990s, however, most of the newsgroups on the Net were unmoderated; no one did editorial screening, and what any user decided to contribute on a given day went out to all members of the group. Although the Internet can be a wild place, online *net-iquette* about the do's and don'ts of Internet behavior has gradually developed. See Figure 2.2.

Worldwide, millions of new participants log onto the Internet each month. Some have access through university accounts or their workplace, while others subscribe to regional hubs or national online services like America Online or Prodigy.

Within the last decade, Internet users have doubled each year, and the Net's environment has become known as *cyberspace*, the mysterious regions where the global networks of computer communication take their users. Transcending geographic borders, the millions of Net users worldwide have generally circumvented the authority of anybody bent on regulating it. In fact, many newsgroups take advantage of the Net's ability to cross borders, circulating banned or controversial writing or art that may have been suppressed by authoritarian governments in other nations.

Figure 2.2 Net-iquette

Source: Eric Gagnon, *What's on the Internet*, Summer/Fall 1995 (Berkeley: Peachpit Press, 1995), 21.

information access on the information highway

What generally distinguishes the information highway is not only the revolutionary ways in which data are stored and retrieved but also the increasing convergence of mass media. Two innovations make the information highway a particularly distinct mass medium. First, it is interactive, enabling receivers to respond almost immediately to senders' messages. Prior to the digital age, traditional print media had few feedback avenues, relying mainly on letters to the editor, which might or might not be acknowledged. Now, however, online print-media editors can respond more quickly to thousands of individual users. Whereas editors have traditionally restricted the number of letters they print due to space limitations, the information highway makes it possible to circulate most feedback letters.

The second way in which the information highway is innovative is that it enables many traditional media to appear on computer screens. Users can call up a magazine story, a music video, a banned book, or a radical newsletter. Previously, one mass media company delivered a product—a newspaper or TV program—to a mass audience. Now, however, the Internet multiplies the channels of delivery, thus transforming consumers' traditional interactions with the mass media. The Internet not only connects consumers to other media but it also personalizes this experience by allowing them to call up mass media on demand.

converging technologies

The information highway has blurred the boundary between point-to-point communication and mass communication. The highway has the potential to link home, school, and business computers, TV sets, telephones, radios, CD players, VCRs, e-mail, video games, newspapers, fax machines, magazines, and communication satellites. This capability makes it possible for many services—from computer software firms to cable TV companies to regional telephone services—to become players on the information highway.

Three key technological developments have made possible today's intersection of mass media along the information highway. The first innovation has involved **digital** communication. In digital technology, an image, text, or sound is converted into electronic signals represented as a series of binary numbers—ones and zeroes —which are then reassembled as a precise reproduction of an image, text, or sound. Used in computer technology since the 1940s, digital signals operate as pieces or *bits* (from *BI*nary digi*TS*) of information representing two values, such as yes/no, on/off, or 0/1. For example, a typical compact-disk track uses a binary code system in which zeroes are microscopic pits in the surface of the disk, while ones are represented on the unpitted surface. Used in various combinations, these digital codes can duplicate, store, and play back the most complex kinds of sounds.

The words in books, the images on television, and the voices over phone lines can all be converted into the digital ones and zeros that computers can "read" or process. With books, magazines, music, TV programs, movies, and phones all beginning to "speak the same language," they are merging onto a congested highway.

The second technological breakthrough, microtechnology, has enabled companies to produce miniature circuits that could process and store electronic signals. In the 1970s, the development of **microchips** and **microprocessors** squeezed or integrated thousands of electronic components into thin strands of silicon along which binary codes traveled. With this innovation, manufacturers could produce computers that were smaller, cheaper, and increasingly more powerful. In the mid-1990s, home computers were doubling in power about every eighteen months, and at the same time their cost was cut in half. Because of microtechnology, a single computer that now fits on a person's lap is more powerful than the bulky computer systems that once occupied entire floors in 1960s office buildings.

In the mid-1980s, the third technological development, **fiber-optic cable**, featured thin glass bundles of fiber capable of transmitting thousands of messages converted to shooting pulses of light. Fiber-optic technology has allowed information to be transported via lasers. With their ability to carry broadcast channels, telephone signals, and all sorts of digital codes, thin fiber-optic cables began replacing the older and bulkier copper wire used by phone and cable companies. Nicholas Negroponte, the founding director of MIT's Media Lab, points out that "a fiber the size of a human hair can deliver every issue ever made of the *Wall Street Journal* in less than one second."[5] With the increased speeds of the new media technology, few limits exist with regard to the amount of information that digital technology can transport. The chief problems now center on what to put on the information highway, who will run it, and who will have access.

Fiber-optic laser beams carry more than 150,000 times as much information as do older copper phone wire and coaxial TV cables. About forty fiber-optic strands together can carry more than a million digitally compressed telephone conversations or two thousand cable TV channels.

converging media

Digital technology now permits multiple and immediate computer access to traditional media such as newspapers, magazines, television programs, movies, and sound recordings. The term for this phenomenon is **media convergence**, whereby old and new media are available via the integration of personal computers and high-speed satellite-based phone links. For example, audio, video, and data technology are mixed in a number of forms, often offered in **CD-ROM** formats. The latest development in storing vast amounts of computer software and information, CD-ROM stands for *Compact-Disc Read-Only Memory*, which means that, unlike a floppy disk or an audio tape, new data cannot be entered or stored on a CD-ROM. A single CD-ROM holds as much information as seven hundred conventional floppy disks. An entire library's collection can now be stockpiled on several CD-ROMs that can fit into a student's backpack. In fact, most CD-ROM encyclopedias today far outsell their bulky print versions and are often included as part of the software package that comes with new computer systems.

A variety of books, magazines, newspapers, sound recordings, movies, and TV programs can also be obtained through various commercial online services and via the Internet. Traditional print media are getting up to speed on the information highway. Publishing companies such as Random House and McGraw-Hill have begun offering thousands of books on the Internet. Hundreds of major daily newspapers and smaller alternative papers not only provide their contents on the Internet but also offer computerized versions of classified ads.

mapping the internet

One of the major problems of the information highway, especially Internet intersections, has been its complexity and disorganization. Originally lacking any basic directory services, the networks were like an enormous free-floating library without a Dewey decimal system. This situation has changed. By the mid-1990s, two major mapping systems existed for negotiating the Internet's sprawling terrain. The first map featured the **World Wide Web,** initially a free and open system for organizing and standardizing information on the Internet. The Web moved the Internet from a message delivery system to a mass medium. The second mapping system was implemented by commercial online services such as America Online (AOL), CompuServe, Prodigy, and the Microsoft Network.

Internet history was made in 1994, when a group of California computer scientists, using a digital system called MBone (short for Multicast Backbone), made twenty minutes of a live Rolling Stones concert from Dallas available worldwide.

The World Wide Web. By the early 1990s, the World Wide Web had become the most frequently visited region of the Internet. Developed in the 1980s, the Web was initially a text-only data-linking system that allowed computer-accessed information to associate with, or link to, other information no matter where it was on the Internet. Known as *hypertext*, this data-linking feature of the Web was a breakthrough for those attempting to use the Internet. Hypertext allows a user to click on a highlighted word or phrase and skip directly to other files related to that subject in other computer systems. By using standardized software, today users can navigate through most features of the Internet, including text data such as e-mail and also photo image files, and video and audio clips. (See "Case Study: The Word and the Web" on page 44.)

By 1996, individuals, groups, and companies worldwide had established hundreds of thousands of "pages" or sites on the Web, promoting everything from a point of view to a job résumé to a wide variety of consumer products. A Web page can be designed on an ordinary word-processing program that has a feature for writing hypertext commands. Almost all national TV commercials now include the product's Web page address, where more information about a company or its product can be found. By early 1996, new pages on the Web were being launched at the extraordinary rate of one per minute.[6] Among the most popular Web sites, **browsers** are search services, like Netscape's Navigator and Microsoft's Explorer, which offer detailed organizational maps of the Web landscape. Many people use browsers to access popular content pages, such as HotWired (the multimedia version of *Wired* magazine), the University of Michigan's weather database, Time Warner's news and information service (Pathfinder), or ESPNET SportsZone (an Internet extension of the popular national cable sports channels).

Online Services. Although most individuals access the Internet through their university or business accounts, home users often purchase a commercial online service. Four or five companies have dominated in providing these services. Begun in the

A computer scientist at CERN, a European physics lab near Geneva, Switzerland, updates pages on the World Wide Web. The Web made the Internet more accessible, allowing users to navigate among computers all over the world.

mid-1980s, America Online (AOL), partially owned by the Tribune Company, is the largest. Late in 1996, when the company dropped its rate to a monthly flat fee of $19, service was so backed up that it took hours for customers to log on, creating a brief public-relations nightmare. By 1997, though, AOL had more than 8 million subscribers. In addition to providing access to the Internet and to thousands of software applications, AOL offers inroads to newspapers, magazines, and the TV networks. Other major online services include CompuServe, begun in the late 1970s by the tax firm H&R Block, and Prodigy, originated by IBM and Sears in the late 1980s. The computer software giant Microsoft entered the online business in 1995. Given the company's control of 80 percent of the home-computer software market, the Microsoft Network (MSN) quickly became a major player. It teamed up with NBC in 1996 to create the first national news channel available simultaneously on cable TV systems and on the World Wide Web. Alongside the national online services, hundreds of local services, many of them operated by regional telephone companies, also compete to offer consumer access to the Internet.

By the mid-1990s, online services offered access not only to other media but also to financial planning, stock information, weather reports, sports scores, computer games, travel and health tips, electronic shopping, and reference works. The availability of online services, accessible with a home computer, a telephone modem, and a monthly fee, has increased dramatically because of digital technology. Even medical information such as X-rays and CAT scans can be retrieved via computer and modem.

As computers and modems have become more affordable, and as fiber-optic connections have replaced copper wire in cable and phone lines, the "side streets" to new information have proliferated. Just as the interstate highway system helped create and expand suburban communities half a century ago, the information highway has produced what are frequently called **virtual communities**. These are users who are separated geographically but connected nationally and globally by their shared interests or business and their access to an online service or the Internet.

> "In less than three years, the Internet's World Wide Web has spawned some **10 million electronic documents** at a quarter million Web sites. By contrast, the Library of Congress has taken 195 years to collect 14 million books."
> —Tim Miller,
>   New Media Resources,
>   1995

The Word and the Web

by Edward Mendelson

When the Benedictine monks at the Monastery of Christ in the Desert, in New Mexico, created a Web site on the Internet, they claimed to be reviving a tradition that began when monastic scribes created the first illuminated manuscripts. One of the monks told a reporter for the *New York Times* that their work "goes back to the ancient tradition of the scribes, taking information and making it beautiful, into art." But the relation between modern Web sites and medieval scriptoria, or writing rooms, is even closer than these monks may have guessed. The technology that connects all the millions of pages on the World Wide Web derives ultimately from techniques invented by the scribes and scholars who copied out the Bible more than a thousand years ago.

The pages of the Web are connected by a system of hyperlinks—words, phrases, or pictures that, when you click on one with a mouse, will summon up another page to your computer screen, perhaps a page on a computer thousands of miles away. Medieval manuscripts of the Bible were the first books to be interconnected by a system of cross-references—marginal notes that directed a reader from one biblical passage to another, perhaps to a passage written at a distance of hundreds of years from the first. The marginal references to the Bible and the hyperlinks of the World Wide Web may be the only two systems ever invented that give concrete expression to the idea that everything in the world holds together, that every event, every fact, every datum is connected to every other. Where the two systems differ drastically is in what their connections mean.

A tenth-century monk reading a manuscript of the Book of Exodus might find a line under the verse "And the Lord went before them by day in a pillar of a cloud, to lead them the way." A note in the margin would refer him to a verse in another manuscript that included Paul's First Letter to the Corinthians: "Our fathers were under the cloud, and all passed through the sea; and were all baptized unto Moses in the cloud and in the sea." This gives a new meaning to the verse from Exodus, but also gives new meaning to verses in the Gospels about baptism, verses that the monk could find by tracing further cross-references in the margin of Paul's letters.

The system of hyperlinks connecting the pages of the World Wide Web suggests a world where connections are everywhere but are mostly meaningless, transient, fragile and unstable. A would-be monk in the twentieth century who visits the Web page of the Monastery of Christ in the Desert will find the exhortation "Don't miss our Thanks page." A few clicks, and he arrives at an image by a local artist, which will be replaced on screen automatically and randomly in a few seconds by another, and then another. You can create a link between your own Web page—the "homepage" that acts as a table of contents for all the pages linked to it—and someone else's homepage, but you have no assurance that the other person's page will display the same content from one day to the next.

In a world without tangible bodies or enduring memories, no one can keep promises. No one can even remember why they might be worth keeping. In the Bible, the connections between early and later books signify covenants that a personal God has already kept and promises that will be kept in the future. The connections between pages of the World Wide Web exist independently of space or time. The World Wide Web is touted by its evangelists as a force that will transform society in ways that no political revolution could ever accomplish. Until now the Web's main social achievement has been to provide a cure for spare time.

Another claim for the Web is that it is uniquely nonhierarchical, that it has no beginning and no end, no top or bottom, that it can be entered anywhere and traveled in any direction. In a strictly technical sense, all this is true, but in all practical and social senses, the Web dutifully reproduces all the hierarchies and inequalities of the world outside. Thousands of links point toward Web sites backed by fame, money, and power. Far fewer scattered links point toward sites posted by the obscure and impoverished. A thousand students can insert in their homepages a link to the page dedicated to a rock group like

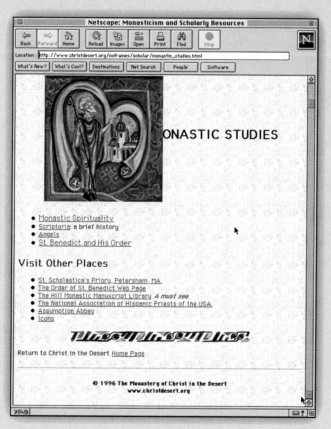

Sonic Youth, but Sonic Youth's homepage contains no link to any of the students' pages.

Biblical cross-references, unlike most of the links on the World Wide Web, always point in both directions. A link from the Old Testament to the New is mirrored by a link from the New to the Old. Some parts of the Bible are more densely cross-referenced than others—the margins of the dietary laws in Leviticus are mostly blank—but the annotators of the Bible believed that every word was equally inspired, that it was their own fault if they had not yet found all the connections that the Bible contained. Some passages of the Bible were more difficult than others, but all were available to be read and studied. The Web, on the other hand, has secret pages accessible only to those who know a password, and others accessible only to those willing to pay....

The greatest difference between the cross-references in the Bible and the links on the World Wide Web is the difference between words written on parchment or paper in books that were meant to last forever and words written on the transient phosphorescence of a computer screen, where they will soon be effaced by others. This may or may not be the same contrast, written down 1900 years ago, between the wise man who built his house upon rock and the foolish man who built his house upon sand.

Source: Edward Mendelson, "The Word and the Web," *New York Times Book Review*, June 2, 1996, p. 35.

During the O.J. Simpson trial in 1995, for instance, one of his attorneys, Harvard law professor Alan Dershowitz, participated in the California proceedings even though he was watching on cable's Court TV in his Boston-area office. Using a fax machine and the Internet, his staff was able to route on-the-spot cross-examination questions and concerns to other defense lawyers in Los Angeles. At the time, Dershowitz told a CNN reporter, "We made *virtual* . . . and *cyber* objections." Although the information highway is able to collapse space and distance to create these virtual places, many of the new technologies remain expensive and consequently unavailable to citizens of more modest means.

ownership issues on the internet

Our contemporary era is distinguished not only by the revolutionary ways in which data are transmitted but also by the increasing convergence of owners and players in mass media industries. Large media firms, such as Disney and Time Warner, are buying up smaller companies and spreading their economic interests among books, magazines, music, movies, radio, television, cable, and Internet channels.

At this point, the economics of newly emerging and converging media remains open and freewheeling. Like the automobile or film industries of an earlier era, many players and companies are jockeying for position. With the passage of the Telecommunications Act of 1996, most regional and long-distance phone companies can now participate in both cable and Internet-access businesses. The phone companies, like cable TV firms, have the added advantage of controlling the wires into most American homes and businesses. As cable and phone companies gradually convert older wiring into high-speed fiber-optic lines, they are wrestling for control of Internet circuitry and intensifying the battle over mass communication delivery systems.

a clash of values

Discussing the economic implications of the information highway, critics Daniel Burstein and David Kline associate the Internet with a series of personality traits: "Free. Egalitarian. Decentralized. Ad hoc. Open and peer-to-peer. Experimental. Autonomous. Anarchic." They contrast these traits to the personality of modern business organizations: "For profit. Hierarchical. Systematized. Planned. Proprietary. Pragmatic. Accountable. Organized and reliable."[7] Given this clash of values, the development of the Internet should remain unstable and dynamic over the next several years, despite the attempts to commercialize access to the Net's vast regions. Unlike phone, movie, broadcast network, and cable TV businesses, where ownership has become increasingly consolidated in the hands of a few powerful firms, many parts of the Internet have so far eluded centralization. In fact, the Internet is less likely to suffer from the same economic limits of other mass media because it was not designed to be an efficiently managed, tightly controlled, and secure system.

future control of the internet

The Federal Communications Commission (FCC) was originally set up in the late 1920s and early 1930s to protect the public's interest in broadcasting. Ultimately, however, this government body mainly served the interests of private entrepreneurs and narrowed access to our public airwaves. This pattern is being repeated with the Internet. In the late 1980s, the government officially bowed out as the Internet's major operator and was superseded by a wide variety of public and private concerns.

With many pathways along the information highway now dictated by corporate and commercial interests, critics predict that Internet programs in particular will increasingly favor those who have the money to develop content or technology. The favored ones are likely to be business firms and university research institutes, which depend on large corporations for funding. By 1994, several noncommercial university consortiums, which had been running regional computer hubs and Internet services, began selling the rights to manage their services to private corporations. Businesses maintain that they can provide improved services at affordable costs. Critics warn, though, that the increasing privatization of Internet services could threaten its continued development as a democratic network of relatively equal individuals and institutions, free from government or corporate control.

Although the government has taken a less central role in developing and maintaining the Internet, what is still to be determined is who will manage the information and communication systems of the future. For instance, some traditional broadcasters and cable operators, often at odds in the past, have joined forces. They are linked by a common purpose: to ensure that telephone companies are seriously challenged in the race to convert copper wire to fiber-optic systems and to sign subscribers to the newest media services.

citizens, cyberspace, and democracy

Throughout the twentieth century, Americans have closely examined emerging mass media for their potential contributions to democracy and culture. As radio became more affordable in the 1920s and 1930s, we hailed the medium for its ability to reach and entertain even the poorest Americans caught in the Great Depression. When television developed in the 1950s and 1960s, it also held promise as a medium that could reach everyone, even those who were illiterate or cut off from printed information. But as broadcasting evolved, the growth of commercial channels far outpaced the emergence of viable nonprofit channels as fewer and fewer corporations gained more and more control. In the 1980s and 1990s, these issues have resurfaced. Many praise the Internet sector of the information highway for its democratic possibilities and for its accessibility. Some advocates even tout it as the most decentralized social network ever conceived.

Unlike many media industries, the Internet has developed from the "bottom up." Just as amateur radio operators influenced the growth of wireless communication in the early twentieth century, the development of the Internet owes a large debt to amateurs—students, engineers, and assorted computer buffs.

There are several disadvantages, however, to the decentralized nature of the Internet. One drawback has been the increased circulation of data and "news," sometimes called *cyberspace litter*—the Internet equivalent of unwanted junk mail or newspaper advertising supplements. Unlike traditional news media, which routinely employ editors as information gatekeepers, many individuals and newsgroups on the Internet send out data that are not checked by anyone. Most news media screen material for accuracy, fairness, appropriateness, and decency, but such screening is more difficult to accomplish on the Internet. With far less editorial interference in cyberspace, far more misinformation tends to leak through. Still, the Internet offers a diverse array of communication models. In such a decentralized system, millions of message groups send out bits of information, allowing millions of other interested users to receive and respond. Instead of the few-to-many model of traditional media, the Internet offers more opportunities for both one-to-one and many-to-many communication encounters.

free expression and security nightmares

In the 1990s, no Internet issue has commanded more attention than arguments about the suitability of cyberspace material. The Communications Decency Act, a controversial provision in the 1996 Telecommunications Act, banned indecent and obscene cyberspace material that children might be able to access. But First Amendment advocates doubted whether the government could enforce such a ban, and in June 1997 the Supreme Court struck down the act as unconstitutional (see "Tracking Technology: Regulating the Internet"). Battles over inappropriate material have been part of the story of most mass media, from debates over lurid pulp fiction in the nineteenth century to opposition to sexually explicit themes and images during film's early years. More recently, the demand for X-rated movies helped drive the VCR–video store boom of the 1980s, and today eliminating some forms of sexual content from television remains a top priority for many politicians and groups.

Although the "back alleys of sex chat" and the "off-road environment" of the Internet have drawn considerable public attention, early studies estimate that less than 1 percent of all communication on the Internet is pornographic.[8] Many commercial online services and some informal newsgroups have instituted rules aimed at curbing inappropriate language and material at sites children might visit. Nonetheless, the Internet's controversial alt.sex stop ranked as its third most visited region in the mid-1990s.

Another key issue involves Internet security. Both private users and public institutions are concerned about government agencies invading their privacy through home and business computers. With the growing use of personal computers in the 1980s, concerns have increased over intrusion into bank accounts, hospital records, and other private matters. A high-profile 1995 case highlighted another problem. A computer hacker stole twenty thousand credit card numbers from a subscriber list of one of the country's largest Internet-access providers. The puzzled FBI called on another computer expert, Tsutmo Shimomura, a San Diego researcher, who tracked down the thief after he broke into Shimomura's home computer. To counter cyberspace theft, MasterCard and BankAmericard joined with the software firm Netscape in the mid-1990s to develop a system that would allow consumers to buy products online without their credit card numbers being hijacked.

Consumers, however, remain concerned. According to surveys on the commercial uses of the Web, conducted periodically by the University of Michigan's Business School, Web sites are used much more often for gathering information than for actually making product purchases. The fall 1995 survey examined responses from twenty-three thousand Web users in seventy-five different countries. The respondents, whose median annual income was $63,000, expressed more anxiety over security issues than they had in earlier surveys. The researchers also found that women (who accounted for 29 percent of the respondent pool) were especially skeptical about buying products on commercial Web sites.

One firm that monitors Internet security problems reported more than 2,200 security breaches in 1994 alone, double the 1993 figure.[9] According to government

TRACKING TECHNOLOGY

Regulating the Internet

By Michael M. Epstein

As the number of Internet users doubled and tripled in the mid-1990s, politicians and social activists were faced with a complicated question: Should the government regulate the flow of information on the Internet and, if so, how? The question is complicated because the laws of the United States have always treated telephone calls, broadcasts, and printed words very differently in terms of the censorship of inappropriate or indecent speech. Although people who make obscene or harassing calls can be prosecuted, the telephone company that carries the call is not held responsible for the misdeeds of the caller. Radio and television broadcasters, however, who are licensed to use government-owned airwaves in the public interest, are subject to greater regulation of speech content. Networks and individual stations are frequently held legally responsible for inaccuracy and indecency under federal law and the rules of the Federal

Communications Commission, even if the transgression was committed by a third party. Printed materials such as books, newspapers, and magazines are virtually free of regular censorship by government, except in the relatively rare instances when obscene statements or images are deemed to have violated local community standards.

Concerned that unrestricted access to the Internet would put children at risk, the U.S. Congress passed the Communications Decency Act (the CDA) in early 1996. This act made it a felony to transmit obscene, indecent, or harassing material on computer networks where children may see it. Because children have the same access to the Internet as everyone else, the CDA was widely viewed as an effort to hold Internet users legally accountable for the adult-oriented content of their speech, whether or not the speech was directed at children. Over the objections of free-speech advocates like the ACLU, the American Library Association, and the Center for Technology and Democracy,

President Clinton signed the CDA into law on February 8, 1996.

With the enactment of the CDA, Congress and the president had finally declared that the Internet should be regulated like a broadcast medium, or so it seemed. On June 12, 1996, a federal court in Philadelphia decided otherwise. Concluding that the CDA violated the First Amendment because it was "overly broad," the court found that the Internet's "unique and democratic nature" required it to be treated differently from broadcast media. Supporters of the CDA began arguing their case before the Supreme Court in 1997. Opponents of the CDA maintained that the Internet should not be treated any differently from bookstores, libraries, and record shops, where most adult-oriented material is available without restriction. In June 1997, the Supreme Court overturned the CDA as unconstitutional.

Michael Epstein is an attorney and writer. His University of Michigan doctoral dissertation is on images of lawyers in popular culture.

estimates, hackers broke into 350 Defense Department security systems in 1994. Some experts estimate that the number of hacker invasions of computer defense systems over the past few years is as high as 300,000.[10] These invasions point to one of the main problems of the Internet: Due to decentralization and the expertise of computer hackers, it is extremely difficult to patrol and police the Internet. The knowledge of hackers often exceeds that of the groups attempting to supervise the system.

competing highways and the knowledge gap

By the mid-1990s, two economic models emerged to represent the future of the information highway. One model features a one-way communication framework with traditional cable and broadcast TV services providing content on vast five-hundred-

■ SCIENCE & SOCIETY

Hatemongering on the data highway

Bigotry carves out a niche in cyberspace

Chicago computer buff Bob Arbetman was happily surfing through cyberspace one night when his attention was drawn to a bulletin board offering titled HOLOHOAX.TXT. Tapping in, Arbetman found himself in touch with a professional Holocaust denier whose message, he says, was rabidly antisemitic. "It was straight neo-Nazi propaganda," recalls the 37-year-old electrical engineer.

Outraged by what he was downloading, Arbetman alerted the Simon Wiesenthal Center, the Los Angeles-based institute that exposes neo-Nazis and other bigots. His tip and calls from others who had encountered similar online, often violent, antiblack, antigay, antisemitic hate messages triggered an extensive three-year investigation by Wiesenthal researcher Rick Eaton. The result, *U.S. News* has learned, is a massive dossier of cyberspace hate-mongering that the Wiesenthal Center has just submitted to FCC Chairman Reed Hundt. "It may be time for the FCC to place a cop on the superhighway of information," says Rabbi Abraham Cooper, Wiesenthal Center associate dean.

A right to hate. But any attempt to police cyberspace is fraught with practical and legal issues.

television or radio, and so subject to control, or more like the telephone system or the mail, which have greater freedoms over the content of the messages. Unless hate mail directly interferes with civil liberties, insists Godwin, "I can't conceive

invitations to violence and hate. A file called HOMOBASH describes shooting a gay person in the face with a handgun. A graphic titled MONKEY pictures blacks copulating with animals and suggests this was the start of the AIDS epidemic. Another shows a bare-chested, hooknosed Jew holding a bloody knife and standing in a sea of gentile blood.

Some commercial networks, such as Prodigy, say they have taken steps to ban the use of their systems by propagandists of bias. Vinton Cerf, president of the Internet Society, a user organization, says he and his colleagues are preparing a set of voluntary norms they hope will put restraints on racists and other objectionable E-mailers. But guidelines may have little effect in a freewheeling venue such

While the Internet has the potential to spread ideas worldwide, it can also be used to spread pornography, hate speech, and other close-minded ideas. Lewis Lapham, editor of *Harper's*, warns us about the digital highway as a place that can *exclude* as often as it *includes*: "We need never see or talk to anybody with whom we don't agree."

channel systems. For example, a viewer at home could watch and monitor congressional proceedings on cable's two C-Span channels. According to this model, consumers and citizens are rather passive players in the mass communication process, choosing from a smorgasbord of available services that others have designed. The second framework offers a telephone or computer model. It has an interpersonal or two-way channel system with users playing more active roles in the information process, often designing their own Web sites and picking their conversational partners. In this model, users participate in producing and delivering program services. Through e-mail or a newsgroup, they can contact representatives in Congress and receive quick responses, either directly from legislators or from an office staffer about a specific issue featured on C-Span. In this model, anyone in the system can theoretically contact anyone else.

From the vantage point of which model best serves democracy, many observers predict that by the year 2000 the best ideas from both models will emerge. In such a scenario, telephone companies, computer services, cable operators, broadcast interests, powerful leaders, elite entrepreneurs, and ordinary citizens would all play roles in extending the highway and ensuring enough entry ramps for everyone who wants to ride. Under a combination model, a large chunk of the highway would operate more like cable public-access channels, in which viewers and citizens actively participate in the development and direction of programming and content.

One key economic issue is whether the cost of the information highway will undermine equal access. For example, converting the system to fiber optics will cost an estimated $15 billion by the end of the twentieth century. Paying for this conversion could result in an ever widening **knowledge gap**. Mimicking the economic disparity between rich and poor that grew more pronounced during the 1980s, the knowledge gap refers to the growing contrast between "information haves," or digital highway users who can afford to acquire multiple media services, and "information have-nots," who cannot afford a computer much less the many options now available on the highway. Although monthly programming services might become relatively inexpensive, the combined costs of computer technology and cable programming may make easy access to the highway less realizable for less-affluent citizens.

Media critic Marc Gunther offers an analogy about access to virtual and real highways: "If the information highway becomes a vital communications link in the 21st Century, who will be able to ride? . . . The interstates of the 1950s helped relocate jobs to the suburbs and beyond, leaving city folks stranded unless they owned cars."[11] Whereas traditional media made the same information available to everyone with a radio or TV set, the information highway could create economic tiers and classes of service. It could become a toll road rather than a freeway, with wealthy users buying many tiers of service. Policy groups, media critics, and concerned citizens continue to debate the implications of media access for democratic societies, which have traditionally valued the equal opportunity to acquire knowledge.

Jeff Stahler, reprinted by permission of Newspaper Enterprise Association, Inc.

problems and possibilities

Current developments on the information highway, including the roles of broadcasting and cable, are at a crossroads comparable to the early development of radio. In the 1920s, corporate interests in radio pushed aside many noncommercial and civic interests. Similarly, in today's digital environment corporate interests, not government agencies, are building and programming the new systems. With the passage of the 1996 Telecommunications Act, the federal government has cleared the way for cable TV systems, computer firms, and telephone companies to merge their interests in advancing communication technology. Companies such as AT&T and the regional Bell phone companies, for instance, have the ready capital to invest in the new information systems.

By the mid-1990s, Internet users were doubling in number every few months, thus greatly increasing its possibilities and intensifying problems for agencies trying to regulate it. If the past is any predictor, it seems realistic to expect that the Internet's potential for wide democratic use could be partially preempted by narrower commercial interests. As media economist Douglas Gomery warns: "Technology alone does not a communication revolution make. Economics trumps technology every time."[12]

With economic interests trumping technological innovation, a major concern about the information highway relates to corporate downsizing. To reduce payroll overhead, many companies are using sophisticated computer technologies, managed by legions of part-time and full-time computer wizards. This change has reduced traditional job possibilities:

> [T]op down corporate hierarchies are flattening into horizontal, decentralized networks of self-governing work teams. But this flattening process is also crushing and marginalizing millions of once productive citizens. Whole strata of blue-collar and white-collar workers are being downsized into oblivion, their work now performed more efficiently by networked information systems or farmed out to cheap-labor production centers in new global markets overseas.[13]

From the early to mid-1990s, U.S. companies eliminated nearly three million jobs under restructuring plans; much of the downsizing was made possible by the speed and efficiency of new communications technologies.[14]

On the more positive side of the ledger, the new technologies offer at least the potential for enriching democratic processes. Books, newspapers, magazines, radio, film, and television widened and expanded the reach of media, but they did not generate equivalent avenues for response and debate. Defenders of the digital age argue that newer media forms—from radio talk shows to televised town-hall meetings to Internet newsgroups—allow more participation. In response to these forms, older print media are using Internet technology to increase their access to and feedback from varied audiences.

Despite the potential of new media forms, skeptics raise doubts about the participatory nature of discussions on the Internet. For instance, critics warn that Internet users may be searching out only those people whose beliefs and values are similar to their own. Although it is important to be able to communicate across vast distances with people who have similar viewpoints, these kinds of cyberspace discussions may not serve to extend the diversity and tolerance that are central to democratic ideals.

> "Unfortunately, there has been far too little discussion of the **deeper citizenship issues** that stir like fault pressures beneath the bedrock surface of the emerging Information Highway."
> —Mitch Kapor,
> founder,
> Lotus software,
> 1993

Access to information also remains a problem. More than 98 percent of all U.S. homes have TV sets, but 7 percent of American households, most of them poor, still do not have basic telephone service, much less the modems and computers needed to join the Internet. By 1997, fewer than 45 percent of American homes had personal computers, and fewer than 30 percent used modems.[15] In addition, even with a computer and modem, connecting to an online service and the Internet generally requires another substantial monthly fee.

Some communities and organizations are beginning to address the access problem. By installing computers with Internet connections in libraries, banks, and other public locations, they give most community members entry to the Internet, thus encouraging public discussions about taxes, homelessness, rent control, unemployment, and other pressing issues of the day.

With serious concerns that the information highway will be available only to the most affluent or educated in society, many communities have begun offering access to Internet and World Wide Web services through public libraries, like this one in Liverpool, New York.

To take a critical position on the information highway debates, we must analyze and judge its possibilities and limitations. Such a position should be grounded in the knowledge that the media are converging nationally and globally, changing the nature of mass communication. One of these changes is *mass customization*, whereby product companies and content providers can customize a Web page or media form for an individual consumer. For example, Individual Inc., a Massachusetts firm, operates a Web site and online service called NewsPage. Potential customers who "hit" the site can choose from among 850 business-related news issues and categories. After a user completes a consumer profile, Individual Inc.'s software scours 15,000 daily and weekly stories generated by 600 magazines, newspapers, and newsletters, and provides "a customized digest on demand for each user."[16] The user cost for this service is between $3 and $7 per month. Such a service blurs the boundary between one-to-one communication, which we generally associate with an office conversation or a telephone call, and mass communication, which we associate with daily newspapers or TV programs.

It is also no longer very useful to discuss print media and electronic or digital media as if they were completely segregated forms. We live in a world where a ten-year-old can simultaneously watch an old TV rerun on cable and read the latest *Fear Street* book, where a twenty-year-old student can make sense of a nineteenth-century poem while wearing a Walkman radio tuned to alternative rock. Moreover, it is now possible to access old reruns, horror thrillers, classic literary texts, and alternative music all through a home computer and modem. Today, developments in word processing, e-mail, books on tape, cable-access channels, children's pictorial literature, magazine advertising, and Internet newsgroups are integrating aspects of both print and electronic culture at the crossroads of everyday life. By 1997, more than 50 million people worldwide had logged on to the Internet, many of them as producers as well as consumers of mass communication.

REVIEW QUESTIONS

1. What are the three stages in the development of a mass medium?

2. How did the Internet originate? What does its development have in common with earlier mass media?

3. What is media convergence? How does this phenomenon distinguish a different phase in mass media history?

4. What three key technological developments have made possible today's intersection of mass media along the information highway?

5. How does the World Wide Web work? Why is it significant in the development of the Internet?

6. What are the differences and similarities between Internet-based services and commercial online computer services?

7. What are the key issues involving the ownership of the Internet? How are these issues different from earlier ownership issues in other mass media?

8. Who are the major players vying for control of the Internet?

9. What are the central concerns about the Internet regarding freedom of expression?

10. What is the knowledge gap, and what does it have to do with the information highway?

11. What are the key problems involving the expansion of the information highway? How can it make democracy work better?

QUESTIONING THE MEDIA

1. If you have been on the Internet, what was your first encounter like? If you have not used the Internet, go to your school or local library and sign on so that you can participate in the other questions that follow.

2. What features of the information highway are you most excited about? Why? What features are most troubling? Why?

3. What are the advantages of an electronic-digital highway that links together televisions, computers, phones, audio equipment, homes, schools, and offices?

4. Do you think virtual communities are genuine communities? Why or why not?

5. As we move from a print-oriented Industrial Age to a digitally based Information Age, what do you think the effects will be on individuals, communities, and nations?

Pick one of the assignments below.

1. Create a one- to two-page profile of a typical Internet user. Interview five to ten people—students, friends, teachers, employers, or other users—who travel the Internet at least two or three times each week. Find out what sites they visit and how much time they spend per day on the Internet. What do these users have in common? Are there different types of Net users? Consider their gender, age, education, occupation, and other pertinent background information. What do the users consider to be the benefits and drawbacks of the Internet?

2. Form teams and use the Internet or World Wide Web to find information about current mass media products. For example, find reviews of movies and compare the Internet information to reviews in traditional print media. Find Internet or Web reviews of a current CD and compare that information with what is available in print media.

   To accompany your findings, create some sort of comparative chart to keep track of the information you or your team collect.

Sound Recording
and Popular Music

There was little in her background to suggest that by her mid-thirties her music would not be welcome in one of the nation's largest retail chains. Born in Kennett, Missouri, in 1962, she twirled batons and ran track in high school. A gifted singer, she learned to play piano, accordion, and guitar. At the University of Missouri, she performed in a band called Cashmere and earned enough credits to land a job teaching music in a St. Louis grade school. At age twenty-four, she left Missouri for Los Angeles, where she worked as a backup singer for Michael Jackson, Don Henley, Eric Clapton, and Rod Stewart.[1]

Then in 1993, Sheryl Crow launched a solo career. In 1994, her single "All I Wanna Do" soared to the top of the pop charts, making her a star. Crow's first album, *Tuesday Night Music Club*, sold nine million copies. In 1995, she won three Grammy Awards, including one for Best New Artist.

In 1996, the singer hit a snag. "Love Is a Good Thing," a song from her new CD, upset executives at Wal-Mart, the nation's largest retail store and biggest seller of popular music. The song contained the following lyrics: "Watch out sister / watch out brother / watch our children as they kill each other / with a gun they bought at the Wal-Mart Discount stores."

Wal-Mart banned the album.

Throughout the 1990s, Wal-Mart had won praise from parents and politicians for banishing music with explicit sexual or violent lyrics. With seventy million customers walking its aisles each year, the retailer decided not to stock recordings that contained advisory labels and even altered questionable covers. But in Crow's case, her *Sheryl Crow* CD contained neither an advisory nor a controversial cover. Although Wal-Mart does not sell guns to minors, in a few incidents involving juveniles police traced weapons and ammunition back to isolated Wal-Mart stores. In fact, in 1994 the company stopped selling handguns in its stores. For her part, Crow worried that without Wal-Mart her family and fans in remote areas would be unable to find her music. In a few cities during the Crow affair, imaginative deejays distributed copies of her CD in Wal-Mart parking lots. Meanwhile, at Crow's concerts fans continued to call out for "the Wal-Mart song."

> "If people knew what this stuff was about, we'd probably **all get arrested**."
> —Bob Dylan, 1966

Throughout history, popular music has been banned by parents, business outlets, radio stations, school officials, and even governments seeking to protect young people from the raw language and corrupting excesses of the music world. At a time when various forms of rock music have become an ever-present annoyance to many, we forget that in the late 1700s authorities in Europe, thinking it immoral for young people to dance so close together, outlawed the waltz as "savagery." A hundred years later, the Argentinian upper class tried to suppress the tango, whose urban roots could be traced to the bars and bordellos of Buenos Aires. The first Latin music and dance to gain international popularity, the tango migrated to Paris in the early nineteenth century where the clergy condemned its impact on French youth. During the 1920s, some adults criticized the Charleston, a dance that featured cheek-to-cheek contact by partners. Rock and roll in the 1950s and rap in the 1990s added their chapters to the age-old battle between generations.

The medium of sound recording has had an immense impact on our culture. The music that helps to shape our identities and comfort us during the transition from childhood to adulthood resonates throughout our lives. It stirs debate among parents and teenagers, teachers and students, politicians and performers. To place the impact of popular music in context, we will begin by investigating the origins of recording's technological "hardware." We will review Thomas Edison's early phonograph, Emile Berliner's invention of the flat disk record, and the development of audiotape and compact disks. We will study radio's early threat to sound recording and the subsequent alliance between the two media when television arrived in the 1950s.

In this chapter, we will also examine the content and culture of the music industry. The predominant role of rock music is a key reference point. Many important forms of music have become popular—including classical, tango, jazz, salsa, country, blues, gospel, rap, and folk—but no other musical form has had such an extraordinary impact on reshaping other mass media forms. With the introduction of music videos in the early 1980s, rock music dramatically changed the cable and TV landscapes. More significantly, rock music simultaneously linked and transformed the fundamental structure of *two* mass media industries, sound recording and radio. Beginning in the 1950s, rock music created an enormous and enduring consumer youth market for sound recordings, and it provided much-needed content for radio at a time when television "borrowed" most of radio's long-time programming. Rock music has influenced a diverse array of international cultures, operating as a kind of common ground for fans worldwide. In this chapter, we will look at rock and other contemporary forms of popular music to survey the growth of sound recording as a mass medium. Finally, we will examine economic and democratic issues facing the recording industry.

early technology and the development of sound recording

New mass media have often been defined in terms of the communication technology that preceded them. For example, movies were initially called *motion pictures*, a term from photography that stuck; radio was referred to as *wireless telegraphy*; and television was often called *picture radio*. Sound recording instruments were initially labeled *talking machines* and later called the *phonograph*, when Thomas Edison made a recording device in 1877 that played back voices. Edison's invention came from tinkering with existing innovations, the tele*phone* and tele*graph*. The origin of *tele-* is the Greek word for far off; *phono-* and *-graph* come from the Greek words for sound and writing. This early blending of technology foreshadowed our contemporary era, in which media as different as newspapers and movies are converging, both now accessible on the information highway. Before the Internet, however, the first major media convergence involved the relationship between the sound recording and radio industries.

wax cylinders and flat disks

In the 1850s, French printer Leo Scott de Martinville conducted the first experiments with sound recording. Using a hog's hair bristle as a needle, he tied one end to a thin membrane stretched over the narrow part of a funnel. When the inventor spoke into the funnel, the membrane vibrated, and the free end of the bristle made grooves on a revolving cylinder coated with a thick liquid material called *lamp black*. Different sounds made different trails in the lamp black. However, de Martinville could not figure out how to play back the sound. That is what Thomas Edison did in 1877. He recorded his voice by using a needle to press his voice's sound waves onto tinfoil wrapped around a metal cylinder about the size of a cardboard toilet-paper roll. After recording his voice, Edison played it back by repositioning the needle to retrace the grooves in the foil, a material he later replaced with wax.

As we discussed in Chapter 2, most new media pass through three developmental stages. The first is the novelty stage, in which inventors experiment to solve a particular problem, such as how to play back recorded music. In the second or entrepreneurial stage, inventors and investors work out a practical and marketable use for the new device. Edison, for example, initially thought of his phonograph as a kind of answering machine; he envisioned a "telephone repeater" that would "provide invaluable records, instead of being the recipient of momentary and fleeting communication."[2]

In the third stage, entrepreneurs figure out how to market the new device as a consumer product. For sound recording, a key breakthrough at this stage came from Emile Berliner, a German engineer who had immigrated to America. In the late 1880s, he began using a flat spinning five-inch disk to trace voices. Through a photo-engraving process, he recorded the sounds onto disks made of metal and shellac. These disks became the first records. Using Edison's ideas, Berliner developed a machine for playing his disks on the first turntable, which he called the *gramophone*.

Berliner also developed a technique that allowed him to stamp and mass-produce his round records. Previously, using Edison's cylinder, performers had to play or sing into the speaker for *each* separate recording. Berliner's technique featured a master recording from which copies could be easily duplicated in mass quantities. In addition, the industry realized that disks needed to have places for labels, so that the music could be differentiated by title, performer, and songwriter. This led to the development of a "star system" because fans could identify and choose their favorite sounds and artists.

Now is the time to select your Victrola for Christmas

Victrola Instruments and Victor Records are so much in demand for gifts that there is a shortage every Christmas. Place your order now while all the twenty-one instrument styles at from $25 up and complete record stocks are available.

Ask your dealer or write to us for illustrated catalogs.

Victrola

Look under the lid and on the labels for these Victor trade marks

Victor Talking Machine Company, Camden, N.J.

This ad for a Victrola ran in magazines in 1922. RCA bought the company in the late 1920s and adopted Victrola's famous "His Master's Voice" trademark, which became one of the most famous trademarks of the twentieth century.

Another breakthrough occurred in the early twentieth century, when the Victor Talking Machine Company placed the hardware, or "guts," of the record player inside a piece of furniture. These early record players, known as Victrolas, were mechanical and had to be primed with a crank handle. Electric record players, first available in 1925, became more widely used in the late 1920s as more homes got electricity.

In the 1940s, since shellac was needed for World War II munitions production, the record industry turned to a polyvinyl plastic record. The vinyl recordings turned out to be more durable than shellac records, which broke easily. In 1948, CBS Records introduced the 33⅓-revolutions-per-minute (rpm) *long-playing record* (LP) with about ten minutes of music on each side. This was an improvement over the three to four minutes of music contained on the existing 78-rpm records. The next year, RCA developed a competing 45-rpm record, featuring a quarter-size hole (best suited for jukebox use). The two new standards were technically incompatible, meaning they could not be played on each other's machines. A five-year marketing battle ensued, similar to the VHS and Beta war over consumer video standards in the 1980s. In 1953, CBS and RCA compromised. The 33⅓ record became the standard for long-playing albums and collections of music, and 45s became the format for two-sided singles. Record players were designed to accommodate 45s, 33⅓ LPs, and for a while 78s. The 78-rpm record, however, eventually became obsolete, doomed to antique collections along with Edison's wax cylinders.

audiotape and cds

Berliner's flat disk would be the key recording advancement until **audiotape** in the 1940s, when German engineers developed plastic magnetic tape (which U.S. soldiers confiscated at the end of the war). Lightweight magnetized strands of ribbon finally allowed sound editing and multiple-track mixing, in which instrumentals or vocals could be recorded at one location and mixed later onto a master recording in another studio.

The first machines developed to play magnetized audiotape were bulky reel-to-reel machines. But by the 1950s, engineers had placed reel-to-reel audiotapes inside small plastic cassettes. Audiotape also permitted "home dubbing": consumers could copy their favorite records onto tape or record cuts off the radio. This practice denied sales to the worried recording industry; during a period from the mid to late 1970s, record sales dropped by 20 percent. Video games hit the market in the late 1970s, adding a new wrinkle to the competition for consumers' dollars. Meanwhile, blank audiotape sales doubled. Some thought audiotape would kill record albums due to its superior sound and editing capability, but commercial sales of albums did not plummet until the compact disk came along in the 1980s.

In 1958, engineers developed stereophonic sound, or **stereo**, which eventually made monophonic (one-track) records obsolete. Stereo permitted the recording of two separate channels or tracks of sound. Recording studio engineers, using audiotape,

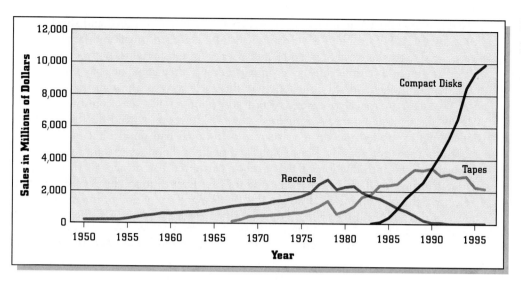

Figure 3.1
Annual Record,
Tape, and CD Sales

could now record many instrumental or vocal tracks, which they "mixed down" to the two stereo tracks. When the channels were played back through two loudspeakers, the sound was fuller and seemed to compete in space apart from the loudspeakers.

The biggest recording advancement came in the 1970s when electrical engineer Thomas Stockham developed **digital recording**, in which music is played back by laser beam rather than by needle or magnetic tape. Digital recorders translate sound waves into computer-like on/off impulses and store the impulses on disks in binary code. When played back, the laser decodes or "reads" the stored impulses; a microprocessor translates these numerical codes into sound and sends them through the loudspeakers. This technique began replacing Edison's **analog recording** technique, which merely captured the fluctuations of the original sound waves and stored those signals on records or cassettes as a continuous stream of magneticism—*analogous* to the actual sound. Incorporating purer, more precise digital techniques (which do not add noise during recording and editing sessions), **compact disks**, or **CDs**, hit the market in 1983.

By 1987, CD sales had doubled LP album sales (see Figure 3.1). Although audio-cassette sales outnumbered CD sales two to one as recently as 1988, by 1994 CDs out-sold cassettes two to one. To compete with CDs, some manufacturers introduced digital cassette tapes with improved sound quality. One such format, *digital audiotape* (DAT), was introduced by Japanese engineers in the early 1990s. DAT featured CD-quality sound on a machine that could record as well as play back tapes. As a consumer product, the new tape format, even with its recording and dubbing capacity, could not overcome the head start of CDs. By 1997, more than 65 percent of all American households had a CD player and seemed reluctant to invest in new incompatible formats.

surviving the threat of radio

By 1915, the phonograph had become a popular form of entertainment. The recording industry sold thirty million records that year, and by the end of the decade, sales more than tripled each year. By 1924, though, record sales were only half of what they had been the previous year. Radio had arrived as a competing mass medium.

To avoid paying the record industry for copyrighted music, many radio stations started their own in-house orchestras. The American Society of Composers, Authors, and Publishers (ASCAP), founded in 1914 to collect copyright fees for publishers and writers, charged that radio was contributing to plummeting record and sheet music sales. By 1925, before radio advertising had fully emerged, small and large stations were asked to pay between $250 and $2500 a week for music rights. Between 1922 and 1925, six hundred stations left the air in part because they could not pay for content.

Radio, though, would ultimately win this early round. Through the late 1920s and the onset of the Depression, record and phonograph sales continued to fall. Meanwhile, music on radio remained "free." However, when the Twenty-First Amendment repealed the thirteen-year constitutional ban on alcohol in 1933, the record industry got a boost. Music clubs and neighborhood taverns mushroomed in popularity. The introduction of the jukebox permitted bar owners to play records without hiring live bands—a hardship during the Depression. The record industry welcomed the new business. Although the 1930s marked a period of intense struggle between the radio and recording industries, the decade also launched the two media on an extended courtship.

By the 1950s, radio turned to the record industry full force. With television pilfering much of radio's programming and advertising revenue, music provided a cheap source of content for radio use. When songs were played on the air, record sales rose. By the end of the 1950s, the adversarial history of recording and radio had come full circle. Once the threatened medium in the 1930s, the music industry saved radio in the 1950s. Their marriage would eventually enable both to prosper economically at record levels.

Just as radio would later improve its sound quality (through FM and stereo) to retain an edge over television, the recording industry survived during radio's golden age by continually improving sound reproduction. With RCA's acquisition of the Victrola company in 1929 came the development of radio-phonograph players. Then, in the 1930s, RCA built *high-fidelity* (*hi-fi*) systems that dramatically improved phonographic sound. Designed to produce the best fidelity (faithfulness to the music or voice without noise or distortion), these systems came in two varieties: *console* and *component*.

A variation on the Victrola, *console systems* combined several elements—radio tuner, turntable, speakers, and amplifier—all hardwired inside a piece of furniture. Hi-fis looked like dining-room sidebars and, based on the market research of the day, were marketed mainly to women. By the 1950s, when this consumer market was saturated, manufacturers "unpacked" the furniture, introducing *component systems*, which allowed consumers to mix and match different models and parts. They also permitted easier replacement of various elements. Once again, based on research that tapped into existing gender stereotypes, component systems featured lots of dials, chrome, and control panels—new marketing ploys aimed at men. Today, companies have created another market by melding the console and component concepts into *entertainment systems*. These systems allow users to stack various components, including a CD and tape player, television, radio, and VCR, in a large piece of furniture.

popular music and the formation of rock

Although popular music today refers to styles as diverse as blues, country, Tejano, salsa, jazz, rock, reggae, and rap, popular American music existed prior to these genres. In general, **pop music** appeals either to a wide cross section of the public or to sizeable subdivisions within the larger public based on age, region, or ethnic background (for example, teenagers, southerners, Mexican Americans). The word *pop* has also been used to distinguish popular music from classical music, which is written primarily for ballet, opera, ensemble, or symphony. Although we sometimes assume that popular music depended on the phonograph and radio for success, it actually existed prior to the development of these media.

the rise of pop music

In the late nineteenth century, the sale of sheet music for piano and other instruments spread rapidly in a Manhattan area along Broadway known as Tin Pan Alley. There, a tradition of song publishing extended from the 1800s to 1950s rock-and-roll writing teams such as Jerry Lieber–Mike Stoller and Carole King–Gerry Goffin. Major influences during the earlier period included the marches of John Philip Sousa, the ragtime piano of Scott Joplin, and the show tunes and vocal ballads of Irving Berlin, Hoagy Carmichael, George Gershwin, and Cole Porter. During the popular ragtime era in the early 1900s, "tin pan" was a derisive label describing the way that quickly produced tunes sounded like cheap pans clanging together.

At the turn of the century, with the new-found ability of song publishers to mass produce sheet music for a growing middle class captivated by a piano craze, popular songs moved from novelty stage to business enterprise. With the emergence of the phonograph, song publishers also discovered that recorded tunes boosted interest in and sales of sheet music. Although sheet music's popularity would decline rapidly with the development of the radio in the 1920s, songwriting along Tin Pan Alley played a key role in transforming popular music into a mass medium.

As sheet music grew in popularity, **jazz** developed in New Orleans. An improvisational and mostly instrumental music form, jazz absorbed and integrated a diverse body of musical styles, including African rhythms, blues, and gospel. Jazz affected many bandleaders throughout the 1930s and 1940s. Groups led by Louis Armstrong, Count Basie, Tommy Dorsey, Duke Ellington, Benny Goodman, and Glenn Miller were among the most popular of the jazz or "swing" bands, whose music also dominated radio and recording in their day.

The first vocal stars of popular music in the twentieth century were products of the vaudeville circuit (which radio and the Depression would kill in the 1930s). In the 1920s, Rudy Vallee wrapped himself in a raccoon coat and sang popular songs into a megaphone. In the 1930s, the bluesy harmonies of a New Orleans vocal trio, the Boswell Sisters, influenced the Andrew

New CDs roll off the assembly line in a French manufacturing plant.

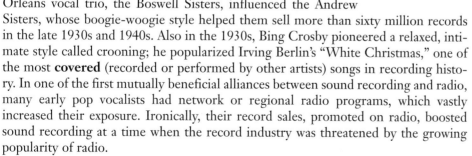

Sisters, whose boogie-woogie style helped them sell more than sixty million records in the late 1930s and 1940s. Also in the 1930s, Bing Crosby pioneered a relaxed, intimate style called crooning; he popularized Irving Berlin's "White Christmas," one of the most **covered** (recorded or performed by other artists) songs in recording history. In one of the first mutually beneficial alliances between sound recording and radio, many early pop vocalists had network or regional radio programs, which vastly increased their exposure. Ironically, their record sales, promoted on radio, boosted sound recording at a time when the record industry was threatened by the growing popularity of radio.

Frank Sinatra arrived in the 1940s. His romantic ballads foreshadowed the teen love songs of rock and roll's early years. Nicknamed "the voice" early in his career, Sinatra, like Crosby, used his music and radio exposure to become a movie star. (Both singers made over fifty films apiece.) Helped by radio, Vallee, the Andrew Sisters, Crosby, and Sinatra were among the first vocalists to become popular with a large national teen audience. Their record sales helped stabilize the industry, and Sinatra's concerts alone caused the kind of audience riots in the early 1940s that would later characterize rock performances.

rock and roll: here to stay

The cultural storm called **rock and roll** hit in the 1950s. (Like the early meaning of *jazz*, *rock and roll* was a blues slang term that sometimes meant sex.) It mixed the vocal and instrumental traditions of popular music with the rhythm and blues sounds of Memphis and the country beat of Nashville. Early rock and roll was therefore considered the first "integrationist music," merging the black sounds of rhythm and blues, gospel, and Robert Johnson-style urban blues with the white influences of country, folk, and pop vocals.[3] Only a few musical forms have ever sprung from such a diverse set of influences, and no new musical form has ever had such a widespread impact on so many different cultures. From an economic perspective, no single musical form prior to rock and roll had ever simultaneously transformed the structure of two mass media industries: sound recording and radio.

Rock and roll germinated from many social, cultural, economic, and political seeds in the 1940s and 1950s. First, radio, which saw its network programs converting to television, was seeking inexpensive forms of content. Radio deejays, particularly Alan Freed in Cleveland (and later on WINS in New York), began exposing more white people to black music. Some white teens, though, cruising the radio dial, had already discovered black-oriented stations and had adopted the different rhythms as dance music. The migration of southern blacks to northern cities in search of better jobs during the Depression and World War II also spread different popular music styles.

During this time, **R&B**, or **rhythm and blues**, developed in various cities. Featuring "huge rhythm units smashing away behind screaming blues singers," R&B merged urban blues and big band sounds.[4] Young listeners, as with rap today, were fascinated by the explicit (and forbidden) sexual lyrics in songs like "Annie Had a Baby," "Sexy Ways," and "Wild Wild Young Men." Although banned on some stations, R&B by 1953 aired on 25 percent of all radio stations for at least a few hours each week. In those days, black and white music forms were segregated: Trade magazines tracked R&B record sales on "race" charts, which were kept separate from white record sales tracked on "pop" charts.

Second, the repressive and uneasy atmosphere of the 1950s—concern over the atomic bomb, the Cold War, and communist witch-hunts—spawned youthful forms of escape from a menacing world created by adults. Traditionally, teens have looked for music with a beat—music they could dance to. This happened in the late 1700s in Europe with the waltz and in America during the 1890s with a dance called the cakewalk. The trend continued during the 1920s with the Charleston, in the 1930s and 1940s with the jazz swing bands and the jitterbug, in the 1970s with disco, and in the 1980s with rap. Each of these twentieth-century musical forms began as dance and party music before their growing popularity eventually energized both record sales and radio formats.

Third, and most significant, the border that had separated white and black cultures began to break down. This process started with music and among the young, but it got a boost in the early 1950s during the Korean War when President Truman signed an executive order integrating the armed forces. Young men drafted into the service were thrown together with others from very different ethnic and economic backgrounds. The biggest legal change, though, came with the *Brown v. Board of*

"Frank Sinatra was categorized in 1943 as 'the glorification of ignorance and **musical illiteracy**.' "
—Dick Clark,
*The First
25 Years
of Rock & Roll*

Education decision in 1954. The Supreme Court officially ended "separate but equal" laws, which had kept white and black schools, hotels, restaurants, restrooms, and drinking fountains segregated for decades. Thus mainstream America began to wrestle seriously with the legacy of slavery and the unequal treatment of its African American citizens. A cultural reflection of the times, rock and roll would burst from the midst of these social and political tensions.

rock muddies the waters

In the 1950s, legal integration accompanied a cultural shift, and the industry's race and pop charts blurred. White deejay Alan Freed had been playing black music for his young audiences since the early 1950s, and white performers like Johnnie Ray and Bill Haley had crossed over to the race charts to score R&B hits. Black artists like Chuck Berry were performing country songs, and Ray Charles even played for a time in an otherwise all-white country band. Revitalizing record sales and changing the sound of radio, rock and roll exploded old distinctions and tested traditional boundaries in five critical ways.

High and Low Culture. In 1956, Chuck Berry's song "Roll Over Beethoven" introduced rock and roll to high culture: "You know my temperature's risin' / The jukebox is blowin' a fuse . . . Roll over Beethoven / and tell Tchaikovsky the news." Although such early rock-and-roll lyrics seem tame today, at the time, rock and rollers were challenging music decorum and the rules about how musicians behave (or misbehave): Berry's "duck walk" across the stage; Elvis Presley's pegged pants and gyrating hips, influenced by blues performers he admired; and Bo Diddley's use of the guitar as a phallic symbol, another old blues tradition. An affront to well-behaved classical music audiences, such acts and antics would be imitated endlessly throughout rock's history. In fact, rock and roll's live exhibitions and the legends about them became key ingredients in promoting record sales.

> "**Listening to my idol** Nat [King] Cole prompted me to sing sentimental songs with distinct diction. The songs of Muddy Waters impelled me to deliver the **down-home blues** in the language they came from, Negro dialect. When I played hillbilly songs, I stressed my diction so that it was harder and whiter. All in all it was my intention to hold both the black and the white clientele. . . . "
>
> —Chuck Berry,
> *The Autobiography,*
> 1987

Masculine and Feminine. Rock and roll was also the first popular music that overtly confused issues of sexuality. Although early rock mostly attracted males as performers, the most fascinating feature of Elvis Presley, according to the Rolling Stone's Mick Jagger, was his androgynous appearance.[5] During this early period, though, the most sexually outrageous rock-and-roll performer was Little Richard (Penniman), who influenced a generation of extravagant rock stars.

Wearing a pompadour hairdo and assaulting his Steinway piano, Little Richard was considered rock's first drag queen, blurring the boundary between masculinity and femininity (although his act had been influenced by a flamboyant six-and-a-half-foot gay piano player named Esquerita, who hosted drag queen shows in New Orleans in the 1940s).[6] Little Richard has said that given the reality of American racism, he feared the consequences of becoming a sex symbol for white girls: "I decided that my image should be crazy and way out so that adults would think I was harmless. I'd appear in one show dressed as the Queen of England and in the next as the pope."[7] By the end of the 1950s, though white parents may not have been too concerned about their daughters falling for Little Richard, most adults did not view rock and roll as harmless.

Black and White. Rock and roll also blurred geographic borders between country and city, between black urban rhythms from Memphis and white country & west-

Among the most influential and innovative American guitarists, Robert Johnson (1911–1938) played the Mississippi delta blues and was a major influence on early rock and rollers, especially the Rolling Stones and Eric Clapton. His intense slide-guitar and finger-style playing also inspired generations of blues artists, including Muddy Waters, Bonnie Raitt, and Stevie Ray Vaughan.

ern music from Nashville. Early white rockers such as Buddy Holly and Carl Perkins combined country or hillbilly music, southern gospel, and Mississippi delta blues to create a sound called **rockabilly**. Raised on bluegrass music and radio's Grand Old Opry, Perkins (a sharecropper's son from Tennessee) mixed these influences with music he heard from black cotton-field workers and blues singers like Muddy Waters and John Lee Hooker, both of whom used electric guitars in their performances. In 1956, Perkins recorded "Blue Suede Shoes." A Presley cover version made the song famous.

Conversely, rhythm and blues spilled into rock and roll. The urban R&B influences on early rock came from Fats Domino ("Blueberry Hill"), Willie Mae Thorton ("Hound Dog"), and Big Joe Turner ("Shake, Rattle, and Roll"). Many of these songs, first popular on R&B labels, crossed over to the pop charts during the mid to late 1950s (although many were performed by better-known white artists). Chuck Berry, who originally played country music to supplement his day jobs as a beautician and carpenter, obliterated these boundaries. His first hit was "Maybellene," modeled on an old country song called "Ida Red." To earn royalties, since the country version was too old for copyright, Chess Records asked Berry to make some changes, and he renamed the song after a popular cosmetic product. Chess gave the record to Alan Freed, who attached his name to the credits in exchange for radio play. "Maybellene" became a No. 1 R&B hit in July 1955 and crossed over to the pop charts the next month, where it climbed to No. 5.

North and South. Not only did rock and roll muddy the urban and rural terrain, but in doing so it combined northern and southern influences as well. In fact, with so much blues, R&B, and rock and roll rising from the South, this region regained some of the cultural standing that it had lost after the Civil War. With many young northern middle-class teens influenced by southern lower-class music, rock and roll challenged stereotypes regarding class as well as race. Just as many white male teens today are fascinated by rap (buying 75 percent of the rap CDs on the commercial market by the late 1980s), Carl Perkins, Elvis Presley, and Buddy Holly—all from the rural south—were fascinated with and influenced by the black urban styles they had heard on radio or seen in night clubs.

But the key to record sales and the spread of rock and roll, according to famed record producer Sam Phillips of Sun Records, was to find a white man who sounded black. Phillips found him in Elvis Presley. Commenting on Presley's cultural importance, one critic wrote: "White rockabillies like Elvis took poor white southern mannerisms of speech and behavior deeper into mainstream culture than they had ever been taken, at the same time he was being reviled for seducing white youth with black music."[8]

Although rock lyrics in the 1950s may not have been especially provocative or overtly political, soaring record sales and the crossover appeal of the music itself represented an enormous threat to long-standing racial and class boundaries. In 1956, the secretary of the North Alabama White Citizens Council bluntly spelled out the racism and white fear concerning the new prominence of African American culture: "Rock and roll is a means of pulling the white man down to the level of the Negro. It is part of a plot to undermine the morals of the youth of our nation."[9]

The Sacred and the Secular. Just as it confronted race, sex, region, and class taboos, the new music for many mainstream adults also constituted an offense against God. Many early rock figures had close ties to religion. As a boy, Elvis Presley had dreamed of joining the Blackwoods, one of country-gospel's most influential groups. As a teen, Jerry Lee Lewis was thrown out of a Bible institute in Texas. Also influenced by church gospel music, Ray Charles changed the lyrics to an old gospel tune: "I've got a Savior / Way over Jordan / He's saved my soul, oh yeah?" became "I got a woman / way over town / she's good to me." A top R&B hit in 1955, "I Got a Woman" became one of Charles's signature songs. The recording drew criticism from many African American church leaders and members who worried about the impact of such worldly music on black youth.

Many people in the 1950s thought that rock and roll violated the boundary between the sacred and the secular. Public outrage in the late 1950s was so great that it even convinced Little Richard and Jerry Lee Lewis, both sons of southern preachers, that they were playing the "devil's music." By 1959, Little Richard left rock and roll to become a minister. Lewis, too, feared that rock was no way to salvation. He had to be coerced to record "Great Balls of Fire," a song by Otis Blackwell that turned an apocalyptic biblical phrase into a highly charged sexual teen love song. The tune, banned by many radio stations, nevertheless climbed to No. 2 on the pop charts late in 1957.

"[Elvis Presley's] kind of music is **deplorable**, a rancid smelling aphrodisiac."
—Frank Sinatra, 1956

"There have been **many accolades uttered** about his talent and performances through the years, all of which I agree with wholeheartedly."
—Frank Sinatra, 1977

Although his unofficial title, "King of Rock and Roll," has been challenged by Little Richard and Chuck Berry, Elvis Presley remains the most popular solo artist of all time. From 1956 to 1962, he recorded seventeen No. 1 hits, from "Heartbreak Hotel" to "Good Luck Charm." According to Little Richard, Presley's major legacy was opening doors for many young performers and making black music popular in mainstream America.

battles in rock and roll

With the blurring of racial lines, performers and producers played a tricky game as they tried to get R&B music accepted in the 1950s. Two prominent white disc jockeys used different methods. Alan Freed, credited with popularizing the term *rock and roll*, played original R&B songs from race charts and the black versions of early rock and roll. In contrast, Philadelphia deejay Dick Clark believed that making black music acceptable to white audiences required cover versions by white artists.

Some music historians point to Jackie Brenston's "Rocket 88" and other R&B songs from the early 1950s as the first rock and roll. But Bill Haley and the Comets, a former country group, scored the first No. 1 rock-and-roll hit on the *Billboard* pop chart in May 1955 with "Rock around the Clock." The record had been an R&B hit in 1954, but it gained popularity and notoriety in the 1955 teen rebellion movie *Blackboard Jungle*. The song became a symbol of juvenile delinquency for many parents and raised concerns about negative influences in the changing recording industry.

Cover Music and Race. Since the 1960s, the integration of popular music has featured a rich history of black and white artists recording and performing each other's original tunes. For example, Otis Redding, an established R&B songwriter, covered the Rolling Stones' "Satisfaction" in 1966. Both the Stones and Eric Clapton covered Robert Johnson's 1930s blues songs, and Clapton had a No. 1 hit in 1974 with Bob Marley's reggae tune "I Shot the Sheriff." More recently, R&B singer Etta James recorded the Eagles' 1976 hit "Take It to the Limit," and in 1994 Nirvana covered an old Leadbelly folk-blues tune, "In the Pines."

Although today we take such rerecordings for granted, in the 1950s cover music was racially coded. Almost all popular covers were attempts by white producers and artists to capitalize on popular songs from the R&B charts and transform them into hits on the pop charts. Occasionally, white producers would list white performers like Elvis Presley, who never wrote songs himself, as a co-writer for the tunes he covered. More often, dishonest producers would buy the rights to potential hits from naive songwriters, who seldom saw a penny in royalties or received credit as the writers.

During this period, black R&B artists, working for small record labels, saw many of their popular songs covered by white artists working for major labels. These cover records, boosted by better marketing and ties to white deejays, usually outsold the original black versions. Covers also slowed sales of the original releases and hampered smaller labels. For instance, the 1954 R&B song "Sh-Boom," by the Chords on Atlantic's Cat label, was immediately covered by a white group, the Crew Cuts, for the major Mercury label. Record sales declined for the Chords, although jukebox and R&B radio play remained strong for their original version. As one rock critic suggested, "With 'Sh-Boom,' the pop establishment had found itself a potent weapon to use against R&B records—whiten them up and use the corporate might of a major label to get them to places a hapless [small label] caught with a hit on its hands could never reach."[10]

By 1955, R&B hits regularly crossed over to the pop charts. LaVern Baker's 1955 hit "Tweedlee Dee" for Atlantic was quickly covered by Mercury's Georgia Gibbs. Baker's version went to No. 14; two weeks later, Gibbs' cover reached No. 2 and stayed in the Top 40 for nineteen weeks. Pat Boone's cover of Fats Domino's "Ain't That a Shame" went to No. 1 and stayed on Top 40's pop chart for twenty weeks, while Domino's original made it to No. 10.

During this time, Pat Boone ranked as the king of cover music, with thirty-eight Top-40 songs between 1955 and 1962. A popular entertainer during this era, his records were second in sales only to Presley. Slowly, however, the cover situation changed. After watching Boone outsell his song "Tutti-Frutti" in 1956, Little Richard wrote "Long Tall Sally," which included lyrics written and delivered in such a way that he believed Boone would not be able to adequately replicate them. "Long Tall Sally" went to No. 6 for Little Richard and charted for twelve weeks; Boone's version got to No. 8 and lasted nine weeks.

Richard Wayne Penniman (Little Richard) was inducted into the Rock and Roll Hall of Fame in 1986. Little Richard played a key role getting black music played on white radio stations and sold in mainstream record stores. His flamboyant style has been a major influence on many performers—including Elton John in the 1970s, Culture Club in the 1980s, and Dennis Rodman in the 1990s.

Overt racism lingered in the music business well into the 1960s. When the Marvelettes scored a No. 1 hit with "Please Mr. Postman" in 1961, their Tamla/Motown label had to substitute a cartoon album cover because many record store owners feared customers would not buy a recording that showed four black women. A turning point, however, came in 1962, the last year that Pat Boone, then twenty-eight, ever had a Top-40 rock-and-roll hit. That year Ray Charles covered "I Can't Stop Loving You," a 1958 country song by the Grand Old Opry's Don Gibson. This marked the first time a black artist, covering a white artist's song, notched a No. 1 pop hit. In Charles's cover, the rock-and-roll merger between gospel and R&B and white country and pop was complete. In fact, the relative acceptance of black crossover music provided a more favorable context for the political activism that spurred important civil rights legislation in the mid-1960s.

Payola, Records, and Radio. Rock and roll helped the recording and radio industries confront racism, but in other ways these two media did not fare well in their partnerships with rock and roll. During the late 1950s, both industries faced the payola scandals. In the music industry, **payola** is the practice of record promoters paying deejays or radio programmers to play particular songs. As recorded rock and roll became central to commercial radio in the 1950s, independent promoters hired by record labels applied pressure to deejays to play the artists whom they represented. In the 1950s, as today, fewer than 10 percent of new releases became hits or sold more than the fifty thousand copies needed for a major label to make money. With the industry releasing a hundred new singles per week by the end of the 1950s, demand for airplay—the key ingredient to establishing hit record sales—was enormous. Although payola was considered unethical and a form of bribery, no laws prohibited its practice.

Following closely on the heals of television's quiz-show scandals, congressional hearings on radio payola began in December 1959. After a November announcement for the upcoming hearings, stations across the country fired deejays, and many others resigned. The hearings were partly a response to general fraudulent business practices and partly an opportunity to blame deejays and radio for rock and roll's negative impact on teens (in the same manner that some politicians today routinely blame television or movies for escalating crime).

In 1959, shortly before the hearings, a Chicago deejay decided to clear the air. He broadcast secretly taped discussions in which a small independent record label acknowledged it had paid $22,000 to ensure that a record would get airplay. The deejay, Phil Lind of WAIT, got calls threatening his life and had to have police protection. At the hearings in 1960, Alan Freed admitted to participating in payola, although he believed there was nothing illegal about such deals. His career soon ended. Dick Clark, then an influential twenty-nine-year-old deejay and the host of TV's *American*

Bandstand, would not admit to payola. But the committee chastised Clark and alleged that a number of his complicated business deals were ethically questionable. Congress eventually added a law concerning payola to the Federal Communications Act, pre-scribing a $10,000 fine and/or a year in jail for each violation of the law. However, given the interdependent relationship between radio and recording, payola scandals persist. Along with MTV, radio still has enormous influence in making or breaking songs, careers, and a record label's investment.

Taming the Music. By late 1959, many key figures in rock and roll had been tamed, partly by mounting social pressure against the music so often accused of undermining America's youth. Jerry Lee Lewis was exiled from the industry, labeled southern "white trash" for marrying his thirteen-year-old third cousin; Elvis Presley was drafted into the army; Chuck Berry was run out of Mississippi and eventually jailed for gun possession and transporting a minor (with a prostitution record) across state lines; and Little Richard left rock and roll to sing gospel music. Then, in February 1959, a plane crash in Iowa killed Buddy Holly ("Peggy Sue"), Richie Valens ("La Bamba"), and the Big Bopper ("Chantilly Lace"), a tragedy detailed in Don McLean's 1971 hit "American Pie" as "the day the music died."

Although rock and roll did not die in the late 1950s, the recording industry decided it needed a makeover. To protect the enormous profits the new music had been generating, record companies began to discipline some of rock's rebellious impulses. In the early 1960s, in particular, the industry tried to clone Pat Boone by featuring a new generation of clean-cut white singers, including Frankie Avalon, who made beach-movie musicals for teenagers, and Ricky Nelson, the youngest son from TV's popular *Adventures of Ozzie & Harriet*. Rock and roll's explosive violations of class and racial boundaries were, for a time, transformed into simpler generation gap problems. By the early 1960s, the music had a milder reputation for merely fostering disagreements among parents and teens.

a changing industry: reformations in popular music

As the 1960s began, rock and roll was tamer and "safer," as reflected in the surf and road music of the Beach Boys and Jan & Dean. Rock music, however, was beginning to spread out like a map in several directions. For instance, the success of producer Phil Spector's so-called all-girl groups—the Crystals ("He's a Rebel"), the Ronettes ("Be My Baby"), and the Shangri-Las ("Leader of the Pack")—challenged the male-dominated world of early rock. In addition, rock music and other popular styles went through cultural reformations that significantly changed the industry. These included the internationalization of sound recording during the "British invasion," the devel-opment of soul and Motown, the political impact of folk-rock, the rejection of music's mainstream by punk and grunge performers, and the reassertion of black urban style in the phenomenon of rap.

the british are coming!

Rock recordings today remain among America's largest economic exports, bringing in more than $15 billion a year from abroad. The seeds of rock's global impact can be traced to England in the late 1950s with the young Rolling Stones listening to the urban blues of Robert Johnson and Muddy Waters and the young Beatles trying to imitate Chuck Berry and Little Richard.

Until 1964, rock-and-roll recordings had traveled on a one-way ticket to Europe. While American artists regularly reached the top of the charts overseas, *no* British performers had yet appeared on any Top-10 pop lists in the States. This changed almost overnight. In 1964, the Beatles invaded with their mop haircuts and pop reinterpretations of American blues and rock and roll. By the end of the year, more than thirty British hits had landed on American Top-10 lists.

Ed Sullivan, who booked the Beatles several times on his TV variety show in 1964, helped their early success. Sullivan, though, reacted differently to the Rolling Stones, who had initially been rejected by British television because lead singer Mick Jagger sounded "too black." Before the Stones performed on Sullivan's program in 1964, he made them change a lyric from "let's spend the night together" to "let's spend some time together"; then he issued an apology to viewers following their performance. The Stones were not invited back. Performing black-influenced music and struggling for acceptance, the band was cast as the "bad boys" of rock in contrast to the "good" Beatles. Despite Sullivan's lack of support, the Stones would go on to inspire harder versions of rock music in the 1970s, what one conservative critic called "a relentless percussive assault on the human ear."[11]

With the British invasion, rock and roll unofficially became *rock*, sending popular music and the industry in two sprawling directions. On the one hand, the Stones, influenced by both blues and 1950s rock and roll, emphasized hard rhythms and vocals in their performances. Their music would influence a generation of hard rock and heavy metal performers, two of the many subgenres of rock that developed in the 1970s. The Beatles, on the other hand, affected by Frank Sinatra as well as rock and roll, more often stressed melody. Their music inspired rock's softer digressions. With the Beatles arriving shortly after the assassination of John F. Kennedy, America welcomed their more melodic and innocent recordings.

> "Hard rock was rock's blues base electrified and upped in volume . . . heavy metal wanted to be the rock music equivalent of a horror movie— **loud, exaggerated, rude,** out for thrills only."   —Ken Tucker,
> *Rock of Ages,*
> 1986

In the end, the British invasion verified what Chuck Berry and Little Richard had already demonstrated, that rock-and-roll performers could write and produce popular songs as well as Tin Pan Alley had. The success of British groups helped change an industry arrangement in which most pop music was produced by songwriting teams hired by major labels and matched with selected performers. Even more important, however, the British invasion showed the recording industry how older American music forms, especially blues and R&B, could be repackaged as rock and exported around the world.

▓ soul music and motown

Ironically, the British invasion, which drew much of its inspiration from black influences, siphoned off many white listeners from a new generation of black performers. Gradually, however, through the 1960s, black singers like James Brown, Sam Cooke, Aretha Franklin, Ben E. King, and Wilson Pickett found large diverse audiences. Transforming the rhythms and melodies of older R&B, pop vocals, and early rock and roll into what became labeled as *soul*, they countered the British invaders with powerful vocal performances. It is hard to define soul music, which mixes gospel, blues, and urban and southern black styles, with slower, more emotional and melancholic lyrics. Soul contrasted sharply with the emphasis on loud fast instrumentals that had become so important to rock music.[12]

SOMEDAY WE'LL BE TOGETHER / CAN'T YOU SEE IT'S ME / YOU GAVE ME LOVE / THE YOUNG FOLKS / SHADOWS OF SOCIETY / LOVING YOU IS BETTER THAN EVER / HEY JUDE / WHEN IT'S TO THE TOP (STILL I WON'T STOP GIVING YOU LOVE) / TILL JOHNNY COMES / BLOWIN' IN THE WIND / THE BEGINNING OF THE END

Born and raised in Detroit, the Primettes changed their name to the Supremes in 1961 when they signed with Motown's Tamla label. They became Motown's most popular singing group, scoring the first of twelve No. 1 hits in 1964 with "Where Did Our Love Go?" The group's lead singer, Diana Ross, left the Supremes in 1969 to begin a successful solo career.

The main independent label to nourish soul and black popular music was Motown, started by former Detroit autoworker and songwriter Berry Gordy with a $700 investment in 1960. (In 1988, Gordy would sell Motown to MCA for $60 million.) Beginning with Smokey Robinson and the Miracles, whose "Shop Around" hit No. 2 late in 1960, Motown groups rivaled the pop success of British bands throughout the decade. Robinson, later a Motown vice president, also wrote "My Girl" for the Temptations and "My Guy" for Mary Wells—both No. 1 hits in the mid-1960s. In the 1960s and 1970s, Motown produced the Four Tops, Martha and the Vandellas, and the Jackson 5. But the label's most successful group was the Supremes, featuring Diana Ross. Between 1964 and 1969, this group scored twelve No. 1 singles. These Motown groups had a more stylized and softer sound than the grittier southern soul (or funk) of Brown and Pickett. Motown producers realized at the outset that by featuring romance and dance over rebellion and politics, black music could attract a young, white audience. But this music did not stay politically quiet. Popular Motown hits like Marvin Gaye's "What's Goin' On" (1970) and Edwin Starr's "War" (1970) directly confronted the Vietnam War.

folk, blues, politics, and drugs

Other forms of black music also had an impact on the 1960s, including the folk-blues of the legendary Leadbelly. In its broadest sense, **folk music** in any culture refers to songs performed by untrained musicians and passed down through oral traditions. Folk encompasses old-time music from the banjo and fiddle tunes of Appalachia to the accordion-led zydeco of Louisiana. Given its rough edges and amateur quality, folk is considered a more democratic and participatory musical form. Unlike most 1960s soul, surfer music, and early Beatles, folk music also had a political edge. Folk, in fact, would inspire a social conscience in many forms of popular music in the 1960s.

In the early 1900s, **blues** music had emerged as a category separate from folk. Influenced by African American spirituals, ballads, and work songs in the rural South, the music of Robert Johnson, Son House, and Charley Patton exemplified early blues. Their sound came from the misnamed Mississippi delta—"a flat, fertile leaf-shaped plain" that stretches south two hundred miles from Memphis, Tennessee, to Vicksburg, Mississippi, but is north of the river's actual delta in Louisiana.[13] The music traveled to northern cities during the migration of black workers looking for industrial jobs in Chicago before and after World War I. In the late 1930s, the electric guitar—a major contribution to rock music—made it easier for musicians "to cut through the noise in ghetto taverns" and gave southern blues its urban style, popularized in the work of Muddy Waters, Howlin' Wolf, B.B. King, and Buddy Guy.

During the 1930s, folk became defined by a white musician named Woody Guthrie ("This Land Is Your Land"). Like many blues singers, Guthrie also brought folk music from the country to the city. He wrote his own songs, promoted social reforms, and played acoustic guitar. Groups such as the Weavers, featuring labor activist and songwriter Pete Seeger, carried on Guthrie's legacy. In 1950, before rock and roll, the Weavers' cover of Leadbelly's "Good Night, Irene" stayed at the top of the pop charts for thirteen weeks. Although the group was regularly blacklisted for their political activism, their comeback concert at Carnegie Hall in 1955 reenergized folk and inspired a new generation of singer-songwriters, including Joan Baez, Bob Dylan, Simon & Garfunkel, James Taylor, Carly Simon, and Joni Mitchell.

Bob Dylan identified folk as "finger pointin'" music that addressed current social circumstances, such as the growing civil rights movement and the Vietnam War. For many folk followers who had grown up on less overtly political rock and roll, acoustic folk music represented both a maturing process and a return to traditional, deamplified values.

Folk-Rock and Dylan. When the Byrds electrified folk recordings in the early 1960s, they invented **folk-rock**, a sound that went on to influence a long list of performers, from the Grateful Dead to R.E.M. and the Indigo Girls. Partly a response to the British invasion, amplified folk-rock earned the Byrds a No. 1 hit in 1965 with a cover of Dylan's folk song "Mr. Tambourine Man."

The Byrds had grabbed the attention of Dylan, who had also been influenced by a British group, the Animals, and their 1964 hit "The House of the Rising Sun." Then, at a key moment in popular music's history, Dylan walked on stage at the 1965 Newport Folk Festival with an electric guitar and took rock music in a more political direction. Often accompanied by a backup group later known as The Band, Dylan was booed by traditional "folkies," who saw amplified music as a sellout to the commercial recording industry (see "Case Study: The Band" on page 76). For many critics, however, Dylan's move to rock was viewed as populist, aimed at reaching a broader and younger constituency. For Dylan, who would later experiment with country and gospel music, it was a matter of changing with the times and finding sounds that matched his interests. By the summer of 1965, Dylan had his first major hit, "Like a Rolling Stone," a six-minute tune boosted by new "progressive rock" radio stations that played longer cuts.

Rock's Psychedelic Turn. Alcohol and drugs have long been associated with the private lives of blues, jazz, country, and rock musicians. These links, however, became much more public in the late 1960s and early 1970s, when authorities busted members of the Rolling Stones and the Beatles. With the increasing role of drugs in youth culture and the availability of LSD (not made illegal until the mid-1960s), more and more rock musicians experimented with and sang about drugs in what were frequently labeled rock's psychedelic years. A number of performers believed, like various writers and artists from other eras, that artistic expression could be enhanced by mind-altering drugs. The music of this era fed on liberal drug laws and a large college student population, the targeted consumers for much of this music. Older musicians had not publicized their drug and alcohol habits. The 1960s drug explorations, however, coincided with the free-speech movement, in which taking drugs was seen by some artists as a form of personal expression and a public challenge to traditional values.

The rock-drug connection was also a cultural response to the perceived failure of institutions to deal with social problems such as racism and the Vietnam War. Students and musicians used drugs not only to experiment or get high, or out of boredom or addiction, but to drop out of conventional society. Some dropped all the way out. During this time, incidents involving drugs or alcohol claimed the lives of several artists, including Janis Joplin, Jimi Hendrix, and the Doors' Jim Morrison.

Looking back, the recording industry generally did little to confront the diseases of drug dependency and alcoholism among musicians. As long as artists produced hits, record companies either ignored the problem or, in a few cases, made sure that musicians were supplied with drugs to sustain their routines and energy levels. With the rise in cocaine and heroin addiction among musicians in the 1980s and 1990s, the industry has faced a new set of challenges. Critics and scholars alike have linked the 80 percent rise in drug use among twelve- to seventeen-year-olds between 1992 and 1996 to its increased use among their rock-group role models.[14] This time around, however, the National Academy of Recording Arts and Sciences, which runs the Grammy Awards, brought together hundreds of industry managers and agents to discuss drug issues. Many critics contend, though, that until record companies are willing to terminate contracts and drop their support for artists unwilling to confront their addictions, problems and tragedies will persist.

Rock as Mainstream Culture. Following the historic Woodstock concert in 1969, which drew over 400,000 fans to a New York farm, the deaths of Joplin and Hendrix in 1970, and the announcement late in 1970 that the Beatles had officially broken up, rock music reached a crossroads. Considered a major part of the rebel counterculture in the 1960s, rock music in the 1970s was increasingly viewed as the centerpiece of mainstream consumer culture. With major music acts earning huge profits, rock was viewed as another product line for manufacturers and retailers to promote, package, and sell.

Nevertheless, some rock musicians carried on the traditions of early rock. In the 1970s, stars like Bruce Springsteen emerged to carry on rock's integrationist legacy, combining the influences of Chuck Berry and Elvis Presley with the folk-rock poetry of Bob Dylan. Britain's Elton John drew upon the outrageous stage performances of Little Richard and the melodic influences of the Beatles. Generally, though, in the 1970s business concerns steered rock and its stars toward a new form of segregation, dividing popular music along class and race lines. Both the recording industry and album-oriented rock formats on radio began to aggressively market and program harder rock music and to aim it primarily toward middle-class white male teens.

▮alternative sounds of punk and grunge

In the United States and Britain in the mid-1970s, **punk rock** challenged the orthodoxy and commercialism of the record business. Punk has generally been characterized by its loud unpolished qualities, jackhammer beat, primal vocal screams, crude aggression, and defiant or comic lyrics. By this time, the glory days of rock's competitive independent labels had ended, and rock music was controlled by six major companies: CBS, Warner, Polygram, RCA, Capitol-EMI, and MCA. This situation gave rise to "faceless rock—crisply recorded, eminently catchy" and anonymous hits by bands with "no established individual personalities outside their own large but essentially discrete audiences" of young white males.[15]

Punk, in avoiding rock's consumer popularity, attempted to recover the early amateurish and offensive energies of rock and roll. Essentially, any teenager with a few weeks of guitar practice could learn the sound, making music that was both more democratic and discordant. In the early 1970s, pre-punk groups like the Velvet Underground set the stage for the Ramones and the Dead Kennedys. In England, the music of the Sex

"Somewhere between calculation and desperation, the music business has decided to get behind . . . **a new female archetype**—uninhibited and smart, bruised and resilient, unorthodox and proud of it. . . . She can, and will, get loud to make her point. . . ."
—Jon Pareles,
New York Times,
1996

In the late 1970s, the Sex Pistols, one of the most controversial groups in rock's history, pioneered British punk music. Together for only two years, the Sex Pistols specialized in nihilistic lyrics and violent performances. The group offered a loud alternative sound that mocked the commercial mainstream, inspiring a generation of young basement and garage musicians. After bad publicity surrounding their first single, the band was dumped by their label, EMI; the group's next single, "God Save the Queen," was banned by the BBC.

Pistols ("Anarchy in the U.K."), one of the most controversial groups in rock history, was eventually banned for offending British decorum.

Punk, of course, was not a commercial success in the United States in the 1970s, lack of popularity being one of punk's goals. Nevertheless, punk made contributions, especially by "defining the big business of the rock industry and then condemning it." Punk also offered women the opportunity "to participate fully in the rock world for the first time in the history of the music."[16] In the United States, for instance, poet and rocker Patti Smith helped pioneer punk in the mid-1970s, and in Britain, Siouxsie & the Banshees assaulted commercial rock's fixation on all-male groups. In the 1990s, women artists in rock and other musical forms continued to become more popular and to gain recognition.

Taking the spirit of punk and infusing it with attention to melody, **grunge** represented a significant development in rock in the 1990s. Grunge's commercial breakthrough can be traced to the "Smells Like Teen Spirit" cut on the album *Nevermind* by Nirvana, led by songwriter and vocalist Kurt Cobain. In 1992, *Nevermind* was the top-selling album in America, its popular success ironically built on satirizing some of the rock music of the 1970s and 1980s. One critic described a Cobain song as "stunning, concise bursts of melody and rage that occasionally spilled over into haunting, folk-styled acoustic ballad."[17] Suffering from stomach problems, drug addiction, and severe depression, Cobain committed suicide in 1994.

The legacy of punk that partly defined grunge offered an alienated performing style that was in direct contrast to the slick theatrics of 1970s and 1980s rock. Taking a cue from low-key folk singers and 1960s' rock bands like the Grateful Dead, grunge spoke the low-maintenance language of the garage: torn jeans, t-shirts, long underwear, worn sneakers, and old flannel shirts. But with the music's success, grunge's anti-style became commercially viable as hundreds of new garage bands emulated it.

Nirvana's influences paved the way for a variety of punk and alternative groups in the 1990s, including Nine Inch Nails, Smashing Pumpkins, Soundgarden, Stone Temple Pilots, and Pearl Jam. In 1993, trying to play down its commercial success, Pearl Jam refused to release any music video singles from its new No. 1 album, *Vs.*, which had sold over five million copies. It chose also to perform in smaller arenas and college campuses rather than the gigantic, impersonal sports stadiums preferred by established rock bands. Then, in 1994, the band canceled a national tour to protest

75

The Band

The Band

The group included four Canadians—Robbie Robertson, a lead guitarist and later the group's main songwriter; Richard Manuel, accomplished at vocals, piano, and drums; Rick Danko, the bass player who played fiddle; and Garth Hudson, the classically trained rock organist who also played sax and accordion—and a hillbilly drummer and mandolin player from Arkansas, Levon Helm. They are best known for "The Weight," a song that symbolizes the rich and enduring history of rock and roll. An attempt to merge musical styles and melt racial barriers, "The Weight" made its mark in the 1960s road film *Easy Rider*. In the 1970s, it showed up in *The Last Waltz*, Martin Scorsese's documentary about the group. In the 1980s, it resurfaced in the soundtrack of *The Big Chill*. Then, in the 1990s, its opening lines were used in a TV ad for Diet Pepsi.

Like many alternative rock musicians today, The Band missed commercial success. The group had only two Top 40 hits of their own, despite appearances on the *Ed Sullivan Show* and the cover of *Time* in 1969. When rock was becoming harder and more psychedelic in the late 1960s, The Band's first album, *Music from Big Pink*, fought upstream, focusing on storytelling and reinterpreting rock's country and gospel roots. With few guitar solos and intentionally rough vocal edges, the album was a departure. But while rock's mainstream moved in one direction, The Band moved in another.

Nevertheless, a number of rock historians and fans believe that The Band serves as an exemplary standard for rock and roll. The question is, why? The answer lies in the group's versatility, their willingness to acknowledge and synthesize all sorts of influences, and their violation of musical boundaries. In their songs, The Band exhibited a spirit that continues to drive some of today's best alternative music: swimming against the cultural mainstream.

Before they became The Band, the group had played backup for Bob Dylan. The Band's interests in rock, folk, country, and storytelling matched Dylan's own. Some of the group had toured with Dylan when he switched from acoustic folk to electric rock in 1965–66, but his acoustic "folkie" fans booed the electric performances so mercilessly that Levon Helm left the tour after a few appearances. The group also influenced the next turn Dylan took in the late 1960s, merging country, folk, and rock in his *John Wesley Harding* and *Nashville Skyline* albums.

Following the Dylan tour in 1966, the group settled in Woodstock, New York, playing and writing occasionally for

the high service charges and alleged monopolistic practices of Ticketmaster, a company that often dictates a concert's ticket prices.

In some critical circles, both punk and grunge are considered subcategories or fringe movements of *alternative rock* music. This vague label describes many types of experimental rock music that offered a departure from the theatrics and staged extravaganzas of 1970s *glamour rock*, which showcased performers like David Bowie and Kiss. Appealing mostly to college students, alternative rock traditionally has opposed the sounds of Top-40 and commercial FM radio. In the 1980s and 1990s, U2 and R.E.M. emerged as successful groups often associated with alternative rock. A key dilemma for successful alternative performers, however, is that their popularity results in commercial success, ironically, a situation that their music often criticizes.

Dylan. They also started to make their own music and picked up the name The Band. While many American bands were rejecting and condemning their country during the late 1960s, the Canadians in the group, so affected by the music from the South, went in search of America. Their early songs were about the land and rural America, the past and the Civil War, traveling carnivals and medicine shows, old-time religion and traditional kinship, displaced people and important transitions. Some of their titles capture this spirit: "The Night They Drove Old Dixie Down," "Tears of Rage" (co-written by Manuel and Dylan), "King Harvest," "Rag Mama Rag," "W.S. Walcott Medicine Show," "Life Is a Carnival," "Acadian Driftwood," and "Up on Cripple Creek."

Perhaps The Band's greatest achievement was their influence on both folk- and country-rock. The four Canadians in the group had

Stage Fright
(courtesy of Capitol Records)

Music from Big Pink
(courtesy of Capitol Records)

Jericho
(courtesy of Pyramid Records)

grown up listening to fifty-thousand-watt country & western stations that were not inhibited by geographical borders.

Mix these elements with The Band's own intriguing Canadian backgrounds (Robertson, for example, is the son of a Toronto "gangster" and Mohawk Indian mother), and you have a cultural salad that defines rock and roll's celebration of both our diversity and our common ties. Critic Greil Marcus sums up why The Band remains a defining group in rock's short history: "Flowing through their music were spirits of acceptance and desire, rebellion and awe, raw excitement, good sex, open humor, a magic feel for history— a determination to find plurality and drama in an America we had met too often as a monolith."[1]

In short, quintessential rock and roll.

**The Band
Key Discography**

Music from Big Pink
(Capitol, 1968)

The Band
(Capitol, 1969)

Stage Fright
(Capitol, 1970)

Cahoots
(Capitol, 1971)

Rock of Ages
(Capitol, 1972)

Moondog Matinee
(Capitol, 1973)

**Northern Lights—
Southern Cross**
(Capitol, 1975)

The Last Waltz
(Capitol, 1977)

To Kingdom Come
(Capitol, 1989)

With Bob Dylan :

Before the Flood
(Asylum, 1974)

The Basement Tapes
(Columbia, 1975)

rap redraws musical lines

With the growing segregation of radio formats and the dominance of mainstream rock by white male performers, the place of black artists in the rock world diminished. No popular black successor to Chuck Berry or Jimi Hendrix had emerged in rock by the mid-1990s. These trends, combined with the rise of "safe" dance disco by white bands (the Bee Gees), black artists (Donna Summer), and integrated groups (the Village People), created a space for the culture that produced rap music.

In some ways a black counterpart to the spirit of white punk, **rap** music also stood in direct opposition to the polished, professional, and less political world of soul. Rap's combination of social politics, male swagger, and comic lyrics carried for-

"We're like
reporters.
We give them [our
listeners] the truth.
People where we
come from hear so
many lies that the
truth stands out
like a sore
thumb."
—Eazy-E,
N.W.A.,1989

ward traditions long-standing in blues, R&B, soul, and rock and roll. Like punk, rap was driven by a democratic, nonprofessional spirit—accessible to anyone who could talk in street dialect and cut (or sample) records on a turntable. Rap deejays emerged in Jamaica and New York, scratching and re-cueing old reggae, disco, soul, and rock albums. As dance music, rap developed MCs (masters of ceremony), who used humor, boasts, and "trash talking" to entertain and keep the peace at parties.

When the Sugarhill Gang released "Rapper's Delight" in 1979, the music industry thought of it as a novelty album, even though the music was rooted in a long tradition of party deejays playing soul and funk music through powerful sound systems. Then, in 1982, Grandmaster Flash and Furious Five released "The Message" and infused rap with a political take on ghetto life. Rap also continued the black musical tradition of elevating the spoken word over conventional instruments, now displaced by turntables. Although rap was considered party music at first, its early political voices like Public Enemy and Ice-T addressed civil rights issues and the worsening economic conditions facing urban America.

Rap exploded as a popular genre in 1984 with the commercial successes of groups like Run-DMC, the Fat Boys, and LL Cool J. That year, Run-DMC's album *Raising Hell* became a major crossover hit, the first No. 1 rap album on the popular charts (thanks in part to a collaboration with Aerosmith on a rap version of their 1976 hit "Walk This Way"). Like punk and early rock and roll, rap was cheap to produce, requiring only a few mikes, speakers, amps, turntables, and some record albums. With CDs displacing LPs as the main recording format in the 1980s, partially obsolete hardware was "reemployed" and restored to use by rap artists, many of whom had trained in vocational colleges for industrial jobs that evaporated in the 1970s and 1980s.

Since most major labels and many black radio stations rejected the rawness of rap, the music spawned hundreds of new independent labels. Although initially dominated by male performers, rap was open to women, and some—Salt-N-Pepa and Queen Latifah (Dana Owens) among them—quickly became major players. Soon white groups like the Beastie Boys and 3rd Bass were also combining rap and punk influences in commercially successful music.

Rap, like punk, defies mainstream culture. Some rap has drawn criticism from both white and black communities for lyrics that degrade women or applaud violence. Rappers respond that punk has often been more explicit and offensive but that punk's lyrics are less discernible under the guitar distortion. The conversational style of rap, however, makes it a forum in which performers can debate such issues as gender, class, and drugs. A few rappers have also fought extended battles over copyright infringement, since their music continues to sample rock, soul, funk, and disco records.

Although rap includes many different styles, including various Latin offshoots, its most controversial subgenre probably is *gangsta rap*. This style developed in Los Angeles in 1987 partly in response to drug news stories that represented, at least for many African American communities, a one-sided portrait of life in urban America. This offshoot of rap drew major national attention in 1996 with the shooting death of

With her 1989 hit debut album, *All Hail the Queen*, Queen Latifah opened doors for many women rappers. Her lyrics were among the first to challenge the misogyny and violence in the music of some male rap stars. Born and raised in New Jersey as Dana Owens, Queen Latifah (an Arabic word for "sensitive and delicate") was the first female rap artist to launch a successful acting career.

Tupac Shakur, a performer, actor, and ex-con who lived the violent life he sang about on albums like *Thug Life*. Although criticized for his criminal lifestyle, Shakur was revered by many fans for telling hard truths about urban problems and street life. In 1997, Notorious B.I.G. (Christopher Wallace a.k.a. Biggie Smalls), whose followers were prominent suspects in Shakur's death, was shot to death in Hollywood. He was considered Shakur's main gangsta-rap rival.

Throughout rap's brief history, artists have occasionally characterized themselves as street reporters who tell alternative stories of city life. Chuck D of Public Enemy has maintained that most rap music operates as the CNN of black youth, offering interpretations of urban experience and the war on drugs that are very different from network news portrayals. Despite the conflicts generated around rap, it remains a major development in popular music. Like early rock and roll, rap's crossover appeal, particularly to white male adolescents, seems rooted in a cultural style that questions class and racial boundaries and challenges status quo values.

the business of sound recording

One key issue raised by alternative movements in the recording industry is the uneasy relationship between music's business and artistic elements. The lyrics of rap or alternative rock, for example, often question the commercial values of popular music. Both rock and rap carry expectations that musical integrity requires a separation between business and art. But, in fact, the line between commercial success and musical style grows hazier each day. When the questioning of commercialism resonates with enough fans, popular artists stand to make a lot of money. In order to understand this situation, we need to look at the business of sound recording.

By the mid-1990s, CD and tape sales surpassed $12 billion a year in the United States and $25 billion worldwide. In economic terms, the music business generates more revenue than all other media except television. It also constitutes a global **oligopoly**: a business situation in which a few firms control most of an industry's production and distribution resources. Such global reach gives these firms enormous influence over what types of music gain worldwide distribution and popular acceptance.

the major labels

As in the 1970s, six companies control popular music today. They produce over 80 percent of all American CDs and cassettes and distribute well over 90 percent of the world's recordings. In addition, while virtually all major labels were once American owned, by the mid-1990s only one major company, Warner Music (a subsidiary of Time Warner), claimed the United States as home. The other five global players are MCA, owned by Canada's Seagram Company; Sony, the Japanese company that bought CBS Records in the 1980s; Polygram, owned by Philips Electronics in the Netherlands; EMI, owned by Britain's Thorn-EMI; and BMG, owned by Bertelsmann in Germany, which bought RCA Records in the 1980s (see Figure 3.2). Each "major" owns and operates several labels, most of them formerly independent companies. Majors produce and distribute some twenty-five hundred CD and cassette albums each year.

Figure 3.2
The Major Labels in the Sound Recording Industry
Source: New York Times, December 6, 1995.

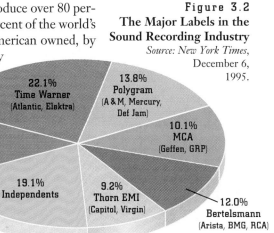

22.1% Time Warner (Atlantic, Elektra)

13.8% Polygram (A&M, Mercury, Def Jam)

10.1% MCA (Geffen, GRP)

13.6% Sony (Columbia, Epic)

19.1% Independents

9.2% Thorn EMI (Capitol, Virgin)

12.0% Bertelsmann (Arista, BMG, RCA)

THE GLOBAL VILLAGE

The International Beat

TOP WORLD MUSIC ARTISTS

1 **GIPSY KINGS** – *France*

2 **THE CHIEFTAINS** – *Ireland*

3 **LOREENA MCKENNITT** – *Canada*

4 **LEBO M** – *South Africa*

5 **CLANNAD** – *Ireland*

6 **CESARIA EVORA** – *Cape Verde*

7 **DEAD CAN DANCE** – *UK & Australia*

8 **BILL WHELAN** – *Ireland*

9 **JAMES GALWAY** – *Ireland*

10 **KEALI'I REICHEL** – *Hawaii*

Source: Billboard Magazine, December 28, 1996.

The 1996 Grammy Awards program, viewed by over one billion people in 172 countries, confirmed the global reach of the popular music industry. Although various forms of rock have become the world's music in terms of popularity and commercial success, other forms of popular music are more central to various cultures worldwide. Since the late 1980s, most good music stores have added a section designated as international, ethnic, or world music, which includes releases from African, Latin American, Indian, Irish, and other international artists. This category incorporates the many styles of popular regional and folk music from cultures throughout the world. Most of this music has neither sought nor achieved the global range of European classical music, Latin tango, or American country and rock music. In the 1990s, however, the world music section has represented the largest growth area in American music stores.

From Africa comes manding music of Mali and Guinea; the highlife and roots rhythms of Ghana; the soukous and dance music of Zaire; and the penny-whistle and bubblegum sounds of South Africa. Europe offers Celtic folk tunes from Ireland, Scotland, and Wales; Magyar and Gypsy traditional music from Hungary; folk and punk sounds from the Alps; and flamenco from southern Spain (music influenced by Morocco, Egypt, India, Pakistan, and Greece). The diverse regions of the Caribbean have produced rumba, salsa, merengue, calypso, and reggae. Regional America offers its own contributions to world folk forms with bluegrass, cajun, zydeco, Tejano, and the traditional music of various Indian tribes.

Although American rock has had a strong impact on global culture since the 1950s, much of this music has in turn been influenced by sounds from around the world. For example, the music of India's famed sitar player, Ravi Shankar, influenced the Beatles' albums recorded in the late 1960s; and in the 1980s South Africa's Ladysmith Black Mambazo changed the sound of folk-rock on Paul Simon's *Graceland* album.

World music has produced its own non-Western stars, but few Americans have ever heard of them: the Dominican Republic's Juan Luis Guerra, whose merengue recordings have sold over five million copies; Cuba's Celia Cruz, the queen of salsa; and East Indian movie star Asha Bhosle, the world's most recorded singer and the star of cable's International Channel.

Celia Cruz

WORLD MUSIC STARS

Juan Luis Guerra

World music critics argue that throughout this century other musical styles have had a larger global impact than have those from the United States, particularly Argentina's tango and Cuba's mambo and rumba music.[1] The bottom line is that almost all musical styles are complex mixes from a variety of cultures. Given the ongoing development of global communication systems, different musical forms will continue to bump into each other, and this democratic tendency will become more pronounced in the twenty-first century.

independent labels

The rise of rock and roll in the 1950s and early 1960s showcased a rich diversity of independent labels all vying for a share of the new music. These labels included Sun, Stax, Chess, Motown, and Atlantic. Today most of these independents have folded or been absorbed by majors. However, in contrast to the six global players, some five thousand large and small production houses—sometimes called *indies*—record less commercially viable music or music they hope will become commercially viable. Often struggling enterprises, indies require only a handful of people to operate them. They identify forgotten older artists and record new innovative performers. To keep costs down, indies depend on wholesale distributors for promoting and selling their music. Producing about 20 percent of America's music in the mid-1990s, indies often enter into deals with majors to gain the widest distribution for their artists. They may also distribute their own recordings or contract with independent distributors who ship new recordings to various retail outlets and radio stations.

In the music business, the majors frequently rely on indies to discover and initiate distinctive musical trends that first appear on a local level. For instance, although rap was and still is rejected by many radio stations and major labels, indies such as Sugarhill, Tommy Boy, and Uptown emerged in the 1980s to produce this music for regional markets. In the early 1990s, punk faced similar problems and relied on labels such as Kill Rock Stars, Liquid Meat, and Aargh! Records. As another example, two small southern companies—Fat Possum Records and Rooster Blues Records—have been scouring the South in the 1990s for forgotten or ignored blues artists. Indies play a major role as the music industry's risk-takers, since major labels are reluctant to invest in lost or commercially unproven artists.

Once indies become successful, the financial inducement to sell out to a major label is enormous. Seattle indie Sub Pop (Nirvana's initial recording label), faced with the commercial success of alternative rock, sold 49 percent of its stock to Time Warner for $20 million in 1994. Polygram, Sony, and EMI aggressively pursued the punk label Epitaph, which once rejected takeover offers as high as $50 million. Today, all six majors are busy looking for and picking off independent labels that have successfully developed artists with national or global appeal (see "The Global Village: The International Beat").

the business of making a recording

Like most mass media, the music business is divided into several areas, including artist development, technical facilities, sales and distribution, advertising and promotion, and administrative operations. Recording companies, whether major or minor, are generally driven by **A&R (artist & repertoire) agents**: the talent scouts of the music business who discover, develop, and sometimes manage artists. A&R executives listen to demonstration tapes, or *demos*, from new artists; they decide who to hire and which songs to record. Before Chuck Berry, Little Richard, and rock's British invasion, few commercially successful performers wrote their own music, so A&R agents had to match them with songs and writers—a practice still prevalent in country music.

The technical group at a recording label oversees the entire production process. A typical recording session is a complex process involving musicians and audio technicians, directed by a session engineer and producer. George Martin, for example, served as both chief engineer and producer for the Beatles' sessions in the 1960s. He is credited with introducing orchestral sounds into rock music, a trend many rock groups copied in the 1970s.

Today, the engineer and producer roles usually fall to different people. A chief engineer oversees the technical aspects of the recording session, everything from choosing recording equipment to arranging microphone placement. In charge of the overall recording process, the producer handles most nontechnical elements of the session, including reserving studio space and hiring musicians. During recording, the producer takes command and in most cases makes the decisions on whether certain vocal or instrumental parts work well or need to be rerecorded.

Most popular CDs and tapes are now produced part by part. Using separate microphones, the vocalists, guitarists, drummers, and other musical sections are digitally recorded onto audio tracks. To produce one song, as many as two or three dozen tracks might be recorded, often at different times and in different studios. Controlling the overall sound quality, the chief engineer mixes the parts onto a two-track stereo master tape. Assistant engineers specialize in other postproduction editing; they mix the multiple tracks after the recording sessions. Mastering engineers prepare the song for transfer to a final version on audiotape and CD. Remix engineers work with tapes that are already mastered, removing flaws or adding new instrumental or vocal parts. Since digital keyboard synthesizers are able to reproduce most instrumental sounds, engineers can now duplicate many instrumental parts without recalling studio musicians.

Throughout the recording and postproduction process, the marketing department plans strategies for packaging, promoting, and selling a recording. In addition to arranging advertising in various media, this department might design point-of-purchase displays that use signs, posters, and other eye-catching gimmicks to encourage in-store impulse buying, which accounts for nearly 15 percent of all CD and audiotape sales.

Selling a Recording. Distributing and selling CDs and tapes is a tricky part of the business. Most recordings are sold by rack jobbers, direct retailers, or record clubs. Accounting for more than 50 percent of all CD and tape sales, *rack jobbers* contract with general retailers like Kmart to stock their stores' music racks or shelves with the latest CDs, audiocassettes, and music videos. Rack jobbers either lease shelf space from the stores or sell recordings directly to them. By managing inventories and orders, rack jobbers perform record-keeping tasks that many retailers prefer to avoid. To earn the highest profits, rack jobbers generally stock the most popular music, screen controversial titles for some of their clients, and ignore obscure music forms.

Direct retail stores offer more variety and account for nearly 30 percent of all recording sales. Like the bookstore business, the major economic trend in music sales leans toward large chain stores such as Musicland–Sam Goody or Tower Records, each of which operates hundreds of stores nationally, mostly in shopping malls or near college campuses. Direct retailers specialize in music, carefully monitoring new releases by major labels and independents. Like chain bookstores, direct music retailers keep a large inventory. Their staffs can also track down and order obscure recordings the store may not have on hand. In addition, used-CD stores and inventories have developed as a by-product of the durability of digital recordings.

Another 10 percent of recording sales each year come from *record clubs* such as BMG and Columbia. Like book clubs, record clubs use direct mail and inserts in Sunday newspapers to promote or advertise new and old releases. They might offer prospective members ten CDs for the price of one as an incentive to join. In exchange, consumers agree to buy three or four CDs at the regular price (about $15 in 1997) over the next three or four years. Like major book clubs, record clubs sort through many possible new releases, identifying the commercial hits or "hot" groups. Through clubs, consumers are generally offered the music of only the most popular and profitable performers.

With the appearance of MTV in the early 1980s, music videos created another level of complexity for the music business. Virtually every artist today who introduces a new CD or cassette also makes an accompanying video for distribution on cable channels such as MTV, the Nashville Network, Black Entertainment Television (BET), or VH1. On average, a music video cost a recording company and its artists between

$75,000 and $300,000 to produce in the mid-1990s. Initially, MTV was particularly important to recording companies and new artists. If they had difficulty getting radio play, the cable channel became another venue for launching performers. MTV has become so influential today, however, that it is often a must: Radio stations may choose not to play a particular rock artist until a demand has been created by MTV airings.

Dividing the Profits. If we look at the various costs and profits from a typical CD, we can see how money circulates in the recording industry. For a CD that retails at Tower Records for $15.99, the wholesale price is about $8—the actual cost of producing the recording. The remaining half constitutes the profit margin, which is split among the record company, the distributor, and retailers. The record company reaps the highest profit (close to $4 on a typical CD) but, along with the artist, bears the bulk of the expenses: manufacturing costs, packaging and CD design, advertising and promotion, and artist royalties (see Figure 3.3).

A singer-songwriter who has negotiated a 12 percent royalty rate would earn just under $1 for a CD or cassette whose wholesale price is $8. So a CD that "goes gold"— sells 500,000 units—would net the artist around $500,000. Out of this amount, the artist repays the record company the money it has advanced to him or her—approximately $150,000—for recording and music video costs, tour expenses, and so forth. Another $150,000 or so might have to be set aside in a reserve account to cover any unsold recordings returned by record stores. This would leave the artist with about $200,000, some of which would be split up among band members.[18]

New artists usually earn a royalty rate of between 5 and 10 percent on the wholesale price of a cassette or CD. A more established performer might negotiate a 10 to 15 percent rate, and popular artists might get more than 15 percent. However, most lesser-known songwriters and performers remain in debt. For every Hootie and the Blowfish (whose debut album, *Cracked Rear View*, sold more than thirteen million copies in 1995), thousands of songwriters and performers cannot overcome their debts to various managers, producers, and record labels.

Independent producers or labels sign songwriters, singers, or groups and then advance them money to cover expenses, hoping for a hit song or album. The Jayhawks, for example, a country-rock group whose 1992 album sold 200,000 copies, had debts in 1995 totaling $1 million. Due to stress over debt, one member left the group to make furniture, which he began selling to wealthy musicians he had met while touring as a Jayhawk. This story is not unusual: More than 95 percent of all musicians who receive advances do not recoup them through recording sales.

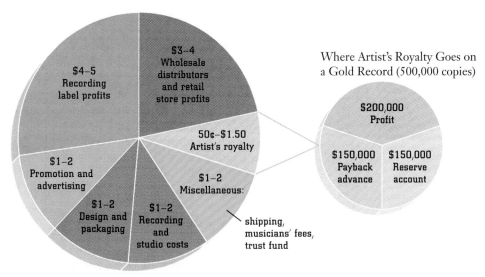

Where Artist's Royalty Goes on a Gold Record (500,000 copies)

$4–5 Recording label profits

$3–4 Wholesale distributors and retail store profits

50¢–$1.50 Artist's royalty

$1–2 Promotion and advertising

$1–2 Design and packaging

$1–2 Recording and studio costs

$1–2 Miscellaneous: shipping, musicians' fees, trust fund

$200,000 Profit

$150,000 Payback advance

$150,000 Reserve account

Figure 3.3
Where Money Goes on a $15.99 CD

In addition to sales royalties received by artists from their recording companies, two other kinds of royalty payments exist: mechanical and performance royalties. Songwriters protect their work by obtaining an exclusive copyright on each song, ensuring that it will not be copied or performed without permission. To protect their copyrights, songwriters assign their creations to a publisher, who represents the songs by trying to sell them in printed form or have them recorded by a major label or indie. Songwriters and publishers receive a *mechanical royalty* when they allow a song to be recorded. They are paid at a rate of about one-half cent for each CD or audiotape sold.

The owner of a song's copyright, which is not always the songwriter, also receives a *performance royalty* whenever the music is used on radio or television. Since songwriters are seldom wealthy enough to underwrite the original costs of producing a CD or tape, they often sell their copyrights to recording companies. On behalf of songwriters and recording labels, performance royalties are collected by several national licensing associations, the largest of which are ASCAP and Broadcast Music, Inc. (BMI). These groups keep track of recording rights, collect copyright fees, and license music for use in TV commercials or films. Radio stations annually pay licensing fees of between 1 and 2 percent of their gross annual revenues, and they generally play only licensed music, which makes it difficult for alternative or independent music to gain a broad following.

bootlegging

In the late 1980s, the collapse of communist governments throughout Eastern Europe and the growth of wide-open economies worldwide led to a flourishing illegal market in the music industry. With no international policing of copyright laws, manufacturing plants were set up, especially throughout China and other parts of Asia, to copy or bootleg unauthorized CDs and cassettes. These illegal firms sold recordings at cut-rate prices with no profits going to the original recording companies or to the artists themselves.

Three forms of **bootlegging** have been a part of the music industry for much of the twentieth century. First, as just described, are *counterfeits*, who duplicate the content of a record as it appeared in its original form. Second are *pirates*, who reissue rare or out-of-print material without official permission from the songwriter or copyright holder.[19] Finally, the most common bootlegging occurs from unauthorized or stolen tape recordings of live concerts, informal studio sessions, or live radio or TV appearances. Individuals duplicate these recordings and then sell them for profit without paying fees to the artists.

Although bootlegging has been part of musical lore ever since tape recorders appeared in the 1930s, it reached its heyday in the sixties. With informal folk and rock concerts increasing, many musicians paid scant attention to those who recorded their performances. The most famous bootleg album from this period was a Bob

In 1996, police in Miyun, China, shoveled pirated CDs and videotapes into the path of a steamroller. However, despite such public acts and a 1996 China-U.S. agreement to protect intellectual property rights, China remains the world's largest producer of pirated CDs and cassettes.

Dylan collection, *The Great White Wonder*, a set of demo tapes and informal sessions that surfaced during the late 1960s as Dylan was recovering from a motorcycle accident. Arguably the most taped artists in music history, The Grateful Dead were unable to stop the illegal recording of their lengthy concerts and eventually encouraged fans to tape their performances.

In general, although the first two forms of bootlegging have often been practiced but seldom condoned, the third type has generated arguments. Record companies and their artists claim that bootlegging denies them a share of revenue that, by law, belongs to them. Bootleggers, however, contend that most fans already own all the "legal" music of the artists and that bootlegging adds a personal touch to fans' music collections. Fans also contend that bootlegging provides free publicity and a commercial payoff for artists since the clandestine music circulates among people who may not otherwise hear it.

recordings, free expression, and democracy

In the mid-1980s, the newly formed Parents Music Resource Center (PMRC) triggered Senate hearings on explicit sexual and violent themes in rock music. Although opposed to the *direct* censorship of music, PMRC sought warning stickers on CDs and tapes. The group appeared at subcommittee hearings that also took testimony from rock and pop figures such as Frank Zappa, Donny Osmond, and John Denver. Opposed to labeling as a violation of free speech, the musicians also argued that advisory warnings would merely attract attention to music that curious adolescents might otherwise overlook. Soon after the 1985 hearings, the record industry established a voluntary system, stamping disks and tapes containing explicit lyrics with parental-advisory stickers. However, gangsta rap came along in the late 1980s and became another lightning rod for free-expression issues. In the 1990s, public pressure forced Time Warner to sell its 50 percent share of the controversial gangsta-rap label Interscope Records.

The battle over popular music's controversial lyrics speaks to the heart of democratic expression. On the one hand, popular recordings have a history of confronting stereotypes (by integrating urban and country styles, for instance) and questioning conventions (by the explicit use of political or sexual lyrics). At the same time, however, popular music has often reproduced old stereotypes: limiting women's access as performers in the recording world, fostering racist or homophobic stereotypes, and celebrating violence or misogyny.

A major issue faces popular music forms that test cultural boundaries: how to uphold a legacy of free expression while facing cooptation by giant companies bent on consolidating independents and maximizing profits. For example, forms of rock music keep going to the edge, pulling back, reemerging as rebellious, becoming commercial, and then repeating the pattern over again. This dynamic between popular music's clever innovations and capitalism's voracious appetite is crucial. Record companies sign a handful of stars, making deals such as Janet Jackson's record-setting $80 million megadeal with EMI's Virgin label in 1996, while other forms of innovative music are never heard by many mainstream audiences.

Still, the major labels need resourceful independents to develop new talent. Ironically, successful commerce requires periodic infusions of the diverse sounds that come from ethnic communities, backyard garages, dance parties, and neighborhood clubs. At the same time, musicians need the major labels if they want wide distribution or national popularity. Such an interdependent pattern is common in contemporary media economics. It is a pattern that consumers and citizens need to monitor and criticize to ensure that new voices and sounds get heard.

"Music should never be **harmless**."
—Robbie Robertson,
The Band

Popular music endures because it speaks to both individual and universal themes, from a teenager's first romantic adventure to a nation's outrage over social injustice. Music often reflects the personal or political anxieties of a society. It also breaks down artificial or hurtful barriers better than many government programs. Despite its tribulations, music at its best continues to champion a democratic spirit. Writer and free-speech advocate Nat Hentoff addressed this in the 1970s when he wrote, "Popular music always speaks, among other things, of dreams—which change with the times."[20] The recording industry continues to capitalize on and spread those dreams globally, but in each generation musicians and their fans keep imagining new ones.

REVIEW QUESTIONS

1. The technological configuration of a particular medium sometimes elevates it to mass-market status. Why did Emile Berliner's flat disk replace Edison's wax cylinder, and why did this reconfiguration of records matter in the history of the mass media? Can you think of other mass media examples in which the size and shape of the technology have made a difference?

2. How did sound recording survive the coming of radio?

3. How did rock and roll significantly influence two mass media industries?

4. Although many rock-and-roll lyrics from the 1950s are tame by today's standards, this new musical development represented a threat to many parents and adults at that time. Why?

5. What moral and cultural boundaries were blurred by rock and roll in the 1950s?

6. Why did cover music figure so prominently in the development of rock and roll and the record industry in the 1950s?

7. Explain the British invasion. What was its impact on the recording industry?

8. How did soul music manage to survive the British invasion in the 1960s?

9. What were the major influences of folk music on the recording industry?

10. Why did rap and punk rock emerge as significant musical forms in the late 1970s and 1980s? What do their developments have in common, and how are they different?

11. What companies control the bulk of worldwide music production and distribution?

12. Why are independent labels so important to the music industry?

13. What accounts for the cost of a typical CD recording? Where do the profits go?

14. Why is it ironic that so many forms of alternative music become commercially successful?

QUESTIONING THE MEDIA

1. Who was your first favorite group or singer? How old were you at the time? What was important to you about this music?

2. If you ran a noncommercial campus radio station, what kinds of music would you play and why?

3. Think about the role of the 1960s drug culture in rock's history. How are drugs and alcohol treated in contemporary and alternative forms of rock and rap today?

4. Is it healthy or detrimental to the music industry that so much of the recording industry is controlled by six large international companies? Explain.

5. Do you think the global popularity of rock music is mainly a positive or a negative cultural influence? What are the pros and cons of rock's influence?

In small groups, take on the investigation of a small independent recording company (of which there are thousands throughout the United States). In your investigation, try to find answers to the following questions:

1. What kind of music does this label specialize in? What is the profile of a typical fan?

2. How does this label go about identifying artists and getting a recording to the consumer?

3. What sorts of commercial obstacles does this independent label face?

4. Is the goal of this label to eventually sell to a major label or to remain independent?

5. From the perspective of those who run the label, what are the major problems facing the recording industry?

6. According to those who work at this label, how easy or difficult is it to enter the industry? Are there student internship possibilities at the label or at other independent labels?

Add other questions and information as you go along. Meet with the members of your group to discuss your findings. Your group might want to prepare a chart or provide information on your label that can be shared with the rest of the class.

(*Note:* This assignment can be adapted to other media industries covered in this text.)

Popular Radio
and the Origins of Broadcasting

CHAPTER 4

When MTV premiered in August 1981, the first video shown was "Video Killed the Radio Star" by the Buggles. The song title's ominous prediction was yet another in a long line of doom-laden forecasts for radio. In the mid-1950s, many critics believed that television's explosion onto the American landscape would ultimately spell radio's demise. That, of course, did not happen.

In fact by late 1996, in a stunning example of media convergence, veteran New York deejay Don Imus struck an unprecedented deal that simultaneously put his syndicated radio show on national television and the Internet via cable channel MSNBC, itself a joint venture between the NBC television network and the computer software giant Microsoft. Imus's New York anchor station, WFAN, and its owner, Infinity Broadcasting, had recently been purchased by another television network, CBS/Westinghouse, now the nation's largest owner of radio stations.

The Imus experiment happened in part because MSNBC wanted to capitalize on a resurgence in radio's stature and popularity. After all, by the mid-1990s two of the nation's most prominent media celebrities were "radio stars" Howard Stern and Rush Limbaugh. Both had published autobiographies that topped best-seller lists (and Stern's was made into a popular 1997 movie). Both drew criticism for their often mean-spirited attacks on people who disagreed with them. Stern's typically sexist performances on his daily syndicated radio program "earned" him a slot on cable's E! channel, and Limbaugh hosted a syndicated television show promoting his conservative political views.

The celebrity status of Limbaugh and Stern illustrates the increased blurring of cultural and political boundaries in contemporary life. Howard Stern briefly ran for governor of New York in 1994, promising to revive the death penalty, repair potholes, and put a bottle of Snapple in every voter's refrigerator. Summoned to Washington by Republican leaders after the GOP election victories in 1994, Rush Limbaugh schooled incoming conservative legislators on the perils of politics, especially on how to handle media pressure. Many Limbaugh fans wanted him to seek public office. But his detractors mounted a campaign to slow him down. In 1996, for example, comedian Al Franken launched a best-selling political book, *Rush Limbaugh Is a Big Fat Idiot and Other Observations*, that capitalized on the radio star's celebrity stature.

> "The telegraph and the telephone were instruments for private communication between two individuals. The radio was democratic; it directed its **message to the masses** and allowed one person to communicate with many.
>
> "The **new medium of radio** was to the printing press what the telephone had been to the letter: it allowed immediacy. It enabled listeners to experience an event as it happened."
>
> —Tom Lewis,
> *Empire of the Air*

The impact of radio in the twentieth century has been immense, and from all indications, it has not faded. From the early days of network radio, which gave us "a national identity" and "a chance to share in a common experience,"[1] to the more customized medium today, radio's influences continue to reverberate through the airwaves. Though television has displaced radio as our most "common experience," radio has specialized and survived. The daily music and persistent talk that resonate from radios all over the world continue to play a key role in contemporary culture.

The story of radio from its invention at the turn of the century to its survival in the age of television is one of the most remarkable in media history, and it is the focus of this chapter. We will examine the cultural, political, and economic factors surrounding radio's development and perseverance. We will explore the origins of broadcasting, from the early theories about mysterious radio waves to the critical formation of RCA as a national radio monopoly. We will then probe the evolution of commercial radio, including the rise of NBC as the first network, the development of CBS, and the establishment of the first federal radio acts. Reviewing the fascinating ways in which radio reinvented itself in the 1950s, we will also examine television's impact on radio programming and its advertising base, focusing on the invention of FM radio, radio's convergence with sound recording, and the influence of formats. Finally, we will survey the economic health and cultural impact of commercial and noncommercial radio today.

the origins and development of broadcasting

The wired and electronic transmissions of media messages have always required three ingredients: power (electricity); symbols (Morse code, music, or language); and a transmission-reception system (such as radio and TV stations and sets). With these requirements, radio did not emerge as a full-blown mass medium until the 1920s, but its recipe had been evolving for a number of years.

the underlying technology

The invention of the telegraph in the 1840s ushered in the modern age of mass media. American artist-inventor Samuel Morse developed the first practical system, sending electrical impulses from a transmitter through a cable to a reception point. Using a

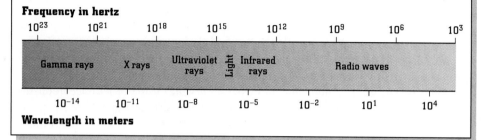

The electromagnetic spectrum extends from short gamma rays through light waves to long radio waves. The spectrum diagrammed below gives the frequency and wavelength for the various waves. Frequencies are given in hertz and wavelengths in meters. The raised figures with the 10's are a way of abbreviating numbers. For example, 10^{15} hertz equals 1 followed by 15 zeros, or 1,000,000,000,000,000 hertz. The numbers with a minus sign tell how many places the decimal point must be moved in front of the number. For example, 10^{-7} meters equals 0.0000001 meter.

Frequency in hertz

| 10^{23} | 10^{21} | 10^{18} | 10^{15} | 10^{12} | 10^{9} | 10^{6} | 10^{3} |

| Gamma rays | X rays | Ultraviolet rays | Light | Infrared rays | Radio waves |

| 10^{-14} | 10^{-11} | 10^{-8} | 10^{-5} | 10^{-2} | 10^{1} | 10^{4} |

Wavelength in meters

**Figure 4.1
The Electromagnetic Spectrum**
Source: The World Book Encyclopedia, Chicago, 1988.

symbol system that became known as Morse code—a series of dots and dashes that stood for letters in the alphabet—telegraph operators transmitted news and messages simply by interrupting the electrical current along a wire cable. By 1844, Morse had set up the first telegraph line between Washington and Baltimore. By 1861, lines ran coast to coast. By 1866, the first transatlantic cable ran between Newfoundland and Ireland along the ocean floor. Although it only transmitted about six words per minute, this cable was the forerunner of global communication embodied in today's Internet, fax, and satellite technologies.

Along with this revolution came a recognition of the telegraph's limitations. For instance, the telegraph dispatched complicated language codes, but it was unable to transmit the human voice. In addition, although armies benefited from telegraphed information, ships were still out of contact with the rest of the world. As a result, navies could not find out that wars had ceased on land and often continued fighting for months. Another problem was that commercial shipping interests lacked an efficient way to coordinate and relay information about South American produce supplies. What was needed was a telegraph without the wires.

The key development in wireless transmissions came from James Maxwell, a Scottish physicist who in the mid-1860s elaborated on some earlier ideas about electricity and magneticism. Maxwell theorized that there existed **electromagnetic waves**: invisible electronic impulses similar to visible light. Maxwell's equations showed that electricity, magnetism, light, and heat are essentially part of the same phenomena and radiate in space at the speed of light, about 186,000 miles per second (see Figure 4.1). Maxwell further theorized that a portion of these phenomena, later known as radio waves, could be harnessed so that their signals could be sent from a transmission point and obtained at a reception point. As one historian commented on the significance of Maxwell's ideas: "Every appliance we have today, from an electric generator to the microwave oven in the kitchen—and, of course, the radio—operate according to his fundamental equations. As Newton revolutionized mechanical science in the seventeenth century, so Maxwell revolutionized electrical science in the nineteenth."[2]

It was German physicist Heinrich Hertz, however, who in the 1880s proved Maxwell's theories. Hertz created a crude device that permitted an electrical spark to jump a small gap between two steel balls. As the electricity jumped the gap, it emitted electromagnetic waves and marked the first recorded transmission and reception of a radio wave. Hertz's experiments had profound influences on two inventor-entrepreneurs, Guglielmo Marconi and Lee De Forest, who at the turn of the century began marketing wireless communication systems for businesses.

Marconi and Wireless Telegraphy. In 1894, a twenty-year-old, self-educated Italian engineer, Guglielmo Marconi, read Hertz's work and set about trying to make wireless technology practical. Marconi understood that developing a way to send high-speed messages over great distances would transform communication, the military, and commercial shipping. Although revolutionary, the telephone and the telegraph were limited by where wires could go.

Marconi improved on Hertz's experiments in a number of important areas. First, to the spark-gap transmitter he attached a Morse telegraph key, which could send out dot-dash signals. The electrical impulses traveled into a Morse inker, the machine telegraph operators used to record the dots and dashes onto narrow strips of paper. Second, Marconi discovered that grounding, connecting the transmitter and receiver to the earth, greatly increased the distance he could send signals.

The Italian government, not understanding what Marconi had accomplished, refused to patent his invention. Thus, in 1896 he left for England, where he quickly received a patent on *wireless telegraphy*, a form of voiceless point-to-point communication. In London in 1897, he formed the Marconi Wireless Telegraph Company, later known as British Marconi, and began installing wireless technology on British naval and private commercial ships. In 1899, he opened a branch in the United States, establishing a company nicknamed American Marconi. That same year he sent the first wireless Morse code signal across the English Channel to France, and in 1901 he relayed the first wireless signal across the Atlantic Ocean.

As successful as Marconi was as an innovator-entrepreneur, his vision was still limited. He saw wireless telegraphy only as point-to-point communication, much like the telegraph and telephone, and not as a one-to-many mass medium. He confined his applications to military and commercial ships. In limiting his patents to Morse code transmission, Marconi left open to others the exploration of voice and music via the wireless.

De Forest and Radio. In 1899, inventor Lee De Forest, who liked to call himself "the father of radio," wrote the first Ph.D. dissertation on wireless technology. Understanding the extent and influence of Marconi's innovations, De Forest decided that his future livelihood and place in history could be realized by going beyond Marconi. In 1901, De Forest challenged the Italian inventor, who had contracted with

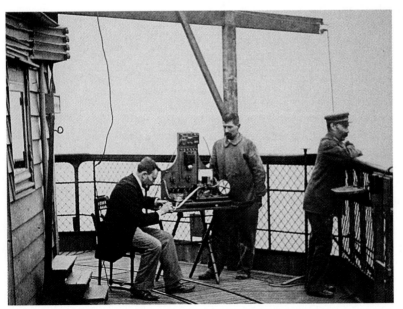

the Associated Press to cover New York's International Yacht Races. De Forest signed up to report the races for a rival news service. The transmitters of the two rivals jammed each other's signals so badly that officials ended up relaying information on the races the premodern way—with flags and hand signals. The event symbolized a prob-

French engineers transmitted an early wireless signal from the Eiffel Tower in 1898. Their Morse code transmission was picked up almost three miles away. Two years earlier, twenty-two-year-old Guglielmo Marconi had sent a signal two miles across his parent's estate in Bologna, Italy.

lem that would become stickier throughout radio's early development: noise and interference from too much competition for a finite supply of radio waves (see "Tracking Technology: Before Satellites, Shortwave Radio" on page 94).

In 1902, De Forest set up the Wireless Telephone Company to compete head-on with American Marconi, by then the leader in the field. A major difference between Marconi and De Forest was the latter's interest in wireless voice and music transmissions, which became known as *wireless telephony* and later as *radio*. The key distinction is that both wireless telegraphy and telephony are forms of point-to-point communication, either wireless operator to wireless operator or phone to phone. Radio or broadcasting, however, became a form of mass communication—one to many. Radio offered the possibility of sending accessible messages to thousands of people who did not need training in Morse code.

Although occasionally accused of stealing ideas, De Forest went on to patent more than three hundred inventions. He claimed as his biggest breakthrough the development of the Audion or triode vacuum tube. The Audion, until the arrival of transistors and solid-state circuits, powered radio by detecting signals and then amplifying them. De Forest's improvements in detection, conduction, and amplification greatly aided listeners' ability to hear dots and dashes and later speech and music on a receiver set. His modifications were essential to the development of voice transmission, long-distance radio, and later television. In fact, many historians consider De Forest's improvements of the vacuum tube the beginning of modern electronics.

The credit for the first voice broadcast belongs to Canadian engineer Reginald Fessenden, former chief chemist for Thomas Edison. Fessenden went to work for the U.S. Navy and eventually for General Electric, where he played a central role in improving wireless signals. Both the navy and GE, however, were interested in the potential for simple voice transmissions that did not require Morse code. On Christmas Eve in 1906, after GE had built Fessenden a powerful transmitter, he gave his first public demonstration of a voice aired from his station at Brant Rock, Massachusetts. A radio historian describes what happened:

> That night, ship operators and amateurs around Brant Rock heard the results: "someone speaking! . . . a woman's voice rose in song. . . . Next someone was heard reading a poem." Fessenden himself played "O Holy Night" on his violin. Though the fidelity was not all that it might be, listeners were captivated by the voices and notes they heard. No more would sounds be restricted to mere dots and dashes of the Morse code.[3]

Ship operators, who had not seen the publicity announcing Fessenden's broadcast, were startled to hear voices rather than the familiar Morse code. (Some operators actually thought they were having a supernatural encounter.)

Broadcasting, once an agricultural term that referred to casting seeds over a large area, would come to mean the transmission of radio waves (and later TV signals) to a broad public audience. Prior to radio broadcasting, the wireless was considered only a form of **narrowcasting**, the kind of person-to-person communication that was possible via the telegraph and telephone. Today, narrowcasting has come to mean any specialized electronic programming or media channel aimed at a target audience, such as cable's Golf Channel or an Internet newsgroup for the medical profession.

In 1907, De Forest followed Fessenden's first broadcast by sending radio voices and music—actually a performance by Metropolitan Opera tenor Enrico Caruso—to his friends in New York. The next year, De Forest and his wife, Nora, played records into a microphone from atop the Eiffel Tower. The signals were picked up four hundred miles away. Radio had passed from inventor's toy to business venture; it was now set to explode as a mass medium.

"I discovered an **Invisible Empire of the Air,** intangible, yet solid as granite."
—Lee De Forest, inventor

Before Satellites, Shortwave Radio

Radio was the first media to fully realize the potential of the world as a global village, where messages could be sent across vast areas instantly. An important step in radio's global reach, shortwave, was initially dismissed because this type of radio wave did not seem to carry as far as standard signals. In the 1910s, however, experiments in Europe and the United States, mostly by licensed amateur ham-radio operators, demonstrated that shortwave signals could travel halfway around the world. Amateurs, confined to shortwaves by the government and commercial wireless interests, bounced a shortwave signal across the Atlantic Ocean as early as 1921.

As is often the case in media history, government and business became interested soon thereafter. Westinghouse engineers, for instance, used shortwave to link three radio stations as a network in 1923. By the end of the 1920s, engineers in England had figured out how to use shortwave signals to send long-distance telephone calls—as satellites do today—to the sprawling colonies of the British Empire. By 1930, the Soviet Union was spreading messages in fifty different languages via shortwave.

By 1935, shortwave radio served most of Europe, sending programs in various languages to the United States and the rest of the world. Shortwave had become the best way for immigrants to keep track of developments in their home countries. As worldwide tension mounted in the 1930s, shortwave use increased, as it always has during global crises. Since many commercial radio sets were once equipped to receive shortwave signals, millions of people in the 1930s and 1940s tracked global news. They relied on the shortwave in the same way that we rely on satellite transmissions today.

During World War II, the United States set up the Voice of America (VOA) to boost the morale of American soldiers and citizens overseas. The government took over privately owned shortwave stations to transmit music, news, commentary, drama, and comedy programs gathered from domestic radio. Sent in a variety of languages, VOA became a primary source of information about the United States for foreign countries—a predecessor to satellite-delivered CNN. Today VOA still dispatches more than forty hours of programming a day in multiple languages.

During the Cold War, shortwave reached its zenith as both the United States and the Soviet Union funded it heavily. Although claiming to be privately supported, America's Radio Free Europe and Radio Liberty, begun in the early 1950s, were CIA-backed operations. In large part, they were programmed by refugees and exiles from communist nations, who aired news that was censored in their native countries. To counter U.S. transmissions, the Soviets built facilities to spread their own propaganda and to jam incoming American signals.

With the collapse of communism, shortwave changed in the 1990s. On the decline, Russian shortwave today sounds more like Western European and American news and commentary. Radio Free Europe and Radio Liberty have also cut back programming. However, shortwave has been growing

early broadcasting regulations

The first international conference on the wireless convened in Germany in 1903. Besides signal interference issues, the conference addressed wireless requirements for ships at sea. The U.S. government had initially refused to ratify international rules because American manufacturers thought this would stifle national growth. But ultimately America passed the Wireless Ship Act in 1910, which required wireless equipment with a one-hundred-mile range for all major U.S. seagoing ships carrying over fifty passengers and traveling more than two hundred miles off the coast.

Then Congress passed the Radio Act of 1912 in response to increased noise and interference on the airwaves and to the tragedy of the *Titanic*. (A brand-new British luxury steamer, the *Titanic* sank in 1912, killing fifteen hundred people; wireless reports had played a critical role in pinpointing the *Titanic*'s location and helping rescue ships save seven hundred lives.) A short policy guide, this first Radio Act required all wireless stations to obtain radio licenses from the Commerce Department. Since radio waves crossed state and national borders, legislators determined that broadcast-in Africa and southern Asia, especially in places where $20 shortwave receiver sets are far cheaper than satellite dishes. The content of programs has also shifted; religious viewpoints mix with politics, news, and entertainment programs.

Today, over sixteen hundred shortwave stations worldwide dispatch programming to and from 160 different countries. In addition, over one million licensed amateurs transmit and receive messages in both voice and Morse code signals. Amateurs often use a transceiver, which combines a shortwave transmitter and a receiver in one unit. By purchasing used equipment for under $100, ham operators today can still bounce a radio signal across an ocean. Functioning in the same way that electronic mail and the Internet operate, ham operators relay messages that are often outside the mainstream. Shortwave stations and amateurs continue to serve their communities and nations. In fact, shortwave is sometimes the only means of mass communication during times of natural disasters or wars, when regular broadcast services are interrupted, destroyed, or captured.

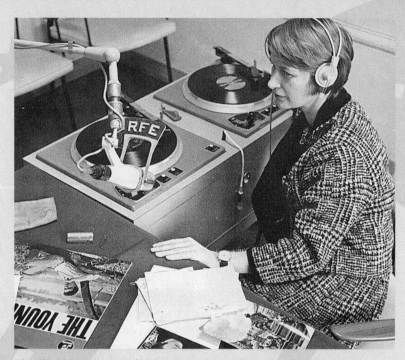

After World War II, covert CIA funding supported Radio Free Europe stations in Munich, Germany. In the 1960s, an RFE deejay broadcasts rock and roll to Czechoslovakia. At the time, rock and roll was banned in Eastern European countries under the influence of the Soviet Union.

ing constituted a "natural resource"—a kind of interstate commerce. With the act, America formally adopted the SOS Morse code distress signal that other countries had been using for several years. The Radio Act of 1912 governed radio's development and regulated the new medium until 1927.

the formation of the rca monopoly

By 1915, more than twenty American companies sold point-to-point communication systems, primarily for ship-to-shore usage. With a reputation for efficiency and honesty, American Marconi was the biggest and best of these companies. But in 1914, with World War I beginning in Europe and with America poised to enter the conflict, the U.S. Navy raised the specter of a foreign-controlled company wielding so much power. American corporations in competition with Marconi, especially General Electric and AT&T, capitalized on the navy's xenophobia and succeeded in undercutting Marconi's influence.

Wireless telegraphy played an increasingly large role in military operations as the navy sought tight controls on information. When the United States entered the war in 1917, the navy closed down all amateur radio operations and took control of key radio transmitters to ensure military security. When the war ended in 1919, corporate heads and government leaders conspired to make sure radio communication would serve American interests. They planned to dominate communication worldwide by controlling the manufacture of radio transmitters and receivers.

At a meeting in May 1919, GE decided not to sell Marconi $5 million worth of vacuum tubes and potent new alternators, the best available power source for long-range radio transmissions. The military, influenced by Franklin Roosevelt, at that time the navy's assistant secretary, did not want such equipment under foreign control. Roosevelt was guided by President Woodrow Wilson's vision of developing the United States as an international power, a position greatly enhanced by American military successes during the war. Wilson believed that in the postwar era, a world power needed international dominion over shipping, or oil, or communication. Great Britain had long controlled the first two and had dominated transatlantic telegraph operations and the world's supply of cable since the 1860s. Wilson and the navy saw an opportunity to slow Britain's influence over communication and to promote a U.S. plan for control of wireless operations.

Some members of Congress and the corporate community opposed federal legislation that would grant the government or the navy a radio monopoly. Consequently, Owen Young, head of GE's legal department (and later GE's chairman), hatched a compromise plan that would pool wireless patents and technology in a new American company. To secure the alternators that it needed, British Marconi was forced to sell its American subsidiary. GE then bought American Marconi at the urging of the navy and formed the Radio Corporation of America (RCA), the chosen instrument for the expansion of American communication technology throughout the world.[4]

With the formation of RCA, the patents pool expanded. Under the new arrangement, wireless patents from the navy, AT&T, GE, and the former American Marconi were combined to ensure U.S. control over the manufacture of transmitters and receivers. Initially, AT&T manufactured most transmitters, while GE (and later Westinghouse) made radio receivers. RCA administered the pool, collecting and distributing patent royalties to pool members. To protect individual profits from existing patents, the government did not permit RCA to manufacture equipment or to operate radio stations under its own name for several years. Instead, RCA's initial function was to ensure that radio parts were standardized by manufacturers and to control frequency interference by amateur radio operators, which became an increasing problem after the war.

At this time, the control of patents, amateurs, and foreigners were among RCA's major concerns. A government restriction mandated that no more than 20 percent of RCA—and eventually any U.S. broadcasting facility—could be owned by foreigners. This restriction, later raised to 25 percent, became a 1934 law that applied to all U.S. broadcasting stocks and facilities. In 1985, this rule would necessitate that Rupert Murdoch, the head of Australia's giant News Corp., become a U.S. citizen so that he could buy a number of TV stations as well as the Fox network.

Even after defusing Marconi's power in 1919, the navy worried that other important patents might come under foreign control. Over the next two years, RCA entered into a series of cross-licensing agreements that brought Westinghouse and a number of smaller companies into the monopoly. These agreements further strengthened the cozy relationship between government and radio's corporate leaders that had begun during World War I. RCA's most significant impact, however, was that it gave America incredible control over the emerging mass medium of broadcasting, which at the time had not been envisioned by most wireless executives. By pooling more than two thousand patents and sharing research developments, RCA launched the United States into global dominance in mass communication, a position it maintained in electronic hardware into the 1960s and in program content through the 1990s.

At the time, the United States was the only country that placed broadcasting under the care of commercial, rather than military or government, interests. RCA's head start and protected status would enable America to become the world's largest exporter of information services and popular culture.

the evolution of commercial radio

When Westinghouse engineer Frank Conrad set up a crude radio studio above his Pittsburgh garage in 1919, placing a microphone in front of a phonograph to broadcast music and news to his friends (whom Conrad supplied with receivers) two evenings a week, he unofficially became the medium's first disc jockey. In 1920, a lightbulb went on in the head of a Westinghouse executive who had become intrigued by Conrad's curious hobby: "The efforts that were being made to develop radio telephone as a confidential means of communication were wrong . . . instead its field was really one of wide publicity."[5] In other words, the executive had realized the potential of radio as a mass medium. Westinghouse then established station KDKA, which aired national returns from the Cox-Harding presidential election on November 2, an event most historians consider the first professional broadcast. Almost overnight, the age of point-to-point wireless became the age of broadcast radio.

In 1921, the Commerce Department officially licensed five radio stations for operation, although a number of engineering schools had been operating experimental stations for several years. By early 1923, more than six hundred commercial and noncommercial stations were operating. Some stations were owned by AT&T, GE, and Westinghouse, but many were run by amateurs or were independently owned by universities or businesses. Later, the government permitted RCA to acquire its own stations. By the end of 1923, 550,000 radio receivers, most manufactured by GE and Westinghouse, had been sold for about $55 each. Just as the "guts" of the phonograph had been put inside a piece of furniture to create a consumer product, the vacuum tubes, electrical posts, and bulky batteries that made up the radio receiver were placed inside stylish furniture and marketed to the home. By 1925, 5.5 million radio sets were in use across America, and radio was a mass medium.

> "I believe the **quickest way to kill** broadcasting would be to use it for direct advertising."
> —Herbert Hoover, Secretary of Commerce, 1924

dissension in the ranks

In 1922, in a major power grab, AT&T, which already had a government-sanctioned monopoly in the telephone business, decided to break its RCA agreements in an attempt to monopolize radio as well. Identifying the new medium as the "wireless telephone," AT&T argued that broadcasting was merely an extension of its control over the telephone. Ultimately, the corporate giant complained that RCA had gained too much monopoly power. In violation of early RCA agreements, the phone company began making and selling its own radio receivers.

Then, in New York in 1922, AT&T started WEAF (now WNBC), the first radio station to sell commercial time to advertisers. The phone company claimed it had the exclusive right under the RCA agreements to sell ads, which AT&T called *toll broadcasting*. Most people in radio at the time recoiled at the idea of using the medium for crass advertising, viewing it instead as a public information service. But by August 1922, AT&T nonetheless sold its first ad to a New York real-estate developer for $50. The idea of promoting the new medium as a public service, along the lines of today's noncommercial National Public Radio (NPR), ended when executives realized that radio ads offered another opportunity for profits. Advertising revenue would in fact ensure profits long after radio-set sales had saturated the consumer market.

The initial strategy behind AT&T's toll broadcasting idea, however, was the phone company's effort to conquer radio. By virtue of its agreements with RCA, AT&T retained the rights to interconnect the signals between two or more radio stations via telephone wires. In 1923, when AT&T aired a program simultaneously on its flagship WEAF station and on WNAC in Boston, the phone company created the first **network**: a cost-saving operation that linked, through special phone lines, a group of broadcast stations that share programming produced at a central location. By the end of 1924, AT&T had interconnected twenty-two stations to air a talk by President Calvin Coolidge. Some of these stations were owned by AT&T, but most simply agreed to become AT&T "affiliates," agreeing to air the phone company's programs. These networked stations became known informally as the *telephone group* and later as the Broadcasting Corporation of America (BCA).

In response, GE, Westinghouse, and RCA interconnected a smaller competing set of stations, known as the *radio group*. Initially, their network linked WGY in Schenectady, New York (then GE's national headquarters), and WJZ in Manhattan. The radio group had to use inferior Western Union telegraph lines when AT&T denied them access to telephone wires. By this time, AT&T had sold its stock in RCA and refused to lease its lines to competing radio networks. The telephone monopoly was now in a battle to defeat RCA for control of radio. This, among other problems, eventually led to a government investigation and an arbitration settlement in 1925. In the agreement, the Justice Department, irritated by AT&T's power grab, redefined patent agreements. AT&T received a monopoly on providing the wires, known as *long lines*, to interconnect stations nationwide. In exchange, AT&T sold its BCA network to RCA for $1 million and agreed not to reenter broadcasting for eight years (a banishment that actually lasted into the 1990s).

sarnoff and nbc

After Lee De Forest, David Sarnoff was among the first to envision the wireless as a modern mass medium. From the time he served as Marconi's fifteen-year-old personal messenger, Sarnoff rose rapidly at American Marconi. He became a wireless operator, helping to relay information about the Titanic survivors in 1912. Promoted to a series of management positions, Sarnoff was closely involved in RCA's creation in 1919, when most radio executives saw wireless merely as point-to-point communication. But with Sarnoff as RCA's first commercial manager, radio's potential as a mass medium was quickly realized. At age thirty, Sarnoff became RCA's general manager in 1921.

After RCA acquired AT&T's telephone-group stations, Sarnoff created a new subsidiary in September 1926 called the National Broadcasting Company (NBC). Its ownership was shared by RCA (50 percent), General Electric (30 percent), and Westinghouse (20 percent). This loose network of stations would be hooked together by AT&T long lines. Shortly thereafter, the original telephone group became known as the NBC-Red network, and the radio group became the NBC-Blue network.

Although NBC owned a number of stations by the late 1920s, many independent stations began affiliating with the networks to receive programming. An **affiliate** station, although independently owned, signs a contract to be part of a network and receives money to carry a network's programs. In exchange, a network reserves time slots, which it sells to national advertisers. By 1933, NBC-Red had twenty-eight affiliates; NBC-Blue had twenty-four.

> "I have in mind a plan of development which would make radio a 'household utility' in the same sense as the piano or phonograph. The idea is to bring **music into the house** by wireless."
>
> —David Sarnoff, 1915

The rationale behind a network is an economic one: to control program costs and avoid unnecessary duplication. As early as 1923, AT&T realized that it would be cheaper to produce programs at one station and broadcast them simultaneously over a network of owned or affiliated stations. Such a network centralized costs and programming by bringing the best musical, dramatic, and comedic talent to one place, where programs could be produced and then distributed all over the country through a network of phone lines (and later satellite relays).

In essence, network radio helped modernize America by deemphasizing the local and the regional in favor of national programs broadcast to nearly everyone. In fact, when Charles Lindbergh returned from the first solo transatlantic flight in 1927, an estimated twenty-five to thirty million people listened to his welcome-home party on the six million radio sets then in use. At the time, it was the largest shared audience experience in the history of any mass medium.

David Sarnoff's leadership at RCA was capped by two other negotiations that solidified his stature as the driving force behind radio's modern development. In 1929, he cut a deal with General Motors for the manufacture of car radios, which had been invented a year earlier by William Lear (designer of the Learjet), who sold the radios under the name Motorola. Sarnoff also merged RCA with the Victor Talking Machine Company. Afterwards, the company was known until the mid-1960s as RCA Victor, adopting as its corporate symbol the famous terrier sitting alertly next to a Victrola radio-phonograph. The merger gave RCA control over Victor's records and recording equipment, making the radio company a major player in the sound recording industry. In 1930, David Sarnoff became president of RCA and ran the company for the next forty years.

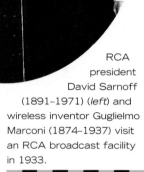

RCA president David Sarnoff (1891–1971) (*left*) and wireless inventor Guglielmo Marconi (1874–1937) visit an RCA broadcast facility in 1933.

the end of the rca monopoly

As early as 1923, the Federal Trade Commission had charged RCA with violations of antitrust laws but allowed the monopoly to continue. By the late 1920s, however, the government intensified its scrutiny, now concerned about NBC's growing control over radio content. Then in 1930, when RCA bought out the GE and Westinghouse interests in the two NBC networks, federal marshals charged RCA/NBC with a number of violations, including too much control over manufacturing and programming. Although the government had originally sanctioned a closely supervised monopoly for wireless communication, RCA products, its networks, and the growth of the new mass medium had dramatically changed the radio industry by the late 1920s. After the collapse of the stock market in 1929, public opinion became increasingly distrustful of big business. In 1932, the government revoked RCA's monopoly status.

RCA acted quickly. In exchange for the government canceling half of the corporation's nearly $20 million debt that had accumulated during the early years of the Depression, Sarnoff's company bought out the remaining GE and Westinghouse shares in RCA's manufacturing business. Now RCA would compete directly against GE, Westinghouse, and other radio manufacturers, but to encourage new competition, Sarnoff agreed not to make radio equipment for thirty months. Ironically, in the mid-1980s, General Electric bought back RCA, a shell of its former self and no longer competitive with foreign electronics firms. GE was chiefly interested in RCA's brand-name status and its still-lucrative subsidiary, NBC.

paley and cbs

Even with its head start and RCA's favored status, the company's two NBC networks faced competitors in the late 1920s. They all found it tough going. One group, United Independent Broadcasters (UIB), even lined up twelve prospective affiliates and offered them $500 a week for access to ten hours of station time in exchange for quality programs. UIB was cash poor, however, and AT&T would not rent the new company line services to link the affiliates. Enter the Columbia Phonograph Company, which was looking for a way to preempt RCA's merger with the Victor Company, then Columbia's major competitor. With backing from the record company, UIB and the new Columbia Phonograph Broadcasting System launched a wobbly sixteen-affiliate network in 1927. But after losing $100,000 in the first month, the record company pulled out. UIB then dropped the word *phonograph* from the title, creating CBS.

In 1928, William Paley, the twenty-seven-year-old son of Sam Paley, owner of a Philadelphia cigar company, bought controlling interest in CBS to sponsor the cigar manufacturer's La Palina brand. One of Paley's first moves was to hire public relations pioneer Edward Bernays, Sigmund Freud's nephew, to polish the new network's image. Paley and Bernays modified a concept called **option time** in which CBS paid affiliate stations $50 per hour for an option on any of their time. The network provided programs to them and sold ad space or sponsorships to various product companies. In theory, CBS now could control up to twenty-four hours a day of its affiliates' radio time. Some affiliates received thousands of dollars per week merely to serve as conduits for CBS programs and ads. Since NBC was still *charging* some of its affiliates as much as $90 a week to carry network programs, the CBS offer was extremely appealing.

By 1933, Paley had over ninety affiliates, many of them defecting from NBC. Paley also concentrated on developing news programs and entertainment shows, particularly soap operas and comedy-variety series. In the process, CBS successfully raided NBC, not just for affiliates but for top talent as well. Throughout the 1930s and 1940s, Paley lured a number of radio stars from NBC, including Jack Benny, Frank Sinatra, George Burns and Gracie Allen, and Groucho Marx. During World War II, Edward R. Murrow's powerful firsthand news reports from bomb-riddled London established CBS as the premier radio news network, a reputation it carried forward to television. In 1949, near the end of big-time network radio, CBS finally surpassed NBC as the highest-rated network. Although William Paley had intended to run CBS only for six months to help get it off the ground, he ran it for more than fifty years.

the mutual broadcasting system

While the major networks were building their dynasties during the 1930s, not all radio stations sought affiliations with them; many stations were content to produce their own regional and local programs. In 1934, four powerful independent stations— WGN in Chicago, WOR in Newark, WLW in Cincinnati, and WXYZ in Detroit— formed the Mutual Broadcasting System. Sharing programs and functioning more as a cooperative venture than as a regular network, three of these stations operated fifty-thousand-watt "clear channels" that reached most of North America.

Mutual offered a small central news service and a few entertainment programs, and it mostly served smaller stations, often in remote areas that were ignored by NBC and CBS. In 1968, Mutual became the first network to offer a news service, the Mutual Black Network, that raised issues aimed primarily at black listeners. Mutual today serves thousands of radio affiliates by providing a variety of national news services and other programs, including rebroadcasts of many old radio programs from the 1930s.

chaos and the radio act of 1927

In the 1920s, as radio moved quickly from narrowcasting to broadcasting, the battle for more frequency space and less channel interference intensified. Manufacturers, engineers, station operators, network executives, and the listening public demanded action. Many wanted more sweeping regulation than the simple licensing function granted under the Radio Act of 1912, which gave the Commerce Department little clout to deny a license or to unclog the airwaves.

Beginning in 1924, commerce secretary Herbert Hoover conducted a series of national radio conferences to fix the channel problems. He ordered radio stations to share time and to set aside certain frequencies for entertainment and news and others for farm and weather reports. To challenge Hoover, a station in Chicago jammed the airwaves, intentionally moving its signal onto an unauthorized frequency. In 1926, the courts eventually decided that, based on the existing Radio Act, Hoover had the power only to grant licenses, not to restrict stations from operating. Within the year, two hundred new stations clogged the airwaves, creating a chaotic period in which nearly all radios had poor reception. By early 1927, sales of radio sets had declined sharply.

In an attempt to restore order to the airwaves, Congress passed the Radio Act of 1927, the precursor to the Federal Communication Act of 1934. The 1927 act stated that licensees did not *own* their channels but could license them as long as they operated in the "public interest, convenience, or necessity." To oversee licenses and negotiate channel problems, the 1927 act created the Federal Radio Commission (FRC), appointed by the president. Although the FRC was intended as a temporary committee, it grew into a powerful regulatory agency. In 1934, with the passage of the Federal Communication Act, the FRC became the Federal Communication Commission (FCC). Its jurisdiction covered not only radio but also the telephone and telegraph (and later television, cable, and the Internet).

In 1941, an activist FCC went after the networks. Declaring that NBC and CBS could no longer force affiliates to carry programs they did not want, the government outlawed the practice of option time that Paley had used to build CBS into a major network. The FCC also demanded that RCA sell one of its two NBC networks. RCA and NBC claimed that the rulings would bankrupt them. The Supreme Court sided with the FCC, however, and RCA eventually sold NBC-Blue to a group of businessmen for $8 million in the mid-1940s. It became the American Broadcasting Company (ABC). These government crackdowns brought long-overdue changes to the radio industry. But they had not come soon enough to prevent considerable damage to noncommercial radio (see "Examining Ethics: NPR and Support for Noncommercial Radio" on page 103).

"Four years ago we were dealing with a **scientific toy**; today we are dealing with a vital force in American life."
—Herbert Hoover, 1925

the golden age of radio

Many ingredients in television today were formulated initially for radio. The term *veejay*, or video jockey, used on cable's MTV and VH-1 derives from *deejay* or *disc jockey*, a term first used in 1941. In addition, the first weather forecasts and farm reports began in the 1920s. Regularly scheduled radio news analysis started the same year with H. V. Kaltenborn, a reporter for the *Brooklyn Eagle*, providing commentary on AT&T's WEAF. The first regular *network* news analysis began on CBS in 1930, featuring Lowell Thomas, who would remain on radio for forty-four years. Thomas's first report began, "Adolph Hitler, the German fascist chief, is snorting fire. There are now two Mussolinis in the world, which seems to offer a rousing time."[6]

Radio, like television today, commanded a central position in most American living rooms in the 1930s and 1940s. At the time, only a handful of stations operated in most large radio markets, and popular stations affiliated with either CBS or one of two NBC networks. Many large stations employed their own in-house orchestras and aired live music daily. Listeners had favorite evening programs, usually fifteen minutes long, which they would tune in each night. Families gathered around the radio to hear such shows as *Amos 'n' Andy*, *The Shadow*, *The Lone Ranger*, *The Green Hornet*, and *Fibber McGee and Molly*, or one of President Franklin Roosevelt's fireside chats.

> "The Shadow, mysterious aide to the forces of law and order is, in reality, Lamont Cranston, **wealthy young man about town** who, years ago in the Orient, learned the hypnotic power to cloud men's minds so that they could not see."
> —opening line,
> *The Shadow*, 1931

Among the most popular early forms on radio, the *variety show* served as the forerunner to popular TV shows. The variety show, developed from stage acts and vaudeville, began with the *Eveready Hour* in 1923 on WEAF. Considered experimental, the program presented classical music, minstrel shows, comedy sketches, and dramatic readings. Stars from vaudeville, musical comedy, and New York theater and opera would occasionally make guest appearances.

By the 1930s, studio audience *quiz shows*—*Professor Quiz* and the *Old Time Spelling Bee*—had emerged. Other quiz formats, used on *Information Please* and *Quiz Kids*, featured guest panelists. The quiz formats were later copied by television, particularly in the 1950s. *Truth or Consequences*, based on a nineteenth-century parlor game, began in 1940 and presented guests performing goofy stunts. It ran for seventeen years on radio and another twenty-seven on television, influencing TV stunt shows like CBS's *Beat the Clock* in the 1950s and cable's *Double Dare* in the 1980s.

Dramatic programs, mostly radio plays that were broadcast live from theaters, developed as early as 1922. Historians mark the appearance of *Clara, Lu, and Em* on WGN in 1931 as the first *soap opera*. One year later, Colgate-Palmolive bought the program, put it on NBC, and began selling the soap products that gave this dramatic genre its distinctive nickname. Early "soaps" were fifteen minutes in length and ran five or six days a week. It wasn't until the 1960s on television that soaps were extended to thirty and sixty minutes. Still a fixture on CBS, the *Guiding Light* actually began on radio in 1937 (the only radio soap to successfully make the transition to television in 1952). By 1940, sixty different soap operas occupied nearly eighty hours of network radio time each week.

The *situation comedy*, a major staple of TV programming today, also began on radio in the mid-1920s. The most popular comedy by the early 1930s was *Amos 'n' Andy*, which started on Chicago radio in 1925 before moving to NBC-Blue in 1929. By today's standards, *Amos 'n' Andy* was a nineteenth-century minstrel show that often stereotyped black characters as shiftless and stupid. Created as a blackface stage act by two white comedians, Charles Correll and Freeman Gosden, the program drew criticism that it was racist. But NBC

In 1942, a family in Provincetown, Massachusetts, listened to a favorite network radio program. In the next decade, television would push radio sets out of most American living rooms and into bedrooms, bathrooms, and cars.

Since Thomas Paine declared government a "necessary evil" in the 1700s, Americans have had a healthy skepticism about government-funded projects. That makes the success of National Public Radio (NPR) a surprise. Supported since 1970 by the federal government and individual donations, NPR is usually touted for fulfilling radio's promise as a mass medium. Most critics argue that NPR programs, particularly its syndicated *All Things Considered* (1971-) and *Morning Edition* (1980-), have outperformed the commercial sector in bringing quality and variety to radio. For example, in 1978 NPR aired the first live coverage of a Senate debate (on the Panama Canal treaties); in 1991, NPR's Nina Totenberg was the first broadcaster to report Anita Hill's sexual harassment charges against future Supreme Court Justice Clarence Thomas; and NPR's many interview and news feature series are considered unrivaled in broadcast news.

So why is it that in every decade since NPR's creation, politicians have threatened to cut off its support? One reason is a perceived liberal bias, which makes NPR a target of political conservatives. Most critics, however, regard NPR as much more even-handed than the commercial news networks. NPR's own audience studies indicate that slightly more than one-third of its listeners are conservatives, just under one-third are liberals, and the other third are moderates.[1]

To get at the real dilemma of NPR's shaky status requires backtracking through radio history. By the late 1920s, corporate interests had wrested the control of radio away from the noncommercial sector: farmers, labor unions, educators, religious leaders, and other citizen groups operating radio stations. Even prior to this time, the government had long been granting favors to commercial radio, including requests for rules to control amateur operators and signal interference. In a bit of slippery reasoning, radio lobbyists representing the networks claimed that the issues of education, religion, and labor (often represented today on NPR) were propaganda serving special interests. They also

claimed, however, that the profit motives of the networks represented the real public interest.

Based on this "logic," the newly created Federal Radio Commission (FRC) forced many nonprofit stations off the air during evening hours, turning their frequencies over to commercial stations. This limited a nonprofit station's air time and diminished its audience reach (since most radio listening occurred after dinner). Many nonprofit stations also had their daytime power severely curtailed. A signal that once traveled thousands of miles now went only a few miles.

In addition, every three months, broadcasters could challenge each other for air space, with network stations and their technical superiority given FRC preference. Slowly, commercial stations began buying up the nonprofits, which struggled to meet expenses during the Depression. Overall, noncommercial stations declined from more than 200 in 1927 to 65 by 1934.[2]

During the last major battle over radio reform, the Wagner-Hatfield Amendment to the 1934 Communication Act would have set aside 25 percent of all broadcast frequencies for a wide range of nonprofit groups. The arguments of commercial lobbyists, however, defeated the measure. By describing capitalism (an economic system) as a simple synonym for democracy (a political system), corporate interests prevailed, curtailing most future debates on broadcast ownership. Commercial broadcasting came to be viewed as natural—as the American way.

NPR has been stained with the residue of these early arguments, which still raise a number of ethical and economic questions. Should NPR receive money from the government? Should NPR get money from commercial broadcasters, as happens in other countries, to ensure that diverse voices are heard—even though such voices many not be profitable to commercial radio? Do citizens have a responsibility to protect NPR from the whims of politicians who periodically threaten to end public radio's government support?

> "Most critics regard NPR as much more even-handed than the commercial news networks."

103

Beginning in 1929, the *Rise of the Goldbergs* was a fixture on CBS Radio. The show tracked the lives of a lower-middle-class Jewish family from the Bronx. In 1949, Gertrude Berg, the show's creator, writer, producer, and star, moved *The Goldbergs* (1949–55) to television. For her role as Molly Goldberg, Berg won television's first Best Actress Emmy in 1950.

and the program's producers claimed that *Amos 'n' Andy* was as popular among black audiences as among white listeners.

A pioneering program in many ways, *Amos 'n' Andy* launched the idea of the weekly *serial* show: a program that featured continuing story lines from day to day. The format was soon copied by soap operas and other radio dramas. *Amos 'n' Andy* aired six nights a week from 7:00 to 7:15. During the show's first year on the network, radio-set sales rose nearly 25 percent nationally. To keep people coming to restaurants and movie theaters, owners broadcast *Amos 'n' Andy* in lobbies, restrooms, and entryways. Early radio research estimated the program aired in over half of all radio homes in the nation during the 1930–31 season, making it the most popular radio series in history. From 1951 to 1953, it made a brief transition to television (Correll and Gosden sold the rights to CBS for $1 million), becoming the first TV series with an entirely black cast.

While *Amos 'n' Andy* was the most popular series in radio, the most famous single broadcast featured an adaptation of the *War of the Worlds* on the radio series *Mercury Theater of the Air*. Orson Welles produced, hosted, and acted in this popular series, which adapted science fiction, mystery, and historical adventure dramas for radio. On Halloween eve in 1938, the twenty-three-year-old Welles aired the 1898 H.

G. Wells' Martian invasion novel in the style of radio news. For people who missed the opening disclaimer, the program sounded like a real news report with eyewitness accounts of pitched battles between Martian invaders and the U.S. Army.

The program created a panic that lasted several hours. In New Jersey, some people walked through the streets with wet towels around their heads for protection from deadly Martian heat rays. In New York, young men reported to their National Guard headquarters to prepare for battle. Across the nation, calls jammed police switchboards. Afterward, Orson Welles, once the radio voice of *The Shadow*, used the notoriety of this broadcast to launch a film career. Meanwhile, the FCC called for stricter warnings both before and during programs that imitated the style of radio news.

On Halloween in 1938, Orson Welles' radio dramatization of *War of the Worlds* created a panic up and down the East Coast, especially in Grover's Mills, New Jersey—the setting for a fictional Martian invasion that many listeners assumed was real. Here, a seventy-six-year-old Grover's Mills resident guards a warehouse against alien invaders.

Radio in this golden age was not the portable medium it would later become. Prior to transistors and solid-state integrated circuits, most radio sets required large glass tubes housed in heavy wooden pieces of furniture. Most programs in those days had a single sponsor who created and produced each show. The networks distributed these programs live around the country, charging the sponsors advertising fees. Many shows—the *Palmolive Hour*, *General Motors Family Party*, the *Lucky Strike Orchestra*, and the *Eveready Hour* among them—were named after the sole sponsor's product.

radio reinvents itself

The history of American mass media reveals that older media forms do not disappear when confronted by newer forms. Instead, mass media adapt. Although radio threatened sound recording in the 1920s, and television threatened radio in the 1950s, both older forms adjusted to the economic and social challenges posed by the arrival of a newer medium. Remarkably, the arrival of television in the 1950s marked the only time in media history in which a new medium virtually "stole" every national programming and advertising strategy from the older medium. Television snatched radio's advertisers, its program genres, its major celebrities, and its large evening audiences. In the process, the TV set physically displaced the radio as the living-room centerpiece across America.

> "There are three things which I shall never forget about America—the Rocky Mountains, Niagara Falls, and **Amos 'n' Andy."**
> —George Bernard Shaw, British playwright

new technologies

The story of radio's change and survival provides a fascinating look at the impact of one medium on another. This is especially important today as newspapers and magazines enter the information highway and as publishers produce Web sites and books on tape for new generations of "readers." In contemporary culture, we have grown accustomed to such media convergence as being the norm. To understand this blurring of the boundaries between media forms, it is useful to look at the 1950s and the ways in which radio responded to the coming of television.

The Transistor. A key development in radio's adaptation occurred with the invention of the *transistor* by Bell Laboratories in 1947. Transistors, like De Forest's vacuum tubes, could receive and amplify radio signals. However, they used less power and heat and were more durable and less expensive. Best of all, they were tiny. Transistors, which also revolutionized hearing aids, represented the first step in replacing bulky and delicate tubes, leading eventually to silicon-chip integrated circuits. Texas Instruments marketed the first transistor radios in 1953 at about $40 apiece. Using even smaller transistors, Sony introduced the pocket radio in 1957. But it wasn't until the 1960s that transistor radios became cheaper than conventional tube and battery radios. For a while, the term *transistor* became a synonym for a small, portable radio.

The development of transistors permitted radio to go where television could not—to the beach, to the office, into bedrooms and bathrooms, and into cars. By the 1960s, most radio listening was actually done *outside* the home. For economic reasons, radio turned to the recording industry for content to replace the shows it had lost to television.

Armstrong and FM. By the time the broadcast industry launched commercial television in the 1950s, many, including David Sarnoff of RCA, were predicting radio's demise. To fund television's development and protect his radio holdings, Sarnoff had even delayed a dramatic breakthrough in broadcast sound, what Sarnoff himself called a "revolution"—FM radio.

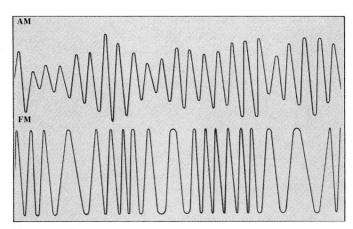

Figure 4.2
AM and FM Waves
Source: Adapted from
David Cheshire,
The Video Manual, 1982.

Edwin Armstrong, who first discovered and developed FM radio in the 1920s and early 1930s, is often considered the most prolific and influential inventor in radio history. He alone understood the impact of De Forest's vacuum tube, and he used it to invent an amplifying system that enabled radio receivers to bring in distance signals. Armstrong's innovations rendered obsolete the enormous 1920s alternators used for generating power in radio transmitters. In 1922, he sold a "super" version of his circuit to RCA for $200,000 and sixty thousand shares of RCA stock, making him a millionaire as well as RCA's largest private stockholder.

Armstrong also worked on the major problem of radio reception—electrical interference. Between 1930 and 1933, the inventor filed five patents on **FM**, or frequency modulation. Offering static-less radio reception, FM supplied greater fidelity and clarity than AM, making FM ideal for music. **AM**, or amplitude modulation, stressed the volume, or height, of radio waves; FM accentuated the pitch, or distance, between radio waves (see Figure 4.2). Although David Sarnoff, by then the chairman of RCA, thought that television would replace the older medium, he helped Armstrong set up the first experimental FM station atop the Empire State Building. Eventually, though, the RCA chief thwarted FM's development (which he was able to do since RCA had an option on Armstrong's new patents). In 1935, Sarnoff threw RCA's considerable weight behind the development of television. With the FCC allocating and reassigning scarce frequency spaces, RCA wanted to ensure that channels went to television before they went to FM. But most of all, Sarnoff wanted to protect RCA's existing AM empire. Given the high costs of converting to FM and the revenue needed for TV experiments, Sarnoff decided to close down Armstrong's station.

Armstrong plunged ahead without RCA. He founded a new FM station and advised other engineers, who started more than twenty experimental stations between 1935 and the early 1940s. In 1941, the FCC approved limited space allocations for commercial FM licenses. Over the next few years, FM grew in fits and starts. Between 1946 and early 1949, the number of commercial FM stations expanded from forty-eight to seven hundred. But then the FCC moved FM's frequency space to a new band on the electromagnetic spectrum, rendering some 400,000 prewar FM receivers useless. Uncertainty loomed over FM's future; by 1954, the number of FM stations had fallen to 560.

On January 31, 1954, Edwin Armstrong, weary from years of legal skirmishes over patents, wrote a note apologizing to his wife, removed the air conditioner from his thirteenth-story New York apartment, and jumped to his death. A month later, David Sarnoff announced record profits of $850 million for RCA with TV sales accounting for 54 percent of the company's earnings. In the early 1960s, the FCC opened up more spectrum space for the superior sound of FM, infusing new life into radio. Although AM stations had greater reach, they could not match the crisp fidelity of FM, which would gradually make FM the preferred medium for music. In the early 1970s, about 70 percent of listeners tuned almost exclusively to AM radio. By the 1980s, however, FM had surpassed AM in profitability. By the 1990s, more than 75 percent of all listeners reportedly preferred FM, and more than five thousand commercial and seventeen hundred noncommercial FM stations were in operation. The expansion of FM represented one of the chief ways radio survived television and Sarnoff's gloomy predictions.

Live and recorded music had long been radio's single biggest staple, accounting for 48 percent of all programming in 1938. Although network affiliates in large markets carried many drama, comedy, and variety series, smaller independent stations had always relied heavily on music. As noted earlier, in the 1920s, many stations even hired their own house bands and studio musicians. In the 1930s and 1940s, lean economic times forced more stations to play recorded music, either older music in the public domain (not under copyright) or music that was marginally popular and not closely monitored by ASCAP (see Chapter 3).

Although live music on radio was generally considered superior to recorded music, early disc jockeys made a significant contribution to the latter. They demonstrated that music alone could drive radio. In fact, when television snatched radio's program ideas and national sponsors, radio's dependence on recorded music became a necessity. Helping radio to survive in the 1950s, the deejay became the norm.

The Rise of Format and Top-40 Radio. As early as 1949, station owner Todd Storz in Omaha, Nebraska, experimented with formula or **format radio**. Under this system, management rather than deejays attempt to control programming each hour. When Storz and his program manager noticed that bar patrons and waitresses repeatedly played their favorite songs from the forty records available in a jukebox, they began researching record sales to identify the most popular tunes. From observing jukebox culture, Storz hit on the idea of *rotation*: playing the top songs many times throughout the day. By the mid-1950s, the management-control idea combined with the rock-and-roll explosion. The *Top-40 format* was born. Although the term Top 40 came from the number of records stored in a jukebox, this format came to refer to the forty most popular hits in a given week as measured by record sales.

As format radio grew, program managers combined rapid deejay chatter with the best-selling songs of the day and occasional *oldies*—popular songs from a few months earlier. By the early 1960s, to avoid "dead air," managers asked deejays to talk over the beginning and the end of a song so listeners would feel less compelled to switch stations. Ads, news, weather forecasts, and station identifications were all designed to fit a consistent station environment. If listeners tuned in at any moment, they would recognize the station by its distinctive sound.

In format radio, management carefully coordinates or programs each hour, much like a lesson plan or a food recipe. Once called a *hot clock* in radio jargon (but now simply referred to as a program log), such recipes dictate what the deejay will do at various intervals throughout each hour of the day (see Figure 4.3). By the mid-1960s, one study determined that in a typical hour on Top 40, listeners could expect to hear about twenty ads; numerous weather, time, and contest announcements; multiple recitations of the station's call letters; about three minutes of news; and approximately twelve songs.

A radio deejay in the mid-1990s depends primarily on digital CDs. Increasingly, the analog LPs that she occasionally still spins on the turntable in the background are becoming obsolete.

```
****************************************************************
*                        KOOL 107                             *
*              * 12 MM  Thursday   01-02-97 *                  *
****************************************************************
CD-TRACK  T I T L E                ARTIST          INTRO  RUN EN
****************************************************************

00:00     BENCHMARK SWEEPER
308-20    ONE                      THREE DOG NIGHT    04  3:03 C

03:03     ACAPELLA JINGLE
   2-05   OH, PRETTY WOMAN          ROY ORBISON       15  2:56 C

05:59     LIVE INTRO
308-27    ON BROADWAY              DRIFTERS           10  2:59 F

09:08     SWEEPER
   408-11 BERNADETTE               FOUR TOPS          00  3:01 F

12:09     JINGLE
   502-08 FEELIN' STRONGER EVERY DA CHICAGO           25  4:13 F

16:22     TALK-OVER MUSIC
405-02    ODE TO BILLY JOE         BOBBIE GENTRY      00  4:17 C

20:39     :25 STOP SET LINER, SPOTS, WEATH
   37-07  FUN, FUN, FUN            BEACH BOYS         17  2:16 F

24:55     SWEEPER
6001-16   STAY                     WILLIAMS, MAURICE & THE Z   1:38

26:33     POSITIONING JINGLE
   2-08   DON'T LET THE SUN CATCH Y GERRY & THE PACEMAKERS  10  2:34 C
```

Figure 4.3
Radio Program Log for an Oldies Station
Source: WQKL-FM, Ann Arbor, MI, 1997.

Radio managers further sectioned off programming into *day parts*, which consisted typically of 6 to 10 A.M., 10 A.M. to 3 P.M., 3 to 7 P.M., and 7 to 12 midnight time blocks. Each day part, or block, was programmed through ratings research according to who was listening. For instance, a Top-40 station would feature its top deejays in the morning and afternoon periods when audiences, many riding in cars, were largest. From 10 A.M. to 3 P.M., research determined that women at home and secretaries at work usually controlled the dial, so program managers, capitalizing on the gender stereotypes of the day, played more romantic ballads and less hard rock. Teenagers tended to be heavy evening listeners, so program managers would often discard news breaks, since research showed that teens turned the dial when news surfaced.

Critics of format radio argued that only the top songs received play and that lesser-known songs, deserving air time, received meager attention. Although a few popular star deejays continued to play a role in programming, many others quit when managers introduced formats. Owners considered programming more of a science, but deejays considered it an art form. Record picks were based on jukebox inventories, record store sales, and trade publication charts. Program managers argued that deejays were probably smarter and more affluent than the average listener and therefore could not be fully trusted to know popular audience tastes. The owners' position, which generated more revenue, triumphed.

Payola. According to management, format radio had another big advantage over deejays who simply played their favorite music. It helped curb **payola**, the practice of record promoters paying deejays to play particular records. As we noted in Chapter 3, payola was rampant during the 1950s as record companies sought to guarantee record sales. When management took control of programming, however, individual deejays had less impact on what records would be played and became less susceptible to bribery. In response to this situation, record promoters often turned their attention to a few influential, high-profile deejays, whose backing could make or break a record nationally, or to key program managers in charge of Top-40 formats in large urban markets.

Despite congressional hearings and new rules to eliminate the problem, payola persisted. In the 1970s, for example, payola scandals involved exchanging airplay for drugs as well as cash. Although a 1984 congressional hearing determined there was "no credible evidence" of payola practices in the recording industry, NBC News broke a story in 1986 about independent promoters with alleged ties to the Mafia. One of NBC's sources on the story, Miami deejay Don Cox, was severely beaten right after the news story aired. Cox had told NBC that he had turned away promoters offering cash and cocaine for guaranteeing airplay. A subsequent investigation led major recording companies to break most of their ties with independent promoters. Prominent record labels had been paying such promoters up to $80 million per year to help records become hits. Format radio eliminated the payola problem on a large scale, but charges of exchanging airplay for money, drugs, and sex continue to haunt both the radio and recording industries.

Contemporary radio sounds very different from its predecessors. In contrast to the few stations per market in the 1930s, most large markets today include more than forty receivable signals that vie for listener loyalty. With the exception of national network-sponsored news segments, most programming is locally produced and heavily dependent on the music industry for content. Although a few radio personalities, such as Howard Stern, Rush Limbaugh, Don Imus, Dr. Laura Schlessinger, and the Fabulous Sports Babe are nationally prominent, local deejays and their music are the stars at most radio stations.

However, unlike listeners in the 1930s who tuned in their favorite shows at set times, listeners today do not say, "Gee, my favorite song is coming on at 8 P.M., so I'd better be home to listen." Instead, radio has become a secondary or background medium that follows the rhythms of daily life. In the 1930s, radio often dictated those rhythms, particularly with its popular evening programs. Today, radio programmers worry about channel cruising, that habit of listeners, especially while in their cars, who search the dial until they find a song they like.

Stations now are more specialized. Listeners in the 1940s were loyal to favorite programs, but today we are loyal to favorite stations and even radio personalities. We generally listen only to four or five stations that target us, usually based on our age, gender, or race. Television long ago took over the role of reaching the larger mass audience. In the 1930s, peak listening time occurred during evening hours—dubbed *prime time* in the TV era—when people were home from work and school. Today, the heaviest radio listening occurs during *drive time*, those periods between 6 and 9 A.M. and 4 and 7 P.M. when people are commuting to and from work or school. All of these changes were well under way by the late 1950s. For a time, critics thought radio might collapse under the weight of TV's growing popularity. In 1944, near the peak of radio's renown, only about a thousand stations were on the air. More than fifty years later, nearly twelve thousand radio stations operate in the United States, customizing their sounds to reach mobile niche audiences.

the economics of broadcast radio

Today, more than 10 percent of all U.S. spending on media advertising goes to radio stations. Like newspapers, radio generates its largest profits by selling local and regional ads. Gross advertising receipts were near $10 billion in 1995, up over 12 percent from the previous year. The industry is economically healthy and employs more than 150,000 people. Unlike television, where the largest chunk—nearly 40 percent—of a station's expenses goes to buy syndicated programs, local radio stations get much of their content free from the recording industry. Therefore, only about 20 percent of a typical radio station's budget goes to cover programming costs.

Network radio, which still generated around $500 million annually in ad sales in the mid-1990s, offers more than twenty different kinds of specialized services. In 1967, for example, ABC pioneered four different services to fit format radio—FM, contemporary, entertainment, and information—each offering particular kinds of news or features. By the 1990s, more than fifty companies offered national program and format services, including 1930s drama and comedy series, special news and features, and national music programs such as Dick Clark's rock and roll retrospectives. In addition, services such as the National Black Network and the Business Radio Network offer programming to local stations in exchange for time slots for national ads.

Commercial Radio and Specialization. Although Top-40 managers pioneered format radio, stations today use a variety of formats arranged according to managed program logs and day parts, as we explained earlier. All told, more than twenty different radio formats, plus variations, serve diverse groups of listeners. To please advertisers who want to know exactly who's listening, formats usually target audiences by their age and income, gender, or race-ethnicity. Radio's specialization allows advertisers to reach smaller target audiences at costs that are much less expensive than television. This process, however, has become extremely competitive because there may be forty or fifty stations available in a large radio market. In the early 1990s, according to the Center of Radio Information, over one thousand stations a year (roughly 10 percent) switched formats, trying to find the formula that would generate more advertising money. Some stations, particularly in large cities, have also been renting blocks of time to various local ethnic and civic groups, allowing them to dictate their own formats and sell ads.

Although Top-40 radio—also called contemporary hit radio (CHR)—is in decline, it still appeals to many teens and young adults, and advertisers continue to buy time from Top-40 stations. Since the mid-1980s, however, these stations have lost steady ground as younger generations have followed music on MTV rather than on radio. In addition, Top-40 music by the mid-1990s had become so diverse, encompassing everything from gangsta rap to children's songs, that "no commercial radio station could ever play it all and hold on to an audience."[7]

In contrast, the nation's fastest growing format through the early and mid-1990s was the *news/talk* format (see "Case Study: The Appeal of Talk Radio" on page 112). In 1987, only 170 radio stations operated formats dominated by either news programs or talk shows, which tend to appeal to adults over thirty-five (except for sports talk programs, which draw both younger and older mostly male sports fans). By 1996, buoyed by the notoriety and popularity of Howard Stern and Rush Limbaugh, more than a thousand stations used some combination of news and talk. A news/talk format, though more expensive to produce than a music format, appeals to advertisers looking to target working- and middle-class adult consumers. Nevertheless, most radio stations continue to be driven by a variety of less expensive musical formats (see Table 4.1).

Contemporary Music Formats. Known first as middle-of-the-road or MOR, the *adult contemporary* (AC) format is among radio's oldest and most popular, reaching

TABLE 4.1
The Twelve Most Popular Radio Formats

September 1987		July 1996	
Format	Number of Stations	Format	Number of Stations
Country	2468	Country	2537
Adult contemporary (AC)	2213	AC	1284
Top 40/CHR	825	News/talk	1074
Nostalgia/adult standards	719	Oldies	702
Religious	554	Religious	567
Easy listening	375	Nostalgia/adult standards	383
Album-oriented rock (AOR)	319	Classic rock	353
Oldies	261	Spanish-language	326
News/talk	171	Top 40/CHR	304
Spanish-language	163	Urban contemporary/black	260
Black/gospel	162	AOR	176
Soft rock	152	Soft rock	165

Source: The Center for Radio Information.

between 17 and 20 percent of all listeners, most of whom are over the age of forty. In the early 1970s, *Broadcasting* magazine described AC's eclectic mix of news, talk, oldies, and soft rock music as "not too soft, not too loud, not too fast, not too slow, not too hard, not too lush, not too old, not too new."

Many formats target by age or gender, but some also appeal to particular ethnic or racial groups. For example, *Spanish-language* radio targets large Cuban populations in Miami, Puerto Rican listeners in New York, and Chicano audiences in California and Texas (where the first all-Spanish-language station, KCOR, originated in San Antonio in 1947). Besides talk shows and news segments in Spanish, these formats feature a variety of Spanish, Caribbean, and Latin American musical styles, including calypso, flamenco, mariachi, merengue, reggae, samba, salsa, and son.

In terms of African American listeners, formats featuring jazz, gospel, rhythm and blues, and dance music have aimed at various audience segments over the years. In 1947, WDIA in Memphis was the first station to program exclusively for black listeners. Now called *urban contemporary* (UC), this format targets a wide variety of African American listeners, mostly in large cities. UC, which typically plays popular dance, rap, and blues music, subdivides also by age, featuring an adult UC category with performers like Luther Vandross and Anita Baker. A number of stations that refuse to play rap use what the industry calls a black/R&B format.

Pitched to older listeners and used as background sound, instrumental radio music is played in many offices, supermarkets, retail stores, and homes. Characterized by critics as "elevator music," the *easy listening* (EZ) format is aimed at adult listeners, predominantly female and white. Sometimes also called *wall-to-wall music* or *musical wallpaper*, these formats were the first to acknowledge that radio had become a secondary activity: background "noise" in the television age. In the past few years, however, EZ formats have declined, losing ground to *nostalgia/big band* formats (also called *adult standards*). Aimed at listeners who care about the original versions of the music from their youth, nostalgia/big band formats emphasize early jazz vocalists and the swing era, including music from Frank Sinatra, Ella Fitzgerald, Louis Armstrong, and Glenn Miller.

The *country* format does not reach as many total listeners as AC or news/talk radio, but country claims by far the most stations. Many of these stations are in tiny markets where country has traditionally reigned as the format of choice for communities with only one radio station. Country music has old roots in radio, starting in 1925 with the influential Grand Old Opry program on WSM in Nashville. Although Top 40 drove country music out of many radio markets in the 1950s, the growth of FM in the 1960s brought it back as station managers looked for market niches not served by rock music. As diverse as rock, country music today includes such subdivisions as old-time, progressive country, country-rock, western swing, country-gospel, and Tejano (a blend of Texas country, Mexican folk melodies, and German accordion music).

Resisting the Top 40. Accompanying the expansion of the FM spectrum in the mid-1960s, *progressive rock* emerged as an alternative to conventional formats. Many of the noncommercial stations broadcast from college campuses, where student deejays and managers, unencumbered by ads and format radio, rejected the commercialism associated with Top-40 tunes. Instead, they began playing lesser-known alternative music and longer album cuts. Until that time, most rock on radio had been consigned almost exclusively to Top-40 AM formats, with song length averaging about three minutes.

The expansion of FM created room for experimenting, particularly with classical music, jazz, blues, and non-Top-40 rock songs. Experimental FM stations, both commercial and noncommercial, served as a venue for Bob Dylan's 1965 song "Desolation Row," which ran eleven minutes. In 1967, the Doors' "Light My Fire," a No. 1 hit, featured a seven-minute version for FM and a three-minute Top-40 AM

The Appeal of Talk Radio

Talk radio, the fastest-growing radio format since Top 40 in the 1950s, comes in two varieties (excluding sports talk): the personal and the political. Much like Rush Limbaugh, Howard Stern, or Don Imus today, the earliest talk shows in radio mixed personal stories and political intrigue, with emphasis on the former. The genre developed in the 1920s around syndicated newspaper columnists Louella Parsons and Walter Winchell. Parsons, who wrote gossip columns about the movie industry for the powerful Hearst newspaper chain, used her position to coerce film stars, who could not afford bad publicity, to appear on radio. Winchell, one of the most popular commentators in radio history, discussed both celebrity culture and the day's top news stories.

The most personal type of early talk show—the forerunner of Dr. Ruth Westheimer and most legitimate talk-therapy programs—was the shady *Medical Question Box* featuring Dr. John Brinkley in the 1920s. Brinkley had purchased a mail-order diploma for $100 from the Eclectic Medical University in Missouri. On his program, which aired out of a powerful Kansas station, a caller would mail in symptoms (at $2 per inquiry), and over the radio Brinkley would diagnose and offer a cure (at $1 per prescription). He also sent out his bottled medicines without ever having

seen the patient. His advertising promoted a surgery that he claimed would restore sexual potency by implanting goat glands in a man's scrotum, an operation that Brinkley performed many times. Not recognizing Brinkley's medical degree, the American Medical Association protested. The Federal Radio Commission eventually revoked his radio license in 1930 for failing to serve the "public interest," whereupon Brinkley took his show across the border to Mexican radio.

Franklin Roosevelt's radio conversations during his thirteen years as president are some of the most important in political talk-radio history. Roosevelt's staff used radio to promote Social Security, rural electrification, and the Tennessee Valley Authority, among other New Deal reforms. FDR's own fireside chats on radio helped a struggling nation survive the Depression, the menace of Hitler, and a second world war. When Roosevelt announced Japan's December 7, 1941, attack on Pearl Harbor, over sixty-two million listeners were tuned in—still the single largest audience for any radio "talk."

Father Charles Coughlin, the "radio priest," began broadcasting from the Shrine of the Little Flower in Royal Oak, Michigan, in the late 1920s. In addition to religion, the charismatic Coughlin discussed politics and economics. He also used his radio pulpit to support FDR. As Coughlin's national reputation expanded and the Depression

version. The same year, some FM stations played Arlo Guthrie's "Alice's Restaurant," an eighteen-minute satiric antiwar folk ballad. FM offered a cultural space for hard-edged political folk and for rock music that commented on the civil rights movement and protested America's involvement in the Vietnam War. By the 1970s, progressive rock had been copied, tamed, and absorbed by mainstream radio under the format label *album-oriented rock* (AOR). By 1972, AOR album sales already accounted for over 85 percent of the retail record business. By the 1980s, as first generation rock and rollers aged and became more affluent, AOR had become less political and played mostly white post-Beatles music featuring groups such as Pink Floyd, Led Zeppelin, Queen, and Cream.

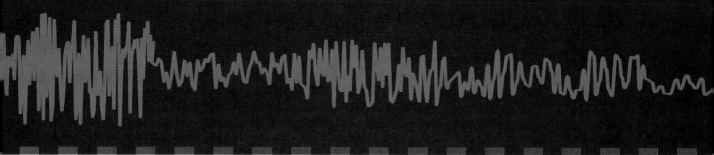

deepened, however, he turned against FDR's New Deal and became more reactionary. He railed against labor unions and began singing the praises of Nazism, using his anti-Semitism to attract donations for his small parish. Although scolded by the Catholic hierarchy, he stayed on the air until 1940 when broadcasters quit selling him time.

Sharing many of Coughlin's early populist views was Louisiana Senator Huey Long. Long, too, turned against Roosevelt in the 1930s and demanded more radical economic reforms to ease the Depression. Using radio to promote his Share-the-Wealth Society, which promised a minimum income for American families, Long soon earned a loyal national following. His populist motto, "Every man a king," and folksy southern charm worked well on radio. In 1935, Long announced his candidacy for the presidency, a move that threatened to split the Democratic party, but he was assassinated later that year.

Today the spirit of Father Coughlin and Huey Long lives on in Rush Limbaugh, a national presence on contemporary radio. Carried by some seven hundred stations by the mid-1990s, Limbaugh has estimated that his listeners, largely working- and middle-class people who are moderate to conservative politically, number three to four million each day. Limbaugh often implores listeners to

Format Favorites

Comparison of audience share for specific formats on average in Arbitron's top 25 metro markets based on listener surveys of people ages 12 and older in fall 1994 and 1995.

FORMAT	% TOTAL AUDIENCE SHARE	
	FALL '94	FALL '95
News/talk	17.2	17.2
Urban	10.0	11.1
Adult contemporary	9.7	9.4
Country	7.9	7.6
Spanish	5.3	6.4
Oldies	6.2	4.8
Album-oriented rock	5.5	4.4
Modern rock	3.9	4.4
Contemporary hits	4.4	3.7
Hot adult contemporary	3.4	3.2
Adult standards	3.0	3.2
Classic rock	3.8	3.0
Jazz	2.7	2.9
Classical	2.2	2.2
Adult alternative	1.2	1.4

Source: The Interep Radio Store.

celebrate their individual status and embrace personal responsibility—a seductive message when bureaucratic social institutions seem in such need of repair.

There are many reasons for the staying power of talk shows. First, broadcast talk represents an electronic extension of an older oral past. As more impersonal forms of print culture displaced the more intimate forms of oral culture, modern societies lost something. Talk shows, although electronically filtered, may be one attempt to recover those important lost traditions of daily conversation. Second, in an age that has become increasingly bureaucratic and impersonal, radio talk at least creates the feel, and frequently the illusion, of intimacy. Although often exploiting the personal pain and problems of individuals, talk radio suggests that someone out there in the world will listen and react to our everyday troubles and anxieties.

Whether the talk is personal or political, whether it takes place in coffee shops, in cars, via e-mail, or over the backyard fence, we tune in to participate. We may be looking for people whose bizarre lives make our daily problems pale in comparison. We may be searching for solutions to larger social dilemmas and ways to make democracy work better. Or we may be seeking some company. When talk radio airs a diversity of viewpoints, it keeps *all* forms of democratic conversation alive.

A number of critics have denounced AOR for limiting the definition of rock music. They argue that the strictly controlled AOR format displaced progressive rock by aiming "programming at an extremely specific, limited listenership," mostly white males in the thirteen to twenty-five age range. AOR programming guidelines initially ignored most black and women performers, whom program directors claimed held little appeal for AOR's target audience. By discouraging certain kinds of music, AOR formats encouraged a type of "institutionalized racism and sexism." These guidelines were later adopted by MTV in its formative years, making it harder for black and women artists to crack the video scene in the early 1980s.[8]

113

"Although noncommercial radio seems to have turned the corner of public awareness, it has not yet overcome **decades of disorganization** and neglect and abuse by the federal government."
—Peter Fornatale and Joshua Mills, *Radio in the Television Age,* 1980

Today there have been several spin-offs from AOR. *Classic rock* serves up rock oldies from the mid-1960s through the 1980s to the baby-boom generation and is aimed primarily at listeners who have outgrown the conventional Top 40. The *oldies* format serves adults who grew up on 1950s and early 1960s rock and roll. Begun in California in the mid-1960s, oldies formats recall the integrationist impulse of early rock as well as emphasize soul and Motown music from the 1960s. Listening habits and record research indicate that most people identify closely with the music they listened to as adolescents and young adults. This partially explains why oldies and classic rock stations have surpassed Top-40 stations today.

nonprofit radio

In the 1930s, the Wagner-Hatfield Amendment was intended to set aside 25 percent of radio for a wide variety of nonprofit stations. When the amendment went down in defeat in 1935, the future of educational and noncommercial radio looked bleak. Many nonprofits had sold out to for-profit owners during the Depression. The stations that remained were often banished from the air during the evening hours or assigned weak signals by federal regulators who favored commercial owners and their lobbying agents. Still, nonprofit public radio survived. More than seventeen hundred such stations now operate, many of them low-wattage stations on college campuses.

During the 1960s, nonprofit broadcasting found a Congress sympathetic to an old idea: radio and television as educational tools. As a result, National Public Radio (NPR) and the Public Broadcasting Service (PBS) were created as the first noncommercial networks. Under the auspices of the Public Broadcasting Act of 1967 and the Corporation for Public Broadcasting (CPB), NPR and PBS were mandated to provide alternatives to commercial broadcasting. NPR's popular news and interview programs, *Morning Edition* and *All Things Considered*, draw three to four million listeners per day. Over the years, however, more time and attention have been devoted to public television than to public radio. When government funding tightened in the late 1980s and 1990s, television received the lion's share. In 1994, a conservative majority in Congress cut financial support and threatened to scrap the CPB, the funding authority for public broadcasting. Consequently, stations became more reliant than ever on private donations and corporate sponsorship. While depending on handouts, especially from big business, public broadcasters steered clear of some controversial subjects, especially those that critically examined corporations.

Like commercial stations, nonprofit radio has also adopted the format style. Unlike commercial radio, however, the dominant style in public radio is a loose variety format whereby a station may actually switch from jazz, classical music, and alternative rock to news and talk during different parts of the day. Some college stations, too small to affiliate, have kept alive the spirit of early 1950s radio, when deejays chose the music. Noncommercial radio still remains the place for both tradition and experimentation, for programs that do not draw enough listeners for commercial success.

By the mid-1990s, *religious, classical music,* and AOR were the primary formats in public and nonprofit radio. Of these, religious broadcasting is the format that most often relies on commercials as a source of revenue. Although about four hundred stations nationally are devoted full time to religious programming, another thousand stations devote at least fifteen hours a week to religious shows, double the number from the early 1980s.[9] Research from 1995 indicated that women constituted about 60 percent of the audience for religious programs and that the average annual income of listeners was about $30,000 a year. Although many religious stations and programs are noncommercial and depend solely on listener donations, roughly half of these broadcasts rely on advertising to pay the bills. In general, religious stations do not advertise controversial products (such as alcohol) that might undercut values promoted on the programs. Major advertisers on religious programs—clothing retailers, department stores, food companies, and car dealers—believe that associating their products with religious values gives their ads a kind of credibility that cannot be found as easily on for-profit, commercial stations.

Although the proposed Wagner-Hatfield Amendment failed to redistribute radio resources in the mid-1930s, public and nonprofit radio have made some minor gains beyond the growth of religious programming. First, in 1948 the FCC approved the 10-watt FM station. Prior to this time, radio stations had to have at least 250 watts to get licensed. A 10-watt station with a broadcast range of only about seven miles took very little capital to operate, so more people could participate in the new FM phenomenon. Not only did these stations promote Edwin Armstrong's invention, but they became training sites for students interested in broadcasting. By the 1990s, more than a thousand 10-watters were in operation.

A second development that aided public radio also occurred in 1948. For the first time, the government authorized a noncommercial license for a noninstitutional operation. In other words, the FCC granted a nonprofit license to a station not affiliated with labor, religion, education, or a civic group. The license went to Lewis Kimball Hill, a radio reporter and pacifist during World War II, who started the Pacifica Foundation to run experimental public stations. Pacifica stations, like Hill himself, have often challenged the status quo in radio as well as in government. Most notably, in the 1950s they aired the poetry, prose, and music of performers—considered radical, left-wing, or communist—who were blacklisted by television and seldom acknowledged by AM stations. Pacifica over the years has also been fined and reprimanded by the FCC and Congress for airing programs that critics considered inappropriate for public airwaves.

> "Radio affects most people intimately, person-to-person, offering a world of **unspoken communication** between writer-speaker and listener. That is the immediate aspect of radio. A private experience.
> —Marshall McLuhan, *Understanding Media*, 1964

radio, ownership, and democracy

In recent years, the rules concerning the ownership of the public's airwaves have changed substantially. With the passage of the 1996 Telecommunications Act, the FCC eliminated most ownership restrictions on radio. As a result, in 1996 alone some 2,100 stations switched owners, as $15 billion changed hands. Previously, any single person or company could own up to twenty AM and twenty FM stations nationwide, and only two of these could be in the same market. The new law allows individuals and companies to acquire as many stations as they wany, with relaxed restrictions on the number of stations a single broadcaster may own in the same city: The larger the market or area, the more stations a company may own within that market. For example, in areas with forty-five or more stations available to listeners, a broadcaster may own up to eight stations, but not more than five of one type (AM or FM). In areas with fourteen or fewer stations, a broadcaster may own up to five stations (three of any one type). In very small markets with a handful of stations, a broadcast company may not own more than half the stations.

There were twice as many radio stations operating in the mid-1990s as in the mid-1980s, but the total number of owners remained the same. Though it had once tried to encourage diversity in broadcast ownership, the FCC has recently pushed a consolidation scheme in which fewer and fewer owners control more and more of the airwaves. For instance, in 1995 its buyout of CBS made Westinghouse the largest single owner of radio stations in the United States. Then, in 1996 Westinghouse/CBS extended its reach by merging its radio holdings with Infinity Broadcasting. The new group now operates more than eighty stations nationwide. Given broadcasters' reluctance to raise questions about these economic arrangements, public debate regarding the national resource that is radio has remained minuscule. Looking to the future, a big question remains to be answered: With a few large broadcast companies now permitted to dominate radio ownership nationwide, will this in any way restrict the number and kinds of voices permitted to speak over public airwaves? To ensure that mass media industries continue to serve democracy, critical scrutiny and public voices need to play a role in the answer.

With its future in the twenty-first century yet to be determined, radio still managed to survive the economic threat posed by television. With its specialized services, radio remains a mass medium where we can find our culture, our history, our politics, and our music represented. Radio's daily doses of news, chatter, and song reverberate through the airwaves, helping to define areas of culture that are not readily acknowledged in mainstream newspapers or on prime-time television.

REVIEW QUESTIONS

1. Why was the development of the telegraph important in media history? What were some of the disadvantages of telegraph technology?

2. How is the concept of the wireless different from radio?

3. What was Marconi's role in the development of the wireless?

4. What were Lee De Forest's contributions to radio?

5. Why was the RCA monopoly formed?

6. How did broadcasting, unlike print media, come to be federally regulated?

7. What was AT&T's role in the early days of radio?

8. How did the radio networks develop? What were the contributions of David Sarnoff and William Paley to network radio?

9. Why did the government-sanctioned RCA monopoly end?

10. What is the significance of the Communication Act of 1934?

11. How did radio adapt to the arrival of television?

12. What was Edwin Armstrong's role in the advancement of radio technology? Why did RCA hamper Armstrong's work?

13. How did music on radio change in the 1950s?

14. What was format radio, and why was it important to radio's survival?

15. Why are there so many radio formats today?

16. Why has Top-40 radio diminished as a format in the 1980s and 1990s?

17. What is the state of nonprofit radio today?

18. What are the current ownership rules governing American radio?

19. Throughout the history of radio, why did the government encourage diversity among radio owners?

QUESTIONING THE MEDIA

1. Describe your earliest memories of listening to radio. Do you remember a favorite song? How old were you? Do you remember the station's call letters? Why did you listen?

2. How much radio do you listen to? When do you listen? What attracts you to a particular station?

3. Count the number and types of radio stations in your area today. What formats do they use? Do a little research and compare today's situation with the number and types of stations available in the 1930s and the 1950s. Describe the changes.

4. If you could own and manage a commercial radio station, what format would you choose and why?

5. If you ran a noncommercial campus radio station in your area, what services would you provide that are not being met by commercial format radio?

6. How might radio be used to improve social and political discussions in the United States?

In small groups (or as a class), listen to a few radio stations and compare two or three types of radio formats for one hour during the day. (This could also be developed as a written project.) Use a chart and break each hour into a program log (see Figure 4.3). Track the time devoted to several categories, including:

- music
- deejay chatter and routines
- community announcements
- contests
- news
- ads
- station promotion
- other

Use a pie graph to demonstrate approximately what percentage of time a station devotes to each category. Then, based on your analysis of the formats, answer the following questions:

1. For each station you analyzed, construct a profile of the kind of listener you think that station is trying to reach. To develop the profile, look at each category carefully. For example, how is news treated during the hour? When Top 40 developed, stations tried to make the news and the ads sound like the music. Was this the case during the hours you listened? Provide evidence to support your position. Call the programming department at each station and ask what audience it is attempting to target. (These departments might also give you information on ad costs and ratings.) Finally, compare your own listener profile to the information each station has given you.

2. According to FCC rules, radio stations are trustees of the public airwaves. Based on the limited hours you listened, were these stations doing a responsible job reaching their public? Did they provide a consistent and identifiable "sound"? What did they do well? In what ways could they improve?

CHAPTER 5

In the late 1980s, the CBS situation comedy *Murphy Brown* featured network news personality Connie Chung in a guest appearance. She plays herself, counseling the fictional Murphy Brown, a network reporter played by Candice Bergen, not to guest star on trivial situation comedies. Such appearances, Chung advises, would undermine Murphy's credibility among real journalists, who might stop taking her seriously. A few years later, after a brief stint coanchoring the *CBS Evening News* with Dan Rather, Connie Chung lost her job—in part because she was not taken seriously as a journalist by television critics and the network news community.

In 1992 during a heated presidential campaign, the fictional Murphy Brown made the real national news. On a spring episode that year, Murphy gives birth to her first child, then rejects two men who offer to marry her, deciding to raise the child as a single mother. The day after the episode aired, Vice President Dan Quayle denounced the program as a mockery of fatherhood, touching off a fierce national debate on "family values." The next day, Quayle's concerns made the front page of the *New York Times* in a story that pitted the lifestyle choices of a fictional reporter against the traditional beliefs of a real vice president.

The blurring of the border between fact and fiction continued. In a 1995 episode of *Murphy Brown*, the characters on the show lament the defections of local television stations to a rival network. Murphy defends the fictional defections, pointing out that her own network's new TV season is nothing but a mediocre "crapfest," featuring a drama about an orangutan who works for an environmental SWAT team. Her comments are quoted in a newspaper. As punishment, she is dispatched by network bigwigs to a convention of local TV managers to dissuade them from deserting.

With *Murphy Brown*, art imitates life. Indeed, in the summer of 1994, the Fox network, owned by media baron Rupert Murdoch, won the four-year broadcast rights to National Football Conference games from CBS for $1.5 billion. In several top markets—including Atlanta, Detroit, Milwaukee, and St. Louis—network-affiliated stations defected shortly thereafter to the upstart six-year-old Fox. Football had been on CBS for thirty years, and the loss shook the network. Even David Letterman, newly arrived at CBS in 1993, began a comic assault on his new employer as his own show began to dip in the ratings due to the station defections.

The Fox raid on CBS programming and station allegiances recalled the offensive that television conducted on the radio industry in the 1950s. Throughout the 1950s, television seduced national audiences with scratchy black-and-white moving images. Television eventually took over radio's national sponsors, program ideas, and even its **prime-time** audience, those tuned in between 8 and 11 P.M. (or 7 to 10 P.M. in the Midwest). Old radio scripts began reappearing in TV form. In 1949, for instance, *The Lone Ranger* rode over to television from radio, where the program had originated in 1933. *Amos 'n' Andy*, a fixture on network radio since 1928, became the first TV series with an entirely black cast in 1951; this circumstance would not be repeated until *Sanford and Son* in 1972. Jack Benny, Red Skelton, George Burns and Gracie Allen, among the most prominent comedians of their day, all left radio for television. Symbolic of the times, the radio news program *Hear It Now* turned into TV's *See It Now*, and *Candid Microphone* became *Candid Camera*.

"[T]elevision artists construct their work by collage, by **pillaging the culture** for pieces of their construction. They exhibit their art—the television series—in our homes, not hung in stately repose on a museum wall, but unfolding within the rhythms of daily life."
—Christopher Anderson, critic, 1985

Since replacing radio in the 1950s as our most popular medium, television's social and cultural impact has repeatedly sparked arguments. Over the last decade, for example, teachers, clergy, journalists, and others have waged a public assault on TV's negative impact on children. A 1995 *New York Times* poll suggested that most Americans blamed television as the biggest single factor underlying teenage sex and violence (although TV viewing during teenage years actually decreases).[1] During election campaigns, television has been a target as well, serving as a lightning rod for frustration regarding what is wrong with American society.

But there is another side to this story. In the 1960s, television was there to expose civil rights violations in the South, and in the 1980s it did the same in Eastern Europe and China. In the early 1990s, the televised Clarence Thomas–Anita Hill hearings triggered public debates about sexual harassment. In times of crisis, our fragmented and pluralistic society has turned to television as a touchstone, as common ground. We did this during the Army-McCarthy hearings on communism in the 1950s, in the aftermath of the Kennedy and King assassinations in the 1960s, during the political turmoil of Watergate in the 1970s, and after the space-shuttle disaster in the 1980s. When President Bush announced America's attack on Iraq in 1991, most U.S. homes tuned in; when 170 people died in the bombing of the Oklahoma City federal building in 1995, we turned to television to try again to make sense of senselessness. For better or worse, television has woven itself into the cultural fabric of daily life.

In this age of increasing market specialization, television is still the one mass medium that delivers content millions can share simultaneously, be it the Superbowl, a network mini-series, or a presidential election debate. In this chapter we will examine television's impact: the cultural, social, and economic factors surrounding the most influential media innovation since the printing press. We will begin by reviewing the early experiments with TV technology that led to the medium's development. We will then focus on the TV boom in the 1950s, including the downfall of sponsor-controlled content and the impact of the quiz-show scandals. Most of TV's major programming trends developed during this period, and we will investigate the most significant ones, including news, comedy, and drama. We will then trace the decline of the major networks. In addition, we will explore television as a prime-time money factory, examining various developments and costs in the production, distribution, and syndication of programs. Finally, we will look at television's impact on democracy.

> **George:** "Gracie, what do you think of **television**?"
> **Gracie:** "I think it's wonderful—I hardly ever watch radio anymore." —*George Burns and Gracie Allen Show*

early technology and the development of television

Television changed social life, and the change was swift and dramatic. In 1948, only 1 percent of America's households had a television set. By 1953, more than 50 percent had one. By the early 1960s, more than 90 percent of all homes had a TV set. With television on the rise throughout the 1950s, many feared that radio—as well as books, magazines, and movies—would become unnecessary. What happened, of course, is that both radio and print media adapted to this new technology. In fact, today more radio stations are operating and more books and magazines are published than ever before; and ticket sales for movies have remained steady since the 1960s.

the formative years

Although television achieved mass media status in the 1950s, inventors from a number of nations had been toying with the idea of televised images for nearly a hundred years. To isolate TV and radio waves, part of the electromagnetic spectrum, required two ingredients: a photoelectric sensing material and a technique for decoding pictures for transmission through the air. Inventors needed a medium like film so that when light struck it, an electric current could be generated. In the late 1800s, the invention of the *cathode ray tube*, the forerunner of the modern TV picture tube, combined principles of the camera and electricity. Since television images cannot physically float through the air, technicians and inventors developed a method of encoding them at a transmission point (a TV station) and decoding them at the reception point (a TV set).

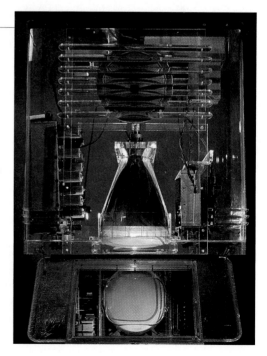

At the 1939 World's Fair in New York, the "guts" of a TV set featured a sealed glass device called a *cathode ray tube*. Such picture tubes were the technical standard in television for more than fifty years. Late in 1996, the FCC approved a new standard—digital, high-definition television.

In the 1880s, German inventor Paul Nipkow developed the *scanning disk*, a large flat metal disk with a series of small perforations organized in a spiral pattern. As the disk rotated, it separated pictures into pinpoints of light that could be transmitted as a series of electronic lines. As the disk spun, each small hole scanned one line of a scene to be televised. For years, Nipkow's disk served as the foundation for experiments regarding the transmission of visual images.

In 1907, Russian physicist Boris Rosing improved the mechanical scanning device, but it was his lab assistant, Vladimir Zworykin, and an Idaho teenager, Philo Farnsworth, who independently pioneered an electronic TV system. Zworykin left Russia for America in 1919 and went to work for Westinghouse, where he developed the *iconoscope*, the first TV camera tube to convert light rays into electrical signals. By breaking down and converting these signals into radio waves, transmitting them through the air, and reconstructing them in a receiver set, inventors made television a possibility by 1923.

At age sixteen, Farnsworth patented an electronic *image dissector* tube and figured out that mechanical scanning systems would not work for sending pictures through the air over long distances. In 1927, at age twenty-one, Farnsworth transmitted the first TV picture electronically—the image of a dollar sign. Finally, in 1930, he patented the first electronic television. RCA, then the world leader in broadcasting technology, challenged Farnsworth, who would have to rely on his high school notebooks as evidence to win a major patents battle against the company. After its court defeat, RCA had to negotiate to use Farnsworth's seventy-three patents. He later licensed these patents to RCA and AT&T for use in the commercial development of television. RCA conducted the first public demonstration of a TV image at the 1939 World's Fair.

Technical Standards. In the late 1930s, the National Television Systems Committee (NTSC), a group representing major electronics firms, began meeting to outline industry-wide manufacturing and technical standards. These meetings were similar to those held in the 1980s and 1990s to develop standards for high-definition television (HDTV) and digital television (see "Tracking Technology: The Digital Revolution"). As a result of the NTSC meetings, in 1941 the FCC adopted a 525-line image, scanned electronically at 30 frames per second (fps), which became the standard for all TV sets produced in the United States (until about 2006 when the new digital standard will make old sets obsolete). About thirty countries, including Japan, Canada, Mexico, Saudi Arabia, and most Latin American nations, adopted the NTSC system. Great Britain and the former Soviet Union, however, waited for the technology to improve and eventually adopted a slightly superior 625-line, 25-fps system, used for decades throughout most of Europe and Asia. A third standard operated in France, Belgium, Algeria, and a few other countries.

The TV Freeze. In 1941, the FCC set aside thirteen channels (1–13) on the **VHF** (very high frequency) band for black-and-white television. At this time, though, most electronic firms were converting to wartime production, so the commercial development of television was limited: Only ten stations were operating when Pearl Harbor was hit. However, by 1948, the FCC had issued nearly a hundred television licenses. Due to growing concern about channel allocation and frequency interference problems, which needed to be reviewed, the FCC declared a freeze on any new licenses from 1948 to 1952.

The Korean War prolonged the freeze. During this time, cities such as New York, Chicago, and Los Angeles had several TV stations, while other areas, including Little Rock, Arkansas, and Portland, Oregon, had none. Cities with TV stations saw

The Digital Revolution

Late in 1996, the Federal Communications Commission initiated the first essential changes in TV technology in more than fifty years.[1] Since the early 1960s, the search had been on to improve the clarity and resolution of the standard NTSC 525-line TV image established in the 1940s. Most experiments focused on improving existing *analog transmission*, in which images are sent as continuous signals through the airwaves on specific frequencies. By the 1980s, Japanese firms had developed *high-definition television* (HDTV) for their own markets; with 1,100-plus lines of resolution, HDTV was far superior to the NTSC standard. HDTV seemed certain to become the new U.S. television standard.

In the late 1980s, however, HDTV ran into the digital revolution. After seeing an impressive Sony HDTV demonstration in 1987, the FCC set up a race among various companies—including Sony—to develop a new American standard that used digital technology, which reduced both images and text to computerized signals. Sony and other Japanese firms created a hybrid of analog and digital HDTV innovations. To meet the Japanese challenge, in 1988 a consortium of broadcasters, electronics and computer manufacturers, and researchers from Europe and America—known as the Grand Alliance—began developing an all-digital system that surpassed the versatility of existing HDTV formats. The digital standard requires much less frequency space to store many more images and holds much more information and computer data than can analog or hybrid systems.

In late 1996, the FCC approved the Grand Alliance digital system. Under this plan, each existing television station will be allocated a second channel for roughly ten years as consumers convert to digital sets. During that time, each station will continue to broadcast programs using traditional analog signals on its old channel. Meanwhile, the same programs, as well as new digitized programs and computer services, will be transmitted on the new digital channel. At the end of the adjustment period, the stations will return their old analog frequencies to the FCC for redistribution, formally ending analog broadcasting.

As we look toward the twenty-first century, several things are clear. Digital television will provide lightweight, flat-screen, and even wall-mounted reception and will eventually replace bulky analog picture-tube sets. But over the short run, the next ten years will feature a marketplace war between the computer industry and the TV electronics industry, each offering its own version of digital television. The predictions of each side, made in 1997 at the outset of this manufacturing battle, appear below.

THE CONSUMER ELECTRONICS INDUSTRY SAYS:

- Past experience has shown that when consumers shop for a new TV, they are most interested in picture quality and cost.
- The Web is not yet a mass medium; there are few regular browsers, and they are concentrated in places like Silicon Valley.
- Viewers want to watch traditional movies, sports, and prime-time programming, not interact with televisions.
- Computers are finicky, difficult devices; most people like the simplicity of their TV sets.

THE COMPUTER INDUSTRY SAYS:

- Consumers, no longer satisfied with plain-vanilla television, want rich, interactive viewing experiences.
- Viewers will be as interested in browsing the World Wide Web as in watching traditional TV programming.
- High-definition pictures, while attractive, will not be enough to sell the new digital TV sets.
- The consumer electronics industry is slow-moving and lacking in imagination and innovation.

Source: Joel Brinkley, "Building Your Next TV: Two Industries Fight for a $150 Billion Prize," *New York Times*, March 28, 1997, pp. C1, C2.

a 20 to 40 percent drop in movie attendance during this period; more than sixty movie theaters closed in the Chicago area alone. But in non-TV cities, movie audiences increased. Taxi receipts and night-club attendance also fell in TV cities, as did library-book circulation. At the same time, radio listening declined; for example, Bob Hope's network radio show lost half its national audience between 1949 and 1951. Sales of television sets by 1951 surpassed sales of radio receivers.

After a second NTSC conference in 1952 sorted out technical problems, the FCC ended the licensing freeze and issued a major report finalizing technical standards, many of which are still used today—and will be until the new digital standard takes over. Among its actions, the FCC set aside seventy new channels (14–83) on an ultrahigh frequency (**UHF**) band, although few manufacturers in the 1950s made TV sets equipped with UHF reception. As a result, UHF license holders struggled for years, until a 1964 law finally required manufacturers to equip sets with UHF reception. With the expansion of UHF slowed by technical snags, the FCC eventually "took back" channels 70–83 and reassigned those frequencies (plus VHF's Channel 1) to other communication services such as cellular phones.

Nearly 250 channels were initially earmarked for educational or nonprofit status, most of them on the newly created UHF band. Commercial interests, as they did in radio, had gobbled up most of the early VHF assignments with the FCC's blessing. Since the FCC did not establish a method for financing nonprofit stations, a long economic struggle followed for many of the educational TV stations. Even with the creation of the Corporation for Public Broadcasting (CPB) in 1967, which funneled federal funds to nonprofit radio and to more than 300 public TV stations, the loose decentralized network of stations that share Public Broadcasting Service (PBS) programming have had to beg listeners for much of their financial support. This has been especially true since the 1990s, when a more fiscally conservative Congress reduced much of the CPB's funding.

In 1952, the CBS color system was tentatively approved by the FCC. Because its signal could not be received by black-and-white sets, however, the system was incompatible with those that most Americans owned. In 1954, RCA's color system, which could also receive black-and-white images, usurped CBS to become the color standard. Although NBC began broadcasting a few shows in color in the mid-1950s, it wasn't until 1966 that all three networks broadcast their entire evening lineups in color.

Almost thirteen hundred communities received TV-channel allocations from the FCC after the freeze ended. Since broadcast signals could interfere with one another, the FCC created a national map and tried to evenly distribute all available channels throughout the country. By the mid-1950s, there were over four hundred television stations operating, a 400 percent surge since the pre-freeze era. Today, about seventeen hundred TV stations are in operation, including more than three hundred nonprofit stations.

> "There's about **three great moments** in a man's life: when he buys a house, and a car, and a new color TV. That's what America is all about."
> —Archie Bunker, *All in the Family*

television booms in the fifties

Like radio in the 1930s and 1940s, television programs were often conceived, produced, and supported by a single sponsor. Many of the top-rated programs in the early 1950s even included the sponsor's name in the title: *Texaco Star Theater, Buick Circus Hour, Camel News Caravan, Colgate Comedy Hour, Gillette Cavalcade of Sports, Kraft Television Theater,* and *Goodyear TV Playhouse.* Today, with the exception of the occasional *Hallmark Hall of Fame* drama, virtually no program on network television is named after and controlled by a single sponsor.

The Collapse of Sponsorship. Throughout the early 1950s, the broadcast networks became increasingly unhappy with the control sponsors exerted over program content. With the growing popularity of television came opportunities to alter prior financial arrangements, especially given the high cost of producing programs on a weekly basis. In 1952, for example, a single one-hour TV show cost a sponsor about $35,000, a figure that rose to $90,000 by the end of the decade. These weekly costs became increasingly difficult for sponsors to bear.

David Sarnoff, then head of RCA/NBC, and William Paley, head of CBS, saw the opportunity to diminish the role of sponsors. Enter Sylvester "Pat" Weaver (father of actress Sigourney Weaver), who was appointed president of NBC by Sarnoff in 1953. A former advertising executive, Weaver was used to controlling radio content for his clients. When he made the switch to television, Weaver sought to retain that control—by forcing advertisers out of the content game. By increasing program length from fifteen minutes (standard for radio programs) to thirty and sixty minutes, Weaver substantially raised program costs for advertisers. In addition, two new programming changes made significant inroads in helping the networks gain control of content. Both strategies involved producing longer programs, thus making it difficult for a single sponsor to foot the bill.

The first strategy featured the concept of the *magazine program*. In January 1952, NBC introduced the *Today* show, which started as a three-hour morning talk-news program. A few years later, in September 1954, NBC premiered the ninety-minute *Tonight Show*. Since both shows ran daily rather than weekly, studio production costs managed by a single sponsor were prohibitive. Rather than selling the whole concept to one sponsor, NBC sold *spot ads* within the shows: Advertisers paid the network for thirty- or sixty-second time slots. The network, not the sponsor, now owned the programs or bought them from independent producers. More than forty years later, shorter versions of the *Today* and *Tonight* shows remain fixtures on NBC.

The second strategy, known originally as the *spectacular*, is today recognized by a more modest term, the *television special*. At NBC, Weaver bought special programs, like Laurence Olivier's filmed version of *Richard III* and the Broadway production of *Peter Pan*, again selling spot ads to many sponsors. The TV version of *Peter Pan* was a particular success, watched by some sixty-five million viewers. More typical specials featured music-variety shows hosted by top singers such as Judy Garland and Frank Sinatra. The combination of these programming strategies—and one juicy television scandal—ended sponsors' control over television content.

Still going strong today, NBC's *Tonight Show* (1954–) has been hosted over the years by Steve Allen, Jack Paar, Johnny Carson, and Jay Leno *(right)*. Comedy sketches, studio bands, and talk segments on the show influenced everything from *Saturday Night Live* (1975–) to the *Rosie O'Donnell Show* (1996–).

The Quiz-Show Scandals. Corporate backers of quiz shows drove the final nail in the coffin of sponsor-controlled TV content. In the mid-1950s, the networks revived the radio *quiz-show* genre. CBS aired the *$64,000 Question*, originally radio's more modest *$64 Question*—symbolic of how much television had raised the economic stakes. Owned by Revlon, which bought a half-hour block of evening prime time from the network in 1955, the program ranked as the most popular TV show in

America during its first year. As one historian has suggested, "It is impossible to explain fully the popular appeal of the *$64,000 Question*. Be it the lure of sudden wealth, the challenge to answer esoteric questions, happiness at seeing other people achieving financial success, whatever the program touched in the American psyche at mid century, this was stunning TV."[2] By the end of the 1957–58 season, twenty-two quiz shows aired on network television.

Revlon followed its success with the *$64,000 Challenge* in 1956. At one point, Revlon's two shows were running first and second in the national ratings, and its name recognition was so effective that the company ran out of products. In fact, its cosmetic sales skyrocketed from $1.2 million before sponsoring the quiz shows to nearly $10 million by 1959.

Compared to dramas and situation comedies (which we'll look at shortly), quiz shows were cheap to produce, with inexpensive sets and mostly nonactors as guests. In addition, these programs offered the corporate sponsor the opportunity to have its name displayed on the set throughout the program.

The problem was that most of these shows were rigged. To heighten the drama and get rid of guests whom the sponsors or producers did not find appealing, key contestants were rehearsed and given the answers. The most notorious rigging occurred on *Twenty-One*, a quiz show owned by Geritol (whose profits climbed $4 million one year after deciding to sponsor the program in 1956). The subject of Robert Redford's 1994 film, *Quiz Show*, *Twenty-One*'s most infamous contestant was Charles Van Doren, a Columbia University English professor from a famous literary family. In 1957, Van Doren won $129,000 during his fifteen-week run on the program; his fame then landed him a job on NBC's *Today* show. In 1958, after a series of contestants accused the morning show *Dotto* of being fixed, the networks quickly dropped twenty shows. Following further rumors of fixing, a *TV Guide* story, a New York grand-jury probe, and a congressional investigation in 1959 (during which Van Doren admitted cheating), big-money prime-time quiz shows ended.

> "I was fascinated by the seduction of [Charles] Van Doren, by the Faustian bargain that lured entirely good and honest people into **careers of deception**."
> —Robert Redford, director, *Quiz Show*

Although often little more than a compelling footnote in many accounts of television's history, the impact of the quiz-show scandals was enormous. First, the pressure on TV executives to rig the programs and the subsequent fraud effectively put an end to any role sponsors might have in creating television content. Sponsors and their ad agencies gradually accepted the networks' economic strategy of several companies buying commercial time during a single program or a TV series.

Second, although many Americans had believed in the democratic possibilities of television—bringing inexpensive information and entertainment into every household—this belief was undermined by the sponsors and TV executives who participated in the quiz-show fraud. During the 1950s, many people trusted that pictures were more honest than words. The quiz-show scandals provided the first dramatic indication that TV images could be manipulated. The seeds, then, for our contemporary cynicism about electronic culture had sprouted full-blown by the late 1950s. At the end of the decade, a growing number of middle-class parents were even refusing to allow their children to watch television.

Third, and most important, quiz shows magnified the separation between the privileged few and the general public, a division between high and low that would affect print and visual culture for at least the next forty years. That Charles Van Doren had come from a literary family of Ivy League intellectuals and "sold his soul" for fame and money drove a wedge between intellectuals and the popular new medium. At the time, many well-educated people had a wary skepticism toward television. This was best captured in the famous 1961 speech by FCC commissioner Newton Minow, who labeled game shows, westerns, cartoons, and other popular genres part of commercial television's "vast wasteland." Critics have used the wasteland metaphor ever since to admonish the TV industry for failing to live up to its potential. More than forty years after the quiz-show scandal, nonnetwork, independently produced programs like *Jeopardy* and *Wheel of Fortune*, now called *game shows*, have made a strong comeback in late afternoon time slots. The networks, however, remain reluctant to put game shows on again in prime time, even though they are profitable and much cheaper to produce than one-hour dramas or half-hour situation comedies.

key programming trends in the tv age

The disappearance of quiz shows marked the end of most prime-time network programs originating from New York. From about 1955 through 1957, the three major networks gradually moved their entertainment divisions to Los Angeles for its close proximity to Hollywood production studios. Network news operations, however, remained in New York. Symbolically, these cities came to represent the two major branches of TV programming: entertainment and information. Although there is much blurring between these categories today, at one time the two were much more distinct.

tv's information culture

In terms of television journalism, many local broadcast stations, TV newsmagazines, and cable's CNN have all made key contributions and generated their own controversies. However, in this section the focus is on the network evening news, which over the years has had the most significant and sustained daily impact on viewers nationwide. Since the 1960s, broadcast journalism has consistently topped print news in national research polls that ask which news medium is more trustworthy. This fact alone makes the evening news a force to be reckoned with in our information culture.

NBC News. Featuring a panel of reporters interrogating political figures, NBC's weekly *Meet the Press* (1947–) remains the oldest news show on television. Daily evening newscasts, though, began on NBC in February 1948 with the *Camel Newsreel Theater*. Actually a ten-minute Fox Movietone newsreel that was also shown in theaters, this filmed news service was converted to a live broadcast one year later. Renamed the *Camel News Caravan* and anchored by John Cameron Swayze (later a spokesperson for Timex watches), the NBC newscast showed Swayze reading short news items in a converted radio studio. Toward the end of the fifteen-minute show, he would announce grandly, "Now let's go hopscotching the world for headlines!" and read a list of one- or two-sentence reports, which were occasionally accompanied by filmed footage.

Sponsored by a cigarette and the first news show to air in color, *Camel News* was succeeded by the *Huntley-Brinkley Report* in 1956. With Chet Huntley in New York and David Brinkley in Washington, this coanchored NBC program became the most popular evening news show on television. To provide a touch of intimacy, the coanchors would sign off their broadcasts, "Good night, Chet." / "Good night, David." This program served as the model for hundreds of local news broadcasts that eventually developed dual anchors to present the news. After Huntley retired in 1970, the program was renamed *NBC Nightly News* and struggled to compete with CBS's emerging star anchor, Walter Cronkite. A series of anchors and coanchors followed before Tom Brokaw settled in as NBC's sole anchor in September 1983.

CBS News. A second regular evening news show, *Television News with Douglas Edwards*, premiered on CBS in May 1948. In 1956, the CBS program became the first news show to be videotaped for rebroadcast on *affiliate* stations (independently owned stations that sign contracts with a network and carry its programs) in western time zones (Ampex had just developed the first workable videotape recorder). Walter Cronkite succeeded Edwards in 1962, starting a nineteen-year run as anchor of the renamed *CBS Evening News*. Once a World War II correspondent for a print wire service, Cronkite in 1963 anchored the first thirty-minute network newscast, which featured a live ocean-side interview with President John Kennedy, twelve weeks before his assassination. In 1968, Cronkite went to Vietnam to cover America's position in that civil war firsthand. Putting aside his role as an objective news anchor, he concluded on the air that the American public had been misled about Vietnam and that U.S. participation in the war was a mistake. With such a centrist news personality now echoing the protest movement, public opinion against American intervention mounted. Partly because of the influence of Cronkite's criticisms, President Lyndon Johnson decided not to seek reelection in 1968.

Retiring from his anchor position in 1981, Cronkite was succeeded by Dan Rather, a former White House correspondent who had starred on CBS's *60 Minutes* since 1975. Despite a $22 million, ten-year contract, Rather could not sustain the program as the highest-rated evening newscast. To woo viewers and exude warmth, he tried wearing colorful sweater vests and briefly signed off the news with the slogan, "Courage." But neither succeeded in increasing the size of his audience. Rather did score a major coup in 1990 when he obtained an exclusive interview in Baghdad with Saddam Hussein shortly after the Iraqi leader ordered his troops to invade Kuwait, triggering the Persian Gulf War. Ratings for the newscast at CBS, however, stayed flat. In the mid-1990s, the network tried an experiment aimed both at recapturing viewers and responding to long-standing criticisms of male anchors controlling the daily network news. Unlike CNN and many local news stations, which routinely use male and female news teams, women anchors on the networks have long been relegated to substitute weekend duty. Bucking this trend, CBS paired Rather with former *Today*-show host Connie Chung in the mid-1990s. Ratings continued to sag, however, and CBS terminated Chung.

ABC News. Initially, ABC struggled to get a daily news program on the air. Over the years, the network tried many anchors and formats as it attempted to cut into the dominance of NBC in the 1960s and CBS in the 1970s. ABC premiered a daily program in 1948, but it folded after few affiliates chose to carry it. The network finally launched a daily news show in 1953, anchored by John Daly, head of ABC News and also the host of CBS's evening game show *What's My Line?* After Daly left in 1960, a series of folks sat behind the anchor desk, including John Cameron Swayze and in 1965 a twenty-six-year-old Canadian, Peter Jennings. Dubbed "anchor boy" by critics at the time, Jennings lasted just over two years before returning to London as a foreign correspondent. Another series of rotating anchors ensued, including Harry Reasoner and Howard K. Smith. Then, in 1976, the network hired Barbara Walters away from NBC's *Today* show, gave her a $1 million annual contract, and made her the first woman to regularly coanchor a network newscast. With Walters and Reasoner (the first reporter chosen in 1968 to launch *60 Minutes*) together, viewer ratings rose slightly, but the network was still behind CBS and NBC. In 1977, ABC sports director Roone Arledge took over as head of the newly combined ABC News and Sports division. In

1978, he launched *ABC World News Tonight* featuring four anchors: Frank Reynolds in Washington, Jennings in London, Walters in New York, and Max Robinson in Chicago. Robinson was the first black reporter to coanchor a network news program. Walters decided to leave her anchor position and focus on doing celebrity and political interviews. In 1983, ABC chose Jennings as the sole anchor. By the late 1980s, the ABC evening news had become the most watched network newscast. It was dethroned, however, in 1996 when Brokaw's NBC program moved ahead.

Contemporary Trends in Network News. Audiences watching the network news contributed to the demise of many afternoon daily newspapers. By the 1980s, though, network audiences also began to decline. Facing competition from VCRs and cable, especially CNN, network advertising revenues flattened out. In response, the networks cut back staffs in the late 1980s and early 1990s, eliminating many national and foreign reporter posts. Trying to duplicate the financial success of *60 Minutes*, the most profitable show in TV history, the networks began developing relatively inexpensive newsmagazines. ABC's *20/20* and *Primetime Live* became moneymakers, and NBC's successful *Dateline* programs appeared three evenings a week by 1996. In addition, a number of syndicated nonnetwork newsmagazines were also developed by independent producers for the local late afternoon and late night markets. These included more than twenty breezy-sometimes-sleazy syndicated tabloids, including *Entertainment Tonight*, *Hard Copy*, and *A Current Affair*. In the newest trend, NBC, which already operated one cable news channel (CNBC), teamed up with Microsoft in 1996 to launch MSNBC, the first national news channel available simultaneously on cable and the World Wide Web.

tv's entertainment culture

While news divisions remained anchored in New York, the networks began to shift their entertainment divisions to Los Angeles, partly due to the success of the pioneering series *I Love Lucy* (1951–57). *Lucy*'s owners and costars, Desi Arnaz and Lucille Ball, began filming the top-rated situation comedy movie-style in California near their home. In 1951, *Lucy* was the first program filmed in front of a live audience. This was before the days of videotape, when the only way to preserve a live broadcast, other than by filming it like a movie, was through a technique called *kinescope*. In this process, a film camera recorded a live TV show off a studio monitor. The quality of the kinescope technique was generally poor, and most series that were filmed this way have not survived.

The Coneheads—*from left to right*, Jane Curtin, Dan Akroyd, Garrett Morris, and Laraine Newman—perform in a 1970s episode of *Saturday Night Live*. A throwback to the live comedies of the 1950s, *SNL* premiered on NBC in 1975. The popularity of the program eventually launched the movie careers of dozens of cast members, and at least two of its popular sketches inspired Hollywood feature films—*Wayne's World* (1992) and *The Coneheads* (1993).

I Love Lucy, Alfred Hitchcock Presents, and *Dragnet* are among a handful of series from the 1950s that endured because they were originally shot and preserved on film.

Televised Comedy. Even during the quiz-show boom of the mid- and late 1950s, the primary staples of television were comedy and drama, both significantly influenced by New York radio, vaudeville, and theater. This period is often referred to as the golden age of television. Television comedy back then (as now) came in three varieties: the situation comedy (or *sitcom*), the domestic comedy, and the sketch comedy, the forerunner of programs such as *Saturday Night Live* and *In Living Color*.

Sketch Comedy. Identified on occasion as *vaudeo*, or the marriage of vaudeville and video, **sketch comedy** was a key element in early vaudeville-like TV variety shows. These programs included singers, dancers, acrobats, animal acts, and ventriloquists as well as comedy skits. The shows "resurrected the essentials of stage variety entertainment" and played to noisy studio audiences.[3] Vaudeville performers dominated television's early history. Stars of sketch comedy included Milton Berle, TV's first major celebrity, in *Texaco Star Theater* (1948–67); Red Skelton in the *Red Skelton Show* (1951–71); and Sid Caesar, Imogene Coca, and Carl Reiner in *Your Show of Shows* (1950–54), for which playwright Neil Simon, filmmakers Mel Brooks and Woody Allen, and writer Larry Gelbart (*M*A*S*H*) all served as sketch writers.

Sketch comedy had major drawbacks. Since skits were an integral part of the hour-long variety series, these programs were more expensive to produce than half-hour sitcoms. In addition, skits on weekly variety shows, such as the *Perry Como Show* (1948–63), the *Dinah Shore Chevy Show* (1956–63), and the *Carol Burnett Show* (1967–79), used up new routines very quickly. Ventriloquist Edgar Bergen (father of *Murphy Brown* star Candice Bergen) once commented that "no comedian should be on TV once a week; he shouldn't be on more than once a month."[4]

With original skits and new sets required each week, production costs mounted, and the vaudeville-influenced variety series faded. The last successful weekly program of this type, *Barbara Mandrell & the Mandrell Sisters*, ended its two-year NBC run in 1982 due to the demanding schedule of doing music and comedy on a weekly basis. In this instance, it was Mandrell, not low ratings, who stopped the production of the show. Mandrell said that musical numbers and sketch comedy, which could be used over and over for different audiences on the nightclub circuit, lasted only one week on television. Since the early 1980s, variety shows have appeared only as yearly specials.

All in the Family (1971–83), starring Carroll O'Connor (*right*) and Jean Stapleton (*left*) as Archie and Edith Bunker, was one of the most popular programs in TV history. Created by Norman Lear, the program explored issues of class, ethnicity, gender, and race, which until then had been considered off-limits in a comedy format.

TABLE 5.1
Selected Situation and Domestic Comedies Rated in the Top 10

The most durable and familiar genre in the history of television has been the sitcom. It is the only genre represented in the Nielsen rating Top-10 lists every year since 1949. Below is a selection of top-rated comedies at five-year intervals, spanning forty years.

1955-56

I Love Lucy (#2)
Jack Benny Show (#5)
December Bride (#6)

1960-61

Andy Griffith Show (#4)
Real McCoys (#8)
Jack Benny Show (#10)

1965-66

Gomer Pyle, U.S.M.C. (#2)
Lucy Show (#3)
Andy Griffith Show (#7)
Bewitched (tie #7)
Beverly Hillbillies (tie #7)
Hogan's Heroes (#9)

1970-71

Here's Lucy (#3)

1975-76

All in the Family (#1)
Laverne & Shirley (#3)
Maude (#4)
Phyllis (#6)
Sanford and Son (tie #7)
Rhoda (tie #7)

1980-81

M*A*S*H (#4)
The Jeffersons (#6)
Alice (#7)
House Calls (tie #8)
Three's Company (tie #8)

1985-86

Cosby Show (#1)
Family Ties (#2)
Cheers (#5)
Golden Girls (#7)
Who's the Boss? (#10)

1990-91

Cheers (#1)
Roseanne (#3)
A Different World (#4)
Cosby Show (#5)
Murphy Brown (#6)
Empty Nest (#7)
Golden Girls (tie #10)
Designing Women (tie #10)

1995-96

Seinfeld (#2)
Friends (#3)
Caroline in the City (#4)
Single Guy (#6)
Home Improvement (#7)
Boston Common (#8)

Sources: Tim Brooks and Earle Marsh, *The Complete Directory to Prime Time Network and Cable TV Shows*, 4th ed. (New York: Ballantine, 1988), 963–75; Susan Sackett, *Prime-Time Hits* (New York: Billboard Books, 1993), 335–48; *The World Almanac and Book of Facts 1997* (Mahwah, NJ: World Almanac Books, 1996), 295; and A. C. Nielsen Media Research.

Situation Comedy. Over the years, the major staple on television has been the half-hour comedy series, the only genre represented in the Top-10-rated programs every year since 1949 (see Table 5.1). One type of comedy series, the **situation comedy**, features a recurring cast and set as well as several narrative scenes. It establishes a situation, complicates it, develops increasing confusion among its characters, and alleviates complications.[5] *I Love Lucy* from the 1950s, the *Beverly Hillbillies* from the 1960s, *Happy Days* from the 1970s, *Night Court* from the 1980s, and *Seinfeld* and *Third Rock from the Sun* from the 1990s are all part of this long tradition.

In most situation comedies, character development is downplayed in favor of wacky plot twists and disruptions. Characters are usually static and predictable; they generally do not develop much over the course of a series. Such characters "are never troubled in profound ways." Stress, the result of external confusion rather than emotional anxiety, "is always funny."[6] While watching situation-driven comedies, viewers usually think of themselves as slightly superior to the characters who inhabit the sitcom world.

Domestic Comedy. One spin-off of the sitcom form is the **domestic comedy**, in which characters and settings are usually more important than complicated predicaments. Although any given show might offer a wacky situation as part of a subplot, more typically the main narrative features a domestic problem or family crisis that characters have to solve. There is a greater emphasis on character development than on reestablishing the order that has been disrupted by confusion. Domestic comedies take place primarily at home (*Leave It to Beaver, Good Times*), at the workplace (*Taxi, Cheers*), or at both (the *Dick Van Dyke Show, Home Improvement, Friends*).

Although funny things happen in domestic comedies, the main emphasis is on how characters react to one another. Family and workplace bonds are tested and strengthened by the end of the show. Generally, viewers identify more closely with the major characters in domestic comedies. One example illustrates the difference between a sitcom and its domestic counterpart. In an early episode of the sitcom *Happy Days* (1974–84), the main characters were accidentally locked in a vault over a weekend. The plot turned on how they were going to free themselves, which they did after assorted goofy adventures. Contrast this with an episode from the domestic comedy *All in the Family* (1971–83) in which archconservative Archie and his ultraliberal son-in-law Mike are accidentally locked in the basement. The physical predicament became a subplot as the main "action" shifted to the characters themselves, who reflected on their generational and political differences.

> "Despite the incredibly hostile treatment she has gotten in the press—because she's four things TV women are not supposed to be, **working-class, loudmouthed, overweight, and a feminist**—Roseanne became a success because her mission was simple and welcome: to take the schmaltz and hypocrisy out of media images of motherhood."
>
> —Susan Douglas,
> *Where the Girls Are*

Today most programs mix comedic elements. An episode of *Friends* (1994–) might offer a character-driven plot about the generation gap and a minor subplot about a pet monkey gone berserk. Domestic comedies also mix dramatic and comedic elements. An episode of *Roseanne* (1988–97), for example, might juxtapose a dramatic scene in which a main character has a heart attack with another in which the Conner family intentionally offends their stuffy neighbors by decorating their home in a "white trash" holiday motif. This blurring of serious and comic themes marks a contemporary hybrid, sometimes labeled *dramedy*, which has included such series as *Moonlighting* (1985–89), the *Wonder Years* (1988–93), *Northern Exposure* (1990–95), and *Picket Fences* (1992–96).

Televised Drama. Another key staple of television has been the drama. Because the production of TV entertainment was centered in New York in its early days, many of its ideas, sets, technicians, actors, and directors came from New York theater. Young stage actors, including Ann Bancroft, Warren Beatty, Ossie Davis, James Dean, Gene Hackman, Grace Kelly, Paul Newman, Sidney Poitier, Robert Redford, and Joanne Woodward, began their professional careers in early television, often because they could not find stage work in New York. The TV dramas that grew from these early influences fit roughly in two categories: the anthology drama and the episodic series.

Anthology Drama. In the early 1950s, television—like cable in the early 1980s—served a more elite and wealthier audience. The **anthology drama**, which brought live dramatic theater to television, entertained and often challenged that audience. Influenced by stage plays, anthologies offered new teleplays, casts, directors, writers, and sets from week to week. Since movie studios owned the rights to major stage plays of the day, anthology television was often based on original material. In fact, this genre launched the careers of writers such as Rod Sterling (*Requiem for a Heavyweight*), William Gibson (*The Miracle Worker*), Reginald Rose (*Twelve Angry Men*), and Paddy Chayefsky (*Marty*). The teleplays of these writers were often later made into movies. Chayefsky, in fact, would go on to write the screenplay for the 1976 film *Network*, a biting condemnation of television.

In the 1952–53 season alone, there were eighteen anthology dramas competing on the networks. Programs such as *Kraft Television Theater* (1947–58), *Studio One* (1948–58), *Goodyear TV Playhouse* (1951–57), the *U.S. Steel Hour* (1953–63), *Alfred Hitchcock Presents* (1955–65), *Playhouse 90* (1956–60), and the *Twilight Zone* (1959–64) mounted original plays each week. However, the demands on the schedule were such that many of these programs alternated slots biweekly with other anthologies or with variety programs.

The commercial networks quit producing anthologies for economic and political reasons. First, although anthologies were popular, advertisers disliked them. Anthologies often presented stories that confronted complex human problems not easily resolved. Chayefsky had referred to these dramas as the "marvelous world of the ordinary."[7] The commercials that interrupted the drama, however, told straightforward stories in which problems were easily solved by purchasing a product: "a new pill, deodorant, toothpaste, shampoo, shaving lotion, hair tonic, car, girdle, coffee, muffin recipe, or floor wax."[8] By probing the psychology of the human condition, complicated anthologies made the simplicity of the commercial pitch ring false. Another aspect of the sponsors' dilemma was that these dramas often cast "non-beautiful heroes and heroines,"[9] unlike the stars of the commercials.

By 1954, sponsors and ad agencies were demanding more input into script revisions. For instance, Reginald Rose's *Thunder on Sycamore Street* was based on a real incident in which a black family moved into an all-white neighborhood and was pressured to leave. CBS, pressured by advertisers who wanted to avoid public controversy, asked that the black family be changed to "something else." For the teleplay to air, Rose had to make the family that of an ex-convict. Faced with increasing creative battles with the writers and producers of these dramas, sponsors began to move toward less-controversial programming, such as quiz shows and sitcoms.

Second, this golden age of television was largely supported by a more affluent audience, particularly in the early 1950s. The people who could afford TV sets at this time could also afford tickets to a play. For these viewers, the anthology drama was an extension of their cultural tastes and simply brought theater directly into their homes. In 1950, fewer than 10 percent of American households had TV sets, with the heaviest concentration of ownership in New York. By 1956, however, 71 percent of households had sets. As the production of sets rose during the post–World War II manufacturing boom, prices dropped as well. Working- and middle-class families were increasingly able to afford televisions. Anthology dramas were not as popular in this expanded market as they were with upscale theatergoers. When the networks began relocating their creative headquarters to Hollywood, such moves also reduced theatrical influences. As a result, by the end of the decade, westerns, which were inexpensively produced by film studios on location near Los Angeles, had become the dominant TV genre.

Third, anthology dramas were expensive to produce—double the price of most other TV genres in the 1950s. In 1949, the average sixty-minute drama cost around $10,000 (compared to $1.5 million today). Although variety series eventually became the most expensive genre, anthologies cost on average $35,000 per hour by 1955. In contrast, a thirty-minute quiz show cost just over $10,000 to produce. Each week meant a completely new story line as well as new writers, casts, and expensive sets. Sponsors and networks came to realize that it would be cheaper to use the same cast and set each week, and it would also be easier to build audience allegiance with an ongoing program. In an anthology series of individual plays, there were no continuing characters with whom viewers could identify over time.

> "Aristotle once said that a play should have a beginning, a middle and an end. But what did he know? Today, a play must have a first half, a second half, and a **station break**."
> —Alfred Hitchcock, director

In addition, anthologies that dealt seriously with the changing social landscape were sometimes labeled "politically controversial." This was especially true during the witch-hunts provoked by Senator Joseph McCarthy and his followers to rid media industries of left-wing influences (see Chapter 16 on blacklisting). Ultimately, sponsors and network executives came to prefer less controversial programming such as quiz shows and westerns. By the early 1960s, this once dominant dramatic form had virtually disappeared from network television, although its legacy continues on American public television, especially with the imported British program *Masterpiece Theater* (1971–).

Episodic Series. Abandoning anthologies, producers and writers increasingly developed the **episodic series**, first used in radio in 1929, as it seemed best suited for the weekly grind of televised drama. In this format, main characters continue from week to week, sets and locales remain the same, and technical crews stay with the program. Story concepts in episodic series are broad enough to accommodate new adventures each week, creating an atmosphere in which there are ongoing characters with whom viewers can regularly identify.

The episodic series comes in two general types: chapter shows and serial programs. Chapter shows employ self-contained stories that feature a problem, a series of conflicts, and a resolution. This structure can be used in a wide range of dramatic genres, including adult westerns like *Gunsmoke* (1955–75); medical dramas like *Marcus Welby, M.D.* (1969–76) and *ER* (1994–); police/detective shows like *Dragnet* (1951–59, 1967–70) and *Magnum, P.I.* (1980–88); family dramas like *The Waltons* (1972–81) and *Little House on the Prairie* (1974–82); and fantasy/science fiction like *Star Trek* (1966–69) and *The X-Files* (1993–).

Culturally, television dramas function as a window into the hopes and fears of the American psyche. In the 1970s, for instance, police/detective dramas became a chapter staple, mirroring the anxieties of many Americans regarding the urban unrest of the late 1960s. The 1970s brought more urban problems, which were precipitated by the loss of factory jobs and the decline of the manufacturing industry. Our popular entertainment reflected the idea of heroic police and tenacious detectives protecting a nation from menacing forces that were undermining our economy and our cities. During this period, shows such as *The F.B.I.* (1965–74), *Ironside* (1967–75), *Mannix* (1967–75), *Hawaii Five-O* (1968–80), the *Mod Squad* (1968–73), *Kojak* (1973–75), and the *Rockford Files* (1974–80) all ranked among the nation's top-rated programs.

A recent spin-off of the police drama has been the law-enforcement reenactment program, sometimes called *cop docs*. Series

The X-Files (1993–), starring David Duchovny (*right*) as Fox Mulder and Gillian Anderson (*left*) as Dana Scully, follows the adventures of two FBI agents assigned to mysterious or unresolved cases involving UFOs, paranormal phenomena, genetic mutants, and government conspiracies. *The X-Files*, the Fox network's biggest hit in the mid-1990s, is also extremely popular in Australia, England, and Japan.

like Fox's *Cops* (1989–) are cheap to produce, with low overhead and a big return on a minimum investment. Instead of hiring actors at $25,000 per episode, producers have their crews tag along with real police, whose supervisors often donate police cars and other equipment that the producers of conventional dramas usually have to rent or buy. While an hour of conventional prime-time drama cost about $1.5 million to produce per episode in the mid-1990s, an hour of crime reenactments cost less than half that amount. Cop docs, like many contemporary daytime talk shows, generally focus their stories on emotional situations and individual pathology rather than on a critical examination of the underlying social conditions that make such problems possible.

Prior to the rise of the cop was the reign of the cowboy, which marked an earlier period of change in America. The western served as one of the most popular chapter genres in television's early history. The network shift to Hollywood made western movie sets immediately available. When studios such as Warner Brothers began dabbling in television in the 1950s, they produced a number of well-received ABC series such as *Cheyenne* (1955–63) and *Maverick* (1957–63). The popular western, with its themes of civilization confronting the frontier, apparently provided a symbol for many middle Americans relocating to the suburbs—between the country and the city. Thirty prime-time westerns aired in the 1958–59 season alone. From this point through 1961, *Gunsmoke* (1955–75), TV's longest-running chapter series, *Wagon Train* (1957–65), and *Have Gun Will Travel* (1957–63) were the three most popular programs in America.

In contrast to chapter programs like westerns and police dramas, *serial programs* are open-ended episodic shows. That is, in these series, most story lines continue from episode to episode. Cheaper to produce, usually employing just a few indoor sets, and running five days a week, daytime soap operas are among the longest-running serial programs in the history of television. Acquiring their name from soap-product ads that sponsored these programs in the days of fifteen-minute radio drama, popular soaps include *Guiding Light* (1952–), *As the World Turns* (1956–), *General Hospital* (1963–), *Another World* (1964–), *Days of Our Lives* (1965–), and *One Life to Live* (1968–).

With their cliff-hanging story lines and intimate close-up shots, which are well suited for television (a personal medium located in our living rooms and bedrooms), soap operas have been good at creating audience allegiance. Soaps probably do the best job of any genre at imitating the actual open-ended rhythms of daily life. The fact that many of them have endured for well over thirty years means that story lines and characters span generations of viewers who stay faithful to their favorite programs for many years.

The success of the daytime soap formula opened a door to prime time. Although the first popular prime-time serial, *Peyton Place* (1964–69), ran two or three nights a week, producers later shied away from such programs because they had less value as syndicated reruns. Most reruns of old network shows are **stripped**—shown five days a week—but serials require that audiences watch every day so that they don't lose track of the story lines. In contrast, chapter programs and sitcoms can be stripped in almost any order and do not require that viewers watch them on a daily basis.

In the 1970s, however, with the popularity of the network *mini-series*—a serial that runs over a two-day to two-week period, usually on consecutive nights—producers and the networks began to look differently at the evening serial. The twelve-part *Rich Man, Poor Man*, adapted from an Irwin Shaw novel, ranked number three in national ratings in 1976. The next year, the eight-part *Roots* mini-series, based on writer Alex Haley's search for his African heritage, became the most-watched mini-series in TV history. Then *Holocaust*, a four-part dramatization of Jewish extermination by the Nazis, drew television's largest audiences in 1978.

These mini-series demonstrated to the networks that viewers would watch a compelling, ongoing story in prime time. The success of such programs spawned soap opera–style series such as *Dallas* (1978–91), *Dynasty* (1981–89), *Knots Landing* (1979–92), and *Falcon Crest* (1981–90), which in the 1984–85 season all ranked among America's Top-10 most-viewed programs. In fact, as the top-rated shows in America in the early 1980s, *Dallas* and *Dynasty* both celebrated and criticized the excesses of the rich and spoiled. These shows reached their popular peak during the early years of the Reagan administration, a time when the economic disparity between rich and poor dramatically escalated.

Another type of contemporary serial is a hybrid form that developed in the early 1980s with the appearance of *Hill Street Blues* (1981–87). Mixing comic situations and grim plots, this multiple-cast show looked like an open-ended soap opera. On occasion, as in real life, crimes were not solved and recurring characters died. As a hybrid form, *Hill Street Blues* combined elements of both chapter and serial television. Juggling multiple story lines, *Hill Street* featured some self-contained plots that were brought to resolution in a single episode as well as other plot lines that continued from week to week. This technique was copied by several successful dramatic hybrids, including *St. Elsewhere* (1982–88), *L.A. Law* (1986–94), *NYPD Blue* (1993–), and *ER* (1994–).

> "I think for a while during the Reagan years it was OK to be **ostentatiously wealthy** and **glitzy**."
> — David Jacobs, executive producer, *Knots Landing*

the decline of the network era

Most historians mark the period from the late 1950s, when the networks gained control over TV's content, to the end of the 1970s as the *network era*. Except for British and American anthology dramas on PBS, this was a time when CBS, NBC, and ABC dictated virtually every trend in prime-time programming (see Figure 5.1). This network dominance was significant because it offered America's rich and diverse ethnic population a cultural center and common points for daily conversation. Television is often credited, for example, with helping to heal the collective national consciousness after the assassination of President Kennedy in 1963 by creating time and space for shared mourning. During this period of supremacy, the networks collectively accounted for 95 percent of all prime-time TV viewing. By 1996, however, this figure had dropped

Figure 5.1

The Fall Prime-Time Schedule toward the End of the Network Era, 1978–79

Programs that are shaded were canceled either during or at the end of the 1978–79 season.
Source: Alex McNeil, *Total Television: A Comprehensive Guide to Programming from 1948 to the Present,* 3rd ed. (New York: Penguin, 1991), 938.

	7	7:30	8	8:30	9	9:30	10	10:30	11 PM	
SUN	THE HARDY BOYS MYSTERIES 3		BATTLESTAR GALACTICA		MOVIE					ABC
	60 MINUTES 11		MARY		ALL IN THE FAMILY	ALICE 9	KAZ 3			CBS
	THE WONDERFUL WORLD OF DISNEY 25		THE BIG EVENT (I)				LIFELINE 2			NBC
MON			WELCOME BACK, KOTTER 4	OPERATION PETTICOAT 2	NFL MONDAY NIGHT FOOTBALL				9	ABC
			WKRP IN CINCINNATI	PEOPLE	M*A*S*H 7	ONE DAY AT A TIME 4	LOU GRANT		2	CBS
			LITTLE HOUSE ON THE PRAIRIE 5		MOVIE					NBC
TUE			HAPPY DAYS 6	LAVERNE AND SHIRLEY	THREE'S COMPANY 3	TAXI	STARSKY AND HUTCH		4	ABC
			THE PAPER CHASE		MOVIE					CBS
			GRANDPA GOES TO WASHINGTON		THE BIG EVENT (II)				2	NBC
WED			EIGHT IS ENOUGH 3		CHARLIE'S ANGELS 3	VEGA$				ABC
			THE JEFFERSONS 5	IN THE BEGINNING	MOVIE					CBS
			DICK CLARK'S LIVE WEDNESDAY		MOVIE					NBC
THU			MORK & MINDY 3	WHAT'S HAPPENING!!	BARNEY MILLER 5	SOAP 2	FAMILY		4	ABC
			THE WALTONS 7		HAWAII FIVE-0 11		BARNABY JONES		7	CBS
			PROJECT U.F.O. 2		QUINCY 3	W.E.B.				NBC
FRI			DONNY AND MARIE 4		MOVIE					ABC
			WONDER WOMAN 3		THE INCREDIBLE HULK 2	FLYING HIGH				CBS
			THE WAVERLY WONDERS	WHO'S WATCHING THE KIDS	THE ROCKFORD FILES 5	THE EDDIE CAPRA MYSTERIES				NBC
SAT			CARTER COUNTRY 2	APPLE PIE	THE LOVE BOAT 2	FANTASY ISLAND			2	ABC
			RHODA 5	GOOD TIMES 6	THE AMERICAN GIRLS	DALLAS			2	CBS
			CHIPS 2		SPECIALS	SWORD OF JUSTICE				NBC

1978–1979

below 55 percent. What happened? To understand the decline of the network era, we will look at three factors: technological changes, government regulations, and the development of new networks.

technological transformations

Two major technological developments contributed significantly to the erosion of network dominance: the arrival of communication satellite services for cable television and the home-video market. Prior to the early 1970s, broadcast lobbyists and local stations, fearing advertising competition, had effectively limited the growth of cable television, which had been around since the late 1940s. But a series of moves by the FCC sprung cable loose in 1972. That same year, when Time Inc. launched HBO into satellite orbit, serving movies to hotels and motels, the first crack in the network dam appeared. In 1975, HBO became available to individual cable markets throughout the country, offering the "Thrilla from Manila"—the heavyweight boxing match between Muhammad Ali and Joe Frazier via satellite from the Philippines.

Then, in December 1976, Ted Turner beamed, or *uplinked*, the signal from WTBS, his **independent station** (not affiliated with a network) in Atlanta, to a satellite where cable systems and broadcast stations around the country could access, or *downlink*, it. To encourage interest, the signal was initially provided free, supported only by the ads Turner sold during WTBS programs. But as Turner expanded services, creating new channels like CNN, he also earned revenue by charging monthly fees for his cable services. In its early days, WTBS delivered a steady stream of old TV reruns, wrestling, and live sports from the Atlanta Hawks and the Atlanta Braves (both teams owned by Turner). Turner and a number of investors would eventually buy the MGM film library to provide additional programming. In the mid-1970s, only about 15 percent of American households received cable. As this figure steadily grew (to more than 65 percent by 1997), the TV networks, for the first time, faced serious competition.

The second technological breakthrough came also in 1975–76 with the consumer marketing of videocassette recorders (VCRs), which allowed viewers to record and play back programs from television. Earlier in the 1970s, Japan's Sony corporation had introduced the TV industry to a three-quarter-inch-wide videocassette format that quickly revolutionized television news; until that time, TV news crews had relied solely on shooting film, which often took hours to develop and edit. Then, in 1975, Sony introduced consumers to a home version, *Betamax*, a half-inch format that allowed viewers for the first time to tape programs off the air. The next year, JVC in Japan introduced a slightly larger half-inch consumer format, *VHS* (Video Home System), which was incompatible with Beta. This triggered a marketing war, which helped drive the costs down and put VCRs in more and more homes.

Beta, though a smaller format and technically superior to VHS, ultimately lost the marketplace battle due to a cultural miscalculation by designers. Early Betamax tapes accommodated only about an hour and a half of programming. However, most American consumers used tapes primarily to record movies, usually two hours in length. This meant that *two* tapes, which cost around $15 apiece in the late 1970s, were necessary. When JVC developed the slightly larger VHS format, one standard tape accommodated two hours of programs, enough for an entire movie. Even with technical improvements that compressed more programming onto a single tape, Betamax could never match the recording time or appeal of the longer VHS tapes.

The VCR also got a big boost from a failed suit brought against Sony by Disney and MCA (now Universal) in 1976: The two film studios alleged that home taping violated their movie copyrights. In 1979, a federal court ruled in favor of Sony and permitted home taping for personal use. In response, the defeated but industrious movie studios quickly set up videotaping facilities so that they could rent and sell movies via video stores, which exploded onto the scene in the early 1980s. By the mid-1980s, VHS had pretty much won the war for the video consumer market, and Sony concentrated on developing *Betacam*, a high-quality half-inch industrial format that in the late 1980s began replacing the bulkier three-quarter-inch format in TV newsrooms.

The impact of videocassettes on the networks was enormous. By 1997, nearly 90 percent of American homes were equipped with VCRs that were used for two major purposes: time shifting and movie rentals. *Time shifting* occurs when viewers tape shows and watch them later, when it is convenient for them. This has been a boon, for example, for daytime soap-opera fans who work outside the home; they record their favorite soaps and watch them on weeknights or weekends. Before VCRs, advertisers and networks worried that consumers used TV ad time to fix a snack or go to the bathroom. After VCRs, they had bigger things to worry about. For example, recording TV programs for viewing at a more convenient time produced more complex audience measurement problems. Along with the remote control that allowed viewers to mute the sound during ads, time shifting let consumers avoid ads altogether, either by *zapping*, or cutting, them out of the program with the pause button during recording or by *zipping*, or fast-forwarding, through the ads during the recorded viewing. Predictably, these practices upset ad and network executives who could no longer assume that "well-behaved" consumers were conscientiously viewing their ads. On top of this was the lure of VCR movies: By the mid-1990s, more than half of all households in America watched a rented movie during prime-time at least once a week. The impact of VCRs and movie rentals shook the TV industry; when viewers were watching a videotape, they weren't watching network shows or network ads.

regulating the networks

By the late 1960s, an activist FCC, increasingly concerned about the monopoly-like impact of the three networks, passed a series of regulations that began undercutting their power. The first, the passage of the *Prime-Time Access Rule* (PTAR) in April 1970, took away the 7:30-to-8:00 P.M. slot (6:30-to-7:00 P.M. central) from the networks and gave it exclusively to local stations in the nation's fifty largest TV markets. With this move, the FCC had hoped to encourage local news and public affairs programs. However, most stations simply acquired syndicated quiz shows (*The Joker's Wild, Wheel of Fortune*) or *infotainment* programs (*P.M. Magazine, Entertainment Tonight*). These shows packaged human interest and celebrity stories in TV news style, during which local affiliates sold lucrative local ads.

In a second move, the FCC in 1970 created the *Financial Interest and Syndication Rules*—called *fin-syn*—which "constituted the most damaging attack against the network TV monopoly in FCC history."[10] Throughout the 1960s, the networks had run their own syndication companies. They sometimes demanded as much as 50 percent of the profits that producers earned from airing older shows as reruns in local TV markets. This was the case even though those shows were no longer on the networks and most of them had been developed not by the networks but by independent companies. The networks claimed that since popular TV series had gained a national audience due to their reach, production companies owed the networks compensation even after shows had completed their prime-time runs. In the 1970s, the FCC banned the networks from reaping such profits from program syndication.

A third and separate action was instituted by the Department of Justice in 1975. Reacting to a number of legal claims against monopolistic practices, the Justice Department limited the networks' own production of nonnews shows to a few hours a week. Initially, the limit was three hours of prime-time entertainment programs per week, but this was raised to five hours by the late 1980s. In addition, ABC, CBS, and NBC were limited to producing eight hours per week of in-house entertainment or nonnews programs outside prime time, most of which was devoted to soap operas (economical to produce and popular with advertisers). This meant that the networks were forced to continue licensing most of their prime-time programs from independent producers and film studios. Given that the networks selected which programs to air, however, they still retained a great deal of power over the content of the prime-time television.

With increasing competition from cable and home video in the 1990s, the FCC gradually phased out the ban limiting network production. In addition, beginning in 1995, the networks once again were allowed to syndicate and profit from rerun programs, but only the ones they produced in-house. The elimination of fin-syn and other rules opened the door for megamerger deals. For example, Disney, which bought ABC in 1995, is able to use its vast movie production resources to produce more entertainment programming for its ABC network. This will certainly cut into opportunities for independent producers to create new shows and compete for prime-time slots on ABC. Many independent companies and TV critics point to the return of a new type of oligopoly. Disney, Westinghouse, and General Electric—multinational corporations that now own the networks—are increasingly dictating the program trends and economic terms for television.

emerging new networks

In addition to the overwhelming number of cable services now available to consumers, the networks, which lost about 25 percent of their audience during the 1980s alone, faced further challenges from the emergence of new networks. Rupert Murdoch, who heads the multinational company News Corp., launched the Fox network in April 1987 after purchasing several TV stations from another company and buying a Hollywood film studio, Twentieth Century Fox. Not since 1955, when the old Dumont network collapsed, had there been another attempt to challenge the Big Three networks.

At first, Fox lost money because it had fewer than a hundred affiliated stations to carry its programs around the country. This was less than half the two-hundred-plus affiliates each contracted to ABC, CBS, and NBC. Originally presenting programs just two nights a week, the Fox network began targeting both young and black audiences with shows like *The Simpsons*, *Beverly Hills 90210*, *In Living Color*, *Martin*, *Roc*, and *Melrose Place*. By 1994, after outbidding CBS for a portion of pro-football broadcasts, Fox was competing every night of the week. It

After *Friends* became the nation's No. 3 program during the 1995–96 TV season, the cast briefly threatened to strike before the 1996–97 season. Each star demanded $100,000 an episode, but they eventually settled for about $60,000 each per episode. These salaries pale in comparison to the contracts signed by the cast of Seinfeld in 1997—a record $600,000 per episode.

had managed to lure more than sixty affiliates away from the other networks or from independent status. Some of these stations were in major markets where traditional networks suddenly found themselves without affiliates. In fact, Fox's poaching forced CBS to spend millions to buy two unknown independent UHF stations—Channel 62 in Detroit and Channel 69 in Atlanta—to satisfy advertisers who expected the network to reach audiences in all major markets. By the early 1990s, Fox was making money. By the mid-1990s, the new network's total affiliations rivaled the Big Three.

Fox's success continued the erosion of network power and spurred others interested in starting new networks as well. Paramount, which had recently been acquired by Viacom, and Time Warner, the world's largest media company, both launched networks in January 1995: UPN (United Paramount Network) and WB (Warner Brothers). Using the strategy initiated by Fox, the new networks offered programs two nights a week in 1995 and added a third night in 1996. Backed by multinational financing, these companies slowly began going after independent outlets and luring other stations from their old network affiliations.

the economics of television

> "By 1960 television had become a mature and streamlined business, a great 'cash cow.' The focus now shifted from invention to convention, from carving out an **acceptable social role** for itself to counting the rewards of investment, planning, and monopoly."
>
> —J. Fred MacDonald,
> *One Nation under Television*

Despite the erosion of their reach and relaxed regulations, the traditional networks have remained attractive investments in the business world. In 1985, General Electric, which once helped start RCA/NBC, bought back NBC. In 1995, Disney bought ABC for $19 billion and Westinghouse acquired CBS for $5.4 billion.

Even though their audiences and profits may have declined, the networks continue to attract larger audiences than any cable or online competitor. To understand the television business today, we need to examine the production and distribution of programming. At stake are billions of dollars in advertising revenue each year. In fact, one way to define TV programming is as a system that delivers viewers to merchandise displayed in blocks of commercials. By the mid-1990s, national advertisers, led by Procter & Gamble and General Motors, were spending more than $25 billion dollars a year in TV advertising.

prime-time production

The key to the television industry's appeal resides in its ability to create programs that American households will habitually tune to on a weekly basis. Producers and film studios spend fortunes telling stories that they hope will keep us coming back. In 1988, while film studios produced a large chunk of network television, more than half of the prime-time schedule was created by independent producers. These companies, such as Carsey-Werner (the *Cosby Show, A Different World, Roseanne, Cybill, Third Rock from the Sun*), license, or rent, each episode to a network for two broadcasts, one in the fall or winter and one in the spring or summer (usually twenty-two to twenty-four episodes are produced in a TV season).

Production costs on network television generally fall into two categories: above-the-line and below-the-line. *Below-the-line* costs account for roughly 40 percent of a program's production budget. They include the technical, or "hardware," side of production: equipment, cameras and crews, sets and designers, carpenters, electricians, art directors, wardrobe, lighting, and transportation. More demanding are the *above-the-line*, or "software," costs, which include the creative talent: actors, writers, producers, editors, and directors. These costs account for about 60 percent of a program's budget.

Independent Programs. Because of their high cost, many prime-time programs today are produced by production companies that are financed or backed by a major film studio. In these arrangements, film studios (if they don't buy out the more successful independent producers) serve as a bank, offering enough capital to carry producers through a season or more. In television, after a network agrees to carry a program, keeping it on the air is done through *deficit financing*. This means that the production company leases the show to a network for a license fee that is actually *less* than the cost of production. (The company hopes to recoup this loss later in lucrative rerun syndication.) Typically, in the mid-1990s, the networks might lease an episode of a new half-hour sitcom for $500,000 to $600,000 for two airings. Each episode, however, cost the producers about $700,000 to $800,000 to make. So on each show, they lose between $100,000 and $200,000. After two years of production (about forty-four episodes), an average half-hour sitcom builds up a $4 to $8 million deficit and the average one-hour drama generates a deficit of $12 to $14 million. This is where film studios have been playing an increasingly crucial role: They finance the deficit. In the early 1990s alone, film studios, which provide production facilities as well as money, covered deficits totaling $350 million annually by bankrolling network prime-time television.

The key to erasing the losses generated by deficit financing is **rerun syndication**: Producers and film studios invest in programs that they hope will stay in a network's lineup long enough to build up enough episodes (usually four seasons'

The *Cosby Show*, the nation's most popular program from 1985 through 1989, featured (*from left to right*) Phylicia Rashad, Bill Cosby, Earle Hyman, Clarice Taylor, and Lisa Bonet. Initially rejected by ABC and CBS, the show eventually was picked up by NBC. As a result, *Cosby* single-handedly took NBC from third to first place in the network prime-time ratings battle.

worth) so that they can be sold, or syndicated, to hundreds of TV markets in the United States and overseas. With a successful program, the profits can be enormous. For instance, when Carsey-Werner's *Cosby Show*, the most-watched show in America from 1985 to 1989, sold its first three years into syndication in 1988, the producers netted more than $800 million. Since a show has already been produced and the original production costs already covered, the syndication market becomes almost pure profit for the producers and their backers. It is for this reason that the practice of deficit financing endures. Although investors rarely hit the jackpot, when they do, it can more than cover a lot of losses. By 1997, the *Cosby Show* had earned a record $1 billion in syndication.[11] Profits from the show (and from *Roseanne*) have allowed Carsey-Werner to function as one of the few remaining independent companies that does not require the financial backing of a film studio.

Network Programs. Although the networks still purchase or license most of their prime-time television, since the relaxation of FCC rules, they create more of their own prime-time fare. The production of newsmagazines, for instance, became one way for networks to save money and control content in the 1990s. Programs such as ABC's *20/20* or NBC's *Dateline* require only about half the outlay (between $500,000 and $700,000 per episode) demanded by an hour's worth of drama. In addition, the networks, by producing projects in-house, avoid paying license fees to independent producers.

Over the years, for example, CBS's highly rated program *60 Minutes* has been a money machine. By 1980, a commercial minute on *60 Minutes*, the nation's highest-rated program that year, sold for a then record $230,000. By the mid-1990s, *60 Minutes*—like other top-rated shows—commanded more than $400,000 per minute for its seven minutes of national ad slots. (By comparison, a low-rated program brought in only a quarter of this amount per minute.) This meant that *60 Minutes* generally earned back its production costs and fees to local stations for carrying the program after selling just a couple minutes of ad time. Even newsmagazines with low ratings still recoup their cheaper production costs fairly easily. Don Hewitt, the creator of *60 Minutes*, estimated that in its first twenty-five years on the air, his program had grossed well over $1 billion for CBS.[12]

prime-time distribution

The networks have always been the main distributors of prime-time TV programs to their affiliate stations around the country. By 1997, ABC, CBS, NBC, and Fox were each allied with approximately two hundred stations. The networks pay a fee to affiliate stations for carrying their programs. In this arrangement, local stations receive quality national programs that attract large local audiences. In addition, local ad spaces are allocated during prime time so that stations can sell their own time during these slots.

A common misconception is that TV networks *own* their affiliated stations. This is not true. Although networks own a few stations in major markets like New York, Los Angeles, and Chicago, throughout most of the country networks merely sign short-term contracts to rent time on local stations. For example, WDIV (Channel 4) in Detroit has a contract to carry NBC programs but is owned by the Washington Post/Newsweek Company based in Washington, D.C. Years ago, the FCC placed restrictions on network-owned-and-operated stations, called **O&Os**. Originally, networks and other companies were limited to owning five VHF and two UHF stations, but the limit was raised to twelve total stations during the 1980s. Hoping to ensure more diversity in ownership, the FCC during this time also mandated that an owner's combined TV stations could reach no more than 25 percent of the nation's ninety-million-plus TV households. Then, in 1996, the sweeping new Telecommunications Act, which will be discussed in Chapter 6, abolished the twelve-station limit and most other ownership restrictions.

Although a local affiliate carries network programs, the station may preempt a network's offering by substituting other programs. According to *clearance rules*, established in the 1940s by the Justice Department and the FCC, all local affiliates are ultimately responsible for the content of their channels and must clear, or approve, all network programming.

Over the years, local affiliates have occasionally rejected the networks. In 1956, Nat King Cole (singer Natalie Cole's father) was one of the first African American performers to host a network variety program. As a result of pressure applied by several white southern organizations, though, the program had trouble attracting a national sponsor. When some southern and northern affiliates refused to carry the program, NBC canceled it in 1957. In another instance, Norman Lear's popular CBS sitcom *Maude* (1972–78) aired two controversial episodes in which the title character, in her late forties, decided to abort an unwanted pregnancy. The episodes topped the ratings when they ran in 1972. However, when the episodes came up for network summer rebroadcast in 1973, a number of Catholic organizations led campaigns that generated seventeen thousand protest letters asking CBS to cancel the second airing. Although CBS refused, 39 of its 217 affiliates did not clear the episodes. Seven national sponsors also pulled their ads. The controversy generated an even bigger audience the second time around, as nearly sixty-five million people watched the two shows in 1973.

how syndication works

Early each year, executives from thousands of local TV stations and cable firms gather at the world's main "TV supermarket" convention, the National Association of Television Program Executives (NATPE). There they buy or barter for programs up for syndication, acquiring the exclusive local market rights, usually for two- or three-year periods, to quiz shows, newsmagazines, talk shows, and *evergreens*—popular old network reruns such as the *Andy Griffith Show* or *I Love Lucy*. In such a competitive arena, TV managers have become less concerned with the quality of programs and more concerned with keeping costs low, delivering viewers to advertisers, and drawing higher ratings than their competitors.

Although the networks have long dominated in selecting and distributing prime-time television, syndicators have played a large role in hours outside of prime time. King World, for example, began in 1972 after the fin-syn rules banished the networks from syndication. Starting out by distributing *Little Rascals* film shorts from the 1930s, King World barely survived its first year. By the end of the 1980s, however, King World was the distributor of the top shows in syndication—*Wheel of Fortune*, *Jeopardy*, and the *Oprah Winfrey Show*—and grossed nearly $400 million per year.

In addition to companies like Viacom and King World, major syndicators of TV programming include film companies such as Twentieth Century Fox, Disney-Touchstone, and Time Warner, all of which are also involved in the production of TV shows. Networks usually select and distribute about three hours of programming each night (four on Sunday) during prime time and another three to four hours of daytime programming, but this still leaves a substantial number of hours to plug. Because it is often cheaper to buy syndicated programs than to produce local programs (other than news), many station managers take the most profitable path rather than originate topical shows that focus on their own communities.

Off-Network and First-Run Syndication. For local affiliate stations, syndicated programs are often used or slotted in what is known as **fringe time**. This includes programming immediately before the evening's prime-time schedule, called *early fringe*, and the time following the local evening news or the network's late night talk shows, called *late fringe*. Syndication to fill these slots comes in two forms.

The *Oprah Winfrey Show* (1986–) is the most popular and influential syndicated daytime talk show in television history. By the 1990s, serious topics on the show triggered national conversations, and guest authors saw their books climb onto best-seller lists.

First, there is **off-network syndication** in which older programs, no longer running during network prime time, are made available for reruns to local stations, cable operators, online services, and foreign markets. A local station may purchase old *Roseanne* or *Home Improvement* episodes as a lead-in to boost the ratings for its late afternoon news, or it may purchase *Cheers* or *Seinfeld* to boost its ratings after the late evening news.

A second type, **first-run syndication**, is any program specifically produced for sale into syndication markets. Quiz programs such as *Jeopardy* and *Wheel of Fortune* and daytime talk shows such as *Ricki Lake* and *Montel Williams* are made *for* syndication. The producers of these programs sell them directly to local markets around the country and the world. When the FCC established the Prime-Time Access Rule in 1971 to turn over more prime time to local stations, it created an immediate market for new nonnetwork programs.

Hybrid Syndication. The new *Star Trek* programs, which include *The Next Generation*, *Deep Space Nine*, and *Voyager*, are examples of a hybrid form of first-run syndication. These new episodes are descended from the original *Star Trek*, which aired on NBC in the mid-1970s but was canceled after three years due to low ratings. Although network rejection ends the lives of most programs, on occasion a producer may decide to make new episodes for syndication.

Besides *Star Trek*, the most famous hybrid programs are probably *Hee Haw* and the *Lawrence Welk Show*. Beginning on CBS in 1969, *Hee Haw* was canceled in 1971 even though it was a Top-20 program in its two years on prime time. CBS, however, thought the show was drawing children and older rural viewers who were not as likely to buy many of the network's advertised products. After cancellation, the show's producers continued making and syndicating *Hee Haw* for more than twenty years. In the late 1970s, it was the most-watched nonnetwork program on television.

Lawrence Welk had a much longer network run, appearing on ABC for sixteen years, before its cancellation in 1971 by executives who determined that the program's audience was too old to attract new ad revenue. Welk's production company, however, made 1,542 new episodes between 1971 and 1982 and sold them into first-run syndication. The show was one of the only series that ran in more TV markets (over 250) in first-run syndication than when it aired originally. In fact, PBS bought the syndication rights in the early 1990s, and *Lawrence Welk* continued to run on more than 270 noncommercial stations.

> "The *Lawrence Welk Show* ran on ABC from July 1955 until September 1971, when the network dropped the broadcasts, claiming its audience was 'too old.' This was probably true, since the sponsors at the time were Geritol and Sominex."
>
> —Susan Sackett, *Prime Time Hits*, 1993

Public television, in picking up programs like *Lawrence Welk*, has often provided programming for viewers who are less attractive to commercial networks and advertisers. Besides programs for the over-fifty viewer, public television has also played an important role in programming for viewers under twelve—another age group not valued by most advertisers and often neglected by the networks. Over the years, children's series such as *Mister Rogers' Neighborhood* (1967–), *Sesame Street* (1969–), the *Electric Company* (1971–76), and *Barney* (1991–) have been fixtures on public television. Except for CBS's long-running *Captain Kangaroo* (1955–84), the major networks have rarely developed educational series aimed at children under twelve. In 1996, however, Congress passed a law ordering the networks to offer a minimum of three hours of children's educational programming a week.

Global Syndication. TV producers can often recoup the high cost of original programming when they sell shows worldwide. In 1994, for instance, Fox had already sold *The X-Files*, which had only premiered a year earlier, into over fifty markets outside the United States. Like American TV markets, the price per episode varies according to the size of the market. By the early 1990s, according to the trade magazine *Variety*, a half-hour American sitcom was airing in Poland for about $450 to $550 per episode, in Peru for $800 to $1,500, and in France for $10,000 to $20,000.

In many countries, the popularity of American television poses a cultural threat: Television industries in these countries cannot always afford to produce original programming; they find it cheaper to buy made-in-the-USA programs than to produce a new series. American producers, who have already paid for production costs and begun earning profits, can undercut most competition in foreign markets. For instance, Malaysia, Jamaica, and Singapore can today purchase some half-hour sitcoms for as little as $200 an episode. As a result, television companies in many developing countries produce few competitive programs. Such countries, in trying to promote their own cultural identities, wrestle with the pros and cons of importing the values of American TV and movie culture. Ultimately, some countries, including Canada, have placed quotas on TV imports from the United States in an effort to encourage original and culture-specific productions.

Barter vs. Cash. Most financing of television syndication is based on either cash or barter. In a *cash deal*, the distributor of a program offers a series for syndication to the highest bidder in a market—typically a station trying to fill a particular time slot. Due to exclusive contractual arrangements, programs air on only one broadcast outlet per market. For example, Viacom, which distributes the *Cosby Show*, offers it in hundreds of television markets around the country. Whichever local station bids the most in a particular market gets the rights to that program, typically for a contract period of two or three years. A small-market station in Fargo, North Dakota, might pay a few thousand dollars to air a week's worth of episodes; in contrast, some Top-10 markets paid well over $150,000 a week for *Cosby* in the late 1980s.

One common variation of a cash deal is called *cash-plus*. For shows that are successful in syndication, distributors may retain some time to sell national commercial spots. When Cosby went into syndication, for example, Viacom, in addition to receiving cash for the show from various local outlets, also sold a minute of ad time to national advertisers. When the two-hundred-plus local stations received the programs, they already contained a minute's worth of national ads. Some syndicators use cash-plus deals to keep down the cost per episode: In other words, stations pay less per episode in exchange for giving up ad slots to a syndicator's national advertisers.

While syndicators prefer cash deals, *barter deals* are usually arranged for new or untested programs. In a straight barter deal, no money changes hands between the local station and the syndicator. Instead, a syndicator offers a new program to a local TV station in exchange for a split of the advertising revenue. The program's syndicator will try to make an arrangement with the station that attracts the largest number of local viewers, though this is not always possible. The syndicator then sells some ads at the national level, charging more money to advertisers if the program has been sold into a large number of markets. This guarantees the wide national distribution that the networks receive for prime-time shows.

As an example, in the early 1990s, *Star Trek: The Next Generation* (before it became a part of the new UPN network) was offered by its producer-distributor, Paramount, in a barter 7/5 deal. Paramount did not charge cash per episode. Instead, during each airing it retained seven minutes of ad time to sell national spots and left stations with five minutes of ad time to sell local spots. The *Jenny Jones Show* also started out as a barter show. As it became a proven product, its syndicator, Time Warner, repackaged the show as a cash-plus deal.

measuring television by ratings and shares

Although the networks wrested control of content from sponsors in the 1950s, advertising still drives the business. TV shows live or die based primarily on whether advertisers are satisfied with the quantity and quality of the viewing audience.

Over the years, the major organization tracking prime-time viewing has been the A. C. Nielsen Market Research Company, which estimates what shows viewers watch in the nation's major markets. During the 1950s and 1960s, before ratings were fine-tuned statistically, firms like Nielsen estimated only the mass numbers of households tuned to particular programs. By the 1970s, ratings services provided advertisers, networks, and local stations with much more detail about those viewers—from their race and gender to age, occupation, and educational backgrounds.

A **rating** in TV measurement is a statistical estimate expressed as a percentage of households tuned to a program in the local or national market being sampled (see Table 5.2). In the mid-1990s, one Nielsen national ratings point represented approximately 960,000 television households. Another audience measure is the **share**, a statistical estimate of the percentage of homes tuned to a program, compared to those actually using their sets at the time of a sample. Let's say, for instance, that on a typical night of the sample of 4,000 metered homes wired by Nielsen across the country, 3,000 of those households have their TV sets *turned on* to assorted networks, pay channels, and cable channels. Of those 3,000, about 1,000 are tuned to *Friends* on NBC. The *rating* estimate for that show is 4,000 (number of sets) divided by 1,000 (number of households watching *Friends*) which equals 25 percent. The *share* estimate is 3,000 (sets actually in use) divided by 1,000, which equals 33 percent.

Share measurements have become increasingly important because they let advertising and TV executives know approximately what percentage of sets in use are tuned to their programs in a competitive market. Shares are also good measures during fringe time, when most sets may be turned off. For example, on a given night, 1,000 sets may still be on for late night viewing. If 400 of that 1,000 are tuned to the *Late Show*, its *rating* would be only 10 percent (4,000 divided by 400), but its *share* of the audience still tuned in would be 40 percent (1,000 divided by 400).

TABLE 5.2
The Top 10 Highest-Rated TV Series, Individual Programs (since 1960)

Program	Network	Date	Rating
1. M*A*S*H (final episode)	CBS	2/28/83	60.2
2. Dallas ("Who Shot J.R.?" episode)	CBS	11/21/80	53.3
3. The Fugitive (final episode)	ABC	8/29/67	45.9
4. Cheers (final episode)	NBC	5/20/93	45.5
5. Ed Sullivan Show (Beatles' first U.S. TV appearance)	CBS	2/9/64	45.3
6. Beverly Hillbillies	CBS	1/8/64	44.0
7. Ed Sullivan Show (Beatles' second U.S. TV appearance)	CBS	2/16/64	43.8
8. Beverly Hillbillies	CBS	1/15/64	42.8
9. Beverly Hillbillies	CBS	2/26/64	42.4
10. Beverly Hillbillies	CBS	3/25/64	42.2

Sources: The World Almanac and Book of Facts 1997 (Mahwah, NJ: World Almanac Books, 1996), 296; Corbett Steinberg, *TV Facts* (New York: Facts on File Publications, 1985); A. C. Nielsen Media Research.

Anatomy of a TV "Failure"

Television shows die early deaths for many reasons. Two of the most common are tough, competitive time slots and poor lead-in shows that fail to attract a big enough following. Then there's the story of *Frank's Place* (1987–88), a critically acclaimed entry in the fall 1987 television lineup.

The series starred Tim Reid as a displaced history professor from Boston who inherited his estranged father's modest restaurant in a working-class area of New Orleans. The winner of three Emmys, *Frank's Place* was canceled by CBS just as it was set to produce new episodes for the 1988–89 TV season.

In fact, most new TV series fail. Even such successful series as *All in the Family*, *M*A*S*H*, *Hill Street Blues*, *Cheers*, and *60 Minutes* started out slowly, some at the bottom of the ratings. But all got second chances. Why not *Frank's Place*—especially after a strong premiere on a Monday night in 1987 when it beat NBC's *Alf* and ABC's *MacGyver* with a rating of 15 and a 25 share? In the first place, the show lacked a patient executive champion at the network level who would allow *Frank's Place* to "find" its audience gradually in a fixed time slot. Over its first year, CBS programmers moved it to six different time slots on four different nights. In fact, the program moved so often that its coproducers, Reid and Hugh Wilson, said that even their own mothers could no longer find it. In addition, the show aired initially at 8:00 P.M. "Kids run the eight o'clock Nielsens," Wilson said at the time, but *Frank's Place* was not aimed at children. He wanted the show in a 9:00 or 9:30 slot.[1]

The cast of *Frank's Place*.

Frank's Place: "the first program since *Roots* to take Black culture seriously"

—Alvin Poussaint,
Harvard psychiatrist and *Cosby* advisor

Bill Cosby as Dr. Cliff Huxtable.

A second problem concerned audience expectations. Shot in film style, *Frank's Place* did not look like *Cosby*, the show that Wilson says paved the way for *Frank's Place*. Instead of viewing *Frank's Place* as a series of short stories, as "individual little movies," viewers perhaps kept looking for, but not finding, a more traditional comedy. Intrinsic to this problem was a question: Was *Frank's Place* too much about black culture to develop an audience among mainstream America? Though it was primarily a comedy, by tackling such issues as drugs, homelessness, corporate greed, alienation, and religion, was it also viewed as *too* serious? No regular network dramatic series featuring a majority black cast had ever succeeded in prime time, although by 1993 there were nine sitcoms on television featuring predominantly black actors.

In one of the show's early episodes, the older bartender Tiger tells a disconsolate Frank, who's not a great businessman, "White folks don't come down here much at night." If we extend that thought, clearly not enough people, white or black, watched or were even aware of the program. Unlike *Cosby*, essentially a show about social class, *Frank's Place* was a show about race as well as class. Safer and less threatening, *Cosby* became one of the most popular shows in the history of television. *Frank's Place*, however, while it lasted, let mainstream America see the viewpoints of characters who lived in a black working-class section of New Orleans—in the margins of America, a place where network prime-time television has never been very comfortable.

In the early 1970s, during the height of the network era, a prime-time series with a rating of 17 or 18 and a share between 28 and 30 was generally a success. By 1997, though, with increasing competition from cable and VCRs, the threshold for success had dropped to a rating of 9 or 10 and a share under 15. Expectations were far less for the new Paramount (UPN) and Time Warner (WB) networks, which had far fewer affiliates in 1995, their first year, than did the four large networks.

The importance of ratings and shares to the survival of specific TV programs cannot be overestimated (see "Case Study: Anatomy of a TV 'Failure'" on page 147). Simply stated, audience measurement tells advertisers roughly how many people are watching. Even more important, it tells them what kind of people are watching. Prime-time advertisers are mainly interested in securing affluent eighteen- to forty-nine-year-old viewers, who account for most consumer spending. If a show is attracting viewers from that group, advertisers then decide if they want to buy time during that particular program and pay the network its asking price. In fact, television operates as an industry in which networks, producers, and distributors target, guarantee, and "sell" viewers in blocks to advertisers. About eight of ten new shows introduced each fall either do not attain the required ratings or fail to reach enough of the "right" viewers. The result is cancellation within the year. (We will return to the economics of ratings in Chapter 13.)

television and democracy

Since the 1950s, television has carried the anti-elitist promise that its technology could reach all members of society, including those who could not read. In such a heterogeneous nation, the idea of a visual, affordable mass medium, giving all citizens entertainment and information that they could talk about the next day, held great appeal. In similar ways, Americans have had this discussion about newspapers in the 1830s, magazines in the 1880s, radio in the 1920s, and the Internet today.

The ideal of "universal" television programming serving as our cultural yardstick has been undercut by the development of cable, the VCR, and new networks that increasingly appeal to individual needs. Supplementing PBS's role, diverse cable channels such as Nickelodeon and the Cartoon Channel appeal to one end of the age spectrum, and Lifetime and Bravo serve the other end; each has built up loyal audiences that were not being targeted during the network era. As new technological changes provide more specialized choices, however, they also weaken television's role as a national touchstone.

Although a greater variety of consumer choices exist today, we still have very little say about what TV programs (or products) we might like to see. To reinvigorate the promise of television, local cable access channels and electronic town-hall meetings—in which citizens participate directly in the programming process—have begun to display TV's democratic potential. Such promising local developments help counter the economic situation in television today in which a few large multinational companies are controlling the bulk of national and international TV programming (see "Examining Ethics: TV Erodes a Sense of Community").

> "Those who complain about **a lack of community** among television viewers might pay attention to the vitality and interaction of TV sports watchers wherever they assemble."
> —Barbra Morris,
> University of Michigan,
> 1997

The future of television is uncertain. Like the other print and broadcast media that it changed, television is also changing. Technologically, digital advances make flat screen, wall-mounted television sets a reality in the next century. However, with on-line services now offering our favorite TV shows via computer screen or CD-ROM, we no longer

EXAMINING ETHICS

TV Erodes a Sense of Community

by Anthony Lewis

When Alexis de Tocqueville sought to explain democracy in America 150 years ago, he pointed to the fact that "Americans are forever forming associations." They get together, he said, for commercial, religious, moral and practical objectives—or to proclaim a truth. Civic groups, he argued, are an essential element of a democratic culture.

The phenomenon that de Tocqueville shrewdly saw—America as a nation of joiners—is now withering away. So we learn from a fascinating article by Professor Robert D. Putnam of Harvard in... *The American Prospect.*

Surveys of average Americans over the last thirty years, the article says, show that participation in voluntary associations is down between 25 percent and 50 percent. That is so of groups as diverse as PTAs, the Elks, the League of Women Voters and the Red Cross.

"Americans today are significantly less engaged with their communities than was true a generation ago," Putnam concludes. And with that has come a decline in what he calls "social trust": belief in one another.

Putnam's purpose is not just to note the decline but to explain it. A clue is that it is generational. Those born between 1925 and 1930 have been "exceptionally civic: Voting more, joining more, reading newspapers more, trusting more."... Those born after World War II participate much less.

Why? Putnam's answer is: television.

The average American spends 40 percent of his free time watching television—and those who watch a lot participate little. Television discourages "social trust and group membership," Putnam writes. "Heavy readers (of newspapers) are avid joiners, whereas heavy viewers are more likely to be loners." Surveys show that readers belong to 76 percent more civic groups than watchers.

The time spent in front of the set is one reason why television may discourage joining groups and participating in the community. Another is the negative picture television usually gives of American society.

"Heavy watchers of TV are unusually skeptical about the benevolence of other people," Putnam says—"overestimating crime rates, for example.... Heavy TV watching may well increase pessimism about human nature."

A final point goes beyond television. It is that the whole electronic revolution in communications, even while it enlarges our opportunities, has a profoundly fragmenting effect on the society. In other words, we can sit alone at our computers and interact only through electronics. Technology, Putnam concludes, "may indeed be undermining our connections with one another and with our communities."

To that provocative analysis I would add another point. The United States today is in the grip of free-market ideology carried to the extreme: a belief that the society will thrive if nearly all decisions are left for individuals to make on economic grounds. That ideology no doubt thrives on the atomization described by Putnam—and feeds it.

But individual decision making cannot give a society clean water or safe drugs, much as the right-wing ideologues in Congress today like to pretend it can as they remove governmental safeguards....

When people in a society care only for themselves, when they are taught by demagogues to sneer at government and the communal good, it cannot be surprising that social bonds and social trust decline. In that process, everyone will eventually lose. In a society where fewer people vote or care or join—a society that has lost its sense of community—individualism will not bring contentment.

Source: Anthony Lewis, "TV Erodes a Sense of Community," *New York Times*, December 21, 1995.

149

even need a traditional TV set. And yet companies are now marketing products that allow access to the World Wide Web through our TV sets. In the digital age, distinctions between computer and TV screens will eventually break down. Most television programs come from a handful of companies, but they rely on independent producers to supply them with the next new idea or story. Although the 1990s featured talk shows and newsmagazines as hot trends (like quiz shows and westerns before them), these genres, too, will fade.

The mainstream allure of television is both its strength and weakness. As a plus, television offers special moments—inaugurations, debates, space conquests, football, *Roots*, the Olympics—that bring large heterogeneous groups together for shared triumphs and mourning, for common experiences. As a drawback, though, television does not easily explore or adapt to territory outside that common ground. When television aims for the great American middle, it often can mute points of view that are at the edges. As cultural activists and TV critics, we need to ensure that many voices and views have access in the media marketplace.

REVIEW QUESTIONS

1. What were the major technical standards established for television in the 1940s?
2. Why did the FCC freeze the allocation of TV licenses between 1948 and 1952?
3. How did the sponsorship of network programs change during the 1950s?
4. What was the impact of the quiz-show scandals on the television industry?
5. How did news develop at the networks in the late 1940s and 1950s?
6. What are the differences among sketch, situation, and domestic comedy on television?
7. Why did the anthology drama fade as a network programming staple?
8. What are the types of episodic TV series? Why did they survive as a TV staple?
9. What were the technological changes that contributed to the decline of network control over television?
10. What rules and regulations did the government impose to restrict the networks' power?
11. How have new networks managed to grow over the last decade?
12. Why has it become more difficult for producers to independently create programs for television?
13. What are the differences between off-network and first-run syndication?
14. Why do syndicated American television shows have advantages in the global marketplace?
15. What is the difference between a rating and a share in audience measurement?
16. How has television served as a national cultural center or reference point over the years?

QUESTIONING THE MEDIA

1. Describe your earliest memories of watching television. What was your favorite show? Which shows did your family watch together? Were there shows that you were not allowed to watch? Which ones?
2. How much television do you watch today? What programs do you try to watch regularly? What attracts you to your favorite program(s)?
3. If you were a network television executive, what changes would you try to make in what America watches?
4. If you ran a public television station, what programming would you provide that isn't being supplied by commercial television? How would you finance such programming?
5. How could television be used to improve social and political life in the United States?
6. Do you think television plays more of a role in uniting us as a culture or separating us as individuals? Explain your answer.

In small groups (or as a class), track two or three TV programs that share the same time period and compete with each other for viewers. Using a chart of your own design, keep track of the following for four to six weeks: (1) the local and national ads in your programs, and (2) the ratings and shares for these shows. (Weekly ratings information can be found in current trade publications like *Variety*, *Broadcasting & Cable*, or *Electronic Media*, or in popular publications such as *Entertainment Weekly* and the Wednesday "Life" section of *USA Today*.) Then, briefly describe each of the programs and analyze them by answering the following sets of questions:

1. During a half-hour block, how many minutes are devoted to advertising? Based on examining the ads in your programs, who do the sponsors think are watching these shows? Can you generalize about the intended audience? Are the sponsors targeting their money wisely? Based on your analysis, are there any discrepancies between the ads themselves and what the programs seem to be about?

2. Offer interpretations as to why you think one show is more popular than the other(s) you have tracked. Consider a number of factors here—the quality of the programs (in terms of production, characters, story themes, etc.); economic factors (costs, placement in the time schedule—what shows your programs follow); social and cultural values and issues raised by the programs (for instance, issues of class, race, age, and gender; whether the programs make you feel included or excluded; how you think other audience groups might respond to the program).

In addition, try to contact the programming and sales departments at local affiliates or at the networks to see if you can get demographic information on who the affiliates or networks think is watching. These departments might also be willing to provide information on ad costs and ratings.

CHAPTER 6

Like a slow-motion earthquake, the upstart cable channel MTV produced early rumblings of changes ahead for television. In 1981, the satellite-delivered service began recycling popular music videos for an audience of suburban teens. Then in the mid-1980s, producer Michael Mann launched the stylized *Miami Vice* (1984–89) and gave millions of network viewers their first major seismic reading of MTV's impact. *Vice* was the first prime-time series to regularly use MTV influences, editing many of its rapid-fire sequences with contemporary rock hits playing as the sound track and casting rock stars as guest villains.

At the same time, MTV-inspired TV commercials began spreading across the cultural landscape. Using the clout and style of MTV, popular musicians, typically confined to radio and records, were suddenly everywhere, from television ads for Diet Pepsi to motion pictures about Eva Perón. MTV's influence has been enormous. As ABC reported in a 1990 *Primetime Live* segment about the music channel, "MTV's style—frenetic, nonverbal, and dazzlingly visual—has influenced everything from movies, to TV drama, to commercials—even campaign ads." For many critics, however, MTV has become a virus, its ceaseless succession of disconnected three-minute mini-musicals and compressed narratives infecting most major sound and visual media.

In the mid-1990s, a music video by the novelty rock band Weezer aired on MTV and captured the spirit of cable television and its growing role in American culture. At first glance, the video, titled "Buddy Holly," looked like a rerun from the 1970s TV series Happy Days. A closer look revealed cleverly intercut images from the situation comedy with performance shots of the band. In recasting an old ABC sitcom, the video combined 1950s rock-and-roll nostalgia with late-1990s new-wave rock and included varied references to the 1970s—the last decade in which the Big Three networks ruled television. In many ways, the Weezer video epitomized how MTV specifically and cable in general have redefined television worldwide. By offering more channels—filled with old network reruns, twenty-four-hour news services, new music videos, and specialized programs on food, sports, history, the weather, and home shopping—cable TV has gradually eroded the status of the once dominant networks.

Although cable is almost as old as network television, broadcasters inhibited its growth throughout its first twenty-five years. Since the mid-1970s, however, when both HBO (Time Warner's premium movie service) and WTBS (Ted Turner's Atlanta TV station) became available to cable companies across the nation, cable's growth has been steady. In 1977, just 14 percent of all homes received cable. By 1985, cabled households reached 46 percent. By the mid-1990s, that figure had leveled off at around 65 percent but was expected to peak at 70 percent by the year 2000.

The cable industry's emergence from the shadow of broadcast television and its rapid rise to prominence was due partly to the shortcomings of broadcast television. For example, cable generally improved signal reception in most communities. In addition, whereas prime-time broadcast television has traditionally tried to reach the largest possible audiences, cable channels—like magazines and radio—focused more on providing specialized services. Furthermore, cable, through its greater channel capacity, has provided access. Various public, education, and government channels have made it possible in many communities for anyone to air a point of view or produce a TV program. When it has lived up to its potential, cable has offered the public greater opportunities to more fully participate in the democratic promises of television.

We will begin this chapter by examining the fallout from "wired" television, beginning with cable's early technological development and traditional broadcasters' attempts to restrict its growth. We will discuss the impact of the various rules and regulations aimed at the cable industry, including the Telecommunications Act of 1996, which was the first major revision of communication law since 1934. We will then turn to various programming strategies, including basic service, premium cable, and pay-per-view, as well as the contributions of CNN, MTV, and HBO. We will also explore an alternative technology—direct broadcast satellite—and its impact on cable. Finally, we will look at business and ownership patterns, particularly the influence of the largest cable operators, Tele-Communications Inc. (TCI) and Time Warner Cable, and investigate cable's role in a democratic society.

early technology and the development of cable

Unlike recording, radio, and television, cable's earliest technical breakthroughs came from a fairly anonymous and practical group of people. Originating in rural and small-town communities in the late 1940s, cable sprang from obstacles that appliance-store owners faced in selling TV sets to curious consumers. In an effort to increase sales in areas where hills and mountains blocked broadcast signals, TV dealers and electronics firms built antenna relay towers on the outskirts of their communities to pick up blocked signals. They strung wire from utility poles and then ran cables from the towers into individual homes. Essentially, these individuals created a market for their products by ensuring clear TV reception for viewers.

Although the technology today is more advanced, cable continues to operate pretty much the same way. The key distinction between cable and broadcasting remains: Programs reach TV sets through a wire rather than over the air. The advantage is that while the airwaves in any given community can accommodate fifteen or so VHF and UHF channels without electrical interference, cable wires can transmit hundreds of channels with no interference. In a cable system, TV signals are processed at a computerized nerve center, or *headend*, which operates various large satellite dishes that receive and process long-distance signals from CNN in Atlanta to MTV in New York. In addition, the headend houses receiving equipment that can pick up an area's local broadcast signals or a nearby city's PBS station. It relays each premium channel (like HBO), local network affiliate, independent station, and public TV signal along its own separate line. These lines are made up of *coaxial cable*, *fiber optics*, or a combination of both. Until fiber-optic technology developed in the 1980s—sending channels along beams of laser light—most cable systems transmitted electronic TV signals via coaxial cable, a solid core of copper-clad aluminum wire encircled by an outer axis of braided wires. These bundles of thin wire could accommodate fifty or more separate channels or lines running side by side with virtually no interference.

After "downlinking" various channels from satellites and pulling in nearby stations from the airwaves, headend computers relay them to a community in the same way that telephone calls and electric power reach the home. Most TV channels are relayed from the headend through *trunk* and *feeder cables* attached to existing utility poles. Cable companies rent space on these poles from phone and electric companies. Signals are then transmitted to *drop* or *tap lines* that run from the utility poles into homes. As TV signals move from drop lines to TV sets, they pass through a cable converter box, which inputs each channel and enables the TV set to receive 30 to 120 signals (see Figure 6.1).

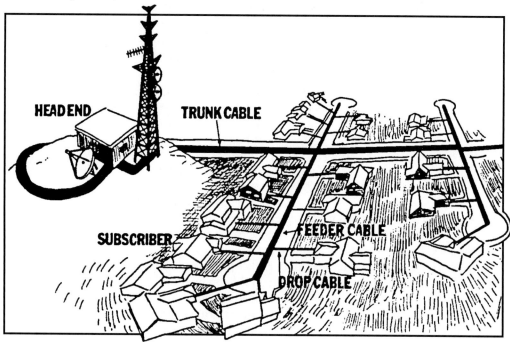

HEADEND   TRUNK CABLE

SUBSCRIBER   FEEDER CABLE

DROP CABLE

**Figure 6.1
A Basic Cable
Television System**
Source: Jennifer Stearns,
A Short Course in Cable
(Office of Communication, United Church
of Christ, 1981), 9.

catv—community antenna television

The first small cable systems—called CATV, or community antenna television—originated in Oregon, Pennsylvania, and Manhattan, where mountains or tall buildings blocked TV signals. Most of the early systems served roughly 10 percent of the country and, due to early technical and regulatory limits, contained only twelve channels. Even at this early stage, though, TV sales personnel, broadcasters, and electronics firms recognized the two big advantages of cable. First, by routing and reamplifying each channel in a separate wire, cable eliminated over-the-air interference. Second, by running signals through coaxial cable, a cable system increased channel capacity.

In the early days, small communities with CATV often received twice as many channels as were available over the air in a much larger city. Since broadcast channels were generally regarded as a limited natural resource, CATV foreshadowed later developments in which cable channel capacity grew dramatically. In combination, the two early technological advantages of cable would soon propel the new cable industry into competition with conventional broadcast television. Unlike radio, which was intended to free mass communication from unwieldy wires, early cable technology sought to restore wires to improve the potential of television.

a threat to broadcasting

Though the technology for cable existed as early as the late 1940s, cable's growth was effectively short-circuited by conventional broadcasters. For nearly thirty years, local broadcasters, the networks, and television's professional organization—the National Association of Broadcasters (NAB)—successfully lobbied to curb cable development in most cities. Throughout the 1950s and 1960s, the FCC operated on behalf of the broadcast industry to ensure that cable would not compete with conventional television. Local broadcasters worried that if towns could bring in distant signals from more "glamorous" cities like Chicago or New York, viewers would reject their local stations—and their local advertisers—in favor of big city signals. Early FCC rules blocked cable companies from bringing distant TV stations into cities and towns with local channels.

There was one exception to these lobbying efforts: CATV service for sparsely populated communities. Since CATV generally served towns with no TV stations of their own, the broadcast industry welcomed the distribution of distant signals to these areas via cable. After all, relaying a commercial signal to rural areas increased the audience reach and potential ad revenue of a broadcast station.

cable's franchising and regulation wars

By the early 1970s, it was clear that cable's growth could no longer be limited to small isolated communities. With cable's capacity for more channels and better reception, the FCC began to seriously examine industry issues. In 1972, the commission updated or enacted a series of rules regarding cable expansion. Established primarily to protect conventional over-the-air broadcasters in the top hundred TV markets, most of these rules did not apply to cable systems with fewer than thirty-five hundred subscribers.

The FCC initially reaffirmed **must-carry rules**, first established in 1965, which required all cable operators to assign channels to and carry all local TV broadcasts on their systems. This rule ensured that local network affiliates, independent stations (those not carrying network programs), and public television channels would benefit from cable's clearer reception. The FCC guidelines also allowed additional noncommercial channels to be introduced into bigger TV markets, but it limited the number of distant commercial TV signals to two or three independent stations per cable system. In addition, it prohibited cable companies from bringing in a network affiliate from another city when a local station already carried that network's programming. This ensured that a network affiliate in one market would not have to compete for viewers against a similar affiliate imported from another market.

The 1972 FCC rules required cable operators to carry their own original programming as well by mandating **access channels** in the nation's top hundred TV markets. In other words, cable operators were thus compelled to provide and fund a tier of nonbroadcast channels dedicated to local education, government, and the public. The FCC required large-market cable operators to assign separate channels for each access service, while cable operators in smaller markets (and with fewer channels) could assign education, government, and the public to share one channel. In addition to free public-access channels, the FCC called for **leased channels**. Citizens could buy time on these channels and produce longer programs or present controversial views.

> "No longer must you be satisfied with programming provided by others. You can **videotape your own shows** and cablecast them to your community on channels set aside for public use. Cable has turned sixth graders, senior citizens, homemakers and clergy into TV producers."
> —Jennifer Stearns,
> "A Short Course in Cable,"
> 1981

franchising frenzy

By the end of the 1970s, competition over obtaining franchises to supply local cable service had become intense. Essentially, a *cable franchise* was a mini-monopoly awarded by a local community to the most attractive bidder, usually for a fifteen-year period. Although a few large cities permitted two companies to build different parts of its cable system, in most cases communities granted franchises to only one company. Cities and states used the same logic that had granted monopoly status to AT&T for more than a hundred years: They did not want more than one operator trampling over private property to string wire from utility poles or bury cables underground.

Local municipalities and, in some instances, state governments got involved in overseeing franchise awards. A number of states, for example, guided the franchising process, and a few even retained the authority to approve a city's cable operator. Eight states—including Alabama, Hawaii, and Vermont—defined cable as a public utility (like the telephone or electric company), so their cable franchises needed approval from public utility commissions at the state level. In states in which cable was not defined as a utility, town councils and city governments selected the cable operator. This period, from the late 1970s through the 1980s, constituted a unique, if turbulent, era in media history, for it was during this time that most of the nation's cable systems were built (see Figure 6.2).

During the franchising process, a city (or state) would outline its cable needs and request bids from cable operators. Then, a number of companies—none of whom could also own broadcast stations or newspapers in the community—competed for the right to install and manage the cable system. In the bid, a company would include a list of promises to the city, including information about construction schedules, system design, subscription rates, channel capacity, types of programming, financial backing, deadlines, and a *franchise fee*: the money the cable company would pay the city annually for the right to operate the local cable system.

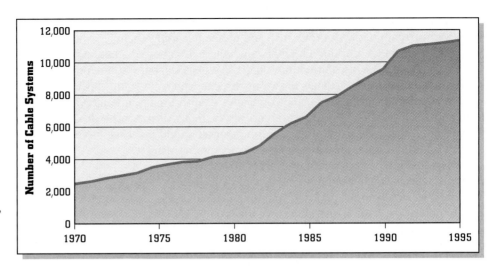

Figure 6.2
**The Rise of Cable
Systems, 1970–95**
Sources: National Cable
Television Association
(NCTA), *Cable Television
Developments* (Fall 1995): 4;
Warren Publishing, Inc.,
Television & Cable Factbook,
Services Volume No. 63, 1995,
1–76. Estimates as of January
1, 1995. Reprinted with per-
mission.

Few rules or laws existed to regulate the process of franchise negotiations. In some cities, cable firms lined up city council members or the mayor's friends to act as advocates for a particular company in exchange for campaign contributions or other perquisites. One practice in major markets became known as *rent-a-citizen:* Competing companies would identify and hire prominent lawyers, politicians, church leaders, and educators as local spokespersons during franchise negotiations. In some cases, these individuals got stock options (for a minimum investment) in the company that eventually received the cable franchise. To win franchises, some companies gave away up to 40 percent of their ownership rights to influential citizens. This occurred even though the companies remained responsible for 80 to 90 percent of the costs of building each cable system, which were $100 million or more in a medium-size city in the early 1980s.

During the franchising process, competing cable companies made attractive offers and promises to gain monopoly rights in certain areas. In the early 1980s, for example, Sammon Communication bid for the Fort Worth, Texas, franchise by offering that city a multimillion dollar community-access package, which included three mobile television vans (for producing community programs), $50,000 for student internship training programs, $175,000 as an annual budget for access channels, and $100,000 to modernize educational buildings and studios. Such offers were typical in large cable markets.

From the late 1970s through the 1980s, lots of wheeling and dealing transpired along with occasional corruption. Cable companies sometimes offered far more than they could deliver, and some cities and suburbs occasionally made unfair demands on the franchise awardees. Often, battles over broken promises, unreasonable contracts, or escalating rates ended up in court. Frequently, courts had to determine whether cities were requesting unfair franchise fees or violating the First Amendment rights of cable operators by demanding various channel services.

regulation nightmares and federal cable laws

From the very beginning of cable, no one seemed to know who held legal jurisdiction over "wired" television. Since the 1934 Communication Act had not anticipated cable, its regulatory status was problematic during these growth years. As late as 1969, the FCC claimed little jurisdiction in this area. However, once cable began importing distant signals into bigger television markets, the FCC's interest perked up. Prior to that time, the FCC functioned primarily to protect the commercial interests of local broadcasters and the national networks.

Common Carrier or Electronic Publisher? Unlike broadcasting, which is under the legal jurisdiction of the federal government, local and state governments are involved in cable, since cable firms rent access rights to property and telephone poles. In those few states where cable is regulated as a public utility, it technically is a *common carrier*, and is required to offer part of its service on a first-come, first-served basis to whomever can pay the rate. Common carriers, like taxi services or phone companies, do not get involved in channel content. Telephone operators, for instance, do not question the topics of personal conversations ("Hi, I'm the phone company, and what are you going to be talking about today?"). Most cable operators, however, view themselves as common carriers only with regard to the one or two leased channels they carry, where customers pay for and control their own programs.

In arguing that they are not common carriers, cable companies instead view themselves as *electronic publishers*, entitled to pick and choose what channels to carry. Historically, the cable industry has sought the same speech or "publishing" freedoms and legal protections that broadcast and print media enjoy in choosing content. In 1979, the Supreme Court agreed, siding with the cable industry in the landmark *Midwest Video* case.[1] In the case, Midwest Video, a cable operator, challenged the FCC's authority to mandate that cable systems carry certain programming, including access channels. Midwest Video's lawyers argued that some of the 1972 rules violated the First Amendment rights of their client. In other words, the government could not tell a magazine what to print and, therefore, should not be able to tell a cable operator what channels to carry. In siding with cable, the Supreme Court upheld the rights of cable operators to dictate their content and defined the industry as a form of "electronic publishing." Although the FCC could no longer mandate channels, the Court said that it was still okay for communities to "request" access channels as part of contract negotiations in the franchising process. Although access channels are no longer a requirement, most cable firms continue to offer them to remain on good terms with their communities.

The Repeal of Syndex Rules. To boost cable from its position as a struggling new industry, the FCC in 1980 repealed its *syndicated exclusivity*, or *syndex*, rules. These rules had given local stations exclusive rights in their area to syndicate TV programs, such as off-network reruns, which they had purchased. In other words, syndex rules had prohibited cable operators from importing reruns like *Happy Days* or *M*A*S*H* from distant markets, thereby offering consumers the same programming available on their local stations. Local broadcasters feared such competition would hurt advertising if consumers chose to watch favorite older shows on a distant cable channel rather than on the station carrying local ads. In exchange for the FCC's repeal of the syndex rules, cable operators agreed to pay copyright fees to broadcasters for imported distant signals. By the late 1980s, these fees amounted to more than $100 million collected from thousands of U.S. cable systems and distributed mostly among the nation's three-hundred-plus independent TV stations. Because of the repeal of syndex, viewers could conceivably watch episodes of *Happy Days* and *M*A*S*H* five or six times a day on five or six different local and distant channels.

The Cable Acts of 1984 and 1992. The first major federal act regarding cable was passed in 1984. Coming during the middle of the Reagan presidency, which had been favorable to deregulating business, it represented a victory for the cable industry and a defeat for local communities. The act capped the annual franchise fee a city could charge a cable operator at 5 percent of the company's gross revenues. The act further protected cable by making it difficult for cities to sign with a new company at the end of the regular fifteen-year franchise period. A more controversial aspect of the act called for a two-year phaseout of must-carry rules, which upset local broadcasters. In addition, it ended rate regulation. This meant that cable operators, while constituting a local monopoly, could set their own unregulated monthly subscriber rates beginning in January 1987.

The 1984 act immediately spurred rate increases. Between 1984 and 1990, the average rate for basic services (excluding premium movie channels like HBO) rose from about $9 to $19 a month. In addition, cable operators had effectively argued in 1984 that must-carry rules violated their free-speech rights (since in many cases they had to assign one-third of their channels to existing broadcast stations). As a result, cable systems began dropping some PBS affiliates and weaker independent stations from their lineups. By the late 1980s, more than 150 public stations had been removed from local cable systems, and some 50 new independent UHF stations, licensed shortly after the 1984 act, were having difficulty getting a cable channel assigned to them. Some large cable operators dropped regular broadcast signals in favor of new satellite-delivered channels on which they run their own ads. Displeased with the act, broadcast lobbyists and consumer watchdog groups began calling for cable reform.

With the growing commercial success of cable and the rapid increase in subscription rates, a less sympathetic FCC and Congress changed the law in 1992, reinstating rate regulation. By the mid-1990s, the FCC had surveyed the twenty-five largest cable companies, which served roughly 75 percent of all cable subscribers, and found that rates had fallen in fourteen of those systems but had increased in the other eleven systems. In most instances, loopholes allowed cable companies to raise rates on basic service but decrease rates for premium channels such as Showtime. By 1995, the FCC's Cable Bureau estimated that rates had dropped about 5 to 10 percent among the nation's systems, but the FCC was still processing a backlog of six thousand complaints about cable rates.

In terms of must-carry, the 1992 act required that commercial broadcasters opt every three years for either must-carry or *retransmission consent*. The latter option meant that broadcasters could now ask cable operators for fees to carry their channels. However, if broadcasters did this, they waived the right to be automatically carried on these cable systems. In other words, local commercial broadcasters who chose must-carry gave up the right to be compensated for their channel, but were assured that

Calvin and Hobbes   by Bill Watterson

Calvin & Hobbes, ©1992 Watterson. Dist. by Universal Press Syndicate. Reprinted with permission. All rights reserved.

they would not be banished from being assigned channels on their local cable system. By June 1993, each of the eleven-hundred-plus commercial U.S. TV stations (noncommercial stations could only choose must-carry) had to inform all cable systems in their broadcast range whether they were opting for must-carry or retransmission. At the time, only low-rated independent stations on the fringes of a market opted for must-carry.

In 1993, the stations that chose retransmission consent did so because they believed cable operators would not risk alienating customers by dropping the popular broadcast stations that carried network programs. In general, a broadcast station either wanted money from cable operators for carrying its signal or the right to advertise on more cable channels. By 1995, the FCC was still processing more than two hundred must-carry complaints. These were from both local stations who were unable to get on cable and from cable operators who sought to eliminate broadcasters from their lineups in favor of new satellite channels. A few large station owners such as ABC struck deals with cable companies that owned a large number of systems. For example, rather than ask for money, ABC requested that cable systems carry its new ESPN2 sports channel.

The Telecommunications Act of 1996. After sixty-two years, Congress finally rewrote the nation's communications laws in 1996, bringing cable fully under the federal rules that had long governed the telephone, radio, and TV industries. In its most significant move, Congress used the Act to knock down regulatory barriers, allowing regional phone companies, long-distance carriers, and cable operators to enter each other's markets. For the first time, owners could operate TV or radio stations in the same market where they owned the cable system. Just as the Act allows cable companies to offer telephone services, the Act also permits phone companies to use fiber-optic wires to offer computer services. Before the passage of the 1996 legislation, the phone and cable industries had long benefited from their regional and national monopoly status. Congress hoped that the new rules would spur competition and lower both phone and cable rates although this did not always happen.

> "If this [telecommunications] bill is a blueprint, it's **written in washable ink.** Congress is putting out a picture of how things will evolve. But **technology is transforming the industry** in ways that we don't yet understand."
> —Mark Rotenberg, Electronic Privacy Information Center, 1996

While broadcasters fought steadily for must-carry rules over the years, cable systems continued to argue that must-carry rules violate their free-speech rights by dictating what signals to include among their cable offerings. The Telecommunications Act appeared to settle the issue by reaffirming broadcasters' need for must-carry rules. However, cable companies with limited channel capacity still objected to having to carry low-rated stations; operators could make more money carrying satellite-delivered movie services and specialty channels on topics such as history or health. The nation's ten-thousand-plus cable operators continued to periodically ask the courts to repeal must-carry rules and free the cable industry to carry whatever channels best serve its commercial interests. In 1997, however, broadcasting won a final victory when the Supreme Court upheld the constitutionality of must-carry rules, assuring that most broadcasters would be carried by their local cable operator.

Among its other features (see Table 6.1), the 1996 Act permits telephone companies to buy or construct cable systems in communities with fewer than fifty thousand residents. The legislation also ended government involvement in rate regulation for all premium movie services and for basic services in small cable systems. For larger systems, however, Congress authorized the FCC to monitor monthly cable rates until 1999 before phasing out federal oversight of regulation entirely.

TABLE 6.1

Impact of the 1996 Telecommunications Act

On Cable	Monthly rates likely to rise Act lifts all federal rate regulations by 1999 for large cable systems Rate regulations eliminated immediately on systems with fewer than 1 percent of the nation's subscribers Cable companies may enter phone business
On Phone Companies	Mergers and alliances likely among cable and phone companies Act allows seven regional Bell companies to offer long-distance services after demonstrating they have opened up their local markets to competition Long-distance companies can compete in local phone-service business Local and long-distance companies can enter cable business Telephone and cable companies can own up to 10 percent of each other
On TV Broadcasting	Act takes limits off number of TV stations one company can own as long as total number of stations reach fewer than 35 percent of population Requires manufacturers to equip TV sets with V-chip to allow parents to block violent or sexually explicit programming
On the Internet	Act tried to make it a crime for online computer services or users to transmit pornographic and indecent material without restricting access by minors. In June 1996, a federal court decided this section of the Act was "overly broad" and unconstitutional. Decision appealed in 1997.

Sources: "Telecom Vote Signals Competitive Free-for-All," *Wall Street Journal*, February 2, 1996, p. B1+; "Who Gets What," *Time*, February 12, 1996, 52.

It is hard to predict the impact of the 1996 Act. New competition will indeed lower rates for some consumers, but in other instances fees might increase, especially as telephone and cable companies merge or form alliances. Such alliances could eliminate rate competition in both the phone and cable businesses, and there will be no government authority to step in and force rate freezes or cuts.

In terms of the Act's impact on cable programs, advances in technology and new commercial players will continue to increase the number of cable channels and add more specialized services, especially for affluent customers. As with other aspects of the information highway, of which cable is now a major section, many new developments are likely to bypass poorer communities. Local governments and citizen advocate groups will need to play a strong role to ensure that new media developments reach the widest cross section of people in their communities.

narrowcasting challenges broadcasting

By the early 1990s, 96 percent of all U.S. households could obtain a basic tier of cable channels for an $18 to $20 monthly fee. However, about one-third of this potential audience, most of them in less affluent central-city areas, chose not to subscribe to cable. Although its audience and advertising revenues remain smaller than those of the major TV networks, cable has emerged as a serious challenger to—and partner with—broadcasting. By 1996, the networks had joined the cable world. NBC operated two cable news services, while both ABC and CBS had agreements with cable channels to share and develop news and sports programming. Fox had also launched a twenty-four-hour news service similar to CNN. The trade magazine for television and an opponent of cable's early growth, *Broadcasting* had become *Broadcasting & Cable* magazine. The O.J. Simpson trials, which might have been covered gavel-to-gavel by the three networks in the 1960s or 1970s, were instead covered in the mid-1990s by three cable channels, CNN, Court TV, and the E! channel.

During the old network era in television, ABC, CBS, and NBC accounted for more than 95 percent of prime-time viewing; independent stations and public television accounted for the rest. By the mid-1990s, however, cable channels drew about 30 percent of the TV-viewing audience during a typical evening, up from only 6 percent in the mid-1980s. On the other hand, the old broadcast networks accounted for just over 50 percent of the prime-time audience, down from 90 percent in the mid-1980s. (Fox, the new UPN and WB networks, PBS, independent stations, and movie videos drew the rest of the audience.) The decline in the networks' viewer base appeared to be healthy for both competition and democracy. In fact, early in its development, especially with the arrival of public access channels, cable was heralded as a voice for the voiceless. In this sense, it offered opportunities to ordinary citizens to deliver messages and produce programs—options that were not available during the network era.

> "The TV game is different now. . . . it's like the magazine business when it shifted from general circulation to specialty publications. You can now choose from six different golfing magazines instead of only one."
>
> —Peggy Ziegler,
> editor,
> *Cable World*

In the new cable era, a redefined concept of **narrowcasting**—providing specialized programming for diverse and fragmented groups—has cut into broadcasting's large mass audience. For the advertising industry, cable programs provide access to specific target audiences that cannot be guaranteed in broadcasting. For example, a golf-equipment manufacturer can buy ads on the Golf Channel and reach only golf enthusiasts. Since the audience is small and specialized, ads are a fraction of the cost of a network ad; they reach only the targeted viewers and not the larger general public. As cable channels have become more and more like specialized magazines or radio formats (see Figure 6.3), they have siphoned off network viewers. As a consequence, the networks' role as the chief programmer of the shared culture has eroded.

Cable consumers usually choose programming from a two-tier structure: a group of **basic channels**, part of one monthly fee, and **premium channels**, available individually to customers at an extra monthly fee. These channels are the production arm of the cable industry, supplying programming to the nation's 11,500 cable operators, who function as program distributors by delivering channels to cable households. In the mid-1990s, a basic service program package of sixty or more channels cost consumers between $24 and $28 a month nationwide, while a single premium channel like HBO cost an additional $8 to $12 per month.

basic cable

A typical basic cable system today includes a thirty-six- to seventy-two-channel line-up composed of local broadcast signals, nonbroadcast access channels (for local government, education, and general public use), a few regional PBS stations, and a variety of services retrieved from national communications satellites (see "Tracking Technology: Communication Satellites Open Doors to the Future" on page 165). These basic satellite services include ESPN, CNN, CNN Headline News, MTV, the USA Network, Bravo, Nickelodeon, Lifetime, the Family Channel, Comedy Central, CNBC, C-Span and C-Span2, Black Entertainment Network, a home- shopping service, the Weather Channel, and ten to thirty additional channels depending on a cable system's capacity and regional interests. Basic services also include **superstations**, which are merely independent TV stations such as WTBS in Atlanta or WGN in Chicago that have uplinked their signal onto a satellite to make themselves available nationwide.

Figure 6.3
The Top 20 Cable
Networks (Ranked by
Number of Subscribers)
Source: National Cable
Television Association, *Cable
Television Developments* (Fall
1996): 16–17. Data provided to
NCTA by the networks,
Aug.–Oct. 1996.
Note: Figures may include non-
cable affiliates and/or sub-
scribers. Broadcast viewership
is not included.

1. CNN
   Affiliates: 11,528
   Subscribers: 69,950,000

2. TBS
   Affiliates: 11,668
   Subscribers: 69,920,000

3. ESPN
   Affiliates: 27,600
   Subscribers: 69,800,000
   THE TOTAL SPORTS NETWORK

4. USA Network
   Affiliates: 12,500
   Subscribers: 69,677,000

5. Discovery Channel
   Affiliates: N/A
   Subscribers: 69,499,000

6. TNT (Turner Network Television)
   Affiliates: 10,406
   Subscribers: 69,075,000

7. C–SPAN
   Affiliates: 5,933
   Subscribers: 68,700,000

8. TNN: The Nashville Network
   Affiliates: 16,411
   Subscribers: 67,000,000
   THE NASHVILLE NETWORK
   The Heart of Country

9. The Family Channel
   Affiliates: 13,352
   Subscribers: 66,900,000

10. A&E (A&E Television Network)
    Affiliates: NA
    Subscribers: 66,880,000
    TIME WELL SPENT

11. Lifetime Television (LIFE)
    Affiliates: 7,600
    Subscribers: 66,000,000
    Lifetime
    Television for Women

12. Nickelodeon/Nick at Nite
    Affiliates: 11,788 (NICK)
    11,711 (N@N)
    Subscribers: 66,000,000

13. MTV: Music Television
    Affiliates: 9,176
    Subscribers: 65,900,000
    MUSIC TELEVISION

14. The Weather Channel
    Affiliates: 6,500
    Subscribers: 64,700,000
    THE WEATHER CHANNEL

15. Headline News
    Affiliates: 6,470
    Subscribers: 62,619,000
    Headline NEWS

16. AMC (American Movie Classics)
    Affiliates: N/A
    Subscribers: 61,000,000
    AMERICAN MOVIE CLASSICS

17. CNBC
    Affiliates: 5822
    Subscribers: 60,000,000
    FIRST IN BUSINESS · FIRST IN TALK

18. QVC
    Affiliates: 5,895
    Subscribers: 57,017,455

19. VH1 (Music First)
    Affiliates: 6,076
    Subscribers: 56,230,000
    MUSIC FIRST

20. The Learning Channel
    Affiliates: N/A
    Subscribers: 52,000,000
    THE LEARNING CHANNEL

"If **Desert Storm** fixed CNN's reputation, and **O.J.** did the same for Court TV, then the blizzard of '96 has put the **Weather Channel** solidly on the map."

—*Newsweek,*
January 1996

Typically, local cable systems pay each of these satellite-delivered services between fifteen and fifty cents a month per subscriber. That fee is then passed along to consumers as part of their basic monthly cable rate. Unlike local broadcasters, who make money almost exclusively through advertising, cable earns revenue in a variety of ways: through monthly subscriptions for basic service, local ad sales, pay-per-view programming, and premium movie channels. Most basic satellite services like ESPN or Arts & Entertainment block out time for inexpensive local and regional ads. These local ads are cheaply produced compared to national network ads and reach a smaller audience than broadcast commercials. Cable, in fact, has permitted many small local companies—from restaurants to clothing stores—that might not otherwise be able to afford TV spots to use television as a means of advertising.

The 1990s witnessed a proliferation of new basic cable networks, increasingly specialized for smaller but more definable audiences. These include the popular Sci-Fi Channel (owned by the USA Network and Viacom/Paramount), the Cartoon Channel (owned by Turner/Time Warner and other investors), Comedy Central (owned by Time Warner and Viacom), and fX (owned by Fox and TCI, the nation's largest cable operator). Newer services featured channels devoted to history, health and fitness, books, games, parenting, pets, therapy, and Indian tribal culture. While more than 160 cable services were offered in 1997, cable systems with thirty-six to seventy-two channels (many of them reserved for local broadcasters) only carried the most popular cable networks.

With the rapid expansion of telephone, television, and radio in the 1950s, a demand developed for more and better ways to send and receive mass communication signals. In the mid-1950s, the Soviet Union and then the United States successfully sent satellites into orbit around the earth. In 1960, the United States launched Echo I, a *passive* metallic sphere that simply received radio signals from an earth station and reflected them back to earth. In 1962, AT&T launched Telstar, the first communication satellite capable of receiving, amplifying, and returning signals. Telstar received transmissions from the ground, beamed into space from an uplink facility, and retransmitted them to a receiving dish called a downlink. An *active* satellite, Telstar was able to process and relay telephone and television signals between the United States and Europe.

The earliest communication satellites worked for only a few hours a day, when they passed over the regions—or *footprints*— they were serving. But in the mid-1960s, scientists figured out how to lock a communication satellite into synchronous or geostationary orbit. In this location—22,300 miles from the equator—satellites traveling at more than 6,800 mph circle the earth at the same speed the earth revolves on its axis.

The first satellites lasted seven or eight years and had twelve to twenty-four *transponders*, the relay points on a satellite that perform the receive-and-transmit functions. Cable and DBS program providers rent these transponders from satellite companies for million-dollar monthly fees. One conventional transponder can process one color TV signal or about three thousand simultaneous long-distance phone calls. By the mid-1990s, the newest satellites had forty-eight transponders. Companies also began experimenting with *digital compression*, a way of increasing the

number of signals transmitted simultaneously without disturbing image quality. This process allowed one transponder to handle four to six TV signals. In 1995, PBS began sending *Sesame Street* to various affiliates using digital compression, hoping to free expensive transponder space that the network could then sublet to other firms.

About 65 percent of satellite use is for television, news, and cable services. Telephone, telegraph, and business communication account for the rest of the transponder market. For example, CNN leases Transponder 5 on the Hughes Galaxy 5 satellite. Many cable channels that operate globally rent two transponders on different satellites to reach receiving dishes in both the western and eastern hemispheres.

One of the more pressing issues regarding communication satellites, particularly in recent years, has involved who gets to occupy synchronous orbit, which technically is a finite resource. (There are only so many available satellite "parking spaces" 22,300 miles from earth.) Formed in 1964, the major global satellite organization INTELSAT, a network of over twenty satellites with more than 120 government members, continues to wrestle with issues of satellite access. Although geostationary orbit has so far accommodated the satellites from industrialized countries, some developing nations worry that by the time they are prepared to launch, there will not be enough room left. Scarce space allocations have generally operated on a common-carrier basis— first come, first served to the highest bidders. But digital compression technology and the new digital TV standard will eventually solve the scarcity problem by increasing transponder capacity the way FM radio increased the radio spectrum and the way cable expanded TV services.

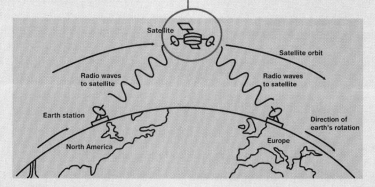

The general success rate of new services, like many mass media products, has been about 10 to 15 percent, which means about 85 to 90 percent of new cable channels fail or are bought out by another cable service. The most difficult challenge new channels face is getting onto enough cable systems—many with limited channel capacity—to become profitable. Although several basic cable services, such as ESPN and the USA Network (both now accessible in seventy million cable households), have been extremely successful, two basic channels—CNN and MTV—have made significant marks on global culture and society.

CNN's Window to the World. Cable News Network (CNN), a twenty-four-hour TV news channel, premiered in June 1980. CNN was the brainchild of Ted Turner, who helped revolutionize cable when he uplinked his small independent Atlanta station, WTBS, to superstation stature in 1976 (see "Case Study: Ted Turner—Cable Power Broker and Global News Maker" on page 168). In 1982, Turner also launched Headline News, adapting the concept of format radio to TV news. Every thirty minutes, Headline News rotates brief versions of the top national and international news stories followed by sports, business, and entertainment segments. Together, these two cable services—CNN and Headline News—lost nearly $80 million before turning a profit of $13 million in 1985. By the early 1990s, the two news channels were making more than $200 million in annual operating profits. In addition, CNN started a radio news service in 1992, which today provides news to five hundred radio affiliates in the United States. By 1997, CNN was available in more than seventy million U.S. homes. It was also carried part-time by more than 250 local broadcasters who were not affiliated with a regular network or who used CNN's twenty-four-hour services to supplement their late night schedules.

> "CNN serves as . . . an instant delivery system for dramatic footage from around the globe. In a crisis it becomes a kind of **video bulletin board** where key players can post messages to one another in full view of the world."
>
> —Jay Rosen,
> *The Nation*,
> 1991

CNN emerged as a serious competitor to ABC, CBS, and NBC during the Persian Gulf War in 1991, when two of its reporters were able to maintain a live phone link from a downtown Baghdad hotel during the initial U.S. bombing of the Iraqi capital. Even Iraq's military leaders watched the channel to get the American point of view. CNN's ratings soared—from 930,000 U.S. households before the crisis to as many as 10,000,000 homes after the war began. About two hundred local broadcast stations with CNN agreements switched to its crisis coverage, including many network affiliates that ordinarily carried regular network coverage. (Many of these local stations had already been carrying CNN during the night when the networks did not offer news to affiliates.) Affecting more than network news, CNN's late evening reports often made morning newspaper accounts obsolete because the newspapers had deadlines the previous evening.

CNN has perhaps made its biggest impact on international news coverage. While the networks were cutting costs by closing foreign news operations in the 1980s, CNN was opening them. By the mid-1990s, it was operating nine

![Christiane Amanpour, Tehran, Iran]

Dubbed the "Chicken Noodle Network" by early critics, the Cable News Network built its reputation by scooping the broadcast networks. CNN was the first to report on the attempted assassination of Ronald Reagan in 1981 and on the explosion of the *Challenger* in 1986. Today, CNN reporter Christiane Amanpour (who also files reports for *60 Minutes*) continues reporting from countries often ignored in mainstream U.S. television news.

bureaus in the United States and nineteen worldwide, stretching from London to Cairo to Moscow to Tokyo—more foreign news bureaus than any U.S. network. Today, CNN appears in more than 150 countries. In 1992, its growing presence in Europe expedited the development of a rival news service, Euronews. A consortium of eleven state-owned European TV groups, Euronews emerged for cultural as well as economic reasons. One of its chief executives argued that "CNN is an American channel, an American point of view. The point of Euronews is to give the viewer back his memories."[2] Though Turner's CNN brought the world its first twenty-four-hour TV news service, it continues to reflect American viewpoints and values.

"I Want My MTV." The second basic cable service to dramatically change the world's cultural landscape has been MTV (the Music Television Network), launched by Warner Communication in 1981 and purchased by Viacom in 1985. Now a highly profitable subsidiary of the merger that joined Paramount and Viacom in 1994, MTV and its global offspring—including MTV Asia, MTV Europe, MTV Brasil, MTV Japan, and MTV Latino—reach nearly 250 million homes worldwide. When Poland escaped Soviet control in the late 1980s, its national television operation immediately began broadcasting MTV. By the mid-1990s, a quarter of MTV's revenue came from international sources.

Although today MTV remains a powerful influence on global culture, it was slow to develop in at least one significant way. In its formative years, MTV gave little airtime to African American artists. This history recalls the 1950s and the problems black rock and rollers faced getting mainstream radio play. In the early 1980s, MTV's reluctance to play music videos by black artists was related to cable's economics. At that time, most cable companies were operating primarily in affluent white communities in U.S. suburbs. These were the areas that could most easily afford cable. Since rock had been dominated by white male groups throughout the 1970s, MTV determined that white suburban teens probably wanted to see similar groups in their music videos. It took Michael Jackson's *Thriller* album in 1982 to break down music video's early color barrier. The album's large crossover appeal, coupled with the expansion of cable into more urban areas, opened the door to far more diverse videos.

"MTV—Music television. You may think of it as the channel that rattles your china . . . and hypnotizes your children, but what you may want to know is that MTV is responsible for a complete revolution in the music business." —Diane Sawyer, *Primetime Live,* 1990

By the end of the 1980s, MTV reported that its annual profits had passed $50 million and that nearly thirty million viewers tuned in at least once during the week. Throughout the 1980s, it sought more and more control over music-video distribution and exhibition, employing two monopoly tactics to ensure dominance. First, MTV paid record companies for exclusive rights to the most popular music videos (for periods ranging from thirty days to one year), thus preventing access by other music-video services. Although this was a form of payola, federal laws prohibiting this practice applied only to broadcasting, not to cable. According to *Billboard* magazine, MTV paid CBS Records $8 million in 1984, covering CBS's total music-video production costs for a two-year period. During the mid-1980s, MTV also signed exclusive deals with RCA Records, MCA, Geffen, Warner Music, Atlantic, Polygram, and Capitol Records.[3]

Second, MTV signed agreements with the major cable systems to ensure that it would become the music-video network in all the main cable markets. Those cable companies with limited channel capacity were often reluctant to carry more than one music channel. Competing services, like Ted Turner's attempt to start a music-video channel in 1984, were quickly countered by VH-1. After MTV launched this second channel, which was geared to the baby-boom generation and the parents of the MTV crowd, it

Ted Turner—Cable Power Broker and Global News Maker

By most accounts, Ted Turner is to cable what David Sarnoff was to broadcasting: a savvy entrepreneur who imagined and realized television's future. After inheriting his father's struggling billboard company, in 1970 Turner bought a small Atlanta UHF station, WHRH, for $500,000. Selling ads for as little as $5 each to attract sponsors, Turner renamed the station WTBS (for the Turner Broadcasting System). In 1976, he changed television forever when he spent more than $1 million for a satellite uplink to lift his independent TV signal to superstation stature. Not stopping there, he bought the Atlanta Braves that same year and in 1977 purchased the Atlanta Hawks, calling them "America's teams." These purchases gave Turner the program content—professional

sports—necessary to lure national audiences with something that only the broadcast networks had controlled before.

Turner's second idea, viewed as a joke by many at the time, was a twenty-four-hour cable news channel. He borrowed $100 million in the late 1970s, and in June 1980 started CNN. Between 1980 and 1985, while Turner's WTBS made good money, he was losing almost $2.2 million a month on his cable news enterprise. In the midst of these losses, he started Headline News, a second cable channel that he programmed like a radio format—repeating Top Stories, Dollars & Sense, Sports, and Entertainment every half hour. When CNN and Headline News turned a profit in 1985, the traditional networks began taking Turner more seriously. ABC even tried to preempt CNN's growing presence by launching its own twenty-four-hour cable news channel, but the venture quickly failed. Although the networks had years of news experience, they could not compete. Cable operators had rallied behind Turner; many refused to carry more than one cable news channel, and that service was almost always CNN.

Although CNN's finest hour came during the Persian Gulf War in 1991, the cable channel laid the groundwork throughout the 1980s. In 1984, it secured an anchor booth alongside the major networks at the Democratic National Convention. In 1985, Shiite Muslims hijacked a TWA passenger jet, and viewers discovered they no longer had to wait for the revered evening network news to find out what was happening. Then, during the 1989 Chinese student uprising in Beijing, CNN was the only news organization that did not depend on government-run earth stations to send signals back to the United States. It had purchased a portable fly-away uplink, which freed the cable channel from attempts by Chinese authorities to muzzle news reports. As a result, CNN was able to transmit key images and information from those historic student-versus-government confrontations.

As CNN's stature grew, so did Ted Turner's ambition. Despite losing $18 million in a failed attempt to purchase ABC in the mid-1980s, Turner targeted the famed MGM movie studio. Critics at the time said Turner wanted to restore his pride after the ABC affair, but Turner was also interested in MGM's old movie libraries, which contained thousands of films that could provide needed programming for WTBS and later TNT (launched by Turner in 1988). Despite advice against the deal, Turner bought MGM when owner Kirk Kerkorian agreed to throw in approximately 1,500 additional films from the old RKO and Warner

Brothers libraries, which he also owned. Turner took on a $1.4 billion debt to complete the deal, which quickly started to unravel, particularly when MGM's new films continued to flop at the box office. Kerkorian's bankers restructured the deal, and Turner had to agree to pay $900 million of his debt back within one year.

With Turner in trouble, the cable industry again came to his aid. At the 1986 national cable convention, TCI chief John Malone announced that the cable industry needed to keep TBS independent—from broadcasters and networks looking to acquire Turner's precarious domain. TCI led a consortium of cable systems that bought $565 million in TBS stock, reducing Turner's control of the company from 81 to 51 percent. The two biggest companies, TCI and Time Inc. (before its merger with Warner), each bought 18 percent stakes in TBS and received seats on the TBS board of directors. Besides WTBS and TNT, TBS's holdings featured a syndication and licensing branch that handled its movie libraries, sports and real-estate ventures, and the news division, which in addition to CNN and Headline News now included CNN International, CNN Spanish-language news, and CNN Radio. In 1995, Time Warner initiated a buyout of Turner's operations for $6.5 billion. Free of debt and much wealthier, Turner stayed on as vice chairman of Time Warner and president of Turner.

Ted Turner's major global legacy, CNN, remains under scrutiny today, even as the news channel appeals to elite leaders throughout the world. News critic Jay Rosen identifies CNN's impact:

> **As CNN begins to constitute—rather than merely inform—the global sphere, its limitations will become global as well. Political deeds that lack a visual dimension may tend to escape world notice because they bore the image-hungry producers at CNN (or its competitors)....**
>
> **In newsrooms, international airports, foreign ministries and financial houses around the world, CNN is left on all the time, becoming the medium of record for people whose business it is to monitor the globe.**[1]

Rosen acknowledges as well that CNN offers much that is progressive, including its refusal to transform news anchors into celebrities and its coverage of live, unedited, and "important news conferences, announcements, and hearings in their entirety." But with CNN taking center stage in 1995 as world viewers tracked the O. J. Simpson criminal trial, one Rosen criticism of CNN from 1991 may be prophetic: "Turner's triumph will do more for the spread of TV culture than for the cultivation of intelligent citizenship around the globe."[2]

Among the most popular programs for pre-teens in the mid-1990s is Nickelodeon's *The Secret World of Alex Mack* (1994–). The show features Larisa Oleynik as a suburban teen who possesses superpowers, such as the ability to levitate objects and morph into a silver blob. The program was so popular that in 1996 Nickelodeon began broadcasting it two nights a week.

was able to buy out Turner within a month. Late in the 1980s, a service called Hit Video USA, trying to compete with MTV, charged that exclusive contracts constituted an MTV monopoly over music-video distribution and exhibition. The case was settled out of court, and by the mid-1990s, MTV remained the only major player in rock videos.

Like Euronews competing with CNN, other countries and companies have tried to challenge MTV. Four major international record companies—EMI, Polygram, Sony, and Warner Music—launched a music channel in Germany in the early 1990s. Mexico in the mid-1990s started Telehit to compete with MTV Latino. German music giant Bertelsmann teamed with TCI to produce a combination music-video/home-shopping channel, which led MTV to plan a similar service. Canada, however, represents MTV's toughest challenge. Its stricter regulations have blocked MTV's access to many of Canada's cable systems while promoting a Canadian music-video network, MuchMusic (which began offering its service in the United States in 1994).

Although the plan was scrapped in mid-1995, for a while the major recording labels contemplated challenging MTV by launching a joint American music-video channel controlled by the recording industry. The Justice Department, however, warned that the major labels' involvement in "exhibition" might constitute a "vertical monopoly": tight control of all three arms of a U.S. media industry—production, distribution, *and* exhibition. Although MTV itself is heavily involved in distributing and exhibiting videos through various deals with cable systems, unlike record companies, it is not involved in actually *producing* videos.

The major recording labels, spending $50 million a year to produce videos by the early 1990s, have grown dependent on MTV's power to certify a hit recording. These companies have also criticized the small group of MTV executives who wade through the hundreds of new videos released each week and judge which 10 to 15 percent are fit for MTV play. The recording companies want to see more of their products on MTV's regular music rotation, which usually accommodates about sixty recordings per week.

As a subsidiary of one of the world's largest media conglomerates, MTV draws more fire for its cultural than for its economic impact. Many critics worry that its influence has eroded local culture-specific traits among the world's youth and substituted an overabundance of U.S. culture in its place. Others argue that MTV has contributed to the decline of conversation and civil discourse through its often sexually suggestive and rapid-fire style. Defenders of the network, however, point out that MTV and cable have created a global village, giving the world's youth a common language. They also applaud a variety of MTV's special programs on issues ranging from drug addiction to racism to social activism. MTV's Rock the Vote campaign, for instance, helped register one million young voters, who may have swung the 1992 presidential election to Bill Clinton. In Hungary, after the decline of Soviet influence, young people started an influential political party that restricted membership to people under thirty years of age, arguing that only young members would not be nostalgic for the return to a more totalitarian regime. Informally, the Hungarians and the press called the new political organization "the MTV party."

One of MTV's major innovations has been the Nickelodeon channel. Tom Freston, chairman of MTV, says Nickelodeon provides "as wide a variety of television for children as exists anywhere." Freston believes that Nickelodeon has changed the way children and teens think about television: "It's interesting—if you talk to kids who are nine years old, they don't see CBS, NBC, and ABC as being the big places. And that generation is going to grow up a generation in whose mind there's more parity between cable networks and broadcast networks."[4] In an era in which the major networks abandoned children's programming—except for cartoons—because they were not lucrative enough, competitors such as PBS and Nickelodeon have tried to fill the gap. As Nick at Nite and MTV kids reach adulthood, they no longer view broadcast programs as superior to cable.

premium cable

Besides basic programming, cable offers a wide range of special or *premium* services. These include movie channels, such as HBO, Showtime, and the Disney Channel; pay-per-view (PPV) programs; and interactive (two-way) services that permit consumers to use their televisions to bank, shop, play games, and access the Internet. Subscribers to such services pay extra fees in addition to their fee for basic cable. In the early days of cable, there was only a single monthly charge, but with HBO providing movies, a new source of revenue—the premium or deluxe tier—was added to the subscription mix. In fact, luring customers to premium channels has plenty of incentives for cable companies: The cost to them is $4 to $6 a month per subscriber to carry a premium channel, but they then charge customers $10 or more per month and reap a nice profit.

The HBO Alternative. By far the oldest and most influential premium service is Home Box Office (HBO), a subsidiary of Time Warner, the nation's second largest owner of cable companies. HBO launched the first premium cable network in 1975, when it began offering services via satellite, mostly to hotel chains. HBO lost money in the beginning. At the time, only two cable systems had invested the $100,000 necessary for the large earth stations that were then technically necessary to retrieve a satellite signal. Between 1975 and 1980, however, the number of cable earth stations grew to seventeen hundred and HBO became a success.

Although HBO reaches less than one-third the audience of a popular basic service, it has remained the dominant premium service, selling monthly subscriptions to nearly twenty million homes by 1996. The next closest competitors were Viacom's two premium services, Showtime and the Movie Channel, which in combination had thirteen million subscribers by 1996. The movie business initially feared that HBO would be a detriment to film attendance in theaters. Eventually, though, HBO and the other premium channels brought a lucrative source of income to the movie studios, which earn roughly a 15 percent share of premium cable's profits. With premium cable locking up rights to feature-length movies after their initial theater runs, film companies recognized that they could recoup losses from a weak theater run by extending a film's life. This could be done not just via television or neighborhood second-run theaters but through lucrative arrangements with premium cable.

In the early 1980s, with little competition, HBO was dictating to movie studios what films it wanted and how much it was willing to pay. HBO and other premium channels ran into trouble, however, as videotapes became the preferred method of viewing movies after their theater runs. Both VCRs and PPV options brought competition to the movie channels. In the mid-1980s, film studios started releasing movies to PPV and to video stores before offering them to movie channels. The new competition forced the movie channels to expand their services. HBO, for example, began developing its own programming—everything from children's shows like *Fraggle Rock* to comedies like the *Larry Sanders Show*, an Emmy-winning satire of late night TV talk shows.

What film studios clearly did not like was HBO's production of its own feature-length films. In 1982, HBO entered into an arrangement with CBS and Columbia Pictures (later bought by Sony) to form a new production house, TriStar Pictures. Many in the movie industry charged that HBO's movie productions constituted vertical integration with involvement in production, distribution, and exhibition. They argued that when Time Inc. (before its merger with Warner) began making movies through HBO and TriStar, the media conglomerate was permitted to do something that film studios were not. A Supreme Court decision in 1948 had broken up the film industry's vertical structure by forcing the major studios to sell their theaters, the exhibition part of their operations. Time Inc., on the other hand, was the second largest owner of cable systems—the movie studio equivalent of owning theaters. Since so many cable companies and services existed, though, the government did not seriously challenge HBO's role in movie production.

Pay-per-View and Interactive Cable. *Pay-per-view* services, which began in 1985, allow customers to select a particular movie for a one-time $3 or $4 charge, payable to the local cable service, or $25 to $40 for a special one-time event, such as a championship boxing match, a professional wrestling event, or a rock concert. When these services started in late 1985, they were available in fewer than 150,000 households. By the mid-1990s, however, Viewer's Choice (a Viacom subsidiary) was available in twelve million households and Request Television in twenty-two million homes. Six other PPV services were also operating. Generally, the movie studios make a hefty profit from PPV companies, asking as much as 50 percent of what the PPV and cable companies earn from subscribers who view the movies. The studios' cut from PPV is substantially higher than their share from home movie rentals (about 20 percent) and premium movie channels (about 15 percent). In the 1990s, studios started buying shares of these services.

Another type of cable service features *interactive*, or two-way, *channels*. When equipped with two-way technology, such systems allow users to send signals upstream or back to the headend. (Most systems are one-way and can only send signals downstream to homes.) Interactive cable can connect households to their banks, where customers can pay bills or transfer money. Some cable services also permit police burglary units and fire stations to monitor homes and apartments. Like the bulk of cable programming, the most frequent type of two-way service involves entertainment. In 1991, Interactive Network began offering video games to cable consumers, including play-along versions of *Wheel of Fortune* and *Jeopardy*. It also provided services that allowed viewers to guess the next play during a football game or the identity of the villain in *Murder, She Wrote*.

Cable Radio. In addition to movies and videos on request, many cable systems now offer CD-quality premium audio services, sometimes called *cable radio*. Routed through a consumer's stereo equipment, cable radio companies like Music Choice and Digital Music Service (DMX) provide twenty-four-hour music channels uninterrupted by ads. Originally known as Digital Cable Radio in the 1980s, Music Choice was the first digital audio service. It featured separate audio channels playing all kinds of prepackaged musical styles ready for home audiotaping. DMX premiered in 1991 and by the mid-1990s offered sixty channels, twenty-four hours a day, ranging from classical to rap. Such satellite-delivered channels are another example of media convergence; they link cable, sound recordings, and home-stereo units for a monthly fee that is less than a new CD. By the mid-1990s, with the consumers' ability to record digital-quality commercial-free music off their stereo, recording industry executives began worrying about cable radio's impact on CD sales.

direct broadcast satellites: cable without wires

Because of its dependence on communication satellites, cable TV has always been on the cutting edge of technological developments. Now many of those advances are posing an economic threat to cable in the same ways that cable challenged traditional broadcasting in the 1970s. Of all the emerging technologies, including the Internet, *direct broadcast satellites* (DBS) present the biggest challenge to the existing cable and television industries.

The earliest earth-station antennas or "dishes"—set up in the mid-1970s to receive cable programming—were large, measuring twenty to forty feet in diameter, and expensive (with FCC license fees adding to their high cost). From the beginning, however, engineers worked on reducing the size and cost of the receiving dishes in order to develop a consumer model. In regions and countries with rugged terrain, the installation of cable wiring was not always easy or possible.

To protect the fledgling cable business through the 1970s and 1980s, the FCC restricted the development of DBS companies, which get their programming from the same satellite channels (such as CNN, MTV, ESPN, and HBO) that supply the regular cable industry. In the United States, rural communities bypassed FCC restrictions by investing in seven- to ten-foot receiving dishes and downlinking, for free, the same channels that cable companies were supplying to wired communities. These home satellite dishes, like early cable systems, appeared mostly in sprawling but sparsely populated areas that were too costly for cable companies to wire. Receiving dishes, visible from many interstate highways, began springing up on farms by the late 1970s. Initially, households could pick up channels once they had invested in a large receiving dish, which ranged from $2,000 to $3,000. Not surprisingly, satellite programmers launched a flurry of legal challenges against farmers and small-town residents who were receiving their signals. Rural communities countered that they had the rights to the airspace above their own property; the satellite firms contended that their signals were being stolen. With the law unclear, a number of cable channels began scrambling their signals. Because of this, most satellite users had to buy or rent descramblers and subscribe to services, just like cable customers did.

From home satellites, the DBS business developed. Signal scrambling spawned companies that provided both receiving dishes and satellite program services for a month-

The dogs in this ad recall a 1902 advertisement for the Victor Talking Machine Co., which featured a similar dog selling Victrola phonographs. RCA later purchased the Victor company, and the dog peering into the phonograph's megaphone-like speaker became RCA Victor's enduring symbol.

Introducing our newest Digital Satellite System. Imitations are sure to follow.

But don't be fooled. For the most advanced DSS® System available, you want the new

[*Separate favorite channel lists make it easier to find something you want to watch.*]

RCA brand DSS System. Its remote has One-Button Record. Highlight a show on

[*One-Button Record means the end of VCR programming as you know it.*]

the program guide, press record* and it programs your VCR for you. And our Personal Profiles feature lets several people create separate favorite channel lists, which you call up by clicking on a picture of yourself. You can also access the most exciting movies and events DIRECTV® and USSB have ever offered,* with laser disc quality picture and CD sound capability.* The new RCA DSS System. We were the first to introduce it, so who better to improve it? **Changing Entertainment. Again.® RCA**

†*Programming sold separately. Model DS4440RA.*

ly fee. Japanese companies had been experimenting with "wireless cable" alternatives for a number of years, and in 1978 they launched the first DBS system in Florida. With gradual improvements in satellite technology, the diameters of satellite receiving dishes decreased from more than twenty feet to three feet in a few years. By 1995, consumers could order satellite dishes the size of a large pizza.

With the emergence of cable as a lucrative industry, the last FCC and technical obstacles gradually fell away, and full-blown DBS services began in 1994. Initially, the FCC authorized a French company to sell DBS dishes, Thomson Consumer Electronics, which had acquired the RCA brand name from General Electric. After Thomson/RCA sold one million units, the FCC permitted Sony to enter the U.S. DBS market. Gradually, the commission let more licensees into the DBS game. Early rapid sales of Thomson/RCA's DBS systems ranked it among the fastest starting technologies in media history.

By the mid-1990s, DBS companies offered consumers all the channels and tiers of service that cable companies carried, often at slightly lower costs (plus the initial investment of $500 to $1,000 for installing the small dish antenna). In addition, DBS systems carried more than fifty channels reserved for a myriad of PPV movies. Thus, DBS presented far more options than what was available on the three or four PPV movie channels offered on most conventional cable systems, which were limited by channel capacity. Buoyed by high consumer interest and competing in large cities as well as rural areas, DBS firms today are challenging the long-standing monopoly status of most cable systems, offering distinct advantages—and disadvantages—compared to cable.

On the upside, DBS's digital technology is superior to standard cable and broadcast signals, providing laser-disk-quality pictures and CD-quality sound. On the downside, along with the initial start-up cost for consumers, DBS dishes do not pick up an area's local broadcast signals, which are not uplinked to satellites. This means that most subscribers have to use either a local cable company, an outside TV antenna, or rabbit-ear antennas on their TV set to get the local PBS, independent, and broadcast network programming. In addition, DBS systems deliver one satellite signal at a time and do not allow consumers to tape a program on a VCR while they watch another show.

In the short run, DBS does not appear to threaten cable, which has a clear advantage in providing the broadcast signals that carry traditional network programming, still the nation's most popular television fare. (In 1997, however, Rupert Murdoch announced plans to provide a DBS system that also carries local broadcast systems.) In addition, telephone companies and TCI are developing prototype cable channels—through digital compression—that transform standard cable services into five-hundred-channel systems (that also includes Internet access). This development would counter DBS's main advantage: offering more channels and better-quality images. In the long run, DBS may pose a bigger threat to the home-video and movie-rental market. For consumers who rent a lot of movies, care about the quality of the image, and want to make their own copies, it may eventually be cheaper and more convenient to subscribe to a DBS service.

> "A buddy of mine with one of them new **satellite dishes** actually gets channels from Neptune."
> —David Letterman, 1996

ownership and business issues in cable

Although there are more than 11,500 cable systems in the United States, most of these systems are controlled by **multiple-system operators (MSOs)**, a shrinking number of large corporations that each own several cable systems. By 1996, the Top 12 MSOs controlled the lines into 70 percent of all households wired for cable (see Table 6.2). Once again, the economic trend points to an industry slouching toward oligopoly, with a handful of megamedia firms controlling programming for future generations. Like the Internet, however, cable and DBS hold the promise of offering more specialized channels on which the diverse needs of individuals and communities might be met.

tci and time warner—
the major players

Since the early 1980s, two giant companies have dominated the acquisition of smaller cable firms and the accumulation of cable subscribers. TCI (Tele-Communications Inc.), under the long tenure of CEO John Malone, accounted for 2.1 million subscribers in 1982; by 1996, TCI's subscriber base was 12.5 million out of nearly 70 million U.S. cable households. The second largest MSO, Time Warner Cable, is a division of the world's largest media company. Time Warner had 1.9 million subscribers in 1982. In 1995, when Time Warner bought Cablevision Industries—the eighth largest MSO—the joint venture meant the control of cable circuits in 11.7 million homes. By the mid-1990s, through a series of acquisitions that had gone on for fifteen years, TCI and Time Warner provided cable to more than 33 percent of U.S. homes.

Beyond their cable-subscriber base, both TCI and Time Warner were also major providers of programming services. For its part, TCI owns or has owned interests in Turner Broadcasting, the Discovery Channel, the Family Channel, a home shopping network, Black Entertainment Television (BET), and American Movie Classics. Actively involved in DBS and PPV developments, TCI also became the world's largest buyer of fiber optic cable in the early 1990s. By the mid-1990s, TCI owned parts of several other cable operations and the United Artists Theatre chain and had ventured into assorted global deals with various telephone companies.

TABLE 6.2
Top 20 U.S. Cable Operators, 1996

Rank	Company	Headquarters	Basic Subscriptions
1	Tele-Communications Inc. (TCI)	Englewood, CO	12,494,000
2	Time Warner Cable	Stamford, CT	11,700,000
3	Continental Cablevision (now MediaOne)	Boston	4,200,000
4	Comcast	Philadelphia	3,600,000
5	Cox Communications	Atlanta	3,282,080
6	Cablevision Systems Corp.	Woodbury, NY	1,915,000
7	Adelphia Communications	Coudersport, PA	1,651,850
8	Jones Intercable	Englewood, CO	1,476,000
9	Marcus Cable	Dallas	1,245,259
10	Viacom Cable	Pleasanton, CA	1,157,600
11	Century Communications	New Canaan, CT	1,100,000
12	Falcon Cable	Los Angeles	1,085,513
13	Charter Communications	St. Louis	900,000
14	Scripps-Howard Cable	Cincinnati	804,464
15	TKR Cable	Warren, NJ	750,121
16	Prime Cable	Austin	657,508
17	InterMedia Partners	San Francisco	571,000
18	Lenfest Group	Pottstown, PA	563,909
19	TCA Cable TV	Tyler, TX	549,000
20	Post-Newsweek Cable	Phoenix	542,000

Source: *Hoover's Guide to Media Companies* (Austin, TX: Hoover's Business Press, 1996), 30; *Cablevision*, April 29, 1996.

In 1995, Time Warner buoyed its position as the world's largest media corporation by offering $6.5 billion to acquire Turner Broadcasting, which included superstation WTBS, CNN, Headline News, TNT, and CNN Radio. Although some FCC staffers raised concerns about sanctioning the extended economic power of Time Warner, the commission formally approved the deal in the fall of 1996. Time Warner—with its magazine, movie, publishing, television, and music divisions—also produces content for its cable services. In addition to acquiring Turner and starting the Warner Brothers television network, Time Warner is the parent company of Cinemax and HBO, two premium movie services, and holds interests in BET, Entertainment Television (E!), Comedy Central, and Court TV.

A number of cable critics worry that the trend toward fewer owners will limit the number of viewpoints, options, and innovations available on cable. The response from the cable industry is that given the tremendous capital investment it takes to run cable, DBS, and other media enterprises, media conglomerates are necessary to buy up struggling companies and keep them afloat. This argument suggests that without today's MSOs many smaller cable ventures in programming would not be possible.

Another view maintains that although cable TV firms compete among themselves, it is a limited type of competition, and it protects them against rivals: "That trend is not only a business marketplace issue. It also concerns the U.S. marketplace of ideas. It puts at risk the principle of open access for all citizens to a broad range of competitive information resources."[5] The 1996 Telecommunications Act does allow phone companies to compete for cable's territory. Concerns have surfaced, though, at least in smaller markets, that cable and telephone services will merge into giant communications overlords, fixing prices without benefit of competition. These concerns raise an important question: In an economic climate in which fewer owners control the circulation of ideas and communication, what happens to new ideas or controversial communication that may not always be profitable to circulate?

the business of cable

In 1970, there were about twenty-five hundred small cable systems operating in the United States; by 1996, more than eleven thousand systems were running. In 1976, there were two basic satellite-delivered services, two premium services, and no such

Launched on cable's Comedy Central channel in 1993, comedian Bill Maher's talk-satire program, *Politically Incorrect*, successfully lured many viewers away from traditional network political coverage. ABC, which bought the rights to the program in 1996, began airing it after *Nightline* in January 1997.

thing as pay-per-view. Twenty years later, more than a hundred basic services were competing for channel space with more than twenty premium services and eight PPV companies. Since 1980, basic cable rates have tripled in price, rising from about $7 per month to more than $25. Monthly prices for premium services, however, have remained about the same—under $9 a month per channel in 1980 and 1996.[6] By the mid-1990s, total revenues from cable rivaled those of broadcasting: $30 billion a year.

The cable industry employed about 23,000 people in 1978 and more than 110,000 by the mid-1990s. As in the movie business, the cable workforce serves the production, distribution, and exhibition sectors of the industry. The production end includes the hundreds of providers who either make original programs or purchase older TV programming for national and global distribution. At the local level, production also includes staffers, volunteers, and student interns who create programming on access channels. The distribution sector includes the delivery systems and PPV services that transmit programming via satellite. The exhibition branch of the industry encompasses the thousands of local cable systems, which require programming, sales, technical, and administrative divisions to operate.

cable, dbs, and implications for democracy

When cable emerged to challenge traditional broadcasting in the 1970s, expectations were high, not unlike today's expectations for the information highway. When cable communication mushroomed in the 1980s, network supremacy over television ended. Offering more than new competition, cable's increased channel capacity provided the promise of access. With more channels, it was believed that access on cable would create vibrant debates, allowing ordinary citizens a voice via television. Access channels have, in fact, provided some opportunities for citizens to participate in democracy and even create their own programs. For the most part, though, cable and DBS have followed the one-way broadcast model: Their operators choose the programming from a few service providers with little input from citizens and consumers.

Most cable channels have become heavily dependent on recycling old television shows and movies to fill up their program schedules. In some ways, this has been beneficial. Cable, particularly through programming like Nickelodeon's Nick at Nite, has become a repository for TV shows that are passed along from generation to generation. Ultimately, however, except for C-Span, local access channels, and some interactive services, cable still has not developed its potential to become a clear alternative to traditional broadcasting services. But with the competition along the information highway and with telephone companies able to deliver TV signals and the Internet through fiber-optic wires, cable's direction seems likely to change.

In the broadest sense, the development of cable has always posed a contradiction. On the one hand, cable has dramatically increased the number of channels and offered previously unserved groups the opportunity to address their particular issues on television. On the other hand, cable has undermined the network era during which television worked as a kind of social adhesive, giving most of the population a common bond, a set of shared programs. The concern remains: Does the onslaught of cable and developments such as the Internet create a fragmented culture in which individuals pursue their narrow personal agendas at the expense of larger social concerns?

By the year 2000, many communities will experience the convergence of computers and modems, satellites, fax machines, and television sets. Such convergence

"It is not conceivable to me that the revolution we're now going through—which is in my view even deeper, and faster, than the **Industrial Revolution**—is going to occur smoothly. It cannot." —Alvin Toffler, futurist, 1993

may make us homebound, freeing us from traditional participation in and travel to workplaces and schools. New technologies have the capacity, of course, to simultaneously bring us together in cyberspace and isolate us physically from one another. Another large question faces democracies in which the control of communication rests increasingly in the hands of a few giant media corporations: How will we direct cable, DBS, and new technologies to serve social agendas while they continue to meet individual needs? As with the Internet, the gulf between the information rich and the information poor remains wide, increasing concerns about who will have access to the cable and other new media technologies.

REVIEW QUESTIONS

1. What is CATV, and what were its advantages?

2. How did cable pose a challenge to broadcasting, and how did the FCC respond to cable's early development?

3. What is the cable franchising process, and how did it work in the 1980s?

4. Why isn't the cable industry treated more like a utility company and a common carrier?

5. What were the syndex rules, and why were they repealed?

6. What were the major differences between the cable acts of 1984 and 1992?

7. How did the Telecommunications Act of 1996 change the economic shape and the future of the cable industry?

8. What are the differences between basic cable service and premium services?

9. How have CNN and MTV influenced culture worldwide?

10. How and why did HBO develop? How has HBO threatened the film industry?

11. What are PPV and interactive cable services?

12. What is DBS? How much of a threat are its services to the cable industry?

13. Who are the two biggest players in the cable business, and what are some of their major holdings?

14. What are the three basic divisions in the organization of the cable business?

15. In terms of fostering democracy, what are cable's main advantages over traditional broadcasting?

QUESTIONING THE MEDIA

1. How many cable channels do you watch regularly? What programs do you watch? What attracts you to a channel?

2. If you controlled a cable public-access channel in your community, what would be your channel's goal? What could we do to make public-, government-, or educational-access programming more appealing? Should we?

3. Do you think the must-carry rules violate a cable operator's First Amendment rights? Why or why not?

4. CNN and MTV have changed our society as well as global culture. Have these changes been positive or negative? Explain.

5. Do you think DBS will be able to compete with cable? Why or why not?

6. Some critics argue that we no longer participate in traditional neighborhoods and that cable has played a role in fragmenting citizens, keeping us in our homes. Do you agree or disagree? What has cable done well, and in what ways has it adversely affected society?

Divide the class into groups of four to six. Each group should prepare an editorial for presentation on public-access cable or public radio. The editorial should be roughly four to five minutes in length (750–1,000 words) and should address a controversial or important public issue. For example, the group might propose an editorial on access to the information highway, the disparity of the knowledge gap, the state of media education, the impact of talk radio and television talk shows, or the advantages of wealth in the legal process.

1. As a group, draft the editorial. Consult with your instructor for topic ideas and writing strategies. Rewrite the final copy of the editorial.

2. Next, divide each group into subgroups of two or three. One subgroup should approach (either by phone, mail, or face-to-face meeting) a local cable access channel or public noncommercial radio station and request time to read the editorial. The other subgroup should approach a local commercial television or radio station with the same editorial. Tell the station manager or news director that you would like to get your idea onto the public airwaves. Ask how your request might be accommodated.

3. Designate a time for your whole group to meet and write a report about how your editorial was treated by the various media you approached. Address the following questions in your report:

   • How easy or difficult was it to get access to traditional broadcasting versus cable?

   • How was your group treated?

   • Based on your experience, do broadcast airwaves and cable services "belong" to the public?

   • How democratic is the process of gaining access on cable or radio?

4. During class, the various groups should share and compare reports and experiences. If you were permitted to cablecast or broadcast your editorial, share it with the class.

(*Note*: Try to ensure that each group approaches different radio or TV stations so that the broadcast people are not inundated with requests. In smaller communities, this might not be possible.)

Movies

and the Impact of Images

Suppose we were to make a movie about going to the movies on a typical summer night in 1997. Our film might well star a group of teenagers gathered at a multiplex near a major highway intersection on the outskirts of a city. Video games line the entrances that lead into twenty or more tiny theaters featuring projection screens not much larger than an oversized double-door garage. There are only a few families in this scene—there would be many more if we were filming on a weekend afternoon. For a more representative family scene, we cut to a family at home watching the 1996 hit *Independence Day*, but on their VCR.

If it were forty years earlier—1957—our movie would tell a very different story. There are no VCRs. The summer cinema experience portrays teens and families heading off to a favorite downtown theater or piling into hot rods and station wagons to go to the drive-in at the edge of town. There they are watching Cecil B. DeMille's sound version of *The Ten Commandments*.

If it were seventy years earlier—1927—there would be no television. Our movie family is enjoying Lillian Gish as Hester Prynne in *The Scarlet Letter*. What's more, the setting is a large downtown movie palace that comfortably seats more than four thousand filmgoers. An organist or even live orchestra accompanies the film, which is silent. In those days, an afternoon or evening at the movies was part of a weekly national ritual that included watching a cartoon, a newsreel, a film short or travel documentary, and a feature-length silent movie.

Throughout their rich history, dating back to the late 1800s, American films have had a substantial social and cultural impact on society. Popular movies such as *Jaws*, *E.T.*, *Jurassic Park*, *The Lion King*, *Forrest Gump*, *Independence Day*, and *The Lost World* represent what Hollywood has become—America's storyteller. Telling cinematic tales that in 1907 drew us to a nickelodeon theater and in 1997 to our local video chain, Hollywood movies have long acted as contemporary mythmakers. At their best, they tell communal stories that evoke and symbolize our best values and basest desires. The most popular films often make the world seem clearer, more manageable, and more commonsensical.

Throughout this century, films have helped moviegoers sort through experiences that either affirm or deviate from their own values. Some movies allow audiences to survey "the boundary between the permitted and the forbidden" and to experience, in a controlled way, "the possibility of stepping across this boundary."[1] Popular movies such as *Silence of the Lambs*, *Menace II Society*, and *Pulp Fiction* examine the distinctions between the normal and abnormal—a moral border repeatedly fought over by religious leaders, politicians, and entrepreneurs as well as by teachers, parents, and the mass media.

> "The movie is not only a supreme expression of mechanism, but paradoxically it offers as product the most magical of consumer commodities, namely dreams."
> —Marshall McLuhan,
> *Understanding Media*,
> 1964

Over and above their immense economic impact (see Table 7.1), movies have always worked on several social and cultural levels. While they distract us from our daily struggles, at the same time they encourage us to take part in rethinking contemporary ideas. We continue to be attracted to the stories that movies tell. It is these stories that keep us going back to movie theaters or to our local video stores.

In this chapter, we will examine the rich legacy and current standing of Hollywood as a national and international mythmaker. We will begin by considering film's early technology and the evolution of film as a mass medium. We will look at the arrival of silent feature films, the emergence of Hollywood, and the development of the studio system with regard to production, distribution, and exhibition. We will then explore the coming of sound and the power of movie storytelling. In the context of Hollywood moviemaking, we will consider major film genres, directors, and alternatives to Hollywood style, including both foreign films and documentaries. Finally, we will look at the movie business today—its major players, economic clout, technological advances, and implications for democracy.

TABLE 7.1
The Top 10 American Box-Office Champions, 1997*

Rank	Title/Date	Domestic Gross** (millions)	Rank	Title/Date	Domestic Gross** (millions)
1	Star Wars (1997)	$459	6	Independence Day (1996)	306
2	E.T.: The Extra-Terrestrial (1982)	407	7	Return of the Jedi (1983)	306
3	Jurassic Park (1993)	357	8	The Empire Strikes Back (1980)	289
4	Forrest Gump (1994)	327	9	Home Alone (1990)	285
5	The Lion King (1994)	313	10	Jaws (1975)	260

*Most rankings of the Top 10 most popular films are based on American box-office receipts. If international box-office receipts counted, *Jurassic Park* would head the list with over $1 billion in worldwide revenues. If these figures were adjusted for inflation, *Gone with the Wind* (1939) would become No. 1 in U.S. theater revenue. With the re-release of the *Star Wars* trilogy in 1997, the original *Star Wars* jumped to No. 1. (Note: This list was compiled before the release of *Lost World*.)

**Gross shown in absolute dollars based on box-office sales in the United States and Canada.

Source: "The 50 All Time Highest Grossing Movies." <http://movieweb.com/movie/alltime.html> (18 April 1997). © 1997 *Movieweb*. All Rights Reserved.

early technology and the evolution of movies

History often credits a handful of enterprising individuals for developing new technologies and mass media. Such innovations, however, are usually the result of extended and simultaneous investigations by a wide variety of people. In addition, the media innovations of both known and unknown inventors are propelled by economic and social forces as well as by individual abilities.[2]

the development of film

Solving the puzzle of making a picture move depended both on advances in photography and on the development of a flexible film stock to replace the heavy metal and glass plates used to make individual pictures in the 1800s. In 1889, an American minister, Hannibal Goodwin, developed a transparent and pliable film—called *celluloid*—which could hold a coating, or film, of chemicals sensitive to light. This breakthrough solved a major problem: It allowed a strip of film to move through a camera and be photographed in rapid succession, producing a series of pictures. In the 1890s, George Eastman (later of Eastman Kodak) bought Goodwin's patents, improved the ideas, and manufactured the first film used for motion pictures.

As with the development of sound recording, Thomas Edison takes center stage in most accounts of the invention of motion pictures. In the late 1800s, Edison initially planned to merge phonograph technology and moving images to create talking pictures (which would not happen in feature films until 1927). Without a breakthrough, though, Edison lost interest. However, he assigned an assistant, William Kennedy Dickson, to combine advances in Europe with the new celluloid to create an early movie camera, called the *kinetograph*, and a viewing system, called the *kinetoscope*. This small projection system housed fifty feet of film that revolved on spools (similar to a library microfilm reader). It was like a peep show in which a person looked through a hole and saw images moving on a tiny plate. In 1894, a kinetoscope parlor, featuring two rows of coin-operated machines, opened in New York.

Founded in Toronto in 1979, Cineplex Odeon is today one of the largest theater chains in North America. In 1986 Cineplex (short for cinema and complex) entered into a partnership with MCA/Universal (now a subsidiary of Seagram). By 1987 the company operated five hundred multiscreen movie complexes in twenty states and six Canadian provinces.

From the start, Edison envisioned movies only as a passing fad or arcade novelty. Meanwhile, in France, Louis and Auguste Lumière (who ran a photographic equipment factory) were hard at work. The brothers developed a projection system so that more than one person at a time could see the moving images on a nine- by six-foot projection screen. In a Paris cafe on December 28, 1895, they projected ten short movies, for viewers who paid one franc each, on such subjects as a man falling off a horse and a child trying to grab a fish from a bowl. Within three weeks, twenty-five hundred people were coming each night to see how, according to one Paris paper, film "perpetuates the image of movement."

With innovators around the world dabbling in moving pictures, Edison's lab and kinetoscope company renewed its interest. Edison patented several inventions and manufactured a new large-screen system called the *vitascope*, which allowed film strips of longer lengths to be projected without interruption. Unlike the kinetoscope, vitascope projection improved viewing for large audiences, hinting at the potential of movies as a future mass medium.

Staged at a music hall in New York in April 1896, Edison's first public showing of the vitascope featured shots from a boxing match and waves rolling onto a beach. The *New York Times* described the exhibition as "wonderfully real and singularly exhilarating." Some members of the audience were so taken with the realism of the film images that they stepped back from the screen's crashing waves to avoid getting their feet wet.

Early movie demonstrations such as these marked the beginning of the film industry. At this point, movies consisted of movement recorded by a single continuous camera shot. Early filmmakers had not yet figured out how to move the camera around or how to edit film shots together. Nonetheless, various innovators were beginning to see the commercial possibilities of film. By 1900, short movies had become a part of amusement arcades, traveling carnivals, wax museums, and vaudeville theater.

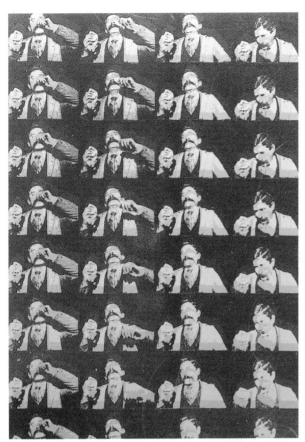

Before the arrival of feature-length movies, audiences in the late 1890s were fascinated by the novelty of any moving image. This Edison kinetoscope reel from 1894 featured one of the first close-up shots ever recorded on film—a man sneezing.

the power of stories
in the silent era

The shift from early development to the mass medium stage came with the introduction of *narrative films:* movies that tell stories. Once audiences understood the illusion of moving images, they quickly tired of waves breaking on beaches or vaudeville acts recorded by immobile cameras. To become a mass medium, the early silent films had to offer what books achieved: the suspension of disbelief. They had to create narrative worlds that engaged an audience's imagination.

Some of the earliest narrative films were produced and directed by French magician and inventor George Melies, who opened the first public movie theater in France in 1896. Melies may have been the first director to realize that a movie was not simply a means of recording reality. He understood that a movie could be artificially planned and controlled like a staged play. By the late 1800s, Melies was producing fairy tales and science-fiction stories—including *Joan of Arc*, *Red Riding Hood*, *Cinderella*, and *A Trip to the Moon*. These film shorts lasted less than ten minutes each. By the early 1900s, he discovered camera tricks and techniques, such as slow motion and cartoon animation, that became key ingredients for future narrative filmmakers.

The first American filmmaker to adapt Melies' innovations to narrative film was Edwin S. Porter. A cameraman who had studied Melies' work in an Edison lab, Porter mastered the technique of editing diverse shots together to tell a coherent story. Early filmmakers plotted and recorded action in a long continuous filmed sequence. But Porter shot narrative scenes out of order (for instance, some in a studio and some outdoors) and reassembled them in the editing process to make a story. In 1902, he made what is regarded as America's first narrative film, *The Life of an American Fireman*.

Porter also pioneered other innovations in filmmaking. First, he moved the camera and varied its distance from subjects and objects. *American Fireman*, for example, contained the first close-up shot in U.S. narrative film history—a ringing fire alarm. Until this time, early movie makers thought that close-ups cheated the audience of the opportunity to see an entire scene. Second, Porter's most important film, *The Great Train Robbery*, introduced the film western as well as chase scenes. In this eleven-minute movie, Porter demonstrated the art of film suspense by alternating shots of the robbers with those of a posse in pursuit.

the arrival of nickelodeons

Another major development was the arrival of movie theaters. They were called **nickelodeons**, a term that combines the admission price with the Greek word for theater. According to media historian Douglas Gomery, these small and uncomfortable makeshift theaters were often converted cigar stores, pawnshops, or restaurants redecorated to mimic vaudeville theaters: "In front, large, hand-painted posters announced the movies for the day. Inside, the screening of news, documentary, comedy, fantasy, and dramatic shorts lasted about one hour."[3] Because they showed silent narrative film shorts that usually transcended language barriers, nickelodeons flourished during the great European immigration at the turn of the century. These theaters filled a need for many newly arrived people struggling to learn English and seeking an inexpensive escape from the hard life of the city. Often managed by immigrants, nickelodeons required a minimal investment: just a secondhand projector and a large white sheet. Usually a piano player added live music, and sometimes theater operators used sound effects to simulate gun shots or loud crashes.

Although vaudeville theaters continued to feature movies, by 1908 nickelodeons had displaced the vaudeville circuit as the main showplace for films. Since they were less expensive than vaudeville shows and drew less well-to-do audiences, nickelodeons were labeled "democracy's theater." Between 1907 and 1909, the number of nickelodeons grew from five thousand to ten thousand. The craze peaked by 1910, when entrepreneurs began to seek more affluent spectators, attracting them with larger and more lavish movie theaters.

the power of the studio system

By the late 1910s the movie industry's three basic economic divisions—production, distribution, and exhibition—were established. In its early phase, control of *production* meant control over camera and projector technology. But as narrative films became central to attracting consumers, production came to mean controlling the making of movies. This is still the case today. *Distribution* constitutes the individuals or companies who deliver films into theaters in various regional, national, and eventually international markets. Finally, *exhibition* refers to where films are displayed—the theaters themselves and the people and companies who own them. Much of film history as well as the current state of moviemaking have been significantly affected by the power struggles of film studios trying to dominate one or all of these industry divisions.

Among the first to try his hand at dominating the movie business, Thomas Edison had been observing the growing popularity of film. He formed the Motion Picture Patents Company, a cartel of major U.S. and French film producers, in 1908. Known as the Trust, Edison's company pooled patents in an effort to control film's major technology and, by default, the production of most movies. In addition, the Trust acquired most major film distributorships and signed an exclusive deal with George Eastman, who agreed to supply movie film only to Trust-approved companies.

Some independent producers refused to bow to the Trust's terms. There was too much demand for films, too much money to be made, and too many ways to avoid the Trust's scrutiny. Some producers began to relocate from the early centers of film production in New York and New Jersey to Cuba and Florida. Ultimately, though, Hollywood became a movie magnet and the film capital of the world. Southern California offered cheap labor, diverse scenery for outdoor shooting, barns that could be converted to studios, and a mild climate suitable for year-round production. Far from the Trust, independent companies could also slip easily over the border into Mexico to escape legal prosecution for patent violations.

Two Hungarian immigrants, Adolph Zukor, who would eventually run Paramount Pictures, and William Fox, who would found the Fox Film Corporation (which later became Twentieth Century Fox), played roles in the collapse of Edison's Trust. Zukor's early companies figured out ways to bypass the Trust, and a suit by Fox, a nickelodeon operator turned film distributor, resulted in the Trust's breakup for restraint of trade violations in 1917.

Ironically, although the Trust's monopoly efforts failed, entrepreneurs like Zukor went on to develop other tactics for controlling the industry. The new strategies, many of which are still used today, were more ambitious than just monopolizing patents and technology. They aimed at dominating the movie business at all three essential levels—production, distribution, and exhibition—in a *vertical integration* of power and control. The new tactics ultimately spawned a system that turned the film industry into an *oligopoly*, in which a few firms controlled the bulk of the business.

> "The American cinema is a **classical art**, but why not then admire in it what is most admirable, i.e., not only the talent of this or that filmmaker, but the genius of the system."
> —André Bazin, film theorist, 1957

controlling production

The first movies were sold or rented by the foot; one product was not differentiated from another. Films were novelties, and people were merely curious about the moving images. Gradually, however, producers and distributors recognized that fans sought not only particular kinds of stories—including dramas, westerns, and romances—but also particular actors and actresses. This was not unlike what would occur in the 1950s as radio-station managers noticed that teenagers listened to favorite songs again and again.

By 1910, film companies were receiving letters from fans inquiring about actors who were not named in the movie credits. (An early practice had been not to list actors in the credits.) Initially, companies were reluctant to identify these individuals because their popularity would force higher salaries; most anonymous film actors were making only $5 to $15 per day. Eventually, though, film studios acknowledged that movie-goers went to certain films because of the performances of favorite actors.

To meet the tastes of discerning audiences and to better compete against Edison's Trust, Adolph Zukor hired a number of popular actors, forming the Famous Players Company in 1912. Zukor's idea was to exert control over movie production, not through patents but through contracts with the most popular actors of the day. By this time, theater owners were already starting to demand films featuring the performers who attracted the largest audiences. Zukor signed these performers to exclusive contracts, ensuring that they would make movies only for his company.

Early on, Zukor also understood the difference between film acting and theater acting, in which actors emphasized "the large gesture" and a "boldly sketched pantomime of emotions."[4] Film acting was more subtle, more intimate, and did not demand that an actor's voice reach the back of a cavernous theater. Film producers began developing talented performers like Mary Pickford, who was "unspoiled" by a theater background and more suited for the new medium. Pickford became one of film's first movie stars. Known as "America's sweetheart" for her portrayal of spunky and innocent heroines, Pickford became so popular that audiences waited in line to see her movies, and producers had to pay her increasingly large salaries to keep her services.

An astute businesswoman, Mary Pickford was the key figure in elevating the financial status and professional role of film actors. Whereas in 1910 Pickford made about $100 a week, by 1914 she earned $1,000 a week. Eventually, Zukor signed her to Famous Players (which later became part of Paramount Pictures). By 1917, Zukor paid Pickford a weekly salary of $15,000. Having appeared in nearly two hundred films, Pickford was so influential that in 1919 she broke from Zukor to form her own company, United Artists. Joining her were actor Douglas Fairbanks (her future husband), comedian-director Charlie Chaplin, and director D. W. Griffith.

By the beginning of the 1920s, film production evolved into the **studio system**. Pioneered by director Thomas Ince and his Hollywood company, Triangle, this system constituted a sort of assembly-line process for moviemaking. It organized a staff of the best technicians and directors schooled in the latest film techniques. Under the system, not only stars but directors, editors, writers, and others worked under exclusive contracts for the major studios. Indeed, those who weren't under contract with some movie company probably were not working at all. To guide multiple movies through various production stages, Ince gave up directing in 1915 and appointed *producers* to handle hiring, logistics, and finances. In this way, Ince could more easily supervise a number of pictures at one time.

Although United Artists represented a brief triumph of autonomy for a few powerful actors, the studio system firmly controlled creative talent in the industry by the 1920s. In 1927, for example, Paramount director Cecil B. DeMille required the actors playing Jesus and Mary in *The King of Kings* to refrain from secular activities such as playing cards or riding in convertibles off the set. The system was so efficient that each major studio was producing a feature film every week—compared to about twelve to fifteen a year today. Pooling talent, rather than patents, was a more ingenious approach for movie studios aiming to dominate film production.

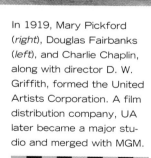

In 1919, Mary Pickford (*right*), Douglas Fairbanks (*left*), and Charlie Chaplin, along with director D. W. Griffith, formed the United Artists Corporation. A film distribution company, UA later became a major studio and merged with MGM.

controlling distribution

One of the early forms of movie distribution, *film exchanges* appeared around 1904 as movie companies provided vaudeville theaters with films and projectors. In exchange for their short films, shown between live acts, producers received a small percentage of the vaudeville ticket gate. Gradually, as the number of production companies and the popularity of narrative films grew, demand for a distribution system serving national and international markets increased as well. Because few regulations existed in these early days, movies were often stolen or copied. Edison's Trust represented, in part, an attempt to prevent film pirating and to manage the industry by withholding equipment from companies not willing to pay the Trust's patent-use fees.

However, emerging film companies and other independent firms looked to distribution strategies to gain a foothold in the fledgling industry. Early independents like Adolph Zukor, who opposed the Trust, developed several distribution techniques, including *block booking*. Under this system, to gain access to popular films exhibitors had to agree to rent new or marginal films with no stars. Zukor would pressure theater operators into taking a hundred movies at a time to get the few Pickford titles they wanted. Such contracts allowed studios to test-market a new star without much financial risk. Although this practice was eventually outlawed as monopolistic, rising film studios used the tactic effectively to guarantee the success of their films in an "open" marketplace.

Another distribution strategy involved the marketing of American films in Europe. When World War I disrupted European film production, only U.S. studios were able to meet the demand. The war thus marked a turning point, making the United States the leader in the commercial movie business. Europe never regained its edge. After the war, no other film industry could compete economically with Hollywood. By the mid-1920s, foreign revenue from U.S. films totaled $100 million. Today, in any given week, when the industry trade magazine *Variety* ranks the top-grossing films in foreign countries, U.S. movies (especially easily translatable action/adventure features) continue to dominate the list. For example, in late March 1997 the rereleased *Star Wars* was the top box-office draw in Germany, Spain, Australia, France, and England.

> "It's still a business where the hits make up for all the losses along the way. *Star Wars* accentuated that. Everyone wants to reproduce that success, even just once. This tells you about the strength of this kind of franchise."
> —Jill Krutick, analyst Smith Barney, 1997

controlling exhibition

When industrious theater owners began forming film cooperatives to compete with block-booking tactics, producers like Zukor conspired to dominate exhibition. By 1921, Zukor's company owned three hundred theaters, solidifying a key ingredient in the film industry. In 1925, a business merger between Paramount and Publix, the country's largest theater chain at the time with over five hundred circuits, gave Zukor enormous influence over movie exhibition.

Zukor and the heads of several major studios understood they did not have to own all theaters to ensure that their movies were shown. Over time, the five major studios (which would eventually include MGM, RKO, Warner Brothers, and Twentieth Century Fox as well as Paramount) merely needed to own about 15 percent of the nation's twenty thousand movie houses. They needed only the first-run theaters, which premiered new films in major downtown areas in front of the largest audiences. Through the 1940s, ticket sales from these venues generated 85 to 95 percent of all film revenue.

Movie Palaces. Entrepreneurs ultimately realized that drawing the middle and upper-middle classes to movies required something more attractive than a sheet hung in an abandoned pawnshop. To provide a more hospitable moviegoing environment, exhibitors converted vaudeville theaters into full-time use as movie theaters. In 1914, the three-thousand-seat Strand Theatre, the first movie palace, opened in New York. With elaborate architecture, movie palaces lured spectators who enjoyed entertainment amid the trappings of high-society opera, ballet, symphony, and live theater.

To work their magic on the outside, these theaters often evoked the grandeur of palaces, with massive electric light displays that announced their presence from blocks away. Linking the moviegoing experience with the trappings of royalty created a powerful attraction. Inside the theater, customers meandered through lavish lobbies, plush promenades, and fancy waiting rooms. Movie exhibitors treated "the movie patron like a king or queen," with ushers, doormen, and services ranging from free child care to "smoking rooms and painting galleries in the basement."[5] Taking advantage of new air-cooling systems developed by Chicago's meatpacking industry, movie palaces also featured the first mechanically air-cooled theaters. This perquisite alone transformed summer moviegoing in Chicago into peak viewing time. Doctors even advised pregnant women to beat the heat by spending their afternoons at the movies.

Mid-City Theaters. Another major innovation in exhibition was the development of mid-city movie theaters. The first wave of middle-class people moved from urban centers to city outskirts in the 1920s, and mass transit systems emerged to shuttle these suburbanites to and from work. Movie theaters soon followed as exhibitors in Chicago began to locate theaters at major transportation intersections in outlying business areas rather than downtown. (For another view of exhibition, see "Case Study: Movie Theaters Display Racism's History" on page 190.) This idea continues today as large *multiplexes* featuring fifteen to twenty-five screens lure middle-class crowds to interstate crossroads.

Throughout the 1920s, movie attendance climbed steadily. But the Great Depression hit the industry hard, and many customers turned to radio, a cheaper form of entertainment. To compete, theaters began holding contests and prize giveaways. They also offered double features—two movies for the price of one—and started selling candy, soda, and eventually popcorn (which, thanks to the movies, became a major farm crop in the late 1930s). With jobs restored during World War II, movie attendance surged during the war years. By 1946—the industry's all-time peak attendance year—ninety million people went to the movies each week.

By the late 1920s, the major studios had clearly established vertical integration in the industry. What had once been a fairly easy and cheap business to enter had become complex and capital-intensive. What had been many small competitive firms in the early 1900s had become a few powerful studios, including the Big Five—Paramount, MGM, Warner Brothers, Twentieth Century Fox, and RKO—and the Little Three (which did not own theaters)—Columbia, Universal, and United Artists. Together these eight companies formed a powerful oligopoly, which made it increasingly difficult for independent companies to make, distribute, and exhibit commercial films.

the triumph of hollywood storytelling

While early filmmakers like Edwin S. Porter and D. W. Griffith demonstrated the appeal of the film narrative, early stars like Mary Pickford and Charlie Chaplin revealed the audience's attraction to movie characters. Meanwhile, the studios searched for the next technical innovation to enliven the industry and further enhance film's storytelling capabilities. They found it by adding sound to moving images, mixing another powerful ingredient into Hollywood-flavored narratives.

Movie Theaters Display Racism's History

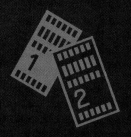

Oscar Micheaux (1884–1951) was one of the only African American filmmakers to own a production company, directing, producing, and distributing forty-six films aimed at black audiences.

Despite inequities and discrimination, a thriving black cinema existed in New York's Harlem district during the 1930s and 1940s. Usually bankrolled by white business executives who were capitalizing on the black-only theaters fostered by segregation, independent films featuring black casts were supported by African American moviegoers, even during the Depression. But it was a popular Hollywood film, *Imitation of Life* (1934), starring Claudette Colbert and Louise Beavers, that emerged as the highest-grossing film in black theaters during the mid-1930s. The film, remade in 1959, told the story of a friendship between a white woman and a black woman, whose young daughter denied her heritage and passed for white, breaking her mother's heart.

Despite African Americans' long support of the film industry, their moviegoing experience has not been the same as that of whites. From the late 1800s until civil rights legislation in the mid-1960s, many theater owners discriminated against black patrons. In large cities, for instance, housing patterns often determined theater

Gordon Parks

Born in 1912; one of fifteen children, worked as *Life* magazine photographer from 1948–68; his son, Gordon Parks Jr., who directed *Super Fly* (1972), died in plane crash in Africa scouting film locations in 1979

Career Achievements

The Learning Tree (1969)— based on his autobiography about growing up poor on a Kansas farm; Parks wrote, produced, directed, and composed musical score

Shaft (1971)—first popular Hollywood action film that featured an African American hero as central character; Isaac Hayes won Oscar for theme song

Shaft's Big Score (1972)— sequel; John Shaft (played by Richard Roundtree) takes on the mob

The Super Cops (1974)

Leadbelly (1976)—biography of black blues and folk singer Huddie "Leadbelly" Ledbetter, best known for songs "Good Night, Irene," "Rock Island Line," and "Midnight Special"

locations. As a result, blacks often had to attend separate theaters where new movies might not appear until a year or two after white theaters had shown them. In smaller towns and in the South, blacks were often able to patronize local theaters only after midnight. In addition, some theaters required black patrons to sit in less desirable areas of the theater. In the South, for example, blacks often had to sit in balconies—away from white patrons—into the 1950s.[1]

Outside large cities, African Americans relied on radio sets, church groups, and social clubs for their cultural entertainment, especially during the Depression. Changes took place during and after World War II, when more middle-class blacks had money to attend movies. When the "white flight" from central cities began during the suburbanization of the 1950s, many downtown and neighborhood theaters started catering to black customers in order to save their businesses. By the late 1960s and early 1970s, these theaters became major venues for popular commercial films, even featuring a few movies about African Americans, including *Guess Who's Coming to Dinner?* (1967), *In the Heat of the Night* (1967), *The Learning Tree* (1969), and *Sounder* (1972).

Based on the popularity of these films, black photographer-turned-filmmaker Gordon Parks, who directed *The Learning Tree* (adapted from his own novel), went on to make commercial action/adventure films, including *Shaft* (1971). Popular in urban theaters, especially among black teenagers, the movies of Parks and his son—Gordon Parks Jr. (*Super Fly*, 1972)—spawned a number of commercial imitators, labeled *blaxploitation* movies. These films were the subject of heated cultural debates in the 1970s; like some rap songs today, these movies were both praised for their realistic

Spike Lee

Born in 1957; raised in Brooklyn; father a jazz musician, mother a teacher

Career Achievements

She's Gotta Have It (1986)—Lee's first feature won him an Independent Spirit Award for "best first feature film" by independent filmmaker

School Daze (1988)—musical score by director's father, Bill Lee

Do the Right Thing (1989)—comic/tragic look at racism

Mo' Better Blues (1990)—story of jazz musician

Jungle Fever (1991)—story of interracial romance

Malcolm X (1992)—chronicles life of famed black activist assassinated in 1965

Crooklyn (1994)—Lee co-wrote story with his sister, Joie Susannah, and brother, Cinque; set in 1970s Brooklyn

Clockers (1995)—based on Richard Price novel

Girl 6 (1996)—story of a phone-sex operator

Get on the Bus (1996)—story of 1995 Million Man March on Washington

depictions of black urban life and criticized for glorifying violence. Nevertheless, they reinvigorated urban movie attendance and reached an audience that had not been well served by the film industry until the 1960s.

Although opportunities for black film directors expanded in the 1980s, by the 1990s mainstream Hollywood was still a formidable place for outsiders to crack. Only one black person, for example, was nominated for any kind of Academy Award in 1995. Still, that same year director Spike Lee asked a number of wealthy black men—from actor Wesley Snipes to pro-basketball player Charles Smith—to bankroll his film, *Get On the Bus*. The film depicted the October 1995 Million Man March on Washington, celebrating the kind of black self-reliance that Lee's own moviemaking had long illustrated. A low-budget film made for one-tenth the $35 million production cost of the average Hollywood movie, the 1996 movie was eventually backed and distributed by Columbia Pictures.

Spencer Williams (1893–1969) was a prolific and respected writer-director-actor of black-audience films, with nine feature films to his directorial credit.

the "sound" of movies

With the studio system and Hollywood's worldwide dominance firmly in place, the next big challenge involved bringing sound to moving pictures. Various attempts at talkies had failed since Edison first tried to link phonograph and moving-picture technologies in the 1890s. During the 1910s, however, technical breakthroughs at AT&T's research arm, Bell Labs, produced prototypes of loudspeakers and sound amplifiers. By the end of the decade, the idea of projecting clear sounds throughout large movie palaces was technically possible, although the cost of outfitting theaters with the necessary equipment remained high.

Experiments with ten-minute sound shorts continued during the 1920s. The four Warner brothers (Harry, Abe, Jack, and Sam), who ran a minor studio at the time, experimented with sound as a novelty, although they did not believe such films would replace silent movies. So Warner Brothers made short "talkers" of vaudeville acts, featuring singers and comedians. The studio packaged them as a novelty along with silent feature films. Over time, Warner Brothers began outfitting theaters with the necessary sound equipment.

In 1927, Warner Brothers produced a feature-length film, *The Jazz Singer*, starring Al Jolson, a popular vaudeville singer. An experiment, *The Jazz Singer* was basically a silent film interspersed with musical numbers and some brief dialogue. At first, there was only modest interest in the movie, which featured just 354 spoken words. But the film grew in popularity as it toured the Midwest, where audiences stood and cheered the short bursts of dialogue. The breakthrough film, however, was Warner Brothers' 1928 release, *The Singing Fool*, which also starred Jolson. Costing $200,000 to make, the film took in $5 million and "proved to all doubters that talkies were here to stay."[6] *Singing Fool* remained the box-office champ for more than ten years until *Gone with the Wind* dethroned it in 1939.

By the mid-1920s, Bell Labs had developed the system used by Warner Brothers, which coordinated sound on records with a film projector. Warner Brothers, however, was not the only studio forging into the technology of sound. In April 1927, five months before *The Jazz Singer* opened, the Fox studio had premiered sound film newsreels. Fox's newsreel company, Movietone, captured the first footage, with sound, of the take-off and return of Charles Lindbergh, who piloted the first plane across the Atlantic Ocean in May 1927. Fox's Movietone system actually "photographed" sound directly onto the film, running it on a narrow film strip that ran alongside the larger image portion of the film. A method superior to the sound-on-record system, Movietone eventually became film's standard sound system.

Meanwhile, Fox was sending camera crews around the world in search of talking news. By 1928, the success of newsreels, as popular as most silent features of the day, led to

In 1927, Warner Brothers released *The Jazz Singer*, featuring vaudeville star Al Jolson in the first "talkie." Basically, it was a silent feature-length film with a musical score and a few spoken words.

the full conversion to talking pictures. Boosted by the innovation of sound, U.S. movie attendance rose from 60 million in 1927 to 110 million in 1929. By 1931, nearly 85 percent of America's twenty thousand theaters accommodated sound pictures, and by 1935 the world had adopted talking films as the commercial standard.

classic hollywood cinema

By the time sound came to movies, Hollywood dictated not only the business but also the style of most moviemaking worldwide. That style, or model, for storytelling developed with the studio system and continues to dominate American filmmaking today. The model comprises three ingredients that give Hollywood movies their distinctive flavor: the narrative, the genre, and the author (or director). The right combination of these ingredients—combined with timing, marketing, and luck—have led to a few blockbuster movie hits, from *Gone with the Wind* to *The Lost World*. Major studios historically have relied on the blockbusters to underwrite the many films that fail at the box office.

Hollywood Narratives. American filmmakers from D. W. Griffith to Steven Spielberg have understood the allure of narrative, which always includes two basic components: the *story*—what happens to whom—and the *discourse*—how the story is told. Most movies, like most TV shows and novels, feature a number of stories that play out within the larger narrative of the entire film. In Quentin Tarantino's 1994 film *Pulp Fiction*, for instance, one major chronological story traces the adventures of two hit men over a few days. However, Tarantino's discourse deliberately disrupts the story's chronology. One hit man, played by John Travolta, is killed midway through the film, but "brought back" to perform other scenes in the larger narrative (via flashbacks of events before the killing) that the director chose to reveal out of order.

Although there are many ways to tell stories, the cultural style that developed during Hollywood's silent and sound eras has a number of markers. Hollywood movies traditionally reveal a series of plausible cause-effect relationships that take place in something approximating real time and real space.[7] Like a 50 mm lens in photography that tries to imitate what the eye actually sees, classic Hollywood films, unlike experimental or nonnarrative cinema, attempt to provide models of a believable world. In such films, problems have particular causes, and characters identify those problems and work to establish credible solutions.

To create believable narrative worlds, some standard techniques have developed over the years. For example, *continuity editing* makes space and time seem continuous and seamless. A shift in scenes or spatial arrangement is marked by *edit points* in which a character appears in a long shot or in an outdoor scene followed by a cut or edit to a close-up or an indoor scene. Viewers have come to understand that edit points function the way punctuation does in writing; they operate as devices for saving time in the interest of moving the narrative along.

In addition, in narrative films dramatic action and conflict spring mainly from individual characters. Although natural disasters or social issues may spark the film's action, the classic narrative typically "centers on personal psychological causes: decisions, choices, and traits of character."[8] Even in stylized Hollywood musicals (such as *Singin' in the Rain*, 1952; *Grease*, 1978; or *Evita*, 1997), artificial song-and-dance sequences are usually motivated by believable psychological and emotional factors that affect particular characters.

With this focus on character, protagonists and antagonists embody sets of competing tensions: good vs. evil, male vs. female, young vs. old, city vs. country, or nature vs. civilization. These conflicts play out against a story that typically moves toward a resolution of the tensions that caused the original problem.

"We tell ourselves stories in order to live."
—Joan Didion, *The White Album*, 1979

Within Hollywood's classic narratives, filmgoers will find an amazing array of intriguing cultural variations. For example, *Jurassic Park*, among the most lucrative films of all time, features the familiar narrative *conventions* of problems, heroes, villains, conflicts, and resolutions. However, the film *differentiates* itself through enhanced *inventions:* computer-animated dinosaurs, which had never been attempted before in a motion picture. This combination of convention and invention—standardized Hollywood stories and differentiated special effects—provides a powerful economic package that satisfies most audiences' appetites for both the familiar and the distinctive.

Hollywood Genres. In general, Hollywood narratives fit a *genre*, or category, in which conventions regarding similar characters, scenes, structures, and themes reoccur in combination. Grouping films by category allows the industry to achieve two related economic goals: *product standardization* and *product differentiation*. By making films that fall into popular genres, the movie industry provides familiar models that can be imitated. It is much easier for a studio to promote a film that already fits into a preexisting category with which viewers are familiar. Among the most familiar genres are comedy, drama, romance, action/adventure, mystery/suspense, fantasy/ science fiction, musical, horror, gangster, western, and film noir (see Table 7.2).

An enduring genre such as the western typically features "good" cowboys battling "evil" bad guys or resolves tension between the natural forces of the wilderness and the civilizing impact of a town. Romances present narratives in which women play more central roles and conflicts are mediated by the ideal of love. Another popular genre, mystery/suspense, usually casts "the city" as a corrupting place that needs to be overcome by the moral courage of a heroic detective; the hero searches for clues of criminal violation; then confronts villains, victims, and bystanders; and, finally, explains and resolves the violation or transgression.[9] A durable genre in novels as well as films, mystery movies rely on the introduction of new plots, stars, and directors to differentiate them from their predecessors.

Besides variations of dramas and comedies, which dominate film's long narrative history, another significant genre, the movie musical, added the innovation of on-screen music. Recently, however, the genre has fallen on hard times. Although musicals such as *Jesus Christ, Superstar* (1973), *Saturday Night Fever* (1977), and *Hair* (1979) were early influences on the music-video era, they have since been overwhelmed by MTV and other forms of popular music. Furthermore, movie musicals became prohibitively expensive. *Annie*, for instance, cost over $40 million in 1982, more than the cost of the average feature in the early to mid-1990s.

Musicals are considered risky investments in the film industry today. Only two musicals—*The Sound of Music* and *Grease*—rank among the Top-100-grossing films in history. Although musicals like *Cats* remain popular as Broadway plays, the staged qualities of such shows actually are a negative when musicals are converted into movies. Since most Hollywood narratives try to create believable worlds, the artificial style of musicals is sometimes a disruption of what many viewers expect. In fact, movie musicals that have done the best at the box office are those with just a few musical numbers that accompany a spoken narrative story.

An interesting and relatively new genre is *film noir* (French for *black film*), which developed in the United States after World War II and continues to influence movies today. Using low lighting techniques, few daytime scenes, and bleak urban settings that generate a chilling mood, films in this genre explore unstable characters and the sinister side of human nature. These films also often resist the conventional closure of the classic narrative. Although the French critics who first identified noir as a genre place these films in the 1940s, their influence resonates in contemporary films— sometimes called *neo-noir*—including *Raging Bull*, *Pulp Fiction*, *Red Rock West*, *Fargo*, and *Leaving Las Vegas*.

TABLE 7.2
Hollywood Genres

Movies, especially contemporary films, are difficult to categorize because they often combine characteristics from different genres. In 1994, for example, *Pulp Fiction* mixed elements from comedy, action/adventure, and film noir, while *Forrest Gump* offered comedy, romance, and action/adventure. Shown below are the categories that are generally used by video stores to sort movies. Films from different decades represent the most familiar major genres.

Comedy

The Gold Rush (1925)
Horse Feathers (1932)
Arsenic and Old Lace (1944)
Some Like It Hot (1959)
Dr. Strangelove (1964)
Annie Hall (1977)*
A Fish Called Wanda (1988)
The Birdcage (1995)
Liar, Liar (1997)

Drama

Grand Hotel (1932)
Gone with the Wind (1939)
Citizen Kane (1941)
On the Waterfront (1954)*
A Man for All Seasons (1966)*
One Flew over the Cuckoo's Nest
   (1975)*
Raging Bull (1980)
Do the Right Thing (1989)
Fried Green Tomatoes (1991)
Dead Man Walking (1996)

Romance

It Happened One Night (1934)*
Casablanca (1943)*
Adam's Rib (1949)
Sabrina (1954)
Dr. Zhivago (1965)
The Graduate (1967)
The Goodbye Girl (1977)
Tootsie (1984)
Beauty and the Beast (1993)
Jerry Maguire (1997)

Action/Adventure

The Adventures of Robin Hood
   (1938)
Sands of Iwo Jima (1949)
Ben Hur (1959)*
The Great Escape (1963)
The Sting (1973)*
Die Hard (1988)
Thelma and Louise (1991)
The Lion King (1994)

Mystery/Suspense

The Lady Vanishes (1938)
Rebecca (1940)*
North by Northwest (1959)
Psycho (1960)
Chinatown (1974)
Witness (1985)
Silence of the Lambs (1991)*
Seven (1996)

Westerns

Cimarron (1931)*
Stagecoach (1939)
The Searchers (1956)
Butch Cassidy and the Sundance Kid
   (1969)
Little Big Man (1970)
The Outlaw Josey Wales (1976)
Silverado (1985)
Unforgiven (1992)*
Posse (1993)
Maverick (1994)

Gangster

Public Enemy (1931)
Scarface (1932)
High Sierra (1941)
Bonnie and Clyde (1967)
The Godfather (1972)*
The Godfather, Part II (1974)*
Scarface (1983)
Goodfellas (1990)
Menace II Society (1993)

Horror

Phantom of the Opera (1925)
Dracula (1931)
Bride of Frankenstein (1935)
The Wolf Man (1941)
The Blob (1958)
The Birds (1963)
The Exorcist (1973)
Nightmare on Elm Street (1985)
Mary Shelley's Frankenstein (1994)

Fantasy/Science Fiction

Metropolis (1926)
The Wizard of Oz (1939)
Invasion of the Body Snatchers
   (1956)
2001: A Space Odyssey (1968)
Star Wars (1977)
The Princess Bride (1987)
Terminator 2: Judgment Day (1991)
Independence Day (1996)

Musicals

Broadway Melody (1929)*
Top Hat (1935)
Meet Me in St. Louis (1944)
An American in Paris (1951)*
West Side Story (1961)*
The Sound of Music (1965)*
Jesus Christ, Superstar (1973)
Annie (1982)
Evita (1997)

Film Noir

Double Indemnity (1944)
Detour (1945)
The Postman Always Rings Twice
   (1946)
The Strange Love of Martha Ivers
   (1946)
Key Largo (1948)
They Live by Night (1948)
Border Incident (1949)

*Won the Academy Award for that year's best picture.

Graham Greene (*right*) and Kevin Costner (*left*) starred in *Dances with Wolves*, winner of the Academy Award for Best Picture in 1990. Along with the 1989 TV mini-series *Lonesome Dove*, the movie resuscitated the western as a viable commercial film genre, taking in more than $180 million at the box office.

Hollywood "Authors." Film has generally been called a director's medium. Although commercial filmmaking requires hundreds of people to perform complicated tasks, from scriptwriting and casting to set design and final editing, the director serves as the main "author" of a film. Certainly the names of Steven Spielberg (*E.T.*, *Schindler's List*, *Jurassic Park*) or Spike Lee (*Do the Right Thing*, *Malcolm X*, *Get on the Bus*) attract many moviegoers to a film today.

D. W. Griffith, among the first "star" directors, paved the way for future filmmakers. Griffith refined many of the narrative techniques that are still used, including varied camera distances, close-up shots, multiple story lines, fast-paced editing, and symbolic imagery. His major work, *Birth of a Nation* (1915), was a controversial three-hour Civil War epic. Although considered a technical masterpiece, the film naively glorified the Ku Klux Klan and stereotyped southern blacks. It is nevertheless the movie that triggered Hollywood's eighty-year fascination with long narrative movies. By 1915, more than 20 percent of films were feature-length (around two hours), and *Birth of a Nation*, which cost a filmgoer a record $2 admission to see, ran for a year on Broadway.

Successful directors, in general, develop a particular cinematic style or an interest in particular topics that differentiate their narratives from those of other directors. Alfred Hitchcock, for instance, redefined the suspense drama through editing techniques that heightened tension (*North by Northwest*, 1959; *Psycho*, 1960); Frank Capra championed romantic characters who stood up for the common person (*Mr. Smith Goes to Washington*, 1939; *It's a Wonderful Life*, 1946).

> "So TV did not kill Hollywood. In **the great Hollywood whodunit** there is, after all, not even a corpse. The film industry never died. Only *where* we enjoy its latest products has changed, forever."
>
> —Douglas Gomery,
> *Wilson Quarterly*,
> 1991

The contemporary status of directors probably stems from two breakthrough films, Dennis Hopper's *Easy Rider* (1969) and George Lucas's *American Graffiti* (1973), which became surprise box-office hits. Their inexpensive budgets, rock-and-roll soundtracks, and big payoffs created opportunities for a new generation of directors. These films exposed cracks in the Hollywood system, which was losing money in the late 1960s and early 1970s. Studio executives seemed lost trying to explain and predict the tastes of a new generation of moviegoers. Yet Hopper and Lucas had tapped into the anxieties of the postwar baby-boom generation—searching for self-realization, longing for an innocent past, and coping with the social turbulence of the late 1960s.

Trained in California or New York film schools and products of the 1960s, Francis Ford Coppola (*The Godfather*), Brian De Palma (*Carrie*), William Friedkin (*The Exorcist*), George Lucas (*Star Wars*), Martin Scorsese (*Taxi Driver, Raging Bull*), and Steven Spielberg (*Jaws, Raiders of the Lost Ark*) represented a new wave of Hollywood directors. Combining news or documentary techniques and Hollywood narratives, they demonstrated not only how mass media borders had become blurred but also how movies had become more dependent on audiences that were products of television and rock and roll. These films signaled the start of a period that Scorsese has called "the deification of the director." A handful of successful men gained the kind of economic clout and celebrity standing that had belonged almost exclusively to top movie stars, and a few of these directors were transformed into big-time Hollywood producers.

Although the standing of directors grew in the 1960s and 1970s, recognition for women directors of Hollywood features remained rare.[10] In the history of the Academy Awards, only two women have ever earned an Academy Award nomination for directing a feature film: Lina Wertmuller in 1976 for *Seven Beauties* and Jane Campion in 1993 for *The Piano* (for which Campion won an Oscar for her original screenplay). When women do get an opportunity, it often comes because their prominent standing as popular actors has given them the power to produce or direct. For example, her cachet as both a movie star and a popular singer allowed Barbra Streisand to produce, co-write, direct, and perform in *Yentl*, a 1983 musical.

Although women have made strong contributions in commercial movies as actors, editors, writers, artists, and designers, critics generally attribute their lack of power to the long history of male executives atop the studio system. With the exception of Mary Pickford, the early studio moguls who ran Hollywood were men. Even by the mid-1990s, among the major studio executives, only a few women held top posts. Independent filmmaker Julie Dash (*Daughters of the Dust*, 1992) argued in the 1995 PBS series *American Cinema* that women's best chances to control the movie process, other than through acting, remained outside the Hollywood system.

In 1993, Jane Campion won an Academy Award for writing the screenplay for *The Piano*. Campion was also nominated as best director for the film, only the second time in sixty-six years that a woman had received an Oscar nomination in the directing category.

alternatives to hollywood

The contemporary film industry tends to focus on feature-length movies that command popular attention and most of the money. However, shorter narrative films and documentaries dominated cinema's first twenty years and continue to account for most movies made today. In addition, movie history has a long tradition in experimental, or avant-garde, films. These types of films, often produced outside the United States, provide opportunities for new filmmakers, both women and men. We will look at two alternatives to Hollywood: foreign films and documentaries.

Foreign Films. Although U.S. films earned more than 90 percent of box-office revenues annually by the mid-1990s, they accounted for only 15 percent of the number of commercial films produced worldwide. Despite Hollywood's domination of global film distribution, other countries have rich histories in producing both successful and provocative short-subject and feature films. For example, German expressionism (1919–24), Soviet realism (1924–30), Italian neorealism (1942–51), French new-wave cinema (1959–60), and post–World War II Japanese cinema have all demonstrated alternative styles to Hollywood.

Americans showed early interest in British and French short films and in experimental films like Germany's *The Cabinet of Dr. Caligari* (1919). The studio moguls, however, held tight reign over the entry of foreign titles into the United States. Foreign-language movies still did reasonably well through the 1920s, especially in ethnic neighborhood theaters in large American cities. Hollywood studios, for a time, even dubbed some popular American movies into Spanish, Italian, French, and German for these theaters. But the Depression brought cutbacks, and by the 1930s, the daughters and sons of turn-of-the-century immigrants—many of them trying to assimilate into mainstream American culture—preferred their Hollywood movies in English.[11]

Postwar prosperity in the 1950s and 1960s saw a rebirth of interest in foreign-language films by prominent directors such as Sweden's Ingmar Bergman (*Wild Strawberries*, 1957), Italy's Federico Fellini (*La Dolce Vita*, 1960), France's François Truffaut (*Jules and Jim*, 1961), Japan's Akira Kurosawa (*Seven Samurai*, 1954), and India's Satyajit Ray (*Apu Trilogy*, 1955–59). In the 1950s, the gradual breakup of the studios' hold over theater exhibition stimulated the rise of art-house theaters, many specializing in foreign titles. Catering to academic audiences, art houses made a statement against Hollywood commercialism as they sought alternative movies.

Art houses numbered close to a thousand during their peak years in the late 1960s. By the late 1970s, though, the home-video market emerged, and audiences began staying home to watch both foreign and domestic films. New multiplex theater owners also rejected the smaller profit margins of most foreign titles, which lacked the promotional hype of U.S. films. In addition, many viewers complained that English subtitles distracted them from devoting their attention to the visual images. As a result, between 1966 and 1990 the number of foreign films released annually in the United States dropped by two thirds, from nearly three hundred to about one hundred titles per year.

With the growth of superstore chains such as Blockbuster in the 1990s, however, more shelf space opened up for diverse kinds of movies, including a larger selection of foreign-language titles. In 1994, the Mexican film *Like Water for Chocolate* became the most successful foreign picture ever marketed in the United States. Then, in 1996, it was surpassed by the Italian film *Il Postino* (*The Postman*), which also became the first foreign-language film since 1973 to earn an Oscar nomination for best picture (see Table 7.3). In Europe, feature filmmaking in the 1990s was on the rise after years of decline. Ireland (20), Great Britain (81), France (129), and Germany (84) all produced more

Massimo Troisi (*right*) and Philippe Noiret (*left*) starred in *Il Postino (The Postman)*. A popular Italian actor, Troisi (who died the day after filming was completed) played a sweet but dimwitted mailman befriended by the exiled Chilean poet Pablo Neruda, played by Noiret. The subtitled Italian film became uncommonly popular in America after it was nominated for an Academy Award for best picture in 1996.

features in 1995 than in 1994.[12] Compare this to the United States, where the major studios distribute about 170 features each year and independent filmmakers annually produce another 300 or so small-budget features. Still, foreign films, unless filmed in cooperative ventures with the major American studios, have difficulty cracking the American market; they accounted for just 2 percent of the U.S. video market in 1995.

TABLE 7.3
The Top 10 Foreign-Language Films in U.S. Theaters

Film (year of U.S. release, director, country of origin)

1. *Il Postino* (1995, Radford, Italy)
2. *Like Water for Chocolate* (1993, Arau, Mexico)
3. *I Am Curious (Yellow)* (1969, Sjoman, Sweden)
4. *La Dolce Vita* (1960, Fellini, Italy)
5. *La Cage aux Folles* (1979, Molinaro, France/Italy)
6. *Z* (1969, Costa-Gavras, France)
7. *A Man and a Woman* (1966, Lelouch, France)
8. *Cinema Paradiso* (1990, Tornatore, Italy/France)
9. *Emmanuelle* (1975, Jaeckin, France)
10. *Das Boot* (1982, Peterson, Germany)

Sources: *People Entertainment Almanac 1995* (Boston: Little, Brown, 1994), 115; Linda Lee, "Nobody Reads a Good Movie These Days," *New York Times*, December 9, 1996, p. C7.

The Documentary Tradition. Both TV news and nonfiction films trace their roots back to the movie industry's *interest films* and newsreels in the late 1890s. In Britain, interest films contained compiled footage of regional wars, political leaders, industrial workers, and agricultural scenes. These films accompanied fiction shorts as part of the early moviegoing experience. Pioneered in France and England, *newsreels* consisted of weekly ten-minute magazine-style compilations of filmed news events from around the world organized in a sequence of short reports. A number of international news services began supplying theaters and movie studios with newsreels, and by 1911 they had become a regular part of the moviegoing menu.

Early filmmakers also produced *travelogues*, which recorded daily life in various communities around the world. Travel films reached documentary status in Robert Flaherty's classic *Nanook of the North* (1922), which tracked a resourceful Eskimo family in the harsh Hudson Bay region of Canada. Flaherty edited his fifty-five-minute film to both tell and interpret the story of his subject. Flaherty's second film, *Moana* (1925), a Paramount-funded study of the lush South Pacific islands and a direct contrast to *Nanook*, inspired the term **documentary** in a 1926 film review by John Grierson, a Scottish documentary producer. Grierson defined Flaherty's work and the documentary form as "the creative treatment of actuality."

Over time, the documentary developed an identity apart from its commercial presentation. As an educational, noncommercial form, the documentary usually required the backing of industry, government, or philanthropy to cover costs. In support of a clear alternative to Hollywood cinema, various governments began creating special units, like Canada's National Film Board, to sponsor documentaries. In the United States, art and film received considerable support from the Roosevelt administration during the Depression. Such funding produced Pare Lorentz's *The Plow That Broke the Plains* (1936), which recounted the ecological abuse and erosion of the Great Plains in the 1930s. During World War II, the government continued to turn to filmmakers and to Hollywood to "sell" patriotism. Director Frank Capra produced the seven-part *Why We Fight* documentary series to inspire support for the war effort against Germany and Japan.

By the late 1950s and early 1960s, the development of portable cameras led to *cinema verité* (a French term for *film truth*). This documentary style allowed filmmakers to go where cameras could not go before and record fragments of everyday life more unobtrusively. Directly opposed to packaged, high-gloss Hollywood features, verité

After cutting a distribution deal with Time Warner, novice independent filmmaker Michael Moore saw his 1989 movie *Roger and Me* become one of the most popular documentaries in film history. The controversial film used humor and satire to document Moore's search for Roger Smith, then CEO of General Motors. The auto giant's plant closings had left thirty thousand unemployed in Moore's hometown of Flint, Michigan, a city still recovering from corporate "downsizing" and economic devastation.

aimed to track reality, employing a rough, grainy look and shaky, handheld camerawork.

Among the key innovators in cinema verité were Drew and Associates, led by Robert Drew, a former *Life* magazine photographer. Through his connection to Time Inc. (which owned *Life*) and its chain of TV stations, Drew shot the documentary *Primary*, which followed the 1960 Democratic presidential primary race between Hubert Humphrey and John F. Kennedy. Drew's portable cameras went everywhere, capturing glimpses of the political process never seen before, including Humphrey directing rehearsals for a TV appearance and Kennedy in a Milwaukee hotel room nervously awaiting the results of his victory. Drew's team went on to work for ABC News, where they produced films for the network's *Closeup* program, influencing the next generation of TV news programs.

Since the late 1960s, a leading American practitioner of cinema verité has been Frederick Wiseman, who has filmed a series of documentaries for public television on the misuses of power in American institutions. Unlike traditional TV news, in which the reporter's voice-over narration organizes the story, Wiseman used careful and clever editing to make his point without a reporter's comments. His work includes *Titicut Follies* (1967), which until 1993 was banned from public viewing in Massachusetts for its piercing look at a state-run mental health facility. Over the years, he also tackled police departments, military training, high schools, animal research labs, department stores, and fashion modeling. Wiseman's films indirectly reveal institutional abuse and waste, and he and the verité tradition have been praised for bringing such corruption to light. They have also been criticized, though, for offering few solutions to the institutional problems they expose.

The documentary form, both inside and outside the United States, extends from turn-of-the-century film shorts to Dziga Vertov's *Man with a Movie Camera* (1927), which demonstrated Soviet-sponsored innovations in film editing. In later eras, the documentary tradition included the French film *Night and Fog* (1955), which reported the atrocities of the Nazi death camps during World War II, and *Hoop Dreams* (1994), a three-hour examination of the rituals of college basketball recruiting.

Perhaps the major contribution of documentaries has been their willingness to tackle controversial or unpopular subject matter. Oscar-winning documentaries such as Peter Davis's *Hearts and Minds* (1974) examined the complex cultural impact of the Vietnam War and paved the way for Hollywood to confront Vietnam in fiction features such as *The Deer Hunter* (1978) and *Platoon* (1986). In addition, Barbara Kopple's Academy Award-winning film, *Harlan County, U.S.A.* (1977), documented the poignant stories and hard lives of Kentucky coal miners and their families. Connie Field's *The Life and Times of Rosie the Riveter* (1980) sparked a renewed interest in gender and labor issues. It also influenced Kopple's award-winning *American Dream*

(1990), which traced a protracted Minnesota labor dispute between meatpackers and the Hormel Corporation. Another film about labor became America's most popular filmed documentary: Michael Moore's *Roger and Me* (1989) presented a comic and controversial look at the complex relationship between the city of Flint, Michigan, and General Motors. To reach a broader audience, Moore and his backers struck a deal with Time Warner to distribute the movie, ensuring audiences beyond college campuses and union halls.

Thousands of independent filmmakers persevere. They operate on shoestring budgets and show their movies in thousands of campus auditoriums and at hundreds of small film festivals. Portable technology, including smaller cameras and digital computer editing, has kept many documentarists and other independent filmmakers in business. They make movies inexpensively, relying on real-life situations, stage actors and nonactors, crews made up of friends and students, and local settings outside the studio environment. Successful independents like Joel and Ethan Coen (*Blood Simple, Raising Arizona, Barton Fink, Fargo*) continue to find substantial audiences in college, neighborhood, and some mall theaters that promote work produced outside the studio system. In fact, four of the five films nominated for Best Picture at the 1996 Academy Awards were produced by independent companies—*Fargo, Shine, Sling Blade*, and *The English Patient* (which received the 1996 award).

the transformation of the hollywood system

Beginning in 1946 and continuing over the next seventeen years, the movie industry lost much of its theatergoing audience. In 1951 alone, more than fifty theaters shut down in New York City. The ninety million people going to movies weekly in 1946 dropped to under twenty-five million by 1963. It seemed that the movie industry was in deep trouble, especially facing the ascent of television. Critics and observers began talking about the death of Hollywood. However, although Hollywood diminished as the geographical heart of the industry, a number of dramatic changes altered and eventually strengthened many aspects of the commercial movie business.

By the mid-1950s, significant cultural and social changes—such as suburbanization and television—began reshaping the moviegoing experience. By the mid-1990s, even though movie attendance per capita had declined dramatically, more indoor theater screens—twenty-five-thousand-plus—were available in the United States than ever before (see Figure 7.1). Theaters, however, have been dramatically downsized from the five-thousand-seat movie palaces that reigned in the 1940s. Despite major social transformations, however, the commercial film industry remains controlled, as it was earlier, by a few powerful companies. We will review the film industry's adjustments to changing conditions, particularly the impact of political and legal challenges, suburbanization, television, and other technological changes such as cable and VCRs.

the hollywood ten

In 1947, in the wake of the unfolding Cold War with the Soviet Union, conservative members of Congress began investigating Hollywood for alleged subversive and communist ties. That year, the aggressive witch-hunts for political radicals in the film industry by the House Un-American Activities Committee (HUAC) led to the famous Hollywood Ten hearings and subsequent trial. At the time, Congressman J. Parnell Thomas of New Jersey chaired HUAC, which included future president Richard M.

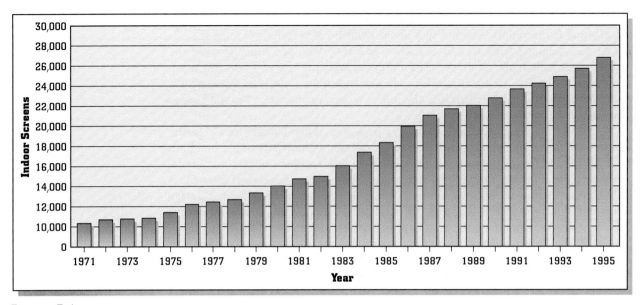

Figure 7.1
Indoor Theater Screens in the United States, 1971–95
Source: ©Motion Picture Association of America, U.S. Economic Review, 1995.

Nixon, then a congressman from California, as one of five members of this powerful committee.

During the investigations, HUAC coerced prominent people from the film industry to declare their patriotism and to list those suspected of politically unfriendly tendencies. Upset over labor union strikes and outspoken writers, many film executives were eager to testify. During the hearings, Jack L. Warner, of Warner Brothers, suggested that whenever film writers made fun of rich men or America's political system, they were engaging in communist propaganda. He reported that movies sympathetic to "Indians and the colored folks" were also suspect.[13] Film producer Sam Wood, who had directed Marx Brothers comedies in the mid-1930s, testified that communist writers could be spotted because they portrayed bankers and senators as villainous characters. Either believing in their patriotic duty or afraid of losing their jobs, many film executives and prominent actors "named names" in 1947.

Eventually, HUAC subpoenaed ten unwilling witnesses who were questioned about their memberships in various organizations. The so-called Hollywood Ten—nine screenwriters and one director—refused to discuss their memberships or to identify communist sympathizers. Charged with contempt of Congress in November 1947, they were eventually sent to prison. Ironically, two Hollywood Ten members went to the same prison as HUAC chairman Thomas, who would later be convicted of conspiracy to defraud the government in a phony payroll scheme. Although jailing the Hollywood Ten clearly violated their free speech rights, in the atmosphere of the Cold War, many seemingly well-intentioned people worried that "the American way" could be sabotaged via unfriendly messages planted in films.

the paramount decision

Coinciding with the political investigations, the government increased its scrutiny of the industry's expanding oligopoly practices. By the mid-1940s, the Justice Department demanded that the five major film companies—Paramount, Warner Brothers, Twentieth Century Fox, MGM, and RKO—end vertical integration. After a series of court appeals, the Supreme Court in 1948 ruled against the film industry in what is commonly known as "the Paramount decision," forcing the studios to gradually divest themselves of their theaters.

Although the government had hoped to increase competition, the Paramount case never really changed the oligopoly structure of the commercial film industry. Initially, the 1948 decision did create opportunities in the exhibition part of the industry. In addition to art houses showing documentaries or foreign films, thousands of new drive-in theaters sprang up in farmers' fields, welcoming new suburbanites who had left the city and embraced the automobile. Although drive-ins had been around since the 1930s, by the end of the 1950s more than four thousand existed. The Paramount decision encouraged other new indoor theater openings as well, but the major studios continued to dominate distribution. By producing the most polished and popular films, they still controlled consumer demand and orchestrated where the movies would play.

moving to the suburbs

Common sense might suggest that television alone precipitated the decline in post–World War II movie attendance, but the most dramatic drop actually occurred in the late 1940s—*before* most Americans even had TV sets.[14] In fact, with the FCC freeze on TV licenses between 1948 and 1952, most communities did not have TV stations up and running until 1954. By then, the theatergoing audience had already dropped by half.

The transformation of a wartime economy and an unprecedented surge in consumer production had a significant impact on moviegoing. With industries turning from armaments to appliances, Americans started cashing in their savings bonds for household goods and new cars. Discretionary income that formerly went to movie tickets now went to acquiring consumer products. And the biggest product of all was a new house in the suburbs, far from the downtown theaters where movies still premiered. Relying on government help through Veterans Administration loans, people left the cities in record numbers to buy affordable houses in suburban areas where tax bases were lower. Home ownership in the United States doubled between 1945 and 1950, while the moviegoing public decreased just as quickly. According to census data, new housing starts, which had held steady at about 100,000 a year since the late 1920s, leaped to more than 930,000 in 1946 and peaked at 1,700,000 in 1950.

After World War II, the average age for couples entering marriage dropped from twenty-four to nineteen. Unlike their parents, many postwar couples had their first children before they turned twenty-one. The combination of social and economic changes meant there were significantly fewer couples dating at the movies. The suburban move altered spending patterns and had a far more profound impact on movie attendance than did television in the early 1950s. In terms of income, there was little left over for movies after mortgage and car payments. When television exploded in the late 1950s, there was even less discretionary income—and less reason to go to the movies.

> "I always wanted to travel—I just never got the opportunity."
> —Thelma, *Thelma & Louise*, 1991

television changes hollywood

In the late 1940s, radio's popularity had a stronger impact than television on film's apparent decline. Not only were 1948 and 1949 high points in radio listenership, but with the shift to the suburbs, radio entertainment (as it had in the 1930s) offered Americans an inexpensive alternative to the movies. Thus, many people stayed home and listened to radio programs until TV assumed this social function in the mid-1950s. Moviegoing was already in steep decline by the time television further eroded the annual number of movie tickets sold, which had peaked at four billion in 1946 but declined and then leveled off at around one billion by 1963.

By the mid-1950s, television had displaced both radio and movies as the medium of national entertainment. With growing legions of people gathering around their living-room TV sets, movie content slowly shifted toward more serious subjects. While this may at first have been a response to the war and an acknowledgment of life's complexity, later movies started to focus on subject matter that television did not encourage. This shift in content began with the rise of film noir in the 1940s but continued into the 1950s as commercial movies, for the first time, explored larger social problems, such as alcoholism (*Lost Weekend*, 1945), anti-Semitism (*Gentleman's Agreement*, 1947), mental illness (*The Snake Pit*, 1948), racism (*Pinky*, 1949), adult-teen relationships (*Rebel without a Cause*, 1955), and drug abuse (*Man with the Golden Arm*, 1955).

Directors even explored sexual relationships that were formerly off-limits to film (in movies such as *Peyton Place*, 1957; *Butterfield 8*, 1960; and *Lolita*, 1962) and certainly off-limits to wholesome family television. Filmmakers also challenged the industry's own prohibitive Motion Picture Production Code (see Chapter 16), which had placed restrictions on film content to quiet public and political concerns about the movie business. Like sound recording executives in the early 1990s, movie administrators who worried about government regulation and public boycotts began planning a self-imposed ratings system. The explicit language and situations of *Who's Afraid of Virginia Woolf?* (1966), based on an Edward Albee play, led in 1967 to the formation of the current ratings system. Nevertheless, filmmakers continued to make movies considered inappropriate for television as a way of holding on to the under-thirty audiences which had become the dominant group of theatergoers. By the 1980s and 1990s, however, with the baby-boom generation growing older and starting families, commercial opportunities emerged for popular feature-length cartoons and family movies, making Disney the most successful contemporary studio.

In terms of technology, Hollywood tried a number of approaches to appeal to the new TV generation (see "Tracking Technology: Advances in Movie Viewing").

Do these "virtual reality" headsets for large-screen viewing used in Sony's I-max Theater in New York represent the future? Or are they just another gimmick, like Smell-O-Vision or 3-D in the 1950s, that audiences will eventually reject?

Technicolor, invented by an MIT scientist in 1917, had gradually improved, and offered images that far surpassed those on a fuzzy black-and-white TV. Color advancement, though, was not enough for studio chiefs increasingly alarmed by the popularity of television. Just as radio in the 1950s worked to improve sound to maintain an advantage over television, the film industry introduced a host of gimmicks to draw attention to the superiority of movie narratives.

In the early to mid-1950s, Cinerama, CinemaScope, and VistaVision all arrived in movie theaters, featuring striking wide-screen images, multiple synchronized projectors, and stereophonic sound. Then 3-D (three-dimensional) movies appeared, including Warner Brothers' horror film *House of Wax*, wildly popular in its first few weeks in theaters. But like other experiments, 3-D required a large investment in new projection technology plus special glasses distributed to all moviegoers. In addition, 3-D suffered from out-of-focus images; it wore off quickly as a novelty. Panavision, which used special Eastman color film and camera lenses that decreased the fuzziness of images, finally became the wide-screen standard throughout the industry. The new gimmicks, however, generally failed to address the movies' primary problem: the middle-class flight to the suburbs, away from downtown movie theaters.

Advances in Movie Viewing

Film delivery has remained largely unchanged from the way movie houses received and projected movies fifty years ago. The distribution arms of the major studios still send most of their films in large reel cans. Distributors have been talking, however, about eliminating expensive film prints by equipping movie theaters with satellite receiving dishes. Theaters would then receive movies the same way that home viewers receive them, via cable or direct broadcast satellite (DBS). Using digital high-definition television technology, movie images look as good as 35 and 70 mm film, the longtime industry standards. Other possibilities include the use of digital laser disks, which also surpass the quality of current film images. However, since film prints are still a minor part of the cost of making and marketing films, it may be some time before there is much incentive to change.

Just as nickelodeons, movie palaces, and drive-ins transformed movie exhibition in earlier times, the key marvel that has transformed contemporary movie exhibition is the videocassette. In 1992, Disney's video and distribution subsidiary, Buena Vista, sold more than twenty million copies of *Beauty and the Beast*, the third-highest-grossing film in 1991, with ticket revenues of $69 million. In video rentals and sales, though, the film earned quadruple that amount—$270 million. Buena Vista's total cassette revenues in 1992 surpassed $1.1 billion, making the subsidiary one of the most profitable business ventures in the entire film industry that year. With VCRs in more than 85 percent of U.S. homes by 1997, consumers spent $14 billion renting or purchasing prerecorded videocassettes. This figure was expected to rise to $19 billion by 1999.

Despite the scope of Technicolor and wide-screen cinema, and despite theaters experimenting with five-story megascreens, most people still prefer the convenience of watching movies on their TV sets. A survey from the early 1990s, conducted by a national electronics association, found that only 22 percent of respondents preferred to see movies at a theater. Aside from cassettes, pay-per-view and premium cable have also stolen parts of the theatergoing crowd. About 10 to 15 percent of the film industry's revenue in a given year now derives from these resources. To keep their edge, TV manufacturers have introduced stereo sets and produced larger TV screens. New digital screens will permit image projection the size of a living-room wall, more closely replicating a theater experience.

Even though theater crowds have dwindled over the years, watching movies is a bigger business than ever. Film studios initially feared the coming of television in the 1950s—to the point of banning film actors from performing on the small screen—but television has ironically become a major second-run venue for many movies. In similar fashion, the movie industry tried to stall the arrival of the VCR in the 1970s—even filing suits to prohibit consumers from copying movies off television. But home-cassette rentals and purchases have turned into a bonanza for the movie business, not only becoming a popular and inexpensive way to exhibit movies, but making money off films that flopped at the box office.

the economics of the movie business

Despite the development of made-for-TV movies as well as the rise of the network era, cable television, pay-per-view, and home video, the movie business has continued to thrive. In fact, since 1963 Americans have purchased roughly one billion movie tickets each year.[15] With the average first-run movie ticket price rising gradually to more than $6 by the mid-1990s, gross revenues from box-office sales climbed to $6 billion a year, up from $3.5 billion annually in the mid-1980s, as shown in Figure 7.2. In addition, video rentals and sales produced another $14 to $15 billion a year, more than doubling box-office receipts. To survive and flourish, the movie industry not only followed middle-class migration to the shopping malls but moved right into their suburban homes. Put another way, by the mid-1990s more people watched commercial films on VCRs in one month than attended movie theaters for the entire year.

production, distribution, and exhibition today

It took until the 1970s for the movie industry to determine where the moviegoers had gone and how to catch up with them. Among the major "stars" in this effort were multiscreen movie complexes, located either in shopping malls or at the crossroads of major highways. Throughout the 1970s, attendance by young moviegoers at the new multiplexes made megahits out of *The Godfather* (1972), *The Exorcist* (1973), *Jaws* (1975), *Rocky* (1976), and *Star Wars* (1977). During this period, *Jaws* and *Star Wars* became the first movies to gross more than $100 million at the box office in a single year.

In trying to copy the success of these blockbuster hits, the major studios set in place economic strategies for the 1980s and 1990s. With 80 to 90 percent of newly released movies failing to make money at the box office, the majors hoped for at least one major hit each year to offset losses on other films. By the 1980s, though, studios were already recouping box-office losses through the lucrative video market.

By 1997, a Hollywood film, on average, cost $35 to $45 million to produce, another $35 million to distribute, and $30 million to advertise and promote world-

Figure 7.2
Gross Revenues from Box-Office Sales, 1980–95
Source: Motion Picture Association of America, Inc.

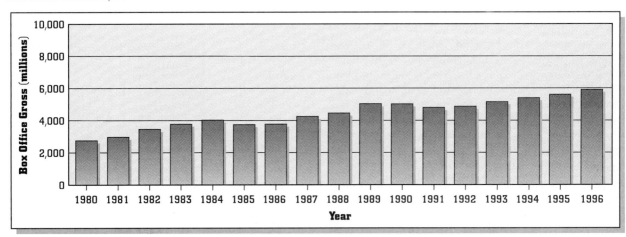

wide. To recover these costs, a studio receives money from at least four sources. First, about 40 percent of the box-office revenues from a film go to the producing studio, with 60 percent going to the theaters. Second, movie-video sales and rentals account for nearly half of what a typical movie earns in overall revenue for a major studio. Third, studios earn profits from distributing films in foreign markets. Finally, studios make money by distributing the work of independent producers and filmmakers, who usually must hire studios to circulate their films widely. Independents pay the studios between 30 and 50 percent of the box-office and video-rental money they make from movies. As distributors, the film studios bear no production costs and charge independents for advertising and promoting their movies. Independents also pay distributors for making copies of the films sent to theaters and video stores. Since producers make money only after all distribution costs are paid, distributors can earn revenue even when the producers don't.

Generally, major stars and directors receive separate fees and percentages totaling another $30 million over and above the production costs for a blockbuster-type movie. Lesser-known actors and directors, assistant producers, screenplay writers, costume and set designers, film editors, music composers, and the cinematographers who physically shoot the movie, however, are paid flat fees for their work and do not usually share in the net profits from a movie (although Dreamworks, Disney, and Warner Brothers now write contracts that give cartoon animators and screenwriters a share of a film's profits). With the *total* cost for producing and distributing many Hollywood movies amounting to as much as $130 million by 1997, the studios claim that little revenue remains to share once the bills are paid.[16]

Film exhibition, like distribution, is now controlled by a handful of theater chains, including General Cinema, Cineplex-Odeon, and United Artists Theatres. All three chains own thousands of screens each in suburban malls and at highway crossroads. Since distributors require access to movie screens, they do business with those chains that control the most screens. In a multiplex, an exhibitor can project a potential hit on two or three screens at the same time; films that do not debut well are relegated to the smallest theaters or bumped quickly for a new release.

the major players

The American commercial film business and the classic Hollywood narrative remained dominant through the mid-1990s. Although MGM/UA (*Get Shorty*, *Goldeneye*, *The Birdcage*) was making a comeback after years of neglect and mismanagement, the industry was ruled primarily by six companies: Warner Brothers, Paramount, Twentieth Century Fox, Universal, Columbia Pictures, and Walt Disney. Except for Disney, all of these companies are owned by large parent conglomerates (see Table 7.4). One new studio, Dreamworks, created in 1994 by Steven Spielberg, former Disney executive Jeffrey Katzenberg, and sound recording tycoon David Geffen, began to rival the production capabilities of the majors. Nevertheless, the six major studios accounted for more than 90 percent of the revenue generated by commercial films. They also controlled half the movie market in Europe and Asia, with nearly a third of the industry's annual box-office profits coming from overseas in the mid-1990s.

To offset losses due to box-office failures, the movie industry in the 1980s began to diversify, to expand into other product lines and other mass media. This expansion included television programming, print media, sound recordings, and home videos as well as cable and computers, electronic hardware and software, videocassettes, and theme parks. Indicative of the effectiveness of this strategy, in 1980 more than 80 percent of movie studio revenue came from box-office receipts; by the mid-1990s, less than 25 percent came from that source.

To maintain the industry's economic stability, management strategies today rely on both heavy advance promotion (which can double the cost of a commercial film) and the process of *synergy*—the promotion and sale of a product throughout the various subsidiaries of the media conglomerate. In other words, companies promote not only the new movie itself but also its book form, soundtrack, toy action figures, and "the-making-of" story for distribution on television, cable, and home cassette. The Disney studio, in particular, has been successful with its multiple packaging of the company's movies, which includes comic books, toys, cable specials, fast food tie-ins, and new theme-park attractions. Since the 1950s, this synergy has been the biggest change in the film industry, and a key element in the flood of corporate mergers.

The first company to change hands in the atmosphere of postwar business mergers was Paramount, which was sold to Gulf & Western Industries in 1966. (Paramount is now owned by Viacom, which originally made its mark by syndicating TV shows.) The next year Transamerica, an insurance and financial services company, bought United Artists (which in 1981 merged with MGM). The biggest mergers, however, have involved the internationalization of the American film business. This began in 1985 when the Australian media conglomerate News Corp. paid nearly $1 billion for Twentieth Century Fox. Along with News Corp., the new players in Hollywood have been large Japanese electronics firms. First purchased by Coca-Cola in 1980, Columbia Pictures was absorbed by Sony for more than $4 billion in 1989. In the deal, Sony acquired a library of twenty-seven hundred films and twenty-three thousand TV episodes. In 1990, Matsushita paid $7 billion for MCA/Universal and in 1995 sold 80 percent of its MCA stock to Seagram, the Canadian beverage company.

Investment in American popular culture by the international electronics industry is particularly significant. This business strategy represents a new, high-tech kind of vertical integration—an attempt to control both the production of electronic

TABLE 7.4
The Major Players in the Movie Business, 1996–97

Studio	Parent Company	Other Subsidiaries
Warner Brothers	Time Warner (USA)	Turner Broadcasting, HBO, cable systems, magazines, records, D.C. Comics, books, Book-of-the-Month Club, theme parks
Walt Disney	Disney (USA)	ABC, theme parks, ESPN, broadcast stations, books, magazines, newspapers, hockey team
Columbia Pictures	Sony (Japan)	TV sets, VCRs, camcorders, CD-ROM drives, CD players, Walkman, videotapes, records, TV programs
Twentieth Century Fox	News Corp. (Australia)	Fox TV network, newspapers, *TV Guide*, cable programs, broadcast stations, books, satellite delivery services
Paramount	Viacom (USA)	Blockbuster Video, records, books, magazines, MTV, Nickelodeon, Showtime, movie theaters, broadcast stations
Universal (formerly MCA)	Seagram (Canada)	MCA Records, books, cable channels, beverages

equipment that consumers buy for their homes and the production/distribution of the content that runs on that equipment. Companies such as Sony or Philips in the Netherlands have sought to increase markets for their electronics hardware by buying "software," especially movies, recordings, and TV shows.

While foreign investment in the U.S. commercial film industry has increased, government policies in many nations have attempted to limit the influence of American films. Restrictions on importing U.S. films and TV programs are intended to encourage the domestic film/TV industries in various countries and blunt the impact of U.S. popular culture. In 1989, for example, twelve European countries placed a 50 percent quota on the amount of time they would allocate for the exhibition of American films and TV shows. With the expansion of cable and satellite-delivered television and movies, however, many countries still depend on inexpensive and abundant U.S. products to fill up channels.

"It is hard to mix **business and culture**. Business is going to **win**."
—Jeremy Thomas, British Film Institute, 1996

popular movies and implications for democracy

Although alternative films may be hard to find, most other movies are readily available today—at the mall, on broadcast and cable television, in campus auditoriums, on videocassettes, on pay-per-view, and in neighborhood theaters. However flawed, most of these are Hollywood films: the common currency in a global market.

At the cultural level, commercial U.S. films function as *consensus narratives*, a term that describes cultural products that become popular and command wide attention. For all their limitations, classic Hollywood movies, as consensus narratives, provide shared cultural experiences, operating across different times and cultures. In this sense, movies are part of a long narrative tradition, encompassing "the oral-formulaic of Homer's day, the theater of Sophocles, the Elizabethan theater, the English novel from Defoe to Dickens, . . . the silent film, the sound film, and television during the Network Era."[17] Consensus narratives—whether they are dramas, romances, westerns, or mysteries—speak to central myths and values in an accessible language that often bridges global boundaries.

At the international level, countries continue to struggle with questions about the influence of American films on local customs and culture. Like other media industries, the long reach of Hollywood movies is one of the key contradictions of contemporary life: Do such films contribute to a global village in which people throughout the world share a universal culture that breaks down barriers? Or does an American-based common culture stifle the development of local cultures worldwide and diversity in moviemaking? Clearly, the steady production of profitable action/adventure movies—whether originating from the United States, Africa, France, or China—continues not only because they appeal to teens and young adults but because they translate easily into other languages.

With the rise of international media conglomerates, it has become more difficult to awaken public debate over issues of movie diversity and America's domination of the film business. In addition, technological innovations—whether they affect radio, television, film, cable, or the Internet—tend to outpace questions of legislation and regulation. Consequently, issues concerning greater competition and a better variety of movies sometimes fall by the wayside. As critical consumers, those of us who enjoy movies and recognize their cultural significance must raise these broader issues in public forums as well as in our personal conversations.

1. How did film go from the novelty stage to the mass medium stage?

2. Why were early silent films popular?

3. What contribution did nickelodeons make to film history?

4. Why did the center of film production end up in Hollywood?

5. Why did Thomas Edison and the patents Trust fail to shape and control the film industry, and why did Adolph Zukor of Paramount succeed?

6. How does vertical integration work in the film business?

7. Why did a certain structure of film—called classic Hollywood narratives—become so dominant in moviemaking?

8. Why are genres and directors important to the film industry?

9. Why are documentaries an important alternative to traditional Hollywood filmmaking? What contributions have they made to the film industry?

10. Why did the Hollywood system change in the 1950s?

11. Explain how television changed the film industry.

12. How do a few large film studios manage to control more than 90 percent of the commercial industry?

13. Why do U.S. movies remain popular worldwide while other countries have had great difficulty getting their films into the United States?

14. Do films contribute to a global village in which people throughout the world share a kind of universal culture? Or do U.S.-based films overwhelm the development of other cultures worldwide? Discuss.

QUESTIONING THE MEDIA

1. Describe your earliest memory of going to a movie. Do some research and compare this with a parent's or grandparent's earliest memory. Compare the different experiences.

2. Do you remember a movie you were not allowed to see? Discuss the experience.

3. How often do you go to movie theaters today? How often do you rent movies on video? Which experience do you prefer and why?

4. If you were a Hollywood film producer or executive, what kinds of films would you like to see made? What changes would you make in what we see at the movies?

5. Look at the international film box-office statistics in the latest issue of *Variety* magazine. Note what films are the most popular worldwide. What do you think about the significant role U.S. movies play in global culture? Should their role be less significant? Explain your answer.

THE CRITICAL PROCESS

Pick a current popular film you have seen or one the class has seen together. Write a three- to four-page (750–1,000 word) movie critique either defending or attacking the movie as a form of popular culture (see Chapter 1). Include plenty of examples to fortify your argument, and focus on three or four significant points. Use the following plan to organize your critique:

1. *Introduction.* In your introduction, identify the *central argument* (the critical stand you are taking) that will help focus and organize your essay.

2. *Body.* Support your argument by drawing on examples from the movie. Think about the first three critical stages: description, analysis, and interpretation. For example, in preparing to write your paper, *describe* important plot, theme, or character points that are relevant to your argument. (This is mostly the note-taking part of your paper; most of your paper should not merely describe plots and character details.) Then *analyze* the particular patterns (the three or four significant points) that you have chosen to examine. Finally, *interpret* what it all might mean based on the evidence you provide.

3. *Conclusion.* In your conclusion, discuss the limits of your critique and offer evaluations of the film industry based on your evidence and interpretations. *Evaluate* the movie by judging whether it works as high art or as popular culture. As part of your evaluation, cite reviews from other publications to support your point of view.

Newspapers

and the Rise of Modern Journalism

In 1887, a young reporter left her job at the *Pittsburgh Dispatch* to seek her fortune in New York City. Although only twenty-three years old, she had grown tired of merely replying to letters and writing for the society pages. She wanted to be on the front page. In those days, however, it was considered unladylike for women journalists to use their real names, so the *Dispatch* editors changed her name from Elizabeth "Pink" Cochrane to Nellie Bly, a name adapted from a Stephen Foster song about the servant daughter of former slaves.

After four months of persistent job-hunting and freelance writing, Nellie Bly earned a tryout at Joseph Pulitzer's *New York World*, the nation's biggest paper. Her assignment: investigate the deplorable conditions at the Women's Lunatic Asylum on Blackwell's Island. Her method: get herself declared mad and committed to the asylum. After practicing the look of a disheveled lunatic in front of mirrors, wandering city streets dazed and unwashed, and terrifying her fellow boarders in a New York rooming house by acting crazy, she succeeded in convincing doctors and officials to commit her. Other New York newspapers even reported her incarceration, speculating on the identity of this "mysterious waif," this "pretty crazy girl" with the "wild, hunted look in her eyes."[1]

Ten days later, an attorney from the *World* went in to get her out. Her two-part story appeared in October 1887 and caused a sensation in New York. She was the first reporter to have pulled off such a stunt. In the days before so-called objective journalism, Nellie Bly's dramatic first-person accounts documented harsh cold baths ("three buckets of water over my head—ice cold water—into my eyes, my ears, my nose and my mouth"); "cruel" attendants who abused and taunted patients; and newly arrived immigrant women, completely sane, who were committed to this "rat trap" simply because no one could understand them. After the series, Bly was famous. Pulitzer gave her a permanent job, and the city of New York committed $1 million toward upgrading asylum conditions.

Within a year, Nellie Bly exposed a variety of shady scam artists, corrupt politicians and lobbyists, and unscrupulous business practices. Posing as an unwed mother with an unwanted child, she uncovered an outfit trafficking in newborn babies. Disguised as a sinner in need of reform, she revealed the appalling conditions at a home for "unfortunate women." And after stealing $50 from another woman's purse, she got herself arrested and reported on how women were treated in New York jails.

A lifetime champion of women and the poor, Nellie Bly also pioneered what was called at the time *detective* or *stunt* journalism. Her work would inspire the whole twentieth-century practice of investigative journalism—from Ida Tarbell's exposés of oil corporations in the early 1900s to the award-winning *Wall Street Journal* investigations of big tobacco companies in the mid-1990s. From the vantage point of both the press and the public, this investigative tradition remains one of journalism's most revered contributions to democracy.

Along with their watchdog role, newspapers serve other key functions in American culture. As chroniclers of daily life, newspapers both inform and entertain. They give assurances that communities are safe and nations are secure. Newspapers also help readers make choices about everything from the kind of food to eat to the kind of leaders to vote for. Comic strips find humor in everyday events. Opinion pages organize public debates and persuade readers to a point of view. Syndicated columnists offer everything from practical advice to political insight.

Despite the importance of newspapers in daily life, in today's digital age the industry is losing both papers and readers at an alarming rate. Newspapers still garner a substantial portion of the nation's advertising dollars. But the loss of papers and readers raises significant concerns in a nation where newspapers have historically functioned to watch over democratic life. To provide some background for the current declines, we will trace the history of newspapers through a number of influential periods and styles. We explore the eras of the early political-commercial press, the penny press, and yellow journalism. Turning to contemporary newspapers, we will examine the influence of the *New York Times* and modern journalism's embrace of objectivity. During this era, interpretive journalism emerged in the 1920s and 1930s to improve news practices; the revival of literary journalism followed in the 1960s. We will also look at the evolution of contemporary newspapers and different ways to categorize them. Finally, we will review issues in chain ownership, new technology, and the role of newspapers in democracy.

"There's almost no media experience sweeter . . . than poring over a good newspaper. In the quiet morning, with a cup of coffee—so long as you haven't turned on the TV, listened to the radio, or checked in online—it's as **comfortable and personal** as information gets."
—Jon Katz,
Wired magazine,
1994

the evolution of american newspapers

The idea of news is as old as language itself. The earliest news was passed along orally from family to family, from tribe to tribe, by community leaders and oral historians. The first written news accounts, or *news sheets*, were probably posted items distributed by local rulers and governments. The earliest known news sheet, *Acta Diurna* (Latin for *daily events*) was developed by Julius Caesar and posted in Rome in 59 B.C. Even in its oral and early written stages, news informed people on the state of their relations with neighboring tribes and towns. The development of the printing press in the fifteenth century greatly accelerated a society's ability to send and receive information. Throughout history, news has satisfied our need to know things we cannot experience personally. Newspapers today continue to document daily life and bear witness to ordinary and extraordinary events.

colonial newspapers and the partisan press

The first newspaper produced in North America was *Publick Occurrences, Both Foreign and Domestick*, published on September 25, 1690, by Boston printer Benjamin Harris. The colonial government objected to Harris's negative tone regarding British rule, and local ministers were offended by a report that the king of France had an affair with his son's wife. Consequently, the newspaper was banned after one issue.

In 1704, the first regularly published newspaper appeared in the American colonies—the *Boston News-Letter*, published by John Campbell. Considered dull, it reported on mundane events that had taken place in Europe months earlier. Because European news took weeks or months to travel by ship, these early colonial papers were not very timely. In their more spirited sections, however, the papers did report local illnesses, public floggings, and even suicides. In 1721, also in Boston, James Franklin, the older brother of Benjamin Franklin, started the *New England Courant*. The *Courant* established a tradition of running stories that interested ordinary readers rather than printing articles that appealed primarily to business and colonial leaders. In 1729, Benjamin Franklin, at age twenty-four, took over the *Pennsylvania Gazette*, which historians rate among the best of the colonial papers. Although a number of colonial papers operated solely on subsidies from political parties, the *Gazette* also made money by advertising products; with a few thousand readers, it had the highest circulation of the time.

Another important colonial paper was the *New York Weekly Journal*, which appeared in 1733. John Peter Zenger had been installed as the printer of the *Journal* by the Popular party, a political group that opposed British rule and ran articles that criticized the royal governor of New York. After a Popular party judge was dismissed from office, the *Journal* escalated its attack on the governor. When Zenger shielded the writers of the critical articles, he was arrested in 1734 for *seditious libel*—defaming a public official's character in print. Championed by famed Philadelphia lawyer Andrew Hamilton, Zenger ultimately won his case in 1735. A sympathetic jury, in

> "**Oral news systems** must have arrived early in the development of language, some tens or even hundreds of thousands of years ago. . . . And the dissemination of news accomplishes some of the basic purposes of language: informing others, entertaining others, **protecting the tribe.**"
>
> —Mitchell Stephens,
> *A History of News*,
> 1988

The *New-England Courant* was founded in 1721 as Boston's fourth newspaper by James Franklin, older brother of Benjamin Franklin. In a time before photography, the elaborate biblical-style engraving, used on this 1722 front page to surround the letter H, helped enhance the dull grayness of printed copy.

revolt against the colonial government, ruled that newspapers had the right to criticize government leaders as long as the reports were true. After the Zenger case, the British never prosecuted another colonial printer. Although the case did not substantially change sedition laws at the time, the Zenger decision would later provide a key foundation for the First Amendment to the Constitution—the right of a democratic press to criticize public officials.

By 1765, about thirty newspapers operated in the American colonies. The first *daily* paper began in 1784. These papers were of two general types: political or commercial. The development of both types was shaped in large part by social, cultural, and political responses to British rule and by its eventual overthrow. The rise of political parties and the spread of commerce also played a significant role in the development of these early papers. Although the political and commercial papers carried both party news and business news, they had different agendas. The political or **partisan press** generally argued one point of view or pushed the plan of the particular party that subsidized the paper. The more commercial press, on the other hand, served the leaders of commerce, who were interested in economic issues such as ship cargoes from Europe.

From the early 1700s to the early 1800s, even the largest of these papers rarely reached a circulation of fifteen hundred. Readership was confined primarily to educated or wealthy men who controlled local politics and commerce. During this time, though, a few pioneering women operated newspapers, including Elizabeth Timothy, the first American woman newspaper publisher. After her husband died of smallpox in 1738, Timothy took over the *South Carolina Gazette*, established in 1734 by Benjamin Franklin and the Timothy family, which included her eight children. Also during this period, Anna Maul Zenger ran the *New York Journal* throughout her husband's trial and after his death in 1746.[2] In general, though, the interests of women readers were not well addressed by either the political or commercial press. By the 1830s, however, the Industrial Revolution and the rise of the middle classes spurred the growth of literacy and set the stage for a more popular and inclusive press.

the penny press era

By the late 1820s, the average newspaper cost six cents a copy and was sold not through street sales but through annual subscriptions priced at $10 to $12. Because that price represented more than a week's salary for most skilled workers, newspaper readership favored the affluent. The Industrial Revolution spawned the conversion from expensive handmade to inexpensive machine-made paper. And when cheaper paper combined with increased literacy, *penny papers* soon began competing with conventional six-cent papers. In the 1820s, breakthroughs in technology, particularly steam-powered presses replacing mechanical presses, permitted publishers to produce as many as four thousand newspapers an hour. Subscriptions remained the preferred sales tool of many penny papers, although they began relying increasingly on street vendors.

In 1833, printer Benjamin Day founded the *New York Sun*. After cutting the price to one penny, he also eliminated subscriptions. The *Sun* (whose slogan was "It shines for all") highlighted local events, scandals, and police reports. It also ran serialized stories, making legends of frontiersmen Davy Crockett and Daniel Boone and blazing the trail for the media's twentieth-century enthusiasm for celebrity news. In the tradition of today's tabloids, the *Sun* fabricated stories, including the famous moon hoax, which reported "scientific" evidence of life on the moon. Within six months, the *Sun*'s lower price had generated a circulation of eight thousand, twice that of its nearest competitor.

The *Sun*'s success initiated a wave of penny papers that favored **human interest stories**: news accounts that focus on the trials and tribulations of the human condition, often featuring ordinary individuals facing extraordinary challenges. These kinds of stories show journalism's ties to literary traditions (which can now be found in the horror or gangster news-story genres of urban drug and crime coverage).

The penny press era also featured James Gordon Bennett's *New York Morning Herald*, founded in 1835. Bennett, considered the first press baron, aimed to free his newspaper from political parties. He wanted to establish an independent paper serving middle- and working-class readers as well as his own business ambitions. The *Herald* concentrated on crime reports, human interest, moral reflections, political scandals, fashion notes, and colloquial tales and jokes. By 1860, it reached nearly eighty thousand readers, making it the world's largest daily paper at the time.

Newsboys and newsgirls sold Hearst and Pulitzer papers on the streets of New York in the 1890s. With more than a dozen daily papers competing, street tactics were ferocious, and publishers often made "newsies," many of them under 12, buy those papers they could not sell.

The penny papers were innovative. They were the first to assign reporters to cover crime. In New York, where the penny press competition was fierce, readers enthusiastically embraced the reporting of local news and crime. Although the *Herald* carried political essays and business stories, it also included a letters section, religious news, play reviews, society news, sports stories, and later, reports from dozens of correspondents sent to cover the Civil War. In an era before modern "objective" journalism, Bennett's paper sponsored yacht and balloon races, financed safaris, and overplayed crime and sex stories. After his first visit to America in the early 1840s, British writer Charles Dickens used the *Herald* as a model for the sleazy *Rowdy Journal*, the fictional newspaper in his novel *Martin Chuzzlewit*.

By gradually separating daily reporting from overt political viewpoints, New York's penny papers shifted their economic base from political party subsidies to the market—to advertising revenue, classified ads, and street sales. Although many partisan papers took moral stands against advertising certain questionable products, the penny press became more neutral toward advertisers and printed virtually any ad. In fact, many penny papers regarded ads as a kind of consumer news. The rise in ad revenues and circulation accelerated the growth of the newspaper industry. In 1830, 650 weekly and 65 daily papers operated in the United States, reaching eighty thousand readers. By 1840, a total of 1,140 weeklies and 140 dailies attracted three hundred thousand readers.

In 1848, six New York newspapers in a cooperative arrangement founded the Associated Press (AP), the first major news wire service. **Wire services** began as commercial organizations that relayed news stories and information around the country and the world using telegraph lines (and eventually radio waves and satellite transmissions). In the case of AP, the New York papers provided access to both their own stories and those from other newspapers. In the 1850s, papers started sending reporters to cover Washington, and in the early 1860s more than a hundred reporters from northern papers went south to cover the Civil War, relaying their reports back to their home papers via telegraph and wire services. The news-wire companies permitted news to travel rapidly from coast to coast and set the stage for modern journalism.

The combination of marketing news as a national and global product and using modern technology to dramatically cut costs made newspapers into a mass medium. By also adapting news content, penny papers captured the middle- and working-class readers who could now afford the paper and also had more leisure time to read it. For newspapers to sustain their mass appeal, news and "factual" reports about crimes and other items of human interest gradually superseded partisan articles about politics and commerce.

the age of yellow journalism

The rise of competitive dailies and the penny press spawned the next significant period in American journalism. Labeled the era of **yellow journalism**, this late 1800s development emphasized profitable papers that carried exciting human interest stories, crime news, large headlines, and more readable copy. This period is generally regarded as the age of sensationalism, the direct forerunner of today's tabloid papers and TV shows. The era of yellow journalism featured two major characteristics. First were the stories about crimes, disasters, scandals, and intrigue. The second, and sometimes forgotten, legacy is that the yellow press provided the roots for investigative journalism: news reports that hunted out and exposed corruption, particularly in business and government. Reporting was viewed as a crusading force for common people, with the press assuming a watchdog role on behalf of the public.

During this period, a newspaper circulation war pitted William Randolph Hearst's *New York Journal* against Joseph Pulitzer's *New York World*. A key player in the war was the first popular cartoon strip, "The Yellow Kid," created by artist R. F. Outcault in 1895. The phrase *yellow journalism* has since become associated with the cartoon strip, which shuttled between the Hearst and Pulitzer papers during their furious battle for readers in the mid-1890s.

> "There is room in this **great and growing city** for a journal that is not only cheap but bright, not only bright but large . . . that will expose all **fraud and sham**, fight all public evils and abuses—that will serve and battle for the people."
>
> —Joseph Pulitzer, publisher, *New York World*, 1883

Pulitzer and the *New York World*. After a brief career in St. Louis politics, Joseph Pulitzer, a Jewish-Hungarian immigrant, became part owner of the *St. Louis Post* newspaper in the early 1870s. He bought the bankrupt *St. Louis Dispatch* for $2,500 at an auction in 1878 and merged it with the *Post*. The *Post-Dispatch* became known for stories that promoted "sex and sin" ("A Denver Maiden Taken from Disreputable House") and satires of the upper class ("St. Louis Swells"). Pulitzer also viewed the *Post-Dispatch* as a "national conscience" that promoted the public good. Pulitzer carried on the legacies of Bennett: making money and developing a "free and impartial" paper that would "serve no party but the people." Within five years, the *Post-Dispatch* became one of the most influential newspapers in the Midwest.

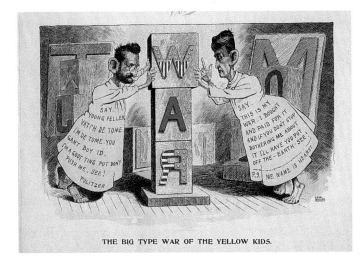

THE BIG TYPE WAR OF THE YELLOW KIDS.

Generally considered America's first comic-strip character, the Yellow Kid was created in the mid-1890s by cartoonist Richard Outcault. The cartoon was so popular that newspaper barons Joseph Pulitzer and William Randolph Hearst fought over Outcault's services, giving yellow journalism its name. A New York street urchin, the Kid became a merchandising marvel, with his image plastered on everything from cracker tins to cigarette packs.

In 1883, Pulitzer bought the *New York World* for $346,000. He encouraged plain writing and the inclusion of maps and illustrations to help immigrant and working-class readers. In addition to running sensational stories on crime, sex, and cannibalism, Pulitzer instituted advice columns and women's pages. Like Bennett, Pulitzer treated advertising as a kind of news that displayed consumer products for readers. Department stores became a major advertising source during this period. The revenue from these stores contributed directly to the expansion of consumer culture and indirectly to the acknowledgment of women as newspaper readers and their eventual employment as reporters.

The *World* reflected the contradictory spirit of the yellow press. It crusaded for improved urban housing, better conditions for women, and equitable labor laws. It campaigned against monopoly practices by AT&T, Standard Oil, and Equitable Insurance. Such popular crusades helped lay the groundwork for tightening federal antitrust laws in the early 1910s. At the same time, Pulitzer's paper manufactured news events and staged stunts, such as sending star reporter Nellie Bly around the world in seventy-two days to beat the fictional record in the popular 1873 Jules Verne novel, *Around the World in Eighty Days*. But in the spirit of contradiction, Pulitzer was also a ruthless businessman, once trying to break a strike by the *World's* newsboys and newsgirls (who believed they should not have to pay Pulitzer for papers they did not sell).

Hearst and the *New York Journal*. By 1887, the *World's* Sunday circulation had soared to more than 250,000, the largest in the world. Eight years later, however, the paper faced its fiercest competition when William Randolph Hearst bought the *New York Journal*. Before moving to New York, Hearst had taken the reins of the *San Francisco Examiner* from his father, George Hearst, who had purchased the paper to further a political career. In 1887, when George was elected to the U.S. Senate, he turned the paper over to his son, who at age twenty-four had recently been expelled from Harvard for a practical joke he played on his professors. With an inheritance from his father, the son in 1895 bought the ailing *New York Journal* (a penny paper founded by Pulitzer's brother Albert) and then raided Joseph Pulitzer's paper for editors, writers, and cartoonists.

Learning from Bennett and Pulitzer, Hearst focused on lurid, sensational stories and appealed (and pandered) to immigrant readers by using large headlines and bold

219

layout designs. To boost circulation, the *Journal* invented interviews, faked pictures, and encouraged conflicts that might result in a story. One account of Hearst's tabloid legacy describes "tales about two-headed virgins" and "prehistoric creatures roaming the plains of Wyoming."[3] In promoting journalism as storytelling, Hearst reportedly said, "the modern editor of the popular journal does not care for facts. The editor wants novelty. The editor has no objection to facts if they are also novel. But he would prefer a novelty that is not a fact to a fact that is not a novelty."[4]

Hearst is remembered as an unscrupulous publisher who once hired gangsters to distribute his newspapers. He was also, however, considered a champion of the underdog, and his paper's readership soared among the working and middle classes. In 1896, the *Journal*'s daily circulation reached 450,000, and by 1897, the Sunday edition of the *Journal* rivaled the 600,000 circulation of the *World*. By the 1930s, Hearst's holdings included more than forty daily and Sunday papers, thirteen magazines (including *Good Housekeeping* and *Cosmopolitan*), eight radio stations, and two film companies. In addition, he controlled King Feature Syndicate, which sold and distributed articles, comics, and features to many of the nation's twenty-five hundred dailies. Hearst, the model for Charles Foster Kane, the ruthless and lonely publisher in Orson Welles' classic 1940 film, *Citizen Kane*, operated the largest media business in the world—the Time Warner of its day.

american print journalism in the modern period

Although objectivity is considered a modern journalistic idea, the early commercial and partisan press was, to some extent, covering important events impartially. These papers often carried verbatim reports of presidential addresses, murder trials, or the annual statements of the U.S. Treasury. In the late 1800s, this journalistic ideal was overshadowed as newspapers pushed for circulation and emphasized sensational news, especially in New York. By the late 1890s, two distinct types of journalism competed for readers: a *story* model, supported by the penny and the yellow press, which emphasized dramatizing important events, and an *information* model, advocated by the six-cent papers, which emphasized a more factual approach.[5]

the advent of modern journalism

As the consumer marketplace expanded during the Industrial Revolution, facts and news became marketable products that could be sold to consumers. The more a newspaper appeared not to take sides, the more its readership base could be extended. In addition, wire-service organizations were serving a variety of newspaper clients in different regions of the country. To satisfy all their clients and the wide range of political views, news had to at least look more impartial.

Ochs and the *New York Times*. The ideal of an impartial or informational news model was reinvented by Adolph Ochs, who bought the *New York Times* in 1896. The son of immigrant German Jews, Ochs grew up in Ohio and Tennessee, where at age twenty-one he took over the *Chattanooga Times* in 1878. Known more for his business and organizational ability than for his writing and editing skills, he transformed the Tennessee paper. Ochs then moved to New York and invested $75,000 in the struggling *Times*. Through wise hiring, Ochs's staff of editors rebuilt the paper around substantial news coverage and provocative editorial pages. To distance themselves from the yellow press, the editors also downplayed entertainment news and sensational features, favoring the documentation of major events or issues.

Such distancing was partly a marketing strategy to counter the large circulations of the Hearst and Pulitzer papers. Ochs offered a distinct contrast to the more sensational newspapers: an *informational* paper that offered stock and real-estate reports to businesses, court reports to legal professionals, treaty summaries to political leaders, and theater reviews to intellectuals. Ochs's promotional gimmicks took direct aim at yellow journalism, advertising the *Times* under the motto, "It does not soil the breakfast cloth." The strategy of the *Times* was similar to many TV marketing plans today, which target upscale viewers who control a disproportionate share of consumer dollars.

With the Hearst and Pulitzer papers capturing the bulk of working- and middle-class readers, managers at the *Times* at first associated their straightforward reporting with people of higher social status. In 1898, however, Ochs lowered the paper's price to a penny. His thinking was that people bought the *World* and *Journal* primarily because they were cheap, not because of their storytelling. As a result, the *Times* began attracting more middle-class readers who gravitated to the paper as a status marker for the educated and well informed. Between 1898 and 1899, its circulation rose from 25,000 to 75,000. By 1921, the *New York Times* had a daily circulation of 330,000 and 500,000 on Sunday. (For contemporary circulation figures, see Table 8.1.)

"**Just the facts, please**." At the dawn of the twentieth century, with reporters adopting a more scientific attitude to news- and fact-gathering, the ideal of objectivity began anchoring journalism. In **objective journalism**, which distinguishes factual reports from opinion columns, modern reporters strive to maintain a neutral attitude toward the issue or event they cover; they also search out competing points of view among the sources for a story. This kind of reporting is often distinguished by the **inverted pyramid style** (see Figure 8.1). War correspondents developed this style by imitating the terse, compact press releases that came from Lincoln's secretary of war, Edwin M. Stanton, during the Civil War.[6] Often stripped of adverbs and adjectives, inverted pyramid reports began with the most dramatic or newsworthy information.

TABLE 8.1
The Nation's Largest Daily Newspapers

Newspaper	1996 Circulation*
Wall Street Journal	1,783,532
USA Today[+]	1,591,629
New York Times	1,071,120
Los Angeles Times	1,029,073
Washington Post	789,198
Daily News (New York)	734,277
Chicago Tribune	680,535
Newsday	564,754
Houston Chronicle	545,348
Chicago Sun-Times	496,030
San Francisco Chronicle	486,977
Dallas Morning News[+]	478,181
Boston Globe	471,024

*Average weekday circulation at the nation's largest newspapers, for the six months ending September 30, 1996.
[+]Fridays excluded.
Source: Audit Bureau of Circulations, Schaumburg, IL.

They answered *who, what, where, when* (and less frequently *why* or *how*) questions at the top of the story and then tailed off with less-significant details. If wars or natural disasters disrupted the telegraph transmissions of these dispatches, the information the reporter chose to lead the story often had the best chance of getting through.

For most of this century, the inverted pyramid style has served as an efficient way to arrange a timely story. As one news critic points out, the wire services that used the inverted pyramid style when distributing stories to newspapers nationwide "had to deal with large numbers of newspapers with widely different political and regional interests. The news had to be 'objective' . . . to be accepted by such a heterogeneous group."[7] Among other things, the importance of objectivity and the reliance on the inverted pyramid signaled journalism's break from the partisan tradition. Although difficult to achieve, the notion of objectivity nonetheless became (and in many ways remains) the guiding ideal of the modern press.

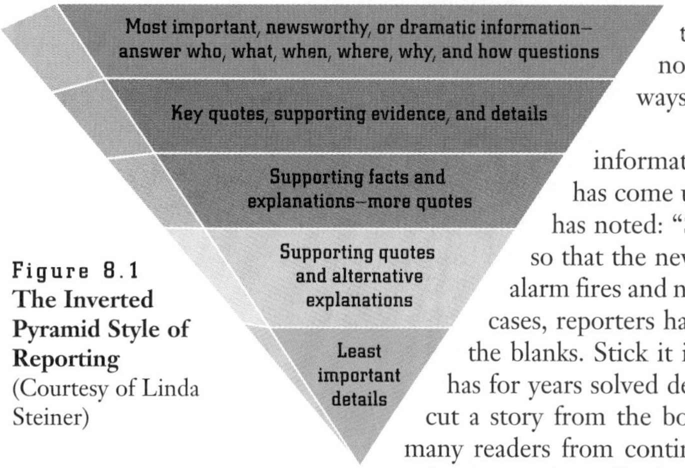
Most important, newsworthy, or dramatic information–answer who, what, when, where, why, and how questions
Key quotes, supporting evidence, and details
Supporting facts and explanations–more quotes
Supporting quotes and alternative explanations
Least important details

Figure 8.1 The Inverted Pyramid Style of Reporting (Courtesy of Linda Steiner)

Despite the success of the *New York Times* and other informational papers, the more factual approach toward news has come under increasing scrutiny. As one newswriting coach has noted: "Some reporters let the pyramid control the content so that the news comes out homogenized. Traffic fatalities, three-alarm fires and new city ordinances all begin to look alike. In extreme cases, reporters have been known to keep files of story forms. Fill in the blanks. Stick it in the paper."[8] Although the inverted pyramid style has for years solved deadline problems for reporters and allows editors to cut a story from the bottom to fit available space, it also has discouraged many readers from continuing beyond the key details in the opening paragraphs. Research studies have demonstrated that the majority of readers do not follow a front-page story when it continues or "jumps" inside the paper.

By the 1920s, the *New York Times* had established itself as the official *paper of record*, the standard that other newspapers emulated and that libraries throughout the country stocked to document important daily occurrences. Filled with the texts of treaties, court reports, political speeches, and other national documents, the *Times* became more than a powerful alternative to the storytelling of earlier papers; it became the official way to do journalism in the 1900s. The modern reporter became, ideally, a detached observer who gathered information and adapted it to the wire-service formula.

interpretive journalism

By the 1920s, the information model of reporting had become the standard for most mainstream journalism. There was still a sense, however, especially after the trauma of World War I, that the impartial approach to reporting was insufficient in explaining complex national and global conditions. Partly as a result of "drab, factual, objective reporting," one news scholar contended, "the American people were utterly amazed when war broke out in August 1914, as they had no understanding of the foreign scene to prepare them for it."[9]

The Limits of Objectivity. Modern journalism had undermined an early role of the partisan press—that of offering analysis and opinion. But with the world becoming more complex in the modern age, some papers started reexploring the analytical function of news. The result was the rise of **interpretive journalism**, which tries to explain key issues or events and to place them in a broader historical or social context. According to one historian, this approach, especially in the 1930s and 1940s, was a viable way for journalism to address "the New Deal years, the rise of modern scientific technology, the increasing interdependence of economic groups at home, and the shrinking of the world into one vast arena for power politics."[10] In other words, journalism took an analytic turn in a world grown more interconnected and complicated.

Noting that objectivity and factuality *should* serve as the foundation for journalism, editor and columnist Walter Lippmann by the 1920s thought the press should do more. He ranked three press responsibilities: (1) "to make a current record," (2) "to make a running analysis of it," and (3) "on the basis of both, to suggest plans."[11] Reporters and readers alike have historically distinguished between informational reports and editorials or interpretive pieces that offer particular viewpoints or deeper analyses of the issues. The boundary between information and interpretation can be somewhat ambiguous. Thus, American papers traditionally have placed news analysis in separate columns and opinion articles on certain pages so that readers do not confuse them with "straight news."

In the 1930s, the extended Depression and the Nazi threat to global stability helped news analysis take root in newsmagazines and radio commentary. Editorial pages also made a strong comeback. More significant, however, was the growth of the political column. Although literary and humor columns existed prior to World War I, the political column was a new form. More than 150 syndicated columns developed between 1930 and 1934 alone. Moving beyond the informational and storytelling functions of news, journalists and newspapers began to extend their role as analysts.

The Press-Radio War. In the 1930s, with the rise of radio, the newspaper industry became increasingly annoyed by broadcasters who took their news directly from papers and wire services. As a result, a major battle developed between radio journalism and the established power of print. Mainstream newspapers attempted to copyright facts reported in the news and even sued radio stations, which routinely used newspapers as their main sources (a common practice today). Editors and newspaper lobbyists argued that radio should only be permitted to do commentary. By conceding to radio this interpretive role, the print press temporarily protected its dominion over "the facts." It was amid the press-radio war that radio analysis began to flourish as a form of interpretive news. Lowell Thomas delivered the first daily network analysis for CBS on September 29, 1930, and attacked Hitler's rise to power in Germany. By 1941, twenty regular network commentators explained the world to millions of listeners.

In the 1930s, many print journalists and some editors believed that interpretive stories, rather than objective reports, could better compete with radio. They realized that interpretation was a way to counter radio's (and later television's) superior ability to report breaking news quickly. In 1933, the American Society of Newspaper Editors (ASNE) supported the idea of interpretive journalism, resolving to "devote a larger amount of attention and space to analytical and interpretative news and to presenting a background of information which will enable the average reader more adequately to understand the movement and the significance of events."[12]

Newspapers, however, did not fill their front pages with probing analysis during the 1930s. Even Walter Lippmann believed that news commentary and interpretation were misdirected without the foundation of facts and a "current record." As he put it, "the really important thing is to try and make opinion increasingly responsible to the facts."[13] Still, by the early 1930s, the ideals of objectivity and impartiality had shifted.

In Europe, interpretive news and partisan papers have long been the norm, but in American dailies explicit interpretation remains relegated to the two editorial and opinion pages in most papers. After World War II, interpretive journalism diminished substantially. It wasn't until the 1950s—with the Korean War, the development of atomic power, tensions with the Soviet Union, and the anticommunist movement—that reporting as analysis resurfaced in a new form on television. Interpretive journalism in newspapers grew at the same time, especially in such areas as the environment, science, agriculture, sports, and business. Today, stories favoring analysis over description frequently find their way onto most front pages, but the interpretive approach has not gained equal footing with the information model.

literary forms of journalism

By the late 1960s, many people were criticizing America's major social institutions. Political assassinations, civil rights protests, the Vietnam War, the drug culture, and the women's movement were not easily explained. Faced with so many unusual situations, many individuals began to lose faith in the ability of institutions to oversee and direct the social order. Members of protest movements as well as many middle Americans began to suspect the privileges and power of traditional authority. As a result, key institutions—including journalism—lost much of the credibility they had previously commanded.

The Attack on Objectivity. Columnist Tom Wicker has argued that in the early 1960s an objective approach to news remained the dominant model. According to Wicker, the "press had so wrapped itself in the paper chains of 'objective journalism' that it had little ability to report anything beyond the bare and undeniable facts."[14]

Throughout the 1960s, attacks on the detachment of reporters escalated. News critic Jack Newfield even indicted journalistic impartiality as "a figleaf for covert prejudice": "Objectivity is believing people with power and printing their press releases. Objectivity is not shouting 'liar' in a crowded country."[15] As a result, the authority of experts and professionals in a variety of fields became suspect along with the ideal of objectivity.

A number of reporters in the late 1960s responded to the criticism by rethinking the framework of conventional journalism. To improve on the older approach, they adapted a variety of alternative techniques. One of these was *advocacy journalism*, an approach in which the reporter actively promotes a particular cause or viewpoint. Following this approach, some women reporters displayed feminist points of view in their writing; they argued

> "Stop them damn pictures! I don't care so much what papers write about me. **My constituents can't read.** But, damn it, they can see pictures!"
>
> —Boss Tweed

An early example of interpretive journalism, political cartoons began appearing in newspapers after the Civil War. Thomas Nast (*see above*), the first prominent editorial cartoonist, combined his artistic and satiric skills to skewer corrupt politicians like New York's William "Boss" Tweed.

that merely recording events in a neutral way failed to confront the unequal arrangements of jobs and power in many institutions. *Precision journalism*, another technique, attempted to push news more in the direction of science. Precision journalists argued that only by applying rigorous social science methods, such as using poll surveys and questionnaires, could they achieve a valid portrait of social reality.

Journalism as Art. Throughout the modern period, the story dimension of news reports was hidden by such conventions as the inverted pyramid and the separation of fact from opinion. Dissatisfied with these approaches, some reporters began reexploring journalism's ties to storytelling. This model of reporting, **literary journalism**—sometimes dubbed *new journalism*—adapted so-called fictional storytelling techniques to nonfictional material and in-depth reporting. In the United States, literary journalism's roots are evident in novelists such as Mark Twain, Stephen Crane, and Theodore Dreiser, who all started out as reporters in the nineteenth century. In the late 1930s and 1940s, new journalism surfaced in literary reports: Journalists began to demonstrate how writing about real events could achieve an artistry often associated only with good fiction.

> "Critics [in the 1960s] claimed that urban planning created slums, **that school made people stupid,** that medicine caused disease, that psychiatry invented mental illness, and that the courts promoted injustice. . . . And objectivity in journalism, regarded as an antidote to bias, came to be looked upon as the most insidious bias of all. For 'objective' reporting reproduced a **vision of social reality** which refused to examine the basic structures of power and privilege."
>
> —Michael Schudson, *Discovering the News*, 1978

A leading proponent and practitioner of literary journalism, Tom Wolfe, saw it mixing the *content* of reporting with the *form* of fiction to create "both the kind of objective reality of journalism" and "the subjective reality" of the novel.[16] Writers such as Wolfe, Truman Capote (*In Cold Blood*), Joan Didion (*Slouching toward Bethlehem*), and Norman Mailer (*Miami and the Siege of Chicago*) turned to literary journalism in the 1960s in an attempt to overcome the weaknesses they perceived in routine reporting. Their often self-conscious treatment of social problems gave their writing a perspective that conventional journalism did not offer.

According to critics, the dilemmas of the sixties demanded a new journalistic form that could deal more effectively with social contradictions. After the tide of intense social upheaval ebbed, however, the new journalism subsided as well. In retrospect, literary reporting has often been criticized for being influenced by television or for blurring the lines between fact and fiction. Nevertheless, the legacy of literary journalism continues. It not only influenced magazines like *Mother Jones* and *Rolling Stone*, but it affected the lifestyle and sports sections of most daily newspapers. In virtually every daily paper, we see longer feature stories on cultural trends and social issues. Many such stories can be attributed to the impact of literary journalism.

contemporary journalism

If the seeds of modern journalism were sown by Adolph Ochs and the *New York Times* in the late 1890s, a postmodern brand of journalism arose from two developments in the early 1980s. First was the electronic newspaper. In 1980, the *Columbus Dispatch* became the first paper to go online and transmit its pages via computers and cable channels. By the mid-1990s, more than two hundred American newspapers were offering some kind of computerized news service. Second, the arrival of the colorful *USA Today* in 1982 radically changed the look of most major U.S. dailies. This new paper incorporated features closely associated with postmodern style, including an emphasis on surface slickness over substantive news and the use of brief news items that appeal to readers' short attention spans. *USA Today* represents the only success-

The colorful national newspaper *USA Today* created a splash when it first appeared in 1982. Founded by the powerful Gannett chain, *USA Today* lost money every year until 1993. Today, the circulation of its Monday through Thursday editions is second only to that of the *Wall Street Journal*, and its Friday edition is the most widely circulated daily paper in the United States.

ful launch of a new major U.S. daily newspaper in the last several decades. A sign of its marketing savvy, *USA Today* was the first paper to pay tribute to network TV's central role in mass culture: The paper designed its vending boxes to look like color TV sets, and it appealed to a national rather than a local or regional audience.

Writing for *Rolling Stone* in March 1992, media critic Jon Katz argued that the authority of modern newspapers was being usurped by a variety of "new news" forms that combined information, entertainment, persuasion, and analysis. Katz claimed that the news authority of most prominent daily papers, such as the *New York Times* and the *Washington Post*, was being challenged by "news" coming from talk shows, television sitcoms, popular films, and even rap music. In other words, we were passing from a society in which the transmission of knowledge depended mainly on books, newspapers, and magazines to a society dominated by a mix of print, visual, electronic, and digital information. In the process, the new forms of news have been taking over the roles of traditional journalism, setting the nation's cultural, social, and political agendas.

Today a fundamental tension exists between print and electronic conceptions of news. With news reading habits among young people in decline, TV magazine programs, talk shows, sitcoms, movies, and popular music are sparking public conversation more often than are traditional newspapers. Add to this the speed at which personal computers can now transmit data. As Jon Katz wrote in *Wired*, "When in January 1994 a RadioMail subscriber used his wireless modem to flash news of the LA earthquake to the Net well before CNN or the Associated Press could report it, a new news medium was born."[17] With radio, television, film, music, and the Internet all competing with newspapers, their traditional roles are being seriously challenged and changed.

categorizing news and u.s. newspapers

Part of the reason for newspapers' decline in the United States stems from the industry's slow response to the electronic and digital revolutions. Yet in spite of this, newspapers have not been abandoned. The nation's fifteen hundred daily papers still reach more than sixty-two million readers each day. This is down from twenty-six hundred dailies in 1910, the highwater mark for daily newspapers in the United States.

In the news industry today, there are several kinds of papers. *National newspapers* (such as the *Wall Street Journal*, the *New York Times*, the *Christian Science Monitor*, and *USA Today*) serve a broad readership across the country. Other papers primarily serve specific geographic regions. Roughly 120 *metropolitan dailies* have circulations of 100,000 or more. About 40 of these papers had circulations of more than 250,000 by the mid-1990s. Most daily newspapers, however, are either medium dailies (50,000 to 100,000 in circulation) or small dailies (under 50,000 in circulation). While dailies serve urban and suburban centers, more than 8,000 nondaily and *weekly newspapers* (down from 14,000 in 1910) serve small towns and communities.

consensus vs. conflict

Smaller nondaily papers tend to play a consensus role in communities, promoting social and economic harmony. Besides providing community calendars and meeting notices, **consensus-oriented papers** carry articles on local schools, social events, town government, property crimes, and zoning issues. Recalling the partisan spirit of an earlier era, small newspapers are often owned by business leaders who occasionally serve in local politics. Because consensus-oriented papers have a small advertising base, they are generally careful not to offend local advertisers, who provide the financial underpinnings for many of these papers.

In contrast, national and metro dailies practice **conflict-oriented journalism** in which news is defined primarily as events, issues, or experiences that deviate from social norms. Under this news orientation, journalists see their role not merely as neutral fact-gatherers but as observers who monitor their city's institutions and problems. These papers offer rival perspectives on issues such as education, government, poverty, crime, and the economy. It would be considered unethical, a conflict of interest, for publishers, editors, or reporters on these papers to play a major role in community politics. In theory, modern newspapers believe their role in large cities is to keep a wary but impartial eye fixed on local and state intrigue and events.

In telling stories about complex and controversial topics, journalists under the conflict model often turn such topics into two-dimensional stories, pitting one idea or person against another. This convention, often called "telling both sides of a story," allows a reporter to take the position of a detached observer. Although this convention offers the appearance of balance, it usually functions to generate conflict and sustain a good news story; and sometimes reporters ignore the fact that there may be *more* than two sides to a story.

ethnic, minority, and oppositional newspapers

Historically, small-town weeklies and daily newspapers have served predominantly white mainstream readers. Exceptions to this include the various minority, foreign-language, and alternative papers, which have played a prominent role for Mexican and Cuban immigrants, Korean Americans, disabled veterans, retired workers, the gay and lesbian communities, and the homeless. Most of these weekly and monthly newspapers serve some of the same functions for their constituencies as the "majority" papers. Minority papers, however, are often published outside the social mainstream. Consequently, they provide viewpoints that are different from the mostly middle- and upper-class white attitudes that have shaped the media throughout much of America's history.

The Immigrant and Ethnic Press. Since Benjamin Franklin launched the short-lived German-language *Philadelphische Zeitung* in 1732, newspapers aimed at ethnic groups have played a major role in initiating immigrants into American society. During the nineteenth century, Swedish- and Norwegian-language papers informed various immigrant communities in the Midwest. The early twentieth century gave rise to papers written in German, Yiddish, Russian, and Polish, which assisted the massive influx of European immigrants. In the 1980s, hundreds of small papers developed to serve immigrants from Cuba, Haiti, Pakistan, Laos, Cambodia, and China. More than sixty small U.S. papers are now printed in Vietnamese. By the 1990s, several hundred foreign-language daily and non-daily presses existed in at least forty different languages. These papers help readers both adjust to foreign surroundings and retain ties to their traditional heritage. Many are financially healthy today, supported by classified ads, local businesses, and increased ad revenue from long-distance phone companies, who see the ethnic press as an ideal place to reach those customers most likely to use international phone services.[18]

African American Newspapers. Between 1827 and the end of the Civil War in 1865, forty newspapers aimed at black readers and opposed to slavery struggled for survival. These papers faced not only higher rates of illiteracy among black slaves and citizens but also hostility from white society and the majority press of the day. The first black newspaper, *Freedom's Journal*, operated from 1827 to 1829 and opposed the racism of many New York newspapers. In addition, it offered a voice for a number of antislavery societies. Other notable papers included the *Alienated American* (1852–1856) and the *New Orleans Daily Creole*, which began a short life in 1856 as the first black-owned daily in the South. The most influential oppositional newspaper at the time was Frederick Douglass's *North Star*, a weekly antislavery newspaper in Rochester, New York, which began in 1847 and reached a circulation of three thousand. Besides writing essays on slavery, Douglass, a former slave, covered a variety of national and international topics.

Since 1827, more than 3,000 newspapers have been edited and owned by blacks. These papers, with an average life span of nine years, took stands against race baiting, lynching, and the Ku Klux Klan. They promoted racial pride long before the civil rights movement of the 1950s and 1960s. More than 170 such papers survive today and remain influential, including Baltimore's *Afro-American*, New York's *Amsterdam News*, and the *Chicago Defender*. The most widely circulated black-owned paper was Robert C. Vann's weekly *Pittsburgh Courier*, founded in 1910. Its circulation peaked at 350,000 in 1947—the year professional baseball was first integrated by Jackie Robinson, thanks in part to relentless editorials in the *Courier* that denounced the color barrier in pro sports. As they have throughout their histories, these papers offer oppositional viewpoints to the mainstream press and record the daily activities of black communities, listing weddings, births, deaths, graduations, meetings, and church functions.

The circulation rates of most black papers have dropped sharply, particularly since the 1960s. The local and national editions of the *Pittsburgh Courier*, for instance, had a combined circulation of only 20,000 by the early 1980s.[19] Several factors contributed to these declines. First, television and specialized black radio stations tapped into the limited pool of money businesses allocated for advertising. Second, some advertisers, to avoid controversy, withdrew their support when the black press started giving favorable coverage to the civil rights movement in the 1960s. Third, the loss of industrial urban jobs in the 1970s and 1980s not only diminished readership but hurt small neighborhood businesses, which could no longer afford to advertise in both the mainstream and black press. Finally, after the enactment of civil rights and affirmative

> "Too long have others spoken for us."
> —*Freedom's Journal*, 1827

Because of the diverse immigrant populations of the United States, ethnic and foreign-language newspapers are available on newsstands in most large American cities. By the 1990s, there were more than thirty-five daily newspapers in ten different languages.

action laws, black papers were raided by mainstream papers seeking to integrate their newsrooms with good black journalists. Black papers could seldom match the offers from large white-owned dailies.

As civil rights legislation improved economic conditions for many working- and middle-class African Americans, the mainstream press began to court them as a consumer group, devoting weekly special sections to black issues and finding advertisers to support those sections. In siphoning off both ads and talent, a more integrated mainstream press diminished the status of many black papers—an ironic effect of the 1960s civil rights laws. By the mid-1990s, 11 percent of the newsroom staffs at the nation's fifteen hundred daily papers were African American, Hispanic, Asian American, and Native American.[20]

Spanish-Language Newspapers. Bilingual and Spanish-language newspapers have long served a variety of Cuban, Mexican, Puerto Rican, and other Latino readerships. New York's *El Diario-La Prensa* has been serving Spanish-language readers since 1914. Los Angeles boasts *La Opinion*, the nation's largest Spanish-language daily. Other prominent publications are in Miami (*La Voz* and *Diario de las Americas*), Houston (*La Informacion*), Chicago (*El Manana Daily News* and *La Raza*), San Diego (*El Sol*), and New York (*El Noticias del Mundo*). By the mid-1990s, more than two hundred Hispanic newspapers reached more than ten million readers nationwide.

Until the late 1960s, Hispanic issues and culture were virtually ignored by mainstream newspapers. But with the influx of Mexican, Haitian, Puerto Rican, and Cuban immigrants over the past two decades, many mainstream papers introduced weekly Spanish-language supplements. The first was the *Miami Herald*'s section, "El Nuevo Herald," introduced in 1976. Other mainstream papers also joined in, but many were folding their supplements by the mid-1990s. In 1995, the *Los Angeles Times* discontinued its supplement, "Nuestro Tiempo," and the *Miami Herald* trimmed budgets and staff for "El Nuevo Herald." Spanish-language radio and television had beaten the papers to these potential customers and to advertisers. While many of the nation's mainstream papers were cutting their Spanish-language sections, TV advertising aimed at Hispanic markets jumped 25 percent.[21]

Native American Newspapers. An activist Native American press has also provided oppositional voices to mainstream American media since 1828, when the *Cherokee Phoenix* appeared in Georgia. Another prominent early paper was the *Cherokee Rose Bud*, founded in 1848 by tribal women in the Oklahoma territory. The Native American Press Association has documented more than 350 different Native American papers, most of them printed in English but a few in tribal languages. Two national papers include *Akwesasne Notes*, a radical paper from the Mohawk nation published a few times a year, and *Wassaja*, a bimonthly paper of the American Indian

229

Historical Society, promoting tribal pride and education. In opposing the lack of coverage of their culture's viewpoints in the mainstream press, Native American newspapers have helped to educate various tribes about their heritage and build community solidarity. In addition, these papers provide forums for debates about tribal conflicts, which are generally ignored in mainstream papers.

The Underground Press. Another important historical development in the mid to late 1960s involved the explosion of alternative newspapers. Labeled the *underground press* at the time, these papers questioned mainstream political policies and conventional values. Generally running on shoestring budgets, they often voiced radical viewpoints and were erratic in meeting publication schedules. Springing up on college campuses and in major cities, underground papers were inspired by the writings of socialists and intellectuals from the 1930s and 1940s and, in their own time, by a number of writers, poets, and musicians. Particularly inspirational were poets and writers (such as Allen Ginsberg, LeRoi Jones, Jack Kerouac, and Eldridge Cleaver) and "protest" musicians and performers (including Bob Dylan, Peter Seeger, Joan Baez, and Lenny Bruce). In criticizing social institutions, alternative papers critiqued the official reports handed out by public relations agents, government spokespersons, and the conventional press (see "Case Study: The Alternative Journalism of Dorothy Day and I. F. Stone" on page 232).

During the 1960s, underground papers played a unique role in documenting social tension by including voices of students, women, blacks, gays, and others whose opinions were often excluded from the mainstream press. The first and most enduring underground paper, the *Village Voice*, was founded in Greenwich Village in 1955. Among campus underground papers, the *Berkeley Barb* was the most influential, developing amid the free-speech movement in the mid-1960s. Other significant underground papers of the 1960s included the *Los Angeles Free Press*, the *Boston Phoenix*, the *Fifth Estate* in Detroit, the *Washington Free Press*, the *Seed* in Chicago, *Kaleidoscope* in Milwaukee, and the *Distant Drummer* in Philadelphia.

Despite their irreverent and often vulgar tone, many underground papers turned a spotlight on racial and gender inequities and, on occasion, influenced mainstream journalism to examine social issues. Like the black press, though, most underground papers either lost circulation or folded after the 1960s. Given their radical outlooks, it was difficult for them to generate sponsors or keep advertisers. In addition, like the black press, the underground press was raided by mainstream papers, which began expanding their coverage of culture by hiring away the underground's best editors and writers.

economic demands vs. editorial duties

Although a weekly paper may employ only two or three people and a major metro daily more than two thousand, most newspapers generally distinguish business operations from editorial or news functions. Although journalists' and readers' praise or criticism usually rests on the quality of a paper's news and editorial components, business and advertising decisions drive the industry.

Business Operations. Most major daily papers devote one-half to two-thirds of their pages to advertisements. Accounting for 20 to 25 percent of all ad dollars spent annually in the United States, newspapers carry everything from expensive full-page spreads for prominent department stores to classifieds, which consumers can purchase for a few dollars to advertise used furniture. In most cases, ads are positioned in the paper first. The space left over after ads are placed is called the *newshole*, which accounts for the remaining 35 to 50 percent of daily newspapers—everything from front-page news reports to horoscopes and advice columns.

In addition to managing a paper's finances, business operations generally include departments of advertising, circulation, and promotion. Advertising staffs sell space to various companies and classified spots to individuals and small businesses. Circulation departments oversee distribution through street-corner boxes and newsstand sales, neighborhood paper routes, mail subscriptions, and, most recently, the Internet. Promotion departments try to attract new readers and advertisers, paying particular attention to younger, hard-to-reach readers. Mechanical departments, supervised by a production manager, generally run the technical and computerized processes of assembling the pages of the paper and operating the printing presses.

News Responsibilities. On the news and editorial side, the chain of command at most larger papers starts at the top, with the publisher and owner, and then moves to the editor-in-chief, the person in charge of the daily news-gathering and writing processes. Under this main editor, assistant editors and news managers run different news divisions, including features, sports, photos, local news, state news, and wire-service reports that contain much of the day's national and international news. In addition, copy editors check each

The VDT (video display terminal) transformed the news business in the late 1960s and early 1970s. The computer allowed reporters to share stories, and editors could lay out the paper electronically rather than manually.

story for accuracy, style, and grammar and write the headlines for each report.

Reporters work for editors and are generally grouped into two broad categories: *general assignment reporters*, who handle all sorts of stories that might emerge in a given day, and *specialty reporters*, who are assigned to particular beats (police, courts, city government) or topics (education, religion, technology, economy, health, environment). On large dailies, *bureau reporters* file reports every day from other major cities—such as Washington or their state's capital. Daily papers also feature columnists and critics; these reporters have usually worked their way up the hierarchy and may review or analyze everything from fashion to foreign policy.

Wire Services and Feature Syndication. Major daily papers might have between 100 and 150 local reporters and writers, but they still cannot cover the world or produce enough material to fill up the newshole each day. Therefore, newspapers rely on wire services and syndicated feature services to supplement local coverage. A few major dailies, such as the *New York Times*, run their own wire services, selling their reprinted stories to other papers. Other agencies, such as the Associated Press and United Press International (UPI), have hundreds of staffers stationed throughout major U.S. cities and the world capitals. They submit stories and photos each day for distribution to newspapers across the country. Some U.S. papers also subscribe to foreign wire services, such as Agence France-Press in Paris or Reuters in London. Daily papers generally pay monthly fees for access to all wire stories, which are relayed by computer, satellite, or Teletype machines. Although they may use only a fraction of what is available over the wires, editors carefully monitor wire services each day for important stories and ideas for local angles. Wire services have greatly expanded the

The Alternative Journalism of Dorothy Day and I. F. Stone

Over the years, a number of unconventional reporters have struggled against the status quo to find a place for unheard voices and alternative ways to practice their craft. James Franklin stubbornly refused to get a news license during the early 1700s; Ida Wells fearlessly investigated violence against blacks for the *Memphis Free Speech* in the late 1800s; and the underground papers of the late 1960s let the voices of many groups be heard. Newspaper lore offers a rich history of alternative journalists and their publications. Two such papers were Dorothy Day's *Catholic Worker* and *I. F. Stone's Weekly*.

In 1933, Dorothy Day (1897–1980) cofounded a radical religious organization with a monthly newspaper, *Catholic Worker*, that opposed war and supported social reforms. Like many young intellectual writers during World War I, Day was a pacifist; she also joined the Socialist party. Quitting college at age eighteen to work as an activist reporter for socialist newspapers, Day participated in the ongoing suffrage movement, which helped pass the Nineteenth Amendment, giving women the right to vote, in 1920. Throughout the 1930s, her Catholic Worker organization invested in thirty hospices for the poor and homeless, providing food and shelter for five thousand people a day. This legacy would endure into the 1980s and 1990s, with the organization continuing to fund soup kitchens and homeless shelters throughout the country.

An advocate journalist, Day used the *Catholic Worker* to defend the rights of working people and to encourage nonviolent social change. For more than sixty years, the *Worker* has consistently advocated personal activism to further social justice, opposing anti-Semitism, Japanese American internment camps during World War II, nuclear weapons, the Korean War, military drafts, and the communist witch-hunts of the 1950s. During the Cold War period, Day was jailed four times for opposing military-style civil-defense drills in public schools. In the early 1970s, at age seventy-five, Day was arrested for supporting migrant workers while she picketed with Cesar Chavez in California. She also used the paper to advocate religious change, urging Catholics to resist consumer culture and return the Church to its early radical teachings. Although the paper's circulation peaked in 1938 at 190,000, it fell dramatically during World War II when Day's pacifism was at odds with much of America. During the

national and international scope of news, but editors often must put their trust in a handful of powerful wire firms when they select a newsworthy issue or event.

In addition, *feature syndicates*, such as United Features, King Features, and Tribune Media Services, are commercial outlets that contract with newspapers to provide work from the nation's best political writers, editorial cartoonists, comic-strip artists, and self-help columnists. These companies serve as brokers, distributing horoscopes and crossword puzzles as well as the columns and comic strips that appeal to a wide audience. When a paper bids on and acquires the rights to a cartoonist or columnist, it signs exclusivity agreements with a syndicate to ensure that it is the only paper in its region to carry Peanuts, Ellen Goodman, Clarence Page, George Will, or Dear Abby. Feature syndicates, like wire services, wield great influence in determining who becomes a prominent national figure.

Vietnam War and the protest movements, however, it climbed again to more than 100,000.

I. F. Stone (1907–1989) shared Dorothy Day's passion for social activism. He also started early, publishing his own monthly paper at the age of fourteen and becoming a full-time reporter by age twenty. He worked as a Washington political writer for the *Nation* in the early 1940s and later for the *New York Daily Compass* until the early 1950s. A lifelong socialist, Stone challenged the conventions and privileges of both politics and journalism. In 1941, for example, he resigned from the National Press Club when it refused to serve his guest, the nation's first African American federal judge. In the early 1950s, he actively opposed Joseph McCarthy's rabid search to rid government and media of alleged communists.

When the *Daily Compass* failed in 1952, the radical Stone was unable to find a newspaper job and decided to create his own newsletter, *I. F. Stone's Weekly*, which he published for nineteen years. Practicing interpretive and investigative reporting, Stone became as adept as any journalist at tracking down government records to discover contradictions, inaccuracies, and lies. Over the years, besides taking on McCarthy, Stone challenged the policies of J. Edgar Hoover's FBI, questioned decisions by the Supreme Court, investigated the substandard living conditions of many African Americans, and criticized political corruption on both the Right and Left. Working only with his wife and an occasional researcher, Stone guided the *Weekly* to a circulation as high as seventy thousand during the 1960s, when he probed American invesments of money and military might in Vietnam.

I. F. Stone and Dorothy Day embodied a spirit of independent reporting that has been threatened by the decline in newspaper readership and the rise of chain ownership. Stone, who believed that alternative ideas were crucial to maintaining a healthy democracy, once wrote that "there must be free play for so-called 'subversive' ideas—every idea 'subverts' the old to make way for the new. To shut off 'subversion' is to shut off peaceful progress and to invite revolution and war."[1]

Alternative newspapers in the United States

San Francisco
Bay Guardian
San Francisco

Willamette Weekly
Portland, OR

Denver Westword
Denver, CO

City Pages
Minneapolis/
St. Paul, MN

New City
Chicago

Boston Phoenix
Boston

Village Voice
New York City

Washington
City Paper
Washington, DC

Independent
Raleigh/Durham/
Chapel Hill, NC

Los Angeles
Independent
L.A.

Private Eye
Salt Lake City, UT

Austin Chronicle
Austin, TX

The RiverFront
Times
St. Louis, MO

Gambit-New
Orleans Weekly
New Orleans, LA

Creative Loafing
Atlanta, GA

Miami New Times
Miami, FL

Some information courtesy Sylvia R. Curtis

issues of ownership, economics, and technology

A number of tough issues face the newspaper industry as it adapts to changes in economics and technology. For publishers and journalists, no issues are more worrisome than the decline in newspaper readers and the failure of many papers to attract younger readers. Other problems persist as well, including the inability of most cities to support competing newspapers and the capability of online computer services to vie with newspapers for lucrative classified advertising. Finally, the newspaper industry struggles to find its place along the information highway, trying to predict the future of printed and digital versions of the news.

circulation woes

Newspaper owners struggle daily with readership concerns. Since the mid-1960s, yearly circulation has flattened out at just over sixty million copies per day. Although the population has increased during that period, the percentage of adults who read the paper at least once a week dropped from 78 percent in 1970 to around 60 percent by the mid-1990s. This decline in readership actually began during the Depression and the rise of radio. Between 1931 and 1939, six hundred newspapers ceased operation. Between the early 1940s and the mid-1990s, the number of daily papers in the United States dropped from nineteen hundred to fifteen hundred.

The biggest circulation crisis for newspapers occurred from the late 1960s through the 1970s. Both the rise in network television viewing and competition from suburban weeklies intensified the decline in daily readership. In addition, with an increasing number of women working full-time outside the home throughout the seventies, newspapers could no longer consistently count on one of their core readership groups. Circulation dropped by more than 20 percent in the nation's twenty largest cities (even though the population declined by only 6 percent in those areas).[22]

> "**Declining readership** is a symptom well understood by the leaders of our industry. Only recently, however, have newspaper people come to agree that content is first among the many reasons readership is in decline."
>
> —Robert Giles,
> editor and publisher,
> *Detroit News*

While some newspapers experienced circulation gains in the 1980s and early 1990s, especially in more affluent suburban communities, readership in the United States generally declined or flattened out during this period. Increases at many suburban weekly papers actually siphoned off readers of large city dailies. By comparison, many other countries did not experience readership declines. For example, for every one thousand people, Sweden sells five hundred papers per day. In the United States, which has more diverse populations, social classes, and cultural choices, that figure is only about 250 copies sold daily for every one thousand people. Countries such as Norway, Finland, Japan, Germany, and Sweden also have higher rates of readership. (See Table 8.2 for a list of the world's most widely circulated newspapers.)

joint operating agreements

Although the FCC once limited the number of TV stations a person or corporation could own, newspaper owners have historically faced few government limitations. Gannett, for instance, owns more than eighty daily papers (and forty more nondailies), ranging from small suburban papers to the *Detroit News* and *USA Today*. In the past, antimonopoly rules prevented a single owner from controlling all the newspapers in a city or town. Today, however, such rules have little impact because just a single paper serves most communities. In addition, prior to the 1996 Telecommunications Act, the FCC prohibited newspaper owners from purchasing broadcast or cable outlets in the same markets where they publish newspapers. Such restrictions once encouraged more voices in the media marketplace.

Although regulation has lessened, in general the government continues to monitor the declining numbers of newspapers in various American cities and mergers in cities where competition among papers might be endangered. The Justice Department has allowed a number of mergers over the years, but it was not until 1970 that Congress passed the Newspaper Preservation Act, which enabled failing papers to continue operating through a **joint operating agreement (JOA)**. Under a JOA, two competing papers keep separate news divisions while merging business and production operations for a period of years.

TABLE 8.2
The Top Fifteen Daily Newspapers in the World (1995 Circulation)

Newspaper	Country	Circulation
Yomiuri Shimbun	Japan	14,573,988
Asahi Shimbun	Japan	12,697,898
Mainichi Shimbun	Japan	5,947,333
Bild	Germany	5,567,100
Nihon Keizai Shimbun	Japan	4,536,561
Chunichi Shimbun	Japan	4,323,142
Sun	England	4,023,548
Sankei Shimbun	Japan	2,882,252
Renmin Ribao	China	2,740,000
Daily Mirror	England	2,568,957
Chosun Ilbo	South Korea	2,225,000
Dong-A Ilbo	South Korea	2,150,000
Al Ahram	Egypt	2,117,399
Hokkaido Shimbun	Japan	1,964,774
Yangcheng Evening News	China	1,900,000

Source: *The Editor & Publisher International Yearbook*, 1996, New York, NY, xii.

JOAs are now in place in seventeen cities, including Nashville, Seattle, and Tucson. Although JOAs and mergers encourage monopolistic tendencies, they have sometimes been the only way to maintain competition between newspapers in the Information Age. For instance, in the mid-1920s about five hundred American cities had two or more newspapers with separate owners. By the mid-1990s, fewer than twenty cities had independent, competing papers. In 1995, the *Houston Post* folded, leaving the nation's fourth largest city with only one paper, the *Houston Chronicle*.

Until the 1990s, Detroit was one of the most competitive newspaper cities in the nation. The *Detroit News* and the *Detroit Free Press* both ranked among the ten most widely circulated papers in the country and sold their weekday editions for just fifteen cents a copy. But in the early 1990s, managers at the two papers began exploring joint ways to stabilize flat circulations and revenue declines. Claiming that in Detroit's depressed economy the death of one newspaper might result in substantial job losses, the papers asked for a JOA, which the government authorized. In the largest JOA to date, the *News*, owned by Gannett, and the *Free Press*, owned by Knight-Ridder, began sharing business and production operations, although the companies remained independently owned and staffed separate news and editorial departments. On Saturday and Sunday, the two papers circulated one edition, which featured special sections from both papers. Beginning in the summer of 1995, a prolonged and bitter strike by several unions sharply reduced circulation, especially at the *News*, which had become a home-delivered afternoon daily under the terms of the JOA. One of the unions' concerns involved reduced competition under the JOA, which had allowed managers at both papers to cut costs and jobs to sustain high profits for stockholders. Before the 1995 strike, Gannett and Knight-Ridder—later accused of trying to break the labor unions in Detroit—had both reported profit margins of well over 15 percent on their other newspaper holdings.[23]

On occasion, the government has allowed one newspaper to buy another struggling paper in the same city. In the early 1960s in Milwaukee, for example, the Justice

Department permitted the locally owned *Milwaukee Journal* to purchase the failing morning paper, the *Milwaukee Sentinel*, owned by the Hearst chain, when no other serious buyers stepped forward. Both papers continued to operate separate editorial staffs while sharing business and production facilities. With declining afternoon circulation, which fell from 375,000 in the mid-1970s to 215,000 in 1994, the more prestigious afternoon *Journal* finally closed down the morning *Sentinel*, which had existed since 1837. Beginning in April 1995, the company issued only a morning paper, renamed the *Milwaukee Journal Sentinel*.

newspaper chains

Another key economic change in the newspaper industry has been the rise of **newspaper chains**, companies that own several papers throughout the country. Edward Wyllis Scripps founded the first newspaper chain in the 1890s. By the 1920s, there were about 30 chains in the United States, each one owning an average of five papers. The emergence of chains parallels the major business trend during the twentieth century: the movement toward oligopolies in which fewer and fewer corporations control each industry. By the 1980s, more than 130 chains owned an average of nine papers each, with the 12 largest chains accounting for 40 percent of the total circulation in the United States. By the mid-1990s, chains controlled nearly 80 percent of all daily newspapers.

Similar to the cable industry, newspapers operate as monopolies in most cities. Furthermore, many newspaper owners, instead of striving for better journalism or new readers, have devoted their energies to buying radio and TV stations. Gannett, for instance, one of the nation's largest chains, owns more than twenty radio and TV stations. Rupert Murdoch's News Corp., among the world's largest chains, now owns twenty-two U.S. television stations, the most in history. Right after the passage of the 1996 Telecommunications Act, the Tribune Company in Chicago paid more than $1 billion to acquire six more TV stations, now reaching into a third of all U.S. households.[24] (See "Tracking Technology: Media Convergence and the *Tribune* Empire.")

A disturbing trend in the 1990s is that daily newspapers are changing hands at a much faster rate than in previous years. For example, between 1993 and 1996, more than 250 of the nation's 1,500-plus daily papers were sold—usually to distant chains not headquartered in the community where the paper operates.[25] News critics fear that fewer chain owners will make it more difficult for multiple viewpoints to be expressed in the news media. They are also concerned about whether out-of-town owners and newly installed editors will put the special needs of their communities above corporate interests and the bottom line.

changes in technology

Modern technology began radically revolutionizing newsrooms in the 1970s. VDTs (video display terminals), for instance, displaced typewriters, enabling reporters to easily change or share stories; editors could also measure headlines or design pages on their personal computer screens. As dramatic as this change was, however, it did not pose the challenges of the information highway and digital news, which brought a kind of competition that newspapers had never seen.

In the spring of 1995, eight of the nation's largest newspaper chains formed an unprecedented alliance to help more than 120 local newspapers make the transition to the World Wide Web. With their Web sites, local papers began luring consumers to

TRACKING TECHNOLOGY

Media Convergence and the *Tribune* Empire

by Christopher Harper

The *Tribune* Co. has been at the forefront of many journalistic innovations—some bad and some good. One publisher instituted a series of spelling changes because he thought the English language was too complicated. "Through" became "thru," for example, a practice that did not die until the 1970s.

While other newspapers worried about the encroachment of radio and television, the *Tribune* added the new media to its holdings. In Chicago, it owns and operates ChicagoLand TV, its own local television news venture. The company has also expanded its radio and television businesses in New York, Denver, New Orleans, Atlanta, Los Angeles, Philadelphia, and Boston. The company has 10 television stations, seven in the top markets; five radio stations; Tribune Entertainment Co., which produces programming such as *Geraldo*; and joint ventures, such as a significant holding of Warner Bros. Television Network.

In 1991, the *Tribune* began to invest in online technology companies, buying a stake in America Online. In 1996, the company also invested $7 million in Excite, a firm that indexes and searches World Wide Web sites on the Internet.

The company has also teamed up with AOL on a variety of projects. The most ambitious is a $100 million plan called "Digital Cities," which will offer news, information and entertainment to more than 100 cities throughout the United States, from Peoria, Illinois, to Portland, Oregon. Only a few sites are up and running, but the venture is a clear signal to Microsoft that big-time daily newspapers are not about to surrender to Bill Gates' similar project, "Cityscape."

Is the next competition going to be Cityscape vs. Digital Cities? "I think that's one of the battlegrounds," says Owen Youngman, director of interactive media at the *Tribune*. "Because we believe their focus is on entertainment and leisure listings and materials newspapers have always presented, we think it's an important battleground. But we're not focusing on any one opponent. We're looking to the opportunities to perform all the traditional functions we provide. If we do provide that information, we think we will be competitive and then the marketplace can decide about the value and content and who's doing the best job."

Digital City Chicago is one of the biggest projects. The *Tribune* will offer 342 different sites for towns, villages and cities in the reading area, similar to what the *Tribune* did two decades ago in zoned editions. In the past, these editions offered specific news and advertising to local communities. Youngman plans to start the online sites with what he describes as "horizontal communities," political and geographical locations throughout the Chicago area. Then he hopes that "vertical communities" sprout up with readers interested in subject areas such as religion, parenting, and politics. "Microsoft, CNN, and the *Chicago Tribune* are all going to cover a bombing at the Olympics," Youngman says. "Not everybody else is going to worry about Fox River Valley Gardens."

A leading Internet research firm is not convinced that Digital Cities will make it into the next century. "We believe the next five years will see a bloody battle for control of the local online market," Forrester Research wrote in October. Ultimately, Forrester thinks that Microsoft will win that battle, but that it will be costly for Gates.

Another ambitious project is the online "New Century Network," to which newspapers nationwide, including the *Tribune*, contribute articles for readers in another part of the country. In its promotional material, the New Century Network says it "aims to marry the interactivity, breadth, and cool conversation of the Net with the credibility and dedicated insight of hometown newspapers across the country... and eventually, maybe, across the world."

Source: Christopher Harper, "The *Tribune* Empire," *American Journalism Review*, December 1996, 29.

237

their digitized versions of the news, offering color photographs, classified ads, and goods and services available from local businesses. Called the New Century Network, the alliance began sharing information about the electronic and digital delivery of news. It also began sharing ideas about reaching new generations of readers, who may be more likely to get their news and information from computer screens than from printed pages.

Even more significant, the alliance was a response to the looming 1996 Telecommunications Act, which was about to spur other alliances among cable television and telephone companies in their quest to deliver digital data into homes via cable, copper, or fiber-optic wires. The newspaper alliance believes that it can provide the best electronic versions of local community news and services, in contrast to the national services offered by cable or phone systems. The alliance also will try to remain competitive with online computer services, cable companies, and phone services, all of which are now vying with newspapers for lucrative local classified advertising.

Because of their local monopoly status, many newspapers have been slower than other media to confront the challenges of the electronic revolution. Into the mid-1990s, however, newspapers were still the leader in collecting advertising revenue. The nation's fifteen hundred daily papers annually attract 20 to 25 percent of all ad revenues spent in the United States, which is down from a 27 percent share in the late 1980s (see Figure 8.2). In 1995 and 1996, the newspaper industry captured more ad dollars than any other mass medium. Nonetheless, newspaper managers have continued to express concern because nearly two-thirds of the nation's sixty largest metro dailies reported circulation declines by the mid-1990s.[26]

Although some observers think newspapers are on the verge of extinction as the digital age eclipses the print era, the industry is no dinosaur. In fact, the history of communication demonstrates that older mass media have always adapted. Actually, as increasing numbers of newspapers go digital, they tackle one of the industry's major economic headaches: the cost of newsprint. After salaries, purchasing newsprint from paper manufacturers is the industry's largest expense, accounting for more than 20 percent of a newspaper's total cost. As we enter the twenty-first century, newspapers will be available in multiple formats—both online and in print—surviving in ever more varied versions and styles, as they have done since the 1700s.

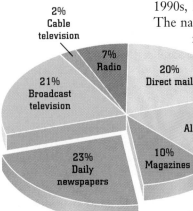

**Figure 8.2
Newspapers' Slice of the Advertising Pie**
Source: The Missouri Group, *News Reporting and Writing*, 5th ed. (New York: St. Martin's Press, 1996), 18; and Newspaper Association of America.

newspapers and democracy

Despite their considerable achievements as investigators of corruption and chroniclers of daily life, newspapers and journalists today are often viewed in a negative light. Seen as jaded or cynical, reporters in the 1990s are sometimes perceived merely as invaders of people's privacy. Yet in some historical periods, newspapers and reporters were more highly regarded. Particularly noteworthy have been the courageous war correspondents, many of whom gave their lives to bear witness to major civil and world wars. Still, the last time that a significant number of Americans viewed the press heroically was in 1974, after newspapers played key roles in forcing Richard Nixon to resign the presidency over the Watergate scandal. Best representing this coverage was the daily reporting in the *Washington Post* by Bob Woodward and Carl Bernstein, who later recounted their Watergate investigations in the book *All the President's Men*.

Certainly, of all mass media, newspapers have played the longest and strongest role in sustaining democracy. As a venue to express ideas and distribute information, newspapers keep readers abreast of issues and events in their communities, their nation, and their world. Over the years, newspapers have fought heroic battles in places that had little tolerance for differing points of view. In the 1990s alone, hundreds of reporters from several countries died or disappeared trying to report sensitive stories that threatened political leaders or military regimes. In 1995 and 1996, 77 reporters from around the world were killed and another 185 were held in prisons for trying to do their jobs. In these settings, reporters and editors continue to articulate unpopular and oppositional ideas even when their right to publish has been threatened.

Although newspapers remain a strong medium of communication, critics have raised a number of concerns about their future. For instance, some charge that newspapers have become so formulaic in their design and reporting styles that they may actually discourage new approaches to telling stories and reporting news. In addition, given the rise of newspaper chains, the likelihood of including new opinions, ideas, and information in mainstream daily papers may be diminishing. Although wealthy and powerful chains may keep smaller struggling papers solvent, such chains sometimes have little commitment to local communities beyond profits. Chain journalism tends not to foster watchdog journalism and the crusading traditions of newspapers. Like other business managers, many news executives prefer not to offend investors or outrage potential advertisers by running too many investigative reports, especially business probes. Indeed, reporters have generally not thoroughly reported the business and ownership arrangements in their own industry.

Critics today have raised some important questions regarding the transformation from a modern print to a postmodern digital culture. For example, does such a transformation represent a cheapening of public discourse? Do "new news" forums and nonprint media offer opportunities to improve democracy by permitting public conversations that are not dependent on major newspapers? Also, what is the role of large corporations in this transformation? Do they allow enough different voices and viewpoints into the market? (We will return to these questions and the *public journalism* movement in Chapter 14.)

By the mid-1990s, the social definition and role of a reporter seemed in question. Reporting the latest White House gossip, weekly supermarket tabloids had readerships three and four times larger than the *New York Times*, which itself had followed up on stories that first appeared in tabloids. Talk-show hosts were also performing news functions by bringing to light controversial issues. Giving third-party candidates like Ross Perot a platform, Larry King's talk show on CNN played a journalistic role in both the 1992 and 1996 presidential elections. In 1994, Rush Limbaugh's radio program became a forum for airing the Republican party's

> "Journalism, and specifically the newspaper, ought to become a support system for public life." —Jay Rosen, 1992

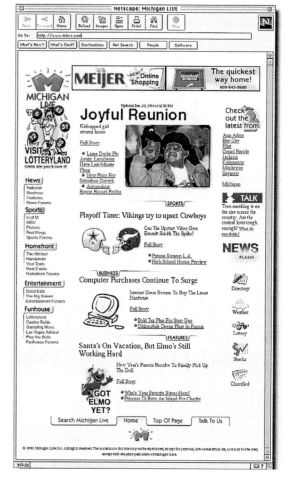

This electronic newspaper is a prime example of the entry of mainstream media to the World Wide Web. *Michigan Live* (http://www.mlive.com), owned by the Newhouse publishing empire, publishes the daily news, sports and feature stories, and photos from eight Michigan newspapers also owned by Newhouse. *Michigan Live* staffers also produce their own content, such as searchable restaurant databases, an interactive crossword puzzle, and a movie finder service listing a year's worth of movie reviews.

Contract with America. The mid-1990s also saw furious competition for younger readers weaned on moving images in a highly visual culture. Since most major newspapers are now available via interactive computer services, the old battle lines between print and electronic culture need to be redrawn. For better or worse, journalism today encompasses a host of resources that perform news and entertainment functions. Newspapers are working to keep up as they compete in a world overloaded with information. The best of them continue to sustain journalism's democratic traditions: They make sense of important events and watch over our central institutions.

REVIEW QUESTIONS

1. What are the limitations of a press that serves only partisan interests? Why did the earliest papers appeal mainly to more privileged readers?

2. How did newspapers emerge as a mass medium during the penny press era? How did content changes make this happen?

3. What are the two main features of yellow journalism? How have Joseph Pulitzer and William Randolph Hearst contributed to newspaper history?

4. Why did objective journalism develop? What are its characteristics? What are its strengths and limitations?

5. Why did interpretive forms of journalism develop in the modern era? What are the limits of objectivity?

6. How would you define literary journalism? Why did it emerge in such an intense way in the 1960s? How is literary journalism an attack on objective news?

7. What is the difference between consensus- and conflict-oriented newspapers?

8. What role have ethnic, minority, and oppositional newspapers played in the United States?

9. Why have African American newspapers struggled to maintain their circulation figures over the past two decades?

10. What is the impact of a JOA (joint operating agreement) on the business and editorial divisions of competing newspapers?

11. Why did newspaper chains become an economic trend in the twentieth century?

12. What are the major reasons for the decline in newspaper circulation figures?

13. What major challenges does new technology pose to the newspaper industry?

14. What is a newspaper's role in a democracy?

QUESTIONING THE MEDIA

1. When you pick up a newspaper, which section do you read first? Why do you make that choice?

2. What kinds of stories, topics, or issues are not being covered well by mainstream papers?

3. Why do you think people aren't reading daily newspapers as frequently as they once did? What could newspapers do to increase circulation?

4. Discuss whether newspaper chains are ultimately good or bad for the future of journalism.

5. Are Geraldo Rivera, Oprah Winfrey, and Ricki Lake practicing a form of journalism on their talk shows? Explain your answer.

6. Do newspapers today play a vigorous role as watchdogs on our powerful institutions? Why or why not?

7. Will television news and online news services eventually replace newspapers? Explain your response.

The purpose of this project is to extend your critical approach to news. Work with a partner or in a small group. Over a period of *three* weekdays, study the *New York Times*, *USA Today*, and one local daily paper. Devise a chart and a descriptive scheme so that you can compare how each of the three papers covered *international* news. You should consider international news any news story that is *predominantly* about a country other than the United States. Exclude sports sections of the papers. Follow these steps as you work on your project:

1. *Description*. Count the total number of international news stories in each paper. Which foreign cities are covered? Which countries? What are the subjects of these stories (civil wars, anti-Americanism, natural disasters, travelogue profiles, etc.)? Prepare a descriptive chart to show the differences among the three papers.

2. *Analysis*. Using your chart as a guide, write two or three paragraphs discussing *patterns* that emerge. What locales seem to get the most attention? What kinds of stories seem to appear most often? In other words, what kind of issue or event makes another country newsworthy? Do not try to summarize your chart here. Instead, just write about three or four intriguing patterns that you noticed.

3. *Interpretation*. Write a two- or three-paragraph critical interpretation of your findings. What does your analysis mean? Why do some countries appear more frequently than other countries? Why do certain kinds of stories seem to get featured?

4. *Evaluation*. Discuss the limitations of your study. Which paper seemed to do the best job of covering the rest of the world? Why? Do you think newspapers give us enough information about other people's cultures?

CHAPTER 9

THE MAGAZINE ABOUT LIFE IN YOUR TWENTIES

SWING

WHAT IS LOVE IN THE '90s?

Exclusive Poll: What We Want From Sex and Relationships

CAN ONE YOUNG GUN SAVE THE NRA?

GEORGE LUCAS' CYBER DISCIPLES

A SPECIAL REPORT: HOLLYWOOD AFTER DARK

Rock 'n' Roll Fantasy Camp

Mardi Gras Vampire Tour

Snowboards Get Graphic

US $2.95 UK £2.25
CANADA $3.95

03457
FEBRUARY 1997
0 272011 7
02

S ay you graduate from college and decide to start a national magazine. It might help to have a rich father, particularly one who will purchase expensive full-page ads in your first issue. After all, of the more than sixteen hundred new magazines launched in 1995 and 1996, fewer than 20 percent will still be publishing two years later in a fickle and jam-packed media marketplace. But if your father is ranked annually among *Forbes* magazine's Top 400 wealthiest Americans and also happens to buy a lot of advertising, the capital investment needed to start and sustain a new magazine might be easier to negotiate.

In November 1994, Duke University graduate David Lauren launched *Swing*, a magazine for the so-called Generation X—the "twentysomething" audience. At age twenty-two, Lauren became the magazine's editor and publisher. David's father, designer Ralph Lauren, bought six full-page ads in that first issue. The magazine's target readership was the market for Ralph's cologne and clothing lines. For *Swing*'s nationwide debut, two hundred thousand copies were printed. The issue sold well in Manhattan, and sixty-five copies of *Swing* shipped to newsstands at Duke sold out within four hours.

According to David Lauren, *Swing* grew from an idea he got while attending Duke: to create a more substantive magazine for people in their twenties. Lauren did not like the association of his generation with lazy slackers interested only in celebrity culture. Covering topics from sex education to voter turnout, the magazine Lauren envisioned highlighted the accomplishments of twentysomethings—young people doing extraordinary things in both their personal and professional lives. The magazine's name came from the economic and political clout of today's twentysomethings and their ability to affect advertising and to swing elections. By the mid-1990s, Gen-Xers constituted more than forty-five million young Americans who spent $125 million annually on consumer products. This group was also largely responsible for helping swing the bulk of the 1992 and 1996 vote to Bill Clinton.

In the beginning, David Lauren refused to put *Swing* online: "I think people generally want something they can hold onto and take with them to the beach or on the subway. I would consider taking *Swing* online. But a magazine online is inaccessible to the masses. Not everyone has the technology or wants the technology."[1] By 1997, *Swing* was still going, with a circulation around a hundred thousand. It also was still not online.

When television was on the rise in the early 1950s, many critics predicted the collapse of the magazine industry. But as the *Swing* story illustrates, it never happened. Like radio, the magazine industry showed remarkable resilience in adapting to a changing media landscape. In fact, by the mid-1990s more than eight hundred new magazines were being launched annually, nearly four times as many as a decade earlier.

Magazines adapted readily to the TV era. The introduction in 1953 of an inconspicuous publication—*TV Guide*—was a significant turning point in modern magazine history. That magazine capitalized instantly on TV's popularity. *TV Guide* was also an early example of media convergence: one medium devoting its content to another medium. It demonstrated one way the magazine industry could survive television, which would soon digest ever-larger portions of the national advertising pie.

Traditional national magazines discovered they would have to retool rapidly; television was snatching away sponsors and displacing general circulation magazines as the dominant family medium. As a result, many magazines started developing market niches, appealing to advertisers who wanted to reach specific audiences defined by gender, age, race, class, or social interests.

Since the 1740s, American magazines have played a key role in our social and cultural lives. More than newspapers, which have been mainly local and regional in scope, magazines became America's earliest national mass medium. They created some of the first spaces for discussing the large social issues of the age, including public education, the abolition of slavery, women's suffrage, literacy, and the Civil War. Early publications provided political forums for debates among the colonial elite. In addition, many leading literary figures used magazines to gain public exposure for their essays and fiction.

In the nineteenth century, magazines became an important educational forum for women, who were barred from higher education and from active participation in the nation's political life. At the turn of the century, magazines contained probing reports that would influence a century of investigative print and broadcast journalism. From an economic perspective, magazines helped reorient households toward advertised products, hastening the rise of a consumer society. From a cultural perspective, magazines pioneered the use of engraving and photography, providing the earliest hints of the visual culture to come.

Today—despite movies, radio, television, and cable—magazines still give us voices that are not readily heard in mainstream electronic culture. Certainly, newsmagazines such as *Time* and *Newsweek* play a pivotal role in determining what consumers think about. But outside the mainstream, numerous specialized magazines cover everything from radical politics to unusual hobbies. These publications bring information and viewpoints to readers who are not being served by the other major media channels.

More than twelve thousand commercial and alternative magazines and an additional thirteen thousand noncommercial publications and newsletters are published in the United States annually. Like newspapers and television, magazines continue to both reflect and construct portraits of American life. They are catalogues for daily events and experiences. They show us the latest products, putting our consumer culture on continuous display. Just as we delve into other forms of culture, we read and view our favorite magazines to learn something about our community, our nation, our world, and ourselves.

In this chapter we will investigate the history and health of the magazine industry, highlighting the colonial and early American eras, the arrival of national magazines, and the development of engraving and photography. Turning to the modern American magazine, we will also focus on the age of muckraking and the rise of general interest publications and consumer magazines. We will then look at the decline of mass-market magazines and TV's impact on the older print medium. We will see how magazines have specialized in order to survive in a fragmented market and adapt in the Information Age. Finally, we will investigate the organization and economics of magazines, and their function in democracy.

the early history of magazines

The first magazines probably developed in seventeenth-century France, originating from bookseller catalogues and notices that book publishers inserted in newspapers. The word *magazine* derives from the French term *magasin*, meaning storehouse. The earliest magazines were indeed storehouses of contemporary writing and reports taken mostly from newspapers. Today, the word *magazine* broadly refers to collections of articles, stories, and advertisements appearing in nondaily (such as weekly or monthly) periodicals that are published in tabloid style rather than newspaper style.

The first political magazine, called the *Review*, appeared in London in 1704. Edited by political activist and novelist Daniel Defoe (author of *Robinson Crusoe*), the *Review* was printed sporadically until 1713. Like the *Nation*, the *National Review*, and the *Progressive* in the United States today, early European magazines were channels for political commentary and persuasion. These periodicals looked like newspapers, but they appeared less frequently and were oriented more toward broad domestic and political issues than toward recent news.

In the eighteenth century, regularly published magazines or pamphlets, such as the *Tatler* and the *Spectator*, also appeared in England. They offered poetry, politics, and philosophy for London's elite, and they served readerships of a few thousand. The first to use the term *magazine* was *Gentleman's Magazine*, which appeared in London in 1731 with reprinted articles from newspapers, books, and political pamphlets. Later, the magazine began publishing original work by writers such as Defoe, Samuel Johnson, and Alexander Pope.

colonial magazines

With neither a substantial middle class nor advanced printing technology, magazines developed slowly in the United States. Like the partisan press, magazines served politicians, the educated, and the merchant classes, interpreting their political, commercial, and cultural world. Paid circulations were slight—between a hundred and fifteen hundred. In the late 1700s, reading magazines was not a habit of the working classes; most adults were illiterate. However, early magazines did document a new nation coming to terms with issues of taxation, state versus federal power, Indian treaties, public education, and the end of colonialism. George Washington, Alexander Hamilton, and John Hancock all wrote for magazines, and Paul Revere worked for a time as a magazine illustrator.

The first colonial magazines appeared in Philadelphia in 1741, about fifty years after the first newspapers. Andrew Bradford started it all with *American Magazine, or A Monthly View of the Political State of the British Colonies*. Three days later, Ben Franklin's *General Magazine and Historical Chronicle* appeared. Bradford's magazine lasted only three months and three issues. It faced circulation and postal obstacles that Franklin, who had replaced Bradford as Philadelphia's postmaster, put in its way. For instance, Franklin mailed his magazine without paying the high postal rates that he subsequently charged others. Franklin's magazine primarily duplicated what was already available in local papers. After six months, he shut it down.

Following the Philadelphia experiments, magazines emerged in other colonies as well. Boston produced several magazines beginning in the 1740s. The most successful publications simply reprinted articles from leading London periodicals, keeping readers abreast of European events. Magazines such as the *Independent Reflector* also sprang up in New York, featuring poetry as well as cultural and political essays. The *Pennsylvania Magazine*, edited by activist Thomas Paine, helped rally the colonies against British rule. While editing the magazine, Paine worked on his famous 1776 pamphlet *Common Sense*, which made the intellectual case for American independence. By 1776, about a hundred colonial magazines had appeared and disappeared. Although historians consider them dull and uninspired, these magazines did launch a new medium that would catch on after the Revolution.

the first u.s. magazines

The early growth of magazines in the United States was steady but slow. Delivery costs remained high, and some postal carriers even refused to carry magazines because they added so much weight to a load. Twelve magazines operated in 1800. By 1825, about a hundred magazines existed, although another five hundred or so had failed in the first twenty-five years of the nineteenth century. By the early 1800s, most communities had their own weekly magazines, but much of the material was still reprinted from other sources. These magazines featured essays on local issues, government activities, and political intrigue. They sold some advertising but were usually in precarious financial situations because of their small circulations.

The idea of specialized magazines devoted to certain categories of readers developed throughout the nineteenth century. Many early periodicals, for instance, were overtly religious. Published by various denominations, religious magazines boasted the largest readerships in their day. The Methodist *Christian Journal and Advocate*, for example, claimed twenty-five thousand subscribers by 1826. Literary magazines also emerged. The *North American Review*, for example, established the work of important writers such as Ralph Waldo Emerson, Henry David Thoreau, and Mark Twain. Besides religion and literature, magazines addressed various professions, lifestyles, and topics, including agriculture (*American Farmer*), education (*American Journal of Education*), law (*American Law Journal*), medicine (*Medical Repository*), and science (*American Journal of Science*). Such specialization spawned the modern trend of reaching readers who share a profession, a set of beliefs, cultural tastes, or social identities.

In 1821, two young Philadelphia printers, Charles Alexander and Samuel Coate Atkinson, launched the *Saturday Evening Post*, which became the longest-running magazine in U.S. history. The printers ran their venture from the same printing plant that once published Franklin's newspaper, the *Pennsylvania Gazette*. Like most magazines of the day, the early *Post* included a few original essays by its own editors but "borrowed" many pieces from other sources. Eventually, the *Post* developed into one of the leading magazines of the nineteenth century, featuring news, poetry, essays, and play reviews. Its editors published prominent popular authors such as Nathaniel Hawthorne and Harriet Beecher Stowe. It was the first prominent magazine to appeal directly to women, starting the "Lady's Friend," a column that addressed women's issues. During the 1800s, the weekly *Post* became the first important general interest magazine aimed at a national audience.

the arrival of national magazines

With increases in literacy and public education and developments in faster printing technology, a market was created for more magazines like the *Post*. Improvements in rail transportation also made it possible to ship magazines and other consumer products easily from city to city. Whereas in 1825 a hundred magazines struggled for survival, by 1850 nearly six hundred magazines were being produced. During this twenty-five-year period, publishers launched as many as five thousand magazines, although most of them lasted less than a year.

Besides the *Saturday Evening Post*, the most influential general magazines of the day were targeted to women. In 1828, Sarah Josepha Hale started the first women's magazine, *Ladies' Magazine*. It advocated women's rights and schools to train women as teachers (Hale did not believe men and women should be educated together). After nine years and marginal success, Hale merged her magazine with its main rival, *Godey's Lady's Book* (1830–98), which she edited for the next forty years. By 1850, *Godey's*, known for its colored fashion illustrations, had a circulation of 40,000, at that time the biggest ever for a U.S. magazine. By 1860, circulation swelled to 150,000. Hale's magazine, a champion of women's property rights, played a central role in educating working- and middle-class women, who were denied access to higher education throughout the nineteenth century.

Other magazines also marked the shift to national periodicals. *Graham's Magazine*, published in Philadelphia from 1840 to 1858, was one of the most influential and entertaining magazines in the country. Also important at the time was the precursor of the *New Yorker*, *Knickerbocker Magazine* (1833–64), which drew from such New York literary talent as Washington Irving, James Fenimore Cooper, and Nathaniel Hawthorne. The magazine introduced the "Editor's Table," a breezy and often humorous column that discussed the topics of the day and would later be imitated

Americanized versions of Paris fashion trends appeared in *Godey's Lady's Book*, the first American magazine for women and a pioneer in colorized illustrations. America's most popular magazine in the mid-nineteenth century, *Godey's* was run for forty years by writer/editor Sarah Josepha Hale, who wrote the children's poem "Mary Had a Little Lamb."

by the *New Yorker*. Also emerging during this period was the *Nation*, founded in 1865 by E. L. Godkin. The oldest surviving American political opinion magazine, the *Nation* continues to serve mostly an educated national readership whose politics are left of center. In addition, the weekly *Youth's Companion* (1826–1929) became one of the first successful magazines for younger readers. It, too, sought to extend the reach of magazines beyond local boundaries.

◼ pictorial pioneers

Like the first newspapers, many early magazines were dull and gray in appearance, totally dependent on the printed word. Beginning in the 1850s, however, some newspapers and magazines started printing elaborate engravings and illustrations. Photographs took a bit longer. Mathew Brady and his employees, whose thirty-five hundred photos documented the Civil War, had popularized photography by the 1860s. But it took newspapers and magazines until the 1890s to figure out how to adapt photos to print media.

By the mid-1850s, drawings, engravings, woodcuts, and other forms of illustration became major features of magazines. During this time, *Godey's Lady's Book* employed up to 150 women to color-tint its magazine illustrations and stencil drawings. *Harper's New Monthly Magazine*, founded in 1850, published top American and British writers but also offered extensive woodcut illustrations with each issue. During the Civil War, many readers relied on *Harper's* for its elaborate battlefield sketches. Publications like *Harper's* married visual language to the printed word, helping to transform magazines into a popular national mass medium.

> "They spring up as fast as mushrooms, in every corner, and like all **rapid vegetation**, bear the seeds of early decay within them . . . and then comes a 'frost, a killing frost,' in the form of **bills due and debts unpaid**. . . . The average age of periodicals in this country is found to be six months."
> —*New-York Mirror*, 1828

the development of modern american magazines

In 1870, about twelve hundred magazines were produced in the United States. By 1890, the number of magazines reached forty-five hundred; by 1905, more than six thousand existed, most of them intended for local and regional audiences. The rate of failure, however, was still high. Although publishers launched approximately seventy-five hundred magazines between 1895 and 1905, more than half of them died or merged with other magazines.[2] Part of this surge in titles and readership had been facilitated by the Postal Act of 1879, which gave magazines cheaper rates and put them on an equal footing with newspapers delivered by mail.

While cheaper postal rates and better rail transportation were reducing magazines' distribution costs, advances in modern technology were lowering production costs. By the end of the nineteenth century, advances in mass-production printing, using conveyor systems, assembly lines, and faster presses, made large-circulation national magazines possible.[3] These technological improvements allowed magazine entrepreneurs to slash the price of magazines, which ran about thirty-five cents a copy in the late 1880s. As prices dropped to fifteen and then to ten cents, the working classes were gradually able to purchase national publications. By 1905, there were about twenty-five national magazines, available from coast to coast and serving millions of readers.[4]

As magazine circulation began to skyrocket, publishers began deriving higher ad revenues from companies eager to sell their wares in this expanding market. Ad pages in national magazines soared. *Harper's*, for instance, devoted only seven pages to ads in the mid-1880s, nearly fifty pages by 1890, and more than ninety pages by 1900.[5] By the turn of the century, advertisers increasingly used national magazines to get consumers' attention and build a national marketplace. In addition, the dramatic growth of drug and dime stores, supermarkets, and department stores offered new venues and shelf space for selling consumer goods, including magazines. As jobs and the population began shifting from farms and small towns to urban areas, magazines helped readers to imagine themselves as part of a nation rather than as individuals with only local or regional identities.

One magazine that took advantage of these changes was *Ladies' Home Journal*, begun in 1883 by Cyrus Curtis. Prior to *LHJ*, many women's magazines had been called *cookie-and-pattern* publications because they narrowly confined women's concerns to baking and fashion. *LHJ* broadened the scope of magazines as its editors and advertisers realized that women consumers were a growing and lucrative market. Publishing popular fiction and sheet music as well as the latest consumer ads, *LHJ* by the early 1890s had a circulation of half a million—the highest of any magazine in the country. In 1903, it became the first magazine to reach a circulation of one million.

social reform and the muckrakers

The economics behind the rise of popular magazines was simple: A commercial publisher could dramatically expand circulation by dropping the price of an issue *below* the actual production cost for a single copy. The publisher recouped the loss through ad revenue, guaranteeing large readerships to advertisers who were willing to pay more to reach more readers. Throughout the twentieth century, many commercial magazines adopted this principle. However, simply lowering costs from twenty-five or thirty-five cents to a dime was not enough. Like the penny press, magazines had to change content as well.

Besides being attracted to the ten-cent price tag, readers were drawn to the changing content of magazines. While printing the fiction and essays of good writers of the day, magazines also engaged in one aspect of yellow journalism—crusading for social reform on behalf of the public good. Curtis's *LHJ* and its editor Edward Bok, for example, led the fight in the early 1890s against unregulated patent medicines (which often contained nearly 50 percent alcohol). Other magazines joined the fight against phony medicines, poor living and working conditions, and unsanitary practices in various food industries.

The rise in overall magazine circulation coincided with the search for better jobs. Moving from farms to factories, hundreds of thousands of Americans and new immigrants poured into cities. Thus, the nation that journalists and magazines wrote about grew increasingly complex at the turn of the century. Some reporters became dissatisfied with conventional journalism and turned from newspapers to magazines, where they were able to write in greater depth about broader issues. They wrote both factual and fictional magazine accounts on topics such as big-business and government corruption, urban problems faced by immigrants, labor-management conflicts, and race relations. Angry with so much negative reporting, President Theodore Roosevelt in 1906 dubbed these reporters *muckrakers*, because they were willing to crawl around in society's muck to uncover a story. **Muckraking** was a label that Roosevelt used with disdain, but it was worn with pride by reporters such as Ray Stannard Baker, Frank Norris, Lincoln Steffens, and Ida Tarbell.

In 1902, *McClure's Magazine* (1893–1933) touched off this investigative era in magazine reporting with a series of probes on business monopolies, life-insurance frauds, political dishonesty in city governments, and the problems of labor and working people. The muckrakers distrusted established institutions and undertook to protect ordinary citizens from corruption. First serialized in *McClure's*, Ida Tarbell's book *The History of the Standard Oil Company* took on John D. Rockefeller's big oil monopoly. Lincoln Steffens' "Shame of the Cities" series for *McClure's* tackled urban problems. Steffens said of his own investigations, "When I set out to describe the corrupt systems of certain typical cities, I meant to show simply how the people were deceived and betrayed."[6]

In 1906 *Cosmopolitan* (1886–), recently purchased by William Randolph Hearst, joined the muckraking parade with a series called "The Treason of the Senate." *Collier's* (1888–1957) developed "The Great American Fraud" series, again focusing on patent medicines (whose ads accounted for 30 percent of the profits made by the American press by the 1890s). Influenced by Upton Sinclair's *The Jungle*, a fictional account of Chicago's meatpacking industry, and *Collier's* and *LHJ's* muckraking reports, Congress passed the Pure Food and Drug Act in 1906.

the rise of general interest magazines

The heyday of the muckraking era lasted into the mid-1910s. Then national social crusades and reforms became less significant as America and journalism were gradually drawn into the first major international war. After World War I, the prominent publications were **general interest magazines**, which offered occasional investigative articles but covered a wide variety of topics aimed at a broad national audience. A key to these magazines, predominant from the 1920s into the 1950s, was the pioneering influence of *photojournalism*, the use of photos to document the rhythms of daily life. National picture magazines gave the industry at least one advantage over radio, which was developing into the most popular medium of the day.

This 1935 Thanksgiving cover from the *Saturday Evening Post* was illustrated by Norman Rockwell (1894–1978). Rockwell created realistic, sentimental, and humorous scenes from small-town life, and over the years more than three hundred of his paintings graced the *Post* cover. His illustrations presented ideals about family values that remain central to American culture to this day.

Saturday Evening Post. As we have noted, the first widely popular general interest magazine was the *Saturday Evening Post*. When Cyrus Curtis bought the *Post* in 1897 for $1,000, it had a circulation of approximately ten thousand. Curtis's strategy to reinvigorate the magazine included printing popular fiction and romanticizing American virtues through words and pictures (a *Post* tradition best depicted in the three hundred cover illustrations by Norman Rockwell). Curtis also featured articles that celebrated the business boom of the 1920s. This reversed the journalistic direction of the muckraking era, in which business corruption was often the focus. The *Post* reached two million in circulation by the 1920s, the first magazine to hit that mark. By 1920, about fifty-five magazines fit the general interest category; by 1946, more than a hundred such magazines competed with radio networks for the national audience.

Reader's Digest. The most widely circulated general interest magazine during this period was *Reader's Digest*. Started in 1922 by Dewitt Wallace and Lila Acheson Wallace for $5,000 in a Greenwich Village basement, *Reader's Digest* championed one of the earliest functions of magazines: printing condensed versions of selected articles from other magazines. In its early years, the Wallaces refused to accept ads and sold the magazine only through subscriptions. The *Digest*'s circulation was just over a hundred thousand by the late 1920s, when it began appearing on newsstands. With its inexpensive costs and price, its circulation climbed to one million in 1935 during the heart of the Depression. By 1946, *Reader's Digest* was the nation's most popular magazine, with a circulation of nine million. Its pocket-size format made it popular both at home and for travel. By 1963, the *Digest* had a circulation of more than fourteen million, five million more than its nearest rival, *TV Guide*.

For years the *Digest* selected articles based on three criteria: "applicability" (articles relevant to readers' daily lives), "lasting interest" (articles that could still be read the next year), and "constructiveness" (articles that had an optimistic and upbeat outlook on life).[7] Although over the years *Reader's Digest* has been both chastised and praised for its conservative viewpoints and occasionally pious moral tone, by the mid-1980s it had become the most popular magazine in the world. At its peak, it reached a circulation of twenty million in America and another ten to twelve million in 160 other countries. (See Table 9.1 for the circulation figures of the top ten U.S. magazines.)

Time. During the general interest era, national newsmagazines such as *Time* were also major commercial successes. Begun in 1923 by Henry Luce and Britton Hadden, *Time* developed a magazine brand of interpretive journalism, assigning reporter-researcher teams to cover stories over a period of several weeks. A rewrite editor would put the whole project together in narrative form and provide an interpretive point of view. Luce believed that journalistic objectivity was a myth and sought instead to be fair. Critics charged, though, that *Time* became increasingly conservative politically as the magazine got more successful in the 1940s and 1950s. *Time* had a circulation of two hundred thousand by 1930, increasing to more than three million by the mid-1960s.

In 1931, *Time* began sponsoring radio's *March of Time* and later a newsreel version, which ran in theaters from 1935 to 1951. These "news" programs, the first so-

TABLE 9.1
The Top 10 Magazines
(ranked by paid U.S. circulation, 1972 vs. 1996)

1972		1996	
Rank/Publication	Circulation	Rank/Publication	Circulation
1 Reader's Digest	17,827,661	1 NRTA/AARP Bulletin	20,716,609
2 TV Guide	16,410,858	2 Modern Maturity	20,673,063
3 Woman's Day	8,191,731	3 Reader's Digest	15,150,822
4 Better Homes and Gardens	7,996,050	4 TV Guide	13,076,790
5 Family Circle	7,889,587	5 National Geographic	9,184,878
6 McCall's	7,516,960	6 Better Homes and Gardens	7,616,270
7 National Geographic	7,260,179	7 Good Housekeeping	5,032,901
8 Ladies' Home Journal	7,014,251	8 Family Circle	5,003,227
9 Playboy	6,400,573	9 Ladies' Home Journal	4,705,020
10 Good Housekeeping	5,801,446	10 Woman's Day	4,501,612

Source: Magazine Publishers of America.

called docudramas, mixed fact and fiction as actors recreated the roles of current politicians and reenacted news events of the day. *March of Time* became the prototype for the popular reenactment shows of the 1990s—syndicated programs such as *A Current Affair*, *Cops*, and *Inside Edition*.

Time's success encouraged prominent imitators, including *Newsweek* (1933–) and *U.S. News & World Report* (1948–). When the major weekly general interest magazines *Life* and *Look* failed in the early 1970s, newsmagazines took over photo-journalism's role in news reporting, visually documenting both national and international events. By the mid-1990s, the three major newsmagazines had circulations ranging from *Time*'s 4 million to *Newsweek*'s 3.1 million to *U.S. News*' 2.2 million.

A South African man speaks out against his country's racism and the second-class status of blacks. The photo, which appeared in *Life* in the 1940s, was taken by Margaret Bourke-White (1906–1971), one of the first staff photographers hired by the magazine.

Life. Despite the commercial success of *Reader's Digest* and *Time*, those two did not come to symbolize general interest publications during this period. That honor belongs to the oversized pictorial weeklies *Look* and, especially, *Life*. More than any other magazine of its day, *Life* developed an effective strategy for competing with popular radio by advancing photojournalism. Launched as a weekly by Henry Luce in 1936, *Life* combined the public's fascination with images (invigorated by the movie industry), the radio journalism of the *March of Time* series, and the popularity of advertising and fashion photography. By the end of the 1930s, *Life* had a *pass-along readership*—the total number of people who come into contact with a single copy of a magazine—of more than seventeen million, rivaling the ratings of popular national radio programs.

Life's first editor, Wilson Hicks, formerly a picture editor for the Associated Press, built a staff of renowned photographer-reporters who chronicled the world's ordinary and extraordinary events from the late 1930s through the 1960s. Among them were Margaret Bourke-White, the first woman war correspondent to fly combat missions during World War II, and Gordon Parks, who would become Hollywood's first African-American director of major feature films. *Life*—"child" of the turn-of-the-century pictorial magazines and "parent" to *People*, *US*, and *Entertainment Weekly*—used an oversized format featuring ninety-six pages of pictures with a minimum of written text.

the fall of general interest magazines

Life's circulation peaked in 1970 at 8.5 million, with an estimated pass-along readership of nearly fifty million. *Life*'s chief competitor, *Look*, founded by Gardner Cowles in 1937, reached 2 million in circulation by 1945 and 4 million by 1955. It climbed to almost 8 million in 1971. Dramatically, though, both magazines suspended publication. The demise of these popular periodicals at the peak of their circulations seems inexplicable. But their fall illustrates a key economic shift in media history as well as a crucial moment in the conversion to an electronically oriented culture.

***TV Guide* Is Born.** While *Life* and *Look* were just beginning to make sense of the impact of television on their audiences, *TV Guide* appeared in 1953. Taking its cue from the pocket-size format of *Reader's Digest* and the supermarket sales strategy used by women's magazines, *TV Guide*, started by Walter Annenberg's Triangle Publications, soon rivaled the success of *Reader's Digest* by specializing in TV listings and addressing the nation's growing fascination with television. The first issue sold a record 1.5 million copies in ten urban markets. The next year, *TV Guide* featured twenty-seven regional editions, tailoring its listings to TV channels in specific areas of the country. Since many newspapers were not yet listing TV programs, *TV Guide's* circulation soared to 2.2 million in its second year. In 1962, the magazine became the first weekly to reach a circulation of 8 million with its seventy regional editions.

 TV Guide would rank among the nation's most popular magazines from the late 1950s into the 1990s. However, with increased competition from newspaper TV supplements and thousands of new magazines, *TV Guide's* prominence and circulation began flattening out in the 1980s. Then in 1988, media baron Rupert Murdoch acquired Triangle Publications for $3 billion. Out of this magazine group (which included *Seventeen* and the *Daily Racing Form*), Murdoch kept only *TV Guide*. Murdoch's News Corp. already owned the new Fox network, and buying *TV Guide* ensured that the fledgling network would have its programs listed. Prior to this move, many predicted that no one would be able to start a new network because ABC, CBS, and NBC exercised so much control over television.

 The *TV Guide* story illustrates a number of key trends in the magazine business. First, in exploiting Americans' shared interest in television, *TV Guide* emerged as a wildly successful magazine just as general magazines like *Life* and *Look* began their economic decline. Second, *TV Guide* demonstrated the growing sales power of the nation's checkout lines, which also sustained the high circulation rates of women's magazines and supermarket tabloids. Third, News Corp.'s ownership of *TV Guide* underscored the fact that magazines were facing the same challenges as other mass media: Large media companies were strategically buying up smaller media outlets and applying economic synergy—using one medium to promote another. By the mid-1990s, Fox was using *TV Guide* to promote the network's programming in the magazine's 115 regional editions. The other networks occasionally complained—even threatening to pull their ads—that their programs were not treated as well.

 Throughout its history, *TV Guide* has been criticized by the networks for an anti-television bias and by TV critics for not being tough enough on the networks. The magazine has also been chastised for Annenberg's conservative viewpoints, which sometimes leaked into editorial copy, particularly when he used the magazine to endorse Ronald Reagan's candidacy for president in 1980. Nonetheless, *TV Guide* became widely circulated, even surpassing *Reader's Digest* for a time in the 1980s with a U.S. circulation of more than eighteen million.

 The rise of *TV Guide* paralleled the decline of the weekly general interest magazines that had dominated the industry for thirty years. In 1956, both *Collier's* (founded in 1888) and *Woman's Home Companion* (founded in 1873) folded. Each had national circulations of more than four million the year they died. No magazines with such high circulations had ever shut down before. Together, they brought in advertising revenues of more than $26 million in 1956. Although some critics blamed poor management, both magazines were victims of changing consumer tastes, rising postal costs, falling ad revenues—and television, which began usurping the role of magazines as the family medium.

Life and Look Expire. Although *Reader's Digest* and women's supermarket magazines were not greatly affected by television, other general magazines were. The weekly *Saturday Evening Post* folded in 1969, *Look* in 1971, and *Life* in 1972. At the time, all three magazines were rated in the Top 10 in terms of paid circulation; each had readerships in excess of six million per issue. To maintain these figures, however, their publishers were selling the magazines for far less than the cost of production. For example, by the early 1970s a subscription to *Life* cost a consumer twelve cents an issue, yet it cost the publisher more than forty cents per copy to make and mail a single issue.

"At $64,200 for a black-and-white [full] page ad, *Life* had the **highest rate of any magazine**, which probably accounts for its financial troubles. . . . If an **advertiser** also wants to be on television, he may not be able to afford the periodical."

—John Tebbel,
historian,
1969

Eventually, the national advertising revenue pie that helped make up the cost differences for *Life* and *Look* had to be shared with network television—and magazines' slices were getting smaller. *Life*'s high pass-along readership meant that it had a larger audience than many prime-time TV shows. But it cost more in 1971 to reach that general audience with a single full-page ad in *Life* than to buy a minute of time during evening television. National advertisers were often forced to choose between the two, and in the late 1960s and early 1970s, television seemed like a slightly better buy to many general advertisers looking for the biggest audience.

The failure of prominent general magazines was complicated by other problems as well. Essentially, both distribution and production costs (especially paper) were rising, while national magazine ad sales had flattened out. Also, the *Saturday Evening Post*, *Life*, and *Look* still relied more on subscriptions than on supermarket and newsstand sales. Dramatic increases in postal rates, however, had a particularly negative effect on oversized publications (those larger than the 8 x 10.5 in. standard for most magazines). In the 1970s, postal rates increased by more than 400 percent for these magazines. The *Post* and *Life* cut their circulations drastically to save money. The *Post* went from producing 6.8 million to 3 million copies per issue; *Life*, which lost $30 million between 1968 and 1972, cut circulation from 8.5 million to 7 million. The economic rationale here was that limiting the number of copies would reduce production and postal costs, enabling the magazines to lower their ad rates to compete with network television. But, in fact, with decreased circulation, these magazines became less attractive than television for advertisers trying to reach the largest general audience.

The general magazines that survived the competition for national ad dollars tended to be women's magazines, such as *Good Housekeeping*, *Better Homes and Gardens*, *Redbook*, *Ladies' Home Journal*, and *Woman's Day*. These publications were in smaller formats and depended primarily on supermarket sales rather than on expensive mail-delivered subscriptions. However, the most popular magazines, *TV Guide* and *Reader's*

Calvin and Hobbes   by Bill Watterson

Reprinted with permission. All rights reserved.

Digest, benefited not only from supermarket sales but from their larger circulations (twice those of *Life*), their pocket sizes, and their smaller photo budgets. Although the *Saturday Evening Post* and *Life* later returned as downsized monthlies, their failures as oversized weeklies ushered in a new era of specialization.

***People* Puts Life Back into Magazines**. In March 1974, Time Inc. launched *People*, the first successful mass-market magazine to appear in decades. *People* showed a profit in two years and reached a circulation of more than two million within five years. By the early 1990s, *People* ranked second behind *TV Guide* in generating revenue from advertising and circulation sales—more than $700 million.

The success of *People* is instructive, particularly since television just two years earlier had helped kill *Life* by draining away national ad dollars. Instead of using a bulky oversized format and relying on subscriptions, *People* downsized and generated most of its circulation revenue from newsstand and supermarket sales. For content, it took its cue from our culture's fascination with celebrities. Supported by plenty of photos, its articles were short, with about one-third as many words as a typical newsmagazine.

Time Inc. used *People* as the model for reviving *Life* in 1978. The magazine came back as a standard-size supermarket monthly and reached a circulation of around 1.5 million by the mid-1990s. Although *People* never achieved the broad popularity that *Life* once commanded, it does seem to defy the contemporary trend of specialized magazines aimed at narrow but well-defined audiences, such as *Tennis World*, *Teen*, or *Hispanic Business*. One argument suggests that *People* is not, in fact, a mass-market magazine but a specialized publication targeting people with particular cultural interests: the agonies and ecstasies of music, TV, and movie stars. If *People* is viewed as a specialty magazine, its financial success makes much more sense in a world dominated by electronic mass media.

the domination of specialization

The general trend away from mass-market publications and toward specialized magazines coincided with radio's move to specialized formats in the 1950s. With the rise of television in that decade, magazines ultimately did what radio did: They adapted, trading the mass audience for smaller, discrete audiences who could be guaranteed to advertisers. Two major marketing innovations also helped ease the industry into a new era: the development of regional and demographic editions.

regional editions

As television advertising siphoned off national ad revenues, magazines began **regional editions**: national magazines whose content is tailored to the interests of different geographic areas. For example, *Reader's Digest* for years had been printing different language editions for international markets. Largely by necessity, *TV Guide* also developed special editions for each major TV market in the country. Produced on a cheaper grade of paper, different regional listings were inserted into a glossy national section that featured the same photos and articles across the country. *TV Guide* today has more than a hundred regional editions to suit various markets.

While magazine content shifted in these regional editions, ads generally remained the same. Other magazines, however, soon adapted this idea to advertising variations and inserts. Often called **split-run editions**, these national magazines tai-

"At one time marketers viewed magazines as a place in which they could rent space for advertising. Today they view them as **real estate holdings**. Once you own real estate, you begin to think about the neighborhood, the surroundings, **changing the shrubbery** and so forth."
—Stuart Ewen, media historian, 1990

lor ads to different geographic areas. Most editions of *Time* and *Newsweek*, for example, contain a number of pages of regional ads. The editorial content remains the same, but the magazine includes a few pages of ads purchased by local or regional companies in various areas of the country. By the end of the 1960s, nearly 250 magazines featured split-run editions. This strategy has been enhanced by the growth of regional printing centers, which allow publishers to download national magazines from communication satellites for printing near their distribution points. The local ads can be inserted at the various regional production sites.

Another recent innovation in computer technology, called **ink-jet imaging**, allows a magazine publisher or advertiser to print personalized messages to individual subscribers. In this technique, a national news story on political elections might contain the individual subscriber's own voting district in a special inset within the larger national story. In other words, the same technology that allows magazines to encode names and addresses on magazine covers makes it possible to print names *inside* the magazine as well. The technique is frequently used to personalize an ad. For more than a decade, Publishers Clearinghouse and other direct-mail advertisers have used this technology to identify consumers by name as potential sweepstakes winners.

demographic editions

Another variation of specialization includes **demographic editions**, which target particular groups of consumers. In this strategy, market researchers identify subscribers by occupation, class, and zip-code address. In an experiment in 1963, *Time* pioneered demographic editions by carrying advertising from a drug company that was inserted into copies of its magazine. These editions were then sent only to sixty thousand doctors who had been chosen from *Time*'s subscription rolls. By the 1980s, aided by developments in computer technology, *Time* had also developed special editions for top management, high-income zip-code areas, and ultrahigh-income professional/managerial households. Certain high-zip-code editions, for instance, would include ads for more expensive consumer products. *Newsweek*, too, began to use demographic specialization. One annual edition, for example, targets college campuses with special inserts featuring articles on college life and ads aimed only at students.

The economic strategy behind regional and demographic editions was to guarantee clients a particular magazine audience at lower rates. Since these ads would run only in special editions, advertisers had to purchase only part of the total audience. Not only is this cheaper than buying access to a publication's entire readership, but it also links a national magazine with local retailers. The magazine can then compete with advertising in regional television and newspaper supplements. Because of the flexibility of special editions, new sources of income opened up for national magazines. Ultimately, these marketing strategies permitted the massive growth of magazines in the face of predictions that television would cripple the magazine industry.

magazine categories and types

Although regional and demographic editions provided specific strategies for financial survival, the magazine industry ultimately prospered by fragmenting into a wide range of choices and categories (see Table 9.2). Given their current variety, magazines do not classify easily by type; but a number of strategies have been used. One method has been

TABLE 9.2
Number of New Consumer Magazine Launches by Interest Categories, 1995

Category	Number	Category	Number
Arts and antiques	7	Health	9
Automotive	35	Home service and home	44
Aviation	8	Horses, riding, and breeding	3
Babies	2	Literary, book reviews, and writing technique	14
Black/African American	8	Mature market	1
Brides and bridal	3	Media/personalities	43
Business and finance	14	Men's	4
Camping and outdoor recreation	5	Metropolitan, regional, and state	48
CD-ROM	8	Military and naval	7
Children's	6	Motorcycle	16
Comics and comic technique	15	Music	19
Computers	48	Mystery, adventure, and science fiction	3
Crafts, games, hobbies, and models	72	Nature and ecology	2
Dogs and pets	3	Photography	7
Dressmaking and needlework	6	Political and social topics	5
Education/teacher	1	Popular culture	18
Entertainment and performing arts	28	Religious and denominational	14
Epicurean	33	Science and technology	8
Fashion, beauty, and grooming	9	Sex	79
Fishing and hunting	20	Special-interest publications	26
Fitness	14	Sports	70
Gaming	6	Teen	4
Gardening	10	Travel	10
Gay publications	6	TV, radio/communications, and electronics	7
General editorial	2	Women's	10
		Total	838

Source: Samir Husni's Guide to New Consumer Magazines, 1996.

to label magazines according to two categories already discussed: *general interest magazines* reaching diverse national audiences and *specialized magazines* appealing to readers' common traits. A second approach is to divide periodicals between mainstream or *mass-market magazines* (such as *Time* or *Reader's Digest*), which appeal to a diverse readership, and *alternative magazines* (such as *In These Times* or *Against the Current*), which target distinct audiences and are generally critical of conventional culture. (See "Case Study: Alternative Magazines and the *Utne Reader*" on page 258). Because magazines are so varied, however, large two-category distinctions are not very helpful in cataloging them.

Another industry strategy for grouping magazines has been to divide them by advertiser type, although this neglects magazines such as *Ms.*, *Mad*, and *Consumer Reports*, which rely solely on subscription and newsstand sales and accept no advertising. Nevertheless, given the influence of the ad industry, magazines are often categorized as *consumer magazines* (*Newsweek*, *Redbook*), which carry a host of general consumer product ads; as *business* or *trade magazines* (*Advertising Age*, *Progressive Grocer*), which include ads for products and services for various occupa-

"Every magazine has its own architecture. *National Geographic* is a Greek revival temple. *TV Guide* is a fruit stand. The *New Yorker* is a men's hat store. The *Atlantic* is a church (Congregational)."
—Roger Rosenblatt, *New Republic*, 1989

Alternative Magazines and the *Utne Reader*

In 1984, Minnesotan Eric Utne founded the *Utne Reader*, widely regarded today as the *Reader's Digest* of alternative magazines. The *Wall Street Journal* once suggested that the task of Utne's *Reader* was to "sift the good from the goofy."

In some ways, Eric Utne was predestined for the job. His name doesn't exactly mean *alternative*, but it's close. In Norwegian, *utne* means "far out." With fewer than eighty of twelve thousand American magazines reaching circulations that exceed one million, the great bulk of "far out" publications struggle to satisfy small but loyal groups of readers. Of these more modest periodicals, alternative magazines number more than two thousand—with many failing and others starting up from month to month.

Alternative magazines used to define themselves only in terms of politics: published either by the Left (the *Progressive*, *In These Times*, the *Nation*) or the Right (*National Review*, the *American Spectator*, *Insight*). In a broad generalization in 1991, media scholars John Tebbel and Mary Ellen Zuckerman detailed the historical development of these two camps: "While the right-wing magazines have grown in number, strength, and power since the Second World War, well financed as many of them are by rich conservatives, the Left clings to the precarious perch it has always occupied, without well-heeled 'public interest' institutions to support it."[1]

One reason that left-oriented alternative journals seem perpetually on the verge of collapse is historical. It dates

from the late 1960s, when the CIA and FBI tried to infiltrate and disrupt such periodicals for protesting the government's undeclared war on North Vietnam. Tebbel and Zuckerman note, "In this unprecedented attack on First Amendment rights, the CIA became the first federal agency to operate against underground publications in the United States."[2]

The debate over the government's authority to curb alternative forms of speech was resurrected in the aftermath of the 1995 bombing of the federal building in Oklahoma City, which killed 168 people. But this time, discussion focused on curbing the speech of far-right extremists. Both alternative publications and right-wing radio were criticized for inflammatory rhetoric that might encourage citizens to take up weapons against their own government. In these discussions, however, many critics and legal scholars cautioned legislators and the public not to weaken the First Amendment by replicating the government tactics used against leftist alternative publications in the 1960s.

Although Oklahoma City refocused attention on extreme alternative politics, what constitutes an alternative magazine has gone far beyond politics. Today, alternative publications include almost any magazine outside the mainstream, from politics to *punkzines*—magazines' answer to punk rock. Eric Utne has defined *alternative* as any sort of "thinking that doesn't reinvent the status quo, that broadens issues you might see on TV or in the daily paper."

Occasionally, alternative magazines have become

marginally mainstream. For example, during the Reagan era in the 1980s, William F. Buckley's *National Review* saw its circulation swell to more than a hundred thousand, enormous by alternative standards. In the late 1980s, the *Review* even ran slick promotional TV ads featuring actors Charlton Heston and Tom Selleck. On the Left, *Mother Jones* (named after labor organizer Mary Harris Jones), which continues to champion the muckraking tradition of investigative journalism, reached a circulation of more than two hundred thousand during this decade.

The all-time circulation champ in the alternative category is *Rolling Stone*, started in 1967 as an irreverent left-wing political-cultural magazine by twenty-one-year-old Jann Wenner. By 1982, *Rolling Stone* had paddled into the mainstream with a circulation approaching eight hundred thousand and half of its ninety-six-plus pages devoted to high-gloss fashion and consumer advertising. By the mid-1990s, *Rolling Stone*, now famous for its personality profiles and still occasional radical articles on economics or politics, had a circulation of well over one million. Many fans of the early *Rolling Stone*, however, who were disappointed with its move to increase circulation and reflect mainstream consumerist values, turned to alternatives such as *Spin*.

Rolling Stone is an exception. Most alternative magazines are content to swim outside the mainstream. The *Utne Reader*, in its bimonthly editions, routinely sifts through

God and Health: The Latest Findings

(UR) **UTNE READER**

THE BEST OF THE ALTERNATIVE MEDIA $4.99 USA $5.99 CAN
                                        MARCH-APRIL 97

SLOW DOWN

Finding your natural rhythm in a speed-crazed world

Milan Kundera on Seduction
Gary Snyder on Wild Mind
Terry Gross on Nasty Media

these small magazines to feature "the best of the alternative media." Typically, the *Reader* reprints alternative articles on a particular theme, such as work, urban life, psychotherapy, or business ethics. The *Reader* prides itself on staying on top of current social, political, cultural, and economic trends. Three months before the stock market crash in October 1987, for instance, the *Reader* announced "The Coming Crash" and reprinted ominous articles from *In These Times*, *Dollars & Sense*, and *Harper's*. The digest reprints articles from mainstream publications like *Harper's*, *Time*, or the *New Republic* only when the viewpoints expressed do not "reinvent the status quo."

In each issue, the *Reader* indeed sifts the good from the goofy, representing alternative magazines such as *Christianity and Crisis*, *Jewish Currents*, *Southern Africa Report*, *Yellow Silk: Journal of Erotic Arts*, *Hysteria: Women, Humor & Social Change*, and *The Journal of Polymorphous Perversity* ("a social scientist's answer to *Mad* magazine").

For readers interested in alternative points of view, the *Utne Reader* provides a valuable service, sorting through thousands of magazines to reprint quality writing. Ironically, the *Reader* itself has become so successful—with a circulation of three hundred thousand and ads for natural cosmetics, health foods, and alternative businesses—that a few critics, who define alternative publications only by their size, no longer count it among America's alternative media.

tional groups; or as *farm magazines* (*Dairy Herd Management, Dakota Farmer*), which contain ads for agricultural products and farming lifestyles. Grouping by advertisers further distinguishes commercial magazines from noncommercial magazine-like periodicals. The noncommercial category includes everything from activist newsletters and scholarly journals to business newsletters created by companies for distribution to employees.

As we have seen, during the 1950s, radio, film, and magazines arrived at a crossroads as they encountered television. In their own ways, all three media shifted to specialization. Radio developed formats for older and younger audiences, for rock fans and classical fans. At the movies, filmmakers focused on more adult subject matter that was off-limits to television's family medium image. The depiction of language, violence, and sexuality all changed as movies sought an identity apart from television.

Magazines also used such strategies as they searched for niche audiences that were not being served by the new medium. In the magazine industry, publications targeted older and younger readers, tennis buffs, and quilting enthusiasts. Magazine content changed, too. *Playboy*, started in 1953 by Hugh Hefner, capitalized on the patriarchal values of pre–World War II America and emphasized subject matter that was taboo on television in the 1950s. Scraping together $7,000, Hefner published his first issue, which contained a nude calendar reprint of actress Marilyn Monroe, together with a less famous attack on alimony payments and gold-digging women. With the financial success of that first issue, which sold more than fifty thousand copies, Hefner was in business. After one year, *Playboy* defined its audience in this 1954 editorial statement:

> *Playboy* is an entertainment magazine for the indoor man—a choice selection of stories, articles, pictures, cartoons, and humor selected from many sources, past and present, to form a pleasure-primer for the sophisticated city bred male. . . . We hoped it would be welcomed by that select group of urbane fellows who were less concerned with hunting, fishing, and climbing mountains than good food, drink, proper dress, and the pleasure of female company.

Circulation gradually climbed, and Hefner introduced advertising in 1956. *Playboy*'s circulation peaked in the 1960s at more than seven million but fell gradually through the 1970s as the magazine faced competition from imitators and video, and criticism for "packaging" women for the enjoyment of men. Through the 1970s and 1980s, government commissions and religious groups succeeded in eliminating the sale of *Playboy* and similar magazines at military bases and many local retail chains.

the fragmented magazine marketplace

Playboy's early financial success demonstrated to the magazine industry that specialty magazines aimed at men could achieve large circulation figures. Women's publications sold in supermarkets had long demonstrated that gender-based magazines were highly marketable and that women carried enormous economic clout. *Better Homes and Gardens, Good Housekeeping, Ladies' Home Journal, Family Circle, Woman's Day*, and *McCall's* have all ranked among the Top 10 for years, with circulations ranging from 4.5 to 8 million by the mid-1990s. But these numbers are the exception rather than the norm. Of the twelve thousand or so consumer magazines published in the United States today, only about eighty have circulations of more than one million. Most contemporary magazines and newsletters aim at smaller communities of readers who share values, interests, or social identities—from Asian Americans to disabled veterans to conservative students. Indeed, in the early 1990s, the Magazine Publishers of America trade organization listed more than forty special categories of consumer magazines, illustrating the fragmentation of the industry. These included magazines organized around sports and leisure activities, travel and geography, lifestyle and age, and race and ethnicity.

Sport and Leisure Magazines. The television age spawned not only *TV Guide* but a number of specialized leisure magazines. For example, *Soap Opera Digest* updates viewers on the latest plot twists and their favorite characters. By the mid-1990s, the four leading soap-opera magazines had a combined circulation of more than two million. In the age of specialization, magazine executives have developed multiple magazines for fans of soap operas, running, tennis, golf, hunting, quilting, antiquing, surfing, and skin diving, to name only a few. Within categories, magazines specialize further, targeting older or younger runners, men or women golfers, duck hunters or bird watchers, and midwestern or southern antique collectors.

The most popular sports and leisure magazine is *Sports Illustrated*, which took its name from a failed 1935 publication. Launched in 1954 by Henry Luce's Time Inc., *Sports Illustrated* was initially aimed at well-educated, middle-class men. It has become the most successful general sports magazine in history, covering everything from baseball strikes, mountain climbing, fox hunts, and snorkeling to Tiger Woods's 12-stroke victory at the 1997 Masters golf tournament. Although frequently criticized for its popular but exploitive yearly swimsuit editions, *Sports Illustrated* over the years has done major investigative pieces on racketeering in boxing and on land conservation. Its circulation climbed from more than half a million in its first year to two million by 1980 and well over three million by 1997.

Travel and Geography Magazines. In 1992 and 1993, capitalizing on the increasing longevity of the American population and retirees interested in travel, publishers introduced thirty new travel magazines. Periodicals such as *Discover*, *Smithsonian*, *AAA World*, *Travel & Leisure*, and the *Condé Nast Traveler* have all ranked among the nation's hundred top magazines. Some accompany subscriptions to museum organizations or travel clubs, like the American Automobile Association (AAA). Others are devoted to exploring distant cultures or planning trips to various locales.

The undisputed champion in this category is *National Geographic*. Boston lawyer Gardiner Green Hubbard and his famous son-in-law Alexander Graham Bell founded the magazine in 1888, along with the National Geographic Society. From the outset, *National Geographic* relied for its content on a number of distinguished mapmakers, naturalists, explorers, geologists, and geographers. Bell, who became the society's director in 1889, referred to the magazine as "a vehicle for carrying the living, breathing human-interest truth about this great world of ours to the people."[8] Promoted as "humanized geography," *National Geographic* helped pioneer color photography in 1910. It was the first publication to publish both undersea and aerial color photographs. It remains one of the few magazines that subscribers save from year to year and also pass along from generation to

National Geographic is one of the few current magazines whose back issues are valued by used-book stores. Saved by faithful subscribers, the magazine is frequently passed along from generation to generation. A pioneer in color photography, the magazine was founded by the National Geographic Society in 1888.

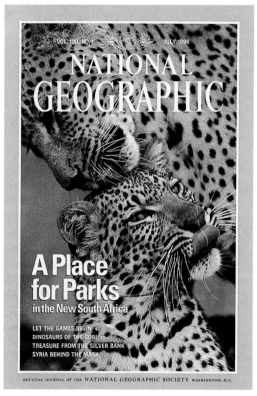

VOL. 190, NO. 1   JULY 1996

NATIONAL GEOGRAPHIC

A Place for Parks in the New South Africa

LET THE GAMES BEGIN 42
DINOSAURS OF THE GOBI 70
TREASURE FROM THE SILVER BANK 90
SYRIA BEHIND THE MASK 106

OFFICIAL JOURNAL OF THE NATIONAL GEOGRAPHIC SOCIETY WASHINGTON, D.C.

generation. *National Geographic*'s popularity grew slowly and steadily throughout the twentieth century, reaching a million in circulation in 1935 and ten million in the 1970s. In the mid-1990s, it still had a circulation of more than nine million, all from paid subscriptions. In addition, many of *National Geographic*'s nature and culture specials on television, which began in 1965, rank among the most popular programs in the history of public television.

Magazines for the Ages. For years, magazines have targeted readers by economic class and lifestyle, usually distinguishing the mass appeal of *Life* and *Reader's Digest* from the more sophisticated appeal of the *New Yorker, Esquire,* or *Vogue.* In the age of specialization, however, magazines have further delineated readers along ever narrowing age lines, appealing more and more to very young and to older readers, groups that have often been ignored over the years by mainstream television.

The first children's magazines appeared in New England in the late 1700s. Ever since, magazines such as *Youth's Companion, Boy's Life* (the Boy Scouts' national publication since 1912), *Highlights,* and *Ranger Rick* have successfully targeted preschool and elementary school children. Helped by its TV connection, *Sesame Street Magazine* was the top children's magazine in the mid-1990s with a circulation of more than one million, followed by *Disney Adventures* with just under a million subscribers. The leading high school education magazines included the *Scholastic* group (*Update, Scope, Voice,* and *Science World*), which totaled more than two million in circulation in the early 1990s. In the popular arena, humor magazines such as *Mad, Cracked,* and *National Lampoon* have had high readerships among male teens and young adults. Overall circulation for the leading female teen magazines showed substantial growth in 1996; the top magazines for thirteen- to nineteen-year-olds included *Seventeen, YM,* and *Teen.* Their loyal fans demonstrated that many young people, in search of their own social and cultural identities, remain avid readers despite the competition from television and computer games.

In targeting audiences by age, the most dramatic success has come from magazines aimed at readers over fifty-five, America's fastest-growing age segment. These publications have tried to meet the cultural interests of older Americans, who historically have not been prominently featured in mainstream consumer culture. The American Association of Retired Persons (AARP) and its magazine, *Modern Maturity,* were founded in 1958 by retired California teacher Ethel Percy Andrus, who eleven years earlier had established the National Retired Teachers Association (NRTA). For years, both groups published newsletters—which they later merged into the *NRTA/AARP Bulletin*—keeping older citizens current on politics, health, and culture.

Subscriptions to six issues per year of *Modern Maturity* and the AARP newsletter have always come with a modest membership fee ($8 in 1997). By the early 1980s, *Modern Maturity*'s circulation approached seven million. However, with the AARP signing up thirty thousand new members each week by the late 1980s, both *Modern Maturity* and the joint newsletter overtook *TV Guide* and *Reader's Digest* as the top circulated magazines. By the mid-1990s, both had circulations of more than twenty million. Not available at newsstands, *Modern Maturity* (like its early competitors *Senior Citizen* and *Harvest Years*) also did not carry advertising during its first ten years. The conventional wisdom in many ad agencies, dominated by staffers under age fifty, suggested that people over fifty were loyal to certain brand names and were difficult to change through ads. Research demonstrated, however, that many in this group are more affluent than eighteen- to forty-nine-year-olds and have consumer interests increasingly in line with the thirty-nine to forty-nine age bracket. Today, *Modern Maturity* still carries few consumer ads, relying mostly on inexpensive subscriptions, the growth of the plus-fifty-five age group, and its readers' continuing interest in the printed word.

elite magazines and cultural minorities

In his important 1964 study, *Magazines in the Twentieth Century*, historian Theodore Peterson devoted a chapter to cultural minorities. In the mid-1960s, though, the term *cultural minorities* meant elite readers who were served mainly by non-mass-market political and literary magazines such as *Atlantic Monthly*, *Kenyon Review*, the *Nation*, *National Review*, the *New Republic*, *Partisan Review*, or *Poetry*. In general, these political and literary magazines appealed to formally educated readers who shared political ideas, aesthetic concerns, or social values. To their credit, the editors and publishers of such magazines have often struggled financially to maintain the integrity of their magazines in an industry dominated by advertising and mass-market publications.

The *New Yorker*. The most widely circulated "elite" magazine in this century has been the *New Yorker*. Launched in 1925 by Harold Ross, the *New Yorker* became the first city magazine aimed at a national upscale audience. In some ways, the *New Yorker* was the magazine equivalent of the *New York Times*, cultivating an affluent and educated audience and excluding general readers. Snubbing the Midwest, Ross once claimed, "the *New Yorker* will be the magazine which is not edited for the old lady in Dubuque. It will not be concerned in what she is thinking about."[9] Over the years, the *New Yorker* featured many of this century's most prominent biographers, writers, reporters, and humorists, including A. J. Liebling, Dorothy Parker, Lillian Ross, John Updike, E. B. White, and Garrison Keillor, as well as James Thurber's cartoons and Ogden Nash's poetry. It introduced some of the finest literary journalism of the twentieth century, devoting an entire issue to John Hersey's *Hiroshima* and serializing Truman Capote's *In Cold Blood*.

By the mid-1960s, the *New Yorker's* circulation hovered around five hundred thousand. Just as the *New York Times* became known as the nation's best newspaper, the *New Yorker* made promotional claims as the country's best magazine. By the 1960s, the magazine even had a hundred subscribers in Dubuque, Iowa, including a number of "old ladies." In 1985, the *New Yorker* was acquired for $168 million by Advance Publications, the Newhouse newspaper publishing conglomerate. By the mid-1990s, the magazine's circulation had reached eight hundred thousand.

Dec. 16, 1996   THE NEW YORKER   Price $2.95

Famous for its inventive cartoons, well-crafted prose, and whimsical covers, the *New Yorker* first appeared in 1925. Originally planned as a local publication, the *New Yorker* over the years developed into one of the nation's most influential magazines, shaping public opinion on everything from national politics to popular culture. (Cover drawing "Christmas Past, Christmas Present" by Edward Sorel © 1996, The New Yorker Magazine, Inc. All rights reserved.)

Redefining Cultural Minorities. By the 1980s and 1990s, the term *cultural minority* had taken on different connotations. It referred to distinctions regarding gender, age, race, ethnicity, and sexual orientation. Since the late 1960s, with attention drawn to many discriminatory practices, a number of magazines have developed to deal with concerns that were often bypassed by mainstream magazines. Historically, one key magazine has been the *Advocate*, which began in 1967 as a twelve-page newsletter addressing issues about homosexuality. By the mid-1980s, the magazine had a circulation of nearly a hundred thousand, and by the early 1990s

Reader's Digest remains the most widely circulated magazine in the world, available in more than 160 countries and 20 languages, including Arabic, Chinese, Greek, Korean, and Hindi. This 1995 Thai edition of the magazine features the Hong Kong skyline and an article titled "What Will Happen to Hong Kong?" (bottom left in yellow). The top title asks, "Should You Have Cosmetic Surgery?" (upper left in white).

more than fifteen new magazines aimed at gay men or lesbians had been launched. The *Advocate* has published some of the best journalism on AIDS, antigay violence, and policy issues affecting homosexual communities. In some instances, its reporting has led to increased coverage of important issues by the mainstream press.

In general, the term *cultural minority* has been more closely associated with racial and ethnic groups that have often been misrepresented or underrepresented in America's popular media. To counter white mainstream conceptions, African American magazines, for example, date to antislavery publications such as the *Emancipator*, *Liberator*, and *Reformer* during the pre–Civil War era. In the modern age, the major magazine publisher for African Americans has been John H. Johnson, a former Chicago insurance salesman who started *Negro Digest* in 1942 on $500 borrowed against his mother's furniture. By 1945, with a circulation of more than a hundred thousand, Johnson and a small group of editors had enough money to start *Ebony*, a picture-text magazine modeled on *Life* but serving chiefly black readers. The Johnson Publishing Company has since successfully introduced *Jet*, a pocket-size supermarket magazine that originally contained shorter pieces left over from *Ebony*. By the mid-1990s, *Jet*'s circulation was near one million.

Johnson's publications were one of the first places where people could see black images on a weekly basis in American popular culture. Originally criticized for favoring light-skinned black faces over dark-skinned black faces, *Ebony* has over the years developed into the leading popular magazine forum for black politics and social life in the United States. In fact, Johnson's publications were among the first forums to help clarify what it meant to be black and middle-class in America after World War II. By the late 1970s, *Ebony*'s circulation reached 1.3 million; by the mid-1990s, it had 2 million paid subscribers and an estimated pass-along readership of 11 million. In 1970, the first successful magazine aimed at black middle-class women, *Essence*, was started by Edward Lewis. It enjoyed a circulation close to one million by 1996.

With increases in Hispanic populations and immigration, magazines appealing to Spanish-speaking readers have developed rapidly since the 1980s. In 1983, the De Armas Spanish Magazine Network began distributing Spanish-language versions of mainstream American magazines, including *Cosmopolitan en Espanol*, *Harper's Bazaar en Espanol*, and *Ring*, the prominent boxing magazine. In 1989, Casiano Communications launched *Imagen*, a glossy upscale publication for middle- and upper-middle-class Hispanic readers. By the early 1990s, however, the best-selling Spanish-language magazine was *Selecciones del Reader's Digest*, with over 150,000 paid subscriptions in the United States alone. In the mid-1990s, Spanish-language magazines began to decline. Research suggested that because many Hispanics had been in the United States more than ten years, Spanish had become their second language.

Thus, entrepreneurs began developing prototypes for English magazines, such as *Latina Style*, aimed at the nation's 9.5 million upwardly mobile Hispanic readers who earned between $30,000 and $120,000 annually in 1997.

supermarket tabloids

After TV star Carol Burnett won a $1.6 million libel judgment (reduced to $800,000 on appeal) against the *National Enquirer* in the 1980s, supermarket tabloids behaved for a time. Although tabloids have usually been protected by the First Amendment, celebrities have sued them frequently over the years. Partly due to tabloids' bad reputations, neither the newspaper nor the magazine industry likes to claim them as part of its domain. But the Audit Bureau of Circulations, which checks newspaper and magazine circulation figures to determine advertising rates, counts weekly tabloids as magazines. Although tabloids trace their history to newspapers' use of graphics and pictorial layouts in the 1860s and 1870s, the modern U.S. tabloid dates from the founding of the *National Enquirer* by William Randolph Hearst in 1926. The *Enquirer* struggled until it was purchased in 1952 by Generoso Pope, who had worked in the cement business and for his father's New York-based Italian-language newspaper, *Il Progresso*. Also a former intelligence officer for the CIA's psychological warfare unit, Pope intended to use the paper to "fight for the rights of man" and "human decency and dignity."[10] In the interest of profit, though, he settled on the "gore formula" to transform the paper's anemic weekly circulation of seven thousand: "I noticed how auto accidents drew crowds and I decided that if it was blood that interested people, I'd give it to them."[11]

> "It's wonderful. I love talking to witches and Satanists and vampire hunters, and people who have been **kidnapped by UFOs**—it sure beats covering zoning board meetings."
> —Cliff Linedecker,
> former associate editor,
> *National Examiner*

By the mid-1960s, Pope had built the *Enquirer's* circulation to one million through the use of bizarre human interest stories, gruesome murder tales, violent accident accounts, unexplained phenomena stories, and malicious celebrity gossip. Later, the *Enquirer* incorporated some of yellow journalism's crusading traditions, reporting government cover-ups and stories of bureaucratic waste. By 1974, the *Enquirer's* weekly circulation topped four million, where it remained for several years. In 1977, its edition covering the death of Elvis Presley included a controversial picture of Presley in his open coffin and sold more than 6.6 million copies, still a tabloid record.

In 1974, Rupert Murdoch's News Corp. launched the *Star*, built on the "circus-poster layout, garish headlines, and steamy prose" traditions of Great Britain's sleazy tabloid press. Among the *Star's* announced objectives: "not be politically committed, not be a killjoy, not be bullied, not be boring."[12] The *Star* and a third major tabloid player, the *Globe* (founded in 1954), cut into the *Enquirer's* circulation and set the tone for current trends in tabloid content, including stories on medical cures, astrological predictions, celebrity gossip, and the occult.

Between 1990 and 1996, the three largest tabloids lost about 30 percent of their circulation. The *National Enquirer* fell from 4 to 2.7 million, the *Star* from 3.6 to 2.5 million, and the *Globe* from 1.3 million to less than 1 million. Not only did imitators like the *National Examiner*, the *Sun*, and the *Weekly World News* offer competition, but *People*, *US*, new entertainment magazines, newsmagazines, and talk shows also began claiming part of the tabloid audience.[13] At the same time, occasional investigative and political stories started appearing in tabloids and influencing coverage by major newspapers and newsmagazines. Tabloid editors, however, have tried to avoid most political stories: Circulation apparently declines when political intrigue graces their front pages.[14] Although their popularity peaked in the 1980s, tabloids continue to specialize in reaching audiences not served by mainstream media.

the organization and economics of magazines

Given the great diversity in magazine content and ownership, it is hard to offer a common profile of a successful magazine. Unlike a broadcast station or a daily newspaper, a small newsletter or magazine can begin cheaply via computer-driven **desktop publishing** technology, which allows one aspiring publisher-editor to write, design, lay out, and even print a modest publication. Such magazines—sometimes called *zines*—are also mushrooming on the World Wide Web and other sectors of the Internet (see "Tracking Technology: The Personal Zine Explosion").

departments and duties

Most major magazines are now available through online computer services, some of which allow readers to interact electronically with writers and editors at various magazines. Other technological advances enable magazines to offer subscribers digital versions of both text and photos. Many magazines today are also available on the information highway through telephone lines, satellite delivery, or CD-ROM. Not surprisingly, great debates persist over whether online and digital magazines, such as Microsoft's *Slate*, will eventually replace traditional printed versions. By the mid-1990s, however, electronic alternatives had not slowed the growth of printed magazines. Despite the rise of zines and desktop publishing, most large commercial firms still operate several departments, which employ hundreds of people.

Production and Technology. The magazine unit most concerned with merging old and new ideas is the production and technology department, which maintains the computer and printing hardware necessary for mass-market production. Unlike daily newspapers, though, magazines do not face daily production deadlines and are therefore able to farm out the final printing to separate companies. Since magazines are usually printed weekly, monthly, or bimonthly, it is not economically practical for most magazine publishers to maintain expensive print facilities. As with *USA Today*, many national magazines are now able to digitally transport magazine copy via satellite to various regional printing sites for the insertion of local ads and for faster distribution.

To attract advertisers and audiences over the years, magazines have deployed other technological innovations: from *National Geographic*'s pioneering 3-D color holograph cover (similar to the technology used in the special effects for the movie *Star Wars*) to digitized full-color versions of magazines on the World Wide Web. Through reader questionnaires and electronic databases, magazines can even develop special inserts, called *selective edits*, for specific customers. For example, in 1993 *Child* magazine began using data from the birth dates of its subscribers' children; it inserted customized monthly editorial and advertising sections on children at a specific age or developmental stage. In 1994, *Sports Illustrated* identified four hundred thousand serious golfers among its readers and began a "Golf Plus" insert for those copies sent to golfing enthusiasts.[15]

Editorial Content. The lifeblood of a magazine is the editorial department, which produces its content, excluding advertisements. Like newspapers, most magazines have a chain of command that begins with the publisher and extends to the editor-in-chief, the managing editor, and a variety of subeditors. These subeditors oversee such editorial functions as photography, illustrations, reporting and writing,

The Personal Zine Explosion

One of the most democratic developments in media history may be those personal, self-published magazines called *zines*. Riding the wave of personal computer programs for designing newsletters and magazines, zines are a grassroots publishing phenomenon. They usually appeal to younger readers and in recent years have found a home on the Internet.

Zines first emerged in the 1930s as part of cult groups who read and then wrote about science fiction. They produced single-copy zines on typewriters and passed them around to friends. In the late 1960s, zines emerged as part of the student protests against the Vietnam War. These zines were still produced on typewriters, but they could be inexpensively copied on Xerox machines, stapled together, and sold on street corners or given away to friends. In the 1970s, newsletter-style zines paid tribute to the alternative lifestyles of punk-rock culture. But zines really took off with the explosion of desktop publishing in the 1980s and Internet sites in the 1990s.

In print versions alone, more than fifty thousand zines celebrate obscure rock performers, promote eccentric religious views, confront the problem of substance abuse, attack politicians, or document an individual's emotional problems. Some are rambling autobiographies, some offer poetry or science fiction, and others sound like letters to close friends.

At the high end of the market is *Might*, a satirical zine started in 1994 by a group of friends in San Francisco with money borrowed on credit cards. In 1995, it cost the group $1 to produce one copy; *Might* carried alcohol ads and sold some thirty thousand copies at $4 apiece at alternative bookstores and record shops. Some national chains—like Borders and Tower Records—now carry a variety of zines, especially those devoted to culture and music. Nevertheless, few zines make money, even though more and more have started to carry ads. A zine titled *Factsheet Five* emerged in the mid-1980s for the purpose of reviewing other zines; it offers capsule summaries of zines such as *Teen Mom*, *Pagan's Head*, *Dishwasher*, and *Pathetic Life*.

Desktop publishing can produce a decent-looking, four-page zine for a few hundred dollars. Zine sites on the World Wide Web cost no more than the fee of a monthly Internet provider. Zines usually find their audiences by word of mouth, and most sell through direct mail. Some are distributed free over the Internet.

Personal zines operate at the extreme edge of magazine specialization; they are often distributed to just a few people besides the publisher and his or her family and friends. Many are designed intentionally to counter mainstream, mass-market publications. These zines focus on topics so narrow or obscure that only a handful of readers may be interested in them.

Zines are sometimes manifestations of loneliness and the desire to connect as well as venues for spreading information about subject matter ignored by mainstream media. Zine publishers may be looking for solutions to larger problems, or they may just be looking for somebody with whom to share a quirky idea.

copyediting, and layout and design. Writing staffs for magazines generally include *contributing writers*, who are specialists in certain fields. These writers may have recurring columns or may cover specific topics, such as medicine, law, or politics. Magazines also hire professional, nonstaff *freelance writers*, who are assigned to cover particular stories or a region of the country. Many magazines, especially those with small budgets, also rely on well-written unsolicited manuscripts to fill their pages. Most commercial magazines, however, reject more than 95 percent of unsolicited pieces.

Advertising and Sales. The advertising and sales department of a magazine secures clients, arranges promotions, and places ads. Industry-wide, this unit has pioneered innovations such as the scent strip in perfume ads, pop-up ads, and voice-activated message ads that emit sounds when a page is turned. Besides stuffing magazines with the ever-present subscription-renewal postcards, this department also conducts market research to study trends and changes in magazine-reading habits. For instance, audience research from the mid-1990s suggested that the average male reader of *GQ* was twenty-nine years of age and lived in a household with an annual income of around $42,000. *Esquire*'s typical reader, on the other hand, was a thirty-seven-year-old male whose household income averaged $40,000 a year.

Magazines generate about half their annual revenue from selling ads, with the remaining money coming from single-copy and subscription sales (see Figure 9.1). Like radio and TV stations, consumer magazines offer *rate cards* to advertisers, which list what a magazine charges for an ad. For example, a top-rated consumer magazine might charge $64,000 for a full-page color ad and $20,000 for a one-third page, black-and-white ad. However, in today's competitive world, most rate cards are not very meaningful: Almost all magazines offer 25 to 50 percent rate discounts to advertisers.[16]

Although fashion and general magazines carry a higher percentage of ads than do political-literary magazines, the average magazine contains about 45 percent ad copy and 55 percent editorial material. This figure has remained fairly constant over the last twenty-five years. Some dispute these categories, though, since many readers of fashion magazines consider the ads the main "editorial" content.

A few contemporary magazines, such as *Mad*, have decided not to carry ads and rely solely on subscriptions and newsstand sales. To protect the integrity of its various tests and product comparisons, for instance, *Consumer Reports* carries no advertising. To strengthen its editorial independence, *Ms.* magazine abandoned ads in 1990 after years of pressure from the food, cosmetic, and fashion industries to carry recipes and more *complementary copy*: positive, upbeat articles that support the ads carried in various consumer magazines. Some advertisers and companies have canceled ads when a magazine featured an unflattering or critical article about a company or industry.[17] In some instances, this practice has put enormous pressure on editors not to offend advertisers. The cozy relationships between some advertisers and magazines have led to a dramatic decline in investigative reporting, once central to popular magazines during the muckraking era (see "Examining Ethics: Sex, Lies, and Advertising" on page 270).

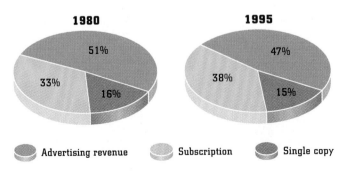

Figure 9.1
Changing Sources of Magazine Revenue
Source: Magazine Publishers of America.

Circulation and Distribution. The circulation and distribution department of a magazine monitors single-copy and subscription sales. Subscriptions, which dominated the industry's infancy, have made a strong comeback. For example, toward the end of the general interest era in 1950, single-copy sales at supermarkets and newsstands accounted for about 43 percent of magazine sales while subscriptions constituted 57 percent. By the 1990s, single-copy sales were just under 20 percent, while subscriptions had risen to over 80 percent. One tactic used by circulation departments is to encourage consumers to renew well in advance of their actual renewal dates. Magazines can thus invest and earn interest on early renewal money as a hedge against consumers who drop their subscriptions each year.

Magazines circulate in two basic ways: paid or controlled. *Paid circulation* simply means consumers either pay for a regular subscription to the magazine or pay for individual copies at a newsstand or supermarket. Most consumer magazines depend on paid circulation as well as advertising. *Controlled circulation* provides the magazine to readers at no charge. This type of circulation generally targets captive audiences such as airline passengers or association members. The *NRTA/AARP Bulletin*, for example, comes with membership in the National Retired Teachers Association or the American Association of Retired Persons. Many business or technical magazines and newsletters, which depend on advertising or corporate sponsorship, are distributed free to members or loyal customers.

Studies by the Magazine Publishers of America suggest that more than 80 percent of all American households either subscribe to a magazine or purchase one on a regular basis. The average household typically purchases at least six different titles during a given year. Although the magazine industry was generally regarded as economically healthy through the 1980s, some signs worry editors and publishers. For instance, in 1990, for the first time since the Depression, the number of consumer magazine titles declined. In addition, a decline in operating pretax profit margins for magazines, which began in the early 1990s, troubled the industry. In part, the decline is attributed to the proliferation of specialized cable television channels and new personal computer and Internet services.

major magazine chains

In terms of ownership, the commercial magazine industry most closely resembles the cable television business, which actually patterned its specialized channels on the consumer magazine market. About twelve thousand commercial magazine titles appear each year—many of them independently owned—just as roughly eleven thousand cable systems now operate in the United States. Also, like the cable industry, large companies or chains increasingly dominate the magazine business. This raises yet unanswered questions about the impact of a handful of powerful magazine owners on the ideas that circulate in the commercial marketplace.

Time Warner, the nation's second-largest cable operator, also runs a magazine subsidiary, Time Inc., a major player among magazine-chain operators with more than twenty titles (see Table 9.3). Other important commercial players include Mortimer Zuckerman, who owns the *Atlantic Monthly* and *U.S. News & World Report*, and the Meredith Publishing Company, which specializes in women's magazines. The Hearst Corporation, the leading magazine chain early in the twentieth century, still remains a formidable publisher.

Long a force in upscale consumer magazines, Condé Nast is now a division of Advance Publications, which operates the Newhouse newspaper chain. The Condé Nast group controls several key magazines, including *Vanity Fair*, *GQ*, and *Vogue*. Advance Publications also owns *Parade* magazine, the popular Sunday newspaper sup-

by Gloria Steinem

What could women's magazines be like if they were as free as books? as realistic as newspapers? as creative as films? as diverse as women's lives? We don't know.

But we'll find out only if we take women's magazines seriously. If readers were to act in a concerted way to change traditional practices of all women's magazines and the marketing of all women's products, we could do it. After all, they are operating on our consumer dollars; money that we now control. You and I could:

- write to editors and publishers (with copies to advertisers) that we're willing to pay more for magazines with editorial independence, but will not continue to pay for those that are just editorial extensions of ads;

- write to advertisers (with copies to editors and publishers) that we want fiction, political reporting, consumer reporting—whatever is, or is not, supported by their ads;

- put as much energy into breaking advertising's control over content as into changing the images in ads, or protesting ads for harmful products like cigarettes;

- support only those women's magazines and products that take us seriously as readers and consumers.

Those of us in the magazine world can also use the carrot-and-stick technique. For instance: pointing out that, if magazines were a regulated medium like television, the demands of advertisers would be against FCC rules. Payola and extortion could be punished. As it is, there are probably illegalities. A magazine's postal rates are determined by the ratio of ad to edit[orial] pages, and the former costs more than the latter. So much for the stick.

"put as much energy into breaking advertising's control over content as into changing the images in ads"

The carrot means appealing to enlightened self-interest. For instance: there are many studies showing that the greatest factor in determining an ad's effectiveness is the credibility of its surroundings. The "higher the rating of editorial believability," concluded a 1987 survey by the *Journal of Advertising Research*, "the higher the rating of the advertising." Thus, an impenetrable wall between edit and ads would also be in the best interest of advertisers.

Unfortunately, few agencies or clients hear such arguments. Editors often maintain the false purity of refusing to talk to them at all. Instead, they see ad sales people who know little about editorial, are trained in business as usual, and are usually paid by commission. Editors might also band together to take on controversy. That happened once when all the major women's magazines did articles in the same month on the Equal Rights Amendment. It could happen again....

Even as I write this, I get a call from a writer for *Elle*, who is doing a whole article on where women part their hair. Why, she wants to know, do I part mine in the middle?

It's all so familiar. A writer trying to make something of a nothing assignment; an editor laboring to think of new ways to attract ads; readers assuming that other women must want this ridiculous stuff; more women suffering for lack of information, insight, creativity, and laughter that could be on these same pages.

I ask you: Can't we do better than this?

Sample pages are from the first issue of *Ms.* magazine, Spring 1972.
Source: Gloria Steinem, "Sex, Lies, and Advertising," *Ms.* (July–August 1990), 18–28.

271

TABLE 9.3
Major Magazine Chains
(selected holdings as of 1996)

Advance Publications (Staten Island, NY)
Condé Nast Group
  Allure
  Architectural Digest
  Bon Appetit
  Bride's
  Glamour
  Gourmet
  GQ
  Mademoiselle
  Vanity Fair
  Vogue
New Yorker
Parade

Bertelsmann (Gütersloh, Germany)
Child
Family Circle
McCall's

Hachette Filipacchi, a subsidiary of Lagardère Groupe (Paris)
Car and Driver
Cycle World
Elle
Family Life
George
Mirabella
Premiere
Road & Track
Video
Woman's Day

Hearst Corporation (New York, NY)
Cosmopolitan
Country Living
Esquire
Good Housekeeping
Harper's Bazaar
House Beautiful
Popular Mechanics
Redbook
Town & Country

K-III Communications (New York, NY)
American Baby
Daily Racing Form
Dog World
Modern Bride
New York
Sail
Seventeen
Soap Opera Digest
Truckin'

Meredith Corporation (Des Moines, IA)
Better Homes and Gardens
Country Home
Golf for Women
Ladies' Home Journal
Motherhood Magazine
Successful Farming

New York Times Company (New York, NY)
Cruising World
Golf Digest
Golf World
Sailing World
Snow Country
Tennis

Reed Elsevier (London)
Lexis-Nexis (online magazine/newspaper search service)
Marie Claire
Publishers Weekly
Variety
Yachting World

Time Inc. (New York, NY)
Asiaweek
Entertainment Weekly
FORTUNE
Life
Martha Stewart Living
Money
Parenting
People
Progressive Farmer
SI for Kids
Sports Illustrated
Sunset
Time
Vibe

Source: Hoover's Guide to Media Companies (Austin, TX: Hoover's Business Press, 1996), 46, 90, 110, 129, 149, 165, 279.

plement that goes to thirty million homes each week. Since Sunday supplements come with newspaper subscriptions, they are not counted among most official magazine tallies. Nevertheless, *Parade* and its closest rival, *USA Weekend*, reached more readers than the leading popular magazines in the mid-1990s.

International companies like Paris-based Hachette Filipacchi are also major players in the U.S. magazine industry. Hachette owns more than twenty consumer magazines with a worldwide readership of more than fifty million. Its holdings include *Mirabella*, *Woman's Day*, and *Car and Driver*. In 1995, Hachette spent $20 million to launch *George*, the political-cultural magazine cofounded by John F. Kennedy Jr. Australia's News Corp. (which owns *TV Guide*) and Britain's Reed Elsevier (owner of *Variety*, the American trade magazine for show business) also play influential roles in American magazine publishing.

In addition, a number of American magazines have carved out market niches worldwide. *Reader's Digest*, *Cosmopolitan*, *Newsweek*, and *Time*, for example, all produce international editions in several languages. In general, though, most American magazines are local, regional, or specialized and therefore less exportable than this country's movies and television. Of twelve thousand titles, only about two hundred magazines from the United States circulate routinely in the world market. Such magazines, however, like exported American TV shows and films, still play a key role in determining the look of global culture.

magazines in a democratic society

Like other mass media whose product lines have proliferated, magazines are a major part of the cluttered media landscape. To keep pace, the magazine industry has become a fast-paced, high-risk industry. Of the eight hundred or so new magazines that start up each year, fewer than two hundred will survive longer than a year.

As an industry, magazine publishing—like advertising and public relations—has played a central role in transforming the United States from a producer to a consumer society. Since the 1950s, though, magazines have not been the powerful national voice they once were, uniting separate communities around important issues such as abolition and suffrage. Today, with so many specialized magazines appealing to distinct groups of consumers, magazines play a much diminished role in creating a sense of national identity.

On the positive side, magazine ownership is more diversified than ownership in other mass media. More magazine voices circulate in the marketplace than do broadcast or cable television channels. Moreover, many new magazines still play an important role in uniting geographically dispersed groups of readers, often giving cultural minorities or newly arrived immigrants a sense of membership in a broader community.

Contemporary commercial magazines provide essential information about politics, society, and culture, thus helping us think about ourselves as participants in a democracy. Unfortunately, however, they have often identified their readers as consumers first and as citizens only secondarily. With magazines' growing dependence on advertising, controversial content sometimes has difficulty finding its way into print. More and more, magazines define their readers merely as viewers of displayed products and purchasers of material goods.

At the same time, magazines arguably have had more freedom than other media to encourage and participate in democratic debates. In addition, because magazines are distributed weekly, monthly, or bimonthly, they are less restricted by the deadline pressures of daily newspapers or evening broadcasts. Released from this burden, good magazines usu-

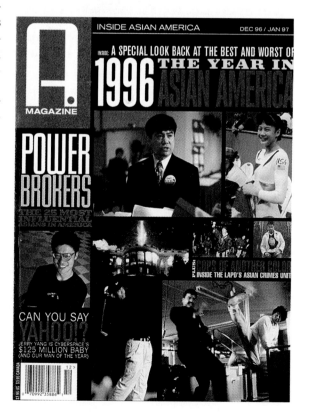

A. Magazine is an example of the increasing diversity of American popular culture. Published since 1990, this bimonthly reviews Asian influences on mass media and covers prestigious Asian Americans in business, politics, law, and sports. In 1997, with a circulation near one hundred thousand, the magazine published its first book, *Eastern Standard Time: A Guide to Asian Influence in American Fad, Food, and Culture.*

ally can offer more analysis of and insight into society than other media outlets. In the midst of today's swirl of images, magazines and their advertisements certainly contribute to the commotion. But good magazines also maintain our connection to words, sustaining their vital role in an increasingly electronic and digital culture.

REVIEW QUESTIONS

1. Why did magazines develop later than newspapers in the American colonies?

2. Why did most of the earliest magazines have so much trouble staying financially solvent?

3. How did magazines become national in scope?

4. What role did magazines play in social reform at the turn of the century?

5. When and why did general interest magazines become so popular?

6. Why did some of the major general interest magazines fail?

7. What triggered the move toward magazine specialization?

8. What are the differences between *regional* and *demographic* editions?

9. What are the most useful ways to categorize the magazine industry? Why?

10. What are the four main departments at a typical consumer magazine?

11. Which are the major magazine chains, and what is their impact on the mass media industry in general?

12. In what ways do magazines serve a democratic society?

QUESTIONING THE MEDIA

1. What are your earliest recollections of magazines? What magazines do you read regularly today? Why?

2. What role did magazines play in America's political and social shift from being colonies of Great Britain to becoming an independent nation?

3. Why is the muckraking spirit—so important in popular magazines at the turn of the century—generally missing from magazines today?

4. Imagine that you are the marketing director of your favorite magazine. What would you do to increase circulation?

5. Think of stories, ideas, and images (illustrations and photos) that do *not* appear in mainstream magazines. Why do you think this is so? (Use the Internet, NEXIS, or the library to compare your list with Project Censor, an annual list of the year's most underreported stories.)

6. Discuss whether your favorite magazines define you primarily as a consumer or as a citizen. Do you think magazines have a responsibility to educate their readers as both? What could they do to promote citizenship?

7. Do you think cable television, the World Wide Web, and other specialized computer technology will eventually displace magazines? Why or why not?

The purpose of this project is to offer a particular type of critical approach to magazines. Work with a partner or in small groups. (This project could also be converted to a formal argument paper.)

1. Take any recent issue of *Time* and *Newsweek*. (Other magazines may be substituted, or contemporary issues may be compared with issues from earlier decades.) Review all photos in the two magazines, counting the males and females represented. Keep a separate count for each magazine of the number of men and women depicted in the *ads* and the number shown in the *news photos* that accompany the stories.

    (Option: You might also break down your count by *race* and by *age*. When these categories are difficult to determine, create a category called *unknown*.)

2. Devise a rough chart to organize your findings. Write a one- or two-paragraph critical interpretation of your findings based on the following questions:

   • What patterns emerge? Are men treated differently from women? If so, in what ways? (Document your evidence.)

   • Do the magazines differ in their treatments of men and women? Explain.

   • Do the content, photos, and ads in these magazines make you think of yourself as a consumer or as a citizen? Who do the magazines think their readers are? Based on your limited analysis, sketch a profile of the typical reader of each magazine.

     (Option: Now call the research department at various magazines and see if they will give you a profile sketch of their typical reader. Compare your profile with theirs.)

   • Explain the limits of simply counting gender depictions in ad and news photos. What issues cannot be addressed by such a method? How might we go about doing a fuller study of issues raised in this project?

CHAPTER 10

Books

and the Power of Print

JOHN
GRISHAM
THE
CLIENT
LARGE
PRINT
EDITION

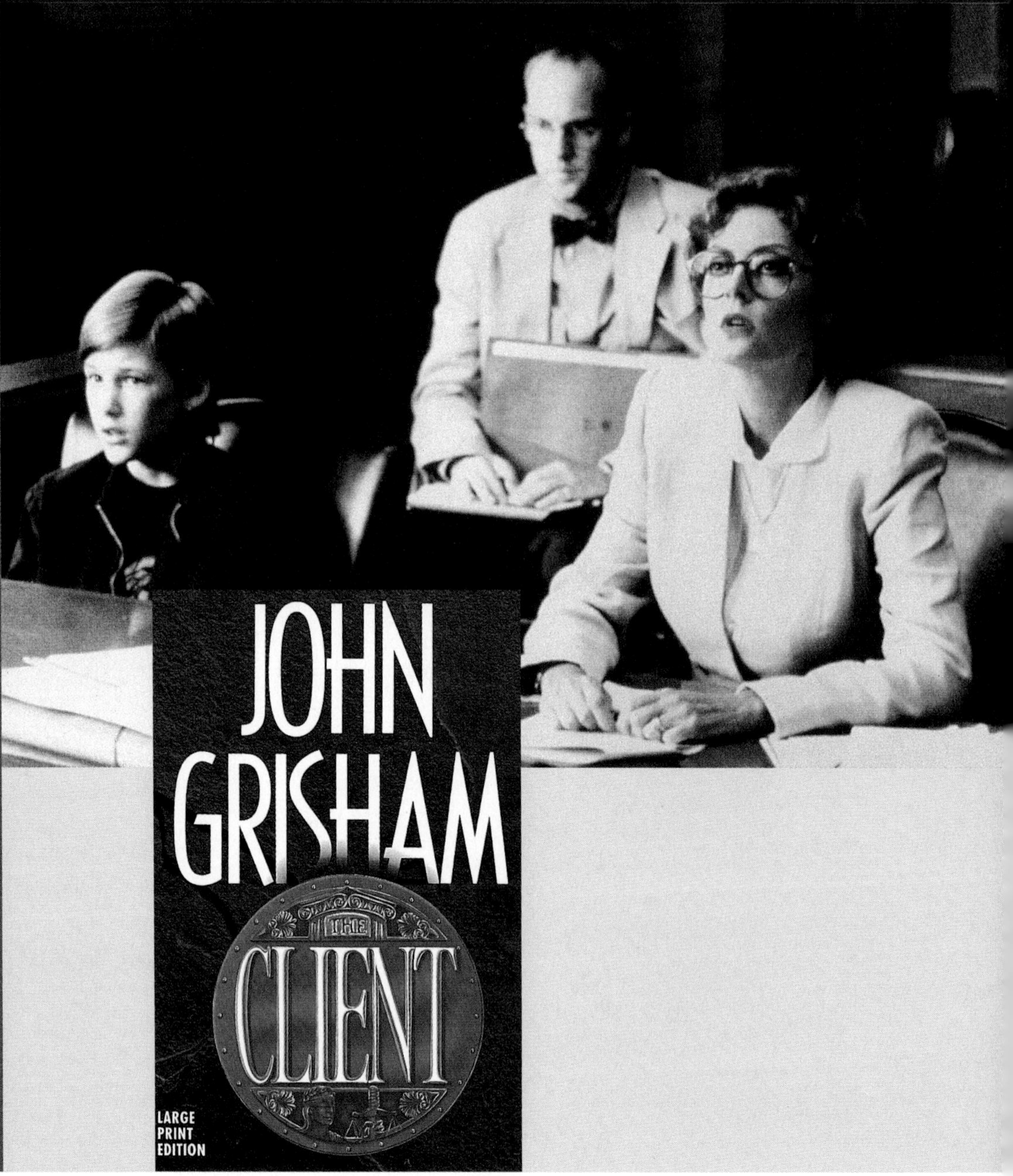

orn in Arkansas in 1955, John Grisham greatly admired Atticus Finch, the
heroic southern lawyer in Harper Lee's *To Kill a Mockingbird*. Grisham became
an attorney, but he never much cared for practicing law. Instead, he enjoyed
reading (including comic books), coaching Little League baseball teams, and writing
about legal cases. He served seven years as a Democrat in the Mississippi legisla-
ture. He also took up writing seriously—so seriously that he shaved just once a
week, before church on Sunday. He also started a comic book company called
Bongo. Then, in the late 1980s, he was inspired by a ten-year-old girl in a
Mississippi courtroom who testified against a man who had raped her and left her
for dead. Grisham's first novel, *A Time to Kill* (1989), was based on the case.

The former criminal lawyer didn't stop there. In 1991 he published *The Firm*,
in 1992 *The Pelican Brief*, in 1993 *The Client*, in 1994 *The Chamber*, in 1995 *The
Rainmaker*, in 1996 *The Runaway Jury*, and in 1997 *The Partner*. All became best-
sellers. The movie versions of *The Firm*, *The Pelican Brief*, and *The Client* earned
$600 million at theaters worldwide. In 1993 and 1994, these three titles also
ranked among the nation's top-selling abridged paperbacks and audio books.

Often labeled formulaic and predictable, Grisham's novels celebrate the individual—the "little guy" winning out over big nasty corporations, scheming lawyers,
organized racketeers, and government bureaucracies. By the mid-1990s,

Grisham's novels had sold nearly sixty million copies. By 1996, Grisham commanded $8 million for the movie rights to one of his novels. By 1997, combined with the initial hardbound sales, the paperback, film, and foreign rights for *The Partner* netted Grisham and his publisher, Doubleday, $90 million. Through it all, he avoided celebrity interviews, making the majority of his public appearances at small southern bookstores that had supported his early writing. Still, he became such a celebrity that he was forced to move from his Oxford, Mississippi, home after tourists started dropping by. (His house had become a stop on a tour that included a visit to Elvis Presley's Graceland.)

In 1995, CBS introduced *John Grisham's "The Client"* as a new fall television drama. By including the author's name in the program's title, the network hoped to capitalize on his popularity. *The Client* had also ranked among 1994's most profitable films. The TV version, though, folded after a year, demonstrating that even Grisham's name and fame could not guarantee high ratings.

Over the past two decades, the interdependence between print and visual forms of popular media has become commonplace. Apart from economics, however, a cultural gulf between the two forms remains. Public debate continues to pit the "superior" quality of print media—usually represented by serious books—against the "inferior" fluff of television. Even within print culture itself, a mini-version of the high-low cultural gulf plays out. It pits high-quality literature against popular forms such as the newest thriller, a supermarket romance novel, or a superhero comic book.

As individuals and as a society, we continue to create cultural classifications that distinguish good from bad, organizing the world through simple black-and-white categories. We also make critical judgments about the kinds of culture that best entertain, inform, and serve a democracy. Because the lines between print and electronic culture have become blurred, we need to look at the developments that have made these media more interdependent. On the one hand, book publishers and video-stocked libraries use talk shows, TV advertising, and public-service announcements to promote reading. On the other hand, the networks follow made-for-TV movies, special mini-series, and even NBA basketball games with promotions for books and libraries.

In the 1950s and 1960s, cultural forecasters thought that the popularity of television might spell the demise of a healthy book industry. It did not happen. In 1950, more than eleven thousand new book titles were introduced, yet in the 1990s, publishers were producing more than four times that number—around fifty thousand titles per year (see Table 10.1). In the first half of the 1990s alone, consumer book sales increased 30 percent. Despite the trend toward the absorption of

Books are portable and compact, and thus have an advantage over other media forms. Despite predictions that books would fade as a mass medium in the face of television, by the 1990s nearly fifty thousand new titles were being published annually, an increase of 400 percent in forty years. Books remain history's main vault, storing information, stories, experience, and knowledge across cultures and generations.

TABLE 10.1
Annual Numbers of New Book Titles Published, Selected Years

Year	Number of Titles	Year	Number of Titles
1778	461	1935	8,766 (drop during the Depression)
1798	1,808		
1880	2,076	1940	11,328
1890	4,559	1945	6,548 (drop during World War II)
1900	6,356		
1910	13,470 (peak until after World War II)	1950	11,022
		1960	15,012
1915	8,202	1970	36,071
1919	5,714 (low point during World War I)	1980	42,377
		1987	56,027 (peak)
1925	8,173	1990	46,473
1930	10,027	1994	51,863

Sources: Figures through 1945 from John Tebbel, *A History of Book Publishing*, 4 vols. (New York: R. R. Bowker, 1978); figures after 1945 from various editions of *The Bowker Annual Library and Trade Book Almanac* (R. R. Bowker).

small publishing houses by big media corporations, more than twenty-two thousand different publishers—most of them small independents—issue at least one title a year. More than twelve thousand bookstores operate today—from user-friendly superstores to cluttered used-book stores—an increase of 75 percent from the 1980s. Still, economic trends are similar to those of other media industries: Several large publishing firms, distribution companies, and bookstore chains control the commercial end of the business and claim the bulk of the profits.

The bottom line is that the book industry has met the social and cultural challenges of television. Books have managed to maintain a distinct cultural identity, partly because of the book industry's willingness to capitalize on TV's reach. As one example, Joseph Campbell, who wrote about the similarity of mythologies across various cultures, published his influential *Hero with a Thousand Faces* back in 1949. By the mid-1980s, the book was still selling about one thousand copies a year. But after Bill Moyers interviewed Campbell in a six-part 1988 series on PBS, the forty-year-old book for a time sold thirty-five thousand copies a month.

Our oldest mass medium is still our most influential and most diverse. The very portability and compactness of books make them a preferred medium in many situations, including relaxing at the beach, passing the lunch hour in the park, resting in bed, and traveling to work on city buses or commuter trains. Most important, books and print culture enable individuals and nations to store knowledge from the past. In their key social role, books are still the main repository of human history and everyday experience, passing along stories, knowledge, and wisdom from generation to generation.

"All good books are alike in that they are truer than if they had really happened and after you are finished reading one you will feel that all that happened . . . belongs to you: the good and the bad, the ecstasy, the remorse and sorrow, the people and the places and how the weather was." —Ernest Hemingway, *Esquire* magazine, 1934

In this chapter, we will trace the history of the book from its earliest roots in Egyptian papyrus plants to its evolution as a paperback and as a CD-ROM. After examining the development of the printing press, we will investigate the rise of the book industry. We will look first at publishing in Europe and colonial America and later at the development of publishing houses in the nineteenth and twentieth centuries. As part of this discussion, we will review the various types of books and the economic issues facing the book industry, particularly the growth of book clubs, bookstore chains, and publishing conglomerates. Finally, we will consider trends in the industry, including books on tape and book preservation. Influencing everything from educational curriculums to popular movies, books continue to play pivotal roles in media culture and democratic life. They are still our central storehouse of personal stories and public knowledge.

the history of books
from papyrus to paperbacks

Since the ancient Babylonians and Egyptians first began experimenting with alphabets some five thousand years ago, people have found ways to preserve their written symbols. Initially, pictorial symbols and letters appeared on wood strips or clay tablets, tied or stacked together to form the first "books." As early as 2700 B.C., the Egyptians wrote on **papyrus** (from which the word *paper* derives) made from plant reeds found along the Nile River. They rolled these writings in scrolls, much as builders do today with blueprints. This method was adopted by the Greeks in 500 B.C. and by the Romans (who imported the papyrus from Egypt) from 300 to 100 B.C. Plato's *Republic* remains the oldest surviving writing collected together in book form, although it was not originally compiled as a book in 400 B.C.

Around 1000 B.C., the Chinese made booklike objects from strips of wood and bamboo tied together in bundles. About the time the Egyptians started using papyrus, the Babylonians pressed symbols and marks into small tablets of clay. These stacked tablets recorded business transactions, government records, favorite stories, and local history. Gradually, **parchment**—treated animal skin—replaced papyrus. Parchment was stronger, smoother, more durable, and less expensive since it did not have to be imported from Egypt.

Although the Chinese began making paper in 105 A.D., paper made by hand from cotton and linen did not replace parchment in Europe until the thirteenth century. Paper was not as strong as parchment, but it was cheaper. The first protomodern book was probably produced in the fourth century by Romans who created the **codex**, a type of book cut into sheets and sewed together along the edge, then bound with thin wood pieces and covered with leather. Whereas scrolls had to be wound, unwound, and rewound, codices could be opened to any page, and their configuration allowed writing on both sides of a page.

manuscript culture

During the Middle Ages (400 to 1500 A.D.), the Christian clergy strongly influenced what has become known as *manuscript culture*. During this time, priests and monks advanced the art of bookmaking; in many ways, they may be considered the earliest professional editors. Known as *scribes*, they "wrote" most of the books of this period, making copies of existing philosophical tracts and religious books, especially versions of the Bible. Through tedious and painstaking work, scribes became the chief caretakers of recorded history and culture.

Many works from the Middle Ages were *illuminated manuscripts*. These books carried decorative, colorful designs and illustrations on each page. Their covers were made from leather, and some were inscribed with precious gems or gold and silver trim. During this period, scribes developed rules of punctuation and distinctions between small and capital letters; they also put space between words, which made reading easier. Older Roman writing had used all capital letters, and words ran together on a page, making reading a tortuous experience.

The oldest *printed* book still in existence is China's *Diamond Sutra* by Wang Chieh from 868 A.D. It consists of seven sheets pasted together and rolled up in a scroll. To make copies of pages, early Chinese printers developed *block printing*, a technique using sheets of paper applied to a block of inked wood with raised surfaces in hand-carved letters and sketches. This constituted the basic technique used in printing newspapers, magazines, and books through much of modern history. Although hand carving each block, or "page," was time consuming, this printing breakthrough enabled multiple copies to be produced and then bound together. In 1295, explorer Marco Polo introduced these techniques to Europe after his excursion to China. The first handmade printed books appeared in Europe during the 1400s, and demand for them began to grow among the literate middle-class populace emerging in larger European cities.

the gutenberg revolution

The next step in printing was the radical development of moveable type, first invented in China around the year 1000. Moveable type featured letters in an alphabet made from reusable pieces of wood or metal. Printers arranged or moved letters into various word combinations, greatly speeding up the time it took to make a page. This process, also used in Korea as early as the thirteenth century, developed independently in Europe in the 1400s. Then, in Germany, between 1453 and 1456, Johannes Gutenberg used moveable type to develop a printing press, which he adapted from a wine press. Gutenberg's staff of printers produced the first so-called modern books, including two hundred copies of a Latin Bible, twenty-one copies of which still exist. The Bible required six presses, many printers, and several months to produce. It was printed on fine handmade paper, a treated animal skin called *vellum*. The pages were hand decorated and used woodcuts to permit illustrations.

Essentially, Gutenberg and his printing assistants had not only found a way to carry knowledge across geographic borders but had also formed the prototype for mass production. Printing presses spread rapidly across Europe in the late 1400s and early 1500s. Chaucer's *Canterbury Tales* became the first English work printed in book form. Many early books were large, elaborate, and expensive, taking months to illustrate and publish. They were usually purchased by aristocrats, royal families, religious leaders, and ruling politicians. Printers, however, gradually reduced the size of books and developed less expensive grades of paper, making books cheaper so more people could afford them.

> "For books, issuing from those primal founts of heresy and rebellion, the printing presses have done more to **shape the course of human affairs** than any other product of the human mind because they are carriers of ideas and it is ideas that change the world." —John Tebbel, *A History of Book Publishing,* 1972

The social and cultural transformations ushered in by the spread of printing presses and books cannot be overestimated. As historian Elizabeth Eisenstein has noted, when people could learn for themselves by using maps, dictionaries, Bibles, and the writings of others, they could differentiate themselves as individuals; their social identities were no longer solely dependent on what their leaders told them or on the habits of their families or communities. The technology of printing presses permitted information and knowledge to spread outside local jurisdictions. Gradually, individuals had access to ideas far beyond their isolated experiences, permitting them to challenge the traditional wisdom and customs of their tribes and leaders.[1]

book production in the united states

In colonial America, English locksmith Stephen Daye set up a print shop in the late 1630s in Cambridge, Massachusetts. In 1640, Daye and his son Matthew printed the first colonial book, *The Whole Booke of Psalms* (known today as the *Bay Psalm Book*). This collection of biblical psalms sold out its printing of 1,750 copies even though fewer than thirty-five hundred families lived in the colonies at the time. By the mid-1760s, all thirteen colonies had printing shops.

In 1744, Benjamin Franklin imported *Pamela; or, Virtue Rewarded*, the first novel reprinted and sold in colonial America. *Pamela* had been written four years earlier by Britain's Samuel Richardson, who helped pioneer the novel as a literary form. *Pamela* and Richardson's second novel, *Clarissa; or, The History of a Young Lady* (1747), connected with the newly emerging and literate middle classes, especially with women who were just starting to gain social identities as individuals apart from the men they were married to or worked for. Still restricted from active participation in politics and professional education, women were drawn to these novels for their glimpses into new social worlds. Richardson's novels, overly long and sentimental by 1990s standards, were among the earliest mass media works to portray women in subordinate roles. Richardson also, however, depicted women triumphing over tragedy, so he is credited as one of the first popular writers to take the domestic life of women seriously.

By the early 1800s, the demand for books among both literate women and men was growing, but the printing process still took time. A page of metal type had to be arranged by hand. The introduction of **linotype** machines in the mid-1880s finally allowed printers to set type mechanically using a typewriter-style keyboard. The introduction of steam-powered machines and high-speed rotary presses also permitted the production of more books at lower costs. Another printing development in the 1800s, **offset lithography**, allowed books to be printed from photographic plates rather than metal casts. Reducing the cost of color and illustrations, offset printing accelerated production and would lead eventually to computerized typesetting.

In the 1830s, machine-made paper supplanted more expensive handmade varieties. Using cloth rather than leather covers also helped reduce book prices. By the mid-1800s, *paperback books* made with cheaper paper covers had been introduced in the United States from Europe. In 1860, Erastus and Irwin Beadle pioneered paperback *dime novels*. Magazine editor-writer Ann Stephens authored the Beadles' first dime novel, *Malaeska: The Indian Wife of the White Hunter*, which was actually a reprint of a serialized magazine story she had written in 1839 for the *Ladies' Companion*.[2] By 1885, one-third of all books published in the United States were popular paperbacks and dime novels, sometimes identified as *pulp fiction*, a reference to the cheap, machine-made pulp paper they were printed on.

No. 1.　　**FRANK STARR'S**　　10 Cts.

TEN CENT POCKET LIBRARY.

Hurricane Nell,

THE QUEEN OF THE SADDLE AND LASSO.

FRANK STARR & CO., 41 PLATT ST., N. Y.

Paperback books, which originated in Europe, were first published in the United States in the early 1830s. In the 1860s, the Beadle brothers helped make paperback "dime novels" into a dominant form of popular culture. By 1870, dime novels had sold seven million copies, with the Beadle line alone producing some six hundred titles—including the "Hurricane Nell" series.

The early history of publishing demonstrated that books could widely disseminate and preserve culture and knowledge over time. Even if a paperback fell apart, another version usually existed in a public library or a personal book collection. Oral culture depended on information and values passed down through the wisdom and memories of a community's elders or tribal storytellers, and sometimes these rich traditions were lost. Print culture and the book, however, gave future generations different and often more enduring records of particular authors' words at particular times in history.

modern publishing and the book industry

Throughout the 1800s, the rapid spread of knowledge and literacy as well as the Industrial Revolution spurred the emergence of the middle class. New professions developed in areas such as the social sciences, business management, and journalism. The demand for books also encouraged the development of a class of publishing professionals, who capitalized on increased middle-class literacy and widespread compulsory education. Many of these early publishers were less interested in skillful marketing strategies than in finding quality authors. But with the growth of advertising and the rise of a market economy in the latter half of the nineteenth century, publishing gradually became more competitive and more concerned with the sales value of titles and authors.

the formation of publishing houses

The modern book industry developed gradually throughout the nineteeth century with the formation of the early prestigious *publishing houses:* companies that tried to identify and produce the work of good writers.[3] These companies professionalized the book industry by dividing into discrete tasks the jobs of acquiring, publishing, and marketing books. Among the oldest American houses established in the 1800s (although most are now part of media conglomerates) were J. B. Lippincott (1792); Harper & Bros. (1817), which became Harper & Row in 1962 and HarperCollins in 1990; Houghton Mifflin (1832); Little, Brown (1837); G. P. Putnam (1838); Scribner's (1842); E. P. Dutton (1852); Rand McNally (1856); and Macmillan (1869). Out of this group, Scribner's, known more for its magazines in the late 1800s, became the most prestigious literary house of the 1920s and 1930s, the publisher of the first novels of F. Scott Fitzgerald (*This Side of Paradise*, 1920) and Ernest Hemingway (*The Sun Also Rises*, 1926).

Between 1880 and 1920, as the center of social and economic life shifted from rural farm production to an industrialized urban culture, the demand for books and bookstores grew. Helped by the influx of European immigrants, the book industry acclimated newcomers to the English language and American culture. In fact, 1910 marked a peak year in the number of new titles produced—13,470—a record that would not be challenged until the 1950s.

The turn of the century also marked the next wave of prominent publishing houses, as entrepreneurs began to better understand the marketing potential of books. These houses included Doubleday (1897), McGraw-Hill (1909), Prentice-Hall (1913), Alfred A. Knopf (1914), Simon & Schuster (1924), and Random House (1925).

> "He was a genius at devising ways to put **books** into the hands of the **unbookish**."
> —Edna Ferber, writer, commenting on Nelson Doubleday, publisher

After World War II, Doubleday became the world's largest firm. Unlike radio and magazines, however, book publishing sputtered from 1910 into the 1950s. Book industry profits were adversely affected by the two world wars and the Depression of the 1930s. Radio and magazines fared better because they were generally less expensive and could more immediately cover topical issues during times of crisis.

types of books

The division of the modern book industry comes from economic and structural categories developed by publishers and by trade organizations such as the Association of American Publishers (AAP) and the American Booksellers Association (ABA). The categories include trade books (both adult and juvenile); professional books; elementary, high school, and college textbooks; mass-market paperbacks; religious books; reference works; and university press books. An additional category—comic books—also exists but is not acknowledged by most conventional publishers (see "Case Study: Comic Books Blend Print and Visual Culture" on page 286).

Trade Books. By far the most lucrative part of the industry, *trade books* include hardbound and paperback books aimed at general readers and sold at various retail outlets (see Figure 10.1). The industry distinguishes between adult and juvenile trade divisions. Adult trade books include hardbound fiction; current nonfiction and biographies; literary classics; books on hobbies, art, and travel; popular science, technology, and computer publications; self-help books; and cookbooks. (*Betty Crocker's Cookbook,* first published in 1950, has sold more than twenty-two million copies in hardcover trade editions.) Like most of the book industry, fiction and nonfiction trade books have experienced healthy growth in the electronic age. Between 1985 and 1990, for example, trade sales doubled, and by the mid-1990s Americans spent an average of $80 a year on books, compared to $56 a year spent on recorded music.[4]

Juvenile book categories range from preschool picture books to young adult or young reader books, such as Bantam's *Sweet Valley* adventure series, Scholastic's *Goosebumps* books, and Pocket Books' *Fear Street* series (the latter two written by R. L. Stine). In the electronic age, juvenile book sales have climbed, although studies show that children's and teenagers' reading scores on national tests have slipped. Nevertheless, according to one industry study, sales of juvenile books between the early 1970s and the early 1980s jumped more than 200 percent. In the 1980s and 1990s, library circulation of books for juveniles also increased sharply.

Professional Books. The counterpart to trade publications in the magazine industry, *professional books* target various occupational groups and are not intended for the general consumer market. This area of publishing mirrors the growth of professional and technical specialties that has characterized the job market, particularly since the 1960s. Traditionally, the industry subdivides professional books into the areas of law, business, medicine, and technical-scientific works. These books are sold mostly through mail order or by sales representatives knowledgeable about various subject areas. This segment of the book industry has found profitable market niches by capitalizing on the expansion of job specialization.

Textbooks. In the mid-1800s, William H. McGuffey, Presbyterian minister and college professor, sold more than a hundred million copies of his *Eclectic Reader*, which taught most nineteenth-century elementary school children to read—and to respect their nation's political and economic systems. Ever since the McGuffey reader, *text-*

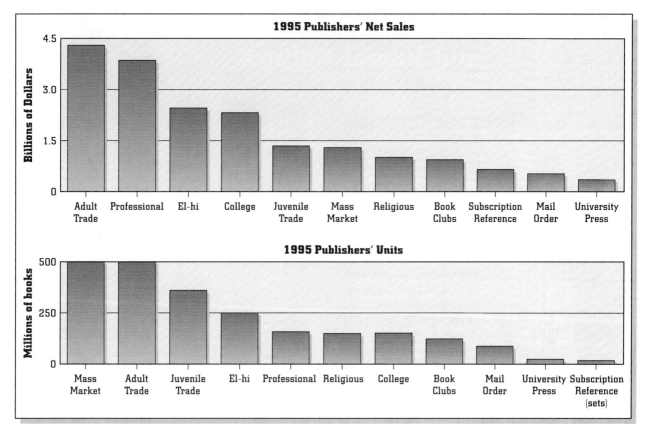

1995 Publishers' Net Sales

Billions of Dollars

Adult Trade | Professional | El-hi | College | Juvenile Trade | Mass Market | Religious | Book Clubs | Subscription Reference | Mail Order | University Press

1995 Publishers' Units

Millions of books

Mass Market | Adult Trade | Juvenile Trade | El-hi | Professional | Religious | College | Book Clubs | Mail Order | University Press | Subscription Reference (sets)

Figure 10.1
A Sales Overview of the Book Publishing Industry
Source: *Book Industry Trends 1996* (Darien, CT: The Book Industry Study Group, 1996).

books have served a nation intent on improving literacy rates and public education. Elementary textbooks found a solid market niche in the nineteenth century, but college textbooks boomed in the 1950s when the GI Bill enabled hundreds of thousands of working- and middle-class men, returning from World War II, to attend college. The demand for textbooks further accelerated in the 1960s as opportunities for women and other minorities expanded.

Textbooks are divided into elementary-high school, known as *el-hi*, vocational education, and college texts. In most states, local school districts determine which el-hi textbooks are appropriate for their students. Texas and California, however, use statewide adoption policies that control text selections. In such situations, only a small number of texts are mandated by the state. If individual schools choose to use books other than those mandated, they are not reimbursed by the state for their purchases. Some teachers and publishers have argued that such sweeping authority undermines the local autonomy of districts, which have varied educational needs and problems. The statewide system of adoptions also allows a few states, which are courted heavily by publishers, to virtually determine the content of the texts sold to every state in the nation. In addition, when publishers aim textbooks at a broad nationwide audience, they tend to water down the content by eliminating regional material or controversial ideas that might offend a group of adopters or a local selection committee.

Unlike el-hi texts, which are subsidized by various states and school districts, hardbound and softcover college texts are paid for by individual students (and parents). At some time during most students' experience, in fact, disputes erupt on campuses about the increasing costs of textbooks and the profit margins of local college bookstores, which in many cases face no on-campus competition. By the mid-1990s, the average textbook cost a college student between $30 and $40—about the price of a pair

285

Comic Books Blend Print and Visual Culture

by Mark C. Rogers

At the precarious edge of the book industry are comic books, which are sometimes called *graphic novels* or simply *comix*. A medium that neither conventional book nor magazine publishers will claim as their own, comics have long integrated print and visual culture. They remain a paradoxical medium, existing as both collectibles and consumables. They are perhaps the medium most open to independent producers; anyone with a pencil and access to a Xerox machine can produce mini-comics. Nevertheless, two companies—Marvel and DC—have dominated the commercial industry for more than thirty years, publishing the routine superhero stories that have been so marketable.

©1996 DC Comics.
All Rights Reserved

Comics are a relatively young mass medium, first appearing in their present format in the 1920s in Japan and in the 1930s in the United States. They began as simple reprints of newspaper comic strips, but by the mid-1930s, most comic books featured original material. Comics have always been published in a variety of genres, but their signature contribution to American culture has been the superhero. In 1938, Jerry Siegel and Joe Shuster created Superman for DC comics. Bob Kane's Batman character arrived the following year. In 1941, Marvel comics introduced Captain America to fight Nazis, and except for a brief period in the 1950s, the superhero genre has dominated the history of comics.

After World War II, comic books moved away from superheroes and experimented with other genres, most notably crime and horror. With the end of the war, the reading public was ready for more moral ambiguity than was possible in the simple good-versus-evil world of the superhero. Comics became increasingly graphic and lurid as they

TM & © Marvel
Characters, Inc.
All Rights Reserved.

tried to compete with other mass media, especially television and mass-market paperbacks.

In the early 1950s, the popularity of crime and horror comics led to a moral panic about their effects on society. Frederic Wertham, a prominent psychiatrist, campaigned against them, claiming they led to juvenile delinquency. Wertham was joined by many religious and parent groups, and Senate hearings were held on the issue in 1954. In October 1954, the Comics Magazine Association of America adopted a code of acceptable conduct for publishers of comic books. One of the most restrictive examples of industry self-censorship in mass media history, the code kept the government from legislating its own code or restricting the sale of comic books to minors.

The code had both immediate and long-term effects on comics. In the short run, the number of comics sold in America declined sharply. Comic books lost many of their adult readers because the code confined comics' topics to those suitable for children. Consequently, comics have only rarely been taken seriously as a mass medium or art form; they remain stigmatized as the lowest of low culture—a sort of literature for the subliterate.

In the 1960s, superhero comics regained their dominance, especially those published by DC and Marvel. This period also gave rise to underground comics, which featured more explicit sexual, violent, and drug themes. These alternative comics, like underground newspapers, originated in the 1960s counterculture and challenged the major institutions of the time. Instead of relying on newsstand sales, underground comics were sold through record stores, alternative

©1996 Mirage Studios.
All Rights Reserved

bookstores, and in a growing number of comic-book specialty shops.

Responding in part to the challenge of the underground form, "legitimate" comics began to increase the political content and relevance of their story lines in the early 1970s. In 1974, a new method of distributing comics developed, which catered to the increasing number of comic-book stores. This direct-sales method involved selling comics on a nonreturnable basis but with a higher discount than was available to newsstand distributors, who bought comics only on the condition that they could return unsold copies. The percentage of comics sold through specialty shops increased gradually, and by 1989 over 80 percent of all comics were sold through direct sales.

The shift from newsstand to direct sales allowed comics to once again approach adult themes. The shift also created an explosion in the number of comics available and in the number of companies publishing comics. Although DC and Marvel still control the majority of this market, worth about $500 million annually, some smaller companies have made significant cuts into their shares. For example, Image and Dark Horse, together with Marvel and DC,

©DC Comics
All Rights Reserved

controlled about 75 percent of the comic-book market in the mid-1990s, leaving another 150 smaller firms to share the remaining quarter share. Between five and six hundred new titles a month are now produced, although Marvel experienced financial trouble in 1996 and decided to focus more on licensing its most famous characters (Spider-Man, Incredible Hulk, X-Men) to help sell consumer products to kids. Despite recent sales declines, superheroes still sell the best. Comics continue to represent virtually every genre, including grim autobiographical sketches (*Self-Loathing Comics*), literate nonfiction overviews (*Introducing Kafka*), and DC's Vertigo line of horror and fantasy comics for "mature readers."

In the wake of the 1980s success of *Teenage Mutant Ninja Turtles* (who began life in an alternative comic book), many independent companies have been purchased by or entered into alliances with larger media firms who want to exploit particular characters or superheroes. DC, for example, is now owned by Time Warner, which has used the DC characters, especially Superman and Batman, to build successful film and television properties. Image, Dark Horse, and other small independents have licensed their properties for both animated cartoons (*The Tick*) and feature films (*The Mask*).

As print media face more competition from electronic media, comics seem well suited in the long run to adapt and survive, appearing frequently in electronic form, on CD-ROM, and underground on the Internet. In 1992, comics' flexibility was demonstrated in *Maus: A Survivor's Tale* by Art Spiegelman, cofounder and editor of *Raw* (an alternative magazine for comics and graphic art). The first comic-style book to win a Pulitzer prize, Spiegelman's two-book fable merged print and visual styles to recount his complex relationship with his father, a Holocaust survivor. As other writers and artists continue to adapt the form to both fictional and nonfictional stories, comics endure as part of popular and alternative culture.

Mark C. Rogers, who studied American culture at the University of Michigan, wrote his doctoral dissertation on the comic book industry.

of new Levis or a few Budweiser twelve-packs. Today some thirty-two hundred college bookstores in the United States sell both texts and trade books.

Mass-Market Paperbacks. Paperbacks represent the prime-time television of the book industry in terms of popular appeal. In fact, about two out of every three books sold in the United States is a **mass-market paperback**.[5] Unlike larger trade paperbacks, which are sold mostly in bookstores, mass-market paperbacks are sold off racks in drugstores, supermarkets, and airports as well as in bookstores. In 1996, John Grisham's 1995 novel *The Rainmaker* sold more than five million copies and ranked No. 1 in paperback sales (see Figure 10.2). The revenue generated in this area of publishing is enormous. Assorted romance book publishers alone, for instance, offer sixty new titles each month.

Paperbacks did not hit it big until the 1870s, when they became popular among middle- and working-class readers. This phenomenon sparked fear and outrage among the professional and educated classes, many of whom thought that reading cheap westerns and crime novels might ruin civilization. Some of the earliest paperbacks ripped off foreign writers, who were unprotected by copyright law and did not receive royalties for the books they sold in the United States. This changed with the International Copyright Law of 1891, which mandated that all authors' works could be reproduced only with their permission.

The popularity of paperbacks hit a major peak in 1939 with the establishment of Pocket Books under the leadership of Robert de Draff. Revolutionizing the paperback industry, Pocket Books dropped the standard book price of fifty or seventy-five cents to twenty-five cents. To accomplish this, de Graff cut bookstore discounts from 30 to 20 percent. The book distributor's share was trimmed from 46 to 36 percent of the cover price, and author royalty rates went from 10 to 4 percent. In its first three weeks in business, the company sold a hundred thousand books in New York City alone. Among its first titles was *Wake Up and Live* by Dorothea Brande, a 1936 best-seller on self-improvement, which ignited an early wave of self-help books. In testing the market with both nonfiction and fiction, Pocket Books also published paperbacks of *The Murder of Roger Ackroyd* by Agatha Christie; *Enough Rope*, a collection of poems by Dorothy Parker; *Five Great Tragedies* by Shakespeare; and *Bambi* by Felix Salten, which became a children's classic three years before Walt Disney released the film version. Pocket Books' success spawned a series of imitators, including Dell, Fawcett, and Bantam Books (see Table 10.2).

A major innovation of paperback publishers was the *instant book*, a marketing strategy that involves publishing a topical book quickly after a major event. Pocket Books produced the first instant book, *Franklin Delano Roosevelt: A Memorial*, six days after FDR's death in 1945. Similar to made-for-TV movies that capitalize on contemporary events, instant books allow the industry to better compete with journalism and magazines. Such books, however, like their TV counterparts, have been accused of exploiting tragedies for quick profits.

Bantam began dominating this field in 1964 with *The Report of the Warren Commission on the Assassination of President*

> "Universally priced at twenty-five cents in its early years, the **paperback** democratized reading in America."
> —Kenneth Davis, *Two-Bit Culture,* 1984

PW's 1996 Longest-Running Paperback Bestsellers

Mass Market	#Wks. on '96 List		#Wks. on '96 List
The Rainmaker. John Grisham. Island/Dell	35	**How the Irish Saved Civilization.** Thomas Cahill. Anchor/Doubleday	38
The Two Dead Girls. (Green Mile #1) Stephen King. Signet	26	**What to Expect When You're Expecting.** A. Eisenberg. H. Murkoff & S. Hathaway. Workman (129)	33
Beach Music. Pat Conroy. Bantam	18	**Dr. Atkins' New Diet Revolution.** Dr. Robert C. Atkins. M. Evans	33
The Mouse on the Mile (Green Mile #2). Stephen King. Signet	17	**Ten Stupid Things Women Do to Mess Up Their Lives.** Laura Schlessinger. HarperPerennial (45)	32
Sleepers. Lorenzo Carcaterra. Ballantine	16	**The Liars' Club.** Mary Karr. Penguin	29
The Lost World. Michael Crichton. Ballantine	15	*A 3rd Serving of Chicken Soup for the Soul.* Jack Canfield & Mark Victor Hansen, eds. Health Communications	22
Trade		**Ladder of Years.** Anne Tyler. Fawcett/Columbine	22
Chicken Soup for the Soul. Jack Canfield & Mark Victor Hansen, eds. Health Communications (73)	52	*There's Treasure Everywhere.* Bill Watterson. Andrews & McMeel	19
Snow Falling on Cedars. David Guterson. Vintage (11)	52	**Dead Man Walking.** Sister Helen Prejean. Vintage	16
Reviving Ophelia. Mary Pipher. Ballantine (36)	52	**A Civil Action.** Jonathan Harr. Vintage	16
7 Habits of Highly Effective People. Stephen R. Covey. S&S/Fireside (255)	50	**Moo.** Jane Smiley. Fawcett/Columbine	16

These titles achieved the No. 1 spot during their 1996 presence on PW's Bestseller list. Numbers in parenthesis show how many weeks the book was on PW's list prior to 1996.

Figure 10.2
***Publishers Weekly*'s List of 1996 Paperback Bestsellers**
Source: *Publishers Weekly*, January 6, 1997, 48.

TABLE 10.2
Mass-Market Paperback Best-Sellers: The First Twenty-Five Years
(approximate sales 1940–65)

Millions of Copies Sold	Title, Author, Year of Publication, Publisher
18.5	*Baby and Child Care*, Benjamin M. Spock, M.D. (1946), Pocket Books
15.5	*The Merriam-Webster Pocket Dictionary* (1947), Pocket Books
10.0	*Peyton Place*, Grace Metalious (1957), Pocket Books
8.0	*God's Little Acre*, Erskine Caldwell (1946), New American Library
6.5	*Webster's New World Dictionary of the American Language* (1958), Popular Library
6.0	*University of Chicago English-Spanish, Spanish-English Dictionary* (1950), University of Chicago
	In His Steps, Charles Sheldon (1960), Advance
5.5	*Exodus*, Leon Uris (1959), Bantam
	To Kill a Mockingbird, Harper Lee (1962), Popular Library
	Roget's Pocket Thesaurus (1946), New American Library
	The Carpetbaggers, Harold Robbins (1962), Pocket Books
5.0	*How to Win Friends and Influence People*, Dale Carnegie (1940), Pocket Books
	Return to Peyton Place, Grace Metalious (1960), Dell
4.5	*The Pocket Cook Book*, Elizabeth Woody (1942), Pocket Books
	Profiles in Courage, John F. Kennedy (1947), Pocket Books
	The Big Kill (1951), *I, The Jury* (1948), *My Gun Is Quick* (1950), Mickey Spillane, New American Library
	1984, George Orwell (1950), New American Library

Source: Kenneth Davis, *Two-Bit Culture: The Paperbacking of America* (Boston: Houghton Mifflin, 1984), 289.

Kennedy, the first Bantam "extra" edition. (*Extra* was a term borrowed from daily newspapers, which produced extra editions to tell important breaking news stories in the pre-TV era.) After receiving the 385,000-word report on a Friday afternoon, Bantam staffers began editing the Warren report on the way to the airport; the book was produced within a week. The publisher, in a joint venture with the *New York Times*, ultimately sold 1.6 million copies.

Today instant books continue to capitalize on a variety of contemporary events, from the arrest of Unabomber suspect Theodore Kaczynski in 1996 to the mass suicide of thirty-nine members of the Heaven's Gate cult in 1997. In the Unabomber case, within thirteen days of Kaczynski's arrest, Pocket Books produced a quickie book. But while it was being reviewed for clearance by the FBI (one coauthor was an ex-agent), Warner Books published *Mad Genius: The Odyssey, Pursuit, and Capture of the Unabomber Suspect* and won the race to market. In the Heaven's Gate deaths, Harper-Paperbacks published the first instant book on the event—*Heaven's Gate: A Cult Suicide in San Diego*—less than three weeks after it happened. Although instant books make fast money for their publishers, they often sacrifice the kind of in-depth analysis and historical perspective that the book medium has generally brought to important social events.

Religious Books. The best-selling book of all time is the Bible, in all its diverse versions. Over the years, the success of Bible sales spawned a large *religious book* industry, now divided into four categories: Bibles, hymnals, and other materials related to religious observances; spiritual or inspirational books aimed at lay readers; professional publications focusing on the work of clergy and theologians; and religious education textbooks.

After World War II, religious book sales soared. Historians attribute the sales boom to economic growth and a nation seeking peace and security while facing the threat of "godless communism" and the Soviet Union.[6] By the 1960s, though, the scene had changed dramatically. The impact of the civil rights struggle, the Vietnam War, the sexual revolution, and the youth rebellion against authority led to declines in formal church memberships. Not surprisingly, sales of some types of religious books dropped as well. To compete, many religious publishers extended their offerings to include serious secular titles on topics such as war and peace, race, poverty, gender, and civic responsibility.

Throughout this period of change, the publication of fundamentalist and evangelical literature remained steady. It then expanded rapidly during the 1980s when the Republican party began making political overtures to conservative groups and prominent TV evangelists. Among the "religious right" in the media, televangelists Jerry Falwell and Oral Roberts inspired a number of successful books. Another televangelist, Pat Robertson, owned the Christian Broadcast Network, TV's *700 Club*, and a college in West Virginia dedicated to placing conservative Christians in the broadcast industry. Robertson grew increasingly influential in the Republican party, although he failed in his bid for the party's presidential nomination in 1992. The popularity of conservative and tradition-bound publications stabilized religious publishing during turbulent social times. From 1994 to 1995, the total book industry grew 6 percent, but the sales of religious and spiritual books—a $1 billion-a-year industry—grew 20 percent.

Reference Books. Another major division of the book industry includes all sorts of reference books, divided typically into three categories: reference works for home and office (accounting for roughly 80 percent of reference sales); those for schools and libraries (about 5 percent); and works distributed through mail-order marketing (about 15 percent). *Reference books* include dictionaries, encyclopedias, atlases, and a number of substantial volumes directly related to particular professions or trades, such as legal casebooks and medical manuals.

The idea of developing encyclopedic writings to document the extent of human knowledge is attributed to Aristotle. Pliny the Elder (23–79 A.D.) wrote the oldest reference work still in existence, *Historia Naturalis*, detailing in Latin thousands of facts about animals, minerals, and plants. But it wasn't until the early 1700s that the compilers of reference works began organizing articles in alphabetical order and relying on specialists to contribute essays in their areas of interest. Between 1751 and 1771, a group of French scholars produced a twenty-eight-volume set of encyclopedias. The circulation of these volumes, full of new and often radical ideas, encouraged support for the French Revolution against aristocratic rule later in that century.

The oldest English-language encyclopedia still in production, the *Encyclopaedia Britannica* (*EB*), was first published in Scotland in 1768. Significant U.S. encyclopedias followed, including *Encyclopedia Americana* (1829), the *World Book* (1917), and *Compton's Pictured Encyclopedia* (1922), bought by *EB* in 1961. *EB* produced its first U.S. edition in 1908. Purchased by Sears in 1920 and later by a U.S. ad agency, *EB* was eventually run as a nonprofit venture for the University of Chicago. *EB* contributed more than $125 million to the univer-

In the 1990s, one of the best examples of media convergence was the proliferation of digitized encyclopedias and other reference works. The sheer volume and weight of these bulky print materials made them prime candidates for digital conversion and storage. A twenty-five-volume encyclopedia occupies far less space and uses far fewer natural resources in its computer hard drive or CD-ROM incarnations.

sity over the years. However, its sales fell from 117,000 sets in 1990 to 51,000 in 1994. Eventually, the company was forced to reorganize and disband its famous door-to-door sales force. *EB* was much slower to adapt to the electronic environment than were other reference firms. In 1995, it finally issued a CD-ROM version that sold for $995 (a traditional bound set ran about $1,500). By this time, though, Microsoft was already selling a CD-ROM Funk & Wagnalls encyclopedia for $99. Most computer packages sold today feature encyclopedias preloaded in the hard drive, and by the mid-1990s digital encyclopedias were outselling print versions by a four-to-one margin. *EB* was sold to a Swiss firm in late 1995.

Dictionaries also have accounted for a large portion of reference sales. Like encyclopedias, the earliest dictionaries were produced by Greek and Roman writers attempting to document specialized and rare words. During the manuscript period in the Middle Ages, however, European scribes and monks began creating glossaries and dictionaries to help people understand Latin. In 1604, a British schoolmaster prepared a three-thousand-word English dictionary. A sixty-thousand-word English dictionary was produced in 1721, followed by Samuel Johnson's *Dictionary of the English Language* in 1755. Describing rather than prescribing word usage, Johnson was among the first to understand that language changes—that words and usage cannot be fixed for all time. Johnson's dictionary served as the model and standard for English dictionaries into the mid-1800s. In the United States in 1828, Noah Webster, using Johnson's work as a model, published the seventy-thousand-word, two-volume *American Dictionary of the English Language*, differentiating between British and American usages and simplifying spelling (for example, *colour* became *color* and *musick* became *music*).

Other reference works include the atlases and almanacs that have become so popular in schools, homes, offices, and libraries. A number of specialty works, such as the *Readers' Guide to Periodical Literature*, are available in libraries. Since 1908, high school and college students have used the *Guide* as a starting point to locate references to magazine articles on virtually any topic. In addition, media trade organizations publish their own reference works, such as *Editor & Publisher Yearbook* and *Broadcasting & Cable Yearbook*. Each year, R. R. Bowker publishes *Books in Print* and *Paperbound Books in Print*, which list all new and available book titles. *The Bowker Annual Library and Trade Book Almanac* reprints articles and compiles statistics on the book industry.

University Press Books. The smallest unit in the book industry is the noncommercial *university press*, which publishes scholarly works for small groups of readers interested in specialized areas. Professors often try to secure book contracts from reputable university presses in order to gain tenure, a lifetime teaching contract. Some university presses are very small, producing as few as ten books a year. The largest, the University of Chicago Press, regularly publishes more than two hundred titles a year. Among the oldest and most prestigious of these presses are Yale University Press, established in 1908, and Harvard University Press, formally founded in 1913 but claiming roots back to 1639 when Stephen Daye published the first colonial book in a small shop behind the house of Harvard's president.

University presses traditionally have not faced pressure to produce commercially viable books, so they can encourage innovative writers and thinkers. Large commercial trade houses are often criticized for encouraging only blockbuster books, but university presses often suffer an opposite criticism—producing subsidized books that only a handful of scholars read. Many social science and humanities professors are content to write for each other; they believe that university presses need to protect narrowly focused, specialized noncommercial publications. Others argue that it is time to declare "an end to scholarly publications as a series of guarded conversations between professors."[7]

University press books typically sell fewer than a thousand copies each, most of which are sold to libraries. Although they bring academic institutions a certain prestige, university presses routinely lose money. Even academic books written in accessible language rarely attract interest from the general public because university presses have little money for marketing and promotion. Increasingly, administrators are reducing subsidies, requiring presses to show more profit. To offset costs and increase revenue, some presses are trying to form alliances with commercial houses to help promote and produce academic books that have wider appeal.

the organization and ownership of the book industry

Compared to the revenues earned by other mass media industries, the steady growth of book publishing has been relatively modest. From the mid-1980s to the mid-1990s, total revenues went from $9 billion to more than $20 billion. Within the industry, the concept of who or what constitutes a publisher varies widely. A publisher may be a large company that is a subsidiary of a global media conglomerate and occupies an entire office building, or a publisher may be a one-person home-office operation using a desktop computer. Unlike commercial television and film, small book publishers can start up relatively easily because of advances in personal computer technology.

the structure of book publishing

Medium-size and large publishing houses employ hundreds of people and share certain similarities. Most of the thousands of small houses, however, have staffs of fewer than twenty. In the larger houses, divisions usually include acquisition and development; copyediting, design, and production; marketing and sales; and administration and business. Unlike newspapers but similar to magazines, most publishing houses contract independent printers to produce their books.

Most publishers employ acquisitions editors to seek out and sign authors to contracts. In the trade fiction area, this might mean discovering talented writers by reading hundreds of unsolicited manuscripts. In nonfiction, editors might examine manu-

Calvin and Hobbes

by Bill Watterson

Reprinted by permission. All rights reserved.

scripts and letters of inquiry or actively match a known writer to a particular topic or project (such as a celebrity biography). Acquisitions editors also handle **subsidiary rights** for an author, that is, selling the rights to a book for use in other media forms, such as a mass-market paperback or CD-ROM, or as the basis for a movie screenplay.

As part of their contracts, writers sometimes receive *advance* money, which is actually an early payment against royalties to be earned later. Newer authors may receive little or no advance from a publisher, but commercially successful authors can receive millions. For example, *Interview with a Vampire* author Anne Rice hauled in a $17 million advance from Knopf for three more vampire novels, and Simon & Schuster advanced Mary Higgins Clark (*I'll Be Seeing You, Remember Me*) more than $30 million for six new mysteries. First-time authors who are nationally recognized, such as political leaders, sports figures, or movie stars, also can command large advances from publishers who are banking on the well-known person's commercial potential. For example, retired general Colin Powell, who directed military operations during the Persian Gulf War and was the first African American to head the Joint Chiefs of Staff, received a $6.5 million advance from Random House for his autobiography. Typically, an author's royalty is between 5 and 15 percent of the net price of the book. But before a royalty check is paid, advance money is subtracted from royalties earned during the sale of the book.

After a contract is signed, an author's manuscript is reviewed by the acquisitions editor. In educational publishing, a major text may also be turned over to a development editor, who provides the author with feedback, makes suggestions for improvements, and obtains advice from knowledgeable academics. After the development stage, copyediting, design, and production people enter the picture. While copy editors attend to specific writing or length problems, production and design managers work on the look of the book, making decisions about type style, paper, cover design, and layout.

Simultaneously, plans are under way to market and sell the book. Decisions generally need to be made concerning numbers of copies to print, how to best reach potential readers, and costs for promotion and advertising. For trade books and some scholarly books, publishing houses may send early or advance copies of a book to appropriate magazines and newspapers with the hope of receiving favorable reviews that can be used later in promotional material. Prominent trade writers typically sign autographs at selected bookstores and travel the radio and TV talk-show circuit to promote their new books. Unlike trade publishers, college textbook firms rarely sell directly to bookstores. Instead, they contact instructors either through direct-mail brochures or sales representatives assigned to various geographic regions. As we noted earlier, el-hi salespeople may be dealing with local school districts or state adoption committees.

Large trade houses spend millions of dollars promoting new books. Viking Penguin routinely spends more than $750,000 to promote each of Stephen King's new books. In the early 1990s, Warner Books spent $600,000 to promote *Scarlett*, Alexandra Ripley's romance sequel to Margaret Mitchell's *Gone with the Wind*, the top-selling fiction trade book in both 1936 and 1937. To help create a best-seller, trade houses often distribute large cardboard bins, called *dumps*, to thousands of stores to display a book in bulk quantity. Like food merchants who buy eye-level shelf placement for their products in supermarkets, large trade houses buy shelf space from

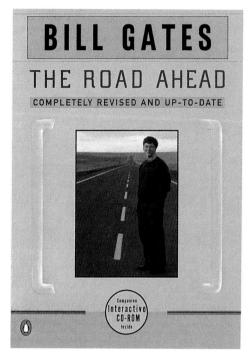

First-time author and America's wealthiest man, Bill Gates of Microsoft scored a $2.5 million advance for *The Road Ahead*, which came packaged with an interactive CD-ROM and was released in thirty countries simultaneously. Heavily promoted, the book sold more than 775,000 copies and ranked No. 5 among 1995's new trade books. Gates donated his proceeds from the book to help finance technological innovation in classrooms.

major chains to ensure prominent locations in bookstores. They also buy ad space on buses and billboards and in newspapers and magazines. Some trade houses now routinely purchase ads on television and radio. To promote *Scarlett*, for instance, Warner Books bought thirty-second spots during talk shows and soap operas shortly before the book was released. *Scarlett* became the top-selling fiction book in 1991.

The final part of the publishing process involves the business and order-fulfillment stages—getting books to market and shipping and invoicing orders to thousands of commercial outlets and college bookstores. Warehouse inventories are monitored to ensure that enough copies of a book will be available to meet demand. Anticipating such demand, though, is a tricky business. No publisher wants to get stuck with books it cannot sell or be caught short if a book becomes more popular than originally predicted. Today, most of these business procedures are managed by computer programs, and bookstores can usually tell customers instantly whether they have a particular book in stock or how long it will take to obtain the book.

book clubs and mail order

In terms of selling books, two alternative strategies have worked for a number of years—book clubs and mail order. In fact, these strategies have often sustained publishers during the changeover from a print-based to an electronically influenced culture. Both tactics also helped the industry in earlier times when bookstores were not as plentiful. Modeled on the turn-of-the-century catalogue sales techniques used by retailers such as Sears, direct-mail services brought books to rural and small-town areas that had no bookstores. Doubleday became the first publisher to introduce direct mail to readers during the early 1900s.

The Book-of-the-Month Club and the Literary Guild both started in 1926. Using popular writers and literary experts to recommend new books, the clubs were successful immediately. By the mid-1990s more than 150 adult book clubs were operating, ranging from the Arts and Crafts Book Society to the Civil Engineers Book Club.[8] Book clubs have long served as editors for their customers, screening thousands of titles and recommending key books in particular genres. Occasionally, though, important books have been overlooked by clubs, such as Steinbeck's *The Grapes of Wrath* and Hemingway's *The Sun Also Rises*.

During the 1980s, as book clubs experienced declining sales, they became more susceptible to pressure from major publishers. Indeed, the outside experts for the clubs began complaining not only that their recommendations were frequently bypassed by club editors but that the clubs were stressing commercially viable authors without regard to literary merit. In 1994, the Book-of-the-Month Club eliminated outside judges altogether.[9]

Besides screening new books for consumers, clubs have offered incentives, such as free books and occasional price reductions, to compete with bookstores. Book clubs offer the same advantages as a cable home-shopping network: You can order from the comfort of your home and avoid "mall madness" or the congestion of downtown shopping. Although Time Warner operates the Book-of-the-Month Club (the largest single club, with more than one million members), Doubleday remains the most active publisher in the book-club business. In the mid-1990s, Doubleday owned and operated both the Literary Guild and Doubleday Book Club as well as several specialty clubs, including the Mystery Guild, the Military Book Club, the Science-Fiction Book Club, and the Audio Book Club. The total membership of the Doubleday clubs was estimated at around three million in 1995.

Mail-order bookselling is used primarily by trade, professional, and university press publishers. The mail-order strategy offers many of the benefits of book clubs in terms of immediately notifying readers about new book titles. Mail-order bookselling was pioneered in the 1950s by magazine publishers. They created special sets of books, such as Time-Life Books, focusing on science, nature, household maintenance, cooking, and so forth. These series usually offered one book at a time (unlike encyclopedias) and sustained sales through direct-mail flyers and newspaper, magazine, radio, and television advertising. To enhance their perceived value and uniqueness, most of these sets could be obtained only through the mail. Although such sets are more costly due to advertising and postal charges, mail-order books still appeal to customers who prefer the convenience of mail to the hassle of shopping. Others like the privacy of mail order (particularly if they are ordering sexually explicit books or magazines).

bookstores

Although the book industry remains the most diverse of all mass media, the same media trend toward large chain ownership prevails. In the mid-1990s, about twelve thousand bookstores in the United States made more than 50 percent of their revenue from the sale of books and magazines. Another fifteen thousand stores, such as department or drug stores, also sell books (see Table 10.3). By the mid-1990s, book sales were dominated by two large chains: Borders-Walden and Barnes & Noble, which includes all B. Dalton and Doubleday stores. These chains operate more than a thousand stores each and account for more than one-fourth of all trade book sales.

Shopping mall bookstores have boosted book sales since the late 1960s. But the current trend reinvigorating the business began in the 1980s with the development of **superstores**. The idea was to adapt to the book trade the large retail-store concept, such as Builders Square in home improvement or Wal-Mart in general retail. Following the success of a single Borders store in Ann Arbor, Michigan, a number of book chains began developing superstores that catered to suburban areas and avid readers. A typical superstore now stocks a hundred thousand titles, compared to the twenty or forty thousand titles found in older B. Dalton or Waldenbook stores. As superstores expanded, they also started to sell recorded music and to feature coffee shops, restaurants, and live performances. By 1996 Borders, which had only fourteen superstores in 1991, and Barnes & Noble were opening two superstores per week around the country.

One benefit to booksellers in the electronic era has been the increased value of used and rare books. Many small cities, especially in college towns, now support half a dozen small used-book stores. For example, Ann Arbor, a city of 110,000 with the University of Michigan at its center, supported twenty-five bookstores in the mid-1990s, and at least twelve of those specialized in used books. As the city where Borders originated, Ann Arbor had the nation's highest books-per-capita ratio: The average Ann

> "There is a public interest at stake in the **fate of bookstores** that quickens the public's appetite for printed words."
> —George Will, *Washington Post*, 1991

One amazing aspect of the enduring popularity of books was the recent emergence of the superstore. By stocking a hundred thousand titles, providing coffee shops, and offering entertainment in their stores, Borders and Barnes & Noble made it increasingly difficult for thousands of small independent booksellers around the nation to remain competitive.

TABLE 10.3
Bookstores in the United States, 1995

Category	Number of Stores	Category	Number of Stores
Antiquarian General	1,414	Gift Shop	388
		Juvenile*	467
Antiquarian Mail Order	630	Mail Order General	438
		Mail Order Specialized	910
Antiquarian Specialized	284	Metaphysics, New Age, and Occult	307
Art Supply Store	76	Museum Store and Art Gallery	586
College General	3,359	Nature and Natural History	172
College Specialized	164	Newsdealer	139
Comics	340	Office Supply	65
Computer Software	363	Other§	2,310
Cooking	164	Paperback‡	465
Department Store	2,372	Religious*	4,026
Educational*	232	Self Help/Development	77
Federal Sites†	313	Stationer	56
Foreign Language*	135	Toy Store	104
General	7,223	Used*	931
		Totals	**28,510**

*Includes Mail-Order Shops for this topic, which are not counted elsewhere in this survey.

†National Historic Sites, National Monuments, and National Parks.

‡Includes Mail Order. Excludes used paperback bookstores, stationers, drugstores, or wholesalers handling paperbacks.

§Stores specializing in subjects or services other than those covered in this survey.

Source: *The Bowker Library and Trade Book Annual, 1996* (New Providence, NJ: R. R. Bowker), 560.

Arborite adult spent more than $230 a year on books (Berkeley, California, and Madison, Wisconsin, also university cities, ranked second and third).

Despite the control that chains have over commercial trade books, the majority of bookstores today remain small and independent. For example, nearly one thousand used- and rare-book stores now operate nationwide. To counter chains, many independents have formed regional or statewide groups to plan survival tactics. In 1992, for instance, independents in Madison, Wisconsin, countered the arrival of a new Borders superstore by redecorating, extending hours and services, creating newsletters, and offering musical and children's performances. Still, many smaller stores fear the rise of superstores, their ability to offer discount prices on best-sellers, and their relationship with large publishers who pay chains for quality shelf space. Chains pose a threat to the continued health of independent booksellers, whose overall sales slipped in the 1990s as the number of superstores expanded to more than six hundred nationwide.

ownership patterns

Like most mass media, commercial publishing is dominated by a handful of major corporations with ties to international media conglomerates such as Viacom/Paramount (which now owns Simon & Schuster), Time Warner, Newhouse's Advance Publications, and Bertelsmann, which began by publishing German Bibles in the

1700s. Since the 1960s and 1970s—when CBS acquired Holt, Rinehart & Winston, Popular Library, and Fawcett—mergers and consolidations have driven the book industry. Germany's Bertelsmann purchased Dell in the late 1970s for $35 million and in the 1980s bought Doubleday for $475 million. Today the Bantam-Doubleday-Dell publishing group ranks among the most successful commercial houses. Random House, the largest trade publisher in the 1990s, has been owned since 1980 by Advance Publications. It now controls Knopf, Vintage, Fawcett Ballantine, Modern Library, and Fodor's Travel Publications, among others. By the mid-1990s, Random House's various imprints collectively were producing more than thirty-four hundred new titles annually (see Table 10.4).

A number of concerns have surfaced regarding conglomerates' control over the publishing industry. The distinctive styles of older houses and their associations with certain literary figures and book types no longer characterize the industry. Of special concern has been the financial struggle of independent publishers and booksellers, who are often undercut in price and promotion by large corporations and bookstore chains. Large houses also tend to favor blockbusters or best-sellers and do not aggressively pursue more modest or unconventional books.

From the corporate point of view, book industry executives argue that large companies can financially support a number of smaller struggling firms and that the editorial ideas of these firms can remain independent from the parent corporation. Executives also tout the advantages of *synergy*: the involvement of several media subsidiaries under one corporate umbrella all working to develop versions of a similar product. One writer commented on these synergistic possibilities when Time and Warner merged in 1990: "Theoretically, this unprecedented corporate fusion makes it possible for a title to be published in hardcover by Little, Brown (a division of Time Inc.), featured as a Book-of-the-Month Club main selection, reviewed by *Time* magazine, issued in paperback by Warner Books, made into a major motion picture and turned into a TV series by Warner television."[10] Still, authors and critics worry that book ideas that lack such "multimedia" potential may be rejected in the trend toward large corporate control.

On one level, the industry appears healthy, with thousands of independent presses still able to make books using inexpensive production techniques and desktop computer publishing. Many independents struggle, however, against the few large

TABLE 10.4
Top 10 U.S. Trade Book Publishers

Rank	Publisher	Parent Company	1995 Revenues ($ mil.)
1	Random House	Advance Publications	1,255.0
2	Simon & Schuster	Viacom	832.7
3	Bantam Doubleday Dell	Bertelsmann	670.0
4	Time Warner	Time Warner Inc.	325.0
5	HarperCollins	News Corp.	317.2
6	Penguin USA	Pearson Inc.	317.0
7	Putnam Berkley	MCA Universal Inc.	300.0
8	Holtzbrinck	Holtzbrinck Publishing Group	267.0
9	Hearst Book Group	Hearst Corp.	160.0
10	Thomas Nelson	Thomas Nelson, Inc.	145.7

Source: Hoover's Guide to Media Companies (Austin, TX: Hoover's Business Press, 1996), 31.

conglomerates that define the direction of much of the industry. By the mid-1990s, the U.S. market share for independents and small bookstores had fallen from 32 percent in 1991 to less than 20 percent,[11] and for the first time more trade books were being sold by chains than by independents.

trends in book publishing

A number of technological changes in the publishing industry demonstrate the blurring of print and electronic cultures. The book industry has adapted successfully in the digital age by using computer technology to effectively lower costs. Today everything from an author's word-processing program to the processes of printing and distribution is computerized.[12] In 1992, the first multimedia books appeared, including electronic versions of Michael Crichton's *Jurassic Park* and Lewis Carroll's *Alice's Adventures in Wonderland* (first published in 1865). These paperless books were produced using Apple Computer software that integrated printed text with animated cartoons and sound effects. Much skepticism remains, however, regarding whether enough consumers will give up the printed page to read a book from a computer screen, even with futuristic visual and audio accompaniment. Reference books have become a primary target for multimedia adaptations on computer hard drives and CD-ROMs. A digitized CD-ROM reference book can easily store more than a hundred thousand pages of text, avoiding the high cost of paper and book production.

> "Electronic text processing marks the next major shift in **information technology** after the development of the printed book. It promises (or threatens) to produce effects on our culture, particularly on our literature, education, criticism, and scholarship, just as radical as those produced by **Gutenberg's moveable type**."
> —George Landow, 1992

In studying various mergers of print and electronic forms, most forecasters suggest that electronic and digital publications are best suited for reference works, some children's literature, and educational materials. Most media observers do not believe that electronic technology will seriously undermine the traditional printed book. Some evidence exists, however, that because of the computerization of bestseller lists and the quicker tracking of inventories, stores may get rid of books before the gradual word of mouth ever has a chance to build up. This slower oral tradition once held much more clout in popularizing book titles. Nonetheless, the book in general remains a sufficiently distinct and personal medium. It stands in sharp contrast to the more visual forms of media as both a cultural form and as a consumer product (see "Tracking Technology: Project Gutenberg Puts Great Literature on the Internet").

influences of television and film

Through their vast television exposure, books by TV celebrities such as Tim Allen (ABC's *Home Improvement*), Ellen DeGeneres (ABC's *Ellen*), or Jerry Seinfeld (NBC's *Seinfeld*) have sold millions of copies—enormous sales in a business where a hundred thousand in sales constitutes remarkable success. In national polls conducted in the 1980s and 1990s, nearly 30 percent of respondents said they had read a book because they had seen the story or a promotion on television.

By the mid-1990s, Oprah Winfrey's afternoon talk show had become a major power broker in selling books. In 1993, for example, Holocaust survivor and Nobel prize recipient Elie Wiesel appeared on *Oprah*. Afterward, his 1960 memoir, *Night*,

TRACKING TECHNOLOGY

Project Gutenberg Puts Great Literature on the Internet

by Elizabeth Weise

San Francisco—Michael Hart is a man with a mission.

"If I had my dream, every Jan. 1, every book that went into the public domain would immediately go out on the net and everyone could have it," he says.

Through his Project Gutenberg, Hart is working toward that vision of a digitally accessible future—one book at a time.

At the stroke of midnight of the last day of every month, Project Gutenberg puts the full electronic text of 16 books out on the Internet—all in "plain vanilla ascii text" that any computer can read.

You don't need fancy programs, you don't need anything special—just an e-mail account and a burning desire to download the entire text of Conrad's *Heart of Darkness*, *The Moon and Sixpence* by Somerset Maugham, *The Return of Sherlock Holmes* or *Caesar's Commentaries*—in Latin?

Why exactly you'd want to download the entire text of Mark Twain's *A Connecticut Yankee in King Arthur's Court* is unclear, but there's something wonderful about the idea that it's just sitting on its virtual shelf, waiting for you.

Project Gutenberg got its start in 1971 when computers took up whole floors. Hart's best friend was a programmer and he used to go hang out with him in the computer room at the University of Illinois.

"It was air-conditioned and private and I could study there," said Hart, 48.

Eventually some of the operators gave him an account on what later became the Internet. Hart wanted to do something to repay the favor.

His first foray into information dissemination for the electronic masses was to make the text of the Declaration of Independence available on the network. It was around the time of

the Bicentennial, and parchment copies of the document were everywhere. Why not an electronic one?

Now his dream is to put 10,000 books out on the Internet by the year 2001. Hart and the gaggle of volunteers devoted to the project hit book No. 238 on Feb. 1, 1995. Each year they double the number of books they do.

"There are little old ladies in the middle of Vermont who type them on ancient Tandy computers and people with quarter of a million dollar scanners," Hart said.

As long as there's someone who wants to input the text and the book has entered the public domain—which means it was published more than 75 years ago and the copyright wasn't renewed—it goes on the list.

Hart works out of Illinois Benedictine College in Lisle, Ill. The entire project lives in one PC on a bookshelf in a little-used office in the computer department at the University of Illinois.

A glance over the complete catalog of books available through the project makes it clear that this is, indeed, a labor of love by volunteers. The February 1992 release of *Paradise Lost* includes the notation "originally all in CAPS," and there's a warning that *Moby Dick* is missing chapter 72.

Hart isn't out to do much—just save the world.

"History was founded on the notion that there wasn't enough for everyone. But the Internet's the opposite. You put a novel up on the net and there's one for everyone. You could spend one week typing in *Winnie the Pooh* if it was your favorite book, and all people for the rest of history will be able to read it."

Source: Elizabeth Weise, "Project Puts Great Literature on Internet," *Associated Press* © 1995.

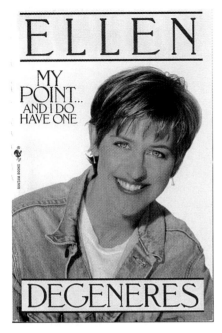

which came out as a Bantam paperback in 1982, returned to the best-seller lists. In 1996, novelist Toni Morrison's nineteen-year-old book *Song of Solomon* became a paperback best-seller after she appeared on *Oprah*. The program exerted similar power for first-time authors. Former reporter Jacquelyn Mitchard saw her first novel, *Deep End of the Ocean*, top the *New York Times* best-seller list and sell more than 840,500 copies in 1996 after her *Oprah* appearance. To promote the habit of reading, Winfrey in 1996 began devoting one program a month to "Oprah's Book Club," during which her audience and writers discussed books.[13]

Television and film continue to get many of their story ideas from books. Michael Crichton's *Jurassic Park* and Winston Groom's *Forrest Gump* became blockbuster movies. Even nineteenth-century novels still translate to the screen. For example, the popular 1994 film version of *Little Women*, written in 1868 by Louisa May Alcott, sent the Random House reissue of the novel to the top of the juvenile best-seller list. In another example from the juvenile book business, the summer of 1995 featured eight of Scholastic's *Goosebumps* books among the Top 10 best-sellers for young readers. Scholastic, the leading publisher of educational magazines, then cut a deal with Fox to produce a TV series based on the books. By 1996, the series had become the most popular children's show on television.

Like the big movie studios, major publishing houses search for best-selling books that allow them to make up for the many titles that do not earn much. Books by television stars like Tim Allen, Jerry Seinfeld, and Ellen DeGeneres, whose TV audiences number between 25 to 35 million viewers, are almost guaranteed best-sellers.

blockbusters and licenses

Since Harriet Beecher Stowe's abolitionist novel, *Uncle Tom's Cabin*, sold fifteen thousand copies in fifteen days back in 1852 (and three million total copies prior to the Civil War), many American publishers have stalked the best-seller. As in the movie business, large publishers are always searching for the blockbuster. To ensure popular success, publishers often pay rights to license popular film and television programs, especially in the juvenile book trade. Books developed from licenses now account for 5 percent of trade industry sales. For instance, the Disney company's resurgence in animated films since the 1980s generated a wave of successful book titles based on their movies. In addition, the popularity of the syndicated TV series *Mighty Morphin Power Rangers* in the 1990s produced millions of dollars in book reincarnations. Despite phenomena such as *Goosebumps*, many critics and publishers believe that it is no longer possible for a book to become popular without television and film support. Consequently, major publishers are often hesitant to develop popular books or series that do not come with a built-in TV or movie audience.

talking books

Another major development in publishing has been the merger of sound recording with publishing. Audio books or **books on tape** generally feature actors or authors reading abridged versions of popular fiction and nonfiction trade books. Indispensable to many sightless readers and older readers whose vision has weakened, talking books are also popular among regular readers who do a lot of commuter driving. A study in 1993 by the Audio Publishers Association reported that nearly 50 percent of all audio-book use took place in cars. Among 1997's audio best-sellers were Grisham's *The Partner* and Patricia Cornwell's *Hornet's Nest* in fiction and Walter Cronkite's *A Reporter's Life* and Frank McCourt's *Angela's Ashes* in nonfiction. Classics such as Charles Dickens' *Christmas Carol* have also done well in audio form. In addition, the number of books on tape borrowed from libraries has soared in the 1990s.

book preservation

Another recent trend in the book industry involves the preservation of older books, especially those from the nineteenth century printed on acid-based paper. Ever since the conversion to machine-made publishing materials during the Industrial Revolution, paper had been produced using chemicals that gradually deteriorate over time. At the turn of the century, research provided evidence that acid-based paper would eventually turn brittle and self-destruct. This research, which had been initiated by libraries concerned with losing valuable older collections, was confirmed by further studies in the 1940s and 1950s. The paper industry, however, did not respond. In the 1970s, leading libraries began developing techniques to de-acidify book pages in an attempt to halt any further deterioration (although this process could not restore books to their original state). Meanwhile, more and more books were removed from circulation and were available to the public only on microfilm and microfiche, which were difficult to read.

Despite evidence that alkaline-based paper was easier on machinery, produced a whiter paper, and caused less pollution, the paper industry did not change. Motivated almost entirely by economics rather than by the cultural value of books, the industry by the early 1990s finally began producing paper that was acid free. Libraries and book conservationists, however, still had to focus attention on older, at-risk books. While clumsy, hard-to-read microfilm remained an option, some institutions began photocopying original books onto acid-free paper to make copies available to the public. Libraries then stored the originals, which had been treated to halt further wear.

More recently, pioneering projects in digital technology by Xerox and Cornell University have produced electronic copies of books through computer scanning. This process allows a computer to safely "read" a book that is deteriorating and to reproduce it in a digitized version. Once transferred to a digital format, the book can be reproduced at any time and stored in a CD-ROM or other digital version.

books and the future of democracy

As we tentatively enter the digital age, the book-reading habits of children and adults are a social concern. After all, books have played an important role not only in spreading the idea of democracy but in connecting us to new ideas beyond our local experience. In surveys in the 1990s, however, only about 27 percent of middle school students indicated that they read for pleasure each day (although they reported watching about three hours of television per day). Adults also reported sporadic reading habits. For instance, only about 50 percent of U.S. adults said that they read at least one book a year. Likewise, 40 percent of young adults between age nineteen and twenty-one reported that they did not read books. Yet studies also suggest that reading habits are generally more evident among the young than among older people; 60 percent of all avid or regular book readers, for example, are under the age of forty. Overall, the share of regular book readers in the population is about 25 percent, a figure that has remained steady since the 1930s.

Although our society is being dramatically influenced by electronic and digital culture, the impact of our oldest mass medium—the book—remains immense. Without the developments of printing presses and books, the idea of democracy would be hard to imagine. From the impact of Stowe's *Uncle Tom's Cabin*, which helped end slavery in the 1860s, to Rachel Carson's *Silent Spring*, which led to reforms in the pesticide industry in the 1960s, books have made a difference. They have told us things that we wanted—and needed—to know.

Over time, the wide circulation of books gave many ordinary people the same opportunities to learn that were once available only to a privileged few. However, as societies discovered the power associated with knowledge and the printed word, books were subjected to a variety of censors (see "Examining Ethics: Censorship Issues in Book Publishing"). Imposed by various rulers and groups intent on maintaining their authority, the censorship of books often prevented people from learning about the rituals and moral standards of other cultures. Political censors sought to banish "dangerous" books that promoted radical ideas or challenged conventional authority. Some versions of the Bible, Karl Marx's *Das Kapital* (1867), *The Autobiography of Malcolm X* (1965), and Salman Rushdie's *Satanic Verses* (1989) have all been banned at one time or another. In fact, one of the triumphs of the Internet is that it allows the digital passage of banned books into nations where printed versions have been outlawed.

> "Most **would-be censors** object to the obvious 's' words—sex, suicide, Satanism and swearing. The novels of J. D. Salinger and John Steinbeck, which deal with self-conscious teenagers and **the rough edge of life**, respectively, are perennial targets."
>
> —Mary B. W. Taylor,
> *New York Times*,
> 1995

Beyond censorship issues, other concerns have surfaced regarding the limits that democratic societies place on books. For example, the economic clout of publishing houses run by large multinational corporations has made it more difficult for new authors and new ideas to gain a foothold in commercial publishing. Often, editors and executives prefer to invest in commercially successful writers or authors who have a built-in television, sports, or movie audience.

Another issue is whether the contemporary book industry, in its own way, has contributed to entertainment and information overload. For example, Alvin Kernan argues, in his book *The Death of Literature*, that serious literary work has been increasingly overwhelmed by the triumph of consumerism. In other words, people accumulate craftily marketed celebrity biographies and popular fiction but seldom read serious work. Kernan's critique reflects the long-standing view that "superior" cultural taste is associated with reading literature. He contends that cultural standards have been undermined by marketing ploys that divert attention away from serious books and toward mass-produced works that are more easily read.[14]

Since democracies generally depend on literate populations to sift through cultural products and arrive at informed decisions, the abundance of media products raises other important questions. Of particular concern is the apparent decline in juvenile reading levels as measured by standardized tests over the last few decades. Indeed, the increase in published book titles since the 1950s does not mean that we have become a more literate society. The adult illiteracy rate has remained fairly constant at about 10 percent over the years. And today, children have multiple electronic and digital distractions and options with regard to how they use their leisure time.

Yet books and reading have survived the challenge of visual and digital culture. Developments such as word processing, books on tape, children's pictorial literature, and online computer services have integrated aspects of print and electronic culture in our daily lives. Most of these new forms carry on the original legacy of books—transcending geographic borders to provide personal stories, world history, and general knowledge to all who can read.

Despite a commercial book industry that has increasingly developed its own star system of authors, approximately a thousand new publishers enter the business each year. Tensions persist, however, between businesspeople who publish books as a money-making enterprise and authors trying to write well and advance knowledge—or between authors who seek fame and fortune and editor-publishers interested in

Over the years, small communities and large nations have successfully kept certain books out of the hands of their citizens. In 1929, for instance, Edgar Rice Burroughs's *Tarzan* series was pulled from the Los Angeles public library system because Tarzan and Jane lived together but were not married. In 1931, China banned Lewis Carroll's *Alice's Adventures in Wonderland* because animal characters used human language. In 1989, the Ayatollah Khomeini of Iran not only banned Salman Rushdie's novel *Satanic Verses* for blaspheming the Islamic religion but also ordered Rushdie killed, forcing the author into hiding for several years.

Books have faced innumerable cultural and social challenges. Censorship campaigns have often attempted to

Banned in Boston, Boise, and Butte? A Selection of Controversial Books

The Scarlet Letter—Nathaniel Hawthorne

Leaves of Grass—Walt Whitman

Alice's Adventures in Wonderland—Lewis Carroll

The Adventures of Huckleberry Finn—Mark Twain

Lady Chatterley's Lover—D.H. Lawrence

Ulysses—James Joyce

Tropic of Cancer—Henry Miller

As I Lay Dying—William Faulkner

To Kill a Mockingbird—Harper Lee

Of Mice and Men—John Steinbeck

Diary of a Young Girl—Anne Frank

Catcher in the Rye—J. D. Salinger

Lolita—Vladimir Nabokov

A Clockwork Orange—Anthony Burgess

Naked Lunch—William S. Burroughs

Tales of a Fourth-Grade Nothing—Judy Blume

In the Night Kitchen—Maurice Sendak

Song of Solomon—Toni Morrison

The Color Purple—Alice Walker

The Satanic Verses—Salman Rushdie

I Know Why the Caged Bird Sings—Maya Angelou

remove certain books from libraries and classrooms. The American Library Association (ALA), which represents over thirty thousand libraries nationwide, documents more than six hundred censorship attempts annually.[1]

One of the most celebrated censorship cases involved Walt Whitman's *Leaves of Grass*. The book-length poem became the center of a legal case in the early 1880s and was eventually banned in Boston. Because of their provocative sexual themes and language, the full versions of D. H. Lawrence's *Lady Chatterley's Lover* and Henry Miller's *Tropic of Cancer* were banned in the United States until the early 1960s.

During the 1980s and 1990s, the books most often challenged in school libraries and curriculums have included either controversial language or sexual themes. Several parent groups challenged the use in schools of children's books that explain gay lifestyles, including Leslea Newman's *Heather Has Two Mommies* and Michael Wilhoit's *Daddy's Roommate*. Books that mention witchcraft and the occult or that appear insensitive to particular minority groups have also been targeted. Censorship campaigns—initiated by both liberal and conservative groups—have sometimes tried to "protect" preteens and teenagers from significant works of literature. Often these books used common street language or introduced adolescents to complex personal and social themes, which some adults believed were inappropriate for young people.

Censorship campaigns have targeted everything from John Steinbeck's *Of Mice and Men* to Roald Dahl's *The Witches*. But the most censored book has been Mark Twain's *Adventures of Huckleberry Finn*, an 1884 classic that still sells tens of thousands of copies a year in paperback. The novel routinely uses the word *nigger* in the way it was used in everyday language in nineteenth-century America. Most high school teachers are taught how to handle the sensitive racial issues raised in the book. Occasionally, though, parent groups and some civil rights organizations have argued that the frequent appearance of the offensive word gives the book racist overtones.

wisdom and the written word. Some argue that the industry balanced these conflicts better before corporate takeovers tipped the scales heavily toward profit motives. As our oldest media institution, the book industry bears the weight of these economic and cultural battles perhaps more than any other medium.

Given our increasing channels of specialized media, people are able to zero in on their own interests. Books, however, are one medium that takes us in other directions. Since the early days of the printing press, books have helped us to understand ideas and customs outside our own experiences. For democracy to work well, we must read. When we examine other cultures through books, we discover not only who we are and what we value but who others are and what our common ties might be.

REVIEW QUESTIONS

1. What distinguishes the manuscript culture of the Middle Ages from both the oral and print eras in communication?
2. Why was the printing press such an important and revolutionary development?
3. Why were books considered so dangerous to colonial rulers and other leaders during the early periods in American history?
4. Why did publishing houses develop?
5. Why have instant books become important to the paperback market?
6. What are the major issues that affect textbook publishing?
7. Why have religious books been so successful historically?
8. What has hampered the sales of subscription reference encyclopedias?
9. What are the general divisions of a typical publishing house?
10. Why have book clubs and mail-order strategies continued to flourish despite the rapid growth of mall stores and superstores?
11. Why have book superstores been so successful over the past few years?
12. What are the current ownership patterns in the book industry? How have these trends affected the small independent store?
13. What role has licensing played in the trade book industry over the past few years?
14. Why did paper manufacturers convert to acid-free paper in the late 1980s and early 1990s?
15. What have book publishers and sellers done to keep pace with changes in technology and society?
16. What have been the major contributions of books to democratic life?

QUESTIONING THE MEDIA

1. What are your earliest recollections of books? Do you read for pleasure? If yes, what kind of book do you enjoy? Why?
2. What can the book industry do better to ensure that we are not overwhelmed by a visual and electronic culture?
3. If you were opening an independent bookstore in a town with a chain, such as a Borders or Barnes & Noble, how would you compete?
4. If you were running a college bookstore, what would you do differently than your local store to improve relations with students?
5. Imagine that you are on a committee that oversees book choices for a high school library in your town. What policies do you think should guide the committee's selection of controversial books?
6. Why do you think television and cable haven't substantially decreased the number of new book titles available each year? What do books offer that television doesn't? Will cable television and specialized computer technology eventually displace books? Why or why not?

In small groups, investigate a small independent publisher or bookseller in your area. In addition to answering questions, a local company might let you observe the publishing or selling process. In your investigation, try to address the following questions:

1. What kinds of books does the firm specialize in? Profile a typical reader.

2. How does the firm identify writers and/or get a book to the customer? List the steps the firm goes through.

3. What kinds of commercial obstacles does this independent firm face?

4. According to the people who own or work at the firm, what are the major problems facing the publishing industry?

5. What strategies does the firm use in marketing or selling a book? Do the large corporate houses or chains hamper this process? If so, in what ways?

6. According to the people at this firm, how easy or difficult is it to enter the industry? Are student internships a possibility at this firm or at other independent houses or sellers?

Add other questions and information as you go along.

Depending on the time allotted by your group and the instructor, meet to discuss your findings. As a group, prepare a chart or provide information on the firm you investigated, so that your findings can be shared with the rest of the class.

Advertising
and Commercial Culture

CHAPTER 11

What do the Jolly Green Giant, Tony the Tiger, the Pillsbury Doughboy, and the Marlboro Man all have in common? These enduring advertising symbols are all the work of Leo Burnett, a Chicago-based advertising firm founded in 1935 with eight staff members and three clients: Hoover vacuum cleaners, a Minnesota canning company, and Realsilk Hosiery. Today, Burnett ranks among the world's top agencies with offices in more than sixty countries. In the 1990s, the company's Rome office even landed Pope John Paul II as a client, helping the Vatican successfully market a line of CDs and cassette tapes featuring the pope reciting the prayers of the rosary. In 1994, Leo Burnett won the A+ Award given by the American Association of Advertising Agencies (AAAA), the ad industry's major trade organization. Annually, AAAA honors the top creative work demonstrated by an agency during the previous year.

Although most product companies now switch ad agencies every few years, many of Leo Burnett's clients have remained loyal. Pillsbury and Kellogg have used Burnett since the 1940s, Maytag since 1955, Allstate Insurance since 1957, United Airlines since 1965, McDonald's since 1982, Kraft Foods since 1984, and Hallmark Cards since 1988. By far the company's major success story was the transformation of a minor cigarette label, Marlboro, into the world's leading brand. Owned by Philip Morris, also the world's top food manufacturer (after its hostile takeover of Kraft in 1988), the Marlboro account has been with Burnett since 1954.

In the summer of 1995, consumer groups and the FCC challenged Philip Morris and Leo Burnett over some of their advertising techniques. Since Congress and the FCC had banned cigarette commercials in 1971, TV viewers asked why they had to see a Marlboro sign every time Ken Griffey Jr. went back to catch a fly ball or Dennis Rodman dove for a loose basketball next to the scorer's table, which had been cleverly converted into a rotating billboard. Philip Morris had paid a premium to sports teams who knew the ads routinely appeared as part of television's background. Under pressure, however, the company agreed to reposition stadium and arena ads so that they would no longer be visible to TV cameras.

Although the tobacco ads backfired, the sponsorship strategies of Philip Morris and its ad agency represent the new wave of commercial advertising: blending ads seamlessly into everyday life so people either barely notice them or accept them as a natural part of the cultural landscape. In 1996, the strategy surfaced on CBS when actress Elizabeth Taylor, playing herself, showed up on four sitcoms one Monday night. In each program, her character was searching for a missing strand of pearls and thus promoting Taylor's real perfume line—Black Pearls—a product of the Elizabeth Arden Company. For arranging her appearances, the company paid no money to CBS, whose audience numbers rose sharply that evening.

Ads today are scattered everywhere—and they are multiplying. Chameleon-like, advertising adapts to many media forms. At local theaters, advertisements now precede the latest Hollywood movies. Corporate sponsors spend millions for **product placement**: buying spaces for their particular goods to appear on a TV or movie set or in the background as supporting props. Ads are also part of every deejay's morning patter, and they routinely interrupt our favorite television and cable programs. In 1996, network television carried more than six thousand ads each week, double the count from the early 1980s. During the 1996 summer Olympics in Atlanta, NBC devoted 170 hours to covering events and 26 hours to airing advertisements. During the 1997 Super Bowl, the Fox network sold 58 minutes of ad time at an average of $1.2 million for each 30-second spot.

Ads take up over half the space in most daily papers and consumer magazines. They are inserted into trade books and textbooks. They fill our mailboxes. Dotting the nation's landscape, billboards promote fast-food and hotel chains, while neon signs announce the names of stores along major streets and strip malls. The Food Marketing Institute reported in 1995 that more than thirty thousand different brand-name packages filled supermarket shelves and functioned like miniature billboards—almost double the number of brands from the mid-1980s.[1] Most recently, consumers have been able to order products displayed on cable home-shopping networks and on the World Wide Web. In sum, each day the average American comes into contact with thousands of different forms of advertising.

Advertising comes in many forms, everything from classified ads to business-to-business ads that provide detailed information on specific products. However, in this chapter we will concentrate on the more conspicuous advertisements that shape product images and brand-name identities. Because so much consumer advertising intrudes into daily life, ads are often viewed in a negative fashion. Although business managers agree that advertising is the foundation of a healthy media economy—far preferable to government-controlled media—citizens routinely complain about how many ads they are forced to endure. Accordingly, the national cynicism about advertising has forced advertisers to become more competitive. And ad agencies, in turn, create ads that not only seem natural but that also stand out in some way. To get noticed, ads routinely employ celebrities, humor, computer animation, and music-video devices. Ad agencies, in fact, often develop ads that are superior in their execution to the print or electronic content they interrupt.

Given the public's increasing sophistication regarding visual culture, companies have to work especially hard to get our attention. The ad industry's annual CLIO awards recognize the best TV commercials as forms of contemporary art. But consumers have found a variety of ways to dodge ads they dislike: remote controls, mute buttons, and VCRs programmed to erase advertising that runs longer than thirty seconds. Advertisers try to counter the new technology with computer tricks and technological wizardry of their own, such as transforming a two-dimensional drawing of an automobile into a real car. To ensure we pay attention, advertisers also pay enormous sums to associate their products with celebrities. In the mid-1990s, for example, Michael Jordan made over $35 million annually from various product endorsements, and in 1996 Nike signed twenty-year-old golf phenomenon Tiger Woods to a multi-year $40 million endorsement contract.

In an unprecedented contract, Nike signed golf phenom Tiger Woods to a long-range $40 million endorsement deal before the twenty-year-old had played in his first professional tournament. Nike not only gambled on Woods's place in golfing lore but also counted on his ability to appeal to young consumers and symbolize global diversity. The son of a part–African American father and an Asian-immigrant mother, Woods did not disappoint the sportswear giant, winning $1 million faster than any golfer in history. In 1997, he won the Masters Tournament by a record 12 strokes. In his partnership with Nike, Woods says that his goal is "to make golf look more like America."

The cultural and social impact of advertising has been extensive. By the early 1900s, advertising had helped to transform American society from agrarian, small-town customs to urban, consumer-driven lifestyles. When Poland escaped Soviet influence in the late 1980s, TV ads and billboards proliferated—announcing Poland's leap into a market-driven economy. For generations, advertisers have informed society about "new and improved" products, both satisfying consumers' desires and creating needs we never knew we had. Advertising has enabled many of us to have a wide choice among consumer products, even though we may have little input into what those products are. Advertising, finally, has taught us to imagine ourselves as consumers before thinking of ourselves as citizens.

Without consumer advertisements, mass communication industries would cease to function in their present forms. Ads are the economic glue that holds the media together. Yet, despite advertising's importance to the economy, many of us remain skeptical about its impact on American life. In this chapter, we will examine the historical development and role of advertising—an industry that helped transform a number of nations into consumer societies. We will look at the first U.S. ad agencies, early advertisements, and the emergence of packaging, trademarks, and brand-name recognition. Then, we will consider the growth of advertising in the twentieth century, scrutinizing the increasing influence of ad agencies and the shift to a more visually oriented culture. In keeping with our goal of developing critical skills, we will outline the key persuasive techniques used in consumer advertising. In addition, we will investigate ads as a form of commercial speech and discuss the measures aimed at regulating advertising. Finally, we will look at political advertising and its impact on democracy.

"You can tell the ideals of a nation by its advertisements."
—Norman Douglas, South Wind, 1917

309

early developments in american advertising

Advertising has existed since 3000 B.C., when shop owners first began hanging outdoor signs carved in stone and wood so that customers could spot their stores in ancient Babylon. Merchants in early Egyptian society hired town criers to walk through the streets, announcing the arrival of ships and listing the goods on board. When archaeologists were searching for Pompeii, the ancient Italian city destroyed when Mount Vesuvius erupted in 79 A.D., they turned up advertising messages painted on walls. By 900 A.D., many European cities featured town criers who not only called out the news of the day but directed customers to various stores.

> "In a mobile society, commercial products with familiar [brand] names provide people with some **sense of identity** and continuity in their lives."
> —Michael Schudson,
> *Advertising, the Uneasy Persuasion,*
> 1984

The earliest media ads were in the form of handbills, posters, and *broadsides* (long newsprint-quality posters). English booksellers printed brochures and bills announcing new books as early as the 1470s, when posters advertising religious books were tacked on church doors. In 1622, print ads imitating the oral style of criers began appearing in the first English newspapers. Announcing land deals and ship cargoes, the first newspaper advertisements in colonial America ran in the *Boston News-Letter* in 1704.

To distinguish themselves from the commercialism of newspapers, early magazines refused to carry advertisements. By the mid-1800s, though, most magazines contained ads and most publishers started magazines hoping to earn advertising dollars. About 80 percent of early advertisements covered three subjects: land sales, transportation announcements (stagecoach and ship schedules), and runaways (ads placed by farm and plantation owners whose slaves had fled). Other ads told about goods available from merchants or described new books for sale at local print shops.[2]

the first advertising agencies

Until the 1830s, little need existed for elaborate advertising. Prior to the full impact of manufacturing plants and the Industrial Revolution, few goods and products were even available for sale. Demand was also low, since 90 percent of Americans lived in isolated areas and produced most of their own tools, clothes, and food. The minimal advertising that did exist usually featured local merchants selling goods and services in their own communities. National advertising, which initially focused on patent medicines, didn't start in earnest until the 1850s. At that point, railroads first linked towns from the east coast to the Mississippi River and began carrying newspapers, handbills, and broadsides—as well as national consumer goods—across the country.

The first American advertising agencies were really newspaper *space brokers*, individuals who purchased space in newspapers and sold it to various merchants. Newspapers, accustomed to a 25 percent nonpayment rate from advertisers, welcomed the space brokers, who paid up front. In return, brokers usually received discounts of 15 to 30 percent and would sell the space to advertisers at the going rate. The discounts from the newspapers represented a broker's profit. In 1841, Volney Palmer opened the first ad agency in Boston; he had been retained by newspaper publishers to sell space to advertisers for a 25 percent commission.

advertising in the 1800s

The first so-called modern ad agency, N. W. Ayer, worked primarily for advertisers and product companies rather than for publishers. Opening in 1875 in Philadelphia, the agency helped to create, write, produce, and place ads in selected newspapers and magazines. To this day, under a payment structure that began in the nineteenth century, the typical agency collects a fee from its advertising client, keeps 15 percent of this fee for itself, and passes the rest on to the appropriate mass media. The more ads an agency places, the larger the agency's revenue. Thus, agencies have little incentive to buy fewer ads on behalf of their clients. Since the beginning of space brokerage in the 1840s, few have seriously challenged this odd relationship, which drives up costs, adds clutter to the media landscape, and does not always represent the best interests of the client.

Trademarks and Packaging. Some historians contend that the Industrial Revolution generated so many new products that national advertising was necessary to sell these goods quickly and keep factories humming. Now, though, other historians point to a more fundamental reason for advertising's development on a national scale: "the need to get control of the price the manufacturer charged for his goods."[3] During the mid-1800s, most manufacturers served retail-store owners, who usually set their own prices by purchasing goods in large quantities. Over time, however, manufacturers came to realize that if their products were distinctive and became associated with quality, customers would ask for them by name; manufacturers would then be able to dictate prices and not worry about being undersold by generic products or bulk items. To achieve this end, manufacturers began to use advertising, establishing the special identity of their products and separating themselves from competitors. Like many ads today, nineteenth-century advertisements for patent medicines and cereals often created the impression of significant differences among products when very few actually existed. But when consumers began demanding certain products—either because of quality or because of advertising—manufacturers seized control of pricing. With ads creating and maintaining brand-name recognition, retail stores had to stock the desired brands.

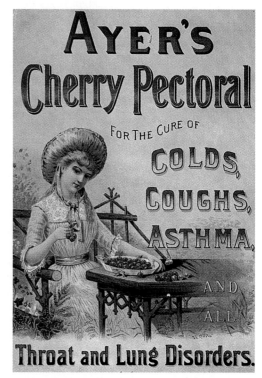

One of the first brand names, Smith Brothers has been advertising cough drops since the early 1850s. Quaker Oats, the first cereal company to register a trademark in 1877, used William Penn, a Quaker who founded Pennsylvania in 1681, to project a company image of honesty, decency, and hard work. The Campbell Soup brand came along in 1869, followed by Levi Strauss overalls in 1873, Ivory Soap in 1879, Chase & Sanborn coffee in 1886, and Eastman Kodak film in 1888. Many of these companies packaged their products in small quantities, thus distinguishing them from the generic products sold in large barrels and bins (not unlike the generic products sold in bulk in many stores today).

Packaging also allowed manufacturers to add preservatives and to claim less contamination and more freshness than might be found in loose food barrels at the local general store. Quaker Oats developed the *folding carton*, which could be printed with color displays and recipes before it was filled with cereal. This marketing strategy represented "the beginning of the end of selling cereal to retailers in bulk."[4] Product differentiation associated with brand-name packaged goods represents the single biggest triumph of advertising. Studies suggest that although most ads are not very effective in the short run, over a period of time they create demand by leading consumers to associate particular brands with quality.

Unregulated patent medicines represented a bonanza for nineteenth-century print media in search of advertising revenue. The problem was, most of these medicines were full of alcohol and other addictive drugs. This innocent-looking ad for Ayer's Cherry Pectoral did not mention that the product's active ingredient was heroin. After a vigorous reporting campaign against patent medicines by magazines like *Ladies' Home Journal*, Congress in 1906 created the Federal Drug Administration.

Not surprisingly, building or sustaining brand-name recognition is the focus of many product marketing campaigns. But the costs that packaging and advertising add to products generate many consumer complaints. The high price of many contemporary products results from advertising costs. For example, designer jeans that today cost $40 or $50 (or more) are made from the same inexpensive denim that has outfitted farm-workers since the 1800s. The difference now is that over 90 percent of the jeans' costs go toward advertising and profit. For years, critics have decried both the price markups by clothing retailers and the overpackaging that creates environmental problems.

Other product lines tell a similar story. For example, the grain in a $4 box of Frosted Mini-Wheats or Cinnamon Toast Crunch costs the manufacturer only a few cents; packaging adds another sixty to seventy-five cents; and the remaining costs go to advertising and profit margins. A dramatic rise in cereal prices in 1995, in fact, led to a congressional investigation, and manufacturers such as Kellogg and General Mills reduced prices to fend off consumer criticism. Meanwhile, generic cereals and less expensive store brands benefited; without the added cost of advertising, these "unknown" cereals have usually sold for half the price of brand-name items.

Patent Medicines and Department Stores. By the end of the 1800s, patent medicines and department stores dominated advertising copy, accounting for half of the revenues taken in by ad agencies. During this period, one-sixth of all print ads came from patent-medicine and drug companies. Such ads ensured the financial survival of numerous magazines as "the role of the publisher changed from being a seller of a product to consumers to being a gatherer of consumers for the advertisers."[5] Bearing names like Lydia Pinkham's Vegetable Compound, Dr. Lin's Chinese Blood Pills, and William Radam's Microbe Killer, patent medicines were often made with water and 15 to 40 percent concentrations of ethyl alcohol. One patent medicine—Mrs. Winslow's Soothing Syrup—actually contained morphine. The alcohol and other powerful drugs in these medicines went a long way toward explaining why people felt "better" after taking them; at the same time, they triggered lifelong addiction problems for many customers.

Many contemporary products, in fact, originated as medicines. Coca-Cola, for instance, was initially sold as a medicinal tonic and even contained traces of cocaine until 1903, when that drug was replaced by caffeine. A Methodist congregation developed Welch's Grape Juice as a substitute for wine. Early Post and Kellogg cereal ads promised to cure stomach and digestive problems. Many patent medicines made outrageous claims about what they could cure, leading ultimately to increasing public cynicism. As a result, advertisers began to police their ranks and develop industry codes to repair customer confidence. Partly to monitor patent-medicine claims, the Food and Drug Act was passed in 1906.

> "The department store did less to provide quality in consumption than to encourage a democracy of aspirations and desires. They contributed to the **democratization of envy**."
> —Michael Schudson, *Advertising, the Uneasy Persuasion,* 1984

Along with patent medicines, department-store ads were also becoming prominent in newspapers and magazines. By the early 1890s, over 20 percent of ad space was devoted to department stores and the product lines they carried. At the time, these stores were frequently reviled for undermining small shops and businesses, which depended on shopkeepers to direct people to store items. The more impersonal department stores allowed shoppers to browse and find brand-name goods themselves. Because these stores purchased merchandise in large quantities, they could generally sell the same products for less. With increased volume and less money spent on individualized service, department-store chains, like Kmart and Wal-Mart today, undercut small local stores and put more of their profits into advertising.

With the advent of the Industrial Revolution, "continuous-process machinery" kept company factories operating at peak efficiency, helping to produce an abundance of inexpensive packaged consumer goods.[6] These companies, which were some of the first to advertise, remain major advertisers today (although many of these brand names have been absorbed by larger conglomerates). They include Procter & Gamble, Colgate-Palmolive, Heinz, Borden, Pillsbury, Eastman Kodak, Carnation, and American Tobacco (see Table 11.1). A few firms, such as Hershey's Chocolate, chose not to advertise initially yet still rose to national prominence through word-of-mouth reputations. By the 1880s, however, the demand for newspaper advertising by product companies and retail stores had significantly changed the ratio of copy at most newspapers. Whereas in the mid-1880s papers featured 70 to 75 percent news and editorial material and only 25 to 30 percent advertisements, by the early 1900s more than half of the space in daily papers was devoted to advertising. This trend continues today as about 60 percent of the space in large daily newspapers is generally consumed by ads.

promoting social change and dictating values

As American advertising became more pervasive, it contributed to major social changes in the twentieth century. First, it significantly influenced the switch from a producer-directed to a consumer-driven society. By stimulating demand for new products, advertising helped manufacturers to create new markets and to recover product start-up costs more quickly. From farms to cities, advertising spread the word—first in newspapers and magazines, later on radio and television. Second, advertising promoted technological advances by showing how new machines, such as

TABLE 11.1
The Top 20 National Advertisers

Rank	Advertiser	1995 Advertising Expenditures (in thousands)
1	Procter & Gamble	$1,507,410.1
2	General Motors	1,499,567.7
3	Philip Morris	1,397,679.0
4	Chrysler	954,727.4
5	Ford	891,757.3
6	Walt Disney	777,777.4
7	Pepsico	730,195.9
8	AT&T	675,233.8
9	Johnson & Johnson	601,321.6
10	Ford Motor Co. (local dealers)	586,444.7
11	Sears Roebuck & Co.	557,847.4
12	Time Warner	542,971.2
13	Toyota Motor	513,392.7
14	General Motors (dealers assn.)	503,744.3
15	McDonald's	490,643.4
16	Nestlé	490,058.3
17	Kellogg Co.	488,205.1
18	General Motors (local dealers)	460,665.7
19	Unilever PLC	442,672.0
20	Sony	430,954.4

Sources: The World Almanac and Book of Facts 1997 (Mahwah, NJ: World Almanac Books, 1996), 297; Competitive Media Reporting and Publishers Information Bureau, New York, © 1996.

vacuum cleaners, washing machines, and cars, improved daily life. Third, advertising encouraged economic growth by increasing sales. To meet the demand generated by ads, manufacturers produced greater quantities, which reduced their costs per unit, although they did not always pass these savings along to consumers.

By the early 1900s, advertisers and ad agencies believed that women, who constituted 70 to 80 percent of newspaper and magazine readers, controlled most household purchasing decisions. (This is still a fundamental principle of advertising today.) Ironically, over 99 percent of the copywriters and ad executives at this time were men, primarily from Chicago and New York. They emphasized stereotyped appeals to women, believing that simple ads with emotional and even irrational content worked best. Thus, early ad copy featured personal tales of "heroic" cleaning products and household appliances. The intention was to help consumers feel good about defeating life's problems— an advertising strategy that endured for much of the twentieth century.

Although ad revenues dropped during the 1930s, World War II marked a rejuvenation for advertising. For the first time, the federal government bought large quantities of advertising space to promote America's involvement in a war. These purchases helped offset a decline in traditional advertising as many industries had turned their attention and production facilities to the war effort. Also during the 1940s, the industry began to actively deflect criticism that advertising created consumer needs that ordinary citizens never knew they had. To promote a more positive image, the industry developed the War Advertising Council—a voluntary group of agencies and advertisers who organized war-bond sales, blood-donor drives, and the rationing of scarce goods.

The postwar extension of advertising's voluntary efforts became known as the Ad Council, praised over the years for its Smokey the Bear campaign ("Only you can prevent forest fires"), its fund-raising campaign for the United Negro College Fund ("A mind is a terrible thing to waste"), and its "crash dummy" spots for the Department of Transportation, which substantially increased seat-belt use. Choosing a dozen worthy causes annually, the Ad Council continues to produce pro bono *public-service announcements* (PSAs) on a wide range of topics, including literacy, homelessness, drug addiction, antismoking, and AIDS education. Independent of the Ad Council, many agencies throughout the nation perform pro bono services in their communities.

After the Depression and World War II, television dramatically altered advertising. With this new visual medium, ads increasingly intruded on daily life. Criticism of advertising grew as the industry appeared to be dictating American values as well as driving the economy. Critics discovered that some agencies used **subliminal advertising**. This term, coined in the 1950s, refers to hidden or disguised print and visual messages that allegedly register on the unconscious and fool people into buying products. Only a few examples of subliminal ads actually exist (for example, a "Drink Coca-Cola" ad embedded into a few frames of a movie, or hidden sexual activity drawn into liquor ads), and research has suggested that such ads are no more effective than regular ads.

early ad regulation

During the early 1900s, the emerging clout of ad agencies and revelations of fraudulent advertising practices led to the formation of several watchdog organizations. Partly to keep tabs on deceptive advertising, advocates in the business community in 1913 created the nonprofit Better Business Bureau, which by the 1990s had more than two hundred branch offices in the United States, Canada, and Israel. At the same time, advertisers wanted a formal service that tracked newspaper readership, guaranteed accurate audience measures, and ensured that papers would not overcharge agencies and their clients. As a result, publishers formed the Audit Bureau of Circulation (ABC) in 1914. That same year, the government created the Federal Trade Commission (FTC), in part to help monitor advertising abuses. Thereafter, the industry urged self-regulatory measures in order to keep government interference at bay. The American Association of Advertising Agencies, for example, established in 1917, tried to minimize government oversight by imploring ad agencies to refrain from misleading product claims.

the shape of american advertising today

Most of modern advertising's history has been influenced by the print media and the facility of copywriters, who create the words in advertisements. Until the 1960s, the shape and pitch of most U.S. ads was determined by a **slogan**: the phrase that attempts to sell a product by capturing its essence in words. With slogans such as Clairol's "Does she or doesn't she?" and "Only her hairdresser knows for sure," the visual dimension of ads was merely a complement. Eventually, however, through the influence of movies, television, and European design, images asserted themselves and visual style began to dictate printed substance in American advertising.

the influence of visual design

Just as a postmodern design phase developed in art and architecture during the 1960s and 1970s, an era of stunning image fragments began to affect advertising at the same time. Part of this visual revolution was imported from non-American schools of design; ad-rich magazines such as *Vogue* and *Vanity Fair* increasingly hired European designers as art directors. They tended to be less tied to America's word-driven radio advertising since most European countries had government-sponsored radio systems with no ads.

> "The cool commercials . . . Nike spots, some Reeboks, most 501s, certainly all MTV promos—flatter us by saying we're too cool to fall for commercial values, and therefore cool enough to want their product."
> —Leslie Savan, *The Sponsored Life*, 1994

By the early 1970s, agencies developed teams of writers and artists: Images and words were granted equal status in the creative process. By the mid-1980s, the visual techniques of MTV, which initially modeled its videos on advertising, influenced many ads and most agencies. MTV promoted a particular appearance—rapid edits, compressed narratives, and staged performances. Video-style ads soon saturated television and featured prominent performers such as Paula Abdul, Ray Charles, Michael Jackson, and Elton John. By the 1990s, a wide range of short polished musical performances were routinely used in TV ads to encourage consumers not to click the remote control.

the mega agency

During the twentieth century, large full-service advertising agencies emerged, and many of those early companies remain major players today (see Table 11.2). Although more than thirteen thousand ad agencies currently operate in the United States, the recent tendency is toward **mega agencies**: large ad firms that are formed by merging several individual agencies that maintain worldwide regional offices. In addition to providing both advertising and public relations services, many of these agencies operate their own in-house radio and TV production studios. In the early 1990s, the two largest agencies were British-based firms, the WPP Group and Saatchi & Saatchi, which later became Cordiant PLC. At the time, Cordiant PLC and its subsidiaries controlled more than 25 percent of all TV ad time purchased worldwide. In 1987, WPP purchased J. Walter Thompson, the largest U.S. firm at the time.

TABLE 11.2
The World's Largest Advertising Agencies, 1997

Rank	Company	Headquarters	1996 Income (in $ millions)
1	WPP Group (includes J. Walter Thompson, Ogilvy & Mather)	London	3,419.9
2	Omnicom Group (includes BBDO, DDB Needham)	New York	3,035.5
3	Interpublic Group (includes McCann-Erickson, Campbell-Ewald)	New York	2,751.2
4	Dentsu (includes DCA)	Tokyo	1,929.9
5	Young & Rubicam (owns Burson-Marsteller; has thirty-year partnership with Dentsu)	New York	1,356.4
6	Cordiant (includes Bates, Saatchi & Saatchi)	London	1,169.3
7	Grey Advertising	New York	987.8
8	Havas	Neuilly-sur-Seine Cedex, France	974.3
9	Hakuhodo	Tokyo	897.7
10	True North Communications	Chicago	889.5
11	Leo Burnett	Chicago	866.3
12	MacManus Group	New York	754.2

Source: *Advertising Age*, April 21, 1997. Reprinted with permission. Copyright, Crain Communications, Inc.

The mega-agency trend has stirred debate among consumer and media watchdog groups. Some consider large agencies a threat to the independence of smaller firms, which are slowly being bought out. An additional concern is that a few firms now control the distribution of advertising dollars globally. Thus, the cultural values represented by American and European ads may undermine or overwhelm the values and products of developing countries, which are still trying to establish their own markets and economic systems.

the boutique agency

The visual revolutions in advertising during the 1960s elevated the standing of designers and graphic artists, who became closely identified with the look of particular ads. Breaking away from bigger agencies, many of these creative individuals formed small **boutique agencies** to devote their talents to a handful of select clients. Offering more personal services, the boutiques prospered, bolstered by innovative ad campaigns and increasing profits from TV accounts. By the 1980s, large agencies had bought up many of the boutiques. Nevertheless, they continued to operate as fairly independent subsidiaries within multinational corporate structures.

One boutique agency in Portland, Oregon, Weiden & Kennedy, made its name by winning the Nike sneaker account in the 1980s and developing the slogan "Just do it" (see "Examining Ethics: Fighting over Sneakers"). Like other boutique agencies at the time, the firm experimented with merging television imagery and popular music to appeal to the baby-boom generation. Weiden & Kennedy gained notoriety with a Nike

During the 1950s and 1960s, most serious basketball players wore simple canvas sneakers—usually Converse or Keds. Encouraged by increasing TV coverage, interest in sports exploded in the late 1960s and 1970s, as did a wildly competitive international sneaker industry. First Adidas dominated the industry, then Nike and Reebok. The Great Sneaker Wars have since continued unabated, although they may have peaked at the 1992 Olympics when pro-basketball stars Michael Jordan and Charles Barkley—Nike endorsers—refused to display the Reebok logo on their team jackets at the awards ceremony. Reebok had paid dearly to sponsor the Olympics and wanted the athletes to fall in line. A compromise was eventually worked out in which the two players wore the jackets but hid the Reebok name.

Although the Olympic incident seems petty, battles over brand-name sneakers and jackets in the 1980s were a more dangerous "game." Advertisers found themselves embroiled in a controversy that, for a time, threw a bright and uncomfortable spotlight on the advertising industry. In many poor and urban areas throughout the United States, kids and rival gangs were fighting over and stealing brand-name sportswear from one another. Particularly coveted and targeted were $100-plus top-of-the-line basketball shoes, especially the Nike and Reebok brands heavily advertised on television. A few incidents resulted in shootings and killings. Articles in major newspapers and magazines, including *Sports Illustrated* ("Your Sneakers or Your Life") took advertisers to task. Especially hard hit was Nike, which by the early 1990s controlled nearly 30 percent of the $5.5 billion world sneaker market. Nike's slogan—"Just do it"—became a rallying cry for critics who argued that while for most middle-class people, the command simply meant get in shape, work hard, and perform, for kids from poorer neighborhoods, "Just do it" was a call to arms: "Do what you have to do to survive."

The problem was exacerbated during the 1980s by underlying economic conditions. As the gap between rich and poor grew, advertisements suggested that our identities came from the products that we own. It is not surprising, then, that the possession of a particular brand-name product became increasingly significant for kids who felt they did not own much. Having the "right" sneaker or jacket came to represent a large part of their identities. For some groups and gangs, such possession became a requirement for membership.

The controversy over brand-name products has raised serious concerns about the moral responsibilities of agencies and advertisers. On one hand, Nike and other advertisers have become a lightning rod for the problems of a consumer culture that promises the good life to everyone who "just does it." On the other hand, criticisms of advertising have often stopped with the ads and have not examined whether they *cause* the violence or are simply *symptoms* of the inequities in contemporary America. Although many critics vilified Nike at the time, few were willing to discuss the drawbacks of capitalism and consumerism in general.

Fights over sneakers and jackets generate significant questions at the heart of our consumer culture. Does brand-name advertising unrealistically raise hopes about attaining the consumer "dreams" that some ads promise? Who should share the ultimate responsibility for violence that takes place in the name of a coveted shoe or jacket? As a society, should we mandate noncommercial messages and public-service announcements that offer alternative visions? While we need to debate these issues vigorously as individuals and as a society, in some communities kids and adults have already acted. Although brand-name products continue to sell well, an alternative attitude rejects such labeling and opts for cheaper generic products and used rummage-sale clothing. Posing a challenge to the advertising industry, this attitude undermines the view that brand-name identification is a requirement of our times.

ad driven by the beat of the 1968 Beatles protest song "Revolution." Nike had bought permission to use the song from Michael Jackson, who owns the copyright to many early Beatles recordings. But Apple Records, the Beatles' old label, objected to commercializing the song and filed a $15 million lawsuit (which it later dropped). Weiden & Kennedy went on to develop the "Bo knows" campaign, using former pro-football and baseball star Bo Jackson; the Michael Jordan spots directed for Nike by Spike Lee; and the comical 1996 ads for ESPN, which featured a number of new Olympic champions.

the structure of ad agencies

The nation's agencies, regardless of their size, generally divide the labor of creating and maintaining advertising campaigns among four departments: market research, creative development, media selection, and account services. A separate administrative unit, besides paying employee salaries, pays each media outlet that runs ads and collects an agency's fees. For instance, a series of full-page, color advertisements in a national magazine may cost an advertiser $100,000. After an agency creates and places the ads on behalf of its advertiser/client, the magazine bills the agency, whose administrative unit then collects the payment from the advertiser. The agency sends $85,000 to the magazine and pockets the standard 15 percent commission—$15,000. Expenses incurred for producing the ads are part of a separate negotiation between the agency and the advertiser. It generally costs most large-volume advertisers no more to use an agency than their own personnel because of this commission arrangement.

Market Research and VALS. Before an agency can pay bills or collect commissions, however, a great deal of planning and research must take place. Since computer technology now lets companies gather intimate data about consumers, the **market research** department plays a significant role in any agency. This department assesses the behaviors and attitudes of consumers toward particular products long before any ads are created. It may study everything from possible names for a new product to the size of the copy for a print ad. Research is conducted not only on toothpastes and cereals but on books, television comedies, and Hollywood action films. In trying to predict customers' buying habits, researchers also test new ideas and products on groups of consumers to get feedback before developing final ad strategies. In addition, some researchers contract with outside polling firms, who are better equipped to conduct regional and national studies of consumer preferences.

As the economic stakes in advertising have grown, agencies have employed scientific methods to study consumer behavior. In 1932, Young &

In 1996, Weiden & Kennedy developed the creative print and TV ad campaigns for ESPN's Sportscenter. These spots were so successful that some ESPN sportscasters were hired to appear in ads unrelated to sports.

Rubicam first used statistical techniques developed by pollster George Gallup. By the 1980s, most large agencies retained psychologists and anthropologists to advise them on human nature and buying habits. The earliest type of market research, **demographics**, mainly documented an audience's age, gender, occupation, ethnicity, education, and income. Early demographic analyses provided advertisers with data on people's behavior and social status but revealed less about feelings and attitudes. Today, demographic data are much more specific. They allow advertisers to locate consumers in particular geographic regions—usually by zip code. Thus, advertisers are able to target ethnic neighborhoods or affluent suburbs for direct mail, point-of-purchase store displays, or specialized magazines and newspaper inserts.

By the 1960s and 1970s, television had greatly increased advertising revenues, allowing agencies to expand their research activities. Advertisers and agencies began using **psychographics**, a research approach that attempts to categorize consumers by their attitudes, beliefs, interests, and motivations. Psychographic analysis often uses the **focus group**: a small-group interview technique in which a moderator leads a discussion about a product or issue, usually with six to twelve people. Because focus groups are small and less scientific than most demographic research, the findings from such groups are often controversial. Many critics wonder whether focus groups can accurately predict future success in the larger marketplace.

> "The best **advertising artist** of all time was Raphael. He had the best client—the papacy; the best art director—the College of Cardinals; and **the best product—salvation**. And we never disparage Raphael for working for a client or selling an idea."
> —Creative Director Mark Fenske, N. W. Ayer, 1996

In 1978, the Stanford Research Institute (SRI), now called SRI International, instituted its **Values and Lifestyles** or **VALS strategy**, which divides consumers into types. Using questionnaires, VALS researchers parceled the public into clusters and measured psychological factors, including how consumers think and feel about products. VALS classified people according to three broad categories: inner-directed, outer-directed, and need-driven. Each of these groups also had several subclassifications, such as achievers, experiencers, societally conscious, belongers, and survivors. Many advertisers adopted VALS to help focus their sales pitch, trying to get the most appropriate target audience for their dollars. VALS research assumed that not every product suited every consumer, encouraging advertisers to vary their sales slants to find their specific market niches.

In the late 1980s, VALS 2 was launched, which not only classified people by values and lifestyles but also considered the ways consumers achieve (or do not achieve) the lifestyles to which they aspire (see Figure 11.1, VALS 2 applied to World Wide Web users). VALS 2 distinguished principle-oriented, status-oriented, and action-oriented consumer types. The principle-oriented group, for instance, includes fulfilleds—"mature, satisfied, comfortable, reflective people who value order, knowledge, and responsibility." These consumers apparently like products that are functional, fairly priced, and durable. Also in this group, believers have "modest but sufficient" income and education; they are generally considered "conservative, conventional people with concrete beliefs based on traditional, established codes." VALS and similar research techniques ultimately provide advertisers with microscopic details about which consumers are most likely to buy which products.

Agencies and clients—particularly auto manufacturers—have relied heavily on VALS to determine the best placements for TV and magazine ads. VALS data suggest, for example, that achievers and experiencers watch more sports and news programs; these groups prefer luxury cars or sports utility vehicles like the Jeep Cherokee and Ford Bronco. Fulfilleds, on the other hand, favor TV dramas and documentaries. In cars, they like the functionality of minivans or the gas efficiency of Hondas. VALS researchers do not claim that most people fit neatly into a category. Many agencies

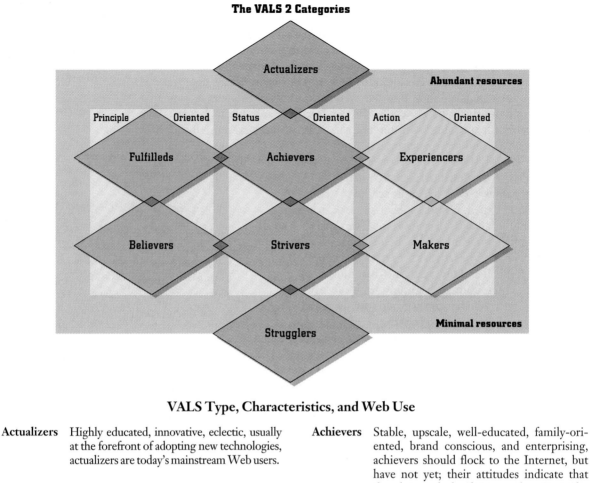

The VALS 2 Categories

Actualizers

Abundant resources

Principle Oriented — Fulfilleds
Status Oriented — Achievers
Action Oriented — Experiencers

Believers | Strivers | Makers

Strugglers

Minimal resources

VALS Type, Characteristics, and Web Use

Actualizers Highly educated, innovative, eclectic, usually at the forefront of adopting new technologies, actualizers are today's mainstream Web users.

Experiencers Impulsive, spontaneous, creative, rebellious, trend conscious, experiencers have healthy Web representation, but their attitudes indicate that their actual use is relatively light.

Fullfilleds Organized, self-assured, intellectual, analytical, and highly information intensive, fullfilleds are key drivers for consumer-information markets in most media; yet fullfilleds only have average representation on the Web, largely due to frustration over the Web's lack of structure and absence of editorial authority.

Achievers Stable, upscale, well-educated, family-oriented, brand conscious, and enterprising, achievers should flock to the Internet, but have not yet; their attitudes indicate that they have a lack of time and patience for much of the Web's triviality and that, in general, achievers perceive computer-based media as overly artificial.

Strivers Eager, social, approval seeking, and image conscious, strivers express high enthusiasm for Web use and exploration.

Believers, Makers, Strugglers Practical, cautious, conservative, traditional, literal, these remaining groups in the VALS 2 system are unlikely near-term Internet candidates due to limited education and financial resources.

Figure 11.1
VALS 2 and World Wide Web Users
Sources: SRI International, Marshall Marketing and Communications; *Channels* Magazine (July/August 1989); PR Newswire Association, © 1995.

believe, though, that VALS research can give them an edge in markets where few differences in quality may actually exist among top-selling brands, whether they are headache medicines or designer jeans. Consumer groups, wary of such research, argue that too many ads promote only an image and provide little information about a product's price, its content, or about the work conditions under which it was produced.

Creative Development. The creative aspects of the advertising business—teams of writers and artists—make up its nerve center. Many of these individuals regard ads as a commercial art form. For print ads, the creative department outlines

the rough sketches for newspaper, magazine, and direct-mail advertisements, developing the words and graphics. For radio, the creative side prepares a working script, generating ideas for everything from narration to sound effects. For television, the creative department develops a **storyboard**: a sort of blueprint or roughly drawn comic-strip version of the potential ad.

Just as tension has always existed between network executives and the creative people who develop TV programs, advertising has its own version of this battle. Often the creative side of the business—the copywriters who create jingles and the graphic artists who design the look of an ad—finds itself in conflict with the research side—the marketers who collect the consumer data to target an ad campaign. In most cases, however, both sides share the responsibility for successful or failed ad campaigns. In the 1960s, for example, both Doyle Dane Bernbach (now DDB Needham) and Ogilvy & Mather downplayed research; they championed the art of persuasion and what "felt right." Yet DDB's simple ads for Volkswagen Beetles in the 1960s were based on weeks of intensive interviews with VW workers as well as creative instinct. The campaign was remarkably successful in establishing the first niche for a foreign car manufacturer in the United States. Although sales of the VW "bug" had been growing before the ad campaign started, the successful ads helped Volkswagen preempt the Detroit auto industry's entry into the small-car field.

A different story resulted from a well-researched and carefully produced Oldsmobile campaign, hatched by Leo Burnett in the 1980s, which attempted to transform the image of the "Olds" into a hip, stylish car for younger people. The clever slogan, "It's not your father's Oldsmobile," was repeated in a series of seemingly persuasive, musically powerful, artistic commercials. Nevertheless, the ad campaign failed. Not only did the ad fail to attract young buyers—difficult to do when the car your father drives is nicknamed Olds—but it alienated older customers, who felt abandoned by the campaign's emphasis on youth.

The costs of advertising, especially on television, grow higher and higher. The average cost of a thirty-second national TV spot in the mid-1980s was under $150,000 but well over $200,000 by the mid-1990s. And, even with their greater emphasis on market research, agencies and advertisers are still not sure which ad pitches will work and which will not. In most cases, both the creative and research sides of the business acknowledge that they cannot predict with any certainty which campaigns will succeed. They say ads work best by slowly creating brand-name identities—by associating certain products over time with quality and reliability in the minds of consumers. Some economists, however, believe that much of the money spent on advertising is ultimately wasted because it simply leads consumers to change from one brand name to another. Such switching may increase profits for a particular manufacturer but has little positive impact on the overall economy.

The 1960s initiated an era of "creative advertising," in which campaigns combined a single-point sales emphasis with bold layouts, humor, and honesty. Bill Bernbach's famous Volkswagen ads, which began in 1959, not only sold many cars, but were also among the most widely read ads ever.

Media Selection. Another integral department in an ad agency, media selection, is staffed by **media buyers**: people who choose and purchase the types of media that are best suited to carry a client's ads and reach the targeted audience. For instance, a company such as Procter & Gamble, the world's leading advertiser, displays its fifty-five major brands, most of them household products, in TV shows viewed primarily by women. Media buyers encourage beer advertisers, however, to spend their ad budgets on network sports coverage, evening talk radio, sports magazines, golf cable channels, or the sports pages in local newspapers to reach male viewers.

"Ads seem to work on the very advanced principle that a small pellet or pattern in a noisy, **redundant barrage of repetition** will gradually assert itself."
—Marshall McLuhan, *Understanding Media*, 1964

Media buyers pay particular attention to the relative strengths and weaknesses of print and electronic forms of advertising. For example, ad campaigns aimed at supermarket shoppers effectively use newspapers, direct mail, and magazine inserts, all of which encourage the tradition of coupon clipping; local news programs, which do not have many teenage viewers, might not be a good buy for a client selling rap music or junk food.

As noted earlier, ad agencies have traditionally received 15 percent of what media outlets charge advertisers. Today, though, this fee is more negotiable, usually ranging from 10 to 15 percent. Another approach, taken by some ad agencies, is to simply charge a client a preset flat fee for every ad they place. Advertisers often add *incentive clauses* to their contracts with agencies, raising the fee if sales goals are met and lowering it if goals are missed. With incentive clauses, it is in the agencies' best interests to conduct repetitive **saturation advertising** in which a variety of media are inundated with ads aimed at target audiences. The initial Miller Lite beer campaign ("Tastes great, less filling"), which used humor and retired athletes to reach its male audience, became one of the most successful saturation campaigns in media history. It ran from 1973 to 1991 and included television and radio spots, magazine and newspaper ads, and billboards and point-of-purchase store displays. The excessive repetition of the campaign helped light beer overcome a potential image problem, that of being viewed as watered-down beer, unworthy of "real" men.

Account and Client Management. Ad agencies also include a department composed of client liaisons or **account executives**: individuals responsible for bringing in new business and managing the accounts of established clients. Generally, this department oversees new ad campaigns in which several agencies bid for the business of a client. Account managers coordinate the presentation of a proposed campaign and various aspects of the bidding process, such as what a series of ads will cost a client. Account executives function as liaisons between the advertiser and the creative team that produces an ad. Since most major companies maintain their own ad departments to handle everyday details, account executives also coordinate activities between their agency and a client's in-house personnel.

The advertising business tends to be volatile, and account departments are especially vulnerable to upheavals. For instance, when Ogilvy & Mather lost its $60 million American Express account ("Don't leave home without it") in the early 1990s, over fifty people were fired, many from account services. Clients routinely conduct **account reviews**: the process of evaluating and reinvigorating a product's image by reviewing an existing ad agency's campaign or by inviting several new agencies to submit new campaign strategies, which may result in the product company switching agencies.[7] One industry study in the mid-1980s indicated that client accounts stayed with the same agency for about seven years, but by the late 1980s clients were changing agencies much more quickly. D'Arcy Masius Benton & Bowles, for example, won the $80 million Maxwell House coffee account in 1989 from Ogilvy & Mather, which then won it back the following year. There are a few exceptions, however: Campbell-

Ewald has held GM's Chevrolet account since 1922—more than seventy-five years, and Leo Burnett has managed the Green Giant (now a subsidiary of Pillsbury) account for more than sixty years.

persuasive techniques in contemporary advertising

Ad agencies and product companies often argue that the main purpose of advertising is to inform consumers straightforwardly about available products. In fact, many types of advertisements, like classified ads in newspapers, are devoted primarily to delivering price information. Most consumer ads, however, merely tell stories about products without telling us much about prices. Since national advertisers generally choose to buy a one-page magazine ad or a thirty-second TV spot to deliver their pitch, consumers get little information about how a product was made or how it compares to similar brands. In managing space and time constraints, advertising agencies engage in a variety of persuasive techniques. We will look briefly at some specific techniques and then focus on the association principle and myth analysis, which serve as strategies for critiquing advertising as well as for explaining how advertisers try to persuade consumers.

conventional persuasive strategies

One of the most frequently used advertising approaches is the **famous person testimonial**, whereby a product is endorsed by a well-known person, such as former football star O.J. Simpson—before his murder trial—running through airports in Hertz rent-a-car ads. Another technique, the **plain folks pitch**, associates a product with simplicity. Over the years, Volkswagen ("Think small"), General Electric ("We bring good things to life"), and AT&T ("Reach out and touch someone") have each used slogans that stress how new technologies fit into the lives of ordinary people. By contrast, the **snob appeal** approach attempts to persuade consumers that using a product will maintain or elevate their social station. Advertisers selling jewelry, perfume, clothing, and luxury automobiles often use snob appeal. For example, Infiniti cars, associated with elegance, are frequently advertised against a backdrop of high-society parties; ads for Mitsubishi sedans use phrases like "a new level of luxury," "superb road manners," "full-size refinement," and "an upscale attitude."

Another approach, the **bandwagon effect**, points out in exaggerated claims that *everyone* is using a particular product. Brands that refer to themselves as "America's favorite" or "the best" imply that consumers will be left out—or that they are not hip—if they ignore these products. A different technique, the **hidden fear appeal**, plays on consumers' sense of insecurity. Deodorant, mouthwash, and dandruff shampoo ads frequently invoke anxiety, pointing out that only a specific product could possibly relieve such embarrassing personal hygiene problems.

A final ad strategy, used more in local TV and radio campaigns than in national ones, has been labeled **irritation advertising**: creat-

WE'RE MAKING SURE OUR RESEARCH

DEVELOPS HEALTHIER FUTURES.

Bayer

WE CURE MORE HEADACHES THAN YOU THINK.

This print ad for Bayer Corporation employs a "plain folks" appeal. Rather than associating Bayer with well-known celebrities, the ad links the company with social concern about health care and ordinary people.

ing product-name recognition by being annoying or obnoxious. Although both research and common sense suggest that irritating ads do not work very well, there have been exceptions. In the 1950s and 1960s, for instance, an aspirin company ran a TV ad showing a hammer pounding inside a person's brain. Critics and the product's own agency suggested that people bought the product, which sold well, to get relief from the ad as well as from their headaches. For years, Charmin tissue used the annoying Mr. Whipple, a fussy store clerk who commanded customers, "Please don't squeeze the Charmin." One study found that people hated the ad but bought the product anyway. On the regional level, irritation ads are often used by appliance discount stores or local car dealers, who yell at the camera or dress in outrageous costumes. Some consumers may purposely avoid companies that engage in irritating ads. A few agencies contend, though, that consumers become so annoyed by the ads that they actually go to the store or dealership to complain—and end up buying a TV set or used car.

the association principle

Historically, American car advertisements have displayed automobiles in natural settings: on winding back roads that cut through rugged mountain passes or across shimmering wheat fields. These ads rarely contain images of cars on congested city streets or in other urban settings where most driving really occurs. Rather, the car—an example of advanced technology—merges effortlessly with the natural world.

This type of advertising exemplifies the **association principle**, a persuasive technique used in many consumer ads. Employing this principle, an ad *associates* a product with some cultural value or image that has a positive connotation but which may have little connection to the actual product. For example, Chevrolet's slogan in the 1980s— "the heartbeat of America"—associated the car with nationalism. In trying "to convince us that there's an innate relationship between a brand name and an attitude,"[8] agencies and advertisers associate products with happy families, success at school or work, natural scenery, and humor. (Some ad agencies contend, however, that viewers do not always remember products associated with funny or quirky situations.) Over the years, the most controversial use of the association principle has been the linkage of products to stereotyped caricatures of women. In numerous instances, women have been portrayed either as sex objects or as clueless housewives who, during many a daytime TV commercial, needed the powerful off-screen voice of a male narrator to instruct them in their own kitchens (see "Case Study: Women, Ads, and Stereotypes" on page 326).

Another strong association used in advertising is nature. In one of the most striking and enduring magazine ad campaigns, Kool cigarettes have been associated with cool mountain waterfalls and tranquil beaches, neither of which has a logical connection to cigarettes. These settings, however, conjure up positive images and link the product to nature. Philip Morris's Marlboro brand also used the association principle to completely transform the product's initial image. In the 1920s, Marlboro began as a fashionable woman's cigarette. Back then, the company's ads equated smoking with emancipation and a sense of freedom, attempting to appeal to women who had just won the right to vote. Marlboro, though, did poorly as a women's product, and new campaigns in the 1950s and 1960s transformed the brand into a man's cigarette. In these campaigns, powerful images of active, rugged men were the central characters. Often, Marlboro associated its product with the image of a lone cowboy roping a calf, building a fence, or riding through a pristine natural landscape. Ironically, over the years two of the Marlboro Man models died of lung cancer associated with smoking. Yet, in 1993 *Financial World* magazine called Marlboro the world's "most valuable brand name," having an estimated worth of $39 billion.

Considered the most successful ad campaign in history, Leo Burnett's Marlboro Country images for Philip Morris began appearing in 1964. Over the years, the Marlboro Man has shown up on everything from highway billboards in remote cornfields to the sides of decaying urban buildings. Associating the cigarette with stoic masculinity and rugged individualism, the campaign helped make Marlboro the world's leading brand for more than thirty years.

As a response to corporate merger mania and public skepticism toward large impersonal companies, the *disassociation corollary* has emerged as a recent trend in advertising. The nation's largest winery, Gallo, pioneered the idea in the 1980s by establishing a dummy corporation, Bartles & Jaymes, to sell jug wine and wine coolers, thus avoiding the Gallo corporate image in ads and on its bottles. The Gallo ads featured Frank and Ed, two low-key, grandfatherly types as "co-owners" and ad spokespersons. This ad concept revealed that simulated entrepreneurship was "a way to connect with younger consumers who yearn for products that are handmade, quirky, and authentic."[9] In contrast, Gallo pitched another label, Turning Leaf, to upscale consumers who wouldn't be caught dead purchasing wine in jugs or twist-cap bottles.

In the 1990s, the disassociation strategy has been used by Miller Brewing Company's Red Dog beer, sold under the quaint Plank Road Brewery logo, and by R. J. Reynold's Moonlight Tobacco Company, which sells local brand cigarettes such as City and North Star. In addition, General Motors, still reeling from the failed Oldsmobile campaign and a declining corporate reputation, "disassociate[d] itself from its innovative offspring, the Saturn"; GM ads have packaged the Saturn as "a small-town enterprise, run by folks not terribly unlike Frank and Ed," who provide caring, personal service.[10] As an advertising strategy, disassociation links new brands in a product line to eccentric or simple regional places rather than to the image conjured up by giant conglomerates.

myth analysis

Another way of looking at ads, **myth analysis** provides insights into how ads work at a general cultural level. According to myth analysis, most ads are narratives with stories to tell and social conflicts to resolve. The term *myth* is not used here in a pejorative sense, referring to an untrue story or outright falsehood. Rather, myths help us to define people, organizations, and social norms. Myths are a society's stories that bring order to the conflicts and contradictions of everyday life.

Three common mythical elements are found in many types of ads:

1. Ads incorporate myths in mini-story form featuring characters, settings, and plots.

2. Most stories in ads involve conflicts, pitting one set of characters or social values against another.

325

Women, Ads, and Stereotypes

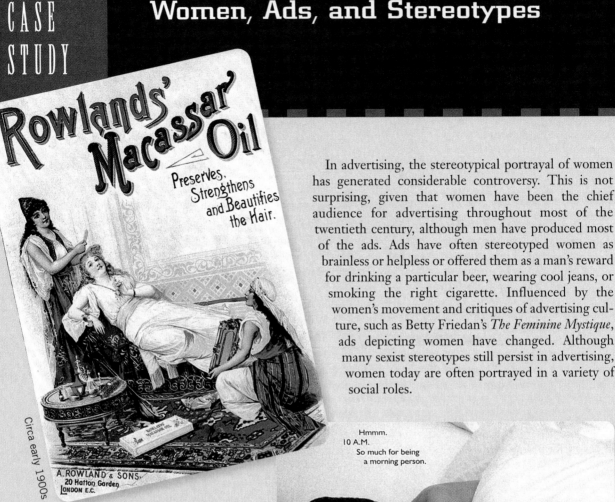

Rowlands' Macassar Oil

Preserves,
Strengthens
and Beautifies
the Hair.

A. ROWLAND & SONS,
20 Hatton Garden
LONDON E.C.

Circa early 1900s

In advertising, the stereotypical portrayal of women has generated considerable controversy. This is not surprising, given that women have been the chief audience for advertising throughout most of the twentieth century, although men have produced most of the ads. Ads have often stereotyped women as brainless or helpless or offered them as a man's reward for drinking a particular beer, wearing cool jeans, or smoking the right cigarette. Influenced by the women's movement and critiques of advertising culture, such as Betty Friedan's *The Feminine Mystique*, ads depicting women have changed. Although many sexist stereotypes still persist in advertising, women today are often portrayed in a variety of social roles.

Over the years, critics and consumers alike have complained about the stereotyping in mainstream advertising. Invisible stereotyping occurs when whole segments of the population are ignored—particularly African, Arab, Asian, Latin, and Native Americans. Visible stereotyping occurs in many ads, as when men are portrayed as stupid, inferior to the heroic products that "save" their lives. Stereotyping robs people of their individuality by assigning them to groups. Members of a group are falsely assumed to act as a single entity and to display certain characteristics, which are usually negative.

Hmmm.
10 A.M.
So much for being
a morning person.

WestPoint Stevens Inc.

MARTEX
THE BARE NECESSITIES

Circa mid-1990s

While the feminist movement helped change the representation of women in advertising, women are still more likely than men to be depicted in passive or horizontal physical positions.

3. Such conflicts are negotiated or resolved by the end of the ad, usually by applying or purchasing a product. In advertising, the product and those who use it often emerge as the heroes of the story.

Even though the stories ads tell are usually compressed into thirty seconds or onto a single page, they still include the traditional elements of narrative. For instance, Marlboro ads often tell the mini-story of a lone and tough cowboy and his horse, dwarfed by towering pines and snow-covered mountains. The ads ask us to imagine his adventure, perhaps returning home after an autumn cattle drive. The cowboy's ability to survive amid the forces of nature is a tribute to rugged individualism, probably America's most powerful cultural value. The conflict is generated by the audience's implicit understanding of what is *not* in the ads—a fast-paced, technology-driven urban world where most smoking actually takes place. This implied conflict between the natural world and the manufactured world is apparently resolved by invoking the image of Marlboro. Although Marlboros are an addictive, manufactured product and advertisers are mandated by the FTC and the Surgeon General to warn us about the lethal dangers of cigarettes, the ads attempt to downplay those facts. Instead, they offer an alternative story about the wonders of nature. The natural is substituted for the manufactured, and the "spirit of Marlboro" becomes the soothing negotiator between these competing worlds.

In an increasingly technology-dependent environment, modern societies have come to value products that claim affiliation with the *real* and the *natural*. Coke sells itself as "the real thing," and the cosmetics industry offers synthetic products that make us look "natural." These twin adjectives, which saturate American ads, almost always describe processed goods.

Most advertisers do not expect consumers to accept without question the stories they tell or the associations they make in their ads; they do not "make the mistake of asking for belief."[11] Rather, ads are most effective when they create attitudes and reinforce values. Then they operate like popular fiction, encouraging us to suspend our disbelief. Although most of us realize that ads create a fictional world, we often get caught up in their stories and myths. Indeed, ads often work because the stories offer comfort about our deepest desires and conflicts—between men and women, nature and technology, tradition and change, the real and the artificial. Most contemporary consumer advertising does not provide much useful information about products. Instead, it tries to reassure us that through the use of familiar brand names everyday tensions and problems can be managed.

commercial speech and regulating advertising

In 1791, Congress passed the First Amendment to the U.S. Constitution, promising, among other guarantees, to "make no law . . . abridging the freedom of speech, or of the press." Over the years, we have developed a shorthand label for the First Amendment, misnaming it the free-speech clause. The amendment ensures that citizens and reporters can generally say and write what they want, but it says nothing directly about speech that is not free. What, then, about **commercial speech**—any print or broadcast expression for which a fee is charged to organizations and individuals buying time or space in the mass media? Whereas freedom of speech refers to the right to express thoughts, beliefs, and opinions in a marketplace of ideas, commercial speech supports the right to circulate goods, services, and images in the marketplace of products. Although most people can buy some commercial speech inexpensively, such as a classified newspaper ad, only wealthy citizens and companies can routinely afford speech that reaches millions.

New forms of commercial speech and advertising continue to crowd the media landscape. Among these are 900 numbers and infomercials (see "Tracking Technology: The 900-Number Industry Makes the Caller Pay"). Long-distance carriers and advertising watchdog groups report rising concern from parents regarding increases in family phone bills due to 900 and other pay numbers. Via late night TV spots, some of these numbers advertise "talk romance" and "talk sex" to the lonely, the young, and the curious.

In addition to the proliferation of cable home-shopping networks, **infomercials** represent a substantial growth area in cable and broadcast television. These thirty-minute late night and daytime programs usually feature fading TV and music celebrities, who advertise a product in a format that looks like a laid-back talk show. Even on regular talk shows, guests generally appear when they have a book to sell or a movie to promote. Paid a fee by the program to boost ratings, such guests use their celebrity status and allotted time as a commercial forum to promote themselves.

critical issues in advertising

In his 1957 book *The Hidden Persuaders*, Vance Packard expressed concern that advertising was manipulating helpless consumers, attacking our dignity, and invading "the privacy of our minds."[12] According to this view, the advertising industry was considered to be all-powerful. Although consumers have historically been regarded as dupes, research reveals that the consumer mind is not as easy to predict as some advertisers once thought. In the 1950s, for example, Ford failed to successfully sell its new mid-size car, the Edsel, which was aimed at newly prosperous Ford customers looking to move up to the latest in push-button window wipers and antennas. After a splashy and expensive ad campaign, Ford sold only sixty-three thousand Edsels in 1958 and just two thousand in 1960, when the model was discontinued. In the 1960s, the Scott paper company predicted that its disposable clothing line would challenge traditional apparel, but this never happened despite heavy advertising. Today, more than ever, most people are not easily persuaded by advertising. Over the years, studies have suggested that between 75 and 90 percent of new consumer products typically fail because they are not embraced by the buying public.[13]

> "The **American apparatus of advertising** is something unique in history. . . . It is like a grotesque, smirking gargoyle set at the very top of America's sky-scraping adventure in acquisition *ad infinitum*."
>
> —James Rorty,
> *Our Master's Voice*,
> 1934

Despite public resistance to many new products and the cynical eye we cast toward advertising, the ad industry has made contributions, including raising the American standard of living and supporting most media industries. Yet serious concerns over the impact of advertising remain. In the mid-1990s, as Congress slashed the budgets of public broadcast stations, these noncommercial stations tried to persuade Congress to approve more commercial advertising for public and educational broadcasting. Watchdog groups worried about expanding advertising's reach, however, and critics continued to condemn ads that associate products with sex appeal, youth, and narrow definitions of female beauty. Some of the most serious concerns involve children, teens, and health.

Children and Advertising. Children and teenagers, living in a culture dominated by TV ads, are often viewed as consumer trainees. For years, groups such as Action for Children's Television (ACT) worked to limit advertising aimed at children.

TRACKING TECHNOLOGY

The 900-Number Industry Makes the Caller Pay

by Michael F. Jacobson and Laurie Ann Mazur

The union of advertising and telecommunications has produced a mutant offspring: the 900-number industry. The 900 number is essentially a marketing device, a way to sell or advertise goods and services over the phone—at the caller's expense.

In the late 1980s, marketers gleefully discovered that some consumers would actually pay to be advertised to through 900-number hotlines. Particularly effective, they discovered, were advertisements disguised as services, contests, or entertainment—especially the recorded voices of celebrities. For instance, actress Alyssa Milano of ABC's *Who's the Boss?* promoted her teen exercise video through a 900 number featuring recorded messages that changed twice a day, which callers paid $2 to hear. Soon, according to one trade publication, marketers were using 900 numbers "to pitch everything from records to laundry detergent, encountering remarkably little resistance even though they were actually charging consumers up to $2 for each call."[1]

The 900-number industry mushroomed in the 1980s, raking in $1.2 billion in revenues by 1991.[2] An astonishing array of products and diversions are now offered over the phone—from kinky sex to papal sermons. Certainly, some 900 numbers provide worthwhile services. For instance, Consumers Union, the group that publishes *Consumer Reports*, maintains a helpful used-car price service that costs $1.75 per minute.

But much of the 900-number industry is fraught with problems. For one thing, the industry is a hotbed of fraud. According to Assistant Chief Postal Inspector K.M. Hearst, "900 numbers have been a very effective billing and collecting system for fraudulent promotions. Classic fraud schemes are thriving under this new technology." Like many scams, 900-number ripoffs are often aimed at people who have fallen on hard times. One 900 number purported to offer tips on getting high-paying jobs in Kuwait, then charged callers up to $100 to hear information that was readily available—for free—from government agencies. Other 900 numbers sold work-at-home schemes, which left their (mostly elderly, unemployed, or handicapped) customers with lots of expensive equipment and unsalable merchandise. "Advance fee" loans are another popular 900-number scam. In one variation on this theme, a 900 number offered $55,000 loans to the families of soldiers serving in the Gulf War. To obtain the loan, however, the families had to pay a $300 advance fee. Couriers came to collect the fees from the unsuspecting families but never paid the loan.[3]

Even legitimate 900 numbers can be booby traps. Advertisements for 900 numbers often downplay or omit information about the cost of the call. Now, however, when people call 900 numbers, they must be told the cost up front. The new regulations frustrate 900-number companies that count on consumer ignorance: After they went into effect in 1992, 900-number revenues fell by almost 50 percent.[4] Still, once a call has been placed, it is easy to lose sight of the fact that the meter is running. In fact, 900-number companies routinely employ tricks to keep callers on the line, such as saving important information for last or speaking so quickly the caller must call back to hear what was said.

The 900-number industry also serves as a powerful tool of the data collectors—marketing firms that are busy compiling electronic portraits of our tastes and buying habits. With Caller I.D., 900-number operators can view the phone number of anyone who calls in. With the right software, they can then match the phone number to the caller's name and address, as well as to information on his or her credit history and buying habits. In addition to a host of disturbing Orwellian possibilities, this capability raises the specter of generating even more junk phone calls.

Source: Michael F. Jacobson and Laurie Ann Mazur, "The 900-Number Industry: Making the Caller Pay," in *Marketing Madness: A Survival Guide for a Consumer Society* (Boulder, CO: Westview Press, 1995), 131.

In the 1980s, ACT fought particularly hard to curb **program-length commercials**: thirty-minute cartoon programs (such as *G.I. Joe*, *My Little Pony*, *Care Bears*, and *He Man*) developed for television syndication primarily to promote a line of toys.

In addition, parent groups have worried about the heavy promotion of sugar-coated cereals during children's programs. Pointing to European countries where children's advertising is banned, these groups have pushed to limit advertising aimed at children. Congress, faced with the protection that the First Amendment offers commercial speech, has responded weakly. The Children's Television Act of 1990 mandated that networks provide some educational and informational children's programming, but the Act has been difficult to enforce and did little to restrict advertising aimed at kids. Most studies on the impact of advertising on children reveal that young children are vulnerable to commercialism, particularly in that ads can pressure children to want products they either do not need or their parents cannot afford.

Advertising in Schools. Among the most controversial developments in recent years was the introduction of Channel One into thousands of schools during the 1989–90 school year. The brainchild of Whittle Communications, Channel One offered "free" video and satellite equipment (tuned exclusively to Channel One) in exchange for a ten-minute package of current-events programming that included two minutes of commercials. If school districts decided to curtail or limit the program, Whittle could reclaim its "free" equipment. In 1994, Channel One was acquired by K-III Communications (publisher of *Weekly Reader*, *Seventeen*, and *Soap Opera Digest*). By the mid-1990s, available in 40 percent of the nation's junior high and high schools, Channel One grossed more than $800,000 each school day.

Over the years, the National Dairy Council and other organizations have also used schools to promote products, providing free film strips, posters, magazines, folders, and study guides adorned with corporate logos. Teachers, especially in underfunded districts, have usually been grateful for the support. Channel One, however, has been viewed as a more intrusive threat, violating the implicit cultural border between an entertainment situation—watching commercial television—and a learning situation—going to school. One study showed that schools with a high concentration of low-income students were more than twice as likely as affluent schools to receive Channel One.[14] Some individual school districts have banned Channel One, as has the state of New York. These school systems have argued that Channel One provides students with only slight additional knowledge about current affairs; but students find the products advertised—sneakers, cereal, and soda, among others—more worthy of purchase because they are advertised in educational environments.[15]

Health and Advertising. We are well aware that advertising has a powerful impact on the standards of youthful beauty in our culture. A long-standing trend in advertising is the association of certain products with ultrathin female models, promoting a style of "attractiveness" that girls and women are invited to emulate. Some forms of fashion and cosmetics advertising actually pander to individuals' insecurities and low self-esteem. Such advertising suggests standards of style and behavior that may be not only unattainable but also undesirable, encouraging eating disorders such as anorexia and bulimia. In fact, some female models became so skinny that critics began referring to the style of their ads as "heroin chic" because the models looked like victims of prolonged drug use. To their credit, many ad agencies refused to do this type of advertising, which was then usually produced by the fashion industry's own in-house staff. Throughout history, however, many companies have capitalized on unhappiness and insecurity by promising relief or the kind of body that is currently fashionable.

Along with criticism of promoting skeleton-like beauty, probably the most sustained criticism of advertising is its promotion of alcohol and tobacco consumption. Opponents of such advertising have become more vocal in the face of grim statistics. Each year, four hundred thousand Americans die from diseases related to nicotine addiction and poisoning, a hundred thousand die from alcohol-related diseases, and another fifteen to eighteen thousand die in car crashes involving drunk drivers.

Tobacco ads disappeared from television in 1971, under pressure from Congress and the FCC, and the hard liquor industry voluntarily banned TV and radio ads for many decades. Still, enormous amounts of money are spent each year to encourage these habits. In the mid-1990s, tobacco companies alone spent nearly $5 billion annually on advertising—about $10 million a day—even though no money went to television.

Although tobacco companies have recently promised not to target young smokers, numerous ad campaigns over the years did appeal to teenage cigarette consumers. In 1988, for example, R. J. Reynolds, a subdivision of RJR Nabisco, revived its Joe Camel cartoon character from an earlier campaign, outfitting him with hipper clothes and sunglasses. Spending $75 million annually, the company put the new Joe on billboards and store posters and in sports stadiums and magazines. One study revealed that before the 1988 campaign fewer than 1 percent of teens under eighteen smoked Camels. After the ad blitz, however, 33 percent of this age group preferred Camels. In response, the ad industry's trade journal, *Advertising Age*, raised some serious questions. For example, shouldn't cigarette advertisers' profit interests be balanced against their "unique social responsibility" in light of the health risks of smoking? Although Canada has long banned cigarette advertising in both print and broadcast forms, the FTC remained reluctant to lead a battle pitting the government against the commercial speech rights of the tobacco industry. This began to change in the mid-1990s as new reports revealed that some tobacco companies knew that nicotine was addictive as early as the 1950s and withheld that information from the public.

In addition to young smokers, the tobacco industry has targeted other groups. In the 1960s, for instance, the advertising campaigns for Eve and Virginia Slims cigarettes (reminiscent of the ads during the suffrage movement in the early 1900s) associated their products with liberation, equality, and slim fashion models. And in 1989, Reynolds introduced a cigarette called Uptown, targeting African American consumers. The ad campaign fizzled, however, due to public protests by black leaders and government officials. When these leaders pointed to the high concentrations of cigarette billboards in poor urban areas and the high mortality rates among black male smokers, the tobacco company withdrew the brand from the market.

Alcohol ads have also targeted minority populations. Malt liquors, which contain higher concentrations of alcohol, have appeared in high-profile television ads for products like Colt 45, PowerMaster, and Magnum. Featuring actors like Billy Dee Williams, these ads have usually been shown during programs appealing to high percentages of black viewers. College students, too, have been heavily targeted, particularly by the beer industry. By the mid-1990s, college students purchased over $4 billion in alcoholic drinks annually. Although colleges and universities have outlawed "beer bashes" hosted and supplied directly by major

How fast am I? Well, I caught a jackrabbit when I was 6, and in 1988, I clocked in at 23.5 mph in the 100-meter. Sure, some of that's natural, but I do train hard and drink milk. 2%. It's loaded with nutrients like calcium and vitamin D, so I drink lots of it. Nice and slow.

MILK
Where's your mustache?"

Countering the "heroin chic" strategy that associates products with gaunt, emaciated female bodies, a competing strategy juxtaposes products with female athleticism and strength. Advertisers such as the National Fluid Milk Processors have used Olympic champions such as Florence Griffith Joyner—"the world's fastest woman"—as well as Hollywood celebrities to promote milk. These kinds of ads portray women as active and physical, and provide a contrast to the long history of featuring women as passive, static figures in visual advertising.

brewers, both Coors and Miller, a unit of Philip Morris, still employ student representatives to help "create brand awareness." These students notify brewers of special events that might be sponsored by and linked to a specific beer label. The images and slogans in alcohol ads often associate the products with power, romance, sexual prowess, athletic skill, or guns. In reality, though, alcohol is a chemical depressant; it diminishes athletic ability and sexual performance, triggers addiction in roughly 10 percent of the U.S. population, and is a factor in many spouse abuse cases.

watching over advertisers

In 1996, Seagram, the Canadian liquor company that bought MCA in 1995, defied the sixty-year voluntary ban by the American liquor industry on hard liquor advertising in broadcasting. (Such ads had been banned from radio since 1936 and from television since 1948.) Faced with declining sales, the company argued that wine and beer, which have long advertised on television and radio, had an unfair market advantage over the hard liquor industry. To promote its Crown Royal whiskey, Seagram began testing regional TV ads in Texas. Executives at Seagram called the old ban "obsolete." They pointed to other countries that featured liquor ads on television and noted the escalating World Wide Web sites devoted to marketing liquor. Following Seagram's lead, the Distilled Spirits Council of the United States, the liquor industry's trade association, voted in 1996 to lift its voluntary ban on broadcast ads. At the time, ABC, CBS, Fox, and NBC executives refused to carry the ads nationally, citing both their efforts to promote responsible drinking and the threat that liquor advertising posed to their beer and wine ad revenue.[16]

> **"Alcohol marketers** appear to believe that the prototypical college student is (1) male; (2) a nitwit; and (3) interested in nothing but **booze and 'babes.'"**
> —Michael F. Jacobson and Laurie Ann Mazur, *Marketing Madness*, 1995

Advertisers and agencies have generally had their commercial-speech rights protected by the First Amendment. But the Seagram move touched off renewed activity at both state and federal levels to pass legislation restricting alcohol advertising. In addition to legislation aimed at controversial products, oversight agencies—such as the Better Business Bureau, the National Fraud Information Center, and the FTC—have long monitored deceptive and false ads. During the Reagan administration in the 1980s, however, the FTC underwent sizeable staff cuts, from over seventeen hundred employees to fewer than nine hundred. With these reductions and a relatively small budget, the FTC has become a less effective watchdog agency over the past fifteen years.

In addition to oversight groups, professions like medicine and law have long had uneasy relationships with advertising and often try to limit ads through their professional organizations. For example, bar associations actually prohibited lawyers from advertising until the Supreme Court ruled in 1978 that lawyers have a First Amendment right to promote their services. (The Supreme Court has since outlined some limits, ruling in 1995 that states may prevent lawyers from sending direct-mail ads within thirty days of an accident for the purpose of soliciting victims or survivors as clients.) Nonetheless, although prestigious law and medical practices have traditionally shunned advertising, many firms advertise to jump-start a new business or to reinvigorate a sagging practice.

Comparative Advertising. For years it was considered taboo for one advertiser to mention a competitor by name in its ads. Industry guidelines discouraged such advertising, and TV networks prohibited it. The government and networks feared that comparative ads would degenerate into unseemly name-calling, and advertisers believed they should not give free time or space to competitors. This led to the development of so-called Brand X products, which identified a competing brand without using a real name. The FTC, however, began encouraging comparative advertising in 1971. The agency thought such ads would help consumers by providing more product information. Subsequently, various food industries started taste-test wars specifically targeting each other in their ads. Burger King took on McDonald's, and Pepsi challenged Coke. As comparative ads became the norm, Japanese and American auto manufacturers even began to compare prices, gas mileage, safety records, and repair and recall rates in their ads.

Puffery and Deceptive Ads. Since the days when Lydia Pinkham's Vegetable Compound promised "a sure cure for all female weakness," false and misleading claims have haunted advertising. Over the years, the FTC has played an investigative role in substantiating the claims of various advertisers. A certain amount of **puffery**—ads featuring hyperbole and exaggeration—has usually been permitted, particularly when a product says it is "new and improved." However, when a product claims to be "the best," "the greatest," or "preferred by four out of five doctors," the FTC has often asked for supportive evidence.

Typical of deceptive advertising over the years were the Campbell Soup ads that used marbles in the bottom of a soup bowl to push more ingredients—and less water—to the surface. In another instance, a 1990 Volvo commercial featured a monster truck driving over a line of cars and crushing all but the Volvo; the company later admitted that the Volvo had been specially reinforced and the other cars' support columns had been weakened. Finally, a more subtle form of deception featured the Klondike Lite ice-cream bar—"the 93 percent fat-free dessert with chocolate-flavored coating." The bars were indeed 93 percent fat-free, but only after the chocolate coating was removed.[17] In 1996, the FTC asked five automakers to stop ads for "no-money down" or "one penny down" car leases because the fine print—virtually impossible for consumers to read on television—required more than $1000 in various fees and taxes before a car could actually be driven off the lot. When the FTC discovers deceptive ads, it usually requires advertisers to change their ads or remove them from circulation. Although the FTC does not have the power to assess financial penalties, it occasionally requires an advertiser to run *corrective ads* to offset deceptive ones.

advertising's threat to journalism

Much of the power advertising wields is subtle and difficult to monitor. One problem, particularly troubling for newspapers during economic recessions, occurs when reporters cover news issues that reflect poorly on a newspaper's major advertisers. Local real-estate firms or car dealers, for instance, are no longer so dependent on newspapers as their main advertising channel. Companies can now take their ad business to direct mail, cable, and the Internet if they are unhappy with negative stories in the local newspaper. With many dailies facing financial difficulties in the 1990s, some editors have turned their investigative eyes away from controversial business stories in order to keep advertisers happy.

In 1992, a report by the nonprofit Center for the Study of Commercialism investigated fifty news stories that were allegedly "killed or downplayed by news media to appease advertisers."[18] The *Portland Oregonian*, for example, Oregon's largest daily paper, destroyed thousands of copies of a Sunday edition in 1989 after a salesperson in the advertising department complained to editors about a real-estate story. The story advised readers on how to sell a home without the help of a real-estate agent. The editor responsible for publishing the article was later demoted. In 1990, car dealers in Hartford, Connecticut, withdrew advertising from the *Hartford Courant* over an article that urged consumers to be wary of shady dealers. After the *Courant's* publisher apologized to the dealers, they ended their boycott, but many readers in the community were upset that the paper backed down. Two years later, one dealer in suburban Hartford reported that he had seen no more negative articles about dealers: "Consumer reporting is virtually nonexistent now."

Nordstrom, a large department-store retailer, reduced its advertising in the *Seattle Times* in the early 1990s, after the paper criticized the company's labor difficulties. In this case, the newspaper did not back down. Michael Fancher, then the executive editor of the *Times*, told the *Wall Street Journal*, "You can't just sell your soul in little bits and pieces and expect that readers will understand it. A lot of newspapers don't understand that."[19] Although the coverage of business at many papers has improved over the years, papers in small communities with fewer advertisers remain more vulnerable to this problem. Large dailies are better able to withstand lost ad revenue from a few disgruntled advertisers.

advertising and democracy

As advertising has become more pervasive and consumers more discriminating, ad practitioners have searched for ways to weave their work more seamlessly into the social and cultural fabric. Products now blend in as props or even as "characters" in TV shows and movies. In addition, almost every national consumer product now has its own site on the World Wide Web, displaying advertising on computers around the globe. With today's video technology and computer graphics, producers can even generate a TV advertising image on a wall or flat surface when in reality no image exists.

Among the most intriguing efforts to become enmeshed in the culture are the ads that exploit, distort, or transform the political meanings of popular music. In the early 1990s, for instance, a number of once-radical or progressive rock songs made their way into TV ads, muddying the boundary between art and commerce. Not only did "Revolution" (1968) promote Nike shoes, but Bob Dylan's "The Times They Are a-Changing" (1964) advertised both an accounting firm and the Bank of Montreal. Crosby, Stills, Nash & Young's "Teach Your Children" (1970) peddled Fruit of the Loom underwear. Buffalo Springfield's "For What It's Worth" (1967) sold Miller beer—with the commercial stopping just short of the band's Vietnam War protest lyric, "There's a man with a gun over there." Even print media got into the act when Time Inc. used the Byrds' version of "Turn! Turn! Turn!" (1965) to market its newsmagazine on television.

A much more straightforward form of cultural blending is **political advertising**: the use of ad techniques to promote a candidate's image and persuade the public to a viewpoint. Since the 1950s, political consultants have been imitating market-research and advertising techniques to sell their candidates. In the early days of television, politicians running for major offices either bought or were offered half-hour blocks of time to discuss their views and the significant issues of the day. As advertising time became more valuable, however, local stations and the networks became reluctant to give away time in large chunks. Gradually, TV managers began selling thirty-second spots to political campaigns just as they sold time to product advertisers.

In the late 1980s, a research team at the University of Pennsylvania's Annenberg School of Communication began critiquing political advertisements that reduce a candidate's ideas to a thirty-second advertising pitch. Using powerful visual images, these ads often attack other candidates and distract viewers from misleading verbal messages. In the early 1990s, the major networks began using the school's techniques in a news segment called Ad Watch. After critiquing a political ad, a commentator labeled it as "true," "correct but . . . ," "misleading," or "false." As a result of Ad Watch, media consultants began paying more attention to the veracity of their ads. Ad Watch pieces, however, usually ran only once, so they were viewed mainly by people who regularly watch the evening news.[20]

During the 1992 and 1996 presidential campaigns, third-party candidate Ross Perot restored the use of the half-hour time block when he ran political infomercials on cable and the networks. However, only very wealthy candidates can afford such promotional strategies because television does not usually provide free airtime to politicians. Questions about political ads continue to be asked. Can serious information on political issues be conveyed in thirty-second spots that many candidates can barely afford? Do repeated *attack ads*, which assault another candidate's character, so discourage citizens about the electoral process that they stop voting?[21] How does a society ensure that alternative political voices, which are not so well-financed or commercially viable, still receive a hearing in a democratic society?

During the 1996 presidential campaign, a bipartisan group of politicians, broadcasters, critics, and activists—the Free TV for Straight Talk Coalition—convinced the major networks to restore a few minutes of free time for candidates every night during the last month of the presidential campaign. The coalition promised, "No tricky images. No unseen narrators. No journalists. No surrogates. Just candidates making their best case to the biggest audience America assembles every night."[22] Critics protested that the process still ignored alternative and third-party candidates, and journalists raised another concern: By taking a probing adversarial reporter out of the loop, the strategy turned the free time into an opportunity for free political advertising.

> "The press enjoys special constitutional protection for being an instrument of self-rule, an educational tool of democracy, not simply to protect the profits of advertisers and the media. But if the citizenry is only told what suits advertisers, the democratic ideal is left in tatters."
> —Michael F. Jacobson and Laurie Ann Mazur, *Marketing Madness*, 1995

Although advertising—for both products and politicians—has generated a culture that is often critical of advertising's pervasiveness, the growth of the industry has not diminished. Ads continue to fascinate. Many consumers buy magazines or watch the Super Bowl just for the advertisements. Adolescents decorate their rooms with their favorite ads. By 1996, more than $350 billion worldwide ($160 billion of that in the United States) was being spent on advertising each year—enough money to finance the operation of several small countries. A number of factors have allowed advertising's largely unchecked growth. Many Americans tolerate advertising as a necessary "evil" for maintaining the economy, but many others dismiss advertising as not believable and even trivial. Thus, because we are willing to downplay its centrality to global culture, many citizens do not think advertising is significant enough to act on or monitor as a group. Such attitudes have ensured advertising's pervasiveness and suggest the need to escalate critical vigilance.

As individuals and as a society, we have developed an uneasy relationship with advertising. Favorite ads and commercial jingles remain part of our cultural world for a lifetime. But we detest irritating and repetitive commercials, using the remote control to mute the offenders on television. We realize that without ads many mass media would need to reinvent themselves. At the same time, we remain critical of what advertising has come to represent: the overemphasis on commercial acquisitions and cultural images, and the disparity between those who can afford new products and those who cannot.

REVIEW QUESTIONS

1. Who did the first ad agents serve?

2. How did packaging and trademarks influence advertising?

3. Explain how patent medicines and department stores figured so prominently in advertising in the late 1800s.

4. What role did advertising play in transforming America into a consumer society?

5. What influences did visual culture exert on advertising?

6. What are the differences between boutique and mega ad agencies?

7. What are the major divisions at most ad agencies? What is the function of each department?

8. What causes the occasional tension between the research and creative departments at some agencies?

9. How do the common persuasive techniques used in advertising work?

10. How does the association principle work, and why is it an effective way to analyze advertising?

11. What is the disassociation corollary?

12. How can myth analysis be used to critique an ad?

13. What is commercial speech?

14. What are three serious contemporary issues regarding health and advertising? Why is each issue controversial?

15. What is comparative advertising?

16. What are some of the major issues involving political advertising?

17. What role does advertising play in a democratic society?

QUESTIONING THE MEDIA

1. What is your earliest recollection of watching a television commercial? Do you have a favorite ad? A most-despised ad? What is it about these ads that you particularly like or dislike?

2. Why are so many people critical of advertising?

3. If you were (or are) a parent, what strategies would you use to explain an objectionable ad to your child or teenager?

4. Should advertising aimed at children be regulated? Support your response.

5. Should tobacco (or alcohol) advertising be prohibited? Why or why not? How would you deal with First Amendment issues regarding controversial ads?

6. Would you be in favor of regular advertising on public television and radio as a means of financial support for these media? Explain your answer.

7. Is advertising at odds with the ideals of democracy? Why or why not?

From a business perspective, magazine ads function to promote advertisers' goods or services over competing brands and to place these goods or services before consumers so that they can make informed buying decisions. We know, however, that ads mean more than what advertisers intend since readers form their own opinions. We know, too, that ads function as popular culture. Ads operate on a symbolic level to affirm cultural values.

In a three- or four-page analysis, compare and critique three magazine ads. The ads should all feature the same *type* of product but should be taken from contrasting magazines (for example, three alcohol ads from women's and men's magazines, or three clothing ads from various kinds of publications). In your critique, use the *association principle* or *myth analysis* to deal with the ads' cultural meanings. In other words, your analysis should go beyond the issue of whether the ads successfully market their products.

Now think about these questions in regard to the ads you have chosen: What different sets of *values* are being sold (for example, ideas about patriotism, family, ethnicity, sex, beauty, femininity, masculinity, age, nature, technology, tradition)? Are the ads selling a particular vision (or stereotype) of what it is to be male or female? Of what it is to be young, old, or middle-class? Of what it is to be a member of a particular race or ethnic group?

Your paper should have a *central thesis*, drawing on evidence from your ads. To this end, organize your paper around an argument that is *worth proving*. For example, to point out that your ads "sell their products in different ways" is not an argument. But if you state that an ad sells "the American Dream as equal opportunity for all," or that it is racist or sexist, these arguments are worth proving. Use the following plan to organize your paper:

1. *Introduction*. Identify the central argument that focuses your essay. Lay out the organization for your paper. Limit your focus to something you can prove in three to four pages.

2. *Body*. Provide evidence (through description and analysis) that supports and defends your central argument. *Analyze* only the significant patterns in the three ads that are appropriate to your argument. *Interpret* or argue what the patterns might mean. Remember to use examples to support your interpretation.

3. *Conclusion*. Avoid summarizing. Instead, develop a new idea. For instance, you may wish to evaluate advertising's role in affirming particular cultural values or myths. Or, you may want to speculate on advertising's role in the postmodern world.

Important: Please include all three ads (or copies of them) with your paper.

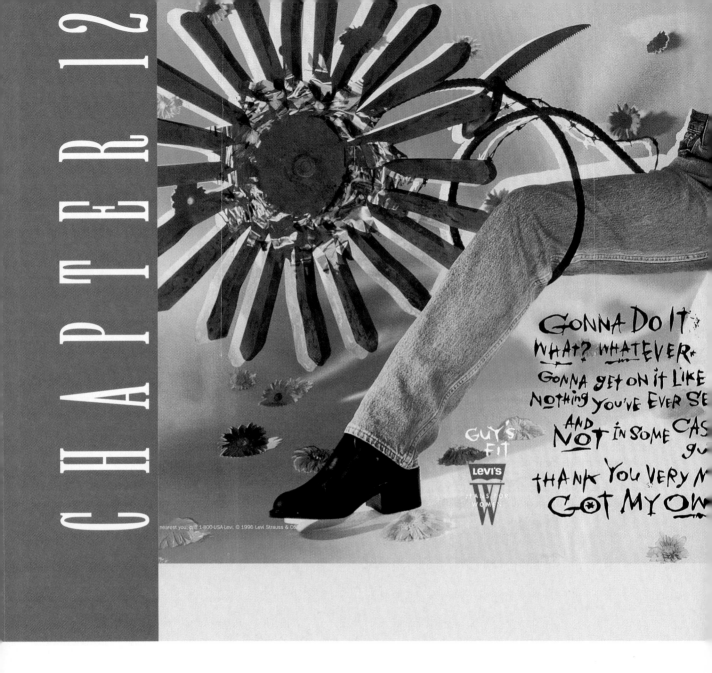

GONNA DO IT
WHAT? WHATEVER·
GONNA GET ON IT LIKE
NOTHING YOU'VE EVER SE
AND NOT IN SOME CAS
G
THANK YOU VERY N
GOT MY OW

GUY'S
FIT
Levi's
W
JEANS FOR WOMEN

nearest you, call 1-800-USA-Levi. © 1996 Levi Strauss & Co

In the mid-1950s, the blue-jeans industry was in deep trouble. After hitting a postwar peak in 1953, jeans sales began to slide. The durable one-hundred-year-old denim product had become associated with rock and roll and teenage troublemakers. Popular movies, especially *The Wild One* and *Blackboard Jungle*, featured emotionally disturbed, blue-jeans-wearing youths terrorizing adult authority figures. A Broadway play about juvenile delinquency was even entitled *Blue Denim*. The worst was yet to come, however. In 1957, the public school system in Buffalo, New York, banned the wearing of blue jeans for all high school students. Formerly associated with farmers, factory workers, and an adult work ethic, jeans had become a reverse fashion statement for teenagers—something many adults could not abide.

In response to the crisis, the denim industry waged a public relations (PR) campaign to eradicate the delinquency label and rejuvenate denim's image. In 1956, the nation's top blue-jeans manufacturers formed the national Denim Council "to put schoolchildren back in blue jeans through a concerted national public relations, advertising, and promotional effort."[1] First the council targeted teens, but its promotional efforts were unsuccessful. The manufacturers soon realized that the problem was not with the teens but with the parents, administrators, teachers, and school boards. It was the adults who felt threatened by a fashion trend that seemed to promote disrespect through casualness. In response, the council hired a public relations firm to turn the image of blue jeans around. Over the next five years, the firm did just that.

The denim public relations team determined that mothers were refusing to outfit their children in jeans due to the product's association with delinquency. To change this perception among women, the team encouraged fashion designers to update denim's image by producing new women's sportswear styles made from the fabric. Media outlets and fashion editors were soon inundated with news releases about the "new look" of durable denim.

The denim PR team next enlisted sportswear designers to provide new designs for both men's and women's work and utility clothes, long the backbone of denim sales. Targeting business reporters as well as fashion editors, the team transformed the redesign effort into a story that appealed to writers in both areas. They also planned retail-store promotions nationwide, including "jean queen" beauty contests, and advanced positive denim stories in men's publications.

The team's major PR coup, however, involved an association with the newly formed national Peace Corps. The brainchild of the Kennedy administration, the Peace Corps encouraged young people to serve their country by working with people from poorer nations. Envisioning the Peace Corps as the flip side of delinquency, the Denim Council saw its opening. It agreed in 1961 to outfit the first group of two hundred corps volunteers in denim. As a result of all these PR efforts, by 1963 manufacturers were flooded with orders, and sales of jeans and other denim goods were way up. The delinquency tag disappeared, and jeans gradually became associated with a more casual, though not antisocial, dress ethic.

The blue-jeans story illustrates a major difference between advertising and public relations: Advertising is controlled publicity that a company or individual buys; public relations attempts to secure favorable media publicity (which is more difficult to control) to promote a company or client. In advertising, clients buy space or time for their products or services, and consumers know who paid for the messages. But with public relations, the process is more subtle, requiring news media to accept a PR campaign and to use it as news. The transformation of denim in the public's eye was achieved primarily without buying advertising. The PR team restyled denim's image mainly by cultivating friendly relations with reporters who subsequently wrote stories associating the fabric with a casual, dedicated, youthful America.

Publicity refers to one type of PR communication: messages that spread information about a person, corporation, issue, or policy in various media. Public relations today, however, uses many communication strategies besides publicity. In fact, much of what PR specialists do involves dealing with negative or unplanned publicity. For example, when documents and audiotapes surfaced in the fall of 1996 revealing that top executives at Texaco had made racist remarks, an intense PR campaign began. It employed a range of tactics, including paid TV advertising, major news conferences, and meetings with regional Texaco distributors. To counter national protests by African American groups and plunging stock market values, Texaco's CEO apologized quickly and initiated broad strategies for improving race relations throughout the company.

Because it involves multiple forms of communication, **public relations** is difficult to define precisely. Its covers a wide array of actions, such as managing complicated issues, shaping the image of a politician or celebrity, repairing the image of a major corporation, establishing two-way communication between consumers and companies, and molding wartime propaganda. Broadly defined, *public relations* refers to the entire range of efforts by an individual, an agency, or any organization attempting to reach or persuade audiences.[2]

The social and cultural impact of public relations, like that of advertising, has been immense. In its infancy, PR helped convince many American businesses of the value of nurturing the public, who had been redefined as purchasers rather than as producers of their own goods. PR also set the tone for the corporate image-building that has characterized the economic environment of the twentieth century. Not only did modern PR pave the way for the public's tacit approval of phone and utility monopolies, but it transformed the profession of journalism by complicating the way "facts" could be interpreted. Perhaps PR's most significant effect, however, has been on the political process in which individuals and organizations—on both the right and the left—hire spin doctors to shape their media images.

Without public relations, the news profession would be hard-pressed to keep up with every upcoming event or complex issue. Although reporters and editors do not like to admit it, PR departments and agencies are a major source of story ideas and information. In this chapter, we will examine the impact of public relations and the historical conditions that affected its development as a modern profession—how it helped to transform America into a more image-conscious society. We will begin by looking at nineteenth-century press agents and at the role that railroads and utility companies played in developing corporate PR. We will then consider the rise of modern PR, particularly the influences of ex-reporters Ivy Lee and Edward Bernays. In addition, we will explore the major practices and specialties of public relations, the reasons for the long-standing antagonism between journalists and the PR profession, and the social responsibilities of PR in a democracy.

> "An **image** . . . is not simply a trademark, a design, a slogan or an easily remembered picture. It is a **studiously crafted personality profile** of an individual, institution, corporation, product or service."
>
> —Daniel Boorstin,
> *The Image,*
> 1961

early developments in public relations

At the beginning of the twentieth century, the United States slowly shifted to a consumer-oriented, industrial society, which fostered the rapid spread of advertising and publicity for new products and services. During this gradual transformation from farm to factory, PR emerged as a profession, partly because businesses needed to fend off increased scrutiny from muckraking journalists and emerging labor unions.[3]

Prior to this time, the first PR practitioners were simply theatrical **press agents**: those who sought to advance a client's image through media exposure, primarily via stunts staged for newspapers. The potential of these early PR techniques soon became obvious to business executives who wanted to boost their companies and to politicians who needed a positive public image to win votes. For instance, press agents were used by people like Daniel Boone, who was involved in various land-grab and real-estate ventures, and Davy Crockett, who was involved in massacres of Native Americans. Such individuals often wanted to repair and shape their reputations as cherished frontier legends or as reputable candidates for political office.

p.t. barnum, buffalo bill, and the railroads

The most notorious theatrical agent of the 1800s was Phineas Taylor (P.T.) Barnum, who used gross exaggeration, fraudulent stories, and staged events to secure newspaper coverage for his clients, his American Museum, and later, his circus. Barnum's best-known acts included the "midget" General Tom Thumb, Swedish soprano Jenny

Lind, Jumbo the Elephant, and Joice Heth, who Barnum claimed was the 161-year-old nurse of George Washington (although she was actually 80 when she died). These performers became some of the earliest nationally known celebrities due to Barnum's skill at using the media for promotion. Decrying outright fraud and cheating, Barnum understood that his audiences liked to be tricked. In newspapers and on handbills, he would often later reveal the strategies behind his more elaborate hoaxes.

From 1883 to 1916, former army scout William F. Cody, who once killed buffaloes for the railroads, promoted himself in his "Buffalo Bill's Wild West and Congress of Rough Riders" traveling show. Cody's troupe—which featured bedouins, cossacks, and gauchos as well as "cowboys and Indians"—re-created dramatic gunfights, the Civil War, and battles of the Old West. The show employed sharpshooter Annie Oakley and Lakota medicine man Sitting Bull, whose own legends were partially shaped by Cody's nine publicity agents. These agents were led by John Burke, who promoted the show for its thirty-four-year run. Burke was one of the first PR agents to use a variety of media channels: promotional newspaper stories, magazine articles and ads, dime novels, theater marquees, poster art, and early films. Burke's efforts successfully elevated Cody's show, which was seen by more than fifty million people in a thousand cities in twelve different countries.[4] Burke and Buffalo Bill shaped many of the lasting myths that developed about rugged American individualism and frontier expansion. Along with Barnum, they were among the first to use publicity to elevate entertainment-centered culture to an international level.

One of the first publicity agents, P. T. Barnum (1810–1891) started his famous circus in 1871. Using poster art, print media ads, and publicity stunts, Barnum made his name synonymous with the circus. In 1881, he merged his traveling show with Joseph Bailey's. Barnum & Bailey called their product the "greatest show on earth." The five Ringling brothers from Baraboo, Wisconsin, bought out Barnum & Bailey in 1907.

During the 1800s, America's largest industrial companies, particularly the railroads, also employed press agents to win favor in the court of public opinion. Initially, government involvement in railroad development was minimal; local businesses raised funds to finance the spread of rail service. Around 1850, however, the railroads began pushing for federal subsidies, complaining that local fund-raising efforts took too long. In its drive for government support, for example, Illinois Central promoted the following public strategy: "The railroad line would be expensive to construct; it would open up new land for economic development; without subsidy, the line might not be built; with subsidy the public interest would be served."[5] Illinois Central was one of the first companies to use government lobbyists to argue that railroads between the North and South would ease tensions, unite the two regions, and prevent a war.

The railroads successfully campaigned for government support by developing some of the earliest publicity tactics. Their first strategy was simply to buy favorable news stories through direct bribes. By the late 1880s, this practice was so common that a Chicago news reporter published his tongue-in-cheek rates: "For setting forth of virtues (actual or alleged) of presidents, general managers, or directors, $2 per line. . . . For complimentary notices of the wives and children of railroad officials, we demand $1.50 per line. . . . Epic poems, containing descriptions of scenery, dining cars, etc., will be published at special rates."[6] In addition to planting favorable articles in the press, the railroads engaged in *deadheading*: the practice of giving reporters free rail passes with the tacit understanding that they would write glowing reports about rail travel. Occasionally, railroads also hired academics to write articles supporting their rationale for subsidies. This was a particularly good way to influence legislators and intellectual readers. Eventually, wealthy railroads received federal subsidies and increased their profits while the public shouldered much of the financial burden for rail expansion.

In terms of power and influence, companies like Illinois Central and the Pennsylvania Railroad in the late 1800s were comparable to American automakers in the 1950s. Having obtained construction subsidies, the larger rail companies turned their attention to bigger game—lobbying the government to control rates and reduce competition, especially from smaller, aggressive regional lines. Any PR strategy used for this purpose would have faced an uphill battle since the entrepreneurial spirit of the times encouraged competition. Consequently, the campaign for regulation tried to convince people that competitive lower rates did not benefit the average citizen and that competition actually encouraged unfair business practices.

"Public relations developed in the early part of the twentieth century as a profession which responded to, and helped shape, the public, **newly defined as irrational**, not reasoning; spectatorial, not participant; consuming, not productive."
—Michael Schudson,
Discovering the News,
1978

Railroad lobbyists argued that federal support would improve service and guarantee quality, since the government would be keeping a close watch. These lobbying efforts, accompanied by favorable publicity, led to the passage of the Interstate Commerce Act in 1881, authorizing railroads "to revamp their freight classification, raise rates, and eliminate fare reduction."[7] Historians have argued that the PR campaign's success actually led to the decline of railroads; artificially maintained higher rates and burdensome government regulations forced smaller firms out of business and eventually drove many customers to other modes of transportation.

the modern public relations agent

Along with the railroads, utility companies such as Chicago Edison and AT&T also used PR strategies in the late 1800s to derail competition and eventually attain monopoly status. In fact, although both local and regional competitors existed at the time, AT&T's PR and lobbying efforts were so effective that they eliminated all telephone competition—with the government's blessing—until the 1980s.

The tactics of the 1880s and 1890s, however, would haunt public relations as it struggled to become a respected profession. In addition to buying the votes of key lawmakers, the utilities used a number of shady practices. These included third-party editorial services, which would send favorable articles about utilities to newspapers; assigning company managers to become leaders in community groups; producing ghostwritten articles (often using the names of prominent leaders and members of women's social groups, who were flattered to see their names in print); and influencing textbook authors to write histories favorable to utilities.[8]

As the promotional agendas of many companies escalated in the late 1800s, a number of reporters and muckraking journalists began investigating these practices. By the early 1900s, with an informed citizenry paying more attention, it became more difficult for large firms to fool the press and mislead the public. With the rise of the middle class, increasing literacy among the working classes, and the spread of information through print media, democratic ideals began to threaten the established order of business and politics—and the elite groups who managed them.

"Poison Ivy" Lee. Most nineteenth-century corporations and manufacturers cared little about public sentiment. By the early 1900s, though, executives realized that their companies could sell more products if they were associated with positive public images and values. Into this public space stepped Ivy Ledbetter Lee, considered one of the founders of modern public relations. Lee understood the undercurrents of social change. He counseled clients that honesty and directness were better PR devices than the deceptive practices that had prevailed in the 1800s, which had fostered a climate of suspicion and anti-big-business sentiment.

A minister's son and once a Princeton economics student, former reporter Lee opened one of the first New York PR firms with a colleague in the early 1900s. Lee quit the firm in 1906 to work for the Penn Railroad, which, following a rail accident, wanted him to help downplay bad publicity. Lee's advice, however, was that Penn admit its mistake, vow to do better, and let newspapers in on the story. These suggestions ran counter to what the utilities and railroads had been practicing. Nevertheless, Lee, who believed in open, frank relationships between the press and business, argued that such a policy would lead to a more favorable public image in an era when companies could no longer afford to alienate customers. In the end, Penn adopted Lee's strategies.

In 1914, Lee went to work for John D. Rockefeller, who by the 1880s controlled 90 percent of the nation's oil industry ("It is my duty to make money and still more money").[9] Rockefeller suffered from periodic image problems, particularly after Ida Tarbell's powerful muckraking series in *McClure's Magazine* on Rockefeller's Standard Oil trust. Despite his philanthropic work, Rockefeller was often depicted in the press as a tyrant, as were other corporate bosses. The Rockefeller and Standard Oil reputations reached a low point in April 1914, when tactics to stop union organizing erupted in tragedy at a fuel and iron company in Ludlow, Colorado. During a violent strike, fifty-three workers and family members, including thirteen women and children, died.

Ivy Lee was hired to contain the damaging publicity fallout. He immediately put out a series of fact sheets to the press, telling the corporate side of the story and discrediting the United Mine Workers who had been trying to organize the Ludlow workers. As he had done for Penn, Lee brought in the press and staged photo opportunities. John D. Rockefeller Jr., who by then ran his father's company, donned overalls and a miner's helmet and posed with the families of workers and union leaders. While Lee helped the company improve conditions for workers, the publicity campaign also kept the union out of the Ludlow coal mines. This was probably the first use of a PR campaign in a labor-management dispute. Over the years, Lee completely transformed the Rockefeller image, urging the discreet family to publicize its charitable work. To improve his image, the senior Rockefeller took to handing out dimes to children wherever he went—a strategic ritual that historians attribute to Lee.

Called "Poison Ivy" by newspaper critics and corporate foes, Lee had a complex understanding of facts. He realized, better than most journalists of his day, that facts were open to various interpretations. For Lee, facts were elusive and malleable, begging to be forged and shaped. Interpreting facts so as to shine the best light on a client was not viewed as a particularly honorable practice. In the Ludlow case, for instance, Lee noted that the women and children who died retreating from the charging company-backed militia had overturned a stove, which caught fire and killed them. His PR fact sheet implied that they had been, in part, victims of their own carelessness.

In the 1930s, Ivy Lee was investigated by Congress for counseling German industries during the Nazi regime and for fraternizing with the Soviet Union under Joseph Stalin. Some critics thought that Lee's interest in a communist nation represented a curious contradic-

John D. Rockefeller (1839–1937) owned the Standard Oil Company, which monopolized the oil industry in the late 1800s. After the 1914 Ludlow labor disaster claimed the lives of fifty-three people, he hired Ivy Lee to repair the Rockefeller reputation. Among other things, the PR agent is credited with advising Rockefeller to hand out shiny new dimes to strangers, a publicity stunt that helped soften his image late in his life.

tion for an avowed capitalist. In Lee's earlier work for railroads and utilities, however, he had advocated an anticompetition, pro-consolidation theme that he believed to be in the best interests of his clients. Lee had argued for corporate-controlled monopolies, which benefited from protective government regulation. Thus, Lee did share some common ground with foreign governments that ran state-controlled, anticompetitive business monopolies.

Edward Bernays. The nephew of Sigmund Freud, former reporter Edward Bernays inherited the public relations mantle from Ivy Lee and dressed it up with modern social science. Bernays, who died in 1995 at age 103, was the first person to apply the findings of psychology and sociology to his corporate clients. He also referred to himself as a "public relations counselor" rather than as just a publicity agent. Over the years, Bernays' client list included General Electric, the American Tobacco Company, General Motors, *Good Housekeeping* and *Time* magazines, Procter & Gamble, RCA, the government of India, and the city of Vienna. In addition, he served as an advisor to President Coolidge in the 1920s, helping the president revamp his stiff formal image.

Bernays made key contributions to public relations education.[10] He taught the first class called *public relations*—at New York University in 1923—and wrote the field's first textbook, *Crystallizing Public Opinion*. For many years, his definition of PR was a standard: "Public relations is the attempt, by information, persuasion, and adjustment, to engineer public support for an activity, cause, movement, or institution." Bernays worked for the Committee on Public Information (CPI) during World War I, developing propaganda that supported America's entry into that struggle. Later, CPI helped create an image of President Woodrow Wilson as a peacemaker, among the first full-scale governmental attempts to mobilize public opinion.

Hired by the American Tobacco Company after World War I, Bernays was asked to develop a campaign that would make smoking more publicly acceptable for newly liberated women who had recently won the right to vote. Among other strategies, Bernays staged an event: placing women smokers in New York's 1929 Easter parade. He labeled cigarettes "torches of freedom" and encouraged women to smoke as a symbol of their newly acquired suffrage and independence from men. He also asked the women he used in the parade to contact newspaper and newsreel companies in advance—to announce their symbolic protest. The campaign received plenty of free publicity from newspapers and magazines. Within five weeks of the parade, men-only smoking rooms in New York theaters began opening up to women.

Through much of his writing, Bernays suggested that emerging forms of social democracy threatened the established hierarchical order. He thought it was important for experts and leaders to keep business and society pointed in the right directions: "The duty of the higher strata of society—the cultivated, the learned, the expert, the intellectual—is therefore clear. They must inject moral and spiritual motives into public opinion."[11] Bernays saw a typical public relations campaign giving shape to public opinion—what he termed the "engineering of consent." Bernays believed that for any PR campaign to work, securing the consent of the people was the crucial ingredient.

Ivy Lee believed that public opinion was based on people's self-interests. Both Lee and Bernays thought that such opinion was pliant and not always rational: In the hands of the right experts, leaders, and PR counselors, public opinion was ready for shaping in forms that people could rally behind.[12] Walter Lippmann, the newspaper columnist who wrote *Public Opinion* in 1922, also believed in the importance of an expert class to direct the more irrational twists and turns of public opinion. But he saw the development of public relations as "a clear sign that the facts of modern life [did] not spontaneously take a shape in which they can be known."[13] Lippmann lamented

"Since crowds do not reason, they can only be organized and stimulated through **symbols and phrases**."
—Ivy Lee, 1917

Beat back the **HUN** with **LIBERTY BONDS**

During World War I, PR pioneer Edward Bernays (1891–1995) worked for the federal Committee on Public Information (CPI). One of the main functions of the CPI was to create the poster art and print ads that would persuade reluctant or isolationist Americans to support the war effort against Germany.

that too often PR professionals with hidden agendas, rather than detached reporters, were giving meaning to the facts.

Through Bernays' most active years, his business partner and later his wife, Doris Fleischman, worked on many joint projects as a researcher and coauthor. Beginning in the 1920s, she was one of the first women to work in advertising and public relations. She edited a pamphlet called *Contact*, which explained the emerging profession of public relations to America's most powerful leaders. Because it was a new quasi-profession, not claimed entirely by men, PR was one of the few accessible professions—other than teaching and nursing—for women who chose to work outside the home. By the mid-1990s, women made up more than half of the sixteen thousand members in the Public Relations Society of America (PRSA), the professional organization that was founded in 1948.

pseudo-events and manufacturing news

Armed with its new understanding of public psychology, modern public relations changed not only the relationship between corporations and the public but among corporations, politics, and journalism. In his influential book *The Image*, historian Daniel Boorstin coined the term **pseudo-event** to refer to one of the key contributions of PR and advertising in the twentieth century. Basically, a pseudo-event is any circumstance created for the purpose of obtaining coverage in the media. In other words, if no news media show up, there is no event. Boorstin extended this idea to argue that any advertisement is a classic example of a pseudo-event since an ad would not exist without collusion between advertisers and various media outlets.[14]

"It was the **astounding success of propaganda** during the war which opened the eyes of the intelligent few in all departments of life to the possibilities of regimenting the public mind."
—Edward Bernays,
Propaganda,
1928

More typical pseudo-events are interviews, press conferences, TV and radio talk shows, the Super Bowl pregame show, or any other staged activity aimed at drawing public attention and media coverage. Such events depend on the participation of clients and performers and on the media recording the performances. In regard to national politics, Theodore Roosevelt's administration set up the first White House pressroom and held the first presidential press conferences in the early 1900s. In the 1990s, Vice President Al Gore championed White House Internet sites, making it possible for larger public audiences to interact with reporters and leaders in electronic press conferences.

As powerful companies, savvy politicians, and activist groups became aware of the media's susceptibility to pseudo-events, these activities proliferated. For example, to get free publicity, companies began staging press conferences to announce new product lines. During the 1960s, antiwar and civil rights protestors began their events only when the news media were assembled. One anecdote from that era aptly illustrates the principle of a pseudo-event: A reporter asked a student leader about the starting time for a particular protest; the student responded, "When can you get here?"

Politicians running for national office have become particularly adept at scheduling press conferences and interviews around 5 or 6 P.M. They realize that local TV news is live during these times, so they stage pseudo-events to take advantage of TV's live remote feeds.

the practice of public relations

By the mid-1990s, more than 150,000 practitioners as well as 5,000 companies offered various types of PR services. In addition, the formal study of public relations, especially since the 1980s, experienced significant growth in college and university settings. As certified PR programs expanded (often featuring journalism as a minor), the profession relied less and less on the ranks of reporters for its workforce. At the same time, new courses in professional ethics and issues management trained future practitioners to be more responsible.

The growth of formal PR education has been fairly dramatic. In the 1970s, the majority of students in communication and journalism programs indicated in surveys that they intended to pursue careers in news or magazine writing. By the late 1980s, however, similar surveys indicated that the majority of students wanted to enter public relations or advertising. By the 1990s, entry-level salaries and opportunities were greater in these latter areas. By 1995, the Public Relations Student Society of America (PRSSA) had over fifty-five hundred members and chapters in nearly two hundred colleges and universities. Such growth parallels the general rise of business schools and majors throughout the 1970s and 1980s.

approaches to organized pr

In 1988, the PRSA offered this useful definition of PR: "Public relations helps an organization and its publics adapt mutually to each other." To carry out this mutual communication process, the PR industry has two major approaches. First, many agencies function as independent companies whose sole job is to provide PR services to various clients. (During the 1980s and 1990s, though, many large ad agencies acquired independent PR firms as subsidiaries.) Second, most companies, which may or may not buy the services of independent PR firms, maintain their own in-house staffs to handle routine PR tasks, such as writing press releases, managing various media requests, and dealing with the public.

Independent Agencies. About sixteen hundred American companies identify themselves exclusively as public relations counseling firms. Two of the biggest, Burson-Marsteller and Hill and Knowlton, are now subsidiaries of global ad agencies (see Table 12.1). Young & Rubicam, an advertising giant, operates Burson-Marsteller, founded in 1953. With billings of $200 million or more annually, Burson-Marsteller has been one of PR's top-ranking firms in the 1990s. It has fifty-eight offices operating in twenty-six countries and more than eighteen hundred employees worldwide. Among its major clients have been Coca-Cola and General Electric.

Hill and Knowlton claimed the title "counsel of choice" in the mid-1990s for "more than one quarter of the world's largest corporations."[15] A unit of the world's largest ad agency, the WPP Group, Hill and Knowlton employs over twelve hundred people in twenty-five offices in sixty countries. Its clients have included IBM, Kodak,

Nintendo, Pepsi, Procter & Gamble, Xerox, former president Richard Nixon, and the royal family of Kuwait. By the mid-1990s, most of the largest PR firms were owned by or affiliated with ad agencies, which have long provided PR as a part of their full-service operations.

In-House Services. In contrast to independent agencies, the most common type of public relations is done in-house by individual companies and organizations. Although about a third of America's largest companies retain an external PR firm, almost every company involved in a manufacturing or service industry has an in-house department. Such departments are also a vital part of many professional organizations, such as the American Medical Association, the AFL-CIO, and the National Association of Broadcasters, as well as large nonprofit organizations, such as the American Cancer Society, the Arthritis Foundation, and most universities and colleges.

performing public relations

Public relations, like advertising, pays careful attention to the various publics that it interacts with or serves. These groups include not only consumers and the general public but company employees, shareholders, media organizations, government agencies, and community and industry leaders. Among potential clients, which constitute another public, are politicians, educational institutions, small businesses, industries, and nonprofit organizations (including hospitals, museums, religious groups, and various charities).

Public relations involves a multitude of practices and techniques. The PRSA identifies a number of general activities associated with PR: publicity, communication, public affairs, issues management, government relations, financial PR, community relations, industry relations, minority relations, advertising, press agentry, promotion, media relations, and propaganda. This last activity, **propaganda,** is communication strategically placed, either as advertising or publicity, to gain public support for a spe-

TABLE 12.1
The Top 15 Public Relations Firms
(by Net Fees)

Firm	1996 Net Fees	Number of Employees	% Change vs. 1995
Burson-Marsteller	$233,344,022	1,863	+10.1
Shandwick	190,700,000	1,969	+11.4
Hill and Knowlton	160,800,000	1,320	+13.9
Porter Novelli International	121,178,280	1,175	+25.0
Edelman Public Relations Worldwide	111,680,350	1,151	+24.8
Fleishman-Hillard	107,494,000	935	+20.0
Ketchum Public Relations	74,836,000	614	+16.3
GCI Group	52,293,330	445	+17.4
Ogilvy Adams & Rinehart	48,544,000	410	+17.7
Manning, Selvage & Lee	47,925,000	370	+25.7
Bozell Sawyer Miller Group	43,900,000	276	+8.0
Ruder Finn	41,870,165	366	+26.6
Cohn & Wolfe	25,034,552	198	+35.9
Financial Relations Board	20,224,882	209	+23.7
Morgen-Walke Assocs.	16,504,604	126	+30.9

Sources: The J. R. O'Dwyer Company, Inc., 1996.

cial issue, program, or policy, such as a nation's war effort. All of these activities are typical of public relations, whether they are carried out by a large PR firm or by the in-house department of a product company, a nonprofit organization, or a politician.

The practice of public relations encompasses a wide range of activities. PR personnel produce employee newsletters, manage client trade shows and conferences, conduct historical tours, appear on news programs, organize damage control after negative publicity, and analyze complex issues and trends that may affect a client's future. Basic among these activities, however, are writing and editing, media relations, special events, research, and community and government relations. PR practice generally divides into two roles: PR technicians, who handle daily short-term activities, and PR managers, who counsel clients and manage activities over the long term.

Writing and Editing. One of the chief day-to-day technical functions in public relations is composing news or **press releases**: announcements, written in the style of news reports, that give new information about an individual, company, or organization and pitch a story idea to the news media (see Figure 12.1). In issuing press releases, often called *handouts* by the news media, PR agents hope that their client information will be picked up and transformed into news. Through press releases, PR firms manage the flow of information; they often control which media get what material in which order. (Sometimes a PR agent will target TV over newspapers or reward a cooperative reporter through the strategic release of information.)

News editors and broadcasters sort through hundreds of releases daily to determine which ones contain the most original ideas or the most currency for their readers and viewers. The majority of large media institutions rewrite and double-check the information in news releases, but small media companies may use them verbatim, especially if their own editorial resources are limited or if they are under deadline constraints. Usually, the more closely a press release resembles actual news copy, the more likely it is to be used, which is why newspaper work is a good training ground for PR.

Since the 1970s and the introduction of portable video equipment, agencies and departments have been using **video news releases (VNRs)**, which are thirty- to ninety-second visual PR stories packaged to mimic the style of a broadcast news report. Many large companies now operate their own TV studios, enabling them to produce training videos for their employees and to create VNRs for their clients. Broadcast news stations in small TV markets regularly use video material from VNRs. Although large stations with more resources may get story ideas from VNRs, their news directors do not like to use video material obtained directly from PR sources; they prefer to assemble their own reports in order to maintain their independence. On occasion, news stations have been criticized for using bits of video footage from a VNR without acknowledging the source. *TV Guide* sharply criticized VNRs as "false news" in 1992 after Hill and Knowlton distributed a pro-Kuwaiti VNR to promote American support for the Desert Storm military offensive in 1991.

In addition to issuing press releases, nonprofit groups also produce **public-service announcements (PSAs)**: fifteen- to sixty-second reports or announcements for radio and television that promote government programs, educational projects, voluntary agencies, or social reform. As part of their requirement to serve the public interest, broadcasters historically have been encouraged to carry free PSAs. Since the deregulation of broadcasting began in the 1980s, however, there is less pressure and no minimum obligation for TV and radio stations to air PSAs. When they do run, PSAs frequently are scheduled between midnight and 6 A.M., a less commercially valuable time slot with relatively few viewers or listeners.

The writing and editing part of PR also involves creating brochures and catalogues as well as company newsletters and annual reports for shareholders. It may

Figure 12.1
Differences between a Press Release and a News Story

News reporters—especially in medicine, science, and technology—are heavily dependent on public relations for story ideas. Here are an excerpt from a medical PR release, written by the in-house PR staff at a suburban Detroit hospital, and a *Detroit News* story, written by a medical reporter, based partly on information in the release.
Source: Courtesy Jim Tobin and Yvette Monet.

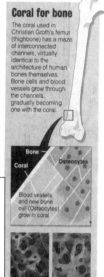

Coral for bone

The coral used in Christian Groth's femur (thighbone) has a maze of interconnected channels, virtually identical to the architecture of human bones themselves. Bone cells and blood vessels grow through the channels, gradually becoming one with the coral.

Bone —
Coral
Osteocytes

Blood vessels and new bone cell (Osteocytes) grow in coral

Human bone   Sea coral
(Magnified)

Source: Interpore International

Chris Willis / The Detroit News

Sea coral bone graft gives teen chance at being a kid again

An amazing coincidence of nature helps put implant patients back on their feet.

By James Tobin
The Detroit News

Because of a gift from the sea — tropical coral harvested in the south Pacific — Christian Groth is swimming again.

The coral rests snugly inside the femur (thigh bone) of his right leg, just above the knee. It fills a hole the size of a large marble, replacing a benign tumor that was making it harder and harder for Chris, 14, to play the sports he loves.

If you used a powerful magnifying glass to compare the coral to Chris' bone, you couldn't tell the difference. The two materials are almost exactly the same.

Groth

Thanks to this remarkable coincidence of nature, Chris — one of the first people in Metro Detroit to have a bone repaired with sea coral — is "doing everything," said his doctor, Ronald Irwin, an orthopedic oncologist affiliated with Beaumont Hospital, Royal Oak. "It looks good," Irwin said. "He'll ski this year."

The material won't work for every bone problem, but for Chris, an eighth-grader from Birmingham, and others, it means less pain and a quicker recovery than with other bone-graft materials, including his own bone.

The new process begins in the Pacific and Indian oceans, where a California company called Interpore International, the only provider so far, harvests a couple tons of coral annually — a yield so small that environmentalists aren't upset.

At Interpore, the coral is blasted with heat and chemicals to convert it to a substance called coralline hydroxyapatite, the strength-giving mineral in bone. Then it's cut into small blocks or crumbled into granules.

The key advantage: It retains the coral's structure — an intricate, three-dimensional maze of tiny channels.

Bone doctors sculpt the blocks to fit the problem — a tumor site, like Chris', or a fracture or shattered bone that needs extra material. Irwin used the granules, since he couldn't get a sculpted block into the cavity inside Chris' femur. The surgery was performed Aug. 20.

Once the coral was in place, bone cells and blood vessels began to creep into the coral's tiny channels, like vines through a trellis. Chris' immune system didn't reject the coral because its structure and substance is so similar to human bone.

Gradually, the coral and bone become one.

Traditionally, doctors have used bone from the patient's own pelvis for such repairs. But that demands two surgeries instead of one, and the pelvic surgery means a lot of pain and difficult recoveries.

Using grafts from cadavers carries a slight risk of infection, and using grafts from living donors sometimes provokes the immune system.

Irwin uses the coral only for benign tumors, not malignancies or fractures. But other doctors are looking to coral for those repairs, too, and it may be useful for some bone breaks in people with osteoporosis.

Beaumont

William Beaumont Hospital   Public Relations
Royal Oak   3601 West Thirteen Mile Road
                              Royal Oak, Michigan 48073-6769
                              (810) 551-0740

News release

Contact:

Colette Stimmell   Dec. 18, 1996
Yvette Monet

FOR IMMEDIATE RELEASE
NEW HOPE EMERGES FROM THE DEEP BLUE SEA FOR PATIENTS WITH BONE TUMORS

Sea coral harvested from vast tropical reefs is surfacing as part of a new technology that enables doctors to rebuild human bones after benign tumors located on or in the bone are surgically removed.

William Beaumont Hospital orthopaedic oncologist Ronald Irwin, M.D., is currently one of just a few tumor surgeons in the United States to use Pro Osteon Implant 500, a coral-based synthetic graft material developed by Interpore International, a biomaterials company in Irvine, Calif.

The implant originates from goniopera coral, which grows abundantly in the Pacific and Indian oceans. Because the pore size and structure of the coral is very similar to human bone, bone cells weave in and through the implant, eventually strengthening the bone and helping to spur new bone growth.

The implant has significant advantages over the alternatives for rebuilding bones,

(more)

---

include writing and editing speeches that aim to boost a politician's image or a company's stature. Major politicians and business leaders today seldom write their own speeches. Instead, they hire speechwriters or PR specialists.

Media Relations. Through publicity, PR managers specializing in media relations promote a client or organization by securing favorable coverage in the news media. Media specialization often requires an in-house PR person to speak on behalf of an organization or to direct reporters to experts who can provide the best, or at least official, sources of information.

Media relations specialists also perform *damage control* or *crisis management* when negative publicity occurs (see "Case Study: GM Trucks and NBC's *Dateline* Disaster" on page 352). Occasionally, in times of crisis—such as a virus outbreak at a hospital, a scandal at a university, or a safety recall by a car manufacturer—a PR spokesperson might be designated as the only source of information available to news media. Although journalists often resent being cut off from higher administrative levels and leaders, the institution or company wants to ensure that rumors and inaccurate stories do not circulate easily in the media. In these situations, a game often develops in which reporters attempt to circumvent the company spokesperson and induce a knowledgeable insider to talk *off the record*, providing background details without being named directly as a source.

PR agents who specialize in media relations also recommend advertising to their clients when it seems appropriate. Unlike publicity, which is sometimes outside a PR agency's control, paid advertising may help to focus a complex issue or a client's image. Publicity, however, carries the aura of legitimate news and thus has more credibility than advertising. In addition, media specialists cultivate associations with editors, reporters, freelance writers, and broadcast news directors to ensure that press releases or VNRs are favorably received. Since the majority of this material goes unused, a PR specialist who can get information accepted as news is especially valuable.

Special Events. Another public relations specialty involves coordinating special events. Since the late 1960s, for instance, the city of Milwaukee has run Summerfest, a ten-day music and food festival that attracts nearly a million people each year. As the festival's popularity grew, various companies sought to become sponsors of the event. Local manufacturers and the beer industry, for example, signed up to support different musical venues. The Miller Brewing Company sponsored a festival stage devoted to jazz. In exchange for sponsorship, the stage carried the Miller name, which also accompanied many items connected with Summerfest. In this way, Miller received favorable publicity by showing a commitment to the city that serves as the company's corporate headquarters.[16]

More typical of special-events publicity is the corporate sponsor who aligns its company image with a cause or organization that has positive stature among the general public. For example, for more than twenty-five years, Mobil Oil has underwritten special programming such as *Masterpiece Theater* on PBS. At the local level, companies often sponsor a community parade or a charitable fund-raising activity. When a new professional sports team arrives in a community, a host of local companies may compete to associate themselves with the new franchise. In this kind of situation, a team's PR specialist attempts to identify those companies that will provide the most favorable publicity for the client.

Many business executives score points with the public by associating their companies with special community events. For example, the city of Milwaukee runs Summerfest, one of the world's largest food and music festivals. Since the late 1960s, the festival has been supported prominently by the region's beer industry.

Research. Just as advertising is driven today by demographic and psychographic research, PR uses similar strategies to project a client's image to the appropriate audience. The research area is PR's fastest growing segment as the profession attempts to bring new social science techniques to its audience studies and image campaigns. Since historically it has been difficult to determine why particular campaigns succeed or fail, research has become the key ingredient in PR forecasting. Like advertising studies, PR research targets specific audiences. It uses mail and telephone surveys to get a fix on an audience's perceptions of a client's reputation.

As in advertising research, focus groups have become prominent in public relations campaigns. Although such groups are often unreliable because of small sample size, they are fairly easy to set up and do not require elaborate statistical designs. In 1990, for example, Gemstar Development Corporation introduced a remote-control technology that helps people program television codes into their VCRs more easily. This device, which employs a one-step recording technique using number codes printed in *TV Guide* and most newspaper TV supplements, was the end product of research initiated by a California PR firm, Rogers and Associates. The firm used three focus groups totaling forty-eight participants to learn that the majority of the nation's then seventy million VCR owners did not know how to tape movies or TV programs because the steps seemed too complicated. The research project concluded that users were most interested in "high-fidelity picture quality," one-step recording, and "a VCR that quickly locates a segment on your recorded tape for playback or editing." The

GM Trucks and NBC's *Dateline* Disaster

On November 17, 1992, NBC's new *Dateline* program aired a report that showed two different full-size Chevy pickup trucks bursting into flames after being hit broadside by small cars. Along with the demonstration, *Dateline* implied that the truck's side-mounted fuel tanks were extremely dangerous.

There was only one problem: The report was phony. For dramatic impact, *Dateline* had rigged the trucks with special igniters. With careful editing, the effect in each case was a big explosion and leaping flames, suggesting that drivers and passengers were at risk. In response, a General Motors crisis-management team fought back. During a thorough investigation, GM got a tip from an area news reporter who had found a witness to the enhanced presentation—a firefighter who had made his own video recording of each crash. GM investigators also located the rigged trucks in an Indiana junkyard.

A GM public relations team wrote a series of letters asking NBC to acknowledge the deception. When NBC executives continued to stand by the report, GM filed a lawsuit in February 1993. The defamation suit was announced at a press conference conducted by Harry Pearce, GM's

general counsel. More than 150 reporters, photographers, and TV camera crews attended Pearce's own two-hour exposé of *Dateline*. Systematically critiquing the sixteen-minute report, Pearce convincingly showed that the only fires in both rigged sequences were brief grass fires ignited mainly by gasoline spurting from ill-fitting gas caps that came loose on impact. At the end of the conference, Pearce called on the assembled members of the news media to monitor the episodes of abuse in their own profession.

The day after the conference, NBC and GM entered negotiations, with GM demanding public repentance. On

February 9, 1993, *Dateline* coanchors Jane Pauley and Stone Philips read a four-minute retraction and apology. Eventually, three *Dateline* producers were fired and an on-air reporter demoted. Michael Gartner, NBC News president, resigned in disgrace. Up until the press conference, Gartner had claimed that NBC's report was accurate and responsible. NBC reimbursed GM $2 million for the costs of the company's investigation. In turn, GM dropped its defamation suit.

During its battle, GM's PR team also had to confront charges from national safety experts, many of whom were on NBC's payroll. GM was able to discredit these officials and also fend off a recall effort by the National Highway Traffic Safety Administration (NHTSA), which raised its own questions about truck safety. The NHTSA asked GM to recall the trucks in question even before the organization had finished its own investigation. GM refused and made convincing public arguments in two additional press conferences about the flawed conclusions of the NHTSA concerning the proficiency of its older trucks.

The NBC deception is a story that might not have been told had GM decided not to challenge the network. After all, it is very difficult for public individuals and companies to win damages in suits against the mainstream news media, which citizens count on to watch for abuses in politics and business. The strategy used by GM now serves as a crisis-management model for handling complicated cases that have both legal and ethical implications. Although GM is one of the world's largest companies and had the resources (and evidence) to fight back in this case, its PR strategy demonstrated that all citizens have a responsibility to watch over the watchdog.

participants not only helped pick the name of the product—VCR Plus+—but 77 percent of them bought or ordered the device after their experience in the focus group.[17]

Community and Consumer Relations. Two other PR activities involve building the relationship between companies and their communities and customers. Companies have learned that sustaining close ties with their neighbors enhances not only their image but the idea that the companies are good citizens. Such ties expose a business to potential customers through activities such as plant tours, town parades and open houses, and special events such as a company's anniversary. Many companies also operate museums—with attached gift shops—that point up their historical importance to the community.

Besides encouraging client employees to get involved in community activities, many PR firms like their clients to make charitable donations that build local bonds. Some companies offer their work sites to local groups for meetings and help in fund-raising efforts. More progressive companies get involved in unemployment and job-retraining programs, and yet others donate equipment and workers to urban revitalization projects such as Habitat for Humanity.

In terms of customer relations, PR has become much more sophisticated since the 1960s, when Ralph Nader's *Unsafe at Any Speed* revealed safety problems concerning the Chevrolet Corvair. Nader's book gave General Motors a corporate migraine that resulted in the discontinuance of the Corvair line. More important, however, Nader's book lit the fuse that ignited a vibrant consumerism movement. During the 1960s, consumers became more sophisticated and consequently unwilling to readily accept the claims of those in power—including corporate leaders. Contributing to this movement was the trend toward large multinational corporate mergers and the rise of impersonal chain stores, both of which signaled a decreasing accountability to consumers.

The consumerism movement for a while drew media attention. Many newspapers and TV stations hired consumer reporters, who tracked down the sources of customer complaints and often embarrassed companies by putting them in the media spotlight. Firms that were PR savvy responded by paying more attention to customers, establishing product and service guarantees, and ensuring that all calls and mail from customers were answered quickly. The smartest companies produced consumer education literature about specific products and developed close ties with local consumer groups.

The impact of the consumer movement today is especially evident in the resources devoted to training employees carefully in good customer relations. Many product and service companies have also developed customer satisfaction questionnaires and "consumer creeds." For example, many restaurants and department stores go beyond asking consumers for advice, outlining for them what treatment to expect and what to do when those expectations are not met. PR professionals routinely advise clients that satisfied customers mean not only repeat business but new business, based on strong word-of-mouth reputation about a company's behavior and image.

Socially conscientious PR firms encourage their employees and their clients to get involved in community projects, donating work and time that pays off by strengthening a firm's image. For example, the efforts of Habitat for Humanity—building low-income housing using volunteers and donated material—are often supported by progressive public relations companies.

Government Relations and Lobbying. Public relations also entails maintaining connections with government agencies that have some say over how companies operate in a particular community, state, or nation. The PR divisions of major firms are especially interested in making sure that government regulation neither becomes burdensome nor reduces their control over their businesses. Specialists in this area often develop self-regulatory practices, which either keep governments at some distance or draw on them for subsidies, as the railroads and utilities did in the nineteenth century. Such specialists also monitor new and existing legislation, create opportunities to ensure favorable publicity, and write press releases and direct-mail letters to educate the public on the pros and cons of new regulations.

In many firms, government relations has developed into **lobbying**: the process of attempting to influence the voting of lawmakers to support a client's or organization's best interests. In seeking favorable legislation, some PR agents lobby government officials on a daily basis. Since lobbyists have generally developed a negative reputation for aggressively hawking special interests, many in public relations are wary of counting lobbying among their activities. Nevertheless, most major firms provide lobbying services. In Washington, D.C., alone, nearly seven thousand registered lobbyists write speeches, articles, and position papers in addition to designing direct-mail campaigns, buying ads, and befriending editors.

Today most major corporations, trade associations, labor unions, consumer groups, professional organizations, religious groups, and even foreign governments employ lobbyists. For instance, prior to the Persian Gulf War, lobbyists representing both the U.S. oil industry and the government of Kuwait had to work extremely hard to deflect that country's image as a privileged oil-rich state. Lobbyists tried to change Kuwait's image in order to justify U.S. and UN military action against Iraq, which had invaded Kuwait in 1990. To that end, the Kuwaiti royal family (who went into exile before Iraq invaded Kuwait) hired Hill and Knowlton to help rally public support for U.S. military intervention. The firm developed the idea of a "congressional human rights caucus," which in October 1990 reported acts of barbarism perpetrated by Iraqis on Kuwaitis. Later it was discovered that one witness, a fifteen-year-old Kuwaiti girl who testified at the caucus to seeing acts of cruelty, was the daughter of the Kuwaiti ambassador to the United States and "had been witness to no such events." In January 1991, the United States invaded Iraq with the majority of Americans, according to opinion polls, supporting the intervention.[18]

tensions between pr and the press

In 1932, Stanley Walker, an editor at the *New York Herald Tribune*, compared public relations agents and publicity advisors to "mass-mind molders, fronts, mouthpieces, chiselers, moochers, and special assistants to the president."[19] Walker added that newspapers and public relations agencies would always remain enemies, even if PR professionals adopted a code of ethics (which they did in the 1950s) to "take them out of the red-light district of human relations."[20] Walker's tone captures the spirit of one of the most mutually dependent—and antagonistic—relationships across mass media.

Much of this antagonism, directed at public relations from the journalism profession, is historical. Reporters have long regarded themselves as part of an older public-service profession, whereas many regard PR as a pseudo-profession created to distort the facts that reporters work so hard to gather. Over time, reporters and editors developed a nationwide derogatory term for a PR agent—**flack**—which continues in usage to this day. The term derives from the military word *flak*, meaning the antiaircraft artillery shells fired from naval ships to deflect aerial attack, and from the related *flak jacket*, the protective military attire worn to ward off enemy fire. For journalists, the word *flacks* has come to mean PR persons who insert themselves between their business or political employers and the "enemy"—members of the press.

In the 1960s, an Associated Press manual for editors defined a flack as "a person who makes all or part of his income by obtaining space in newspapers without cost to himself or his clients." The AP depiction continued: "A flack is a flack. His job is to say kind things about his client. He will not lie very often, but much of the time he tells less than the whole story. You do not owe the PR man anything. The owner of the newspaper, not the flack, pays your salary. Your immediate job is to serve the readers, not the man who would raid your columns." This description, however, belies journalism's dependence on public relations. Many editors, for instance, admit that more than half of their story ideas each day originate with PR people. Since reporting staffs are limited, they are not privy to all the potential news ideas in a community. Therefore, they rely heavily on PR professionals for suggestions. Throughout the twentieth century, this growing interdependent relationship has come to shape both professions.

elements of professional friction

The relationship between journalism and PR is an important and complex one. Although journalism lays claim to independent traditions, the news media have become increasingly reliant on public relations because of the increasing amounts of information now available. Staff cutbacks at many papers and television's need for local newscast events have also increased the news media's need for PR story ideas.

Further depleting journalism, PR firms routinely raid the ranks of reporting for new talent. Since most press releases are written in a style that imitates news reports, the PR profession has always sought good writers who are well connected to sources and savvy about the news business. For instance, the fashion industry likes to hire former style or fashion news writers for its PR staff, and university information offices seek reporters who once covered higher education. It is interesting to note that although reporters frequently move into PR, public relations practitioners seldom move into journalism. The news profession also rarely accepts prodigal sons or daughters back into the fold once they have left reporting for public relations. According to many reporters and editors, any profession that shapes images is considered manipulative or self-serving—and its practitioners may not be redeemable. Nevertheless, the professions remain co-dependent: PR needs journalists for publicity, and journalism needs PR for story ideas. Several historical explanations shed light on the discord and on the ways in which different media professions interact.

> "Tabloid journalists, no matter how pleasant, are not your friends. They are often there to trick or trap your client."
> —Fran Matera, *Public Relations Journal*, 1990

Undermining Facts and Blocking Access. Modern public relations redefined and complicated the notion of facts. PR professionals demonstrated that the same set of facts may be spun in a variety of ways, depending on what information is emphasized and what is downplayed. As Ivy Lee noted in 1925, "The effort to state an absolute fact is simply an attempt to achieve what is humanly impossible; all I can do is to give you *my interpretation of the facts*."[21] With practitioners like Lee showing the emerging PR profession how facts and news could be manipulated, the journalist's role as a custodian of accurate information became much more difficult.

Journalists also have objected to PR flacks who block press access to key leaders. At one time, reporters could talk directly to such leaders and obtain quotable information for their news stories. Now, however, PR people insert themselves between the press and the powerful, thus disrupting the old ritual in which reporters would vie for interviews with top government and business leaders. With the rise of PR, the news media began to receive more carefully controlled information, much of it sent out simultaneously to all media outlets. If PR agents today want to manipulate or use reporters, they may give information to journalists who are likely to cast a story in a favorable light in return for getting the information first. On rarer occasions, a reporter's access to key sources might be cut off altogether if that journalist has written unfavorably about a client.

Promoting Publicity and Business as News. Another explanation for the professional friction between the press and PR involves simple economics. The trade journal *Editor & Publisher* once called public relations agents "space grabbers"; what editors and publishers feared actually became a reality: PR agents helped companies "promote as news what otherwise would have been purchased in advertising."[22]

As Ivy Lee wrote to John D. Rockefeller after the oil magnate gave money to Johns Hopkins University: "In view of the fact that this was not really news, and that the newspapers gave so much attention to it, it would seem that this was wholly due to the manner in which the material was 'dressed up' for newspaper consumption. It seems to suggest very considerable possibilities along this line."[23] Many newspeople react strongly to this sort of manipulation. Critics and journalists alike worry that public relations is taking media space and time away from other voices, especially from those that do not have the financial resources or the sophistication to become readily visible in the public eye. Beyond this lies another issue. If public relations can secure publicity for clients in the news, the added credibility of a journalistic context gives clients a status that the purchase of advertising cannot confer.

Today, however, something more subtle underlies journalism's contempt for public relations: Much of journalism actually functions the same way. For instance, politicians, celebrities, and PR firms with abundant resources are clearly afforded more coverage by the news media than their lesser-known counterparts. For example, workers and union leaders have long argued that the money that corporations allocate to PR leads to more favorable coverage for management positions in labor disputes. Standard news reports may feature subtle language choices, with "rational, cool-headed management making *offers*" and "hot-headed workers making *demands*." Walter Lippmann saw such differences in 1922 when he wrote: "If you study the way many a strike is reported in the press, you will find very often that [labor] issues are rarely in the headlines, barely in the leading paragraph, and sometimes not even mentioned anywhere."[24] Most newspapers now have business sections that focus on the work of various managers, but few have a labor, worker, or employee section. In fact, most large metro papers have eliminated the specialty beat of labor reporting.[25]

Business, economic, and stock "news" reports generated by corporate PR agents inundate newspapers. A single business reporter at a large metro daily sometimes receives as many as a hundred press releases a day—far outnumbering the fraction of handouts generated by organized labor or grassroots organizations. This imbalance is particularly significant in that the great majority of workers are neither managers nor CEOs, and yet these workers receive little if any media coverage on a regular basis. Essentially, as a number of critics have pointed out, mainstream journalism best serves managers and the status quo.

managing the press

Public relations, by making reporters' jobs easier, has often enabled reporters to become lazy. PR firms now supply what reporters used to work hard to gather for themselves. Instead of going out to beat the competition, many journalists have become content to wait for a PR handout or a good tip before following up on a story. Small community groups, social activists, and nonprofit organizations often cannot afford elaborate publicity. These groups argue that because of PR, large corporations and connected politicians enjoy easier access to reporters and receive more frequent news coverage. Occasionally, also due to PR, powerful firms and individuals receive less critical scrutiny. Some members of the news media—grateful for the reduced workloads that occur when handouts are provided to them—may be hesitant to criticize PR firms' clients.

Dealing with a tainted past and journalism's hostility have often preoccupied the public relations profession, leading to the development of several image-enhancing strategies. Over the years, for example, as public relations has subdivided itself into specialized areas, it has used more positive descriptive terms, such as institutional relations, corporate communications, and news and information services. With the development of its own professional organization, PRSA, the PR industry has also increased its standing among the public and even the news media.[26] PRSA functions as an internal watchdog group that accredits individuals, maintains a code of ethics, and publishes newsletters and trade publications. Most PRSA local chapters and national conventions also routinely invite reporters and editors to speak to PR practitioners about what the news media expects from their rival professionals. In addition, independent agencies, devoted to uncovering shady or unethical public relations activities, publish their findings in publications like *PR Tactics* or *PR Watch* (see Table 12.2). Ethical issues have become a major focus of the PR profession, with self-examination of these issues routinely appearing in PR textbooks as well as various professional newsletters.

TABLE 12.2
PRSA Ethics Code

The public relations profession first established an ethics code more than forty-five years ago, yet fewer than 10 percent of individual practitioners and firms formally subscribe to today's PRSA code. Listed here are the first ten points of the current code.

Public Relations Society of America Code of Professional Standards for the Practice of Public Relations

These articles have been adopted by the Public Relations Society of America to promote and maintain high standards of public service and ethical conduct among it members.

1. A member shall conduct his or her professional life in accord with the **public interest**.
2. A member shall exemplify high standards of **honesty and integrity** while carrying out dual obligations to a client or employer and to the democratic process.
3. A member shall **deal fairly** with the public, with past or present clients or employers, and with fellow practitioners, giving due respect to the idea of free inquiry and to the opinions of others.
4. A member shall adhere to the highest standards of **accuracy and truth**, avoiding extravagant claims or unfair comparisons and giving credit for ideas and words borrowed from others.
5. A member shall not knowingly disseminate **false or misleading information** and shall act promptly to correct erroneous communications for which he or she is responsible.
6. A member shall not engage in any practice which has the purpose of **corrupting** the integrity of channels of communications or the processes of government.
7. A member shall be prepared to **identify publicly** the name of the client or employer on whose behalf any public communication is made.
8. A member shall not use any individual or organization professing to serve or represent an announced cause, or professing to be independent or unbiased, but actually serving another or **undisclosed interest**.
9. A member shall **not guarantee the achievement** of specified results beyond the member's direct control.
10. A member shall **not represent conflicting** or competing interests without the express consent of those concerned, given after a full disclosure of the facts.

Source: PRSA.

Public relations' best press strategy, however, may be the limitations of the journalism profession itself. For most of the twentieth century, many reporters and editors have clung to the ideal that journalism is, at its best, an objective institution that gathers information on behalf of the public. Reporters have only occasionally turned their pens, computers, and cameras on themselves to examine their own practices or their vulnerability to manipulation. Thus, by not challenging PR's more subtle strategies, many journalists have allowed PR professionals to interpret "facts" to their clients' advantage.

Limited in its ability to identify and evade savvy public relations tactics, conventional journalism remains vulnerable. Take this hypothetical situation: A wealthy and powerful development corporation decides to raze a homeless shelter to build a condo. The firm uses public relations resources that overwhelm the protests of a few homeless activists. The major newspaper in town attempts to remain neutral on the issue. However, the strength of the PR unit of the corporation has already tipped the balance via an abundance of PR handouts. To recenter the scales, the newspaper in this case would have to take an advocacy position on behalf of the activists. But in conventional journalism, detachment prohibits this, and thus the corporate point of view triumphs—or at least gains most of the space and time in the news. Although many alternative newspapers and advocacy reporters do a fine job critiquing the limits of various public relations activities, conventional journalism has few mechanisms for rebalancing the scales tipped by PR embellishment, whether advanced by government or business leaders. Journalists have rarely challenged "the routines of government news management and the creation of pseudo-events."[27]

public relations, social responsibility, and democracy

"The **Exxon**
Valdez Story: How
to Spend a Billion or
Two and Still Get a
Black Eye in Public"
—Business school
conference title,
Fordham
University,
1990

Although public relations professionals may not have a public image as negative as that of advertisers, a cynical view of the profession nonetheless exists beyond the field of journalism. Given the history of corporate public relations, many concerned citizens believe that when a company or individual makes a mistake or misleads the public, too often a PR counsel is hired to alter the image rather than to admit the misdeed and correct the problem. An anecdote about a lawn-service/weed-control company illustrates this scenario: "A PR manager for a company named ChemLawn complained that the entire city of Columbus, Ohio, its headquarters, hated the company because it makes . . . chemicals. 'But what can you do?' she asked a couple of colleagues. They replied immediately—and in unison—'Change the name.'"[28] Although ChemLawn did not change its name, a company's decision to simply alter an image rather than deal with a problem highlights a dilemma for many PR agencies and their clients.

Let's look at a more familiar PR dilemma. In the aftermath of one of the largest natural disasters of this century—the Exxon *Valdez* oil spill along the Alaskan coast in 1989—the multinational corporation eventually changed the name of the tanker *Valdez* to the *Mediterranean* in the 1990s. The name change was just a small tactic in a series of damage-control strategies that Exxon enacted to cope with the oil spill. Such disaster management may reveal the worst—or best—attributes of the profession. How to enhance a company's image and, at the same time, encourage the company to be a socially responsible corporate citizen remains a major challenge for public relations.

The Exxon *Valdez* case was a corporate as well as a natural disaster, despite the company's outlay of $2 billion to clean up both its image and the spill. When eleven million gallons of crude oil were dumped into Prince William Sound, contaminating fifteen hundred miles of Alaskan coastline and killing countless birds, otters, seals, and fish,

Exxon was slow to react to the crisis and accept responsibility. Although its PR advisors had encouraged a quicker response, the corporation failed to send any of its chief officers immediately to the site to express concern. Many believed that Exxon was trying to duck responsibility by laying the burden of the crisis on the shoulders of the tanker's captain. A former president of NBC News, William Small, maintained that Exxon "lost the battle of public relations" and suffered "one of the worst tarnishings of its corporate image in American history."[29]

A decidedly different approach was taken in the 1982 tragedy involving Tylenol pain-relief capsules. Seven people died in the Chicago area after someone tampered with several bottles and laced them with poison. Like the oil spill, the case was a major news story. Discussions between the parent company, Johnson & Johnson, and its PR and advertising representatives focused on whether withdrawing all Tylenol capsules might send a signal that corporations could be intimidated by a deranged person. Nevertheless, Johnson & Johnson's chairman, James E. Burke, and the company's PR agency, Burson-Marsteller, opted for full disclosure to the media and the immediate recall of the capsules nationally, costing the company an estimated $100 million. Before the incident, Tylenol had a market share of 37 percent, making it the leading pain-relief medicine. After the capsule withdrawal, Tylenol's share was cut nearly in half.

As part of its PR strategy to restore Tylenol's market share, Burson-Marsteller tracked public opinion nightly through telephone surveys and organized satellite press conferences to debrief the news media. In addition, emergency phone lines were set up to take calls from consumers and health-care providers, who altogether sent two million messages to Johnson & Johnson. When the company reintroduced Tylenol three months after the tragedy began, it did so with tamper-resistant bottles that were soon copied by almost every major drug manufacturer. Burson-Marsteller, which received PRSA awards for its handling of the crisis, found that the public thought Johnson & Johnson had responded responsibly to the crisis and did not hold Tylenol responsible for the deaths. In less than three years, Tylenol had recaptured its former share of the market.

The Exxon and Tylenol examples demonstrate both dim and bright aspects of public relations, a profession that continues to provoke concern (see "Examining Ethics: Levi Strauss and Anti-Sweatshop Public Relations" on page 360). The bulk of criticism leveled at public relations argues that journalism is at the mercy of the crush of information produced by PR professionals. In one example, former president Richard Nixon, who resigned from office in 1974 to avoid impeachment hearings regarding his role in the Watergate scandal, hired Hill and Knowlton to restore his post-presidency image. Through the firm's guidance, Nixon's writings, mostly on international politics, began appearing in Sunday op-ed pages.

"The media make **heavy use of handouts** (press releases) and other information provided free by public relations people. Clearly, this is **not fair** and does not serve the American people very well." —Everette E. Dennis, *Media Debates*, 1991

"PR expands the public discourse, helps provide a wide assortment of news, and is essential in explaining the **pluralism** of our total communication system." —John C. Merrill, *Media Debates*, 1991

In 1982, several people in the Chicago area died after ingesting Tylenol—someone had tampered with the store-bought medicine's containers. Superb crisis management and the introduction of tamper-resistant packaging helped turn around Johnson & Johnson's fortunes. Four years later, when a New York woman died after taking a poisoned Tylenol capsule, Johnson & Johnson offered to exchange all capsules for caplets and stopped the production of over-the-counter capsules. The second tragedy cost Johnson & Johnson $150 million, but once again, the company's timely and honest response earned high marks from the public.

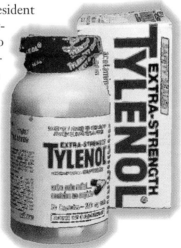

In 1996, both Wal-Mart and Nike faced major public relations scandals over the practice of *outsourcing*: using the production, manufacturing, and labor resources of foreign companies to produce American brand-name products.

Outsourcing drew major media attention that year when morning talk-show host Kathie Lee Gifford discovered that part of her clothing line, made and distributed by Wal-Mart, came from sweatshops in New York and Honduras. The sweatshops paid less than minimum wages and some employed child laborers. In the overseas sweatshops, in particular, human rights activists claimed that children were being exploited in violation of international child labor laws.

Then, during an NBA press conference in June 1996, Michael Jordan was questioned about allegations that Nike, which had long employed the basketball star as a spokesperson, used sweatshops in its global production of athletic shoes. Jordan promised to look into the charges.

Many global companies now conform to international guidelines that protect children and pay living wages to workers. Many countries, however, including the United States, still tolerate sweatshop conditions in which workers take home minimal pay, sometimes as little as a dollar an hour for working ten- to twelve-hour shifts six days a week.

Levi Strauss & Co. pioneered a program to guard against sweatshop practices.

As labor unions, the national media, and human rights groups began tracking the problem of sweatshops, stories about worker exploitation were exposed. One U.S. firm, Levi Strauss & Co., pioneered an institutional public relations program to guard against sweatshop practices. With more than seven hundred sewing contractors making jeans and other clothing in fifty countries, Levi Strauss developed the first set of international, anti-sweatshop guidelines for its contractors. The guidelines were the company's response to early criticism about moving some of its manufacturing overseas in search of low-cost labor markets.

The Levi Strauss plan focused on balancing "the company's merchandising and production needs with corporate social responsibility." Managers at Levi Strauss studied various ways of dealing with the cultural values and differences in the countries where they had manufacturing interests.[1]

To execute the plan, Levi Strauss instituted a training

He started showing up on *Nightline* and spoke frequently before groups such as the American Newspaper Publishers Association and the Economic Club of New York. In 1984, after a media blitz by Nixon's PR handlers, the *New York Times* announced, "After a decade, Nixon is gaining favor" and *USA Today* trumpeted, "Richard Nixon is back." Before his death in 1994, Nixon, who never publicly apologized for his role in Watergate, saw a large portion of his public image shift from that of an arrogant, disgraced politician to that of a revered elder statesman.[30] Many media critics have charged that the press did not balance the scales and treated Nixon too reverently after the successful PR campaign.

In terms of its immediate impact on democracy, the information crush delivered by public relations is at its height during national election campaigns. In fact, PR's most significant impact may be on the political process, especially when organizations hire spin doctors to favorably shape or reshape a candidate's media image. During the 1996 presidential campaign, for instance, Republican candidate Bob Dole, drawing on advice from his PR handlers, decided to resign from the Senate to distance himself from his negative image as a dull but capable government bureaucrat. After Dole left Washington, his PR strategists were able to remind voters of his small-town roots and

program involving more than a hundred "in-country" managers who understood the language, culture, and values of their workforces. The company met with apparel workers' unions to get input and support; the trained managers then regularly monitored and audited their plants. The Levi Strauss media plan succeeded in positioning the company as a leader in global business practices, while "distinguishing itself from other companies as the 'bright spot' in otherwise negative sourcing stories."[2]

By 1993, all of Levi Strauss's worldwide contractors had been audited. About 70 percent met the anti-sweatshop standards set by company policy. About 25 percent of the contractors promised to make mandated improvements in the treatment of their workers. Five percent of the contractors were dropped for violating anti-sweatshop agreements. The company withdrew outsourcing from both Burma and China after human rights violations persisted. It also suspended its contract with Peruvian plants due to employee safety concerns. In 1993, *Fortune* magazine ranked Levi Strauss as "America's most admired apparel company," and *Business Ethics* magazine honored the jeans company with its Award for Excellence in Ethics.

A number of companies have used Levi's outsourcing policies as a model. In 1996, J. C. Penney declared that it would sever ties with any of its sixty-six hundred worldwide suppliers who were found to be operating sweatshops. While Nike launched a study of its overseas manufacturing facilities, Wal-Mart executives, still smarting from the Kathie Lee Gifford incident, started special training programs for buyers and contractors based on the Levi Strauss public relations model.

his contributions as a war hero during World War II, in which he was seriously injured. To put a counterspin on Dole's campaign strategy, the PR tacticians serving President Clinton's reelection effort sent out the word that Dole was "abandoning" his civic duties and extensive Washington experience at a time when the nation needed them most.

Though public relations often provides political information and story ideas during an election, the PR profession probably bears only part of the responsibility for manipulating the news media; after all, it is the job of an agency to spin the news favorably for its candidate. PR professionals should certainly police their own ranks (and usually do) for unethical or irresponsible practices, but the news media should also monitor the public relations industry, as they do other government and business activities. This media vigilance should be on behalf of citizens, who are entitled to robust debates on important social and political issues. When these debates are overwhelmed by public relations blitzes, journalism is discredited and citizens are poorly served.

In a democracy, journalism and public relations need to retain their guarded posture toward one another. But journalism itself may need to make changes that will make it less dependent on PR and more conscious of how its own practices play into

"In politics, image [has] replaced action."
—Randall Rothenberg, *Where the Suckers Moon*, 1994

the hands of spin strategies. Especially during local and national elections, journalists need to become more vigilant in monitoring questionable PR tactics. A positive example of change on this front is that many major newspapers and news networks now offer regular critiques of the facts and falsehoods contained in political advertising.

Like advertising and other forms of commercial speech, publicity campaigns that result in free media exposure raise a number of questions regarding democracy and the expression of ideas. Large PR agencies and product companies, like well-financed politicians, have money to invest to figure out how to obtain favorable publicity. The question is not how to prevent that but how to ensure that other voices, less well-financed and less commercial, receive an adequate hearing. To that end, journalists need to become less-willing conduits in the distribution of publicity. PR agencies, for their part, need to show clients that participating in democracy as responsible citizens can serve them well and enhance their images.

REVIEW QUESTIONS

1. What did people like P.T. Barnum and Buffalo Bill Cody contribute to the development of modern public relations in the twentieth century?

2. How did railroads and utility companies give the early forms of corporate public relations a bad name?

3. What contributions did Ivy Lee make toward the development of modern PR?

4. How did Edward Bernays affect public relations?

5. What is a pseudo-event? How does it relate to the manufacturing of news?

6. What are two approaches to organizing a PR firm?

7. What are press releases, and why are they important to reporters?

8. What is the difference between a VNR and a PSA?

9. What special events might a PR firm sponsor to build stronger ties to its community?

10. Why have research and lobbying become increasingly important to the practice of PR?

11. Explain the historical background of the antagonisms between journalism and public relations.

12. How did PR change old relationships between journalists and their sources?

13. In what ways is conventional news like public relations?

14. How does journalism as a profession contribute to its own manipulation at the hands of competent PR practitioners?

15. What are some socially responsible strategies that a PR specialist can use during a crisis to help a client manage bad publicity?

16. In what ways does the profession of public relations serve democracy? In what ways can it hamper democracy?

QUESTIONING THE MEDIA

1. What do you think of when you hear the term *public relations*? What images come to mind? Where did these impressions come from?

2. What could a college or university do to improve public relations with home owners on the edge of a campus who have to deal with noisy weekend student parties and a shortage of parking spaces?

3. What steps can reporters and editors take to monitor PR agents who manipulate the news media?

4. Can and should the often hostile relationship between the journalism and PR professions be mended? Why or why not?

5. Besides the Exxon *Valdez* and Tylenol cases cited in this chapter, investigate and research an international PR crisis (such as the Union Carbide disaster in India or the Perrier contamination story in France). How was the crisis handled?

Split the class into groups of three or four for a bit of investigative work to be done over a three- to four-week period. Each group should try to identify one or two press releases that were converted into a *substantial* news story by a local paper. In the newspaper, look for articles that highlight a particular organization or that profile a prominent business or government leader. The business section of most papers is a particularly good source for PR-influenced stories.

The goal is to get a copy of the original press release and compare it to the article that appears in the paper. Here are a couple of strategies your group might use:

- Call a local reporter (ideally the person who wrote the story), explain the assignment, and see if he or she will provide your group with the original release to compare against the news story.

- Call a public relations department at a local company, explain your assignment, and see if someone will provide your group with a copy of the original release.

- Call a local PR agency or the PR department at a local bank or business, explain your assignment, and ask to be put on the mailing list for some of the firm's news releases. Track the releases to see if any newspapers use them.

Another part of this assignment is to interview both a PR agent and a reporter about the use and success of news releases. Your group should devise a questionnaire for each professional. The questions listed here may be helpful.

To the reporter:
1. What determines whether a PR release will be used?

2. How does a reporter go about rewriting press releases? What information should be kept? Eliminated?

3. What is the importance of public relations to the journalism profession?

4. What is the newspaper's policy on rewriting press releases? Does the paper ever print releases verbatim? Why or why not?

To the PR agent:
1. What determines whether a PR release will be used? What are some writing tips for composing a good release?

2. Do newspapers ever print releases verbatim? Should they?

3. How important are newspapers to the PR profession?

Feel free to develop other questions. After the releases and news stories have been gathered and the subjects interviewed, your group should wrestle with the following questions:

- What significant changes, if any, were made between each public relations release and the corresponding news story? Why do you think these changes were made?

- Which version represented the best story—the press release or the news story? Why? (Keep in mind that each story has a different purpose and audience.)

Each group should report its findings to the entire class or prepare a written report that critiques the news and PR strategies discovered in this project.

Media Economics
and the Global Marketplace

ROLLING STONES
VOODOO LOUNGE

Featuring "Love Is Strong"

Produced by Don Was and The Glimmer Twins

A global-size rock-and-roll extravaganza is a fitting symbol of blending popular culture and economic virtuosity. Take the Rolling Stones' 1994-95 Voodoo Lounge tour (topping their successful Steel Wheels tour in the late 1980s). Each week's performance cost $1 million to mount, but the tour netted the Stones more than $100 million by its finale. Once a London School of Economics student, lead singer Mick Jagger told *60 Minutes* during the tour that economists now considered his group's traveling rock show a *virtual corporation*—touring for a brief lucrative run and then disappearing, virtually into thin air. These same economists consider Jagger the CEO of this mobile, global enterprise, which took in $250 million in ticket sales in twenty-five countries—the top musical tour in history.

The Voodoo Lounge tour illustrates at least two features of contemporary media economics. First, the rise of the Stones in the 1960s coincided with the first significant corporate media mergers. These mergers produced the now-familiar type of transnational media corporation—such as Sony, Time Warner, Bertelsmann, or News Corp.—that the Stones would later become on a mini-scale. Second, the Stones built their economic fortune by merging various kinds of popular music, especially Celtic folk music, blues, R&B, and early rock and roll. Along with the Beatles, the Stones capitalized globally on popular Americanized rock music in the same way that film barons internationalized American movies in the 1920s. By the 1990s, popular media products from the United States alone raked in a trade surplus of more than $10 billion, rivaling the food and aerospace industries as America's most successfully exported global products.

Ironically, the prestige of American culturalized software, especially movies and music, has risen in inverse proportion to the decline of the United States as a manufacturer of electronic hardware. In 1995, for instance, the LG (Lucky-Goldstar) group, a South Korean conglomerate, paid over $350 million to acquire Zenith, the last American-owned firm to make TV sets (though most of those were actually being produced in Mexico). A few U.S. manufacturers continue to make televisions and VCRs, but these firms are no longer American-owned. Globally, since the 1980s, electronic hardware firms such as Sony and Matsushita in Japan, Philips in the Netherlands, and Thomson in France have been acquiring American companies and prestigious historical brand names such as Zenith and RCA.

More significant, however, is the fact that these companies have been buying up American cultural software. Today American television, music, and films—among the world's most marketable products—bring in billions of dollars a year. To enter this market, Sony paid $2 billion for CBS Records in 1988 and $4.9 billion for Columbia Pictures in 1989. Australia's News Corp. paid $2.8 billion in 1988 for three American magazines, including *TV Guide*. Among the six largest recording companies, only Time Warner remained a U.S.-based firm by the mid-1990s.

The influence of American popular culture has created considerable debate in international circles. On the one hand, the notion of freedom that is associated with innovation and rebellion in American culture has been embraced internationally. The global spread of media software and electronic hardware has made it harder for political leaders to secretly repress dissident groups since so much police and state activity, such as the 1989 student uprising and massacre in China, can now be documented on video and dispatched by satellite around the world. On the other hand, American media are shaping the cultures and identities of other nations. American styles in fashion and food, as well as media fare, dominate the global market—what many critics have identified as *cultural imperialism*.

The rash of global media mergers over the last decade has made our world—at least in economic terms—very distinct from earlier generations. In this chapter, we will explore the issues and tensions that have contributed to current economic conditions. We will look at the rise of the Information Age, distinguished by its flexible, global, and specialized markets. We will discuss the breakdown of economic borders, focusing on media consolidation, corporate mergers, synergy, deregulation, and the emergence of an economic global village. We will also take up ethical and social issues in media economics, investigating the limits of antitrust laws, the concept of consumer control, and the threat of cultural imperialism. Finally, after examining the role of journalism in monitoring media economics, we will consider the impact of media consolidation on democracy and on the diversity of the marketplace.

analyzing the media economy

Given the sprawling scope of the mass media, the study of their economic conditions poses a number of complicated questions. For example, does the government need to play a stronger role in determining who owns what mass media and what kinds of media products should be manufactured? Should the government step back and let competition and market forces dictate what happens to mass media industries? Should citizen groups play a larger part in demanding that media organizations help maintain the quality of social and cultural life? Does the rapid spread of American culture smother or encourage the growth of democracy and local cultures? Does the increasing concentration of economic power in the hands of several international corporations restrict or expand the number of players and voices in media markets? Answers to such questions roam the economic spectrum. On the one hand, critics express concerns about the increasing power and reach of large media conglomerates. On the other hand, many free-market advocates maintain that as long as these structures ensure efficient operation and generous profits, they measure up as quality media organizations. In order to probe economic issues from different perspectives, we need to understand key economic concepts in two broad areas: media structure and media performance.[1]

> "Unlike American automobiles, television sets, and machine tools, **American cultural products**—movies, TV programs, videos, records, cassettes, and CDs—are sweeping the globe."
> —Richard J. Barnet
> and John Cavanagh,
> *Global Dreams*, 1994

the structure of
media organizations

In economic terms, three common organizational structures characterize the media business: monopoly, oligopoly, and limited competition. First, a **monopoly** occurs when a single firm dominates production and distribution in a particular industry, either nationally or locally. At the national level, for example, until the mid-1980s, AT&T ran a rare government-approved-and-regulated monopoly—the telephone business. On the local level, monopoly situations are more plentiful, occurring in any city with only one newspaper or one cable company. Until the 1996 Telecommunications Act, the government historically had encouraged owner diversity by prohibiting a newspaper from operating a broadcast or cable company in the same city. Many individual local media monopolies, though, have been purchased by large national and international firms. For instance, TCI and Time Warner—the nation's largest cable operators—own hundreds of small local cable monopolies. Likewise, in the newspaper business, chain operators like Gannett own more than a hundred daily and weekly papers, most of which constitute monopolies in their communities.

Second, an **oligopoly** describes an economic situation in which just a few firms dominate an industry. The commercial sound recording and feature film businesses are both oligopolies. Each has six major players who control the production and distribution of more than 90 percent of that industry. As of 1997, three multinational firms—Seagram of Canada, Sony of Japan, and Time Warner of the United States—were major players in *both* the movie and music oligopolies. Usually conducting business only in response to each other, such companies face little economic competition from small independent firms. Oligopolies often add new ideas and product lines by purchasing successful independents.

Third, **limited competition**, sometimes called *monopolistic competition*, characterizes a media market with many producers and sellers but only a few differentiable products within a particular category.[2] For instance, although the 1996 Telecommunications Act encouraged consolidation by lifting ownership restrictions on radio, hundreds of independently owned stations still operate in the United States. (CBS/Westinghouse, which recently bought Infinity Broadcasting, now owns more than eighty stations and dominates radio advertising nationwide.) Most of these commercial stations, however, feature a limited number of formats—such as country, classic rock, and contemporary hits—from which listeners may choose. Since commercial radio is now a difficult market to enter, requiring an FCC license and major capital investment, most station managers play the few formats that attract sizeable audiences. Under these circumstances, fans of blues or classical music may not be able to find the radio product that matches their interests. Given the high start-up costs of launching a commercial media business, diverse players and alternative products were becoming rarer in the late twentieth century.

the performance of media organizations

A second important area in media economics is analyzing the behavior and performance of media companies. Economists pay particular attention to the two ways the media collect revenues, through direct and indirect methods. **Direct payment** involves media products supported primarily by consumers, who pay directly for a book, a music CD, a movie, an online computer service, or a cable TV subscription. **Indirect payment** involves media products supported primarily by advertisers, who pay for the quantity or quality of audience members that a particular medium delivers. Over-the-air radio and TV broadcasting, daily newspapers, and consumer magazines rely on indirect payments for the majority of their revenue. Through direct payments, consumers communicate their preferences immediately. Through indirect payments of advertiser-supported media, "the client is the advertiser, not the viewer or listener or reader."[3] Advertisers, in turn, seek media that persuade customers with discretionary income to acquire new products. Many forms of mass media, of course, generate revenue both directly and indirectly, including newspapers, magazines, World Wide Web services, and cable systems, which charge subscription fees in addition to selling commercial time to advertisers (see Table 13.1).

In reviewing other behaviors of the media, economists look at many elements of the commercial process, including program or product costs, price setting, marketing strategies, and regulatory practices. For instance, marketers and media economists determine how high a local newspaper can raise its weekly price before enough disgruntled readers drop their subscriptions and offset the profits made from the price increase. Let's look at another example. In 1996, critics and government agencies began reviewing the artificially inflated price of CDs. They demonstrated that the **economies of scale** principle, which refers to the increasing production levels so as to reduce the overall cost per unit, should have driven down the price of a CD in the same way that videotape prices dropped in the 1980s. By 1997, however, CD prices remained inflated—determined largely by the oligopoly formed by the six major recording conglomerates.

In a final example, when citizen groups and the FCC determined in the 1980s that the TV networks were not meeting the needs of children, the government began placing regulatory limits on the minutes per hour of commercial time during Saturday morning programs. By 1996, the FCC had also mandated that local broadcast TV stations and networks carry three hours of children's educational programs each week. This regulation was unusual in that major media have a history of instituting self-regulatory measures (like ratings systems) to keep the government out of their business. In most cases, media companies try to respond to citizen pressure. Businesses, after all, want to maintain good public images that encourage sales and limit government regulation.

Economists, media critics, and consumer organizations over the years have asked the mass media to meet certain performance norms. Following are some of the key expectations of media organizations: introducing new technologies to the marketplace; making media products and services available to all economic classes; facilitating free expression and robust political discussion; acting as public watchdogs over wrongdoing; monitoring times of crisis; playing a positive role in education; and maintaining the

TABLE 13.1
Average Annual Consumer Spending on Selected Media

Year	Cable Television and Other Subscription Services	Recorded Music	Daily Newspapers	Consumer Books	Consumer Magazines	Home Video	Movies in Theaters	Consumer Online Internet-Access Services
1989	$77.86	$32.25	$45.71	$61.24	$31.49	$50.71	$24.67	$2.22
1990	87.90	36.64	47.55	63.90	33.14	56.35	24.40	2.93
1991	94.44	37.73	46.56	68.18	33.45	58.69	23.13	3.61
1992	101.28	43.05	48.54	71.37	34.26	63.23	23.24	4.39
1993	108.54	47.42	48.25	74.90	35.27	68.42	24.33	5.35
1994	110.00	56.35	49.28	79.22	36.36	72.97	25.20	7.44
1995	117.84	62.36	52.67	84.20	38.79	78.19	25.13	11.23
1996	128.65	65.07	55.78	88.89	40.53	81.47	24.83	16.34

Source: *Hoover's Guide to Media Companies* (Austin, TX: Hoover's Business Press, 1996), 8.

quality of culture.[4] Although media industries live up to some of these expectations better than others, economic analyses permit consumers to examine the instances when the mass media fall short. For example, when corporate executives at the networks trimmed TV news budgets in the early 1990s to make their businesses leaner, their decision jeopardized the networks' role as watchdog on the rest of society.

the transition to an information economy

A number of key economic changes have affected the media during the last half of the twentieth century. The 1950s, for instance, marked a transition period in which the machines that drove the modern Industrial Age shifted into the high gear of the Information Age. With offices displacing factories as major work sites, centralized mass production gave way to decentralized and often temporary service work. Indeed, by the early 1990s, the temporary-employment agency Manpower had surpassed General Motors as the largest U.S. private employer.

A major global change, which continues to unfold, accompanied this transformation. Bolstered by the passage of NAFTA (North American Free Trade Agreement) and GATT (General Agreement on Tariffs and Trade) in the 1990s, global cooperation fostered the breakdown of economic borders. Transnational media corporations executed business deals across international terrain. Global companies took over high-profile brand-name industries, particularly the electronic equipment once associated with the United States. In 1995, for example, Matsushita, the world's seventeenth largest company according to *Fortune* magazine, produced VCRs in the United States under the General Electric, Magnavox, Sylvania, and J. C. Penney labels.

The first half of the twentieth century emphasized mass production, the rise of manufacturing plants, and the intense rivalry of one country's products against another. The contemporary era, however, emphasizes information distribution and retrieval as well as transnational economic cooperation. The major shift to an information-based economy began in the 1950s as various mass media industries were able to market music, movies, television programs, and computer software on a global level. During this time, the emphasis on *mass* production shifted to the cultivation of specialized *niche* markets. In the 1960s, the first waves of national media consolidation began, escalating into the global media mergers of the 1980s and 1990s.

deregulation trumps regulation

During the rise of industry in the nineteenth century, entrepreneurs such as John D. Rockefeller in oil, Cornelius Vanderbilt in shipping and railroads, and Andrew Carnegie in steel created giant companies that monopolized their respective industries. In 1890, Congress passed the Sherman Antitrust Act, thus outlawing the monopoly practices and corporate trusts that often fixed prices to force competitors out of business. In 1911, the government used the Act to break up both the American Tobacco Company and Rockefeller's Standard Oil Company, which was divided into thirty smaller competing firms. In 1914, Congress passed the Clayton Antitrust Act, prohibiting manufacturers from selling only to dealers and contractors who agreed to reject the products of business rivals. The Celler-Kefauver Act of 1950 further strengthened antitrust rules by limiting any corporate mergers and joint ventures that reduced competition. These laws today are enforced by the Federal Trade Commission and the antitrust division of the Department of Justice.

New high-definition television (HDTV) sets in production in France's Thomson Consumer Electronics facility. New digital HDTV sets will be available from most manufacturers by late 1998 or early 1999.

In recent decades, government regulation has often been denounced as a barrier to the more flexible flow of capital. Although the Carter administration (1976–80) actually initiated deregulation, under Reagan (1980–88) most controls on business were drastically weakened. Sometimes the deregulation had severe consequences—such as the savings and loan industry scandal, which cost consumers billions of dollars—but many businesses flourished in this new pro-commerce climate. Deregulation also led to easier mergers, corporate diversification, and increased tendencies in some sectors (airlines, energy, communications, and financial services) toward oligopolies.[5]

In the broadcast industry, the Telecommunications Act of 1996 lifted most restrictions on how many radio and television stations one corporation could own. The Act further welcomed the seven powerful regional telephone companies, known as the Baby Bells, into the cable TV business. In addition, cable operators not only regained the right to raise cable rates with less government oversight but were also authorized to compete in the local telephone business (although high entry costs in 1996 and 1997 kept most cable companies out of the phone business). Economists thought the new competition would bring down consumer prices for a time but would also encourage more mergers and eventually a powerful oligopoly controlling *both* the telephone and cable industries.

> "Had anyone in 1975 predicted that the two oldest and most famous corporate producers and marketers of American recorded music [the RCA and CBS labels] would end up in the hands of German printers and publishers [Bertelsmann] and Japanese physicists and electronic engineers [Sony], the reaction in the industry would have been astonishment."
> —Barnet and Cavanagh, *Global Dreams*, 1994

Since the 1980s, a spirit of deregulation and special exemptions has guided communication legislation. For example, in 1995, despite complaints from NBC, Rupert Murdoch's Australian company News Corp. received a special dispensation from the FCC and Congress, allowing the firm to continue owning and operating the Fox network and a number of local TV stations. The Murdoch decision ran counter to the government decisions made in the early days of Marconi and RCA—right after World War I. At that time, the government feared outside owners and limited foreign investment in U.S. broadcast operations to 20 percent. However, in today's global business climate, special exemptions for foreign media owners have become acceptable.

Deregulation has also returned media economics to nineteenth-century principles that believe markets take care of themselves with little government interference. In this context, one of the ironies in broadcast history is that seventy years ago commercial radio broadcasters demanded government regulation to control technical interference and amateur competition. By the mid-1990s, however, the original impetus for regulation had reversed course. With new cable channels and Internet sites, broadcasting was no longer regarded as a scarce resource—once a major rationale for government funding of noncommercial and educational stations. Roughly ten thousand U.S. commercial AM and FM stations and twelve hundred commercial VHF and UHF television stations now operate in U.S. cities.

consolidation and mergermania

In spite of the strong antitrust laws of the twentieth century, these rules have been unevenly and curiously applied, especially in terms of the media. When International Telephone & Telegraph (ITT) tried to acquire ABC in the 1960s, loud protests and government investigations sunk the deal. But when General Electric purchased RCA/NBC in the 1980s, the FTC, FCC, and Justice Department found few problems. Other actions have been even more significant. When the government broke up AT&T's century-old monopoly in the mid-1980s—creating telephone competition—it also authorized a number of mass media mergers that consolidated power in the hands of a few large companies.

Although the original Big Three TV networks—ABC, CBS, and NBC—constituted a prime-time oligopoly from the 1950s into the 1980s, competition from cable and VCRs changed the economic terrain. Eventually, the government allowed GE to buy back RCA for its NBC network in 1985. Then, in 1996, the software giant Microsoft joined with NBC to create a CNN alternative, MSNBC: a twenty-four-hour interactive news channel available on both cable and the World Wide Web.

Among the world's biggest media deals, Disney in 1995 acquired ABC, which itself had been taken over by Capital Cities in the mid-1980s. Disney paid $19 billion. Shortly thereafter, Westinghouse, another global electronics firm, purchased the last remaining independent network, CBS, for $5.4 billion. To ensure its rank as the world's largest media conglomerate, Time Warner made an offer for Turner Broadcasting in 1995 for $7.5 billion. Although this merger was questioned by FTC officials, who raised concerns about the concentration of too much power over cable in too few hands, the deal went through in 1996.

Until the 1980s, antitrust rules historically had attempted to ensure diversity of ownership among competing businesses. Sometimes this happened, as in the breakup of AT&T, and sometimes it did not, as in the cases of local newspaper and cable monopolies. What has occurred consistently, though, is that media competition has been usurped by media consolidation. Today, the same anticompetitive spirit exists that once allowed a few utility and railroad companies to control their industries—in the days before antitrust laws.

"Big is bad if it **stifles competition** . . . but big is good if it produces quality programs." —Michael Eisner, CEO, Disney, 1995

"It's a small world, after all."
—theme song,
Disney theme parks

Most media companies have skirted monopoly charges by purchasing diverse types of mass media rather than trying to control just one medium. For example, Disney, rather than trying to dominate one area, provides programming to a TV network, to a cable channel, and to movie theaters. The company evades charges of monopoly by scattering products across many media outlets. In 1995, Disney CEO Michael Eisner defended the ABC takeover on a number of ABC News shows. According to Eisner, as long as large companies remain dedicated to quality—and as long as Disney did not try to buy the phone lines and TV cables running into homes—such mergers benefit America. But Eisner's position raises questions: If companies cannot make money on quality products, what happens? How should the government and citizens respond?

flexible markets

In addition to the trend toward consolidation, today's information culture is also characterized by flexibility. It emphasizes "the new, the fleeting . . . and the contingent in modern life, rather than the more solid values implanted" during Henry Ford's day, when relatively stable mass production drove mass consumption.[6] The new elastic economy features the expansion of the service sector (most notably in health care, banking, real estate, fast food, video rental, and computer software) and the search for products to serve individual consumer preferences. This type of economy relies on cheap labor, often exploiting poor workers in sweatshop conditions, and on quick high-volume sales to offset the costs of making so many niche products for specialized markets.

Given that 80 to 90 percent of most consumer and media products fail, a flexible economy demands fast product development and market research. Companies need to score a few hits to offset investments in their failed products. For instance, during the peak summer movie season, studios premier dozens of new feature films. A few are hits but many more miss, and studios hope to recoup their losses via video rentals. Similarly, the networks introduce scores of new programs in the fall and then quickly replace those that fail to attract high numbers or the "right" kinds of affluent viewers. At the same time, new music recordings are released daily on radio and in stores, while magazines vie for attention on supermarket shelves and through direct-mail solicitation. This flexible media system, of course, favors large companies with greater access to capital over small businesses that cannot so easily absorb the losses incurred from failed products.

In the 1970s, when VCRs made it possible for consumers to watch videos at home, Hollywood at first tried to hamper the new industry's development. Today, however, film studios earn far more money on video rentals than they do on theater receipts. In fact, a movie that fails at the box office can recoup its losses after the video is released.

global markets and specialization

Labor unions made strong gains on behalf of workers after World War II and through the 1950s. In response, manufacturers and other large industries began to look for ways to cut the rising cost of labor. With the shift to an information economy, many jobs, such as making CD players, TV sets, and VCRs, were exported to avoid the higher price of unionized labor. As large companies bought up small companies across national boundaries, commerce developed rapidly at the international level.

By the mid-1990s, as global firms sought greater profits, they looked to less economically developed countries that were short on jobs. But in many cases, global expansion by U.S. companies ran counter to America's early-twentieth-century vision. Henry Ford, for example, followed his wife's suggestion to lower prices so workers could afford Ford cars. (In fact, with assembly-line production, Ford managed to drop the price of the average Model T from $850 in 1908 to $260 by 1925.) In many countries today, however, most workers cannot afford the stereo equipment and TV sets they are making.

The new globalism has coincided with the rise of specialization. The magazine, radio, and cable industries sought specialized markets both in the United States and overseas, in part to counter television's mass appeal at the national level. By the 1980s, however, even television—confronted with the growing popularity of home video and cable—began niche marketing, targeting eighteen- to thirty-five-year-old viewers who controlled the bulk of consumer spending (see "Case Study: Consumer Ratings and TV Economics" on page 374). Younger and older audiences were increasingly abandoned by the networks but were sought by other media outlets and advertisers. Magazines such as *Seventeen* and *Modern Maturity* flourished. Cable channels such as Nickelodeon served the under-eighteen market, while Lifetime addressed the over-fifty viewer.

Beyond specialization and national mergers, though, what really distinguishes current media economics is the extension of synergy to international levels. In Henry Ford's day, national companies competed against one another, and national pride was at stake. "Made in Japan," for instance, went from being a label of inferiority in the 1950s to a mark of superiority in the 1980s, especially in the automobile and electronics industries. Major foreign electronics firms began purchasing American popular culture by the boatload—to guarantee content for their TV, VCR, and CD-ROM technologies.

The global extension of America's vast popular media output occurred for a couple of key reasons. First, media technologies became cheaper and more portable, allowing proliferation both inside and outside national boundaries. Audiocassettes and CDs became compact enough to fit in a Sony Walkman, transportable to every room in the house and beyond. Thus, even when U.S. radio stations were not heard outside national borders, American music went everywhere. Furthermore, the transmission of visual images via satellite made North American and European TV available at the global level. Cable services such as CNN and MTV quickly took their national acts to the international stage, and by the mid-1990s, CNN and MTV were available in more than 150 countries.

Second, as we have noted, VCR, CD, and TV manufacturers lowered costs by moving plants outside the country. In addition, global manufacturing permitted companies that lost money on products at home to profit in the international market. About 80 percent of American movies, for instance, do not earn back their costs in the United States and depend on foreign circulation to recoup their early losses.

In the global television market, consider these examples of programs that were not particularly successful in the United States but became hits internationally. When MGM/United Artists produced *Fame*, a TV drama about talented students from a New York performing-arts high school, NBC canceled it after one year. However, the program continued to be produced for national and international syndication from 1983 through 1987. In fact, at one point in the mid-1980s, *Fame* was the most popular program in Great Britain. More amazing is the phenomenon of *Baywatch*, which went into first-run syndication in 1991, also after being canceled by NBC. The program's producers claimed that by the mid-1990s, *Baywatch*, about the adventures of underdressed lifeguards who make the beaches of Los Angeles safer for everyone, was

Consumer Ratings
and TV Economics

Whether TV shows live or die today depends on whether advertisers are satisfied that enough young, affluent viewers are watching particular programs. Indeed, television has been defined as an industry in which networks, producers, and distributors target and "sell" viewers in guaranteed blocks to advertisers.

The major organization tracking prime-time TV viewers has been the A. C. Nielsen Market Research Company. Nielsen provides overnight estimates in thirty-five major TV markets on the programs that viewers watched the night before. Each month, broadcast stations across the nation pay thousands of dollars for such ratings data, which ultimately determine the fate of most television programs.

Nielsen surveys national audiences through written weekly diaries kept by viewers, through phone surveys, and through computerized boxes called *people meters*, which are hooked up to four thousand households in the country. Measurements are most important during *sweeps:* month-long measurement periods conducted four times a year (six times in larger markets). During sweeps, both local and national ad rates are determined. Although the connections between ratings and ad rates may seem straightforward, the relationship is complicated. During sweeps, the networks pack their schedules with new programs, special events, and Hollywood movies, which is a distortion of their regular listings.

Many viewers question the power of ratings. After all, how can 4,000 Nielsen families represent the tastes and desires of 260 million Americans? In theory, however, statistical samples are fairly accurate estimates. To use a medical analogy, a doctor does not have to draw all the blood from someone's body to get a fix on that person's health.

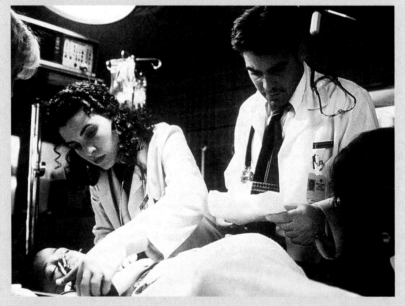

Similarly, to get a representative idea of TV viewing, statisticians do not have to ask *everyone* what they have been watching.

Theoretically, a perfect representative random sample gives each TV household an equal chance to be chosen. In reality, this rarely occurs. In broadcast ratings, researchers have trouble getting adequate representation from people with lower incomes and less formal education, from homes in rural areas and central cities, and from non-English-speaking communities. As a result, ratings services offer small cash bonuses to entice viewers to complete diaries. When this fails, statisticians have to juggle the numbers through *weighting*: assigning more weight to a particular respondent in an attempt to correct the underrepresented group in the original sample.

Ratings suffer from other problems as well. Prior to the installation of people meters in 1987, Nielsen's original rating method could not determine if people were actually sitting in front of their TV sets. In fact, research in the 1980s suggested that about 13 percent of the time, the TV set was on but no one was watching. In addition, written weekly diaries are not always filled out or are filled out inaccurately. A *halo effect* occurs when diary keepers write down not what they actually watched but what they think they *should have watched*.

The people meter, instituted in 1987, has its own limitations. One problem with the early models was *button fatigue*. All household members and guests were assigned a number and asked to log on or off the people meter whenever they watched TV, but weary viewers sometimes stopped punching in.

When people meters were first instituted, early data suggested a dramatic drop in network prime-time viewership. This meant losses in ad revenue to networks. After the 1988 season, the networks had to return $200 million in ad money to make up for the apparent audience decline. Upset network executives authorized an independent study, which severely criticized Nielsen. The study found that the initial rate of cooperation for the Nielsen families selected for people-meter hookup was under 50 percent.

The study led to experiments with a passive people meter. With this system, computerized surveillance equipment "sensed" who was watching TV. The sensors, however, sometimes mistook wind blown curtains and family pets for people watching television.

Ratings are used as guidelines for advertisers in negotiating prices with local stations and networks. The cost of advertising to sponsors has soared dramatically in recent years. In the mid-1960s, a thirty-second spot on national television during a highly rated series cost between $20,000 and $25,000. By 1997, a thirty-second spot during the Super Bowl cost well over $1 million. In regular prime-time television, a thirty-second spot was much less expensive, ranging from $75,000 to $85,000 for a new or low-rated program to $500,000 to $600,000 for NBC's top-rated *ER* in 1997. In addition, clients often paid between $300,000 and $400,000 to film a sixty-second spot for national television.

Many TV and ad executives argue that the ratings system, though admittedly imperfect, is nevertheless a democratic measure that represents "the people" who "vote" for their favorite television shows. Yet it is clear that the votes of some segments of the population count much more than the votes of others. In fact, some programs, like Fox's *Beverly*

Nielsen TV Ratings, May 14, 1997

Top 20

1.	**ER** (NBC)	23.6		* **60 Minutes** (CBS)	
2.	**Seinfeld** (NBC)	20.9	15.	**NYPD Blue** (ABC)	11.5
3.	*Mario Puzo's The Last Don,* Pt. 1 (CBS)	17.8	16.	**Primetime Live** (ABC)	11.0
4.	**Fired Up** (NBC)	15.6	17.	**Spin City** (ABC)	10.9
	* **Friends** (NBC)		18.	*Robin Cook's Invasion,* Pt. 2 (NBC)	10.8
6.	**Suddenly Susan** (NBC)	14.8	19.	*Tidal Wave: No Escape* (ABC)	10.7
7.	**Touched by an Angel** (CBS)	13.8	20.	**Frasier** (NBC)	10.5
8.	**20/20** (ABC)	13.7			
9.	**Home Improvement** (ABC)	13.0			

Evening News

For the week:

NBC 7.5
ABC 7.3
CBS 6.6

10.	**Ellen** (ABC)	12.7
11.	**Walker, Texas Ranger** (CBS)	12.0
12.	**The X-Files** (Fox)	11.8
13.	**The Drew Carey Show** (ABC)	11.6

Last Week:

ABC 7.7
NBC 7.6
CBS 6.7

Using This Chart

➤ A ratings point represents 921,000 TV households; shares are the percentage of sets in use; number of viewers is in millions.

➤ (*) indicates a Nielsen ratings tie.

Ratings Information from the A. C. Nielsen Co.

One ratings point represents approximately 1% of U. S. homes with television sets.

Chart courtesy of *USA Today.*

Hills 90210 and *Melrose Place*, are seldom rated among the top 30 shows. They stay on the air because they attract the "right" viewers: affluent eighteen- to thirty-five-year-olds. In May 1994, for instance, NBC ran *Lois & Clark* on Sunday evening opposite CBS's *Murder, She Wrote*. *Murder*, which ranked No. 16 that month, had an audience that was nearly twice as large as *Lois & Clark*, which ranked No. 94, near the bottom for all prime-time shows. Yet NBC was able to charge sponsors over $130,000 for a thirty-second commercial, while *Murder, She Wrote* commanded just over $115,000.

Lois & Clark reached more viewers between the ages of eighteen and thirty-five; *Murder, She Wrote* drew viewers whose median age was well over fifty. Although people over fifty are usually more affluent than younger viewers, research suggests they are harder to influence in their buying habits—and quicker to mute the remote control during commercials.

In 1994, CBS actually lost a number of affiliates to Fox partly because Fox's prime-time schedule was more appealing to younger, urban viewers. Two decades earlier, this same reasoning led to the "great rural series purge," a group of popular programs tossed off the air by CBS in the early 1970s, including *Hee Haw* (ranked No. 16 in 1970–71), the *Red Skelton Show* (No. 7 in 1969–70), and *Green Acres* (No. 19 in 1968–69).

Since that time, the ratings system has further refined the numbers and defined consumers to the point where popular shows with the "wrong" viewers (too young or too old) are canceled and less popular shows with the "right" numbers are renewed.

the most-watched program in the world, with over a billion viewers. The dialogue in the series, like that of action movies, was limited and fairly simple, so it was not a very expensive program to translate into other languages.

disney: a postmodern media conglomerate

To understand the story of media economics in the twentieth century, we need only examine the transformation of Disney from a struggling cartoon producer to one of the world's largest media conglomerates (see Table 13.2). Walt Disney's first cartoon company, Laugh-O-Gram, went bankrupt in 1922 when he was twenty-one years old. But when Disney moved to Hollywood, he found his niche. After inventing and starring Mickey Mouse (originally named Mortimer) in the first sound cartoons in the late twenties, Disney developed the first feature-length cartoon, *Snow White*, completed in 1937.

The first economic period for Disney—roughly from the late 1920s to the late 1940s—set the standard for popular cartoons and children's culture for much of the twentieth century. The *Silly Symphonies* series (1929–39), which featured classic cartoon shorts like "The Three Little Pigs," established the studio's reputation for quality cartoons. The series ran before feature movies throughout the Great Depression, providing escape, humor, and morality tales. Although the Disney company remained a minor studio during this period, *Fantasia* and *Pinnochio*—the two top-grossing films of 1940—each made more than $40 million. Nonetheless, the studio barely broke even because cartoon projects took time and commanded the company's entire attention. *Snow White*, for example, took four years to complete.

The second Disney period, encompassing the 1950s and early 1960s, was marked by corporate diversification. With the demise of the cartoon film short, Disney expanded into other areas. In 1949, for example, the studio made its first nature documentary short, *Seal Island*, and in 1953 its first feature documentary, *The Living Desert*. In 1950, Disney also produced its first live-action feature, *Treasure Island*.

Disney was also among the first film studios to embrace television. In 1954, the company launched a long-running prime-time show, an even more popular venue than theatres for displaying its products. Then, in 1955, Disneyland opened. Eventually, the theme parks would produce the bulk of the studio's revenues (Walt Disney World in Orlando began in 1971).

In 1953, Disney had also started Buena Vista, its own distribution company. This was the first step in making the studio into a major player. In addition, the company began fully exploiting the box-office power of its early cartoon features. *Snow White*, for example, was successfully rereleased in theaters to many new generations of children before finally going to videocassette. Throughout the 1960s, successes came with *101 Dalmatians* (1961), *Mary Poppins* (1964), and *The Jungle Book* (1967). *Swiss Family Robinson*, a live-action adventure, even beat out Alfred Hitchcock's *Psycho* as the No. 1 box-office hit in 1960.

Disney's death in 1966 triggered a period of decline for the studio. But in 1984 a new management team, led by Michael Eisner, initiated the third Disney era. Eisner inherited Disney's newly created Touchstone division, and *Splash* (1984), starring Tom Hanks, became the first of many hits. However, it was *Who Framed Roger Rabbit?* (1988) that reinvented the live-action cartoon for adults as well as children. A string of animated hits followed, including *The Little Mermaid* (1989), *Beauty and the Beast* (1991), *The Lion King* (1994), and *The Hunchback of Notre Dame* (1996). Along with opening a chain of merchandise mall outlets, the studio began releasing its classic cartoons on video. Disney movies have dominated videocassette sales since 1988.

Although some critics regard synergy as a monopolistic practice, Disney epitomizes the synergistic possibilities of media consolidation. By 1997, Disney could pro-

TABLE 13.2
The World's Fifteen Largest Media Companies

Rank	Company	Headquarters	1995 Revenue ($ mil.)
1	Time Warner Inc.	New York, NY	17,696
2	Bertelsmann AG	Gütersloh, Germany	14,761
3	The Walt Disney Company	Burbank, CA	12,112
4	Viacom Inc.	New York, NY	11,689
5	Havas S.A.	Neuilly-sur-Seine, France	9,118
6	Sony Corporation	Tokyo, Japan	*8,726
7	The News Corporation Limited	Sydney, Australia	8,641
8	THORN EMI plc	London, UK	7,306
9	The Thomson Corporation	Toronto, Canada	7,225
10	R. R. Donnelley & Sons Company	Chicago, IL	6,512
11	Lagardère Groupe	Paris, France	*5,800
12	MCA Inc.	Universal City, CA	5,772
13	Reed Elsevier plc	London, UK	5,646
14	PolyGram N.V.	Baarn, The Netherlands	5,499
15	Aegis Group plc	London, UK	5,262

*Note: Media revenue only

Source: Hoover's Guide to Media Companies (Austin, TX: Hoover's Business Press, 1996), 24.

duce an animated feature for both theatrical release and home-video distribution. With its ABC network, it could spin off a cartoon version of the movie and place it on ABC's Saturday morning schedule. A book version could be released through Disney's publishing arm, Hyperion, and "the-making-of" versions could appear—on cable's Disney Channel as well as in *Disney Adventures*, the company's popular children's magazine. Characters from the movie eventually could become attractions at Disney's theme parks or incentives for buying a Happy Meal at McDonald's. With the 1996 release of the live-action remake of *101 Dalmatians*, Disney licensed or sanctioned seventeen thousand different products, including clothing, candy, dinnerware, shoes, CD-ROM games, dolls, rugs, stuffed toys, and lamp shades.

Along with the international appeal of its cartoon features, in 1983 Disney extended its global reach by opening a successful theme park in Japan. In 1992, the studio also signed a ten-year deal with Russian television, which began showing six hours of Disney programming each week. In exchange, Disney received exclusive rights to sell ads during those programs. In 1986, the company started marketing cartoons to Chinese television, attracting an estimated three hundred million viewers per week. This stopped in 1990 because of the rampant counterfeiting of popular Disney-trademark products, but the studio resumed the deal in 1992 with plans for a Disney magazine in Chinese and the opening of several Disney merchandise boutiques.

George Lucas's *Star Wars* trilogy has grossed more than $4 billion by licensing toys and other merchandise to manufacturers who use the movies' labels and images. In 1996, Disney licensed some seventeen thousand products to supplement the release of the live-action version of *101 Dalmatians*. By the mid-1990s, licensed products accounted for more than 20 percent of Disney's annual operating income.

In the early 1990s, EuroDisney opened outside Paris. The French, though, did not eagerly embrace the theme park. It lost millions each month, well into the mid-1990s, before finally making money. Many Europeans continued to criticize the company for pushing out and vulgarizing classical culture. On the home front, a proposed historical park in Virginia, Disney's America, suffered defeat at the hands of citizens, historians, and politicians who raised concerns about Disney sanitizing, misinterpreting, or vulgarizing American history. Meanwhile, in 1995, shortly after the company purchased ABC, Disney suffered criticism for running a flattering company profile one evening on ABC's evening news program.

Despite criticism, little has slowed Disney's expansion. Indeed, in 1997, Orbit—a Saudi-owned satellite relay station based in Rome—introduced Disney's twenty-four-hour premium cable channel to twenty-three countries in the Middle East and North Africa. In the book *Global Dreams*, the authors set forth a formula for becoming a "great media conglomerate," a formula Disney exemplifies: "Companies able to use visuals to sell sound, movies to sell books, or software to sell hardware would become the winners in the new global commercial order."[7]

social issues in media economics

In recent years, we have witnessed billion-dollar takeovers and mergers between Time Inc. and Warner Communication, Viacom and Paramount, Disney and ABC, Westinghouse and CBS, and Time Warner and Turner. This mergermania accompanied stripped-down regulation, which has virtually suspended most ownership limits on media industries. As a result, a number of consumer advocates and citizen groups have raised questions about deregulation and ownership consolidation.

One long-time critic of media economics, Ben Bagdikian, questions ownership structure in his book, *The Media Monopoly*. Bagdikian worries that although there are abundant products in the market—"1,700 daily papers, more than 8,000 weeklies, 10,000 radio and television stations, 11,000 magazines, 2,500 book publishers"—only a limited number of companies are in charge of those products.[8] Bagdikian and others fear that this represents a dangerous antidemocratic tendency in which economic power is commanded by a handful of media moguls.

the limits of antitrust laws

The current consolidation of media owners has limited the number of independent voices being heard. Although meant to ensure multiple voices, American antitrust laws have been easily subverted since the 1980s. As we have noted, most media companies diversify among different product lines, never completely dominating a particular media industry. Time Warner, for example, spreads its holdings among television programming, cable, film, music, and publishing.

Such diversification strategies, of course, encourage oligopolies in which a few behemoth companies control media production and distribution. This kind of economic arrangement makes it difficult for many products—especially those offered outside an oligopoly—to compete in the marketplace. For instance, in broadcast programming, the few networks that control prime time offer several competing programs at any given time. These programs are selected from known production companies that the networks either contract with on a regular basis or own outright. Thus, even with a very good program or series idea, an independent production company, especially outside Los Angeles or New York, has a very difficult time entering the national TV market.

Since antitrust laws aim to curb national monopolies, most media monopolies today operate locally. For instance, although Gannett owns ninety or so daily newspapers, it controls less than 10 percent of daily U.S. newspaper circulation. Nonetheless, most Gannett papers are monopolies: the only papers in their various towns. Virtually every cable company has been granted monopoly status in its local community; these firms alone decide what channels are made available and what rates are charged. Furthermore, antitrust laws have no teeth globally. Although in late 1996 representatives from 160 countries met to discuss enforcing international copyright laws to protect the work of musicians and writers, no international antitrust rules exist to prohibit transnational companies from buying up as many media companies as they can afford.

" . . . This merger of Time and Warner has gone too far!"

consumer choice vs. consumer control

During the wave of mergers in the 1980s and 1990s, a number of consumer critics pointed to the lack of public debate surrounding the tightening oligopoly structure of international media. This lack of public involvement dates from the 1920s and 1930s. In that era, commercial radio executives succeeded in portraying themselves as operating in the public interest, while labeling their noncommercial counterparts as mere voices of propaganda. In these early debates, the political ideas of democracy became closely allied with the economic structures of capitalism. As one media historian has noted of this period, "by implicitly defining 'democracy' in terms of equal access to consumer products," political and business leaders created the appearance of running a fair society in which everyone has equal access to products and services.[9]

Through the Cold War period in the 1950s and 1960s, it became increasingly difficult to even criticize capitalism, which had become a synonym for democracy in many circles. In this context, any criticism of capitalism became a criticism of the free marketplace. This, in turn, appeared to be a criticism of free speech, since the business community often sees its right to operate in a free marketplace as an extension of its right to commercial speech. As long-time CBS chief William Paley told a group of educators in 1937, "He who attacks the fundamentals of the American system" of commercial broadcasting "attacks democracy itself."[10] One broadcast historian, discussing the rise of commercial radio in the 1930s, has noted that leaders like Paley "equated capitalism with the free and equal marketplace, the free and equal marketplace with democracy, and democracy with 'Americanism.'"[11] The demise of the Soviet Union's communist economy in the early 1990s is often portrayed as a triumph for democracy. It was more accurately a victory for capitalism and free-market economies.

As many economists point out, capitalism is arranged vertically, with powerful corporate leaders at the top and hourly-wage workers at the bottom. But democracy, in principle, represents a more horizontal model in which each individual has an opportunity to have his or her voice heard and vote counted. In discussing free markets, economists also distinguish between *consumer control* over marketplace goods and freedom of *consumer choice*: "The former requires that consumers participate in deciding what is to be offered; the latter is satisfied if [consumers are] free to select among the options chosen for them by producers."[12] Most Americans and the citizens of other developed nations clearly have options among a range of media products. Yet consumers and even employees have limited power in deciding what kinds of media get created and circulated.

379

cultural imperialism

When Disney bought ABC in 1995, Yale literary scholar Harold Bloom called the deal a cultural "disaster" and told one newspaper, "At the end of this road lies cultural homogenization of the most ghastly kind." Bloom was not alone in his criticisms. Today numerous international observers contend that the idea of consumer control or input is even more remote in countries inundated by American fashion, food, movies, music, and television. Even mainstream U.S. newspapers report with skepticism on the 470,000 Brazilian Avon "beauty consultants," many of whom travel the backwaters of the Amazon jungle selling American cosmetics to women who can barely afford shoes.

Although many indigenous forms of media culture—such as Brazil's *telenovela* (a TV soap opera) and Ireland's Riverdance—are extremely popular, U.S. leadership in producing and distributing mass media puts a severe burden on countries attempting to produce their own cultural products. For example, American TV producers generally recoup the costs of production in national syndication by the time their TV shows are exported. This allows American distributors to offer these programs to other countries at bargain rates, thus undercutting local production companies trying to create original programs in their own languages. In Poland, for instance, the national TV station began producing a soap opera set in 1990 Warsaw. Although the program was extremely popular, it was still cheaper for station managers to buy *Dynasty* and *Santa Barbara* reruns from the United States than to develop more new series of their own. In the mid-1990s, Polish TV was paying a mere $500 to $700 for airing one half hour of U.S. programming.

> "The perfect world of **Disney** has replaced the biblical **Garden of Eden** as the American vision of paradise."
>
> —Judith Adams,
> *The American
> Amusement
> Park Industry, 1991*

Defenders of American popular culture argue that because some of our culture challenges authority, national boundaries, and outmoded traditions, this creates an arena in which citizens can raise questions. Supporters also argue that a universal popular culture creates a global village and fosters communication across national boundaries. Critics believe, however, that although American popular culture often contains protests against social wrongs, such protests "can be turned into consumer products and lose their bite. Protest itself becomes something to sell."[13] The harshest critics have labeled American culture in the international arena a form of *cultural imperialism*, which both hampers the development of native cultures and negatively influences teenagers, who abandon their own rituals to adopt the tastes of their American counterparts. The exportation of U.S. entertainment media is sometimes viewed as "cultural dumping" because it discourages the development of original local products.

The opening up of markets in Asia, Africa, and Eastern Europe, particularly after the failure of various totalitarian regimes in the 1980s, spurred the growth of global popular culture. At the same time, an economic form of piracy developed worldwide with the unlicensed pilfering and duplicating of cassettes, CDs, videos, and movies. According to one estimate, by 1990 85 percent of the thirty thousand video stores in South Korea alone stocked bootlegged tapes. Although heavy fines and jail sentences are on the books to stop pirating, many governments have been reluctant to act against their own bootleggers, especially since pirating remains a source of jobs. In certain situations, U.S.-based companies have withdrawn distribution deals to put pressure on governments to end pirating and enforce copyright laws.

Perhaps the greatest concern regarding a global economic village is elevating expectations among people whose standards of living are not routinely portrayed in contemporary media. In the mid-1990s, about two-thirds of the world's population could not afford most of the products advertised on American, Japanese, and European television. Yet more and more of the world's populations were able to glimpse consumer abundance and middle-class values through satellite technology and magazine distribution. Media managers as early as the 1950s feared political fallout—"the revolution of rising expectations"—in that ads and products would raise the hopes of poor people but not keep pace with their actual living conditions.[14] Furthermore, the conspicuousness of consumer culture makes it difficult for many of us to even imagine other ways of living that are not heavily dependent on the mass media and brand-name products.

the media marketplace and democracy

We have been and will continue to be involved in major global transformations of economies, cultures, and societies. The best way to monitor the impact of transnational economies is through vigorous news attention and lively public discussions on fundamental issues. Clearly, however, this process is hampered. In the 1990s, for example, news organizations, concerned about the bottom line, cut back the number of reporters assigned to cover international developments. This occurred just as global news became critical to an informed citizenry. We live in a society in which consumer concerns and profit aspirations, rather than broader citizen issues, increasingly dominate the media agenda. In response, critics have posed some key questions. As consumers, do we care who owns the media so long as most of us continue to have a broad selection of products? Do we care who owns the media so long as multiple voices *appear* to exist in the market?

Merged and multinational media corporations will continue to control more aspects of production and distribution. Of pressing concern is the impact of mergers on news operations, particularly the influences of General Electric, Westinghouse, Disney, Time Warner, and News Corp. on their news subsidiaries—NBC, CBS, ABC, CNN, and Fox, respectively. These companies have the capacity to use major news resources not only to promote their products but to determine the kinds of national coverage that many issues will receive in the future.

In Cairo, a group of Egyptian men watch a rerun of the CBS program *Falcon Crest* (1981–90). Research suggests that many international viewers enjoy programs portraying decadence and shallowness in American life.

In spite of (and perhaps because of) the growth in channels of communication, it has become increasingly difficult to sustain a public debate on economic and ownership issues. The promises of multichannel cable systems and the information highway, which would potentially give voices to the voiceless, may be in jeopardy because these systems are being bought at a rapid pace by large conglomerates. Whether these companies will open up their systems to alternative points of view and to people who cannot afford access is still to be determined.

One promising spot in the current economic atmosphere concerns the role of independent and alternative producers, artists, writers, and publishers. Despite the movement toward economic consolidation, there remains in the media a diversity of opinions and ideas. In fact, when independent views become even marginally popular, they are often pursued by large media companies who seek to make them subsidiaries or capitalize on their innovations. Alternative voices in the mass media often tap into social concerns that are not normally discussed in corporate boardrooms. In fact, business needs independent ideas in order to generate new product lines. A number of transnational corporations encourage the development of local artists—talented individuals who might have the capacity to transcend the regional or national level and become the next global phenomenon.

One key paradox of the Information Age is that for economic discussions to be meaningful and democratic, they must be carried out in the popular media as well as in educational settings. Yet public debates about the structure and ownership of the media are often not in the best economic interests of media owners. Nonetheless, in some places, local groups and consumer movements are addressing media issues that affect individual and community life. Such movements may be united by geographic ties, by common ethnic background, or by shared concerns about technology. The Internet has made it possible for such groups to form globally, united around issues such as contesting censorship or monitoring the activities of large multinational corporations.

Another hopeful sign is similar to what took place around radio in the early 1930s. Given the collapse of so many anticapitalist totalitarian states, no "natural" economic enemy now exists to challenge American, Japanese, and European capitalism. However, because capitalism and democracy became fused in political discussions in the twentieth century, sometimes our economic systems were left unexamined. Perhaps we are ready to question some of our hierarchical and undemocratic arrangements. Even in the face of so many media mergers, the public arena seems open today to such examinations, which might improve the global economy and also serve the public good. By understanding media economics, critics and students can make a contribution to critiquing media organizations and evaluating their impact on democracy.

REVIEW QUESTIONS

1. How are the three basic structures of mass media organizations—monopoly, oligopoly, and limited competition—different from one another?

2. What are the differences between direct and indirect payments for media products?

3. What are some of society's key expectations about its media organizations?

4. Why has the federal government emphasized deregulation at a time when so many media companies are growing so large?

5. How have media mergers changed the economics of mass media?

6. How do global and specialized markets factor into the new media economy?

7. Using Disney as an example, what is the role of synergy in the current climate of media mergers?

8. What are the differences between freedom of consumer choice and consumer control?

9. What is cultural imperialism, and what does it have to do with the United States?

10. What do critics and activists fear most about the concentration of media ownership? How do media managers and executives respond to these fears?

11. What are some promising signs regarding the relationship between media economics and democracy?

QUESTIONING THE MEDIA

1. Are you exposed to popular culture from other countries? Why or why not? Give some examples.

2. Do you read international news? Why or why not?

3. What steps can reporters and editors take to cover media ownership issues better?

4. How does the concentration of media ownership limit the number of voices in the marketplace? Do we need rules limiting media ownership?

5. Is there such a thing as a global village? What does this concept mean to you?

Split the class into three groups and stage a mock public forum on the issue of media mergers. Specifically, groups should examine whether it would be beneficial for a media corporation (for example, Sony, Seagram, Viacom, or Bertelsmann) to buy a television network. Students may volunteer for one of the following groups:

- *Group 1*: the pro-business team that supports the globalization of media and mergers as healthy steps for the American and world economy

- *Group 2*: the pro-consumer or citizens' activist group that worries about the increasing concentration of media ownership

- *Group 3*: journalists who cover the forum and ask key questions

The class should check *Hoover's Handbook* for a list of what the takeover company already owns. Then each group should meet and prepare for the forum. Groups 1 and 2 should appoint two or three spokespersons as "specialists" on various issues. Groups 1 and 2 should also anticipate the questions that reporters might ask and prepare answers. Group 3 should brainstorm and devise a list of questions to be asked.

After the groups plan their strategies, the class should reconvene. Groups 1 and 2 should then briefly state their positions before opening the forum up to questions from reporters.

After the forum and toward the end of class, *each group* should gather and write the first *two* sentences of a news story that reports on the forum. The news reports should highlight the key moments or findings of the forum. The groups should then share their abbreviated news stories, tell why they chose their particular story openings, and comment on each other's story. How do the stories of Groups 1 and 2 differ from those of Group 3? What is the agenda of each group? Can compromises be achieved that satisfy both business and democracy?

The Culture of Journalism
Values, Ethics, and Democracy

In 1994, someone fired bullets into the Dublin home of an Irish investigative reporter as she put her five-year-old son to bed. In 1995, a man forced his way into the reporter's home, held a gun to her head, lowered his aim, and shot her in the thigh. For Veronica Guerin, journalism had become a dangerous business.

Guerin was the first reporter to cover Ireland's escalating organized crime and drug problem. She worked for Dublin's *Sunday Independent*. A few days after the 1995 assault, she wrote about the incident, vowing to continue her reporting despite her fears about safety. Later that year, she was punched in the face by the suspected head of Ireland's gang scene. He threatened to hurt Guerin's son and kill her if she wrote about him. She kept writing. In December 1995, she flew to New York to receive the International Press Freedom Award from the Committee to Protect Journalists.

When she returned to Dublin, she continued her investigations, which went into more and more depth. She began naming names of gang members suspected of masterminding drug-related crimes and a string of eleven unsolved contract murders. Then, in June 1996, waiting in her car at a suburban Dublin intersection, she was shot five times by two hired killers on a motorcycle. Veronica Guerin had become contract murder victim number twelve. Ireland mourned Guerin's death for three days. After her funeral, which was held at the church where she had gone to Mass each Sunday, the government invoked her name and passed a series of laws. The legislation allowed judges to deny bail to dangerous suspects and created a special bureau to confiscate money and property from suspected drug criminals and gang members.

In an *Independent* article after a 1995 incident, Guerin had discussed the danger she faced: "I have already said, and I will continue to say it again now, that I have no intention of stopping my work. I shall continue as an investigative reporter, the job I believe I do best. My employers have offered alternatives—any area I wish to write about seems to be open to me—but somehow I cannot see myself reporting from the fashion catwalks or preparing a gardening column."[1]

In contrast to modern American journalism, there is something unusual about the openness and directness of Guerin's writing. After all, U.S. journalism for much of the twentieth century has operated on the premise that reporters should be detached from the turmoil they report about. Guerin, however, became centrally involved in Ireland's crime and drug world. Her tough reports and tragic death connected her to her readers. Her powerful first-person stories were far different from the neutral third-person accounts that dominate most American news coverage.

> "A journalist is the lookout on the bridge of the **ship of state**. He peers through the **fog and storm** to give warnings of dangers ahead. . . . He is there to watch over the safety and the welfare of the people who trust him."
>
> —Joseph Pulitzer, 1904

With the gradual decline in news audiences and growing criticism of an elite corp of east coast journalists, the news media are searching for ways to reconnect with consumers and citizens. In this chapter, we will examine the changing definition of news. We will look at the implicit values underlying news practice and the ethical dilemmas confronting journalists. Next, we will study the legacy of print-news conventions and rituals. We will then turn to the impact of television and images on news. Finally, we will take up recent controversial developments in journalism and democracy, specifically examining the rise and role of public journalism.

modern journalism in the information age

In modern America, the reporter's main job has been to provide information to enable citizens to make intelligent decisions. Today this guiding principle has been derailed. First, in a world engulfed in media outlets and computer highways, we may be producing too much information. According to social critic Neil Postman, as a result of developments in media technology by the mid-1990s, society had developed an "information glut," transforming news and information into "a form of garbage."[2] Postman believes that scientists, technicians, managers, and journalists have merely piled up mountains of new data, which add to the problems of everyday life. As a result, too much unchecked data and too little thoughtful debate radiate from too many channels of communication.

A second and related problem suggests that the wealth of information the media now provide has made little impact on improving public and political life. In fact, many people feel cut off from our major institutions, including journalism. Many citizens, however, are looking for ways to take part in public conversations and civic debates—to renew a democracy in which many voices participate. We will look at both of these issues—information overload and public alienation—as we explore the culture of news in this chapter.

With the proliferation of information channels, new technology, and converging media forms, critics worry that the *quality* of news and information necessary in a democratic society is being overwhelmed by sheer quantity.

what is news?

In a 1963 NBC staff memo, news president Reuven Frank outlined the narrative strategies integral to all news: "Every news story should . . . display the attributes of fiction, of drama. It should have structure and conflict, problem and denouement, rising and falling action, a beginning, a middle, and an end."[3] Despite Frank's candid insights, most journalists today are not comfortable thinking of themselves as storytellers. Instead, they view themselves mainly as information gatherers.

Over time, most journalists and journalism textbooks have come to choose and define news by a set of criteria for determining *newsworthiness*. Although other elements could be added to the list, news criteria generally include timeliness, proximity, conflict, prominence, human interest, consequence, usefulness, novelty, and deviance.[4] Journalists select and develop news stories based on these criteria.

Most issues and events that journalists select as news are *timely* or new. Reporters, for example, cover speeches, meetings, crimes, or court cases that have just happened. In order to rate as news, most of these events also have to occur close by or in *proximity* to readers and viewers. Although local papers usually offer some national and international news, readers and viewers expect to find the bulk of news devoted to their own towns and communities. In addition to being new and near, most news stories are narratives and thus contain a healthy dose of *conflict*—a key ingredient in narrative writing. In fact, in developing news narratives, reporters are encouraged to seek contentious quotes from those with opposing views. For example, a story on a local tax hike might feature Republican and Democratic positions; it might also include a tax expert and a homeowner who espouse competing viewpoints.

Though timeliness, proximity, and conflict are the most common criteria for determining news topics, *prominence* and *human interest* play a role as well. Reader and viewer surveys indicate that most people identify more closely with a person than with an abstract issue. Therefore, the news media tend to report stories on powerful or influential people. Since these individuals often play a role in shaping the rules and values of a community, journalists have traditionally been responsible for keeping a watchful eye on them. Prominent celebrities, politicians, business leaders, and journalists themselves often dominate news. But reporters also look for human interest: extraordinary incidents that happen to "ordinary" people. In fact, good reporters can often relate a story about a complicated issue (such as unemployment or homelessness) by illustrating its impact on one person or family.

Two other news criteria, found less often in news stories, are *consequence* and *usefulness*. Stories about isolated or bizarre crimes, while they might be new, near, and notorious, often have little impact on our daily lives. To balance these kinds of stories, many editors and reporters believe that some news must also be of consequence to a majority of readers or viewers. For example, stories that affect a family's income or change a community's laws have consequence. Likewise, many people look for stories with a practical use: hints on buying a used car or choosing a college, advice on a political candidate or the stock market, strategies for training a pet or removing a troublesome stain.

> "The 'information' the **modern media** provide leaves people feeling useless not because it's so bleak but because it's so trivial. It doesn't inform at all; it only **bombards with random data bits**, faux trends and surveys that reinforce preconceptions."
> —Susan Faludi, the *Nation*, 1996

Finally, news is often about the *novel* and the *deviant*. When events happen that are outside the routine of daily life, such as a spectacular warehouse fire or a seven-year-old girl trying to pilot a plane across the country, the news media are there. Reporters also cover events that appear to deviate from social norms, including murders, rapes, fatal car crashes, political scandals, and gang activities. Part of the allure of these occurrences is not only their deviation from norms but the fact that they meet other newsworthiness criteria—especially conflict.

Although newsworthiness criteria are a useful way to define news, they do not reveal much about the cultural aspects of news. As culture, news is both a product and a process. It is both the morning paper or evening newscast *and* a set of subtle values and rituals that have been adapted to historical and social circumstances, such as the partisan press of the 1700s and the informational reports of the 1900s. As culture, then, **news** in the twentieth century has become the process of gathering information and making narrative reports—edited by individuals in a news organization—which create selected frames of reference; within those frames, news helps the public make sense of prominent people, important events, and unusual happenings in everyday life.

neutrality and other values in american journalism

In 1841, Horace Greeley described the newly founded *New York Tribune* as "a journal removed alike from servile partisanship on the one hand and from gagged, mincing neutrality on the other."[5] Greeley feared that too much neutrality would make reporters look like wimps, who stood for nothing. Yet the neutrality Greeley warned against is today a major value of conventional journalism. Such a value, ironically, is in the spirit of value-free science, with reporters behaving as detached and all-seeing observers of social experience. Reporting, however, is seldom scientific; it remains essentially a literary or writing activity: "Reporters . . . have no special method for determining the truth of a situation nor a special language for reporting their findings. They make sense of events by telling stories about them."[6]

Even though journalists transform events into stories, they generally believe that they are—or should be—neutral observers who present facts without passing judgment on them. Conventions such as the inverted pyramid news lead, the careful attribution of sources, the miserly use of adverbs and adjectives, and a detached third-person point of view all help reporters perform their work in a supposedly neutral way.

Like lawyers, therapists, and other professionals, modern journalists believe that their credibility derives from personal detachment. Yet the roots of this view reside in less noble territory. Jon Katz, media critic and former CBS News producer, discusses the history of the neutral pose:

> The idea of respectable detachment wasn't conceived as a moral principle so much as a marketing device. Once newspapers began to mass market themselves in the mid-1880s, after steam- and rotary-powered presses made it possible to print lots of papers and make lots of money, publishers ceased being working, opinionated journalists. They mutated instead into businessmen eager to reach the broadest number of readers and antagonize the fewest. . . .
>
> Objectivity works well for publishers, protecting the status quo and keeping journalism's voice militantly moderate.[7]

To reach as many people as possible across a wide spectrum, publishers and editors realized as early as the 1840s that abandoning partisanship would boost sales.

Neutral journalism remains a selective process. Reporters and editors turn some happenings into reports and discard many others. This process is governed by a deeper set of subjective beliefs that are not neutral. Sociologist Herbert Gans, who studied the newsroom cultures of CBS, NBC, *Newsweek*, and *Time* in the 1970s, has generalized that several basic "enduring values" are shared by most American reporters and editors. The most prominent of these values are ethnocentrism, responsible capitalism, small-town pastoralism, and individualism.[8] By **ethnocentrism** Gans means that in most news reporting, especially foreign coverage, reporters automatically judge other countries and cultures based on how "they live up to or imitate American practices and values." Critics outside the United States, for instance, point out that CNN's

> "Ads are *news*. What is wrong with them is that they are **good news**. In order to balance off the effect and to sell good news, it is necessary to have a lot of bad news."
>
> "Real news is **bad news**—bad news *about* somebody, or bad news *for* somebody."
> —Marshall McLuhan, *Understanding Media*, 1964

The major symbol of twentieth-century investigative journalism, Bob Woodward and Carl Bernstein's coverage of the Watergate scandal for the *Washington Post* helped topple the Nixon White House. In *All the President's Men*, the newsmen's book about their investigation, Woodward and Bernstein championed reporters as tenacious individuals locked in a bitter battle with corrupt and heartless institutions.

international news channels see world events and cultures primarily from an American point of view rather than through a more expansive global lens.

Gans also identified **responsible capitalism** as an underlying value, contending that journalists sometimes naively assume that businesspeople compete with each other not primarily to maximize profits but "to create increased prosperity for all." Gans points out that although most reporters and editors condemn monopolies, "there is little implicit or explicit criticism of the oligopolistic nature of much of today's economy."[9] In fact, by the mid-1990s, many journalists worked in monopoly newspaper towns or for oligopoly parent companies. Thus, writing about the limitations of such economic structures constituted biting the hand that feeds you.

Another value that Gans found was a nostalgia for **small-town pastoralism**: favoring the small over the large and the rural over the urban. Reporters and editors, like most Americans, tend to prefer natural settings to their municipal counterparts. Many journalists equate small-town life with innocence and harbor deep suspicions of cities, their governments, and daily urban experience. Consequently, stories about rustic communities with drug or crime problems are usually framed as if the purity of small-town life has been contaminated by brutish city values.

Finally, **individualism**, according to Gans, remains the single biggest value underpinning daily journalism. Many idealistic reporters are attracted to this profession because it rewards the rugged tenacity needed to confront and expose corruption. Beyond this, individuals who overcome personal adversity are the subjects of many investigative news stories. Often, however, journalism that focuses on personal triumphs fails to explain how large institutions work or waver. Conventional journalism lacks a larger framework for understanding complex institutions. Many reporters and editors, for instance, are unwilling or unsure of how to tackle the problems raised by institutional decay. In addition, since they are accustomed to working alone, journalists distrust working on team projects or participating in citizen forums in which community members discuss their own interests.[10]

> "There's a **fine line** between show biz and news biz. The trick is to walk up to that line and **touch it with your toe** but don't cross it. And some people stay so far away from the line that nobody wants to watch what they do. And other people keep crossing the line. . . . But there has to be a line because **the line is called truth**. And the difference between what we do is, we tell true stories and other people tell make believe stories."
> —Don Hewitt, executive producer, *60 Minutes*

Reporters historically have aligned *facts* with an objective position and *values* with subjective feelings.[11] Within this context, news reports offer readers and viewers details, data, and description. It then becomes the citizen's responsibility to judge and take a stand about the social problems represented by the news. Given these assumptions, reporters are responsible only for adhering to the traditions of the trade—"getting the facts." As a result, many reporters view themselves as neutral "channels" of information rather than as citizens actively involved in public life.

ethics and the news media

In late April 1992, a not-guilty verdict was returned in a suburban Simi Valley courtroom, acquitting four Los Angeles police officers who had been charged with excessive force against Rodney King, an ex-con who had led police on a three-mile, high-speed chase through Los Angeles in 1991. According to police reports, King first refused to get out of his car and then resisted arrest; officers used batons and stun guns to subdue him. Without police knowledge, the incident was captured by a bystander on a home video. Played over and over on news programs, the video showed King on the ground offering little resistance as several officers kicked and beat him. The subsequent not-guilty verdict against the officers triggered fighting, looting, and arson fires in South Central L.A. Fifty-eight people died. Officials estimated more than $1 billion in property damages. After the tragedy, the federal government filed a civil case against the four officers, charging them with deliberately depriving Rodney King of his civil rights. In 1993, two of the officers were found guilty and sentenced to thirty months in prison.

In the spring of 1992, between Rodney King's criminal and civil cases, Ted Koppel abandoned his command desk at ABC's *Nightline* and relocated to a church in South Central Los Angeles for a special *Nightline* show. Featuring interviews with gang members, church leaders, community activists, and neighbors, this *Nightline* looked a lot like Oprah and her talk program when she has visited urban housing projects. On the program, one older minister challenged Koppel's authority by accusing *Nightline* of pitting gang members against religious leaders to generate conflict for a more dramatic news story. Koppel, used to the more detached stance of the contemporary news reporter, was visibly uncomfortable and quickly changed the subject.

ethical predicaments

Ted Koppel's dilemma raises an ethical question: What is the moral and social responsibility of journalists, not only for the stories they report but for the actual events or issues they are shaping for millions of people? Wrestling with such *media ethics* involves determining the morality of a situation through critical reasoning. Koppel's ethical jam was more subtle than many faced by journalists on a daily basis. He "solved" it by avoiding it, but media professionals respond in a variety of other ways to a variety of ethical problems. The most frequent ethical dilemmas involve intentional deception, privacy invasions, and conflicts of interest.

Deploying Deception. In 1996, ABC News lost a series of court cases in which the network was charged with misrepresentation and using false credentials to infiltrate private businesses (see "Examining Ethics: Why Those Hidden Cameras Hurt Journalism" on page 392.). The verdicts sent a chill through the newsmagazine business. After all, ever since Nellie Bly faked insanity to get inside an 1880s asylum, investigative journalists have used deception to get stories. Today journalists continue to use disguises and assume false identities to gather information on social transgressions. Beyond legal considerations, though, a key ethical question comes into play: Does the end justify the means? For example, can a newspaper or TV newsmagazine go undercover to expose a suspected fraudulent clinic that promises miracle cures at a high cost? By posing as clients desperate for a cure, are news professionals justified in using deception?

In terms of ethics, there are at least two major positions and multiple variations. First, *absolutist ethics* suggest that a moral society has laws and codes, including honesty, that all must live by. This means citizens, including members of the news media, should tell the truth at all times and in all cases. In other words, the ends (exposing a phony clinic) never justify the means (using deception to get the story). At the other end of the spectrum are *situational ethics*, which promote ethical decisions on a case-by-case basis. If a greater public good is served by using deceit, many journalists would sanction deception as a practice. Absolutists, however, would shun deceptive measures. Instead, they might cover this story by finding victims who have been ripped off by the clinic and telling the story through their eyes.

Should a journalist withhold information about his or her professional identity to get a quote or a story from an interview subject? Many sources and witnesses are reluctant to talk with journalists, especially about a sensitive subject that might jeopardize a job or hurt another person's reputation. Journalists know they can

by Paul Starobin

When a North Carolina jury took a swipe at hidden-camera television exposés [in January 1997], the press mostly circled the wagons and declared it a travesty. But what the Fourth Estate is defending is shoddy journalism, unworthy of the best tradition of investigative reporting.

The jury found ABC liable for $5.5 million in punitive damages for using deceptive research tactics, amounting to fraud, in a 1992 *Primetime Live* broadcast that accused the Food Lion supermarket chain of selling spoiled food. The show's producers faked résumés to get jobs at Food Lion stores and then used hidden cameras to catch workers prettying up tainted meat.

ABC's lawyer, Bill Jeffries, says the Primetime crew was punished "for being journalists." Nonsense. It was punished for trickery and deception.

Hidden cameras? That's the easiest call. Their growing use by TV news-magazine shows, including *Primetime Live* and NBC's *Dateline*, is part of a ratings-driven descent by the major networks into the swamp of tabloid journalism. Teaser promos for the programs hype concealed-camera feats to snag viewers who like to watch people who don't know they're being watched. But good journalism is not about sensationalizing how the story was obtained.

The more difficult is the use of undercover practices to get a story that might otherwise be difficult to report. So what if a few producers falsified their résumés to land jobs at Food Lion: Isn't this part and parcel of muckraking journalism?

Subterfuge does have a long tradition in investigative reporting, but it is a dubious one. The pioneer was Nellie Bly, who in 1887 feigned insanity to gain admission to the New York City Lunatic Asylum.

Bly's report in the *New York World* on her ten days in the asylum exposed horrors that spurred needed reforms. But was that the only way to get the story? Probably not. The flamboyant Bly was an artful practitioner of what was known back then as "stunt journalism." She also posed as a prostitute and a thief and was regarded by some peers as a self-promoting sensationalizer and an embarrassment to the craft.

Broadsheet newspapers hyped derring-do disguise feats just as the TV newsmagazine shows now tout hidden-camera tricks. The headline for a front-page story on Bly's asylum exploit in the rival *New York Sun* blared "Playing Mad Woman," and the subhead declared, "Nellie Bly Too Sharp for the Island Doctors."

The greatest muckrakers shunned such ruses. Ida Tarbell brought down John D. Rockefeller's Standard Oil monopoly by the tireless bird-dogging of court records and other documents—a righteous tradition later upheld by I. F. Stone and honored these days by the crusaders who are following the money to expose the fund-raising practices of Newt Gingrich and Bill Clinton. And *Fortune* magazine didn't need to go undercover for its 1993 report on the exploitation of child labor in garment-industry sweatshops in New York City and Los Angeles.

Indeed, ABC could have done a devastating story on Food Lion without the tricks. Diane Sawyer, the *Primetime Live* anchor, said seventy current and former employees of the chain had attested to unhealthful food-handling practices in on-the-record interviews with the show's researchers. But that wasn't sexy enough, so ABC went undercover to dramatize the tale. A commercial imperative, not a journalistic one, drove this piece.

ABC points out that Food Lion sued for fraud, not libel, and so did not challenge the substance of the story. But news organizations should not be untruthful in their search for the truth. The North Carolina jury has fired a well-deserved warning shot. Stunt journalism saps the credibility of the press and makes life tougher for honest snoops.

Source: Paul Starobin, "Why Those Hidden Cameras Hurt Journalism," *New York Times*, January 28, 1997, p. A13.

sometimes obtain information by posing as someone other than a journalist, such as a curious student or a licensed therapist. Most newsrooms frown on such deception. In particular situations, though, such a practice might be condoned if reporters and their editors believed that the public needed the information. The ethics code adopted by the Society of Professional Journalists is fairly silent on issues of deception. The code "requires journalists to perform with intelligence, objectivity, accuracy, and fairness," but it also says that "truth is our ultimate goal."[12] Furthermore, it does not offer much specific guidance on the ethical means to be used to reach the truth. Honesty, for example, is not a word that appears in the code.

Invading Privacy. To achieve the truth, journalists routinely straddle a line between the public's right to know and a person's right to privacy. For example, journalists are often sent to hospitals to gather quotes from victims or from relatives of individuals who have suffered some injury. In many of these cases, there is very little the public might gain from such a quote, but journalists worry that if they don't get the quote, a competitor might. In these instances, have the news media responsibly weighed the protection of individual privacy against the public's right to know? Although the latter is not constitutionally guaranteed, journalists invoke the public's right to know as justification for many types of stories.

In regard to privacy, do the news media always ask the ethical questions: What public good is being served here? What significant public knowledge will be gained through the exploitation of a tragic private moment? Although journalism's code of ethics says, "The news media must guard against invading a person's right to privacy," this clashes with another part of the code: "The public's right to know of events of public importance and interest is the overriding mission of the mass media."[13] In general, when these two ethical standards collide, journalists usually err on the side of the public's right to know.

Conflict of Interest. Journalism's code of ethics also warns reporters and editors not to place themselves in positions that produce a **conflict of interest**, that is, any situation in which journalists may stand to benefit personally from stories they produce. "Gifts, favors, free travel, special treatment or privileges," the code states, "can compromise the integrity of journalists and their employers. Nothing of value should be accepted."[14] For instance, at large mainstream news media that subscribe to the code, newspapers or broadcast stations pay for the game tickets of their sports writers and for the meals of their restaurant critics. Small newspapers, however, with limited resources and poorly paid reporters, might accept such freebies from a local business or interview subject. This practice may be an economic necessity, but it is one that can increase the likelihood of conflict of interest.

On a broader level, ethical guidelines at many news outlets attempt to protect journalists from compromising positions. For instance, in most cities journalists do not actively participate in politics or support social causes. Some journalists will not reveal their political affiliations and occasionally will even refuse to vote. For these journalists, the rationale behind their decisions is straightforward: Journalists should not place themselves in a situation in which they might have to report on the misdeeds of an organization or political party with which they are actively involved. If a journalist has a tie to any group, and that group is later discovered to be involved in shady practices or criminal activity, the reporter's ability to cover that group would be compromised—along with the credibility of the news medium for which he or she works. Conversely, other journalists believe that *not* actively participating in politics or social causes is abandoning one's civic obligations.

resolving ethical problems

When a journalist is criticized for ethical indiscretions or questionable reporting tactics, a typical response might be, "I'm just doing my job" or "I was just getting the facts." In retrospect, such explanations are troubling because reporters are transferring personal responsibility for the story to a set of institutional rituals. Journalists who disclaim personal or ethical responsibility can become mere extensions of a business enterprise.

There are, of course, ethical alternatives to comments like "I'm just doing my job" that force journalists to think through complex issues. Broad ethical horizons used throughout history establish common ground and offer perspectives beyond narrow reference frames. With the crush of deadlines and daily duties, most media professionals deal with ethical situations only on a case-by-case basis as dilemmas arise. However, examining major ethical models and theories provides a common strategy for addressing ethics on a general rather than situational basis. Ethical and philosophical guidelines also offer universal measures for testing individual values and codes.

Although we cannot address here all major moral codes, a few key precepts can guide us. One principle entails the "categorical imperative," developed by German philosopher Immanuel Kant (1724–1804). A moral imperative or command argues that a society must adhere to moral codes that are universal and unconditional, applicable in all situations at all times. For example, the Golden Rule—do unto others as you would have them do unto you—operates as such an absolutist moral principle. The First Amendment, which prevents Congress from abridging free speech, has served likewise as a national unconditional law.

Another ethical principle, derived from British philosophers Jeremy Bentham (1748–1832) and John Stuart Mill (1806–1873), promotes "the greatest good for the greatest number," directing us "to distribute a good consequence to more people rather than to fewer, whenever we have a choice."[15] The most well-known ethical standard, the Judeo-Christian command to "love your neighbor as yourself," also provides the basis for constructing ethical guidelines.

Arriving at ethical decisions involves several stages. These include laying out the case; pinpointing the key issues; identifying involved parties, their intent, and their competing values; studying ethical models; presenting strategies and options; and formulating a decision. In terms of privacy issues, for instance, the goal would be to develop an ethical policy that the news media might implement in covering the private lives of people who have become prominent in the news.

Consider Richard Jewell, the Atlanta security guard who, for eighty-eight days, was the FBI's prime suspect in the park bombing at the 1996 Olympics. The FBI never charged Jewell with a crime, and he later sued several news organizations for libel. Putting legal issues aside, the Jewell story involved a rivalry among various news media to report unusual or important developments before the competition could do so. The battle for newspaper circulation and broadcast ratings added a complex dimension. As has occurred in other instances, editors were reluctant to back away from the story once it had begun circulating in the major media.

At least two key ethical questions emerged from the Jewell story: Should the news media have named Jewell as a suspect even though he was never charged with a crime? Should they have camped out daily in front of his mother's house in an attempt to interview him and his mother? The incidents surrounding the Richard Jewell case pit the media's right to tell stories and earn profits against a citizen's right to be left alone.

Journalists' livelihoods partly depend on using stories that attract audiences and keep up with their competition. To defend their behavior toward the Jewells, for example, the news media might invoke their constitutional right to free expression or

Atlanta Journal EXTRA
TUESDAY, JULY 30, 1996
50 CENTS

FBI suspects 'hero' guard may have planted bomb

OCT. 27, 1996

Jewell is cleared in bomb case

For almost three months, security guard Richard Jewell was the FBI's main suspect in the July 1996 Olympic Park bombing that killed one person. When the FBI finally exonerated Jewell, he filed a libel suit against an Atlanta newspaper and NBC. Both settled with Jewell's lawyers out of court.

argue that their intent was to serve the public's right to know. To criticize such media behavior, however, we might ask whether any significant public knowledge is gained by stalking a potential interview subject. The news media need to balance principles and profit motives against an individual's right to privacy, especially when someone has not been charged with a crime.

As journalists formally work through various ethical stages, they eventually formulate policies and ground them in an overarching moral principle, such as the command to "love your neighbor as yourself."[16] Would reporters, for instance, be willing to treat themselves, their families, or their friends the same way they treated the Jewells? Ethical reporters could also invoke Aristotle's golden mean: seeking moral virtue between extreme positions. In Richard Jewell's situation, this might have entailed developing guidelines that would attempt to balance the interests of the suspect and the news media. For example, during his eighty-eight day ordeal, in reparation for using Jewell's name in early accounts, reporters might have called off their stakeout and allowed him to set interview times at a neutral site. At such a location, he might have talked with a small pool of journalists designated to relay information to other media outlets.

reporting rituals and the legacy of print journalism

Unfamiliar with being questioned themselves, many reporters are uncomfortable discussing their personal values or their strategies for getting stories. Nevertheless, a stock of rituals, derived from basic American values, underlie the practice of reporting. These include focusing on the present, relying on experts, balancing story conflict, and acting as adversaries toward leaders and institutions.

focusing on the present

Historians mark the 1830s as the beginning of the transition between the partisan and modern press eras. Though American journalism began as a venue for partisan politics (encouraging debate over issues such as constitutional amendments, slavery, and states' rights), in the nineteenth century publishers figured out how to sell news as a product. They used modern technology to substantially cut their costs; they also changed news content to appeal to the emerging middle and working classes, who could now afford a paper and had the leisure time to read it. Publishers realized that they needed more practical content because most readers were not particularly interested in the intricacies of partisan politics.

When the telegraph enabled news to instantly crisscross America, modern journalism was born. Its news agenda called for a dogged focus on the present. Modern print journalism de-emphasized political discussions and historical context, instead accenting the new and the now.

As members of an emerging modern profession, many journalists and newspapers ignored Joseph Pulitzer's call for news that maintained a continuity with the past. As a result, the profession began drawing criticism for failing to offer historical analyses of important phenomena. In news stories about drugs, for example, individual characters—dealers, addicts, abusers, police, medical experts—pass through the frame of news, but only up to a point. Once these characters are no longer timely, they no longer meet the narrative requirements of daily news. Urban drug stories heavily dominated print and network news during the 1986 and 1988 election years. Such stories, however, virtually disappeared from the news in 1992 and 1994, although the nation's serious drug and addiction problems had not diminished.[17] Drug stories simply became "yesterday's news." Modern news tends to reject "old news" for whatever new event or idea disrupts today's routines. In the mid-1990s, when new statistics revealed drug use among middle-class high school students was rising, reporters again latched onto new versions of the drug story during the 1996 elections, but their reports made only limited references to the 1980s. Given the space and time constraints of current news practice, reporters infrequently link stories to the past or to the flow of history.

Getting a Good Story. Early in the 1980s, the Janet Cooke–Pulitzer prize hoax demonstrated the difference between a reporter merely telling a good story and her social responsibility for the actual experience.[18] The major criticism against the former *Washington Post* reporter focused on her fabrication of an investigative report (for which she won a Pulitzer that was later taken away). She had created a cast of characters featuring a mother who contributed to the heroin addiction of her eight-year-old son. At the time the hoax was exposed, Chicago columnist Mike Royko criticized conventional journalism for allowing narrative conventions—getting a good story—to replace journalism's responsibility to the daily lives it documents: "There's something more important than a story here. This eight-year-old kid is being murdered. The editors should have said forget the story, find the kid. . . . People in any other profession would have gone right to the police."[19] Had editors at the *Post* demanded such help, Cooke's hoax would never have gone as far as it did.

In the pursuit of such dramatic and timely accounts, reporters act out two rituals: getting a good story and getting a story first. These rituals, which motivated reporters during the nineteenth century's yellow journalism phase, still inspire reporters today. According to Don Hewitt, the creator and executive producer of *60 Minutes*, "There's a very simple formula if you're in Hollywood, Broadway, opera, publishing, broadcasting, newspapering. It's four very simple words—tell me a story."[20] For most journalists, the bottom line *is* getting a story—an edict that overrides most other concerns. Getting a timely story fills up a journalist's day and meets routine deadline demands. It is the standard against which reporters measure each other and their profession (see "Case Study: Reporters as Detectives on *60 Minutes*" on page 398).

Getting a Story First. In a discussion on public television about the press coverage of a 1980s fatal plane crash in Milwaukee, a news photographer was asked to discuss his role in covering the tragedy. Rather than take up the poignant aspects of witnessing the aftermath of such an event, the excited photographer launched into a dramatic recounting of how he had slipped behind police barricades to snap the first grim photos, which later appeared in the *Milwaukee Journal*. Typically, reporters enjoy recounting how they evaded a PR flack or an authority figure to secure a story ahead of the competition.

The photojournalist's retelling points up the important role journalism plays in calling public attention to serious events and issues. Yet he talked about the newsgathering process also as a game that journalists play. Indeed, it has become routine for local television stations and newspapers today to run self-promotions about how they beat competitors to a story. In addition, during political elections local television stations and networks project winners in particular races and often hype their projections when they are able to forecast results before the competition does.

Such journalistic *scoops* and exclusive stories often portray reporters in a heroic light: They have won a race for facts, which they have gathered and presented ahead of their rivals. It is not always clear, though, how the public is better served by a journalist's claim to have gotten a story first. Certainly, enterprising journalists can get a story started by calling attention to an important problem or issue. But on occasion, as with the O.J. Simpson trials or investigations into political corruption, scoop behavior has led to *herd journalism*, which occurs when reporters stake out a house or follow a story in such large groups that the entire profession comes under attack for invading people's privacy and exploiting their personal tragedies. Although readers and viewers might value the tenacity of adventurous reporters, the earliest reports are not necessarily better than stories written days later with more hindsight and perspective.

The public's distrust of journalism today is partly due to the news media's tendency to chase a story in packs and invade the privacy of individuals. Particularly annoying are photographers and broadcast news crews who often seem to be stalking their subjects.

Reporters as Detectives on *60 Minutes*

If the *New York Times* is the preeminent model of print journalism in the twentieth century, *60 Minutes* has served a similar role for broadcast reporting. The only show ever rated No. 1 in three different decades, *60 Minutes* is the most popular TV program in history, finishing among the Nielsen Top 10 for twenty consecutive years—another record. From the mid-1970s to the mid-1990s, a typical episode of *60 Minutes* reached a bigger audience—sometimes as large as forty million viewers—than any other single news form in American journalism.

Over the years, critics have tried to explain *60 Minutes'* standing as America's first popular news program. Was it CBS's decision to counter Sunday evening kids' shows on other networks by appealing to male viewers winding down from an afternoon of pro sports? Was it the arrival in 1975 of Dan Rather, fresh from the CBS White House beat, and the news media's rising stature after Watergate?

Early on, Don Hewitt, the program's creator and executive producer, pointed to storytelling as the key to the program's popularity: "I said to myself, 'I'll bet if we made it multi-subject and we made it personal journalism—instead of dealing with issues we told stories; if we packaged reality as well as Hollywood packages fiction, I'll bet we could double the rating."[1] Hewitt rightly predicted that personal journalism, starring reporters in mini-news dramas, would dislodge institutional news documentaries in which the network point of view—what Hewitt called "the voice of the corporation"—seemed distant and aloof.

The secret of *60 Minutes* involved its adaptation of a familiar story form long associated with fiction—the detective mystery.[2] Through this dominant frame, the reporters of *60 Minutes* have performed not as detached journalists but as dramatic characters. Their mission: To make sense of the world through stories.

"*60 Minutes* is the adventures of five reporters," Hewitt has said, "more fascinating to the American public being themselves than Robert Redford and Dustin Hoffman were playing Woodward and Bernstein."[3] Cast as detectives, *60 Minutes* reporters each week have championed American individualism in the face of insensitive corporations and heartless bureaucracies.

On any given Sunday, at least one episode features the detective news frame. In these stories, the reporters introduce the alleged injustices, which may range from political intrigue to murder. After identifying the major characters, the setting, and the crime, the reporters rely on their rational instincts and abilities to expose other characters to solve the mystery. Like tidy Columbos, they look like detectives, often wearing trench coats when searching for clues. Like Sherlock Holmes, *60 Minutes* detectives often succeed where traditional, and sometimes inept, investigative agencies fail. In the end, they put the puzzle together and pose in front of the program's trademark storybook frame, explaining to us—armchair Dr. Watsons—the missing evidence, the fate of the villains, and any leftover disparities.

As in conventional journalism, social reform is not the stated goal of the program. However, Mike Wallace has written that viewers regard the show as an unofficial ombudsman, mediating between the people and the powerful. He reveals his own perceptions of the detective role he has performed since 1968: "by the late 1970s... I kept bumping into people who jumped at the chance to alert me to some scandal or outrage....They would give me vivid accounts of foul deeds and the culprits perpetrating them, and urge me to take appropriate action: 'You really should look into this, Mike.'"[4] Certainly, many powerful segments over the years have concluded with *60 Minutes* serving explicitly as a mediating ombudsman—with reporters calling for congressional investigations, redressing government oversights or wrongly accused prisoners, and championing individual rights in the face of bureaucratic ineptitude. These stories portray a heroic news medium monitoring abuses of power and breakdowns in basic values.

The legacy of *60 Minutes* is full of controversies, including a trail of alleged wrongly accused villains. The Illinois Power Company, the apple industry, the MSG/food industry, and the Audi automobile company have all launched campaigns against what these organizations regarded as unfair and misleading stories by *60 Minutes*. Nevertheless, through 1996, the program had never lost a libel case (although at least one lawsuit was settled out of court).

Critics of *60 Minutes* have argued that most of the program's topics should not be portrayed as simplified detective stories. Such journalism often turns experience into melodrama, making it appear that the world is transparent and soluble. Detective stories celebrate individual heroes and villains. But as in conventional journalism, stories about the inner workings of mundane and complex institutions are not well suited to *60 Minutes*.

Even the production techniques on the program contribute to the image of the reporters as detectives. For instance, they typically receive more visual or frame space: They are almost always shown at a greater distance than the characters they interview.

Frequently, in a reaction shot, an interview subject appears in an extreme close-up, usually with the top of the head cut from the frame. This is in contrast to the medium shot of the reporter, usually shown from midwaist with space overhead. On one level, the greater space granted to reporters may be seen as TV's counterpart to print's neutrality. On another level, the greater distance endows the *60 Minutes* reporters with more authority. The reporters seem to be in greater control, whereas the victims and villains, appearing to squirm, often seem to be in less control.

Over the years, *60 Minutes* has penetrated deeply into America's consciousness. The reporter-detectives have tapped into our desires for truth, honesty, and intrigue. Each week, *60 Minutes* locates us in its world and gives us characters to identify with and take exception to. The program's stories inform and affirm individualism and common sense. These are powerful attractions that have drawn viewers back to this same place Sunday after Sunday.

relying on experts

Another ritual of modern print journalism—relying on outside sources—has made reporters heavily dependent on experts. Reporters, although often experts themselves in certain areas by virtue of having covered them over time, are not typically allowed to display their expertise. Instead, they must seek outside authorities to give credibility to their neutral reports. What daily reporters know is generally subordinate to knowing whom to ask.

During the early 1900s, progressive politicians and leaders, such as Theodore Roosevelt, William Jennings Bryan, Woodrow Wilson, and Walter Lippmann, believed in cultivating strong ties among national reporters, government officials, natural scientists, business managers, and academic researchers. They wanted journalists supplied with expertise across a variety of areas. Today a widening gap exists between those citizens with expertise and those without it, creating a need for public mediators. Reporters have assumed this role, becoming surrogate citizens who represent both leaders' and readers' interests. Unlike experts, however, most reporters are generalists, lacking specialized knowledge in any particular field. But with their access to experts, reporters are able to act as agents for citizens, taking specialized knowledge and transforming it into the everyday language of news stories.

In the quest for facts, reporters frequently use experts to create narrative conflict by pitting a series of quotes against one another. Reporters also use experts to support their own particular positions (which, because of neutrality requirements, they are not allowed to state overtly). In addition, the use of experts allows journalists to distance themselves from daily experience; they are able to attribute the responsibility for the events or issues reported in a story to those who are quoted.

In the ritual use of experts, journalists are required to make direct contact with a source—by phone or e-mail or in person. Journalists do not, however, heavily cite the work of other writers; that would violate the reporters' obligation to not only get a story first but on their own. Telephone calls and face-to-face interviews are the stuff of daily journalism. More carefully researched interpretation often is assumed to rest in the hands of academics or magazine writers. News reporters are trained to believe that their credibility springs from their ability to stalk sources and obtain in-person, fresh—though not necessarily more illuminating—quotes.

Of expert sources in general, *Newsweek*'s Jonathan Alter calls them the "usual suspects." Alter contends that "the impression conveyed is of a world that contains only a handful of knowledgeable people. . . . Their public exposure is a result not only of their own abilities, but of deadlines and a failure of imagination on the part of the press."[21] In addition, expert sources historically have been predominantly white and male. For example, based on a forty-month analysis of guests on ABC's *Nightline* between 1985 and 1988, Fairness and Accuracy in Media (FAIR) found that "89 percent of the U.S. guests were men, 92 percent were white, and 80 percent were professionals, government officials, or corporate representatives."[22] Beginning in 1995, coverage of the O.J. Simpson trials helped change this profile somewhat. Legal sources, especially on CNN and CNBC, featured a far more diverse array of expert participants. Nevertheless, as journalists have increased their reliance on experts over the years, they have inadvertently alienated many readers who feel they no longer have a stake in day-to-day social and political life. After all, authoritative experts and knowledgeable journalists seem to be handling things.

"The public will begin to reawaken when they are addressed as a conversational partner and are encouraged to join the talk rather than **sit passively as spectators** before a discussion conducted by journalists and experts."
—James Carey,
Kettering Review,
1992

balancing story conflict

Embedded deep within journalism is a belief in the two-dimensionality of news. A reporter sent to cover property-tax increases might be given this editorial advice: "Interview Republican and Democratic leaders from the district and have them fight it out in the story." Such balance is a narrative device that helps generate story conflict. For most journalists, balance means presenting all sides of an issue without favoring any one position. Unfortunately, since time and space constraints do not always permit representing *all* sides, this value in practice has often been reduced to "telling *both* sides of a story." In recounting news stories as two-sided dramas, however, reporting often misrepresents social issues of multifaceted complexity. The abortion controversy, for example, is often treated as a story pitting two extreme positions (pro-life vs. pro-choice) against one another. Yet people whose views do not fall at one end of the spectrum are seldom represented; they are outside the bounds of a two-dimensional narrative conflict.

Although journalists often claim to be detached, they actually stake out a middle-of-the-road position between the two sides represented in a story. In claiming neutrality and inviting readers to share in their detached point of view, journalists circumvent their own values. The authority of their distant, third-person, all-knowing point of view (a narrative device that scientists and novelists use as well) enhances the impression of neutrality by making the reporter appear value-free (or value*less*).

The claim for balanced stories, like the claim for neutrality, masks journalism's narrative functions. After all, when reporters choose quotes for a story, these are usually the most dramatic or conflict-oriented words that emerge from an interview, press conference, or public meeting. The balance claim also speaks to mainstream journalism's economic agenda; it is in the financial interest of modern news organizations to stake out the middle ground. William Greider, a former *Washington Post* editor, makes the connection between good business and balanced journalism: "If you're going to be a mass circulation journal, that means you're going to be talking simultaneously to lots of groups that have opposing views. So you've got to modulate your voice and pretend to be talking to all of them."[23]

acting as adversaries

Complementing the search for conflict, the value that journalists take the most pride in is their adversarial relationship with the prominent leaders and major institutions they cover. The prime narrative frame for portraying this relationship is sometimes called a *gotcha story*, which refers to the moment when the reporter nabs an evildoer. This narrative strategy—also known as the *tough-question style*—is frequently used in political reporting. Many journalists assume that leaders are hiding something and that the reporter's job is to ferret out the truth through tenacious fact-gathering and gotcha questions. An extension of the search for balance, this stance locates the reporter in the middle, between "them" and "us," between political leaders and the people they represent.

Critics of the tough-question style of reporting argue that it fosters a cynicism among journalists that actually harms the democratic process. Although journalists need to guard against becoming too cozy with their political sources, they sometimes go to opposite extremes. By constantly searching for what politicians may be hiding, reporters may miss other issues and ideas that are important to readers and viewers.

News scholar Jay Rosen argues that "the essential problem is that the journalist's method of being critical is

THE FAR SIDE By GARY LARSON

Mike Wallace interviews the Devil

not disciplined by any political vision."[24] In other words, the bottom line for conventional journalists, who claim to have no political agenda, is maintaining an adversarial stance rather than improving the quality of political discussions. When journalists employ the gotcha model to cover news, being tough often becomes an end in itself. Thus, reporters believe they have done their job just by roughing up an interview subject or by answering the limited "What is going on here?" question. Yet the Pulitzer Prize, the highest award honoring journalism, often goes to the reporter who asks the open-ended "Why is this going on?" and "What ought to be?" questions.

journalism in the age of television

The rules and rituals governing American journalism started shifting in the 1950s. At the time, former radio reporter John Daly began hosting the CBS game show *What's My Line?* When he began moonlighting as the evening TV news anchor on ABC, the fledgling network blurred the entertainment and information border, foreshadowing what in the 1990s has become a central criticism of journalism.

In those early days, the most influential and respected television news program was CBS's *See It Now*. Coproduced by Fred Friendly and Edward R. Murrow, *See It Now* practiced a kind of TV journalism lodged somewhere between the neutral and narrative traditions. Serving as the conscience of TV news in its early days, Murrow also worked as the program's anchor and main reporter, introducing the investigative model of journalism to television—a model that programs like *60 Minutes*, *20/20*, and *Dateline NBC* would later imitate.

Generally regarded as "the first and definitive" news documentary on American television, *See It Now* sought "to report in depth—to tell and show the American audi-

Probably the most revered figure in television news history, CBS newsman Edward R. Murrow (*center*) is pictured here on a 1950s *See It Now* program, interviewing the U.S. ambassadors to Nationalist China and the Philippines. Murrow and *See It Now* set a standard for TV journalism that has been eroded by the increased blending of news-documentary style with dramatic packaging in most of today's newsmagazine shows.

ence what was happening in the world using film as a narrative tool."[25] In the early 1960s, *CBS Reports* carried on the traditions of *See It Now*, and as that decade unfolded, the literary model of reporting played a more significant role in the program. Friendly hinted at the importance of the narrative tradition to *CBS Reports*: "Though based on truth, the programs still have to have stories of their own, with the basic outline of beginning, middle and end."[26]

■ differences between print and television news

Although TV news reporters share many values, beliefs, and conventions with their print counterparts, television has transformed journalism in a number of significant ways. First, broadcast news is often driven by its technology. If a camera crew and microwave-relay van (which bounces a broadcast signal back to the station) are dispatched to a remote location for a live broadcast, reporters are expected to justify such expense by developing a story, even though one may not exist. This happens, for instance, when a national political candidate does not arrive at the local airport in time for an interview on the evening news, leaving the reporter and crew standing on an empty tarmac to report live on a flight delay. Print reporters, however, slide their notebooks or laptop computers back into their bags and report on the story when it actually occurs.

Second, although print editors must cut stories to fit a physical space around the slots allocated for ads, TV news directors have to time stories to fit news in between commercials. They are under pressure to condense the day's main events into a visual show. Despite the fact that a much higher percentage of space is devoted to print ads (more than 60 percent at most dailies), TV ads (which take up less than 25 percent of the time in a typical thirty-minute news program) generally seem more intrusive to viewers, perhaps because TV ads take up time rather than space.

Third, whereas print journalists are expected to behave as detached reporters, TV news derives its credibility from live on-the-spot reporting, believable imagery, and viewers' trust in the reporters and anchors who read the news. In fact, since the early 1970s, the annual Roper polls have indicated that the majority of viewers find television news a more credible resource than print news. Viewers tend to feel a personal regard for the anchors who appear each evening on sets in their homes. Many print journalists have even come to resent operating in the relative anonymity of newspaper work while their TV counterparts become mini-celebrities.

By the mid-1970s, the public's fascination with the Watergate scandal and the improved quality of television journalism helped local news departments realize profits. In an effort to retain high ratings, stations began hiring consultants, who advised news directors to invest in one of the national packaged formats such as Action News or Eyewitness News. Consultants also suggested that stations lead their newscasts with *crime blocks*: a group of stories recounting the worst transgressions of the day. A cynical slogan soon developed in the industry: "If it bleeds, it leads." Traveling the country, viewers noticed that similar theme music and opening visuals were available from market to market. By the 1980s, local news broadcasts—especially in the Midwest, where late evening news airs at 10 rather than at 11—often were the most popular programs during the summer, when networks play reruns.

Sound Bitten. Beginning in the 1980s, the term **sound bite** became part of the public lexicon. The TV equivalent of a quote in print news, a sound bite is the part of a news report in which an expert, celebrity, victim, or person-on-the-street responds in an interview to some aspect of an event or issue. With the 1988 national elections,

sound bites became the focus of intense criticism. Various studies revealed that during political campaigns the typical sound bite from candidates shrunk from an average duration of forty seconds in the 1950s and 1960s to less than ten seconds by the 1990s. With shorter comments from interview subjects, TV news sometimes seemed like dueling sound bites, with reporters creating dramatic tension by editing competing viewpoints together as if the individuals had actually been in the same location speaking to one another. Of course, print news also pits one quote against another in a story, even though the actual interview subjects may never have met. Once again, these reporting techniques are evidence of the profession's reliance on storytelling devices to replicate or create conflict.

Pretty-Face and Happy-Talk Culture. In the early 1970s at a Milwaukee TV station, consultants advised the station's news director that the evening anchor looked too old. Showing a bit of gray, the anchor was replaced and went on to serve as the station's editorial director. He was thirty-two years old at the time. In the late 1970s, a woman reporter at the same station was fired because of a weight problem, although that was not given as the official reason. Earlier that year, she had given birth to her first child. In 1983, Christine Craft, formerly a Kansas City television news anchor, initially won $500,000 in damages in a sex-discrimination suit (she eventually lost the monetary award on appeal) against station KMBC. She had been fired because consultants believed she was too old, too unattractive, and not deferential enough to men.

Such stories are rampant in the annals of TV news. They have helped create a stereotype of the half-witted but attractive news anchor, reinforced by popular culture images (such as Ted Baxter on the *Mary Tyler Moore Show*, Corky Sherwood and Miller Redfield on *Murphy Brown*, and the William Hurt character in the 1987 movie *Broadcast News*). Although the situation has improved slightly, a generation of national news consultants set the agenda for what local reporters should cover—lots of local crime—as well as what they should look like—young, attractive, pleasant, and usually white, with no regional accent. Essentially, news consultants (also known as *news doctors*) tried to replicate in local TV news the predominant advertising images of the 1960s and 1970s.

Another news strategy favored by news consultants has been *happy talk*: the ad-libbed or scripted banter that goes on among local news anchors, reporters, meteorologists, and sports reporters before and after news reports. During the 1970s, consultants often recommended such chatter to create a more relaxed feeling on the news set and to foster conversational intimacy with viewers. Some news doctors also believed that happy talk would counter much of that era's "bad news," which included coverage of urban riots and the Vietnam War. A strategy still used in the 1990s, happy talk often appears forced and occasionally creates awkward transitions, especially when anchors have to report on events that are sad or tragic.

visual language and critical limits

The brevity of a televised report is often compared unfavorably to the length of print news. However, newspaper reviewers and other TV critics seldom discuss the visual language of TV news and the ways in which images may capture events more powerfully than words.

In contemporary America, the shift from a print-dominated culture to an electronic-digital culture requires thoughtful scrutiny. Instead, the complexity of this shift is often reduced to a two-dimensional debate about information vs. entertainment. Yet over the past forty-five years, television news has dramatized America's key events and provided a clearinghouse for shared information—a function that CNN is

Television has served as the main stage for America's biggest news stories, such as the Army-McCarthy hearings in 1954 and the assassination of John F. Kennedy in 1963. In April 1995, television played the roles of both reporter and healer as America and the world tuned in to coverage of the bombing of an Oklahoma City federal building that killed more than one hundred and sixty people.

now performing on a global level. Civil rights activists, for instance, acknowledge that the movement benefited enormously from televised pictures that documented the plight of southern blacks in the 1960s. Other enduring TV images, unfurled as a part of history to each new generation, are embedded in our collective memory: the Kennedy-King assassinations in the 1960s; the turmoil of Watergate in the 1970s; the space-shuttle disaster and the Chinese student uprisings in the 1980s; the Persian Gulf War, the bombing of the Oklahoma City federal building, and the Centennial Olympics in the 1990s. During these critical events, TV news has been a cultural reference point marking the strengths and weaknesses of a nation.

In contrast, many print critics overlooked a disturbing TV news strategy that developed in the mid- to late 1980s. In their coverage of crack cocaine, news operations formulated a visual shot in which news photographers, or *shooters* (using shaky, handheld cameras), leapt from the back of police vans and followed gun-wielding authorities as they broke down the doors of various crack houses. At the time, few critics mentioned that in such a shot TV news actually represented the police or state's point of view. A profession that prides itself on neutrality and watching over the police on society's behalf apparently did not question whether it was appropriate for reporters to implicitly tell these stories from the police viewpoint. Many critics, untrained in visual language, failed to comment.

conventional news, public journalism, and democracy

In 1990 Poland was experiencing growing pains as it shifted from a state-controlled economic system to a more open market economy. The country's leading newspaper, *Gazeta Wyborcza*, the first noncommunist newspaper to appear in Eastern Europe since the 1940s, was also undergoing challenges. Based in Warsaw with a circulation of about 350,000 at the time, *Gazeta Wyborcza* had to report on and explain the new economy and the new crime wave that accompanied it. Especially troubling to the news staff and to Polish citizens were gangs preying on American and Western European tourists at railway stations. Apparently, an inner circle of thieves snatched purses, wallets, and luggage, sometimes assaulting tourists in the process. The stolen goods would then pass to an outer circle whose members transferred the goods to still another outer ring of thieves. Even if police caught the original inner-circle members, the loot disappeared.

These developments triggered heated discussions in the newsroom. A small group of young reporters, some of whom had worked in the United States, argued that the best way to cover the story was to describe the new crime wave and relay the facts to readers in a neutral manner. Another group, many of whom were older and more experienced, felt that the paper should take an advocacy stance and condemn the criminals through interpretive columns on the front page. The older guard won this particular debate, and more interpretive pieces appeared.[27]

the future of news

The Polish newsroom story illustrates the two competing models that have influenced American and European journalism throughout the twentieth century. The first—the *informational* or *modern model*—emphasizes describing events and issues from a neutral point of view. The second—a more *partisan* and *European model*—stresses analyzing occurrences and advocating remedies from an acknowledged point of view. In most American newspapers today, the informational model dominates the front page while the partisan model remains confined to the editorial pages and an occasional front-page piece. Supplementing both models, photographs in newspapers and images on television tell parts of a story not easily captured in words. An alternative model—often labelled "public journalism"—has recently emerged to challenge modern journalistic ideals.

What Is Public Journalism? Since the late 1980s, a number of newspapers have been experimenting with ways to involve readers more actively in the news process. These experiments have surfaced primarily at midsize daily papers, including the *Charlotte Observer*, the *Wichita Eagle*, the *Virginian-Pilot*, and the *Minneapolis StarTribune*. Davis "Buzz" Merritt, editor and vice president of the *Wichita Eagle*, has defined key aspects of civic or **public journalism**:

- It moves beyond the limited mission of "telling the news" to a broader mission of helping public life go well, and acts out that imperative. . . .
- It moves from detachment to being a fair-minded participant in public life. . . .
- It moves beyond only describing what is "going wrong" to also imagining what "going right" would be like. . . .
- It moves from seeing people as consumers—as readers or nonreaders, as bystanders to be informed—to seeing them as a public, as potential actors in arriving at democratic solutions to public problems.[28]

Public journalism might best be imagined as a conversational map for journalistic practice. Modern journalism draws a distinct line between reporter detachment and community involvement; public journalism—driven by citizen forums, community conversations, and even talk shows—redraws this line.

> "We need to see people not as readers, nonreaders, endangered readers, not as customers to be wooed or an audience to be entertained, but as a public, **citizens capable of action**." —Davis "Buzz" Merritt, *Wichita Eagle*, 1995

The impetus behind public journalism is the realization that many citizens feel alienated from politics, from decision making, and from participating in public life in a meaningful way. This alienation arises, in part, from watching passively as the political process plays out in the news media. The process stars the politicians who run for office, the spin doctors who manage the campaigns, and the reporters who dig into every nook and cranny. Meanwhile, readers and viewers serve as spectators, watching a play that does not seem to involve them.

The public journalism movement has drawn both criticism and praise as it has attempted to be taken seriously as another approach to journalism. Though not a substitute for investigative reporting or the routine coverage of daily events, public jour-

Despite criticism of the bland uniformity of most local news programs and their overemphasis on crime, television journalism does occasionally offer viewers the immediacy of seeing an event unfold live and unedited, such as this 1990s anti-nuke rally in New Hampshire.

nalism is a way to involve both the public and journalists more centrally in civic and political life. Editors and reporters interested in addressing citizen alienation—and reporter cynicism—began devising ways to engage people as conversational partners in determining the news. In an effort to draw the public into discussions about community priorities, these journalists began sponsoring reader and citizen forums as one part of the news process. Through such forums, readers are supposed to have a voice in shaping aspects of the news that directly affect them.

Although isolated citizen projects and reader forums are sprinkled throughout the history of journalism, the current public journalism movement began in earnest in the late 1980s. In 1987 and 1988, as Columbus, Georgia, suffered from a depressed economy, an alienated citizenry, and unresponsive leadership, a team of reporters from the *Columbus Ledger-Enquirer*, part of the Knight-Ridder chain, surveyed and talked with community leaders and other citizens about the future of the city. Based on the findings, the paper published an eight-part series.

When the provocative series evoked little public response, the paper's leadership realized there was no mechanism or forum for continuing the public discussions about the issues raised in the series. Consequently, the paper created such a forum by organizing a town meeting. Three hundred citizens showed up. The editor of the paper, Jack Swift, organized a follow-up cookout at his own home at which seventy-five concerned citizens created a new civic organization called United Beyond 2000, led by a steering committee with Swift as a leading member. Staffed by community volunteers, task forces formed around recreation, child care, racial tension, and teenage behavior. The committees spurred the city's managers and other political leaders into action. The Columbus project had generated public discussion, involved more people in the news process, and eased race and class tensions by bringing various groups together in public conversations. In the newsroom, the *Ledger-Enquirer* reimagined the place of journalists in politics: "Instead of standing outside the political community and reporting on its pathologies, they took up residence within its borders."[29]

Another important public journalism project began in Wichita, Kansas, after the 1988 elections. Davis Merritt was so discouraged by the paper's typical and conventional political coverage that he led a campaign to use public journalism as a catalyst for reinventing political news. The *Eagle's* first voter project during the 1990 governor's election used reader surveys and public forums to refocus the paper around a citizens' agenda. This involved dropping the tired horse-race metaphor—who's winning, who's losing—that usually frames political coverage. Merritt argues that "public life cannot regain its vitality on a diet of information alone." He believes that a new direction for journalism must "reengage citizens in public life" through two steps: "(1) Add to the definition of our job the additional objective of helping public life go well, and then (2) Develop the journalistic tools and reflexes necessary to reach that objective."[30] The *Eagle's* project partially revitalized regional politics in Kansas in the early 1990s. It influenced other papers as well, including the *Charlotte Observer*, which created a citizens' agenda to determine key issues for its election coverage throughout the 1990s.

A final example involves editors at Norfolk's *Virginian-Pilot*, which has been on a mission to change the culture of the newsroom since the early 1990s (see Figure 14.1). Defying the long-standing tradition of lone reporters covering beats and topics on their own, the paper reorganized reporters into teams. The editors also began using deliberative citizen forums, called *community conversations*, to discover not what people want to read but how "to name and frame issues" central to the community. These issues then became the driving force motivating some of the paper's coverage. According to the leading theorist of public journalism, New York University's Jay Rosen, "The idea is to frame stories from the citizen's view, rather than inserting man-in-the-street quotes into a frame dominated by professionals."[31]

Criticizing Public Journalism. By the mid-1990s, more than a hundred newspapers, many teamed with local television and public radio stations, had practiced a form of public journalism. Yet many critics and journalists remain skeptical of the experiment, which they often compare to a passing fad or a religious movement.[32] They are primarily concerned about civic journalism projects undermining reporters' long-standing role as neutral watchdogs.

Critics of public journalism have raised a number of other issues. First, some editors and reporters argue that such journalism merely panders to what readers want and takes editorial control away from the newsrooms. They believe that very small focus-group samples and poll research—tools of the marketing department—blur the boundary between the editorial and business functions of a paper. Journalists traditionally have viewed their work as public service and rarely think of the news as a product or commodity. Some fear that as they become more active in the community they may be perceived as community boosters rather than as community watchdogs. These journalists raise legitimate concerns that their work may be compromised if later they are required to report on the wrongdoings of other civic organizations.

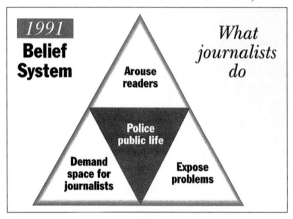

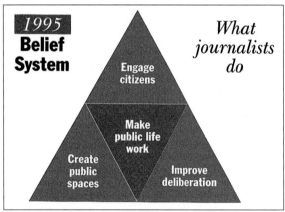

Figure 14.1
Changing the Culture of the Newsroom: Two Models at the *Virginian-Pilot*
In 1995, in the spirit of public journalism, the editors at the *Virginian-Pilot* attempted to transform the "belief system" of their newsroom, imagining themselves primarily as citizens helping to improve public life.
Source: Used by permission of the *Virginian-Pilot*.

Second, some critics worry that public journalism might compromise the profession's credibility, which today derives from detachment. They argue that public journalism turns reporters into participants rather than observers. However, as Merritt points out, professionals who have credibility are regarded as "honest, intelligent, well-intentioned, trustworthy" and "share some basic values about life, some common ground about common good." Yet conventional journalists insist they "don't share values, with anyone; that [they] are value-neutral."[33] He argues that modern journalism, as a result, actually has little credibility with the public. This view is buoyed by polls and studies that reveal the public's basic distrust of most major news media. Research studies in 1988, for instance, indicated that 50 percent of surveyed respondents said they had "a great deal of confidence in newspapers"; by 1993, similar polls showed that the confidence factor had dropped to 20 percent.[34] Still, many journalists believe that neutrality is a worthy ideal and the main source of a journalist's credibility.

Third, some reporters and editors argue that public journalism projects remove their control over both stories and the writing process. They are concerned that conversational models of reporting may undermine their narrative voices as well as their independence, especially if they are placed in reporting teams. Defenders of public journalism, however, respond that its goal is merely to create more frames and narrative models—not to eliminate reporters' control over stories or to eradicate traditional investigative forms of journalism. Public journalists say that their critics

Experiments in public journalism are now going on at newspapers around the country. In rethinking the role of American journalism, many editors and publishers have tried to address the public cynicism directed at both politics and the press. Public journalism asks reporters to become more involved with—rather than detached from—the communities they serve.

The Virginian-Pilot

COMMUNITY CONVERSATION

LESSONS OF LAKE GASTON

Tom Aiken
"If this had been handled regionally from the beginning . . . we would have had a lot more clout."

Joseph M. Donnelly
"As members of this family, we have an obligation to other family members."

Gary F. Russell
Hampton Roads cities should do something for each other when they can, with the expectation of long-range returns.

Mark Yatrofsky
"No relationship depends on a single part, a single issue."

Eloise Collins-Hall
"It's ridiculous to go out and say I'm going to do a project such as water, a subject this large, by myself."

Jerry M. Foley
"If we (in Norfolk) cooperate with Virginia Beach on the water, are they going to cooperate with us on the railway?"

F. Mason Gamage
The initial decision to pursue water from Lake Gaston was a political one, which meant citizens

Vincent D. Carpenter
Regionalism "seems to have multiple meanings for different people, and it seems to be a word that's

Robert M. King
Norfolk should get money from Virginia Beach for agreeing to limit the places it can sell

Norfolk and Virginia Beach have been squabbling for the past month over several aspects of a proposed Lake Gaston pipeline settlement that Virginia Beach negotiated with North Carolina.

AT ISSUE
Quest for Water

The settlement, which must be approved by both state legislatures by June 27, calls for a regional water authority and requires Norfolk to agree never to sell its surplus water to the Eastern Shore or the Peninsula.

Both cities have agreed Norfolk deserves some long-term financial compensation for agreeing to restrict its sales areas, but as of last week, they were still more than $100 million apart.

If the settlement falters ...
to the Federal Energy Re...
agency that must approv...
issue its ruling by July 1...

If FERC sides with Virg...
it would, North Carolina ...
reopening the decade of ...
resolve and delaying furt...

BY KAREN WEINTRAUB
AND MIKE KNEPLER
STAFF WRITERS

CONSENSUS
Think Regional

It was a hot day in mid-July when Gary F. Russell's ancient Chrysler Newport gave out in a shopping center parking lot.

He got sympathy from passers-by — "Oh, you've got a problem," and "Wow, I'd hate to be you." But they continued on their way.

One guy, though, walking out of a store with his son, stopped to help. He ended up splicing a hose to fix the leak in Russell's radiator.

Are you a regional citizen?/13

Russell offered to pay the man, but he refused.

"And what he said to me has remained with me to this day and always will," Russell said. "He said 'No. That's OK. Thank God that I'm in a position to help you today and perhaps you'll be in a position to help someone tomorrow.'"

To Russell, that's the way the cities of Hampton Roads should be acting toward one another in the current Lake Gaston water dispute and in other regional issues. They should do something for each other when they can, with the expectation of long-

but it's true," said Russell, a Portsmouth resident who manages a bank branch in Hampton.

Russell and a dozen other Hampton Roads residents who responded to an invitation from The Virginian-Pilot and The Ledger-S... a roundtable disc... day, had differen... the water issue... political leaders ... ginia Beach.

● The citizens standing why the incapable of work... mutual problems.

Municipal board them in their dai... Donnelly lives ...

The Wichita Eagle

Star Tribune

The Charlotte Observer

mistakenly believe that they merely give readers what they want, when in fact public journalists want to place more citizens at the table to help determine a more inclusive news agenda.

Fourth, critics contend that public journalism undermines the both-sides-of-a-story convention by constantly seeking common ground and community consensus. Public journalists counter that they are trying to set aside more room for centrist positions. Such positions are often representative of many in the community but are missing in the mainstream news, which is more interested in the extremist views that make a gripping news story. Many journalists, who seek to portray conflict by means of extreme viewpoints, worry that such views will become muted in public journalism. They charge that in seeking a middle ground, public journalism runs the risk of dulling the rough and robust edges of democratic speech.

public journalism reimagines reporting's role

Conventional journalism will fight ferociously for the overt principles that underpin its basic tenets—freedom of the press, the public's right to know, and two sides to every story—though it generally does not acknowledge any moral or ethical duty for improving the quality of daily life. Rather, journalism values its news-gathering capabilities and the well-constructed news narrative, leaving the improvement of civic life to political groups, nonprofit organizations, business philanthropists, and individual citizens.

Social Responsibility. Although reporters have traditionally thought of themselves first and foremost as observers and recorders, some journalists have occasionally acknowledged social responsibility. Among them was James Agee in the 1930s. In his

In *Let Us Now Praise Famous Men*, which begins with haunting photos taken by Walker Evans, author James Agee questioned the basic honesty of daily journalism in the late 1930s. He thought that professional journalists could too easily exploit interview subjects as simply news stories that serve a business enterprise without actively engaging in changing the conditions of social life.

book *Let Us Now Praise Famous Men*, which was accompanied by the Depression-era photography of Walker Evans, Agee regarded conventional journalism as dishonest, partly because the act of observing intruded on people and turned them into story characters.

Agee also worried that readers would retreat into the comfort of his writing—his narrative—instead of confronting what for many families was the horror of the Great Depression. For Agee, the question of responsibility extended not only to journalism and himself but to the readers of his stories as well: "The reader is no less centrally involved than the authors and those of whom they tell." Agee's self-conscious analysis provides insights into journalism's hidden agendas and larger social duties. Foreshadowing public journalism, Agee spoke to the responsibility of all citizens for making public life go better.

Deliberative Democracy. According to advocates of public journalism, when reporters are chiefly concerned with maintaining their antagonistic relationship to politics, and are less willing to improve political discourse, news and democracy suffer. *Washington Post* columnist David Broder thinks that national journalists—through rising salaries, prestige, and formal education—have distanced themselves "from the people that we are writing for and have become much, much closer to people we are writing about."[35] Broder believes that journalists need to become activists, not for a particular party but for the political process and for reenergizing public life. This might involve the news media spearheading voter registration drives or setting up pressrooms in public libraries or even shopping malls.

> "Neither journalism nor public life will move forward until we actually rethink, redescribe, and **reinterpret what journalism is;** not the science or information of our culture but its poetry and conversation."
> —James Carey,
> *Kettering Review,*
> 1992

By advocating a more active role for reporters and the news media, public journalism intends to reinvigorate both reporting and politics. Most of all, it offers people models for how to deliberate in forums, and then it covers those deliberations. Public journalism aims to improve our standard *representative democracy*, in which most of us sit back and watch elected officials act on our behalf, by reinvigorating *deliberative democracy*, in which citizen groups, local government, and the news media together take a more active role in shaping social and political agendas. In a more deliberative democracy, a large segment of the community discusses public life and social policy before advising or electing officials who represent the community's interests.

In 1989, the historian Christopher Lasch argued that "the job of the press is to encourage debate, not to supply the public with information."[36] Although he overstated his case—journalism does both and more—Lasch made a cogent point about how conventional journalism has lost its bearings. Adrift in data, mainstream journalism has lost touch with its partisan roots. The early mission of journalism—to advocate opinions and encourage public debate—has been relegated to alternative magazines, the editorial pages, an occasional TV documentary, and Sunday morning news programs, starring Washington's elite reporters and prominent politicians. Ironically, Lasch connected the gradual decline in voter participation, which began in the 1920s, to more responsible conduct on the part of professional journalists. With a modern "objective" press, he contended, the public increasingly began to defer to the "more professional" news media to watch over civic life on its behalf.

As the advocates of public journalism acknowledge, people have become used to letting their representatives think and act for them. Public journalism and other civic projects offer citizens an opportunity to deliberate and to influence their leaders. Public journalism asks the mainstream press to reconsider its role in deliberative democracy. This may include broadening the story frames that journalists use to recount experiences; paying more attention to the historical context of their stories;

doing more reports that analyze both news conventions and social issues; taking more responsibility for their news narratives; and participating more fully in the public life of their communities.

Arguing that for too long journalism has defined its role only in negative terms, news scholar Jay Rosen notes, "To be adversarial, critical, to ask tough questions, to expose scandal and wrongdoing . . . these are necessary tasks, even noble tasks, but they are negative tasks." In addition, he suggests, journalism should assert itself as a positive force, not merely as a watchdog or as a neutral information conduit to readers but as "a support system for public life."[37]

REVIEW QUESTIONS

1. What are the drawbacks of the informational model of journalism?

2. What is news?

3. What are some of the key values that underlie modern journalism?

4. How do issues such as deception and privacy present ethical problems for journalists?

5. Why is getting a story first important to reporters?

6. What are the connections between neutral journalism and economics?

7. Why have reporters become so dependent on experts?

8. Why do many conventional journalists believe firmly in the idea that there are two sides to every story?

9. How is credibility established in TV news as compared to print journalism?

10. With regard to TV news, what are sound bites and happy talk?

11. What is public journalism? How does it propose to make journalism better?

12. What are the major criticisms of the public journalism movement, and why do the mainstream national media have concerns about public journalism?

13. How do public and conventional journalists differ when it comes to maintaining credibility with their audience?

14. What is deliberative democracy, and what does it have to do with public journalism?

QUESTIONING THE MEDIA

1. What are your main criticisms of the state of news today? In your opinion, what are the news media doing well?

2. As a reporter or editor, should you quit voting to demonstrate your ability to be neutral? Why or why not?

3. How would you go about formulating an ethical policy with regard to using deceptive means to get a story?

4. For a reporter, what are the dangers of both detachment from and involvement in public life?

5. What steps would you take to make journalism work better in a democracy?

The purpose of this project is to extend your critical approach to the news. With a partner, choose for reading and viewing one local daily paper, the *New York Times*, and one network or CNN newscast—*all from the same weekday*.

Devise a series of charts and a descriptive scheme that will allow you to compare who gets quoted as expert sources in the stories for that particular day. For example, devise one chart that compares the occupations of the sources. Are they from academic, business, or government sectors? Or are they "ordinary" people? Throughout this project, *limit your focus to local, national, or international news*.

1. *Description*. Count the total number of sources used by each newspaper or network program. Look for quotes in news articles and for sound bites on television. Are all sources identified? How are they identified? Can you tell which area of the country these sources are from? What kinds of experts are quoted in the news? What jobs do they seem to hold? What gender are the news sources?

2. *Analysis*. After completing your charts, write one or two paragraphs discussing patterns that emerge. Who seems to get quoted most often? Among those quoted, what kinds of occupations appear most frequently? Do male or female sources dominate?

3. *Interpretation*. Write a one- or two-paragraph critical interpretation of your findings. How are the sources used? Why do you think certain sources appear more frequently than other sources in this day's news? Why do reporters seek out certain types of sources rather than others? Does the gender of sources mean anything?

4. *Evaluation*. Discuss the limitations of your study and whether you think print or television handles sources best. Did circumstances on the particular day you chose suggest why one type of expert appears more often than other types?

(*Note*: This assignment works either as an in-class presentation or as a written project. Either way, it should include charts that help organize the material.)

CHAPTER 15

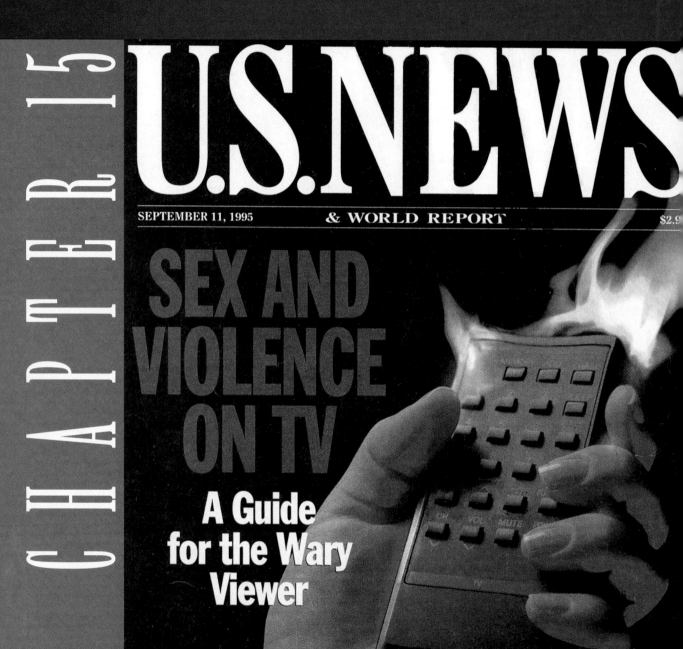

U.S.NEWS

SEPTEMBER 11, 1995   & WORLD REPORT $2.9

SEX AND VIOLENCE ON TV

A Guide for the Wary Viewer

In 1966, NBC showed the Rod Serling made-for-television thriller *The Doomsday Flight*, the first movie to depict an airplane hijacking. In the story, a man plants a bomb and tries to extract ransom money from an airline. In the days following the telecast, the nation's major airlines reported a dramatic rise in anonymous bomb threats, some of them classified as teenage pranks. The network agreed not to run the film again.

In 1993, the Walt Disney Company released a movie called *The Program*. The film included a controversial scene showing a troubled college quarterback who believes he has to place his life in danger to test his "courage" and maintain his leadership status among his peers. The test required lying down on the dividing line of a busy highway as cars zoomed past on either side. Shortly after the film's release, a rash of real-life copycat incidents occurred. After one teenager died, Disney recalled the film and cut the scene from the movie.

When they took place, both movie incidents renewed long-standing cultural debates over the suggestive power of visual imagery and screen violence. Since the emergence of movies and television as influential mass media, the relationship between make-believe stories and real-life imitation has drawn a great deal of attention. Concerns have been raised not only by parents, teachers, and politicians but by several generations of mass communication researchers as well.

When it comes to government- or university-sponsored mass media research, no social groups have been pondered and probed more than children and teens. The dominant strain of this research—known in shorthand as *media effects*—has focused on a particular area: the connection between aggressive behavior and violent media stories. In the late 1960s, government leaders—reacting to the social upheavals of that decade—first set aside $1 million to examine this connection. Since that time, thousands of studies have told us what most kindergarten teachers believe instinctively: Violent scenes on television and in movies stimulate aggressive behavior in children—especially young boys. Over the years, children have imitated fight scenes from the *Mighty Mouse Playhouse*, *Batman*, *Teenage Mutant Ninja Turtles*, and the *Mighty Morphin Power Rangers*, leading generations of adults to suspect the effects of mass media.

In this chapter, we will examine the evolution of media research over time. After looking at some early research efforts, we will focus on two major strains in media research: effects research and cultural studies. We will investigate the strengths and limitations of these two approaches. Finally, we will consider how media research interacts with democratic ideals.

early developments in media research

In the early days of the United States, philosophical and historical writings tried to explain the nature of news and print media. For instance, Frenchman Alexis de Tocqueville, author of *Democracy in America*, noted differences between French and American newspapers in the early 1830s:

> In France the space allotted to commercial advertisements is very limited, and . . . the essential part of the journal is the discussion of the politics of the day. In America three quarters of the enormous sheet are filled with advertisements and the remainder is frequently occupied by political intelligence or trivial anecdotes; it is only from time to time that one finds a corner devoted to the passionate discussions like those which the journalists of France every day give to their readers.[1]

During the mid- to late nineteenth century, the major models of media analysis were based on moral and political arguments, as suggested in de Tocqueville's writings.[2] More scientific approaches to mass media research did not begin to develop until the late 1920s and 1930s.

It was in 1920 that Walter Lippmann, in his book *Liberty and the News*, called on journalists to operate more like scientific researchers in gathering and analyzing factual material. Lippmann's next book, *Public Opinion*, published in 1922, applied psychology to journalism. It is considered by many academics to be "the founding book in American media studies."[3]

In America, the emphasis on applied research led to an expanded analysis of the effects of the media, emphasizing data collection and numerical measurement. According to media historian Daniel Czitrom, by the 1930s "an aggressively empirical spirit, stressing new and increasingly sophisticated research techniques, characterized the study of modern communication in America."[4] Czitrom traces four early trends between 1930 and 1960 that contributed to the rise of modern media research: propaganda analysis, public opinion research, social psychology studies, and marketing research.

Propaganda Analysis. After World War I, some media researchers became interested in the ways in which propaganda had been used to advance the American war effort. They found that, during the war, governments routinely relied on propaganda divisions as part of their "information" apparatus. Though propaganda was considered a positive force for mobilizing public opinion during the war, researchers after the war labeled propaganda as "partisan appeal based on half-truths and devious manipulation of communication channels."[5] Harold Lasswell's important 1927 study, *Propaganda Techniques in the World War*, focused on media representations, defining propaganda as "the control of opinion by significant symbols, . . . by stories, rumors, reports, pictures and other forms of social communication."[6] *Propaganda analysis* became a major early strain in mass media research.

Public Opinion Research. Researchers soon extended the study of war propaganda to include general concerns about how the mass media filtered information and shaped public attitudes. In the face of growing media influence, Walter Lippmann distrusted the public's ability to function as knowledgeable citizens as well as journalism's ability to help the public separate truth from lies. In promoting the place of the expert in modern life, Lippmann celebrated the social scientist as part of a new expert class that could best make "unseen facts intelligible to those who have to make decisions."[7]

Today, Lippmann's expert class conducts citizen surveys in the form of *public opinion research*, which has become especially influential during political elections. On the upside, research on diverse populations has provided insights into citizen behavior and social differences, especially during election periods or following major national events. For example, election polls demonstrated that Bill Clinton's 1996 victory over Bob Dole was partly the result of the president's heavy support among women voters. In another example, polls conducted after the first O.J. Simpson verdict convincingly documented a wide disparity among white and black citizens regarding their relative trust or suspicion of police officers. A number of research studies—informally copied by network newsmagazines such as ABC's *Primetime Live*—also demonstrated that a group of young white males cruising a city's main thoroughfare in a car was far less likely to be routinely stopped by police than was a similar car occupied by young black males driving the same route.

On the downside, the journalism profession has become increasingly dependent on political polls. Some critics ask whether this heavy reliance on measured public opinion has begun to adversely affect active political involvement. For example, stories and studies abound about citizens who decide not to vote because they have already seen poll projections on television and decided that their votes would not make a difference in the outcome. Furthermore, since the public does not design a CBS News or Gallup poll, it is just passively responding to surveys that mainly measure what interests business, government, academics, and the mainstream news media. As one critic notes, "rather than offer governments the opinions that citizens want them to learn, polls tell governments—or other sponsors—what they would like to learn about citizens' opinions."[8]

Social Psychology Studies. Whereas opinion polls measure public attitudes, *social psychology studies* measure individual behavior and cognition. Conducted by social

One of the earliest forms of U.S. mass communication research—propaganda analysis—was prominent during this century's two world wars. Researchers studied the impact of war posters and other government information campaigns to determine how audiences could be persuaded to a position through stirring media messages about patriotism and duty.

Figure 15.1

TV Rating Labels and the Impact of Media Research

Parents and politicians harshly criticized the new 1997 television rating labels for revealing too little about a particular program's actual content. The TV industry continues to study its self-imposed system, promising to fine-tune it to ensure that the government keeps its distance. However flawed, these standards are one example of a policy that was shaped in part by media research. Since the 1960s, a stockpile of accumulated evidence has pointed to links between violent TV images and increased levels of aggression among children and adolescents.

Source: The New York Times, December 20, 1996, p. A12.

AT A GLANCE

Should the Children Watch?

The new television ratings and how they would apply.

TV-Y
All children
This program is designed to be appropriate for all children.
EXAMPLES "The Flintstones," "Scooby Doo," "Bugs Bunny"

TV-Y7
Directed to older children
This program is designed for children age 7 and above.
EXAMPLES "Mighty Morphin Power Rangers," "Teen-Age Mutant Ninja Turtles"

TV-G
General Audience
Most parents would find this program suitable for all ages.
EXAMPLES "The Cosby Show," "Dr. Quinn Medicine Woman," "Touched by an Angel"

TV-PG
Parental Guidance suggested
This program may contain some material that many parents would find unsuitable younger children.
EXAMPLES "Lois and Clark," "Third Rock From the Sun"

TV-14
Parents strongly cautioned
This program may contain some material that many parents would find unsuitable for chilren under 14.
EXAMPLES "NYPD Blue," "Cybill," "Walker Texas Ranger"

TV-M
Mature audience only
This program is specifically designed to be viewed by adults and therefore may be unsuitable for children under 17.
EXAMPLES "Dream On", "Red Shoe Diaries"

psychologists, the most influential of these early investigations, the Payne Fund, grew out of a 1925 project examining the reading habits and learning behavior of juveniles. Backed by Standard Oil money, Payne Fund researchers also investigated radio as a force for education and the effects of movies—especially gangster films—on children and teenagers. These trailblazing studies, which were used by politicians to attack the movie industry, linked frequent movie attendance to juvenile delinquency and antisocial behavior, arguing that movies took "emotional possession" of young filmgoers.[9] The forerunners of today's TV violence and aggression research, these studies became the staple of media research beginning in the late 1960s. (See Figure 15.1 for one example of a contemporary policy that has developed from media research.)

Marketing Research. A fourth influential area of media research, primarily private, developed through the efforts of advertisers, book publishers, and product companies. They began conducting surveys on consumer buying habits, known as *marketing research*. Specialized researchers, using improved audience sampling and statistical techniques, began selling their services to advertisers and media firms in the 1920s. The emergence of commercial radio led to the first ratings systems that measured how many people were listening on a given night. By the 1930s, radio networks, advertisers, large stations, and advertising agencies all subscribed to ratings services. However, compared to print media, whose circulation departments kept careful track of customer names and addresses, radio listeners were more difficult to trace. This problem precipitated the development of increasingly sophisticated direct-mail diaries, phone surveys, and eventually the telemarketing industry, tracking consumer preferences and measuring media use worldwide.

> "Research is formalized **curiosity**. It is poking and prying with a purpose."
> —Zora Neale Hurston, writer

research on media effects

As concern about public opinion, propaganda, and the impact of the media merged with the growth of journalism and mass communication departments, media researchers looked more and more to behavioral science as a model. Between 1930

IF YOU KEEP WATCHING THAT VIOLENCE YOUR HEAD IS GOING TO EXPLODE, SPLATTERING YOUR MUSHY BRAINS ALL OVER MY NICE, CLEAN CARPET.

COOL!

Rob Rogers
Pittsburgh Post-Gazette
United Feature Syndicate

and 1960, "who says what to whom with what effect" became the key question "defining the scope and problems of American communications research."[10] Answering this question activated the major strain in media research, usually identified as **media effects**: research that attempts to understand, explain, and predict the impact—or effects—of mass media on individuals and society. For example, if children watch a lot of TV cartoons (stimulus or cause), will this repeated act influence their behavior toward their peers (response or effect)?

For most of the twentieth century, both media researchers and news reporters have used different methods and routines to answer similar sets of questions—who, what, when, and where—about our daily experiences. In the practice of their professions, researchers and reporters have typically remained suspicious of concepts such as interpretation, subjectivity, and values, seeing them as problems to be avoided or even as dangerous contaminators of their work. A major difference exists, however, between the two fields. Whereas daily news reporters *describe* what happens when teenagers watch violent movies, media researchers not only describe but try to *explain* what happened and often *predict* whether it will happen again.

Media research generally comes from the private or public sectors—each type differing from the other in important ways. *Private research*, sometimes called *proprietary research*, is most often conducted for a business or a corporation. It is usually applied research in the sense that the information it uncovers typically addresses some real-life problem or need, such as determining consumer buying habits or market trends. *Public research*, on the other hand, usually takes place in academic and government settings. It involves information that is often more *theoretical* than applied; it tries to clarify, explain, or predict the effects of mass media rather than to address a consumer problem. Most public research is subject to examination and refutation by other academics. In contrast, private research is seldom shared, although the results of some private opinion polls or broadcast ratings may be released to the public with the owners' permission.

By the 1960s, media studies became synonymous with effects research and with the statistical measurement of audiences. Funding for this type of research was also easier to obtain since it coincided with the interests of both the government and the media: Federal agencies were interested in monitoring various populations, and media industries were interested in the psychology and behavior of consumers.

"My idea of a **good time** is using jargon and citing authorities."
—Matt Groening, *School Is Hell*, 1987

key phases in research approaches

A major goal of scientific research is to develop theories or laws that can consistently explain or predict human behavior. The varied impacts of the mass media and the diverse ways in which people make popular culture, however, tend to defy predictable rules. Historical, economic, and political factors influence media industries, making it difficult to develop systematic theories that explain communication. What has developed instead are a number of small theories or models that help explain individual behavior rather than the impact of the media on large populations. But before these small theories began to emerge in the 1970s, mass media research used several other models. Developing between the 1930s and the 1970s, these major models included the hypodermic needle, minimal effects, and uses and gratifications.

Hypodermic Needle Model. One of the earliest and least persuasive media theories attributed powerful effects to the mass media. A number of intellectuals and academics were particularly fearful of the popularity of film and radio, which had become powerful cultural forces in the 1920s and 1930s. Some of these observations were made by social psychologists and sociologists who arrived in this country to flee Hitler and Nazism in the 1930s. Having watched Hitler use radio, film, and print media as propaganda tools for Nazism, they worried that the popular media in America also had a strong hold over vulnerable audiences. This concept of powerful media affecting weak audiences has been labeled the **hypodermic needle model**, sometimes also called the *bullet theory* or *direct effects model*. It suggests that the media shoot their potent effects directly into unsuspecting victims. Although this theory has been disregarded or disproved by social scientists, many people still attribute such direct effects to the mass media, particularly in the case of children.

> **"Theories abound, examples multiply,** but convincing facts that specific media content is reliably associated with particular effects have proved quite elusive."
> —Guy Cumberbatch,
> *A Measure of Uncertainty,*
> 1989

Minimal Effects Model. With the rise of empirical research techniques, social scientists began demonstrating that the media alone do not cause people to change their attitudes and behaviors. At this point, the limited or **minimal effects model** emerged. Based on tightly controlled experiments and surveys, researchers generally argued that people engage in **selective exposure** and **selective retention** with regard to the media. That is, we selectively expose ourselves to media messages that are most familiar to us, and we retain messages that confirm values and attitudes we already hold. In other words, minimal effects researchers argued that in most cases the mass media reinforce existing behaviors and attitudes rather than change them.

The findings from the first comprehensive study of children and television, by Wilbur Schramm, Jack Lyle, and Edwin Parker in the late 1950s, best captures the minimal effects tradition:

> For *some* children, under *some* conditions, *some* television is harmful. For *other* children under the same conditions, or for the same children under *other* conditions, it may be beneficial. For *most* children, under *most* conditions, *most* television is probably neither particularly harmful nor particularly beneficial.[11]

Joseph Klapper's important 1960 research review, *The Effects of Mass Communication*, found that the mass media influenced individuals who did not already hold strong views on an issue and that the media also had a greater impact on poor and uneducated heavy users. Solidifying the minimal effects argument, Klapper concluded that media effects occur largely at an individual level and do not appear to have large-scale, measurable and direct effects on society as a whole.[12]

Uses and Gratifications Model. Aside from difficulties in proving direct cause-effect relationships, the effects tradition usually assumed that audiences were passive and acted upon by the media. As early as the late 1950s, Schramm, Lyle, and Parker suggested problems with this position:

> In a sense the term "effect" is misleading because it suggests that television "does something" to children. The connotation is that television is the actor, the children are acted upon. Children are thus made to seem relatively inert; television, relatively active. Children are sitting victims; television bites them. Nothing can be further from the fact. It is the children who are most active in this relationship. It is they who use television, rather than television that uses them.[13]

Indeed, as the authors observed, numerous studies have concluded that viewers—especially young children—are often *actively* engaged in the media, using various forms to guide their play.

A response to the minimal effects theory, the **uses and gratifications model** began developing in the 1940s to contest the notion of audience passivity. Under this model, researchers—usually using in-depth interviews to supplement survey questionnaires—studied the ways people used the media to satisfy various emotional or intellectual needs. The uses and gratifications model represented a middle position between the hypodermic needle and minimal effects models. This research focused on audience use and the functions of the media. Instead of asking "What effects do the media have on us?" researchers asked "Why do we use the media?" Using this approach, one study found, for instance, that a majority of people said they read newspapers primarily for entertainment and that getting information was a less important function of news reading.[14]

Asking the *why* question allowed media researchers to develop inventories cataloguing how people employed the media. For example, individuals used the media to see authority figures elevated or toppled, to seek a sense of community and connectedness, to fulfill needs for drama and stories, and to confirm moral or spiritual values.[15] Though the uses and gratifications model addressed the *functions* of the mass media for individuals, it did not address the important questions related to the *impact* of the media on society. Once researchers had accumulated substantial lists of uses and functions, they often did not move in new directions. Consequently, the uses and gratifications model never became a dominant strain in media research.

approaches to media effects

Most media research, whether conducted in universities or in public policy institutes, has focused on the effects of the media on issues such as learning, attitudes, aggression, and voting habits. This research employs the **scientific method**, a blueprint long used by scientists and scholars for studying phenomena in systematic stages. These steps include:

1. identifying the research problem

2. reviewing existing research and theories related to the problem

3. developing working hypotheses or predictions about what the study might find

4. determining an appropriate method or research design

5. collecting information or relevant data

6. analyzing results to see if the hypotheses have been verified

7. interpreting the implications of the study to determine if they explain or predict patterns in human behavior

The scientific method relies on *objectivity* (eliminating bias and judgments on the part of researchers); *reliability* (getting the same answers or outcomes from a study or measure during repeated testing); and *validity* (demonstrating that a study actually measures what it claims to measure).

In scientific studies, researchers pose one or more **hypotheses**: tentative general statements that predict a relationship between a *dependent variable* that is influenced by an *independent variable*. For example, a researcher might hypothesize that a person's level of formal education (independent variable) influences higher instances of reading print media (dependent variable). That is, the more formal education acquired, the more print material consumed. Or, a researcher might predict that heavy levels of TV viewing among adolescents (independent variable) cause poor performances (dependent variable) in traditional school settings. Broadly speaking, the methods for studying media effects on audiences have taken two forms—experimental studies and survey research. To supplement these approaches, researchers also use content analysis as a technique for counting and documenting specific messages in mass media. We will look at all three.

Experimental Research. Like all studies that use the scientific method, **experiments** in media research isolate some aspect of content, suggest a hypothesis, and manipulate variables to discover a particular medium's impact on attitude, emotion, or behavior. To test whether a hypothesis is true, researchers expose an *experimental group*—the group under study—to a selected media program or text. To ensure valid results, researchers use a *control group*, which serves as a basis for comparison; this group has *not* been exposed to the selected media content. Subjects are picked for each group through **random assignment**, which simply means that every subject has an equal chance of being placed in either group. Random assignment generally ensures that the variables researchers want to control are distributed in the same way to each group.

For instance, researchers might take a group of ten-year-old boys and randomly assign them to two groups. They expose the experimental group to a violent action movie that the control group does not see. Later, both groups are exposed to a staged fight between two other boys so that the researchers can observe how each group responds to an actual physical confrontation. Researchers then determine whether there is a statistically measurable difference between the two groups' responses to the fight. For example, perhaps the control subjects tried to break up the fight but the experimental subjects did not.

Experimental research demonstrating the link between aggressive behavior and fictional violence has inspired a variety of projects that show the media's impact in more practical terms. *Media Mayhem*, a visual literacy project developed by the University of Wisconsin–Green Bay, looks at how visual images glamorize violence.

Since the groups were randomly selected and since the only measurable difference between them was the introduction of the movie, researchers may conclude that under these conditions the violent film caused a different behavior.

When experiments carefully account for variables through random assignment, they generally work well in substantiating direct cause-effect links. Such research takes place both in laboratory settings and in field settings, where people can be observed using the media in their everyday environments. In field experiments, however, it is more difficult for researchers to control variables. In lab settings, researchers have more control, but other problems may occur. For example, when subjects are removed from the environments in which they regularly use the media, they may act different-ly—often with less inhibitions—than they would in their everyday surroundings.

Experiments have other limitations as well. For instance, they are not general-izable to a larger population; they cannot tell us whether cause-effect results can be duplicated outside the laboratory. In addition, most academic experiments today are performed on college students, who are convenient subjects for research but are not representative of the American public. Although experiments are fairly good at pre-dicting short-term media effects under controlled conditions, they do not predict how subjects will behave months or years later in the real world.

Surveys. For long-term studies of the media, surveys usually work best. In its sim-plest terms, **survey research** is a method of collecting and measuring data taken from a group of respondents. Using random sampling techniques that give each potential subject an equal chance to be included in the survey, this research method draws on much larger populations than those used in experimental studies. Surveys are simply measuring instruments and do *not* control variables through randomly assigned groups. Survey investigators cannot account for all the variables that might affect media use; therefore, they cannot show cause-effect relationships. Survey research can, however, reveal *correlations*—or associations—between two variables. For example, a random questionnaire survey of ten-year-old boys might demonstrate that a correlation exists between aggressive behavior and watching violent TV programs, but it does not explain which causes which. Unlike experimental research, how-ever, surveys are usually generalizable to the larger society; they can approximate what percentage of a population exhibits certain media-induced behaviors.

> "Writing survey questions and gathering data are easy; writing good questions and collecting useful data are not."
> —Michael Singletary,
> *Mass Communication Research*, 1994

Surveys are also useful measures for comparing voting behavior and levels of media use. To aid survey research, subjects are sometimes assigned to panel studies in which smaller groups of people are interviewed in-depth on several occasions. In addi-tion, surveys allow researchers to investigate various populations in long-term studies. For example, survey research might measure subjects when they are ten, twenty, and thirty years old to track changes in how frequently they watch television and what kinds of programs they prefer at different ages.

Survey researchers usually locate people by using direct mail, personal inter-views, and telephone calls. They can also accumulate large amounts of information by surveying diverse cross sections of people. These data allow researchers to examine demographic factors such as educational background, income levels, race, gender, age, lifestyle profiles, political affiliations, and attitudes. Large government and academic survey databases are now widely available to researchers for doing analyses and com-parisons worldwide. This may lead to the development of more long-range—or lon-gitudinal—studies, which allow social scientists to compare new studies to those con-ducted years earlier. In general, however, it is cheaper and easier to do short-term experimental and survey research, analyzing the effects of the media on particular individuals. Effects research focused on a large community or societal responses to the media over time is much more difficult to conduct and sustain.

Content Analysis. Over the years, researchers recognized that traditional media-effects studies generally ignored specific media messages. As a corrective, researchers developed a method known as **content analysis** to study the messages of print and visual media. Such analysis is a systematic method for coding and measuring media content.

Although content analyses were first used during World War II, more recent studies have focused on television, tracking the numbers of male and female, black and white, and blue- and white-collar characters in daytime and prime-time programming. Probably the most influential content analyses have been conducted by George Gerbner and his colleagues at the University of Pennsylvania; since the late 1960s, they have coded and counted acts of violence on network television. Combined with survey methods, these annual "violence profiles" have shown that heavy watchers of television, including both children and retired Americans, tend to overestimate the amount of violence that exists in the actual world.[16]

The limits of content analysis have been well documented. This technique does not measure the effects of the media or explain why a particular media message gets produced in the first place. Because content analysis is basically descriptive, it is often used in combination with other research techniques. This allows researchers to analyze and interpret the figures produced by content counts. For example, a 1997 study showed that, although women make up a majority of the U.S. population, 63 percent of movie characters, 55 percent of TV characters, and 78 percent of music video performers were men.[17] Content analysis alone, however, cannot tell us exactly what this means to viewers who regularly watch media fare. Problems of definition also occur. For instance, in coding and counting acts of violence, how do researchers distinguish slapstick cartoon aggression from the violent murders or rapes in an evening police drama? Critics point out that such varied depictions may have diverse and subtle effects on viewers that are difficult to measure or quantify.

Throughout the 1990s, the syndicated afternoon children's program *Mighty Morphin Power Rangers* attracted the attention of millions of young viewers and the anger of many adults. Acknowledging the positive verbal messages in the shows, parent and teacher groups nevertheless complained that children mostly remembered and imitated the violent action scenes. The program's producers defended their morphing rangers, arguing that TV programs help children wrestle with the aggressive feelings that everyone has.

As content analysis grew as a primary research tool in media research, it sometimes pushed to the sidelines other ways of thinking about television and media content. Broad questions concerning the media as a popular art form, as a democratic influence, or as a force for social control are difficult to address through strict measurement techniques. Critics of content analysis, in fact, have objected to the kind of social science that reduces culture to acts of counting. Such criticism has addressed the tendency by some researchers to favor measurement accuracy over intellectual discipline.[18] In response, many social scientists have come to regard content analysis as simply one of many techniques that can be used to understand the complex issues that abound in the mass media.

By the 1960s, the first schools of mass communication began graduating Ph.D.-level researchers schooled in experimental or survey techniques and content analysis. These researchers began documenting consistent patterns found in mass communication. Two of the most influential contemporary frameworks that help explain media effects have been agenda-setting and the cultivation effect.

Agenda-Setting. A key phenomenon posited by media-effects researchers has been **agenda-setting**: the idea that when the mass media pay attention to particular events or issues, they determine—set the agenda for—the major topics of discussion for individuals and society. Like uses and gratifications, agenda-setting research has tried to strike a balance between the views of the mass media as all-powerful and the mass media as barely powerful. Essentially, agenda-setting researchers have argued that the mass media do not so much tell us what to think but rather *what to think about*. Traceable to Walter Lippmann's notion in the early 1920s that the media "create pictures in our heads," the first social science investigations of agenda-setting began in the 1970s.[19]

Over the years, agenda-setting research has demonstrated that the more stories the news media do on a particular subject, the more importance audiences attach to that subject. For instance, when the media began seriously covering ecology issues after the first Earth Day in 1970, a much higher percentage of the population began listing the environment as a primary social concern in surveys. When *Jaws* became the top box-office movie in 1975, the news media started featuring more shark-attack stories; even landlocked people in the Midwest began ranking sharks as a problem despite the rarity of such incidents worldwide.

During the 1986 elections, local and national candidates often spoke about the problems of crime and illegal drugs. At the time, researchers documented a big leap in the media's attention to drugs, especially to crack cocaine; they found more than four hundred news stories over a forty-week period dealing with cocaine in America's major papers, newsmagazines, and newscasts.[20] Not surprisingly, the big jump in drug stories was accompanied by a parallel rise in public opinion polls. In April 1986, only 2 percent of the respondents to a *New York Times*/CBS News poll picked drugs as the nation's most important problem. By early September 1986, however, a survey found that drugs topped the list with 13 percent of 1,210 adults interviewed choosing drugs as the nation's most important problem. This shift occurred even though government statisticians showed that illicit drug use—despite rises in the use of crack cocaine—had generally dipped and leveled off since peaking in 1979–80.[21] Although many people's attitudes toward drugs were not affected by increases in news stories, the marked shift in public opinion is a good example of the agenda-setting effect of the news media.

The Cultivation Effect. Another mass media phenomenon—the **cultivation effect**—suggests that heavy viewing of television leads individuals to perceive reality in ways that are consistent with the portrayals they see on television. In essence, this area of effects research attempts to push researchers past the focus on individual behavior and toward larger ideas about the media's impact on society. One study in the late 1960s, for instance, suggested that teens from low-income families tended to view television as more true-to-life than did their middle-income peers. The major research in this area grew from the TV-violence profiles of George Gerbner and his colleagues, who attempted to make larger generalizations about the impact of televised violence on real life. The basic idea suggests that the more time an audience spends viewing television and absorbing its viewpoints, the more likely it is that the audience's own views of social reality will be "cultivated" by the images and portrayals they have seen on television.[22]

According to this view, media messages interact in complicated ways with personal, social, political, and cultural factors; they are one of a number of important factors in determining individual behavior and defining social values. Some critics have charged that cultivation research has provided limited evidence. The cultivation framework, however, deserves close attention, especially with regard to findings about heavy television viewers who believe that the world is a meaner place than it actually is.

evaluating research on media effects

The mainstream models of media research have made valuable contributions to our understanding of the mass media, submitting content and audiences to rigorous testing. This wealth of research exists partly because funding for studies regarding the effects of the media on young people remains popular among politicians and draws ready government support. Because science is systematic and cumulative, we have substantial data—more than fifteen hundred studies—that clearly link aggression in children to violent images and actions in media.

> "Many studies currently published in mainstream communication journals seem filled with **sophisticated treatments of trivial data**, which, while showing effects . . . make slight contributions to what we really know about human mass-mediated communication."
>
> —Willard Rowland and Bruce Watkins, *Interpreting Television*, 1984

Although the potential for government funding restricts the scope of some media research, other limits also face researchers, including the inability to address how the media affect communities and social institutions. Since most media research operates best in examining media and individual behavior, fewer research studies exist on media's impact on community and social life. Research has begun to address these limits and to turn more attention to the increasing impact of media technology on national life and international communication.

cultural approaches to media research

During the rise of modern media research, approaches with a stronger historical and interpretive edge developed as well, often in direct opposition to the scientific models. In the late 1930s, some social scientists began to warn about the limits of "gathering data and charting trends," particularly when research served advertisers and media organizations. Such private market research tended to be narrowly focused on individual behavior, ignoring questions like "Where are institutions taking us?" and "Where do we want them to take us?"[23]

It is important here to distinguish directions in American media studies from British-European traditions. In Europe, media studies have favored interpretive rather than scientific approaches; in other words, researchers approached media questions and problems more like literary critics than experimental or survey researchers. Such approaches built on the writings of political philosophers such as Karl Marx and Antonio Gramsci; researchers investigated how the mass media have been used to maintain existing hierarchies in society. They examined, for example, the ways in

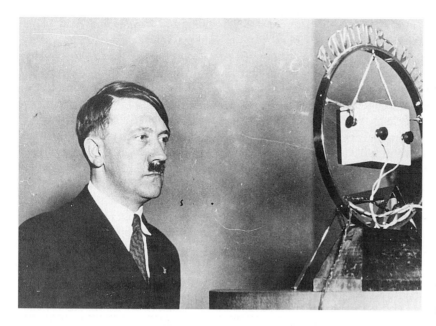

Early media researchers were concerned about Hitler's use of national radio to control information and indoctrinate the German people throughout the 1930s. Germany's wartime international broadcasts, however, were considered failures. Trying to undermine morale in broadcasts aimed at Allied soldiers and the British people, Germany hired British defector William Joyce ("Lord Haw Haw") and Ohioan Mildred Gillars ("Axis Sally"). Because so many media messages competed with Nazi propaganda in democratic countries, these radio traitors had little impact.

which popular culture or sports distracted people from redressing social injustices. They also studied the subordinate status of some social groups in attempting to address some of the deficiencies of emerging social science research.

In the United States, early criticism of modern media research came from the Frankfurt School, a group of European researchers transplanted from Germany to America after they fled Nazi persecution in the 1930s. Under the leadership of Max Horkheimer, T. W. Adorno, and Leo Lowenthal, the school pointed to at least three inadequacies of traditional scientific approaches, arguing that they (1) reduced large "cultural questions" to measurable and "verifiable categories"; (2) depended on "an atmosphere of rigidly enforced neutrality"; and (3) refused to place "the phenomena of modern life" in a "historical and moral context."[24] The Frankfurt School researchers did not reject outright the usefulness of measuring and counting data. They contended, however, that historical and cultural approaches would focus critical attention on the long-range processes of the mass media and their complex relations with audiences.

cultural studies

Since the Frankfurt School, criticisms of the effects tradition and its methods have continued, with calls for more interpretive studies of the rituals of mass communication. Academics who have embraced a cultural approach try to understand how media and culture are tied to the actual patterns of communication in daily life. An important body of research—loosely labeled **cultural studies**—began challenging the mainstream media-effects models in the 1960s. These studies generally have focused on how people make meanings, understand reality, and order experience through their use of cultural symbols in print and visual media. This research has attempted to make everyday culture the centerpiece of media studies, focusing on the subtle ways that mass communication shapes and is shaped by history, politics, and economics. For example, in the 1970s, Stuart Hall and his colleagues studied the British print media and the police as forms of urban surveillance. In *Policing the Crisis*, the authors revealed how political, economic, and cultural constraints aided the news media's success at mobilizing public opinion about crime.[25]

Most cultural researchers assume that all culture and its meanings both shape and are shaped by diverse relations of power among different groups in society. Mainstream social science research, however, has often treated culture—particularly popular culture—as a by-product or an afterthought. Cultural research, though, targets the important role of culture as a link between individuals and society—as a force in organizing daily life and in maintaining social norms.

For example, in *Reading the Romance*, Janice Radway studied a group of midwestern women who were fans of the romance novel. Using her training in literary criticism but also employing interviews and questionnaires, Radway investigated the meaning of romance reading. She argued that this cultural activity functioned as personal time for some women whose complex family and work lives provided very little time for themselves. The study also suggested that these particular romance-novel fans identified with the active, independent qualities of the romantic heroines they most admired. As a cultural study, Radway's work did not claim to be scientific, and her findings are not generalizable to a large group of women. Rather, Radway was interested in investigating and interpreting the relationship between reading popular fiction and ordinary life.[26]

As Radway's study demonstrated, cultural research uses a variety of interpretive methods and displays some common features. Most important, these studies define *culture* in broad terms, made up of both the *products* a society fashions and the *processes* that forge those products. As we discussed in Chapter 1, culture consists of the symbols of expression that individuals, groups, and societies use to make sense of daily life and articulate their values. Within this context, culture is viewed in part as a struggle over who controls symbols and meaning in society. For example, the battles over the meaning of rock and roll in the 1950s or rap in the 1980s were important cultural wars that addressed issues of race, class, region, and religion, as well as generational differences.

Cultural research focuses on the investigation of daily experience, especially on issues of race, gender, class, and sexuality, and the unequal arrangements of power and status in contemporary society. Cultural research highlights the nature of cultural differences, emphasizing how some social groups have been marginalized and ignored throughout history. Cultural studies have attempted to recover lost or silenced voices, particularly among African American, Native American, Asian and Asian American, Arabic, Latino, gay, and women's cultures.

textual analysis

In cultural research, the equivalent to measurement methods and content analysis has been labeled **textual analysis**: the close reading and interpretation of the meanings of culture, including the study of books, movies, and TV programs. Whereas content analysis approaches media messages with the tools of modern social science—replicability, objectivity, and data—textual analysis looks at rituals, narratives, and meanings.

Although textual analysis has a long and rich history in film and literary studies, a significant shift came in 1974 with Horace Newcomb's *TV: The Most Popular Art*, considered the first serious academic analysis of television stories. Newcomb analyzed and interpreted why certain TV programs became predominant, especially comedies, westerns, mysteries, soap operas, news, and sports. Newcomb took television programs seriously, examining patterns in the most popular programs, such as the *Beverly Hillbillies*, *Bewitched*, and *Dragnet*, which traditional researchers had usually snubbed or ignored. Trained as a literary scholar, Newcomb argued that content analysis and other social science approaches often ignored artistic traditions and social context. For Newcomb, "the task for the student of the popular arts is to find a technique through which many

"I take culture . . . and the analysis of it to be therefore not an experimental science in search of law but an interpretive one **in search of meaning**."
—cultural anthropologist Clifford Geertz, 1973

In *TV: The Most Popular Art* (1974), a groundbreaking textual analysis of prime-time television, author Horace Newcomb critiques *Dragnet* (1952–70), whose creator and director, Jack Webb, played LAPD police sergeant Joe Friday. Newcomb analyzes the program's documentary or "factual" look, its lack of ambiguity, and its simple rule of law.

different qualities of the work—aesthetic, social, psychological—may be explored" and to discover "why certain formulas . . . are popular in American television."[27]

Prior to Newcomb's work, textual analysis had generally focused on "important" debates, films, poems, and books—either significant examples of democratic information or highly regarded works of art. But by the end of the 1970s, a new generation of media studies scholars, who had grown up on television and rock and roll, had become interested in less elite forms of culture. They extended the notion of what a "text" is to architecture, fashion, tabloid magazines, Madonna, rock music, soap operas, movies, cockfights, shopping malls, TV drug news, rap, and professional wrestling, trying to make sense of the most taken-for-granted aspects of everyday culture.

evaluating cultural approaches

In opposition to media effects research, textual analysis and cultural studies involve reading written texts and visual programs as a sequence of spoken or written symbols that contain interpretation. As James Carey has put it, a more cultural approach "does not seek to explain human behavior, but to understand it. . . . It does not attempt to predict human behavior, but to diagnose human meanings."[28] In other words, a cultural approach does not provide explanations for the laws that govern the mass media. Rather, it offers interpretations of the stories, messages, and meanings that circulate throughout our culture.

One of the major strengths of a cultural approach is the freedom to broadly interpret the impact of the mass media. Since cultural work is not bound by the precise control of variables, researchers can more easily examine the ties between media messages and the broader social, economic, and political scene. For example, effects research on politics has generally concentrated on election polls and voting patterns, whereas cultural research has broadened the meanings of politics to include class and income differences and the various uses of power by individuals and institutions in authority. Following Horace Newcomb, cultural investigators have also expanded the

Supermarket tabloids have declined in popularity during the 1990s, but they continue to stir controversy. Although most media researchers steer away from "lower" forms of popular culture, some cultural scholars specialize in their study.

study of media content beyond "serious" works. They have studied many popular forms, including music, movies, and prime-time television.

Just as social science measurement has limits, so do cultural studies. Sometimes such studies have focused too heavily on the meanings of media programs or "texts," ignoring their effects on audiences. More recent cultural studies, however, have tried to address this deficiency. For example, Elizabeth Bird's *For Enquiring Minds: A Cultural Study of Supermarket Tabloids* set up a three-part analysis that included (1) interviews with the writers and editors of popular tabloids, (2) in-depth discussions with tabloid readers, and (3) an analysis of the form and content of tabloids. Bird's research demonstrated how individuals make their own diverse meanings from this one ordinary form of popular culture.

Both media-effects and cultural researchers today have begun looking more closely at the limitations of their work, borrowing ideas from each other to better assess the complexity of the media's impact. For instance, in *Democracy without Citizens*, political scientist Robert Entmann employed both perspectives to examine journalism and politics. He used cultural theories about economics and politics to reveal how journalists slant the news and oversimplify complex issues. He supplemented his cultural inquiry with surveys that measured the impact of slanted reports on public opinion. By combining both approaches, Entmann strengthened his argument, which called for substantial journalistic reform. (For another example of research that combines scientific and cultural approaches, see "The Global Village: Television Promotes Literacy and Mutes Class Divisions in Brazil.")

media research, ivory towers, and democracy

One charge frequently leveled at academic studies is that they fail to address the everyday problems of life; they often seem to have little practical application. With the growth of mass media departments in universities has come an increase in special terminology and jargon, which tend to intimidate nonacademics. Although media research has built a growing knowledge base and dramatically advanced what we know about individuals and societies, the academic world has paid a price. That is, the larger public has often been excluded from access to the research process. Researchers themselves have even found it difficult to speak to one another across disciplines due to the obscure language used to report findings.

Television Promotes Literacy and Mutes Class Divisions in Brazil

by Laurie Fenlason

Television in the United-States has been blamed for numerous social ills, including low literacy levels, social isolation, reduced attention spans, increased violence, and a general decline in culture. Using both scientific and cultural approaches, a study of Brazilian television in the 1980s countered many of these claims. The study also documented a number of television's beneficial effects in that country, such as softening class barriers and improving attitudes toward reading.

Anthropologist Conrad Kottak, author of *Prime Time Society: An Anthropological Analysis of Television and Culture*, spent three years in Brazil, interviewing Brazilian network executives, actors, censors, and politicians, and watching Brazilian programming.

Kottak combined research in rural Brazilian communities with investigations of national and local programming. His study revealed high correlations between long-term exposure to television and reduced corporal punishment of children; reduced stereotyping of jobs on the basis of sex; less sexist views on social issues; increased reading; and greater use of print media. As Kottak explained, "In Brazil, a much more illiterate society than America and one in which literacy is not as trusted or valued, television makes literacy respectable. Brazilians even in rural, undeveloped areas now see literate people who come into their homes every evening, on a regular basis."

In addition, Kottak found that television reduced divisions between social classes by familiarizing rural people with urban life and reducing "obsequious and fearful behavior." In the last twenty years, for example, Brazilians' use of the formal "you" when addressing elders or those of a higher social class—on television and in real life—has declined substantially.

According to Kottak, Brazil was a unique laboratory for television research:

I was able to do something in Brazil that you can't do in the United States any more, because almost any American under forty has been exposed to television since birth. Because Brazilians have been exposed to television in their homes for widely different lengths of time, I could separate the cumulative effect of watching television from the effects of normal life experiences— getting older, maturing, acquiring more education.

Beginning in January 1985, Kottak and a team of researchers interviewed Brazilians in four communities. After determining basic information such as age, sex, race, years of television exposure, and hours watched each day, they asked questions such as "Is your community safe?" "Do you trust the government?" "Is it okay for women to go to bars?" In each case, length of exposure to television was one of the strongest predictors of the citizen's response.

"The only stronger indicator of a Brazilian's views on most of the social issues we examined was education," Kottak noted. "Television exposure and gender were the next best predictors, and each explained more than income, social class, religiosity, age or race."

Kottak was cautious about generalizing his findings to include cultures other than Brazil, especially when discussing television's impact on literacy. Kottak speculated that the widely held belief in the United States that television reduces literacy—not supported by any study—arises partly from the importance that Americans place on reading. Television is seen as supplanting solitary, industrious pursuits such as reading.

"The stigma that Americans place on television is almost matched by the Brazilians' traditional disdain of reading," Kottak explained. "In Brazil, reading is held suspect because it is seen as a solitary pursuit. Watching television, on the other hand, is seen as an opportunity to spend more time with friends and family."

Source: Adapted from Laurie Fenlason, *News & Information Services*, University of Michigan, November 9, 1989.

431

BRAZIL

The acceleration of jargon arrived with the splintering of academic life into narrow areas of specialization in the 1970s. We understand why chemistry, physics, math, and engineering require special symbols and languages. It is not as clear, however, why this practice extends to so many social science and humanities disciplines. Although cultural research has affected academics in English, history, sociology, anthropology, and communication, they do not talk easily to one another about their work. Most social science research is intended only for other social scientists with similar training and experience. For example, the elaborate statistical analyses used to document media effects require special training to understand. This kind of research advances knowledge, but it does not generally engage a larger public.

Even in cultural research, the language used is often incomprehensible to students and to other audiences who use the mass media. Cultural research tends to identify with marginalized groups, yet this scholarship can be self-defeating if its complexity is too far removed from the daily experience of those groups and students. Although it may be necessary for academics to construct special languages to dissect popular culture, the language that explains the research should be accessible to an informed general public.

In addition to the issue of specialized language, other problems have arisen involving media research and democracy. By the mid-1990s, lawmakers and the public had become increasingly concerned about the emphasis on research over teaching at most major universities. Throughout the early 1990s, as the government slashed support for student loans and university research, universities escalated their campaigns to raise money and become affiliated with corporations. The late historian Christopher Lasch, however, warned of the dangers "of corporate control of the universities" and the potential for "corruption" in higher education: "It is corporate control that has diverted social resources from the humanities into military and technological research, fostered an obsession with quantification that has destroyed the social sciences, replaced the English language with bureaucratic jargon, and created a top heavy administrative apparatus whose educational vision begins and ends with the bottom line."[29]

> "In many ways the modern university has replaced its function as a **creative/ subversive institution** with a fondness for structure and organization among its parts, and the rigid compartmentalization of knowledge within these structures."
>
> —David Scholle and Stan Denski,
> *Media Education*, 1994

By the mid-1990s, it was also becoming more difficult for middle- and working-class students to attend college, which seemed to contradict the democratic progress that had been going on in higher education since the 1950s. After World War II, many students gained access to college through the government GI loans to war veterans. By the 1960s, spurred on by the women's and civil rights movements, universities opened up further, allowing far greater access to students who were formerly excluded. These democratic movements also ushered in the study of popular culture and the mass media. The news media's coverage of the Watergate scandal alone raised interest in journalism as an undergraduate major throughout the country.

Ironically, while campuses were becoming more democratic, increasing specialization in the 1970s began isolating many researchers from life outside the university. Academics were once again locked away in their ivory towers. As a remedy, education critics began reemphasizing the role and responsibility of teachers and researchers in public life. By the 1990s, in fact, the *Chronicle of Higher Education* reported renewed interest in the idea of public intellectuals: "Bruised after years of attack, professors in the humanities and related fields are working to answer their critics and to speak and write in a public voice. Their work marks a turn away from high literary theory toward autobiography, journalism, and the essay form, styles that in recent years were seen as popularizing and old-fashioned."[30] Earlier in the twentieth century, it was common for academics to operate as public intellectuals. But the proliferation of specialized fields widened the gap between the public and the university. Fortunately, a few researchers, such as paleontologist Stephen Jay Gould and the late astronomer Carl Sagan, made their academic work more accessible to a broader public.

An unprecedented television study at UCLA in 1994 pointed up the increasing effort to connect media research and public life. Funded by ABC, CBS, Fox, and NBC, the UCLA study tracked the depiction of violence in prime-time TV series through the 1994–95 TV season. Faced with the possibility of government-imposed restrictions on content, the networks authorized the study to respond to concerns over violent TV images. Finding high levels of violence in Hollywood films shown on cable channels and relatively low levels in prime-time television, the researchers worked hard to make their analyses and interpretations accessible. In fact, a CBS executive at the time praised the independent report for being "written in English" and "for presenting qualitative rather than quantitative analysis," suggesting that the study had set up a "legitimate debate" on the subject of TV violence (see "Case Study: Violence Study Shows Television's Mental Block"on page 434).[31]

Facing a number of critical problems in higher education, more academics in the 1980s and 1990s began stepping forward to broaden their ideas of research and to become active in political and cultural life. For example, literary scholar Henry Louis Gates began writing essays for *Time* and the *New Yorker* magazines. Popular academic books ranging from conservative accounts—Allan Bloom's *Closing of the American Mind*— to progressive accounts—Cornel West's *Race Matters*—extended academic ideas beyond the boundaries of the university.

In the early 1990s, the TV coverage of the Persian Gulf War included many political scientists, military historians, and religion professors, who interpreted the war in the larger context of ongoing Middle Eastern struggles. In 1992 and 1996, Kathleen Hall Jamison, dean of the communication college at the University of Pennsylvania, made regular appearances on PBS—and guest appearances on the *Tonight Show*—to analyze the presidential elections and perform textual analyses of political advertising. The biggest surge among academics, however, came during the O.J. Simpson trials from 1994 to 1997. During this period, scores of law professors made regular TV appearances and tried to place the trial in a larger historical and legal context.

E S S A Y

Barbara Ehrenreich

Where the Wild Things Are

If it's middle-aged urban women vs. bears, bet on the bears

T WOULD BE NICE TO GO ON A VACATION WHERE I DIDN'T have to worry about being ripped limb from limb by some big ursine slob. But there it is, at any trailhead worth carting your trail mix up to—the National Park Service sign

Inevitably, a few miles up the trail, where the tree trunks all cunningly disguised as hungry sows with cubs, the thou comes to me—evil, unbidden, seductive—Why not just exter nate the pests? This. after all. is the human way: if you don't

Considered a model of the contemporary public intellectual, Barbara Ehrenreich, who has a Ph.D. in biology, has spent a large part of her career communicating her ideas on social issues to both academic communities and the larger public. A *Time* magazine essayist and self-described democratic socialist, Ehrenreich also makes appearances on radio and TV news and talk programs.

Violence Study Shows
Television's Mental Block

by Ellen Goodman

Santa Barbara, California—Ed Donnerstein is not a cultural coroner. He doesn't believe that you can understand the problem of violence on television by merely doing a body count. Or a bullet count.

As one of the lead researchers on a study done at this oceanside campus of the University of California, he wants to make it perfectly clear that not all the violence on television is equally harmful nor are all young viewers equally harmed.

No, he would not oppose televising "Romeo and Juliet" despite the bodies in the last act. And no, he does not believe that violence on television is the sole or primary cause of violence in America.

But he says, "We can no longer deny that violence on television contributes to the problem." He offers this message slowly and distinctly, as if trying to be heard over the din.

The National Television Violence Study that he and his colleagues labored over for three years was released [in 1996] into the middle of heated political debate. It made page one just as the Telecommunications Act became law with its controversial provision for a V-chip, a device to help parents block out programs rated too violent. It hit the evening news just as broadcasters were pondering the president's invitation for a February 29 trip to the White House woodshed.

Rep. Ed Markey, the man with the V-chip on his mind, immediately praised the study as a Perry Mason Moment, the perfect evidence against an industry in the throes of denial. An NBC executive called the research "ridiculous." *Variety* suggested a lobotomy.

What the analysis of 2,693 television programs from twenty-three channels showed is that a majority of programs contain what the researchers call "harmful violence." These were programs that posed three distinct threats to public health: "learning to behave violently, becoming more desensitized to the harmful consequences of violence and becoming fearful of being attacked."

"The issue for us," Donnerstein says, "is not just that there was violence but how it was presented." In analyzing the plots, images and programs, the team asked, what makes violence a public health problem? What contexts should we worry about?"

For one thing, violence turns out to do a lot of harm when it looks harmless. One of the lessons children learn watching television is that there are few consequences to the person who commits violence, or to the victim.

In 73 percent of the scenes, the violence went unpunished. In nearly half of the programs with slugfests and shootouts, the victims miraculously never appeared harmed. In 58 percent they showed no pain. In fact, only 16 percent of the programs showed any long-term problems— physical, emotional, or financial.

Add to this "positive" portrayal of negative behavior the fact that children's programs were least likely to show the bad effects of violence and most likely to make it funny. As Donnerstein says, "We're showing children violence that goes unpunished, is unrealistic and humorous."

As for other messages? Only a minuscule 4 percent of violent programs had an anti-violent theme. Or showed any alternative to the gym, the fist, the fight.

It's not surprising that this study is being touted in Washington as a sound basis for rating television violence. After all, if the V-chip is to become what Clinton called the "parents' power chip," we need a ratings system that's more sophisticated than one that counts dead bodies.

Indeed, selling the V-chip to an audience of Virginia parents, Clinton not only quoted the dark facts of the violence research, he promised that "new technologies can put you back in the driver's seat in your life...." It's an appeal to parents who want to regain some modest control over the messages coming into their houses and to their children.

But the same National Television Violence Study also hints at the limits of a technological fix to what is not really a technological problem.

The portrait that emerges from this analysis, after all, is not just of the television environment. It's a profile of an industry that narrowly equates entertainment with violence. It's a profile of a galaxy of broadcasters, producers, and programmers who have shown more imagination in claiming their programs are harmless than in changing the destructive plots.

The V-chip is a violence block. But the real problem in the television industry is a creative block. Soon we'll have the V-chip. Does anyone know how to get rid of the C-chip?

Source: Ellen Goodman, "Violence Study Shows TV's Mental Block," reprinted in *Ann Arbor News* (February 16, 1996), p. A9.

Other popular voices from the academic world have tried to help the public see university research as both less distant and less corporate. Like public journalists, public intellectuals based on campuses help to carry on the conversations of society and culture, actively circulating the most important new ideas of the day and serving as models for how to participate in public life.

REVIEW QUESTIONS

1. What were the earliest types of media studies, and why weren't they more scientific?

2. What were the major influences that led to scientific media research?

3. What are the differences between experiments and surveys as media research strategies?

4. What is content analysis and why is it significant?

5. What are the differences between the hypodermic needle model and the minimal effects model in the history of media research?

6. What are agenda-setting and the cultivation effect?

7. What are some strengths and limitations of modern media research?

8. Why did cultural approaches to media studies develop in opposition to media-effects research?

9. What are the features of cultural studies?

10. How is textual analysis different from content analysis?

11. What are some strengths and limitations of cultural research?

12. How has specialization in academic research influenced universities?

13. How can public intellectuals and academics improve the relationships between campuses and the general public?

QUESTIONING THE MEDIA

1. What are your main concerns or criticisms about the state of media studies at your college or university?

2. One charge that has been leveled against a lot of media research—both effects and cultural models—is that it has very little impact on changing our media institutions. Do you agree or disagree and why?

3. Can you think of an issue that a media industry and academic researchers could study together? Explain.

4. In looking at media courses in a college curriculum, what do you think is the relationship between theory and practice? Do hands-on practical skills courses such as news reporting, advertising copywriting, or TV production belong in a liberal arts college or in a separate mass communication college? Explain your answer.

The purpose of this project is to extend your critical approach to media research and to the academic culture that has developed various research strategies over the years. Here are three assignments that can work either as group projects in class or as individual writing assignments—or both.

1. Create your own hypothesis with regard to the media *or* test *one* of the following arguments:

   • College students are less informed about current news events than their parents are.

   • Watching late night TV talk-show monologues makes us more cynical about issues in the news.

   Come up with two or three different plans for testing either your own hypothesis or one of the hypotheses just listed. What types of research would you use? Why?

2. Choose an issue from two contemporary media research journals—one devoted mostly to mainstream research (such as *Journalism & Mass Communication Quarterly*) and one devoted to cultural research (such as *Critical Studies in Mass Communication*). Make a list or chart of the topics that each particular issue covers. Pick one article from each issue, and write a paragraph critiquing how well you think the researchers made and supported their arguments. How accessible was the language in each article, and how important was the research? As a journalist, what would you report about these media research projects?

3. Choose one well-established media research journal—*Journalism & Mass Communication Quarterly*, *Public Opinion Quarterly*, or *Film Quarterly*—and read an issue of the journal for each decade from the 1930s or 1940s to today. In your group or in an essay, document the subject matter and explain how the journal has changed over the years. Which issues did you find the best and why?

Legal Controls
and Freedom of Expression

In the fall of 1990, a record store owner in Florida was convicted on obscenity charges for selling a 2 Live Crew rap album to minors. Responding to citizen complaints earlier that year, a court in Florida's Broward County said the recording, *As Nasty as They Wanna Be*, met the test for obscenity. The store owner had apparently ignored county sheriffs who had warned local retailers about selling the controversial album. The conviction was the first of its kind in U.S. legal history.

The 2 Live Crew ruling was also the first time a U.S. court had declared a musical recording obscene. The record contained references to oral sex, group sex, sadomasochism, and violence against women. Two years later, after 2 Live Crew appealed, a federal appellate court reversed the decision. The appeals court determined that the sheriff's office had the burden of proof to demonstrate that the recording was obscene. The court also decided that the sheriff's office had submitted no evidence to counter the band's claim that the work had merit as satire and comedic art. Under obscenity law, a work that demonstrates socially redeeming merit does not meet the obscenity test. The earlier conviction of the record store owner was eventually overturned.

Meanwhile, during the same week in 1990 that the Florida store owner was convicted, an Ohio jury acquitted Dennis Barrie, the head of Cincinnati's Contemporary Art Center. Barrie and his museum had been charged with obscenity for exhibiting sexually explicit photographs. This was the first such criminal trial involving an art museum director. In the spring of 1990, the Cincinnati museum had shown 175 photographs by the late artist Robert Mapplethorpe. The case focused on seven of the photos: two featuring nude minors and five with adult men in sado-masochistic poses. During the controversy, city officials discussed closing the exhibit. Defense lawyers for the museum claimed the pictures contained serious artistic merit, which meant they did not violate obscenity standards. After art experts defended the pictures, eight jurors found Barrie and the museum not guilty.

The Florida and Ohio cases ignited legal and cultural fireworks. They raised important questions about the role of art, popular culture, legal limits, and free expression in a democracy. Should every kind of artistic or musical expression be protected by the First Amendment? How do we protect children from controversial works? Should we punish certain kinds of expression or art that offend or demean adults? Who decides?

With the battle over expression and pornography escalating in the 1990s, conservatives in the U.S. Congress protested the federal funding of sexually explicit art projects. Legal activists Andrea Dworkin and Catharine MacKinnon aided the conservative cause; their legal writings influenced local ordinances and a new Canadian law against pornography, which redefined obscenity to include any "materials that subordinate, degrade or dehumanize women." In affecting Canada's highest court, the Dworkin-MacKinnon strategy involved dodging the long history of protecting even repulsive or pornographic material. The attorneys argued that pornography itself was an act of violence and a violation of women's civil rights.

Although Dworkin and MacKinnon's efforts have many supporters, among their opposition are a number of feminist groups, including some leaders in the National Organization for Women (NOW). These groups argue that they do not need the police or state governments intervening for them—that women are strong enough to fight the battles over pornography with other kinds of free speech. This position grudgingly defends pornographers' speech rights and is closely associated with an absolutist position on free-expression issues, which reaffirms the First Amendment: "Congress shall make *no* law . . . abridging the freedom of speech." To protect *all* forms of expression, this argument contends that even hateful, demeaning, and pornographic speech have to be tolerated—and fought against by using speech rather than censorship. Former Supreme Court Justice Hugo Black supported this absolutist view. Often taking a minority position on speech issues, he contended that even current libel and obscenity laws were unconstitutional.

> "Congress shall make no law respecting an establishment of religion, or prohibiting the free exercise thereof; or **abridging the freedom of speech,** or of the press; or the right of the people to peaceably assemble, and to petition the government for a redress of grievances."
> —First Amendment, U.S. Constitution, 1791

The cultural and social struggles over free speech and press freedom have defined the nature of American democracy. When Supreme Court Justice William Brennan Jr. was asked in 1989 to comment on his "favorite part of the Constitution," he replied, "The First Amendment, I expect. Its enforcement gives us this society. The other provisions of the Constitution really only embellish it." Of all the issues that involve the mass media and popular culture, none are more central, or explosive, than freedom of expression and the First Amendment. Our fundamental development as a nation can often be traced to how much or how little speech we tolerated during particular historical periods.

In 1985, rock musicians like the late Frank Zappa appeared before the Senate to protest warning labels on CDs and tapes as a First Amendment violation. By the late 1980s, though, to ward off government regulation, the music industry voluntarily agreed to place parental-advisory stickers on controversial recordings.

We live in a volatile time for free-speech issues. As a society, we have debated hate-speech codes on campuses, explicit lyrics in music, and violent images in film. In this chapter, we will examine expression issues, focusing primarily on the implications of the First Amendment for a variety of mass media. We will investigate the origins of *free* expression and the standard models that underlie press freedoms. We will look at the definition of censorship and corresponding legal cases. Next, we will study the types of expression that are not always protected as speech. Focusing on the impact of cameras in the courtroom, we will examine some of the clashes between the First and Sixth Amendments. With regard to film, we will review the social and political pressures that gave rise to early censorship boards and the current film ratings system. We will turn to issues in broadcasting and why it has been treated differently than print media. Among other topics, we will inspect the idea of *indecency* in broadcasting and the demise of the Fairness Doctrine. Finally, we will explore the newest frontier in speech—expression in cyberspace and concerns about speech on the information highway.

the origins of free expression and a free press

When students from other cultures attend school in the United States, many are astounded by the number of books, news articles, editorials, cartoons, films, and TV shows that make fun of the president. When writer-director Hugh Wilson toured Spain after his comedy film *Police Academy* (1984) had appeared there, he was astonished to discover that many Spanish citizens regarded him as a hero for "criticizing" the police. Many countries throughout history have jailed, even killed, their citizens for such speech "violations." In the 1990s, more than fifty journalists a year were still dying in the line of duty.[1] In the United States, however, we have generally taken for granted our right to criticize and poke fun at elected officials, politicians, and the police. Many of us are unaware of the ideas that underpin the freedoms we actually have. Indeed, when reporters have surveyed unwitting Americans about the First Amendment to the U.S. Constitution, the majority of respondents, unfamiliar with the amendment's wording, have usually indicated that its freedoms are far too generous.

To understand the development of free expression in the United States, we must understand a key idea underlying the First Amendment. In Europe throughout the

441

1600s, in order to monitor—and punish if necessary—the speech of editors and writers, governments controlled ideas by requiring printers to obtain licenses. In 1644, English poet John Milton, author of *Paradise Lost*, published his essay *Areopagitica*, which opposed government licenses for printers and defended a free press. Milton argued that all sorts of ideas, even false ones, should circulate freely in a democratic society and that truth would eventually emerge. In 1695, England stopped licensing newspapers, and most of Europe followed. In many democracies today, publishing a newspaper, magazine, or newsletter remains one of the few public or service enterprises that requires no license.

models for expression and speech

In 1996, an international survey of the news media in 187 countries, conducted by Freedom House, reported that although more than half the world's population lived under some form of democratic government, fewer than 45 countries offered a relatively free press. The survey related that 58 nations had virtually no press freedom; those governments exercised tight control over the news media, which included jailing, intimidating, and even executing journalists. Championing the Internet as a way to bypass restrictive governments, the survey looked to new technologies to help improve the free flow of information worldwide.[2]

Since the mid-1950s, four models for speech and journalism have been used to categorize the widely differing ideas underlying free expression.[3] These models include the authoritarian, communist, libertarian, and social responsibility concepts. They are distinguished by the levels of freedom they each allow and by the attitudes of the ruling and political classes toward the freedoms granted to the average citizen. Given the diversity among nations, the experimentation of journalists, and the collapse of many communist press systems, these categories no longer hold up as well. Nevertheless, they offer a good point of departure for discussing the press and democracy.

> "Consider what would happen if—during this 200th anniversary of the Bill of Rights—**the First Amendment** were placed on the ballot in every town, city, and state. The choices: **affirm, reject, or amend.**
>
> "I would bet there is no place in the United States where the First Amendment would survive intact."
>
> —Nat Hentoff,
> writer,
> 1991

The **authoritarian model** developed about the time the printing press arrived in sixteenth-century England. Its advocates held that the general public, largely illiterate in those days, needed guidance from an elite and educated ruling class. Government criticism and public dissent were not tolerated, especially if such speech undermined what authorities had determined was "the common good." Censorship was frequent, and the government issued printing licenses primarily to publishers who were sympathetic to government and ruling-class agendas.

Today, many authoritarian systems operate in developing countries throughout Asia, Latin America, and Africa, where journalism often joins with government and business to foster economic growth, minimize political dissent, and encourage social stability. The leaders in these systems generally believe that too much outspoken speech and press freedom would undermine the delicate stability of their social and political infrastructures. In these societies, criticizing government programs may be viewed as an obstacle to keeping the peace, and both reporters and citizens may be punished if they attack the status quo too fiercely.

Under most authoritarian models, the news is still controlled by private enterprise. But under the **communist** or **state model**, press control sits in the lap of government. Speaking for ordinary citizens and workers, state leaders believe they are enlightened and that the press should serve the common goals of the state. Although some state systems encourage media and government cooperation, political and military leaders still dictate the agendas for newspapers and the broadcast media. Some government criticism is tolerated, but ideas that challenge the basic premises of state authority are not. Although state media systems were in decline by the mid-1990s, they were still operating in China, Cuba, Iran, Iraq, and North Korea, among other countries.

The **libertarian model**, the flip side of state and authoritarian systems, encourages vigorous government criticism and supports the highest degree of freedom for individual speech and news operations. In a strict libertarian model, no restrictions are placed on the mass media or on individual speech. Libertarians tolerate the expression of everything from pornography to advocating anarchy. In America and Europe, many political and alternative newspapers and magazines operate on such a model. Placing a great deal of trust in citizens' ability to sort truth from fabrication, libertarians maintain that the best way to fight outrageous lies or repulsive speech is not to suppress them but to speak out and write against them.

Along with the libertarian model, a **social responsibility model** characterizes one ideal of mainstream journalism in the United States. The ideas behind this model coalesced in the controversial 1947 Hutchins Commission, which was formed to examine the increasing influence of the press. Henry Luce, then head of the Time-Life magazine empire, funded the commission with a large grant to his friend Robert Maynard Hutchins, chancellor of the University of Chicago. Hutchins used the grant to assemble a committee to study the press. Luce hoped the commission would endorse free-press ideals and keep outsiders from watching over the press. But to Luce's dismay, the commission's report called for the development of press watchdog groups. The report argued that the mass media had grown too powerful and needed to become more socially responsible. Key recommendations encouraged comprehensive news reports that put issues and events in context, more news forums for the exchange of ideas, better coverage of society's range of economic classes and social groups, and stronger overviews of our nation's social values, ideals, and goals.

A socially responsible press is usually privately owned (although the government technically operates the broadcast media in most European and Scandinavian democracies). In this model, the press functions as a **Fourth Estate**, that is, as an unofficial branch of government that monitors the legislative, judicial, and executive branches for abuses of power. In theory, private ownership keeps the news media independent from government. Thus, they are better able to watch over the system on behalf of citizens. Under this model, which is heavily influenced by the libertarian view, the press supplies information to citizens so they can make wise decisions regarding political and social issues; the press also operates without excessive government meddling in matters of content.

censorship as prior restraint

In the United States, the First Amendment has theoretically prohibited censorship. Over time, Supreme Court decisions have defined censorship as **prior restraint**. This means that courts and governments cannot block any publication or speech before it actually occurs, on the principle that a law has not been broken until an illegal act has been committed. In 1931, for example, the Supreme Court determined in *Near v. Minnesota* that a Minneapolis newspaper could not be stopped from publishing "scandalous and defamatory" material about police and law officials who were negligent in arresting and punishing local gangsters.[4] However, the Court left open the idea that the news media could be ordered to halt publication in exceptional cases. During a declared war, for instance, if a U.S. court judged that the publication of an article threatened national security, such expression could be restrained prior to its printing. In fact, during World War I, the U.S. Navy seized all wireless radio transmitters. This was done to ensure control over critical information about weather conditions and troop movements that might inadvertently aid the enemy. In the 1970s, though, the Pentagon Papers decision and the *Progressive* magazine case tested important concepts underlying prior restraint.

The Pentagon Papers Case. In 1971, with the Vietnam War still in progress, Daniel Ellsberg, a former Defense Department employee, stole a copy of a forty-seven-volume document, "History of U.S. Decision-Making Process on Vietnam Policy." A thorough study of U.S. involvement in Vietnam since World War II, the papers were classified by the government as top secret. Ellsberg and a friend leaked the study—nicknamed the Pentagon Papers—to the *New York Times* and the *Washington Post*. In June 1971, the *Times* began publishing articles based on the study. To block any further publication, the Nixon administration received a temporary restraining order to prepare its case, arguing that publishing the documents posed "a clear and present danger" to national security. The Nixon government had five national security experts testify that publicizing the Pentagon Papers would hamper the war effort.

A lower U.S. district court supported the newspaper's right to publish, but the government's appeal placed the case in the Supreme Court less than three weeks after the first articles were published. In a six to three vote, the Court sided with the newspapers. Justice Hugo Black, speaking for the majority, attacked the government's attempt to suppress publication: "Both the history and language of the First Amendment support the view that the press must be left free to publish news, whatever the source, without censorship, injunctions, or prior restraints."[5]

In 1971, Daniel Ellsberg surrendered to government prosecutors in Boston. Ellsberg was a former Pentagon researcher who turned against America's military policy in Vietnam and leaked information to the press. He was charged with unauthorized possession of top-secret federal documents. Later called the Pentagon Papers, the documents contained evidence on the military's bungled handling of the Vietnam War. In 1973, an exasperated federal judge dismissed the case when illegal government-sponsored wiretaps of Ellsberg's psychoanalyst came to light during the Watergate scandal.

The *Progressive* Magazine Case. The issue of prior restraint ominously surfaced again in 1979, when an injunction was issued to block publication of the *Progressive*, a national left-wing magazine; the editors had announced they were running an article entitled "The H-Bomb Secret: How We Got It, Why We're Telling It." The dispute began when the editor of the magazine sent a draft to the Department of Energy to verify technical portions of the article. Believing that the article contained sensitive data that might damage U.S. efforts to halt the proliferation of nuclear weapons, the Energy Department asked the magazine not to publish it. When the magazine said it would proceed anyway, the government sued the *Progressive* and asked a federal district court to block publication.

Judge Robert Warren sought to balance the *Progressive*'s First Amendment rights against the government's claim that the article would spread dangerous information and undermine national security. In an unprecedented action, Warren sided with the government, deciding that "a mistake in ruling against the United States could pave the way for thermonuclear annihilation for us all. In that event, our right to life is extinguished and the right to publish becomes moot."[6] During appeals and further litigation, several other publications, including the *Milwaukee Sentinel* and *Scientific American*, published articles related to the H-bomb, getting much of their information from publications already in circulation. None of these articles, including the one published in the *Progressive*, contained the precise technical details needed to actually design a nuclear weapon nor did they provide information on where to obtain the sensitive ingredients necessary. Although the government dropped the case, Warren's injunction stands as the first time in American history that a prior restraint order imposed in the name of national security actually stopped the *initial* publication of a controversial news report.

unprotected forms of expression

Early in our nation's history, the Federalist party, which controlled Congress, enacted the Sedition Act to silence opposition to an anticipated war against France. The Act tried to curb criticism by the opposition Democratic-Republican party. Many anti-Federalists supported France and America's newly arrived French immigrants. Led by President John Adams, the Federalists believed that defamatory articles could stir up discontent against the elected government and undermine its authority. Adams signed the Act in 1798. Over the next three years, twenty-five individuals were arrested and ten convicted under the Act, which was also used to prosecute anti-Federalist newspapers. After failing to curb opposition, the Sedition Act expired in 1801 during Thomas Jefferson's presidency. A Democratic-Republican who had challenged the Act's constitutionality, Jefferson pardoned all defendants convicted under the Sedition Act.[7]

Despite the First Amendment's order that "Congress shall make no law" restricting speech and press freedoms, the federal government has made other laws like the Sedition Act, especially during times of war. For instance, the Espionage Acts of 1917 and 1918, which were enforced during World Wars I and II, made it a federal crime to disrupt the nation's war effort. These acts also authorized severe punishment for seditious statements. Beyond the federal government, state laws and local ordinances have on occasion curbed expression, and the court system over the years has determined that some kinds of expression do not merit protection as speech under the Constitution. Today, for example, false or misleading advertising is not protected by law nor are expressions that intentionally threaten public safety.

In the landmark *Schenck v. United States* appeal case during World War I, the Supreme Court upheld the conviction of a Socialist party leader, Charles T. Schenck, for distributing leaflets urging American men to protest the draft, a violation of the newly passed Espionage Act. In upholding the Act, Justice Oliver Wendell Holmes wrote two of the more famous interpretations and phrases in the First Amendment's legal history:

> But the character of every act depends upon the circumstances in which it is done. The most stringent protection of free speech would not protect a man in falsely shouting fire in a theater and causing a panic.

> The question in every case is whether the words used are used in such circumstances and are of such a nature as to create a clear and present danger that they will bring about the substantive evils that Congress has a right to prevent.

In supporting Schenck's sentence—a ten-year prison term—Holmes noted that the Socialist leaflets were entitled to First Amendment protection, but only during times of peace.

"Pretty Woman," Rap, and Copyright Law

by Michael Epstein

The protection of copyright has long helped writers, artists and filmmakers control where, when, and how their creative works are used by others. Under U.S. copyright law, the original creators can sue people who imitate or adapt their works commercially without permission. In most cases, the rule is as follows: If you make money off of someone else's creative material, that money belongs to the person who owns the copyright to the material unless you have obtained his or her prior approval. One exception to copyright protection, known as *fair use*, allows journalists, critics, scholars, and students to excerpt limited portions of other peoples' creations for a variety of purposes.

Until recently, parody was usually considered to be covered by copyright's fair-use exception, yet the Supreme Court did not rule on the issue until March 7, 1994. The Court unanimously found that the rap group 2 Live Crew did not violate U.S. copyright law

2 Live Crew members Luther R. Campbell, Christopher Wong Won, Mark Ross, and David Hobbs

when it released its 1989 song "Pretty Woman." A subversive, cynical, and controversial parody of Roy Orbison's 1964 anthem of hope and fulfillment, "Oh, Pretty Woman," the 2 Live Crew version developed a huge and profitable following among hip-hop audiences. Although the rap group had sought permission to use the song's signature first line for its parody, the owner of the song's copyright, Acuff-Rose Music, decided not to let the group use the famous ballad. When 2 Live Crew went ahead and used the song anyway, Acuff-Rose filed suit in federal court.

2 Live Crew members argued that their version of "Oh, Pretty Woman," was intended to be a parody of Orbison's song. As author Luther R. Campbell explained in a letter to Acuff-Rose, the group's purpose was "through comical lyrics, to satirize the original work." These lyrics, considered offensive and sexist by many, transformed Orbison's pretty woman into a "big hairy woman," "a bald-

In establishing the "clear and present danger" criterion for expression, the Supreme Court demonstrated the limits of the First Amendment. Appropriating a writer's or artist's words or music without consent or payment is another form of expression that is not protected as speech. Rap performers, in fact, have faced a number of court battles for copyright infringement; they have been accused of stealing other musicians' work by sampling their music, a technique fundamental to rap (see "Case Study: 'Pretty Woman,' Rap, and Copyright Law"). A **copyright** legally protects the rights of authors and producers for their published or unpublished writing, music and lyrics, TV programs and movies, or graphic art designs. Beyond copyright protections, several kinds of controversial expression historically have had a great impact on print and other forms of mass media. These include libel, invasion of privacy, and obscenity.

satire? freedom? parody? fair? theft?

headed woman," and a "two-timin' woman." Although 2 Live Crew gave credit for "Oh, Pretty Woman" to Roy Orbison and his co-author William Dees on their album *Clean as They Wanna Be*, Acuff-Rose argued that Campbell's creation was nothing more than a commercial rip-off that made money for the rap group at the copyright owner's expense. Lawyers for the rappers argued, however, that "Pretty Woman" was a legitimate parody and thus exempt from copyright claims.

Although the federal district court in Nashville decided in favor of 2 Live Crew, a U.S. court of appeals later reversed the lower court's ruling, causing a furor in the creative community. The appellate court concluded that by "taking the heart of the original and making it the heart of a new work," the band had borrowed too much of the original song. The court also ruled that "Pretty Woman" could not be protected as fair use under copyright law because the rappers had recorded their version for "blatantly commercial purposes."

Justice David Souter, writing for a unanimous Supreme Court, rejected the ruling of the appellate court. Souter suggested that the rap version could be understood "as a comment on the naivete of the original of an earlier day, as a rejection of its sentiment that ignores the ugliness of street life and the debasement it signifies." Stating that parody's "art lies in the tension between a known original and its parodic twin," the Supreme Court ruled that works that adapt or transform an original creation "lie at the heart of the fair-use doctrine's guarantee of breathing space within the confines of copyright." Souter noted that Campbell's parody deserved credit for both "shedding light on an earlier work and…creating a new one."

In a media-saturated world that has seen the sampling by rap artists of previous recordings and the composite imaging of archival photos and films by computer, it is no wonder that the "Pretty Woman" case attracted wide attention. Satirists as diverse as *Mad Magazine* and political humorist Mark Russell filed friend-of-the-court briefs on behalf of 2 Live Crew. On the other hand, many song writers and composers filed briefs in support of the music company.

It is still too early to tell whether the composers have lost the copyright protection war. Indeed, since the ruling in *Campbell v. Acuff-Rose Music*, instances of copyright infringement are still decided on a case-by-case basis. Whether a parodist, or anyone else, is granted protection under copyright law is still subject to the general rules governing fair use. For example, if a parody is likely to damage the market for the original work, then the creator may be able to collect damages from the parodist. As the courts see it, imitation is still the sincerest form of flattery—but only up to a point.

Michael Epstein is an attorney and Ph.D. candidate in the American Culture Program at the University of Michigan.

Libel. The biggest single legal worry that haunts editors and publishers is the issue of libel, another form of expression that is not protected as speech under the First Amendment. Whereas **slander** constitutes spoken language that defames a person's character, **libel** refers to defamation of character in written expression. Inherited from British common law, libel is generally defined as a false statement—either printed or broadcast—that holds a person up to public ridicule, contempt, or hatred, or injures a person's business or occupation. Examples of potentially libelous statements include falsely accusing someone of professional dishonesty or incompetence (such as medical malpractice); falsely accusing a person of a crime (such as drug dealing); falsely charging a person with mental illness or unacceptable behavior (such as public drunkenness); or falsely accusing a person of associating with a disreputable organization or cause (such as the Mafia or a neo-Nazi military group).

To protect the news media's right to aggressively pursue wrongdoing and stories, courts since the mid-1960s have tried to make it more difficult for public officials to win libel suits. This has not, however, deterred some individuals and organizations from intimidating the news media by either threatening or actually filing libel suits. Such legal actions in civil law can prove costly, particularly to a small newspaper or magazine, even when the defendant wins the case. As a result, over the years many small news organizations have avoided tough probing stories, and large organizations have hired more lawyers to advise them on the libel implications of their more controversial investigative stories.

Juries, too, have traditionally been hostile to the media, often siding with plaintiffs and granting generous mental anguish awards. Prior to the 1960s, libel awards rarely exceeded $25,000, but initial awards averaged nearly $500,000 by 1987–88 and $8 million by 1991. Due to legal reform movements in the 1990s, the complexity of libel law, and the fact that some juries overlooked the letter of the law to sympathize with a wronged celebrity, many libel awards have been reduced in size or dismissed on appeal. Nevertheless, plaintiffs have won the majority of libel cases. In the 1980s, for example, of the twenty-five libel cases tried in U.S. civil courts against newspapers, the news media lost sixteen times.[8]

Since 1964, the *New York Times v. Sullivan* case has served as the standard for libel law. The case stems from a 1960 full-page advertisement placed in the *New York Times* by the Committee to Defend Martin Luther King and the Struggle for Freedom in the South. Without naming names, the ad criticized the general law-enforcement tactics of southern cities, including Montgomery, Alabama, for the methods used to break up civil rights demonstrations. The ad condemned "southern violators of the Constitution" bent on destroying King and the movement. Taking exception, the city commissioner of Montgomery, L. B. Sullivan, sued the *Times* for libel, claiming the ad had defamed him indirectly. Although Alabama civil courts awarded Sullivan $500,000, the newspaper's lawyers appealed to the Supreme Court, which unanimously reversed the ruling, holding that Alabama libel law violated the *Times*' First Amendment rights.[9]

Heed Their Rising Voices

> "The growing movement of peaceful mass demonstrations by Negroes is something new in the South, something understandable.... Let Congress heed their rising voices, for they will be heard."
>
> —New York Times editorial
> Saturday, March 19, 1960

Your Help Is Urgently Needed ... NOW!!

COMMITTEE TO DEFEND MARTIN LUTHER KING AND THE STRUGGLE FOR FREEDOM IN THE SOUTH
312 West 125th Street, New York 27, N. Y.

This is the 1960 *New York Times* advertisement that triggered one of the most influential and important libel cases in American history.

In the Sullivan decision, the Supreme Court asked future civil courts to distinguish whether plaintiffs are *public officials* or private individuals. (In later cases, *public figures* such as entertainment or sports celebrities were also added to this mix.) Within this framework, to successfully argue a libel case, *private* individuals have to prove three things:

1. that the public statement about them was false

2. that damages or actual injury occurred, such as the loss of a job, harm to reputation, public humiliation, or mental anguish

3. that the publisher or broadcaster was negligent

But if a court determines that a plaintiff is a *public* official or figure, that person has to prove falsehood, damages, negligence, *and* **actual malice** on the part of the news medium. This latter test means that the reporter or editor knew the statement was false and printed or broadcast it anyway, or acted with a reckless disregard for the truth. Again, since actual malice is difficult to prove, it is hard for public figures to win libel suits. The Court's rationale for the principle of actual malice not only protects the First Amendment rights of the media but, in theory, allows news operations to aggressively pursue legitimate news stories without fear of continuous litigation. In practice, however, the mere threat of a libel suit still scares off many in the news media.

Under current libel law, civil courts determine, on a case-by-case basis, whether plaintiffs are public or private persons. In general, public officials must have substantial responsibilities in conducting government affairs; therefore, presidents, senators, mayors, police detectives, and city managers count as examples of public officials. Citizens with more "ordinary" jobs, such as city sanitation employees, undercover police informants, nurses, or unknown actors, are normally classified as private individuals.

Judges often have a tough time deciding who is a public figure. Many fuzzy categories exist, such as public high school teachers, police officers, and court-appointed attorneys. Individuals from these professions have ended up in either category depending on a particular court's ruling. The Supreme Court has distinguished two categories of public figures: (1) public celebrities or persons who "occupy positions of such pervasive power and influence that they are deemed public figures for all purposes," and (2) individuals who have thrown themselves—usually voluntarily but sometimes involuntarily—into the middle of "a significant public controversy," such as a lawyer defending a prominent client, an advocate for an antismoking ordinance, a labor-union activist, or a security guard like Richard Jewell. Made famous by the news media, Jewell was initially suspected of setting off the pipe bomb that killed a woman at the 1996 Olympics in Atlanta. (After he was cleared by the FBI, NBC News settled a libel case with Jewell. His lawyers had charged that after news media reports named him as the only suspect, he could not find work, even though he was never charged with the crime.)

Defenses against Libel Charges. As far back as the 1730s, the best defense against libel in an American civil court has been the truth. In most cases, if libel defendants can demonstrate that they printed or broadcast statements that were essentially true, such evidence usually bars plaintiffs from recovering any damages—even if their reputations were harmed. To this end, the news media are particularly careful about using any direct quotes in which a source may have lied, employing legal staffs to check the veracity of controversial stories before publication. If a source, for instance, libels a private person in a news report, the paper may also be held accountable. Even if the reporter did not know the quote was false, he or she might be considered negligent for not checking the truthfulness of the statement more carefully.

Beyond the truth, there are other defenses against libel. Prosecutors, for example, receive *absolute privilege* in a court of law when they make potentially damaging statements about a defendant's reputation. When prosecutor Marcia Clark accused O.J. Simpson of being a murderer and he was later acquitted, she was protected from libel on the legal theory that in public courtrooms the interests of an individual are overridden by the larger common good of the legal process. The reporters who printed or broadcast her statement

Even though prosecutor Marcia Clark called O.J. Simpson a killer in his 1994–95 criminal trial, she was protected by *absolute privilege* from any potential slander suit filed by Simpson, who was eventually acquitted. Journalists, too, who reported Clark's accusations, were protected from a libel suit under a concept called *qualified privilege*.

were also protected against libel. Entitled to conditional or **qualified privilege**, journalists are allowed to report judicial or legislative proceedings even though the public statements being reported may be libelous.

When police detectives, judges, or prosecutors make unsubstantiated claims about a defendant, or when legislators verbally attack each other during a session, reporters are allowed to report those incidents—even when potentially libelous statements are relayed secondhand by the reporter. As a condition for qualified privilege, the reporting of these public events must be fair and accurate. If a reporter, for instance, has prior knowledge that a public statement is untrue and still reports it as the truth, a judge may suspend qualified privilege and hold the reporter accountable for libel.

Another defense against libel concerns the area of *opinion and fair comment*. For example, after O.J. Simpson was acquitted of murder in October 1995, many legal commentators and talk-show hosts continued to suggest that, in their *opinion*, he was guilty of killing his ex-wife, Nicole Brown, and her friend, Ron Goldman. Generally, however, libel applies only to misstatements of factual information rather than opinion, although the line between fact and opinion is often hazy. Some libel cases turn on a plaintiff's ability to persuade a judge or jury that a defendant's statement was a factual error and not merely opinion or fair comment. For this reason, lawyers advise journalists to first set forth the facts on which a viewpoint is based and then to state their opinion based on those facts. In other words, journalists should make it clear that a statement is a criticism and *not* an allegation of fact. Libel laws protect satire, comedy, and opinions expressed in reviews of books, plays, movies, or restaurants. Such laws may not, however, protect malicious statements in which plaintiffs can prove that defendants used their free-speech rights to mount a damaging personal attack.

One of the most famous tests of opinion and fair comment came in a case pitting conservative minister and political activist Jerry Falwell against Larry Flynt, publisher of *Hustler* magazine. The case became the subject of a major Hollywood movie, *The People vs. Larry Flynt* (1996). The actual *Falwell v. Flynt* case developed after a November 1983 issue of *Hustler* made an outrageous reference to Falwell. In a spoof of a Campari vermouth ad, the magazine asked readers to recall their "first time" drinking Campari. The parody stated that Falwell needed to be drunk before he could preach; it also described his "first time" as an incestuous encounter with his own mother. In fine print at the bottom of the page, a disclaimer read: "Ad parody—not to be taken seriously."

On Larry King's cable talk show in 1997, Moral Majority leader Rev. Jerry Falwell (*right*) discusses pornography and forgiveness with *Hustler* magazine publisher Larry Flynt (*center*)—their first face-to-face meeting since their 1984 libel trial.

Often a target of Flynt's irreverence and questionable taste, Falwell sued for libel, asking for $45 million in damages. In the verdict, the jury rejected the libel suit but found that Flynt had intentionally caused Falwell emotional distress, awarding him $200,000. It was an unprecedented verdict in American legal history. Flynt's lawyers appealed, and in 1988 the Supreme Court unanimously overturned the verdict. Although the Court did not condone the *Hustler* spoof, the justices did say that it was entitled to constitutional protection. The case drew enormous media attention and raised concerns about the erosion of the media's right to free speech. In affirming *Hustler*'s speech rights, the Court suggested that while parodies and insults of public figures might indeed cause emotional pain, denying the right to publish them would undermine a key democratic principle and violate the spirit of the First Amendment.[10]

The Right of Privacy. Whereas libel laws safeguard a person's character and reputation, the right of privacy protects an individual's peace of mind and personal feelings. Any public figure who has ever been subjected to intense scrutiny by the media has experienced invasions of privacy. When British actor Hugh Grant and a prostitute were arrested for public indecency in California in 1995, tabloid photographers and TV cameras kept constant vigil over the actor's every move until the event gradually lost its immediacy and allure. In general, the news media have been granted wide protections under the First Amendment to subject public figures to the spotlight. Local municipalities and states, however, have passed laws that protect most individuals from unwarranted surveillance. During her lifetime, for instance, Jacqueline Kennedy Onassis successfully sought court orders to keep photographers at a minimum distance, although the technology of powerful zoom lenses often overcame this obstacle. Public figures have received some legal relief, but every year brings a few stories of a Hollywood actor or sports figure punching a tabloid photographer or TV cameraman who got too close.

In the simplest terms, **invasion of privacy** addresses a person's right to be left alone, without his or her name, image, or daily activities becoming public property. Invasions of privacy occur in different situations, the most common of which are listed here.

1. intrusion, in which unauthorized tape recorders, wiretaps, microphones, or other surveillance equipment are used to secretly record a person's private affairs

2. the publication of private matters, such as the unauthorized disclosure of private statements about an individual's health, sexual activities, or economic status

3. the unauthorized appropriation of a person's name or image for advertising or other commercial benefit

As we have noted, the courts have generally given the news media a lot of leeway under the First Amendment. For instance, the names and pictures of both private individuals and public figures can be used without their consent in news stories. If private citizens become part of public controversies and subsequent news stories, the courts have allowed the news media to record their quotes and use their images without the individuals' permission. In regard to these situations, the courts have argued that the greater public good served by news coverage outweighs the individuals' right to privacy. The courts have even ruled that accurate reports of criminal and court records, including the identification of rape victims, do not normally constitute privacy invasions. Nevertheless, most newspapers and broadcast outlets use their own internal guidelines and ethical codes to protect the privacy of victims and defendants, especially in cases involving rape victims and abused children.

Obscenity. Privacy and libel issues are part of civil or private law: Individuals file personal lawsuits against another individual or a media organization. Obscenity issues, though, are often guided by federal law and can be prosecuted as criminal offenses: A prosecutor makes a case against a purveyor of obscene material on behalf of "the people."

For most of this nation's history, it has been generally argued that obscenity does not constitute a legitimate form of expression. The problem, however, is that little agreement has existed on how to define an obscene work. In the 1860s, a court could judge an entire book obscene if it merely contained a single passage believed capable of corrupting a person. In fact, throughout the 1800s, certain government authorities outside the courts—especially U.S. post office and customs officials—held the power to censor or destroy written material they deemed obscene.

This began to change in the 1930s during the trial involving the celebrated novel *Ulysses* by Irish writer James Joyce. Portions of *Ulysses* had been serialized in the early 1920s in an American magazine, which was later seized and burned by postal officials. The publishers of the magazine, *Little Review*, were fined $50 and nearly sent to prison. Because of the four-letter words contained in the novel and the book-burning incident, British and American publishing houses backed away from the book, which was eventually published in Paris in 1922. In 1928, the U.S. Customs Office officially banned *Ulysses* as an obscene work. Ultimately, Random House agreed to publish the work in America only if it was declared "legal." Finally, in 1933, a U.S. judge ruled that *Ulysses* was an important literary work and removed it from its unprotected status.

Battles over obscenity continued. In a key landmark case, *Roth v. United States*, the Supreme Court in 1957 offered this test for obscenity: whether to an "average person," applying "contemporary standards," the major thrust or theme of the material, "taken as a whole," appealed to "prurient interest" (in other words, was intended to "incite lust"). By the 1960s, based on *Roth*, expression no longer constituted obscenity if only a small part of the work lacked "redeeming social value." Refining *Roth*, the current legal definition of **obscenity** derives from the 1973 *Miller v. California* case, which involved sanctions for using the mail to promote or send pornographic materials. After a series of appeals, the Supreme Court argued that an obscene work had to meet three criteria:

1. The average person, applying contemporary community standards, would find that the material as a whole appeals to prurient interest.

2. The material depicts or describes sexual conduct in a patently offensive way.

3. The material, as a whole, lacks serious literary, artistic, political, or scientific value.

Since this decision, courts have granted great latitude to printed and visual pornography. By the 1980s and 1990s, major cases prosecuting obscenity had become rare in the United States, as the legal system advanced the concept that a free society must tolerate even repulsive kinds of speech for a democracy to work.

The *Miller* refinement of the *Roth* precedent contained two important ideas. First, it acknowledged that different communities and regions of the country have different values and standards; what is considered obscene in Fargo, North Dakota, for example, may not be judged obscene in Miami. The ruling sent various municipalities and states scrambling to develop lists of obscene acts and language that violated their communities' standards. (Some of these lists, when tested, were declared unconstitutional and had to undergo numerous revisions.) Second, the *Miller* decision also required that a work had to be judged as a whole. This removed a loophole in which some publishers would insert a political essay or literary poem to demonstrate in court that their publications contained redeeming features.

first amendment vs.
sixth amendment

Over the years, First Amendment protections of speech and the press have often clashed with the Sixth Amendment, which guarantees an accused individual in "all criminal prosecutions . . . the right to a speedy and public trial, by an impartial jury." In 1954, for example, the Sam Sheppard case, loosely the inspiration for the TV series *The Fugitive* and the subsequent 1994 film, involved enormous publicity. Featuring lurid details about the murder of Sheppard's wife, the Cleveland press editorialized in favor of Sheppard's quick arrest; some papers even pronounced him guilty. A prominent and wealthy osteopath, Sheppard was convicted of the murder. Twelve years later, though, Sheppard's new lawyer, F. Lee Bailey, argued before the Supreme Court that his client had not received a fair trial because of prejudicial publicity. The Court overturned the conviction and freed Sheppard.

Gag Orders and Shield Laws. One of the major criticisms of the O.J. Simpson criminal case in 1994–95 concerned the ways in which defense lawyers used the news media to comment publicly on court matters outside the presence of a sequestered jury. After the Sheppard reversal in the 1960s, the Supreme Court had suggested safeguards—some used in the Simpson case—that judges could employ to ensure a fair trial in a heavily publicized case. These included sequestering juries (Sheppard's jury was not sequestered), moving cases to other jurisdictions, limiting the number of reporters, seating reporters in a particular place in courtrooms, and placing restrictions, or **gag orders,** on lawyers and witnesses. Historically, gag orders have been issued to prohibit the press from releasing preliminary information that might prejudice jury selection. In most instances, however, especially since a Supreme Court review in 1976, gag rules have been struck down as a prior restraint violation of the First Amendment.

In opposition to gag rules, **shield laws** have favored the First Amendment rights of reporters, protecting them from having to reveal their sources for controversial information used in news stories. The news media have argued that protecting the confidentiality of key sources maintains a reporter's credibility, protects a source from possible retaliation, and serves the public interest in that a source gives readers or viewers information they might not otherwise receive. In the 1960s and early 1970s, when the First Amendment rights of reporters clashed with Sixth Amendment fair trial concerns, judges usually favored the Sixth Amendment arguments. In 1972, a New Jersey journalist became the first reporter jailed for contempt of court for refusing to identify sources in an investigative probe of the Newark housing authority. After this case, a number of legal measures developed to protect the news media. By the 1990s, twenty-eight states had enacted some type of shield law, and many other states recognized the reporters' First Amendment rights not to divulge sources. In a few states, however, shield laws do not protect reporters who have been subpoenaed in grand-jury investigations. In the mid-1990s, for instance, a reporter from Warren, Ohio, was jailed for contempt of court after she refused to testify before a grand jury investigating a public official who she had recently interviewed.

Cameras in the Courtroom. When Sam Sheppard was originally convicted in the 1950s, television news was in its infancy and did not play a major role in that trial. But by

"Has TV done irreparable damage to the criminal justice system by laying claim to a **camera in the courtroom?** I doubt it. Has it made itself look foolish and unfeeling by turning a murder trial into TV's longest running entertainment special? I think so."
—Don Hewitt, executive producer of *60 Minutes*, commenting on the first Simpson trial, 1995

In 1935, the news media created a circus atmosphere at the trial of Bruno Hauptmann, the man eventually tried and executed for the kidnap-murder of the infant son of Anne and Charles Lindbergh. The behavior of radio reporters and photographers with flash cameras led to bans on electronic equipment in most courtrooms throughout much of this century.

the mid-1990s, particularly during the Simpson criminal trial, TV cameras in the courtroom had become central to public discussions of our legal system. More and more judges and lawyers had come to believe that cameras made the judicial system more accountable and helped the public learn how U.S. law operated.

This view, however, took a long time to evolve. The debates over intrusive electronic broadcast equipment and photographers actually date to the sensationalized coverage of the Bruno Hauptmann trial in the mid-1930s. Convicted and executed for the kidnap-murder of the nineteen-month-old son of Anne and Charles Lindbergh (the aviation hero who made the first solo plane trip across the Atlantic Ocean in 1927), Hauptmann and his attorney had complained that the circus atmosphere fueled by the presence of radio and flash cameras prejudiced the jury and turned the public against him.

After the trial, the American Bar Association amended a professional ethics code, Canon 35, stating that electronic equipment in the courtroom detracted "from the essential dignity of the proceedings." Calling for a ban on photographers and radio equipment, the Bar believed that lawyers would begin playing to audiences and negatively alter the judicial process. For years after the Hauptmann trial, almost every state banned photographic, radio, and TV equipment from courtrooms.

As broadcast equipment became more portable and less obtrusive, however, and as TV news became the major news source for most Americans, courts gradually reevaluated their bans on broadcast equipment. In fact, in the early 1980s, the Supreme Court ruled that the presence of TV equipment did not make it impossible for a fair trial to occur, leaving it up to each state to implement its own system. Today, some states allow television coverage of trials; some states leave it up to the discretion of the judge. A few states still ban coverage outright; others allow the televising of civil but not criminal trials. In 1991, U.S. federal courts began allowing limited coverage of trials, although in 1997 the Supreme Court still banned TV and radio from its own proceedings.

The judicial system got its very own national cable service when the Courtroom Television Network—Court TV—debuted in 1991. By the mid-1990s, the channel was available in nearly twenty-five million homes, carrying both live and taped coverage of trials from around the United States. Anchored by experienced legal reporters, a prime-time lineup of programs developed on Court TV, including *Prime Time Justice*, a daily wrap-up of key court testimony from around the country; *Lock & Key*, a program covering parole and sentence hearings; and *Trial Story*, a summary and history of the cable channel's most important trial coverage. Similar to daytime talk shows, the channel often focused on private family cases. In the trials of the Menendez brothers, for instance, juries had to decide whether children abused by their parents could use that behavior as justification for murder. Although the first trial ended in a hung jury, the brothers were convicted of murdering their parents during a second trial in 1996.

The Simpson criminal trial—the most publicized case in history—gave Court TV its greatest boost in 1994. The channel was picked to provide the one "pool" camera allowed at the trial, supplying all local news channels and the networks with the only footage from inside the courtroom. Before and during the criminal trial, a number of national discussions took place regarding the impact of the courtroom camera. Judge Lance Ito threatened to pull the plug on at least two occasions—once when the camera briefly panned across an alternate juror, and another time when he thought the camera had zoomed in too tightly on the defendant taking notes. (In Simpson's civil trial, which ended in 1997, the judge banned TV coverage.)

Critical analysis of the first Simpson trial continued long after the outcome. In retrospect, many legal analysts thought that the nine-month duration of the trial—the longest in California history—resulted from too many lawyers overacting for a national audience. Certainly, such intense focus on the case took attention away from other issues that the news media might have covered more fully had the trial not occurred. Still, televising the criminal trial contributed to the democratic process in at least two important ways. First, the Simpson criminal trial gave many people their first sustained glimpse into the strengths and weaknesses of the American legal system. Second, the TV trial focused national attention on the problems of spousal abuse, judicial reform, and racial tension, creating national debates on these issues that went on for months after the trial ended. To capitalize on these and other issues, Geraldo Rivera's program on CNBC focused on the civil suit later filed against Simpson by Ron Goldman's and Nicole Brown's families. To compete with Geraldo and Court TV, CNN also spun off a new legal show, *Burden of Proof*, starring two of its analysts from the criminal trial. In addition, Simpson's main criminal defense lawyer, Johnnie Cochran, began hosting a legal-political talk show—*Cochran & Company*—which premiered on Court TV in 1997.

Curbing the Law's Chilling Effect. As libel law and the growing acceptance of courtroom cameras indicate, the legal process has generally, though not always, tried to ensure that print and other news media are able to cover public issues broadly without fear of reprisals. Since the 1960s especially, legislators have sculpted laws that would not have a chilling effect on the news media; that would not curb their ability to actively pursue and report stories that are in the public interest. In a democracy, we expect journalists to act as watchdogs on public issues of vital importance. Such an expectation necessitates broad speech and press freedom. Because of this First Amendment freedom, as a society we occasionally tolerate pornography, hate speech, and other forms of expression that we may not support personally. We can, however, exercise our own free-speech rights and speak out against—or even boycott—language and expression that we find offensive, demeaning, or hateful.

film and the
first amendment

When the First Amendment was ratified in 1791, even the most enlightened leaders of our nation could not have predicted the coming of visual media such as film and television. Consequently, new communication technologies have not always received the same kinds of protection granted to speech, pamphlets, newspapers, magazines, and books. For example, movies, in existence since the late 1890s, earned speech protection under the law only after a 1952 Supreme Court decision. In addition, broadcast stations, unlike newspapers or magazines, are licensed by the federal government and subject to legislation that does not affect print media.

social and political pressure on the movies

During the early part of the twentieth century, movies rose in popularity among European immigrants and others from modest socioeconomic groups. This, in turn, spurred the formation of censorship groups, who believed that the popular new medium would threaten children, incite violence, and undermine morality. The number of nickelodeon theaters—often housed in ramshackle buildings—surged in 1905 and drew attention from public health inspectors and city social workers. During this time, criticism of movies converged on four areas: "the effects on children, the potential health problems, the negative influences on morals and manners, and the lack of a proper role for educational and religious institutions in the development of movies."[11]

Film Review Boards. Public pressure on movies came both from conservatives, who saw them as a potential threat to the authority of traditional institutions, and from progressives, who worried that children and adults were more attracted to movie houses than to social organizations and urban education centers. Afraid that movies created an illusory dream world, civic leaders publicly escalated their pressure, organizing local review boards that screened movies for their communities. In 1907, the Chicago City Council created an ordinance that gave the police authority to issue permits for a movie's exhibition. By 1920, over ninety cities in America had some type of movie censorship board made up of vice-squad officers, politicians, or citizen groups. By 1923, twenty-two states had established such boards.

Pressure began to translate into law as politicians, wanting to please their constituencies, began to legislate against films. Support mounted for a federal censorship bill. When Jack Johnson won the heavyweight championship in 1908, boxing films became the target of the first federal law aimed at the motion picture industry. In 1912, the government outlawed the transportation of boxing movies across state lines. The laws against boxing films, however, had more to do with Johnson than with concern over violence in movies. The first black heavyweight champion, he was perceived as a threat to the white community.

The first Supreme Court decision regarding film's protection under the First Amendment was handed down in 1915 and went against the movie industry. In *Mutual v. Ohio*, the Mutual Film Company of Detroit sued the state of Ohio, whose

Calvin **and** Hobbes

by Bill Watterson

Reprinted with permission. All rights reserved.

review board had censored a number of the Michigan distributor's films. On appeal, the case arrived at the Supreme Court, which unanimously ruled that film was not a form of speech but "a business pure and simple" and, like a circus, merely a "spectacle" for entertainment with "a special capacity for evil." This ruling would stand for thirty-seven years. Although the U.S. movement to create a national censorship board failed, legislation to monitor and control movies, especially those from America, has passed in many other countries.

Industry Self-Regulation. As the film industry expanded after World War I, the impact of public pressure and review boards began affecting movie studios and executives who wanted to ensure control over their economic well-being. In the early 1920s, a series of scandals rocked Hollywood: actress Mary Pickford's divorce and quick marriage to actor Douglas Fairbanks; director William Desmond Taylor's unsolved murder; and actor Wallace Reid's death from a drug overdose. The most sensational scandal involved aspiring actress Virginia Rappe, who died a few days after a wild San Francisco hotel party hosted by popular silent-film comedian Fatty Arbuckle. After Rappe's death, the comedian was indicted for rape and manslaughter. After two hung juries, Arbuckle's career was ruined. Censorship boards across the country banned his films, even though he was acquitted at his third trial in 1922. Despite his exoneration, the movie industry tried to send a signal about the kind of values and lifestyles it would tolerate: Arbuckle was banned from acting in Hollywood. He later directed several films under the name Will B. Goode.

In response to the scandals, particularly the first Arbuckle trial, the movie industry formed the Motion Picture Producers and Distributors of America (MPPDA) and hired as its president Will Hays, former Postmaster General and Republican National Committee chair. Hays was paid $100,000 annually to clean up "sin city." Known as the Hays Office, the MPPDA attempted to smooth out problems between the public and the industry. Hays blacklisted promising actors or movie extras with even minor police records. Later, he developed an MPPDA public relations division, which successfully lobbied against a movie censorship rule in Massachusetts and stopped a national movement for a federal law censoring movies.

the motion picture production code

During the 1930s, the movie industry faced a new round of challenges. First, various conservative and religious groups—including the influential Catholic Legion of Decency—increased their scrutiny of the industry. Second, deteriorating economic conditions during the Depression forced the industry to tighten self-regulation to keep harmful public pressure at bay. In response, the Hays Office developed a list of "Don'ts and Be Carefuls" in 1927 to steer producers and directors away from questionable sexual, moral, and social themes. Nevertheless, pressure for a more formal and sweeping code mounted. In the early 1930s, the Hays Office established the Motion Picture Production Code, whose overseers officially stamped almost every Hollywood film with a moral seal of approval.

> "No approval by the Production Code Administration shall be given to **the use of . . . *damn* [or] *hell*** (excepting when the use of said last two words shall be essential and required for portrayal, in proper historical context, of any scene or dialogue based upon historical fact or folklore, or for the presentation in proper literary context of a Biblical, or other religious quotation, or a quotation from a literary work provided that no such use shall be permitted which is intrinsically objectionable or **offends good taste**)."
> —Motion Picture Production Code, 1934

The Code laid out its mission in its first general principle: "No picture shall be produced which will lower the moral standards of those who see it. Hence the sympathy of the audience shall never be thrown to the side of crime, wrong-doing, evil or sin." The self-regulatory Code dictated how producers and directors should handle "methods of crime," "repellent subjects," "illegal drug traffic," and "sex hygiene." A section on profanity outlawed a long list of phrases and topics, including "toilet gags" and "traveling salesmen and farmer's daughter jokes." In the late 1930s, the producers of *Gone with the Wind* had to seek a special dispensation so that actor Clark Gable could say "damn." Under "scenes of passion," the Code dictated that "excessive and lustful kissing, lustful embraces, suggestive postures and gestures are not to be shown," and the Code required that "passion should be treated in such a manner as not to stimulate the lower and baser emotions." The section on religion revealed the influences of Jesuit priest Daniel Lord and Catholic publisher Martin Quigley, who helped write the Code: "No film or episode may throw ridicule on any religious faith" and "ministers of religion . . . should not be used as comic characters or as villains."

Adopted by 95 percent of the industry, the Code influenced nearly every commercial movie made between the mid-1930s and the early 1950s. It also gave the industry a relative degree of freedom, allowing the major studios to remain independent from outside regulation. When television arrived, however, competition from the new medium forced movie producers to explore more-adult subjects.

In 1952, the Supreme Court heard the *Miracle* case—officially *Burstyn v. Wilson*—named for the movie distributor who sued the head of the New York Film Licensing Board for banning Roberto Rossellini's film *Il Miracolo (The Miracle)*. A few New York City religious and political leaders considered the 1948 Italian film sacrilegious and pressured the film board for the ban. In the film, an unmarried peasant girl is impregnated by a scheming vagrant (played by Federico Fellini, who also wrote the story). In simple faith, she believes the tramp's story: He is St. Joseph and she has conceived the baby Jesus. The importers of the film argued that censoring it constituted illegal prior restraint; since such an action could not be imposed on a print version of the story, the same freedom should attach to the film. The Supreme Court eventually agreed, declaring movies "a significant medium for the communication of ideas." The decision granted films the same protections as the print media and other forms of speech. Even more important, the decision rendered the activities of film review boards unconstitutional, since they had generally been engaged in prior restraint. Although a few local boards survived into the 1990s to handle complaints about movies that were considered obscene, most had disbanded by the 1970s.

rating movie content

The current voluntary movie rating system—the model for the advisory labels the music business and television now use—developed in the late 1960s after another round of pressure over movie content. *The Pawnbroker* in 1965, for instance, contained brief female nudity, and in 1966, *Who's Afraid of Virginia Woolf?* featured a level of profanity that had not been heard before in a major studio film. In 1966, the movie industry hired Jack Valenti to run the MPAA (Motion Picture Association of America, formerly the MPPDA), and in 1968 he established an industry board to rate movies. Eventually, G, PG, R, and X ratings emerged as guideposts for the suitability of films for various age groups. In 1984, PG–13 was added and sandwiched between PG and R to distinguish slightly higher levels of violence or adult themes in movies that might otherwise qualify as PG (see Figure 16.1).

The MPAA copyrighted all ratings designations as trademarks except for the X rating, which was gradually appropriated by the pornographic film industry. In fact,

What Everyone Should Know About The Movie Rating System.

GENERAL AUDIENCES

G

Nothing that would offend parents for viewing by children.

G GENERAL AUDIENCES

PARENTAL GUIDANCE SUGGESTED

PG

Parents urged to give parental guidance. May contain some material parents might not like for their young children.

PG PARENTAL GUIDANCE SUGGESTED

PARENTS STRONGLY CAUTIONED

PG-13

Parents are urged to be cautious. Some material may be inappropriate for pre-teenagers.

PG-13 PARENTS STRONGLY CAUTIONED

RESTRICTED

R

Contains some adult material. Parents are urged to learn more about the film before taking their young children with them.

R RESTRICTED

NO ONE 17 AND UNDER ADMITTED

NC-17

Patently adult. Children are not admitted.

NC-17 NO ONE 17 AND UNDER ADMITTED

Figure 16.1
The Voluntary Movie Rating System
Source: © 1996 Motion Picture Association of America, Inc.

459

Legal
Controls

between 1972 and 1989, the MPAA stopped issuing the X rating. In 1990, however, based on protests from filmmakers over movies with adult sexual themes that they did not consider pornographic, the industry copyrighted the NC–17 rating—no children under age seventeen—and awarded the first NC–17 to *Henry & June*. In 1995, *Showgirls* became the first movie to intentionally seek an NC–17 to demonstrate that the rating was commercially viable. However, many theater chains in the mid-1990s refused to carry NC–17 movies, fearing economic sanctions and boycotts by their customers, religious groups, and other concerned citizens. Many newspapers also refused to carry ads for NC–17 films. Panned by the critics, *Showgirls* flopped at the box office. Although it did fairly well later in video release, commercial pressures forced the development of a separate, reedited R-rated version for those video stores that would not carry NC–17 or X-rated movies.

expression over the airwaves

During the Cold War, a vigorous campaign led by Joseph McCarthy, the ultra-conservative senator from Wisconsin, tried to rid both government and the media of communist subversives who were allegedly challenging the American way of life. In 1950, a publication called *Red Channels: The Report of Communist Influence in Radio and Television* aimed "to show how the Communists have been able to carry out their plan of infiltration of the radio and television industry." *Red Channels*, inspired by McCarthy and produced by a group of former FBI agents, named 151 performers, writers, and musicians who were "sympathetic" to communist or "left-wing" causes. Among those named were Leonard Bernstein, Will Geer (who later played the grandfather on *The Waltons*), Dashiell Hammett, Lillian Hellman, Lena Horne, Burgess Meredith, Arthur Miller, Dorothy Parker, Pete Seeger (the labor folksinger who in 1994 received a Kennedy Center Honors Award from President Clinton), Irwin Shaw, and Orson Welles. For a time, all were banned from working in television and radio even though no one on the list was ever charged with a crime.[12]

In 1950, the 215-page *Red Channels*, published by American Business Consultants (a group of former FBI agents), placed 151 prominent writers, directors, and performers from radio, movies, and television on a blacklist, many of them simply for sympathizing with left-wing democratic causes. Although no one on the list was ever charged with a crime, many of the talented individuals targeted by *Red Channels* did not work in their professions for years.

Although the First Amendment protects an individual's right to hold controversial political views, network executives either sympathized with the anticommunist movement or feared losing ad revenue. At any rate, the networks did not stand up to the communist witch-hunters. For a blacklisted or "suspected" performer to work required the support of the program's sponsor. Though *I Love Lucy*'s Lucille Ball, who in sympathy with her father once registered to vote as a communist in the 1930s, retained Philip Morris's sponsorship of her popular program, other performers were not as fortunate. Philip Loeb, who played the father on *The Goldbergs*, an early 1950s TV sitcom that came over from radio, found his name listed in *Red Channels*. Gertrude Berg, who owned and starred in the series, supported him. Nevertheless, boycott pressure on the program's sponsor, Sanka coffee, a General Foods brand, forced the company to abandon the program, which was dropped from CBS in 1951. After several months, it resurfaced on NBC, but Loeb had been replaced. Four years later, he committed suicide because he could no longer find work. Although no evidence was ever introduced to show how entertainment programs circulated communist propaganda, by the early 1950s the TV networks were asking actors and other workers to sign loyalty oaths denouncing communism—a low point for the First Amendment.

The communist witch-hunts demonstrated key differences between print and broadcast protection under the First Amendment—differences that are perhaps best illustrated in legal history. On the one hand, licenses for printers and publishers have been outlawed since the eighteenth century. On the other hand, in the late 1920s, commercial broadcasters themselves asked the federal government to step in and regulate the airwaves. At that time, they wanted the government to clear up technical problems, channel noise, noncommercial competition, and amateur interference. Ever since, most broadcasters have been trying to free themselves from the government intrusion they once demanded.

fcc rules, broadcasting, and indecency

Drawing on the scarcity argument (that limited broadcast signals constitute a scarce national resource), the Communications Act of 1934 mandated in Section 309 that broadcasters operate in "the public interest, convenience, and/or necessity." Since the 1980s, however, with cable increasing signal capacity, station managers have lobbied for "ownership" of their airwave assignments. Although the 1996 Telecommunications Act did not grant such ownership, stations continue to challenge the "public interest" statute. They argue that since the government is not allowed to dictate content in newspapers, it should not be allowed to control licenses or mandate any broadcast programming.

Print vs. Broadcast Rules. Two cases—*Red Lion Broadcasting Co. v. FCC* (1969) and the *Miami Herald Publishing Co. v. Tornillo* (1974)—demonstrate the historic legal differences between broadcast and print. In the *Red Lion* decision, the operators of the small-town station in Red Lion, Pennsylvania, refused to give airtime to Fred Cook, author of a book that criticized Barry Goldwater, the Republican party's presidential candidate in 1964. Cook had been criticized by a conservative radio preacher, the Reverend Billy James Hargis, and asked for response time from the two hundred stations that carried the Hargis attack. Most stations complied, granting Cook free reply time. But WGCB, the Red Lion station, offered only to sell Cook time. He appealed to the FCC, which ordered the station to give Cook free time. The station refused, claiming that its First Amendment rights granted it control over its program content. On appeal, the Supreme Court sided with the FCC, deciding that whenever a broadcaster's rights conflict with the public interest, it is the public interest that is paramount. Interpreting broadcasting as different than print, the Supreme Court in 1969 upheld the constitutionality of the 1934 Communications Act by reaffirming that broadcasters' responsibilities to program in the public interest can outweigh their rights to program whatever they want.

In contrast, five years later in *Miami Herald Publishing Co. v. Tornillo*, the Supreme Court sided with the newspaper in a case in which a political candidate, Pat Tornillo Jr., requested space to reply to an editorial opposing his candidacy. Previously, Florida had enacted a right-to-reply law that permitted a candidate to respond to editorial criticisms from newspapers. Counter to the *Red Lion* decision, the Court in this case struck down the Florida state law as unconstitutional. The Court argued that mandating that a newspaper give a candidate space to reply violated the paper's First Amendment rights to publish what it chose. The two decisions demonstrate that for most of the twentieth century, the unlicensed print media have received protections under the First Amendment that are not always available to licensed broadcast media.

June 9, 1969 It is the right of the viewers and listeners, not the right of the broadcasters, which is paramount. . . .
—Supreme Court decision in *Red Lion Broadcasting Co. v. FCC,* 395 U.S. 367

June 25, 1974 A responsible press is an undoubtedly desirable goal, but press responsibility is not mandated by the Constitution and like many other virtues it cannot be legislated.
—Supreme Court decision in *Miami Herald Publishing Co. v. Tornillo,* 418 U.S. 241

Dirty Words and Indecent Speech. Although considered tame in a culture that now includes "shock jock" Howard Stern's lurid sexual innuendos, *topless radio* in the 1960s featured deejays and callers discussing intimate sexual subjects in the middle of the afternoon. The government curbed the practice in 1973 when the chairman of the FCC denounced topless radio as "a new breed of air pollution . . . with the suggestive, coaxing, pear-shaped tones of the smut-hustling host."[13] After an FCC investigation, a couple of stations lost their licenses, some were fined, and topless radio was checked temporarily. It reemerged in the 1980s, only with modern doctors and therapists—instead of deejays—offering intimate counsel over the airwaves.

In theory, communication law prevents the government from censoring broadcast content. Accordingly, the government may not interfere with programs or engage in prior restraint, although it may punish broadcasters after the fact. Over the years, a handful of radio stations have had licenses suspended or denied after an unfavorable FCC review of their past programming records. Concerns over indecent broadcast programming probably date from 1937. That year NBC was scolded by the FCC after running a sketch featuring comedian-actress Mae West on ventriloquist Edgar Bergen's network program. West had the following conversation with Bergen's famous wooden dummy Charley McCarthy:

WEST: That's all right. I like a man that takes his time. Why don't you come home with me? I'll let you play in my woodpile . . . you're all wood and a yard long. . . .

CHARLEY: Oh, Mae, don't, don't . . . don't be so rough. To me love is peace and quiet.

WEST: That ain't love—that's sleep.[14]

After the sketch, West did not appear again on radio for years. Ever since, the FCC has periodically fined or reprimanded stations for indecent programming, especially during times when children might be listening.

The current precedent for regulating radio indecency stems from one complaint to the FCC in 1973. Pacifica's WBAI in New York, in the middle of the afternoon, aired George Carlin's famous comedy album about the seven dirty words that could not be uttered by broadcasters. A father, riding in a car with his fifteen-year-old son, heard the program and complained to the FCC, which sent WBAI a simple letter of reprimand. Although no fine was involved, the station appealed on principle and won its case in court. The FCC persisted, however, appealing all the way to the Supreme Court. Although no court has legally defined indecency, the Supreme Court's unexpected ruling in 1979 sided with the FCC and upheld the agency's authority to require broadcasters to air adult programming at later times. The Court ruled that so-called indecent programming, though not in violation of federal obscenity laws, was a nuisance (like a pig in a parlor, the Court said) and could be restricted to late evening hours to protect children. The commission has effectively banned indecent programs from most stations between 6 A.M. and 10 P.M. In 1990, the FCC tried to ban such programs entirely. Although a federal court ruled this move unconstitutional, it still upheld the time restrictions intended to protect children. This ruling lies at the heart of the indecency fines—totaling over $1 million—that the FCC has leveled over the last several years against Howard Stern's syndicated morning program.

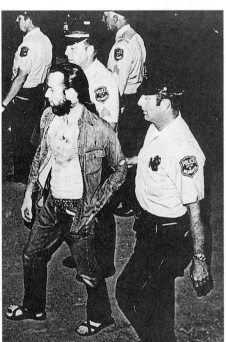

In the summer of 1972, comedian George Carlin was arrested by Milwaukee police after performing a routine about the seven words that cannot be said on radio or television. The subject of a comedy monologue called "Filthy Words," Carlin's routine later was the centerpiece in a 1978 Supreme Court decision regarding a radio broadcast of the twelve-minute monologue. The Court upheld the FCC's authority to regulate indecent speech on the nation's airwaves.

political broadcasts and equal opportunity

In addition to indecency rules, another law that the print media do not encounter is **Section 315** of the 1934 Communications Act, which mandates that during elections broadcast stations must provide equal opportunities and response time for qualified political candidates. In other words, if broadcasters give or sell time to one candidate, they must give or sell the same opportunity to others. Local broadcasters and networks have fought this law for years, since it has often required them to include obscure third-party and fringe candidates in political discussions. Broadcasters claim that since no Section 315–type rule applies to newspapers or magazines, the law violates their First Amendment right to control their content. In fact, because of this rule, many stations have avoided all political programming. Ironically in these cases, a rule meant to serve the public interest by increasing communication backfired as stations decided to skirt the law.

The TV networks managed to get the law amended in 1959 to exempt newscasts, press conferences, and other events—such as political debates—that qualify as news. For instance, if a senator running for office appears in a news story, candidates running against him or her cannot invoke Section 315 and demand free time. Due to this provision, many stations from the late 1960s through the 1980s pulled TV movies starring Ronald Reagan. Since his film appearances did not count as bona fide news stories, candidates opposing Reagan could demand free time in markets that ran an old Reagan movie. Supporters of the equal opportunity law argue that it has provided forums for lesser-known candidates representing views counter to those of the Democratic and Republican parties. They further note that one of the few ways for alternative candidates to circulate their messages widely is to buy political ads, thus limiting serious outside contenders to wealthy candidates, such as Ross Perot and Steve Forbes in 1996.

the demise of the fairness doctrine

Considered an important corollary to Section 315, the **Fairness Doctrine** was to controversial issues what Section 315 is to political speech. Initiated in 1949, this FCC rule required stations to air and engage in controversial issue programs that affected their communities, and when offering such programming, to provide competing points of view. Antismoking activist John Banzhaf ingeniously invoked the Fairness Doctrine to force cigarette advertising off television in 1971. When the FCC mandated antismoking public-service announcements to counter "controversial" smoking commercials, tobacco companies decided to accept an outright ban rather than tolerate a flood of antismoking spots authorized by the Fairness Doctrine.

With little public debate, the Fairness Doctrine ended in 1987 after a federal court ruled that it was merely a regulation rather than an extension of Section 315 law. Broadcasters had argued over the years that the doctrine forced many of them to play down controversial issues; they claimed that mandating opposing views every time a program covered a controversial issue was a burden not required of the print media. Since 1987, there has been periodic interest in reviving the Fairness Doctrine. Its supporters argue that broadcasting is fundamentally different from—and more pervasive than—the print media, requiring greater accountability to the public. Although many broadcasters disagree, supporters of fairness rules insist that as long as broadcasters are licensed as public trustees of the airwaves—unlike newspaper or magazine publishers—legal precedent permits the courts and the FCC to demand responsible content and behavior from radio and TV stations.

"There is no doubt about the unique impact of radio and television. But this fact alone **does not justify government regulation.** In fact, quite the contrary. We should recall that the printed press was the *only* medium of mass communication in the early days of the republic—and yet this did not deter our predecessors from passing the First Amendment to prohibit abridgement of its freedoms."
—Chief Judge David Bazelon, U.S. court of appeals, 1972

By the mid-1990s, broadcast and cable operators were increasingly demanding the same First Amendment rights as the print media. This pressure, combined with a growing belief that a free market can solve most economic problems, allowed a relaxation of the rules governing broadcasting and cable. Still, public concerns about visual violence and children's programming kept regulatory issues prominent during the presidential campaigns of 1992 and 1996. But questions about the negative impact of concentrated media ownership rarely surfaced. They were raised most frequently by fringe conservative candidate and TV pundit Pat Buchanan.

Should deregulation accelerate, however, the remaining public and noncommercial broadcast outlets are at risk. Public broadcasting already faced severe revenue cutbacks in the mid-1990s, so more deregulation of the communication industry might cause a recurrence of the problems of the late 1920s and early 1930s. As we noted in Chapter 4, the Depression crippled noncommercial broadcasters because many of them were forced to sell or transfer their licenses to commercial interests. Although Congress in 1996 mandated that the broadcast networks carry three hours of educational programs a week, public radio and television still offer the bulk of programming that is not commercially viable.

cyberspace, expression, and democracy

Although the United States has tolerated a wide variety of speech and expression, critics charge that such tolerance has generally favored corporate interests and media industries. For example, it is far easier for large corporations and advertisers like Disney or General Motors to buy commercial speech than it is for small grassroots organizations that have important messages but limited finances. As a result, messages that counter mainstream culture might appear only in alternative magazines or on cable access channels, where entry is cheap but audience reach is limited.

communication policy in cyberspace

> "We must make sure that we direct technology in a way that will **lead to democracy**."
> —Mischa Schwartz, Columbia University, 1992

Another arena that increases the voices—and noise—circulating in culture is the Internet. Its current global expansion is comparable to the early days of broadcasting, when economic and technological growth outstripped law and regulation. At that time, noncommercial experiments by amateurs and engineering students provided a testing ground that commercial interests later exploited for profit. Indeed, before the Radio Act of 1927, many noncommercial groups experimented with the possibilities of the new broadcast medium.

In much the same way, "amateurs," students, and various interest groups have explored and extended the communication possibilities of the Internet. They have experimented so successfully that commercial vendors are now racing to buy up pieces of the information highway. Like radio in the 1920s, the Internet's noncommercial developers in the 1990s have been selling off services to commercial entrepreneurs. This is especially true of university consortiums, which had been running most of the regional Internet services. Like radio, experimenting and risk-taking took place at the noncommercial level before commercial adventurers stepped in to explore the profit possibilities.

The last serious widespread public debate on mass media ownership occurred in the early 1930s and ended with the passage of the 1934 Communications Act and the defeat of the Wagner-Hatfield Amendment (which would have reserved 25 percent of the spectrum for noncommercial radio). In recent years, public conversations about the Internet have not typically been about ownership questions. Instead, the debates—often triggered by the news media—have focused on First Amendment issues such as civility and pornography in cyberspace. Reporters, in fact, tend to view Internet issues as entrepreneurial business stories ("What company is marketing the next software breakthrough?") with free-speech implications ("Who is using the highway for pornographic purposes?"). Not unlike the public's concern over television's sexual and violent images, the scrutiny of the Internet is mainly about harmful images in cyberspace, not about who controls it and for what purposes.

In 1995, for example, a male University of Michigan student was arrested and dismissed from school for creating a violent pornographic cyberspace story in which he named and fantasized about a female student. This incident received widespread news coverage. As the federal court case against the student evolved, it became clear that few existing laws applied to speech in cyberspace. Federal attorneys eventually dropped the case against the student as Congress frantically hurried to extend existing obscenity and speech prohibitions to the Internet in the Telecommunications Act of 1996. However, this part of the new Act was quickly challenged as unconstitutional. During this time, little public discussion has taken place over ownership of the Internet even though its hub sites began to pass gradually from the public domain to private entrepreneurs.

As we watch the rapid expansion of the Internet worldwide, an important questions confronts us: Will the Internet continue to develop democratically rather than hierarchically, evading government or corporate plans to contain it, change it, and closely monitor who has access? In the early days of broadcasting, commercial interests became dominant partly because the companies running radio (like the Hearst Corporation, which also owned chains of newspapers and magazines) did not report on ownership questions as serious news stories. It was not in their economic interest to do so. Today, once again, it has not been in the news media's economic interest to organize or lead the ownership debate; the major print and broadcast owners, after all, have heavily invested in the Internet.

Critics and observers hope that a vigorous debate develops on new communication technologies—a debate that goes beyond First Amendment issues. The promise of the Internet as a democratic forum—adding millions of new users each month—encourages the formation of all sorts of regional, national, and global interest groups. Whether such cyber communities could eventually help to frame and solve society-level problems remains at issue.

A positive sign is that global movements abound that use the Internet to fight political forms of censorship. The Digital Freedom Network, for example, circulates material that has been banned in certain countries, including excerpts from dissident Chinese writer Wei Jingsheng and Indonesian novelist Pramoedya Ananta Toer. In another instance, the International Freedom of Expression Exchange (IFEX)—a Toronto-based clearinghouse that documents nearly two thousand international press-freedom violations each year—relayed the 1994 story of a journalist from the former Yugoslavia who had been jailed

Since 1992, the Canadian Committee to Protect Journalists has operated IFEX—the International Freedom of Expression Exchange—based in Toronto. With more than twenty member organizations worldwide, IFEX has documented in print and on its Web site an average of two thousand attacks on free expression each year.

Canadian Committee to Protect Journalists

Working to Protect Freedom of Expression Worldwide

Breaking News

CCPJ News

Freedom of Expression

Journalist Resources

Breaking News | About Us | CCPJ News
Freedom of Expression | Journalist Resources

© The Canadian Committee to Protect Journalists (ccpj@web.net)

This site has been accessed 777 *times since August 24, 1996*

In June 1995, shortly after presidential candidate Bob Dole criticized Hollywood and Time Warner, *Time* magazine itself criticized its parent company in a fourteen-page cover story entitled "Are Music and Movies Killing America's Soul?" Three months later, Time Warner decided to sell its share of the major gangsta-rap label Interscope.

This incident contrasted sharply with another *Time* magazine decision under a different editor in 1989. When Time Inc. and Warner Communications announced their plans to join forces—the largest media merger in history at the time—the editor of *Time* decided *not* to cover the story.

Both decisions raise concerns about the relationship of the national news media to their larger parent companies. Although *Time* magazine was generally praised for its hard-hitting self-examination in 1995, the decision not to cover the billion-dollar merger in 1989 troubled many critics. The two incidents confirmed that a double standard exists between covering popular-culture issues and covering media business concerns.

Media business stories have always made the news media nervous. The modern journalism culture has taught reporters to focus on facts in the "outside" world. So when the story becomes the business of journalism's "inside" world, some news media and editors balk. The rules of a neutral, detached press do not prepare most journalists for turning the lens or pen on themselves. As the *Time* editor did in 1989, many look away.

Even in *Time*'s 1995 story, the CEO of Time Warner declined to comment. The current editor of *Time*, Norman Pearlstine, was disappointed with his boss. He told the *New York Times*, "I think it always looks strange when the chief executive of Time Warner isn't available for comment in the pages of *Time*." The *New York Times* also revealed that a number of reporters and staffers at *Time* were not happy with the role its parent company was playing in harder-edged rap music, some of which featured violent images and sexually degrading lyrics.

The Time Warner dilemma raises important questions for our democracy. Do we have the right to know the inner workings of our large media conglomerates? With media companies growing larger and larger, how will the network news divisions cover their parent companies? Ultimately, who's watching the watchdog? In such a media world, will we be at the mercy of news media that may determine it is not in their best interest to reveal the inside workings of their parent companies— even though such revelations may be in the nation's best interest?

SPECIAL REPORT

ARE MUSIC AND MOVIES
KILLING
AMERICA'S
SOUL?

Bob Dole's attack on the entertainment industry

TIME Forum: Free speech vs. family values

Inside Time Warner, the battle over standards

in Serbia. IFEX sent notices to its members by e-mail; within days, Serbian officials, inundated with faxes and calls, released the reporter. In this example, the digital highway works as a global freeway—a democratic communication "weapon," bypassing both government bans and political restrictions. By 1997, more than twenty organizations around the world had joined the IFEX network, which has been operated by the Canadian Committee to Protect Journalists since 1992. Just as fax machines, satellites, and home videos helped to document and expedite the fall of totalitarian regimes in Eastern Europe in the late 1980s, information highway and Internet services help to spread the word and activate social change.

watchdog citizens

For most of our nation's history, citizens have counted on journalism to monitor abuses in government and business. During the muckraking period in the early part of the twentieth century, writers like Ida Tarbell and Sinclair Lewis made strong contributions in reporting corporate expansion and social change. Unfortunately, however, stories on business issues have usually been reduced to consumer affairs reporting. In other words, when a labor strike or a factory recall are covered, such stories mainly try to answer the question, "How do these events affect consumers?" Although this is an important news angle, other questions remain: "How does the strike affect the families and future of workers and managers?" and "What is the role of unions and manufacturing industries as we move into the twenty-first century?" At this point, citizen discussions about media ownership or labor-management ethics are not part of the news frame that journalists typically use. When companies announce mergers, reporters do not routinely question the economic wisdom or social impact of such changes. Instead, they tend to tell stories about how individual consumers will be affected.

At one level, journalists have been compromised by the frenzy of media mergers involving newspapers and TV stations (see "Examining Ethics: How *Time* Covers Time Warner"). As Bill Kovach, curator of Harvard's Nieman Foundation for Journalism, pointed out after the Disney-ABC and Westinghouse-CBS mergers, "This rush to merge mainly entertainment organizations that have news operations with companies deeply involved in doing business with the government raises ominous questions about the future of watchdog journalism."[15] In other words, how can journalists adequately cover and lead discussions on issues of media ownership when the very news companies they work for are the prime buyers and sellers of major media outlets?

With the news media increasingly compromised by their complex relations to their corporations, it becomes important that the civic role of watchdog be shared by citizens as well as journalists. After all, the First Amendment protects not only the news media's free-speech rights but all of our rights to speak out. Mounting concerns over who can afford access to the media go to the heart of *free* expression.

As we struggle to determine the future of converging print, electronic, and digital media and to broaden the democratic spirit underlying media technology, we need to stay engaged in spirited public debates about media ownership and control, about commercial speech and free expression. As citizens, we need to pay attention to who is included and excluded from the opportunities not only to buy products but to speak out and shape the cultural landscape. To accomplish this, we need to challenge our journalists and our leaders. Even more important, we need to challenge ourselves to become watchdogs—critical consumers and engaged citizens—who learn from the past, care about the present, and map mass media's future.

"For the past decade and a half, **journalism has been slowly squeezed** into a smaller and smaller corner of the expanding corporations that make up the communications industry."
—Bill Kovach, Nieman Foundation, 1995

REVIEW QUESTIONS

1. What is the basic philosophical concept that underlies America's notion of free expression?

2. Explain the various models of the news media that exist under different political systems.

3. How has censorship been defined historically?

4. What is the significance of the Pentagon Papers and the *Progressive* magazine cases?

5. Why is the *New York Times v. Sullivan* case so significant in First Amendment history?

6. What does a public figure have to do to win a libel case? What are the main defenses that a newspaper can use to thwart a charge of libel?

7. What is the legal significance of the *Falwell v. Flynt* case?

8. How does a court determine, in a legal sense, if a magazine article constitutes obscenity?

9. Why were films not constitutionally protected as a form of speech until 1952?

10. Why did film review boards develop and why did they eventually disband?

11. How did both the Motion Picture Production Code and the current movie rating system come into being?

12. The government and the courts view print and broadcasting as different forms of expression. What are the major differences?

13. What is the significance of Section 315 of the Communications Act of 1934?

14. Why didn't broadcasters like the Fairness Doctrine?

15. What are the similarities and differences between the debates over broadcast ownership in the 1920s and Internet ownership in the 1990s?

16. Why is the Internet a potentially more democratic form than broadcasting?

QUESTIONING THE MEDIA

1. Have you ever had an experience in which you thought personal or public expression went too far and should be curbed? Explain. How might you remedy this situation?

2. If you owned a community newspaper and had to make a policy for your editors about which letters from readers appear in a limited space on your editorial page, what kinds of letters would you eliminate and why? Are you acting as a censor in this situation? Why or why not?

3. As owner of this same community newspaper, what would your policy be on accepting advertising for pornographic movie theaters and movies rated NC-17? Justify whatever policy you develop.

4. The writer A. J. Liebling once said that freedom of the press belonged only to those who owned one. Explain why you agree or disagree.

5. What do you think of the movie rating system the industry now uses? Should it be changed? Why or why not?

6. Should the Fairness Doctrine be revived? Why or why not?

The purpose of this exercise is to examine free-speech and press issues. These two assignments can be developed either as group projects in class or as individual writing projects—or both.

1. Do some research on a major obscenity case that is not discussed in the chapter. Ask your instructor for some suggestions, or consult the Internet or computer database services such as Lexis (legal cases) or Nexis (news stories) for ideas. Write a summary of the case and be prepared to discuss the case in class.

   As part of your project, obtain a copy of a local or state obscenity ordinance. Do you think the ordinance would be considered constitutional in a Supreme Court test? Why or why not?

2. Do some research on a major libel case involving the news media, other than the *New York Times v. Sullivan*. Ask your instructor for suggestions or consult the Internet or computer database services such as those listed in the preceding assignment. Write a summary of the case and be ready to talk about what you learned.

   Discuss whether you think libel laws give too much or too little protection to the news media. Do you think public figures, especially Hollywood celebrities, deserve more protection than libel laws currently allow? Why or why not?

NOTES

CHAPTER 1

1. J. Mac McClellan, quoted in "'Fly Till I Die,'" *Time*, April 22, 1996, 38.
2. Neil Postman, *Amusing Ourselves to Death: Public Discourse in the Age of Show Business* (New York: Penguin Books, 1984), 19.
3. James W. Carey, *Communication as Culture: Essays on Media and Society* (Boston: Unwin Hyman, 1989), 203.
4. Postman, *Amusing Ourselves to Death*, 65. See also Elizabeth Eisenstein, *The Printing Press as an Agent of Change*, 2 vols. (Cambridge, England: Cambridge University Press, 1979).
5. See Plato, *The Republic*, Book II, 377B.
6. For a historical discussion of culture, see Lawrence Levine, *Highbrow/Lowbrow: The Emergence of Cultural Hierarchy in America* (Cambridge: Harvard University Press, 1988).
7. For an example of this critical position, see Allan Bloom, *The Closing of the American Mind: How Higher Education Has Failed Democracy and Impoverished the Souls of Today's Students* (New York: Simon & Schuster, 1987).
8. For overviews of this position, see Postman, *Amusing Ourselves to Death*; and Stuart Ewen, *Captains of Consciousness: Advertising and the Social Roots of the Consumer Culture* (New York: McGraw-Hill, 1976).
9. See Carey, *Communication as Culture*.
10. For more on this idea, see Cecelia Tichi, *Electronic Hearth: Creating an American Television Culture* (New York: Oxford University Press, 1991), 187–188.
11. See Jon Katz, "Rock, Rap and Movies Bring You the News," *Rolling Stone*, March 5, 1992, 33.

Examining Ethics: Teens and TV Talk Shows, pp. 14–15

1. For reference and guidance on media ethics, see Clifford Christians, Mark Fackler, and Kim Rotzoll, *Media Ethics: Cases & Moral Reasoning*, 4th ed., (White Plains, NY: Longman, 1995); and Thomas H. Bivins, "A Worksheet for Ethics Instruction and Exercises in Reason," *Journalism Educator* (summer 1993): 4–16.

Case Study: The Material Girl as Postmodern Icon, pp. 22–23

1. Luc Sante, "Unlike a Virgin," *The New Republic* (August 20 and 27, 1990), 25–29.
2. Camille Paglia, quoted in Joseph Sobran, "Sign of the Crotch: Sex and the Single Girl," *National Review* (August 12, 1991), 32.
3. Michael McWilliams, "Why the Rock World Hates Madonna," *Detroit News* (April 21, 1990), p. C1.
4. Bell Hooks, "Madonna: Plantation Mistress or Soul Sister?" in *Black Looks: Race and Representation* (Boston: South End Press, 1992), 157–158.

Global Village: Bedouins, Camels, Transistors, and Coke, p. 28

1. Vaclav Havel, "A Time for Transcendence," *Utne Reader* (January/February 1995), 53.
2. Dan Rather, "The Threat to Foreign News," *Newsweek* (July 17, 1989), 9.

CHAPTER 2

1. Warren Susman, *Culture as History: The Transformation of American Society in the Twentieth Century* (New York: Pantheon, 1984), 32.
2. Daniel Burstein and David Kline, *Road Warriors: Dreams and Nightmares along the Information Highway* (New York: Dutton, 1995), 8.
3. Ibid., 105.
4. Ibid., 101–130.
5. Nicholas Negroponte, *Being Digital* (New York: Alfred A. Knopf, 1995), 23.
6. Evan I. Schwartz, "Advertising Webonomics 101," *Wired*, February 1996, 74.
7. Burstein and Kline, *Road Warriors*, 104.
8. Ibid., 106–107.
9. Amy Cortese, "Warding Off the Cyberspace Invaders," *Business Week*, March 13, 1995, 42.
10. Neil Munro, "New Info-War Doctrine Poses Risks, Gains," *Washington Technology*, December 22, 1994, 11.
11. Marc Gunther, "What's Your Stake in It All: Information Highway Looks Like a Rough Road," *Detroit Free Press*, November 18, 1993, p. D1.
12. Douglas Gomery, "In Search of the Cybermarket," *Wilson Quarterly* (summer 1994): 10.
13. Burstein and Kline, *Road Warriors*, 20.
14. See the *New York Times'* seven-part series, "The Downsizing of America," March 3–10, 1996. These articles and related discussion forums are available on both the *Times'* World Wide Web site (http://www.nytimes.com/downsize) and the AOL commercial service (@times).
15. See "Cable Television over the Net," 1995 Fall Supplement to *Cable Television Developments* (Washington, DC: NCTA, 1995).
16. Schwartz, "Advertising Webonomics 101," 77.

CHAPTER 3

1. See Fred Schruers, "Sheryl: She Only Wants to Be with You," *Rolling Stone*, November 14, 1996, 64–71.
2. Thomas Edison, quoted in Marshall McLuhan, *Understanding Media* (New York: McGraw-Hill, 1964), 276.

471

3. See Bruce Tucker, "'Tell Tchaikovsky the News': Postmodernism, Popular Culture and the Emergence of Rock-'n'Roll," *Black Music Research Journal* 9, no. 2 (fall 1989): 280.

4. LeRoi Jones, *Blues People* (New York: Morrow Quill, 1963), 168.

5. See Mick Jagger, quoted in Jann S. Wenner, "Jagger Remembers," *Rolling Stone*, December 14, 1995, 66.

6. See Mac Rebennack (Dr. John) with Jack Rummel, *Under a Hoodoo Moon* (New York: St. Martin's Press, 1994), 58.

7. Little Richard, quoted in Charles White, *The Life and Times of Little Richard: The Quasar of Rock* (New York: Harmony Books, 1984), 65–66.

8. B. Tucker, "'Tell Tchaikovsky the News,'" 287.

9. Quoted in Dave Marsh and James Bernard, *The New Book of Rock Lists* (New York: Fireside, 1994), 15.

10. Ed Ward, in Ward, Geoffrey Stokes, and Ken Tucker, *Rock of Ages: The* Rolling Stone *History of Rock & Roll* (New York: Rolling Stone Press, 1986), 89.

11. Stuart Goldman, "That Old Devil Music," *National Review*, February 24, 1989, 29.

12. See Gerri Hershey, *Nowhere to Run: The Story of Soul Music* (New York: Penguin Books, 1984).

13. See Robert Palmer, *Deep Blues* (New York: Penguin Books, 1981), 8.

14. See Karen Schoemer, "Rockers, Models and the New Allure of Heroin," *Newsweek*, August 26, 1996, 50–54.

15. K. Tucker, in Ward, Stokes, and Tucker, *Rock of Ages*, 521.

16. Ibid., 560.

17. Stephen Thomas Erlewine, "Nirvana," in *All Music Guide: The Best CDs, Albums, & Tapes*, 2nd ed., Michael Erlewine, ed. (San Francisco: Miller Freeman Books, 1994), 233.

18. See Anita M. Samuels and Diana B. Henriques, "Going Broke and Cutting Loose," *New York Times*, February 5, 1996, pp. C1, C6.

19. See Richie Unterberger, "Bootleg Overview," in M. Erlewine, ed., *All Music Guide*, 1381.

20. Nat Hentoff, "Many Dreams Fueled Long Development of U.S. Music," *Milwaukee Journal*/United Press International, February 26, 1978, p. 2.

Case Study: The Band, pp. 76–77

1. Greil Marcus, *Mystery Train: Images of America in Rock-'n'Roll Music* (New York: Penguin Books/Plume, 1990), 40.

Global Village: The International Beat, p. 81

1. See Simon Broughton et al., eds., *World Music: The Rough Guide* (London: Rough Guides/Penguin Books, 1994).

CHAPTER 4

1. Tom Lewis, *Empire of the Air: The Men Who Made Radio* (New York: HarperCollins, 1991), 181.

2. Ibid., 32.

3. Ibid., 73.

4. For a full discussion of early broadcast history and the formation of RCA, see Eric Barnouw, *Tube of Plenty* (New York: Oxford University Press, 1982); Susan Douglas,

Inventing American Broadcasting 1899–1922 (Baltimore: Johns Hopkins University Press, 1987); and Christopher Sterling and John Kitross, *Stay Tuned: A Concise History of American Broadcasting* (Belmont, CA: Wadsworth, 1990).

5. Harry P. Davis, quoted in Mitchell Stephens, *History of the News: From the Drum to the Satellite* (New York: Viking, 1988), 276.

6. Lowell Thomas, quoted in Lawrence Lichty and Malachi Topping, *American Broadcasting: A Source Book on the History of Radio and Television* (New York: Hastings House, 1975), 299.

7. Neil Strauss, "Birth and Rebirth on the Airwaves," *New York Times*, July 21, 1996, pp. 26–27.

8. See Ed Ward, Geoffrey Stokes, and Ken Tucker, *Rock of Ages: The* Rolling Stone *History of Rock & Roll* (New York: Rolling Stone Press, 1986), 484.

9. See Gustav Nieburh, "Number of Religious Broadcasters Continues to Grow," *New York Times*, February 12, 1996, p. C7.

Examining Ethics: NPR and Support for Noncommercial Radio, p. 103

1. See the foreword in Linda Wertheimer, ed., *Listening to America: Twenty-Five Years in the Life of a Nation, as Heard on National Public Radio* (Boston: Houghton Mifflin, 1995).

2. For a detailed discussion, see Robert McChesney, *Telecommunications, Mass Media & Democracy: The Battle for Control of U.S. Broadcasting, 1928–1935* (New York: Oxford University Press, 1993).

CHAPTER 5

1. See Elizabeth Kolbert, "Americans Despair of Popular Culture," *New York Times*, August 20, 1995, sec. 2, pp. 1, 23.

2. J. Fred MacDonald, *One Nation under Television: The Rise and Decline of Network TV* (Chicago: Nelson-Hall Publishers, 1994), 132.

3. Ibid., 70.

4. Edgar Bergen, quoted in MacDonald, *One Nation under Television*, 78.

5. See Horace Newcomb, *TV: The Most Popular Art* (Garden City, NY: Anchor Books, 1974), 31, 39.

6. Ibid., 35.

7. Paddy Chayevsky, quoted in Eric Barnouw, *Tube of Plenty: The Evolution of American Television*, rev. ed. (New York: Oxford University Press, 1982), 163.

8. Barnouw, *Tube of Plenty*, 163.

9. Ibid., 163.

10. MacDonald, *One Nation under Television*, 181.

11. See Bill Carter, "Cadillac-Sized Hits by the VW of Producers," *New York Times*, January 22, 1996, p. C1.

12. See Richard Campbell, "Don Hewitt's Durable Hour," *Columbia Journalism Review* (September–October 1993): 25.

Tracking Technology: The Digital Revolution, p. 123

1. See Joel Brinkley, "F.C.C. Clears New Standard for Digital TV," *New York Times*, December 25, 1996, pp. C1, C15.

Case Study: Anatomy of a TV "Failure," p. 147

1. All Tim Reid and Hugh Wilson quotes from Jimmie L. Reeves and Richard Campbell, "Misplacing Frank's Place:

Do You Know What It Means to Miss New Orleans?" *Television Quarterly* 24 (1989): 45–57.

CHAPTER 6

1. *Midwest Video Corp. v. FCC*, 571 F. 2d 1025 (8th Cir. 1978).
2. Pierre Brunel-Lantena, quoted in "Top of the News," *Economist*, May 9, 1992, 89.
3. T. Seideman, "Four Labels Ink Vidclip Deals with MTV," *Billboard*, June 23, 1984, 1, 67. See other issues of *Billboard* and *Variety* throughout this time period.
4. "Tom Preston: The Pied Piper of Television," *Broadcasting & Cable*, September 19, 1994, 40.
5. Wilson Dizard, Jr., *Old Media New Media: Mass Communication in the Information Age* (White Plains, NY: Longman, 1994), 124.
6. For statistics on cable performance, see National Cable Television Association, *Cable Television Developments* (Washington, DC: NCTA, 1996).

Case Study: Ted Turner–Cable Power Broker and Global News Maker, pp. 168–169

1. Jay Rosen, The Whole World Is Watching CNN," *The Nation*, May 13, 1991, 623, 625.
2. Ibid., 625.

CHAPTER 7

1. John Cawelti, *Adventure, Mystery, and Romance: Formula Stories as Art and Popular Culture* (Chicago: University of Chicago Press, 1976), 35.
2. See Charles Musser, *The Emergence of Cinema: The American Screen to 1907* (New York: Scribner's, 1991).
3. Douglas Gomery, *Shared Pleasures: A History of Movie Presentation in the United States* (Madison: University of Wisconsin Press, 1992), 18.
4. Richard Schickel, *Movies: The History of an Art and an Institution* (New York: Basic Books, 1964), 44.
5. Douglas Gomery, *Movie History: A Survey* (Belmont, CA: Wadsworth, 1991), 53.
6. Ibid., 167.
7. See David Bordwell and Kristin Thompson, *Film Art: An Introduction*, 5th ed. (New York: McGraw-Hill, 1996); and David Bordwell, Janet Staiger, and Kristin Thompson, *The Classic Hollywood Cinema: Film Style & Mode of Production to 1960* (New York: Columbia University Press, 1985).
8. Bordwell and Thompson, *Film Art*, 70.
9. See Cawelti, *Adventure, Mystery, and Romance*, 80–98.
10. See Barbara Koenig Quart, *Women Directors: The Emergence of a New Cinema* (New York: Praeger, 1988).
11. See Gomery, *Shared Pleasures*, 171–180.
12. See John Tagliabue, "Film Redux in Europe: Action!" *New York Times*, February 24, 1996, p. B17.
13. See Eric Barnouw, *Tube of Plenty: The Evolution of American Television*, rev. ed. (New York: Oxford University Press, 1975, 1982), 108–109.
14. See Douglas Gomery, "Who Killed Hollywood?" *Wilson Quarterly* (summer 1991): 106–112.
15. See Gomery, *Movie History*, 429.
16. See Reed Abelson, "The Shell Game of Hollywood 'Net Profits,'" *New York Times*, March 4, 1996, pp. C1, C4.
17. David Thorburn, "Television as an Aesthetic Medium," *Critical Studies in Mass Communication* (June 1987): 168.

Case Study: Movie Theaters Display Racism's History, pp. 190–191

1. Douglas Gomery, *Shared Pleasures: A History of Movie Presentation in the United States* (Madison: University of Wisconsin Press, 1992), 155–170.

CHAPTER 8

1. See Brooke Kroeger, *Nellie Bly: Daredevil, Reporter, Feminist* (New York: Times Books/Random House, 1994).
2. See Kay Mills, *A Place in the News: From the Women's Pages to the Front Page* (New York: Dodd, Mead, 1988).
3. Piers Brendon, *The Life and Death of the Press Barons* (New York: Atheneum, 1983), 136.
4. William Randolph Hearst, quoted in Brendon, *The Life and Death of the Press Barons*, 134.
5. Michael Schudson, *Discovering the News: A Social History of the American Newspapers* (New York: Basic Books, 1978), 23.
6. See David T. Z. Mindich, "Edwin M. Stanton, the Inverted Pyramid, and Information Control," *Journalism Monographs*, no. 140 (August 1993).
7. John C. Merrill, "Objectivity: An Attitude," in Merrill and Ralph L. Lowenstein, eds., *Media, Messages and Men* (New York: David McKay, 1971), 240.
8. Roy Peter Clark, "A New Shape for the News," *Washington Journalism Review* (March 1984): 47.
9. Ibid., 143, 189.
10. See Edwin Emery, *The Press and America: An Interpretative History of the Mass Media*, 3rd ed. (Englewood Cliffs, NJ: Prentice-Hall, 1972), 562.
11. Walter Lippmann, *Liberty and the News* (New York: Harcourt, Brace and Howe, 1920), 92.
12. American Society of Newspaper Editors, *Problems of Journalism* (Washington, DC: ASNE, 1933), 74.
13. Lippmann, *Liberty and the News*, 64.
14. Tom Wicker, *On Press* (New York: Viking, 1978), 3–5.
15. Jack Newfield, "The 'Truth' about Objectivity and the New Journalism," in Charles C. Flippen, ed., *Liberating the Media* (Washington, DC: Acropolis Books, 1973), 63–64.
16. Tom Wolfe, quoted in Leonard W. Robinson, "The New Journalism: A Panel Discussion . . . ," in Ronald Weber, ed., *The Reporter as Artist: A Look at the New Journalism Controversy* (New York: Hastings House, 1974), 67. See also Tom Wolfe and E. E. Johnson, eds., *The New Journalism* (New York: Harper & Row, 1973).
17. Jon Katz, "Online or Not, Newspapers Suck," *Wired*, September 1994, 5.
18. See Sreenath Sreenivasan, "As Mainstream Papers Struggle, the Ethnic Press Is Thriving," *New York Times*, July 22, 1996, p. C7.
19. See Phyl Garland, "The Black Press: Down but Not Out," *Columbia Journalism Review* (September–October 1982): 43–50.
20. See Iver Peterson, "Hiring of Minorities Again Rises in Newsrooms, but Barely," *New York Times*, April 17, 1996, p. A12.
21. See Allen R. Myerson, "Newspapers Cut Spanish-Language Publications," *New York Times*, October 16, 1995, p. C7.

22. Michael Emery and Edwin Emery, *The Press and America: An Interpretive History of the Mass Media*, 7th ed. (Englewood Cliffs, NJ: Prentice-Hall, 1992), 536.
23. See Philip Meyer, "Learning to Love Lower Profits," *American Journalism Review* (December 1995): 40–44.
24. See Douglas Gomery, "In TV, the Big Get Bigger," *American Journalism Review* (October 1996): 64.
25. See William Glaberson, "Newspaper Owners Do the Shuffle," *New York Times*, February 19, 1996, pp. C1, C4.
26. See Glaberson, "Circulation Losses Go on at New York Papers," *New York Times*, October 24, 1994, p. D10.

Case Study: The Alternative Journalism of Dorothy Day and I. F. Stone, pp. 232–233

1. Stone, quoted in Jack Lule, "I. F. Stone: Professional Excellence in Raising Hell," *QS News* (summer 1989): 3.

CHAPTER 9

1. See Bill Carter, "After a Positive Article on Fox Show, *TV Guide* Learns Other Networks Are Watching," *New York Times*, December 11, 1995, p. C5.
2. John Tebbel and Mary Ellen Zuckerman, *The Magazine in America, 1741–1900* (New York: Oxford University Press, 1991), 68.
3. See Theodore Peterson, *Magazines in the Twentieth Century* (Urbana: University of Illinois Press, 1964), 5.
4. See Richard Ohmann, *Selling Culture: Magazines, Markets, and Class at the Turn of the Century* (New York: Verso, 1996).
5. See T. Peterson, *Magazines*, 5.
6. Lincoln Steffens, quoted in Justin Kaplan, *Lincoln Steffens: A Biography* (New York: Simon & Schuster, 1974), 106.
7. See discussion in T. Peterson, *Magazines*, 228; and Tebbel and Zuckerman, *The Magazine in America*, 223.
8. Alexander Graham Bell, quoted in William H. Taft, *American Magazines for the 1980s* (New York: Hastings House, 1982), 60.
9. Harold Ross, quoted in John Tebbel, *The American Magazine: A Compact History* (New York: Hawthorn Books, 1969), 234.
10. Generoso Pope, quoted in Taft, *American Magazines for the 1980s*, 226–227.
11. See S. Elizabeth Bird, *For Enquiring Minds: A Cultural Study of Supermarket Tabloids* (Knoxville: University of Tennessee Press, 1992), 24.
12. See Taft, *American Magazines*, 229.
13. See Iver Peterson, "Media: Supermarket Tabloids Lose Circulation," *New York Times*, September 9, 1996, p. C5.
14. Ibid.
15. See Deirdre Carmody, "Magazines Go Niche-Hunting with Custom-Made Sections," *New York Times*, June 26, 1995, p. C7.
16. See Robin Pogrebin, "The Number of Ad Pages Does Not Make the Magazine," *New York Times*, August 26, 1996, p. C1.
17. See Gloria Steinem, "Sex, Lies & Advertising," *Ms.*, July–August 1990, 18–28.

Case Study: Alternative Magazines and the *Utne Reader*, pp. 258–259

1. John Tebbel and Mary Ellen Zuckerman, *The Magazine in America, 1741–1900* (New York: Oxford University Press, 1991), 331–332.
2. Ibid., 332.

CHAPTER 10

1. See Elizabeth Eisenstein, *The Printing Press as an Agent of Social Change*, 2 vols. (Cambridge, England: Cambridge University Press, 1980).
2. See Quentin Reynolds, *The Fiction Factory: From Pulp Row to Quality Street* (New York: Street & Smith/Random House, 1955), 72–74.
3. For a comprehensive historical overview of the publishing industry and rise of publishing houses, see John A. Tebbel, *A History of Book Publishing in the United States*, Vol. 1, 1630–1865; Vol. 2, 1865–1919; Vol. 3, 1920–1940; Vol. 4, 1940–1980 (New York: R. R. Bowker, 1972–1981).
4. See Mary B. W. Taylor, "Two Studies See a Bull Market for Book Industry," *New York Times*, August 7, 1995, p. C7.
5. For a historical overview of paperbacks, see Kenneth Davis, *Two-Bit Culture: The Paperbacking of America* (Boston: Houghton Mifflin, 1984).
6. See John P. Dessauer, *Book Publishing: What It Is, What It Does* (New York: R. R. Bowker, 1974), 48.
7. Patricia Nelson Limerick, "Dancing with Professors: The Trouble with Academic Prose," *New York Times Book Review*, October 31, 1993, p. 3.
8. See Doreen Carvajal, "Triumph of the Bottom Line: Numbers vs. Words at the Book-of-the-Month Club," *New York Times*, April 1, 1996, pp. C1, C5.
9. Ibid., p. C5.
10. James Kaplan, "Inside the Club," *New York Times Magazine*, June 11, 1989, p. 62.
11. See Doreen Carvajal, "Restlessness among Nation's Booksellers," *New York Times*, June 17, 1996, p. C5.
12. See Wilson Dizard, Jr., *Old Media New Media: Mass Communication in the Information Age* (White Plains, NY: Longman, 1994), 164.
13. See Doreen Carvajal, "Marriage of Interests Bonds TV Shows, Book Publishers," *New York Times*, November 10, 1996, pp. 1, 12.
14. See Alvin Kernan, *The Death of Literature* (New Haven: Yale University Press, 1990).

Examining Ethics: Censorship Issues in Book Publishing, p. 303

1. See Mary B. W. Taylor, "Publishing: On Both Sides of the Political Spectrum, the Battle over Censorship . . . Continues to Rage," *New York Times*, April 3, 1995, p. C8.

CHAPTER 11

1. See Mary Kuntz and Joseph Weber, "The New Hucksterism," *Business Week*, July 1, 1996, 77.
2. For a written and pictorial history of early advertising, see Charles Goodrum and Helen Dalrymple, *Advertising in America, the First 200 Years* (New York: Harry N. Abrams, 1990), 13–34.
3. Ibid., 18.

4. Michael Schudson, *Advertising, the Uneasy Persuasion* (New York: Basic Books, 1984), 165. See also Arthur Marquette, *Brands, Trademarks, and Good Will* (New York: McGraw-Hill, 1967).

5. Goodrum and Dalrymple, *Advertising in America*, 31.

6. See Schudson, *Advertising*, 164.

7. Randall Rothenberg, *Where the Suckers Moon: An Advertising Story* (New York: Alfred A. Knopf, 1994), 20.

8. Leslie Savan, "Op Ad: Sneakers and Nothingness," *Village Voice*, April 2, 1991, p. 43.

9. Kuntz and Weber, "The New Hucksterism," 79.

10. Ibid.

11. Schudson, *Advertising*, 210.

12. Vance Packard, *The Hidden Persuaders* (New York: Basic Books, 1957, 1978), 229.

13. See Schudson, *Advertising*, 36–43; and Andrew Robertson, *The Lessons of Failure* (London: MacDonald, 1974).

14. See Jay Mathews, "Channel One: Classroom Coup or a 'Sham'?" *Washington Post*, December 26, 1994, p. A1+.

15. See Michael F. Jacobson and Laurie Ann Mazur, *Marketing Madness: A Survival Guide for a Consumer Society* (Boulder, CO: Westview Press, 1995), 29–31.

16. See Stuart Elliott, "Liquor Industry Ends Its Ad Ban in Broadcasting," *New York Times*, November 8, 1996, pp. A1, C5; and "Seagram Flouts Ban on TV Ads Pitching Liquor," *Wall Street Journal*, June 11, 1996, pp. B1, B5.

17. For a discussion of deceptive ads, see Jacobson and Mazur, *Marketing Madness*, pp. 143–148.

18. G. Pascal Zachary, "Many Journalists See a Growing Reluctance to Criticize Advertisers," *Wall Street Journal*, February 6, 1992, pp. A1, A6.

19. Ibid., p. A6.

20. Kathleen Hall Jamieson, "Truth and Advertising," *New York Times*, January 27, 1996, p. 15.

21. See Stephen Ansolabehere and Shanto Iyengar, *Going Negative: How Attack Ads Shrunk and Polarized the Electorate* (New York: Free Press, 1996).

22. See Walter Goodman, "Prime Time, Politics and the Public's Right to Tune Out," *New York Times*, May 5, 1996, Arts & Leisure section, p. 28.

Tracking Technology: The 900-Number Industry Makes the Caller Pay, p. 329

1. Art Kleiner, "Brave New Audiotext," *Adweek's Marketing Week* (April 10, 1989).

2. Laurie Petersen, "900 Numbers: A Mixed Blessing for Marketers," *Adweek's Marketing Week* (October 7, 1991).

3. National Consumers League, "National Consumers League Advisory: Warning to Be Issued on Outbreak of Recession-Related Phone Scams," Press Release (April 1991).

4. Christopher Stern, "Expectations Lowered for 900 Numbers," *Broadcasting & Cable* (October 25, 1993).

CHAPTER 12

1. Matthew J. Culligan and Dolph Greene, *Getting Back to the Basics of Public Relations & Publicity* (New York: Crown Publishers, 1982), 90.

2. Ibid., 100.

3. See Stuart Ewen, *PR! A Social History of Spin* (New York: Basic Books, 1996).

4. Suzanne Heck, "Multimedia Sharpshooter Brought Buffalo Bill Fame," *Public Relations Journal* (October–November 1994): 12.

5. Marvin N. Olasky, "The Development of Corporate Public Relations, 1850–1930," *Journalism Monographs*, no. 102 (April 1987): 3.

6. Quoted in Alfred McClung Lee, *The Daily Newspaper in America* (New York: Macmillan, 1937), p. 436.

7. Olasky, "The Development of Corporate Public Relations," 14.

8. Ibid., 15.

9. See Ewen, *PR!*, 47.

10. See Scott M. Cutlip, *The Unseen Power: Public Relations—A History* (Hillsdale, NJ: Lawrence Erlbaum, 1994).

11. Edward Bernays, *Crystallizing Public Opinion* (New York: Horace Liveright, 1923), 217.

12. Michael Schudson, *Discovering the News* (New York: Basic Books, 1978), 136.

13. Walter Lippmann, *Public Opinion* (New York: Harcourt Brace, 1922), 345.

14. See Daniel Boorstin, *The Image: A Guide to Pseudo-Events in America* (New York: Atheneum, 1961), 11–12, 205–210.

15. Leonard Mogel, *Making It in Public Relations: An Insider's Guide to Career Opportunities* (New York: Collier Books/Macmillan, 1993), 34.

16. The author worked briefly as the assistant PR director for Milwaukee's Summerfest in the early 1980s.

17. Susan Lucarelli, "Public Relations Research," in Michael Singletary, ed., *Mass Communication Research* (New York: Longman, 1995), pp. 357–359.

18. See Ewen, *PR!*, 28–29; and John R. McArthur, *The Second Front: Censorship and Propaganda in the Gulf War* (New York: Hill & Wang, 1992), 58–59.

19. Stanley Walker, "Playing the Deep Bassoons," *Harper's*, February 1932, 365.

20. Ibid., 370.

21. Ivy Lee, *Publicity* (New York: Industries Publishing, 1925), 21.

22. Schudson, *Discovering the News*, 136.

23. Ivy Lee, quoted in Ray Eldon Hiebert, *Courtier to the Crowd: The Story of Ivy Lee and the Development of Public Relations* (Ames: Iowa State University Press, 1966), 114.

24. See Lippmann, *Public Opinion*.

25. See Jonathan Tasini, "Lost in the Margins: Labor and the Media," *Extra!* (summer 1992): 2–11.

26. See J. David Pincus et al., "Newspaper Editors' Perceptions of Public Relations: How Business, News, and Sports Editors Differ," *Journal of Public Relations Research* 5, no. 1 (1993): 27–45.

27. Schudson, *Discovering the News*, 171.

28. Bill Walker, "Green Like Me," in Ray Eldon Hiebert, ed., *Impact of Mass Media: Current Issues*, 3rd ed. (White Plains, NY: Longman, 1995), 177.

29. William Small, quoted in Walker, "Playing the Deep Bassoons," 174–175.

30. See Alicia Mundy, "Is the Press Any Match for Powerhouse PR?" in Hiebert, ed., *Impact of Mass Media*, 179–188.

Case Study: Levi Strauss and Anti-Sweatshop Public Relations, pp. 360–361

1. Public Relations Society of America, *PRSA Silver Anvil Awards* (New York: PRSA, 1994), 9–10.
2. Ibid., 10.

CHAPTER 13

1. For this section I am indebted to the ideas and scholarship of my former teacher Douglas Gomery, a media economist and historian from the University of Maryland.
2. Douglas Gomery, "The Centrality of Media Economics," in *Defining Media Studies*, Mark R. Levy and Michael Gurevitch, eds. (New York: Oxford University Press, 1994), 202.
3. Ibid., 200.
4. Ibid., 203–204.
5. David Harvey, *The Condition of Postmodernity: An Enquiry into the Origins of Cultural Change* (Oxford: Basil Blackwell, 1989), 171.
6. Ibid., 158.
7. Richard J. Barnet and John Cavanagh, *Global Dreams: Imperial Corporations and the New World Order* (New York: Simon & Schuster, 1994), 131.
8. Ben Bagdikian, *The Media Monopoly*, 4th ed. (Boston: Beacon Press, 1992), 222.
9. Roland Marchand, *Advertising the American Dream: Making Way for Modernity, 1920–1940* (Berkeley: University of California Press, 1985), 218.
10. William Paley, quoted in Robert W. McChesney, *Telecommunications, Mass Media, & Democracy: The Battle for Control of U.S. Broadcasting, 1928–1935* (New York: Oxford University Press, 1993), 251.
11. McChesney, *Telecommunications, Mass Media, & Democracy*, 264.
12. Edward Herman, "Democratic Media," *Z Papers* (January–March 1992): 23.
13. Barnet and Cavanagh, *Global Dreams*, 38.
14. Richard J. Barnet and Ronald E. Muller, *Global Reach: The Power of Multinational Corporations* (New York: Simon & Schuster, 1974), 175.

CHAPTER 14

1. Veronica Guerin, quoted in Warren Hoge, "Reporter Roused Ireland's Conscience," *New York Times*, November 23, 1996, pp. 1, 4.
2. Neil Postman, "Currents," *Utne Reader*, July–August 1995, 35.
3. Reuven Frank, "Memorandum from a Television Newsman," reprinted as Appendix 2 in A. William Bluem, *Documentary in American Television* (New York: Hastings House, 1965), 276.
4. For another list and alternative analysis of news criteria, see Brian S. Brooks et al., *The Missouri Group: News Reporting and Writing* (New York: St. Martin's Press, 1996), 2–4.
5. Horace Greeley, quoted in Christopher Lasch, "Journalism, Publicity and the Lost Art of Argument," *Gannett Center Journal* 4, no. 2 (spring 1990): 2.

6. David Eason, "Telling Stories and Making Sense," *Journal of Popular Culture* 15, no. 2 (fall 1981): 125.
7. Jon Katz, "AIDS and the Media: Shifting out of Neutral," *Rolling Stone*, May 27, 1993, 32.
8. Herbert Gans, *Deciding What's News* (New York: Pantheon, 1979), 42–48.
9. Ibid., 42–48.
10. Ibid., 48–51.
11. See Michael Schudson, *Discovering the News* (New York: Basic Books, 1978), 3–11.
12. Code of Ethics, reprinted in Melvin Mencher, *News Reporting and Writing*, 3rd ed. (Dubuque, IA: Wm. C. Brown, 1984), 443–444.
13. Ibid.
14. Ibid., 443.
15. For reference and guidance on media ethics, see Clifford Christians, Mark Fackler, and Kim Rotzoll, *Media Ethics: Cases & Moral Reasoning*, 4th ed. (White Plains, NY: Longman, 1995); and Thomas H. Bivins, "A Worksheet for Ethics Instruction and Exercises in Reason," *Journalism Educator* (summer 1993): 4–16.
16. Christians, Fackler, and Rotzoll, *Media Ethics*, 15.
17. See Jimmie Reeves and Richard Campbell, *Cracked Coverage: Television News, the Anti-Cocaine Crusade, and the Reagan Legacy* (Durham, NC: Duke University Press, 1994).
18. See David Eason, "On Journalistic Authority: The Janet Cooke Scandal," *Critical Studies in Mass Communications* 3, no. 4 (December 1986): 429–447.
19. Mike Royko, quoted in "News Media: A Searching of Conscience," *Newsweek*, May 4, 1981, 53.
20. Don Hewitt, interview conducted at *60 Minutes*, CBS News, New York, February 21, 1989.
21. Jonathan Alter, "News Media: Round Up the Usual Suspects," *Newsweek*, March 25, 1985, 69.
22. William Hoynes and David Croteau, "All the Usual Suspects: *MacNeil/Lehrer* and *Nightline*," *Extra!* Special Issue 3, no. 4 (winter 1990): 2. This article reports on the original *Nightline* study and offers a follow-up study on both *Nightline* and *MacNeil/Lehrer*, which reveals roughly the same gender patterns. See Hoynes and Croteau, "Are You on the *Nightline* Guest List?" *Extra!* 2, no. 4 (January–February 1989): 2–15.
23. William Greider, quoted in Mark Hertsgaard, *On Bended Knee: The Press and the Reagan Presidency* (New York: Farrar, Straus, and Giroux, 1988), 78.
24. Jay Rosen, "Politics, Vision, and the Press: Toward a Public Agenda for Journalism," in Rosen and Paul Taylor, *The New News v. the Old News: The Press and Politics in the 1990s* (New York: Twentieth Century Fund, 1992), 6.
25. Bluem, *Documentary in American Television*, 94.
26. Fred Friendly, quoted in Joseph Michalak, "*CBS Reports* Covers Assortment of Topics," *New York Times*, December 13, 1959, sec. 2, p. 21.
27. Based on notes made by the author's wife, Dianna Campbell, after a visit to Warsaw and discussions with a number of journalists working for *Gazeta Wyborcza* in 1990.
28. Davis "Buzz" Merritt, *Public Journalism & Public Life: Why Telling the News Is Not Enough* (Hillsdale, NJ: Lawrence Erlbaum, 1995), 113–114.

29. Rosen, "Politics, Vision, and the Press," 14.

30. Davis Merritt and Jay Rosen, "Imagining Public Journalism: An Editor and a Scholar Reflect on the Birth of an Idea," Roy W. Howard Public Lecture (Bloomington: Indiana University), no. 5, April 13, 1995, 11.

31. Ibid., 15.

32. See Jonathan Cohn, "Should Journalists Do Community Service?" *American Prospect* (summer 1995): 15.

33. Merritt and Rosen, "Imagining Public Journalism," 12.

34. Poll statistics cited in Merritt, *Public Journalism & Public Life*, xv–xvi.

35. David Broder, quoted in "Squaring with the Reader: A Seminar on Journalism," *Kettering Review* (winter 1992): 48.

36. Christopher Lasch, "Journalism, Publicity and the Lost Art of Argument," *Gannett Center Journal* 4, no. 2 (spring 1990): 1.

37. Jay Rosen, "Forming and Informing the Public," *Kettering Review* (winter 1992): 69–70.

Case Study: Reporters as Detectives on *60 Minutes*, pp. 400–401

1. Hewitt, quoted in "Father of *60 Minutes*: Taking the Heat as No. 1," *Chicago Tribune*, April 3, 1981, sec. 2, p. 15.

2. For more detail, see Richard Campbell, 60 Minutes *and the News: A Mythology for Middle America* (Urbana: University of Illinois Press, 1991).

3. Hewitt, quoted in William A. Henry, "Don Hewitt: Man of the Hour," *Washington Journalism Review* (May 1986): 26.

4. Mike Wallace and Gary Paul Gates, *Close Encounters: Mike Wallace's Own Story* (New York: Berkley Books, 1984), 420.

CHAPTER 15

1. Alexis de Tocqueville, *Democracy in America* (New York: Modern Library, 1835, 1840, 1945, 1981), 96–97.

2. Steve Fore, "Lost in Translation: The Social Uses of Mass Communications Research," *AFTERIMAGE*, no. 20 (April 1993): 10.

3. James Carey, *Communication as Culture: Essays on Media and Society* (Boston: Unwin Hyman, 1989), 75.

4. Daniel Czitrom, *Media and the American Mind: From Morse to McLuhan* (Chapel Hill: University of North Carolina Press, 1982), 122–125.

5. Ibid., 123.

6. Harold Lasswell, *Propaganda Technique in the World War* (New York: Alfred A. Knopf, 1927), 9.

7. Walter Lippmann, *Public Opinion* (New York: Macmillan, 1922), 18.

8. Benjamin Ginsberg, *The Captive Public: How Mass Opinion Promotes State Power* (New York: Basic Books, 1986), 82–83.

9. See W. W. Charters, *Motion Pictures and Youth: A Summary* (New York: Macmillan, 1934); and Garth Jowett, *Film: The Democratic Art* (Boston: Little, Brown, 1976), 220–229.

10. Czitrom, *Media and the American Mind*, 132. See also Harold Lasswell, "The Structure and Function of Communication in Society," in Lyman Bryson, ed., *The Communication of Ideas* (New York: Harper and Brothers, 1948), 37–51.

11. Wilbur Schramm, Jack Lyle, and Edwin Parker, *Television in the Lives of Our Children* (Stanford, CA: Stanford University Press, 1961), 1.

12. See Joseph Klapper, *The Effects of Mass Communication* (New York: Free Press, 1960).

13. Schramm, Lyle, and Parker, *Television*, 1.

14. See, for example, Mark Levy, "The Audience Experience with Television News," *Journalism Monographs*, no. 55 (April 1978).

15. For an early overview of uses and gratifications, see Jay Blumler and Elihu Katz, *The Uses of Mass Communication* (Beverly Hills, CA: Sage, 1974).

16. See George Gerbner et al., "The Demonstration of Power: Violence Profile No. 10," *Journal of Communication* 29, no. 3 (1979): 177–196.

17. Dinitia Smith, "Study Looks at Portrayal of Women in Media," *New York Times*, May 1, 1997, p. A17.

18. Robert P. Snow, *Creating Media Culture* (Beverly Hills, CA: Sage, 1983), 47.

19. See Maxwell McCombs and Donald Shaw, "The Agenda-Setting Function of Mass Media," *Public Opinion Quarterly* 36, no. 2 (1972): 176–187.

20. See Stephen D. Reese and Lucig H. Danielton, "A Closer Look at Intermedia Influences on Agenda Setting: The Cocaine Issue of 1986," in Pamela J. Shoemaker, ed., *Communication Campaigns about Drugs: Government, Media, and the Public* (Hillsdale, NJ: Lawrence Erlbaum, 1989), 47–66; and Peter Kerr, "Anatomy of the Drug Issue: How, After Years, It Erupted," *New York Times*, November 17, 1986, p. A12.

21. See Craig Reinarman and Harry G. Levine, "Crack in Context: Politics and Media in the Making of the Drug Scare," *Contemporary Drug Problems* (winter 1989): 546; see also Adam Clymer, "Public Found Ready to Sacrifice in Drug Fight," *New York Times*, September 2, 1986, pp. A1, D16.

22. See Nancy Signorielli and Michael Morgan, *Cultivation Analysis: New Directions in Media Effects Research* (Newbury Park, CA: Sage, 1990).

23. Robert Lynd, *Knowledge for What?: The Place of Social Science in American Culture* (Princeton, NJ: Princeton University Press, 1939), 120.

24. Czitrom, *Media and the American Mind*, 143; and Leo Lowenthal, "Historical Perspectives of Popular Culture," in Bernard Rosenberg and David White, eds., *Mass Culture: The Popular Arts in America* (Glencoe, IL: Free Press, 1957), 52.

25. See Stuart Hall, et al., *Policing the Crisis: Mugging, the State, and Law and Order* (London: Macmillan, 1978).

26. See Janice Radway, *Reading the Romance: Women, Patriarchy and Popular Literature* (Chapel Hill: University of North Carolina Press, 1984).

27. Horace Newcomb, *TV: The Most Popular Art* Garden City, NY: Anchor Books, 1974), 19, 23.

28. James Carey, "Mass Communication Research and Cultural Studies: An American View," in James Curran, Michael

Gurevitch, and Janet Woollacott, eds., *Mass Communication and Society* (London: Edward Arnold, 1977), 418, 421.

29. Christopher Lasch, "Politics and Culture," *Salmagundi* (winter–spring 1990): 33.

30. Scott Heller, "Humanists Renew Public Intellectual Tradition, Answer Criticism," *Chronicle of Higher Education*, April 7, 1993, p. A6.

31. Lawrie Mifflin, "Study of TV's Violence Points to Films," *New York Times*, September 20, 1995, pp. B1, 4.

CHAPTER 16

1. See Newspaper Association of America, *Facts about Newspapers* (Reston, VA: The Newspaper Center, 1994), 27.

2. See "No Free Press," *Quill*, June 1996, 11.

3. Fred Siebert, Theodore Peterson, and Wilbur Schramm, *Four Theories of the Press* (Urbana: University of Illinois, 1956).

4. See Douglas M. Fraleigh and Joseph S. Tuman, *Freedom of Speech in the Marketplace of Ideas* (New York: St. Martin's Press, 1997), 125.

5. Hugo Black, quoted in "*New York Times* Company v. U.S.: 1971," in Edward W. Knappman, ed., *Great American Trials: From Salem Witchcraft to Rodney King* (Detroit: Visible Ink Press, 1994), 609.

6. Robert Warren, quoted in "U.S. v. *The Progressive*: 1979," in Knappman, ed., *Great American Trials*, 684.

7. See Fraleigh and Tuman, *Freedom of Speech*, 71–73.

8. See Newspaper Association of America, *Facts*, 27.

9. See Knappman, ed., *Great American Trials*, 517–519.

10. Ibid., 741–743.

11. Douglas Gomery, *Movie History: A Survey* (Belmont, CA: Wadsworth, 1991), 57.

12. See Eric Barnouw, *Tube of Plenty: The Evolution of American Television*, rev. ed. (New York: Oxford University Press, 1982), 118–130.

13. Dean Burch, quoted in Peter Fornatale and Joshua Mills, *Radio in the Television Age* (Woodstock, NY: Overlook Press, 1980), 85.

14. See "Dummy and Dame Arouse the Nation," *Broadcasting-Telecasting*, October 15, 1956, 258; and Lawrence Lichty and Malachi Topping, *American Broadcasting: A Source Book on the History of Radio and Television* (New York: Hastings House, 1975), 530.

15. Bill Kovach, "Big Deals, with Journalism Thrown in," *New York Times*, August 3, 1995, p. A17.

GLOSSARY

A&R agents short for artist & repertoire agents, these talent scouts of the music business discover, develop, and sometimes manage performers.

absolutist ethic the principle that in a moral society legal or ethical codes must be followed without exception: No one is above the law or a society's fundamental moral principles.

access channels in cable television, a tier of nonbroadcast channels dedicated to local education, government, and the public.

account executives in advertising, client liaisons responsible for bringing in new business and managing the accounts of established clients.

account reviews in advertising, the process of evaluating or reinvigorating an ad campaign, which results in either renewing the contract with the original ad agency or hiring a new agency.

actual malice in libel law, to act with a reckless disregard for the truth, such as when a reporter or editor knows that a statement is false and prints or airs it anyway.

affiliate any radio or TV station, although independently owned, that signs a contract to be part of a network and receives money to carry the network's programs; in exchange, the network reserves time slots, which it sells to national advertisers.

agenda-setting a media research argument that says when the mass media pay attention to particular events or issues, they determine—set the agenda for—the major topics of discussion for individuals and society.

alternative rock nonmainstream rock music, which includes many types of experimental music and some forms of punk and grunge.

AM amplitude modulation, a type of radio and sound transmission that stresses the volume or height of radio waves.

analog recording a recording that is made by capturing the fluctuations of the original sound waves and storing those signals on records or cassettes as a continuous stream of magneticism—*analogous* to the actual sound.

analysis the second step in the critical process, it involves discovering significant patterns that emerge from the description stage.

anthology drama a popular form of early TV programming that brought live dramatic theater to television; influenced by stage plays, anthologies offered new teleplays, casts, directors, writers, and sets from week to week.

association principle in advertising, a persuasive technique that *associates* a product with some cultural value or image that has a positive connotation but which may have little connection to the actual product.

attack ads a type of political ad that uses repeated negative assaults on another candidate's character.

audiotape lightweight magnetized strands of ribbon that allow sound editing and multiple-track mixing; instrumentals or vocals can be recorded at one location and mixed later onto a master recording in another studio.

authoritarian model a model for journalism and speech that tolerates little government criticism or public dissent; it holds that the general public needs guidance from an elite and educated ruling class.

bandwagon effect an advertising strategy that incorporates exaggerated claims that *everyone* is using a particular product so you should, too.

barter deal in TV syndication, an arrangement in which no money changes hands between the local station and the syndicator; instead, a syndicator offers a new program to a local TV station in exchange for a portion of the advertising revenue.

basic cable in cable programming, a tier of channels composed of local broadcast signals, nonbroadcast access channels (for local government, education, and general public use), a few regional PBS stations, and a variety of popular channels downlinked from communication satellites.

bits a computer term coined from *BI*nary digi*TS*, which refers to information representing two values, such as yes/no, on/off, or 0/1.

blues originally a kind of black folk music, this music emerged as a distinct category in the early 1900s; it was influenced by African American spirituals, ballads, and work songs in the rural South, and by urban guitar and vocal solos from the 1930s and 1940s.

books on tape audiotape books generally featuring actors or authors reading abridged versions of popular fiction and nonfiction trade books.

bootlegging the illegal counterfeiting or pirating of CDs, cassettes, and videos that are produced and/or sold without official permission from the original songwriter, performer, or copyright holder.

boutique agencies in advertising, small regional ad agencies that offer personalized services.

broadcasting the transmission of radio waves or TV signals to a broad public audience.

browsers information search services, such as Netscape's Navigator and Microsoft's Explorer, that offer detailed organizational maps to the World Wide Web.

button fatigue in TV audience measurement, the phenomenon of weary viewers failing to log on and report their viewing.

cable franchise in cable television, a local monopoly business awarded by a community to the most attractive cable bidder, usually for a fifteen-year period.

cash deal in TV syndication, an arrangement in which the distributor of a program offers a series to the highest bidder in a TV market or to a station trying to fill a particular time slot.

cash-plus deal in TV syndication, an arrangement in which the distributor of a program offers a series to the highest bidder in a TV market but retains some time to sell national commercial spots.

CATV (community antenna television) an early cable system that originated where mountains or tall buildings blocked TV signals; due to early technical and regulatory limits, CATV contained only 12 channels.

CD-ROM a computer term coined from *Compact-Disc Read-Only Memory*; a CD technology that permits the storage of vast amounts of computer software and information (one CD-ROM can store as much information as seven hundred conventional floppy disks).

cinema verité French term for *film truth*, a documentary style that records fragments of everyday life unobtrusively; it often features a rough, grainy look and shaky, handheld camera work.

clearance rule established in the 1940s by the Justice Department and the FCC, this rule mandated that all local affiliates are ultimately responsible for the content of their channels and must *clear*, or approve, all network programming.

coaxial cable a system for transmitting TV signals via a solid core of copper-clad aluminum wire encircled by an outer axis of braided wires; these bundles of thin wire accommodate fifty or more separate channels running side by side with virtually no interference.

codex an early type of book in which paper-like sheets were cut and sewed together along the edge, then bound with thin wood pieces and covered with leather.

commercial speech any print or broadcast expression for which a fee is charged to the organization or individual buying time or space in the mass media.

common carrier a communication or transportation business, such as a phone company or taxi service, that is required by law to offer service on a first-come, first-served basis to whoever can pay the rate; such companies do not get involved in content.

communication the process of creating symbol systems that convey information and meaning (for example, language, Morse code, film, computer codes).

communist or **state model** a model for journalism and speech that places control in the hands of an enlightened government, which speaks for ordinary citizens and workers in order to serve the common goals of the state.

compact disks (CDs) playback-only storage disks for music that incorporate pure and very precise digital techniques, thus eliminating noise during recording and editing sessions.

complementary copy positive, upbeat articles—often about food, fashion, and cosmetics—that support the ads carried in various consumer magazines.

conflict of interest considered unethical, a compromising situation in which a journalist stands to benefit personally from the news report he or she produces.

conflict-oriented journalism found in metropolitan areas, newspapers that define news primarily as events, issues, or experiences that deviate from social norms; journalists see their role as observers who monitor their city's institutions and problems.

consensus-oriented papers found in small communities, newspapers that promote social and economic harmony by providing community calendars and meeting notices and carrying articles on local schools, social events, town government, property crimes, and zoning issues.

content analysis in social science research, a method for studying and coding media texts and programs.

continuity editing an editing technique that makes space and time seem continuous and seamless; it is used in most traditional Hollywood films.

control group in social science research, the group that serves as a basis for comparison to the experimental group; the control group has *not* been exposed to the particular phenomena or media content being studied.

controlled circulation the process of earning magazine revenue from advertising or corporate sponsorship by targeting captive audiences, such as airline passengers or association members, who receive the publications free.

copyright the legal right of authors and producers to own and control the use of their published or unpublished writing, music and lyrics, TV programs and movies, or graphic art designs.

cover music songs recorded or performed by musicians who did not originally write or perform the music; in the 1950s, cover music was an attempt by white producers and artists to capitalize on popular songs by blacks.

crisis management in public relations, the strategic response to uncontrolled negative publicity about an individual, client, or company; also known as *damage control*.

cultivation effect in media research, the idea that heavy viewing of television leads individuals to perceive reality in ways that are consistent with the portrayals they see on television.

cultural studies in media research, the approaches that try to understand how the media and culture are tied to the actual patterns of communication in daily life; these studies focus on how people make meanings, understand reality, and order experience through the use of stories and symbols.

culture the symbols of expression that individuals, groups, and societies use to make sense of daily life and to articulate their values; a process that delivers the values of a society through products or other meaning-making forms.

cyberspace   the region where the networks of computer communication transport their users—a territory that does not recognize conventional geographic boundaries or social hierarchies.

day parts   in radio programming, the division of each day into time blocks—usually 6 to 10 A.M., 10 A.M. to 3 P.M., 3 to 7 P.M., and 7 to 12 midnight—in order to reach various listening audiences.

DBS (direct broadcast satellites)   home-satellite dishes that for a monthly fee downlink hundreds of satellite channels and services.

deficit financing   in television, the process whereby a TV production company leases its programs to a network for a license fee that is actually *less* than the cost of production; the company hopes to recoup this loss later in rerun syndication.

deliberative democracy   a political culture in which citizen groups, local government, and the news media join together to actively shape social and political agendas.

demographic editions   national magazines whose advertising is tailored to subscribers and readers according to occupation, class, and zip-code address.

demographics   in market research, the study of audiences or consumers by age, gender, occupation, ethnicity, education, and income.

description   the first step in the critical process, it involves paying close attention, taking notes, and researching the cultural product to be studied.

desktop publishing   a computer technology that allows one aspiring publisher-editor to inexpensively write, design, lay out, and even print a small newsletter or magazine.

digital audiotape (DAT)   a tape format that features CD-quality sound on a machine that records as well as plays back tapes.

digital communication   images, texts, and sounds that use pulses of electric current or flashes of laser lights and are converted (or encoded) into electronic signals represented as varied combinations of binary numbers, usually ones and zeroes; these signals are then reassembled (decoded) as a precise reproduction of a TV picture, a magazine article, or a telephone voice.

digital recording   music recorded and played back by laser beam rather than by needle or magnetic tape.

direct payment   in media economics, the payment of money, primarily by consumers, for a book, a music CD, a movie, an online computer service, or a cable TV subscription.

disassociation corollary   in advertising, a persuasive technique that tries to distance the consumer from a large product manufacturer or parent company by linking new brands to eccentric, intimate, or regional places.

distribution   the individuals or companies in the mass media business who deliver media products into various regional, national, and international markets.

documentary   a movie or TV news genre that documents reality by recording actual characters and settings.

domestic comedy   a TV hybrid of the sitcom in which characters and settings are usually more important than complicated situations; it generally features a domestic problem or work issue that characters have to solve.

dramedy   in TV programming, a narrative that blurs serious and comic themes.

drive time   in radio programming, the periods between 6 and 10 A.M. and 4 and 7 P.M. when people are commuting to and from work or school; these periods constitute the largest listening audiences of the day.

economies of scale   the economic process of increasing production levels so as to reduce the overall cost per unit.

electromagnetic waves   invisible electronic impulses similar to visible light; electricity, magnetism, light, broadcast signals, and heat are part of such waves, which radiate in space at the speed of light, about 186,000 miles per second.

electronic publisher   a communication business, such as a broadcaster or cable TV company, that is entitled to pick and choose what channels or content to carry.

episodic series   a narrative form well suited for television because main characters continue from week to week, sets and locales remain the same, and technical crews stay with the program; episodic series feature new adventures each week, but a handful of characters emerge with whom viewers can regularly identify.

ethnocentrism   an underlying value held by many U.S. journalists and citizens, it involves judging other countries and cultures according to how they live up to or imitate American practices and ideals.

evaluation   the fourth step in the critical process, it involves arriving at a judgment about whether a cultural product is good, bad, or mediocre; this requires subordinating one's personal taste to the critical assessment resulting from the first three stages.

evergreens   in TV syndication, popular old network reruns such as the *Andy Griffith Show* or *I Love Lucy*.

exhibition   the individuals or companies in the mass media business who exhibit media products; the term most often refers to companies who control movie theaters.

experiment   in regard to the mass media, research that isolates some aspect of content, suggests a hypothesis, and manipulates variables to discover a particular medium's impact on attitudes, emotions, or behavior.

experimental group   in social science research, the group under study that has been exposed to particular phenomena or media content.

Fairness Doctrine   repealed in 1987, this FCC rule required broadcast stations to air and engage in controversial issue programs that affected their communities and, when offering such programming, to provide competing points of view.

famous person testimonial   an advertising strategy that associates a product with the endorsement of a well-known person.

feature syndicates   commercial outlets or brokers, such as United Features and King Features, that contract with newspapers to provide work from well-known political writers, editorial cartoonists, comic-strip artists, and self-help columnists.

fiber-optic cable thin glass bundles of fiber capable of transmitting thousands of messages converted to shooting pulses of light along cable wires; these bundles of fiber are able to carry broadcast channels, telephone signals, and all sorts of digital codes.

film noir French for *black film*, this film genre usually is shot in black and white, uses low lighting techniques, shows few daytime scenes, displays bleak urban settings, and explores the sinister side of human nature.

Financial Interest and Syndication Rules (fin-syn) FCC rules that prohibited the major networks from running their own syndication companies or from charging production companies additional fees after shows had completed their prime-time runs; most fin-syn rules were rescinded in the mid-1990s.

first-run syndication in television, the process whereby new programs are specifically produced for sale into syndication markets rather than for network television.

flack a derogatory term journalists use to refer to a public relations agent.

FM frequency modulation, a type of radio and sound transmission that offers static-less reception and greater fidelity and clarity than AM radio by accentuating the pitch or distance between radio waves.

focus group a common research method in psychographic analysis in which a moderator leads a small-group discussion about a product or issue, usually with six to twelve people.

folk music music performed by untrained musicians and passed down through oral traditions; it encompasses a wide range of music, from Appalachian fiddle tunes to the accordion-led zydeco of Louisiana.

folk-rock amplified folk music, often featuring politically overt lyrics; influenced by rock and roll.

format radio the concept of radio stations developing and playing specific styles (or formats) geared to listeners' age, race, or gender; in format radio, management, rather than deejays, controls programming choices.

Fourth Estate the notion that the press operates as an unofficial branch of government, monitoring the legislative, judicial, and executive branches for abuses of power.

franchise fees the money a cable company pays a city annually for the right to operate the local cable system; these fees are limited by law to no more than 5 percent of the company's gross annual revenue.

fringe time in television, the time slot either immediately before the evening's prime-time schedule (called *early fringe*) or following the local evening news or the network's late night talk shows (called *late fringe*).

gag orders legal restrictions prohibiting the press from releasing preliminary information that might prejudice jury selection.

gatekeepers editors, producers, and other media managers who function as message filters, making decisions about what types of messages actually get produced for particular audiences.

general interest magazine a type of magazine that offers a wide variety of topics and is aimed at a broad national audience.

gotcha stories news reports in which journalists nab evildoers or interview subjects caught in deceit.

grunge rock music that takes the spirit of punk and infuses it with more attention to melody.

halo effect in TV audience measurement, the phenomenon of viewers reporting not what they actually watched but what they think they should have watched.

happy talk in TV journalism, the ad-libbed or scripted banter that goes on among local news anchors, reporters, meteorologists, and sports reporters before and after news reports.

headend a cable TV system's computerized nerve center, where TV signals from local broadcast stations and satellites are received, processed, and distributed to area homes.

herd journalism a situation in which reporters stake out a house or follow a story in such large groups that the entire profession comes under attack for invading people's privacy or exploiting their personal tragedies.

hidden fear appeal an advertising strategy that plays on a sense of insecurity, trying to persuade consumers that only a specific product can offer relief.

high culture symbolic expression that has come to mean "good taste"; often supported by wealthy patrons and corporate donors, it is associated with "fine art" (such as ballet, the symphony, painting, and classic literature), which is available primarily in theaters or museums.

high-definition television (HDTV) a new digital standard for U.S. television sets that has more than twice the resolution of the system that served as the standard from the 1940s through the 1990s.

human interest stories news accounts that focus on the trials and tribulations of the human condition, often featuring ordinary individuals facing extraordinary challenges.

hypertext a data-linking feature of the World Wide Web, it allows a user to click on a highlighted word or phrase and skip directly to other files related to that subject in other computer systems.

hypodermic needle model an early model in mass communication research that attempted to explain media effects by arguing that the media shoot their powerful effects directly into unsuspecting or weak audiences; sometimes called the *bullet theory* or *direct effects* model.

hypotheses in social science research, tentative general statements that predict a relationship between a *dependent variable* that is influenced by an *independent variable*.

independent station a TV station, such as WGN or WTBS, that finds its own original and syndicated programming and is not affiliated with one of the major networks.

indies independent music production houses that are outside music's mainstream oligopoly; they often produce less commercially viable music.

indirect payment in media economics, the financial support of media products by advertisers, who pay for the quantity or quality of audience members that a particular medium attracts.

individualism an underlying value held by most U.S. journalists and citizens, it favors individual rights and responsibilities over institutional or bureaucratic mandates.

infomercials thirty-minute, late night and daytime programs that usually feature fading TV and music celebrities, who advertise a product in a format that looks like a talk show.

information highway the circulation of both personal communication and mass media on personal computers and modems, high-speed telephone links, communication satellites, and television screens.

ink-jet imaging a computer technique that allows a magazine publisher or advertiser to print personalized messages to individual subscribers.

instant book in the book industry, a marketing strategy that involves publishing a topical book quickly after a major event.

interactivity a communication process that allows immediate two-way communication (as via telephones or e-mail) between senders and receivers of media messages.

Internet the vast central network of high-speed telephone lines designed to link and carry computer information worldwide.

interpretation the third step in the critical process, it asks and answers the "What does that mean?" and "So what?" questions about one's findings.

interpretive journalism a type of journalism that involves analyzing and explaining key issues or events and placing them in a broader historical or social context.

invasion of privacy the violation of a person's right to be left alone, without his or her name, image, or daily activities becoming public property.

inverted pyramid style a style of journalism in which news reports begin with the most dramatic or newsworthy information—answering who, what, where, and when (and less frequently why or how) questions at the top of the story—and then tail off with less-significant details.

irritation advertising an advertising strategy that tries to create product-name recognition by being annoying or obnoxious.

jazz an improvisational and mostly instrumental music form that absorbs and integrates a diverse body of musical styles, including African rhythms, blues, big band, and gospel.

joint operating agreement (JOA) in the newspaper industry, an economic arrangement, sanctioned by the government, that permits competing newspapers to operate separate editorial divisions while merging business and production operations.

kinescope before the days of videotape, a 1950s technique for preserving television broadcasts by using a film camera to record a live TV show off a studio monitor.

knowledge gap the growing contrast between "information haves," or digital highway users who can afford to acquire multiple media services, and "information have-nots," who cannot afford a computer much less the many options now available on the highway.

leased channels in cable television, channels that allow citizens to buy time for producing programs or presenting their own viewpoints.

libel in media law, the defamation of character in written expression.

libertarian model a model for journalism and speech that encourages vigorous government criticism and supports the highest degree of freedom for individual speech and news operations.

limited competition in media economics, a market with many producers and sellers but only a few differentiable products within a particular category; sometimes called *monopolistic competition.*

linotype a technology introduced in the nineteenth century that allowed printers to set type mechanically using a typewriter-style keyboard.

literary journalism news reports that adapt fictional storytelling techniques to nonfictional material; sometimes called *new journalism.*

lobbying in government public relations, the process of attempting to influence the voting of lawmakers to support a client's or organization's best interests.

low culture symbolic expression allegedly aligned with the questionable tastes of the "masses," who enjoy the commercial "junk" circulated by the mass media, such as soap operas, rock music, talk radio, comic books, and monster truck pulls.

market research in advertising and public relations agencies, the department that uses social science techniques to assess the behaviors and attitudes of consumers toward particular products before any ads are created.

mass communication the process of designing and delivering cultural messages and stories to diverse audiences through media channels as old as the book and as new as the Internet.

mass customization the process whereby product companies and content providers customize a Web page, print ad, or other media form for an individual consumer.

mass media the cultural industries—the channels of communication—that produce and distribute songs, novels, newspapers, movies, online computer services, and other cultural products to large numbers of people.

mechanical royalty the copyright fee, usually about one-half cent for each CD or audiotape sold, received by songwriters and publishers when they allow their music to be recorded.

media buyers in advertising, the individuals who choose and purchase the types of media that are best suited to carry a client's ads and reach the targeted audience.

media convergence the process whereby old and new media are available via the integration of personal computers and high-speed satellite-based phone links.

media-effects research the mainstream tradition in mass communication research, it attempts to understand, explain, and predict the impact—or effects—of the mass media on individuals and society.

mega agencies in advertising, large firms or holding companies that are formed by merging several individual agencies and that maintain worldwide regional offices; they provide both advertising and public relations services and operate in-house radio and TV production studios.

microchips/microprocessors miniature circuits that process and store electronic signals, integrating thousands of electronic components into thin strands of silicon along which binary codes travel.

minimal effects model a mass communication research model based on tightly controlled experiments and survey findings; it argues that the mass media have limited effects on audiences, reinforcing existing behaviors and attitudes, rather than changing them.

mini-series a serial television program that runs over a two-day to two-week period, usually on consecutive nights.

modern period a historical era spanning the time from the rise of the Industrial Revolution in the eighteenth and nineteenth centuries to the present; its social values include celebrating the individual, believing in rational order, working efficiently, and rejecting tradition.

monopoly in media economics, an organizational structure that occurs when a single firm dominates production and distribution in a particular industry, either nationally or locally.

muckraking a style of early-twentieth-century investigative journalism that referred to reporters who were willing to crawl around in society's muck to uncover a story.

multiplexes contemporary movie theaters that exhibit many movies at the same time on multiple screens.

must-carry rules rules established by the FCC in 1965 requiring all cable operators to assign channels to and carry all local TV broadcasts on their systems, thus ensuring that local network affiliates, independent stations (those not carrying network programs), and public television channels would benefit from cable's clearer reception.

myth analysis a strategy for critiquing advertising that provides insights into how ads work at a cultural level; according to this strategy, ads are narratives with stories to tell and social conflicts to resolve.

narrative the structure underlying most media products, it includes two components: the *story*—what happens to whom—and the *discourse*—how the story is told.

narrowcasting any specialized electronic programming or media channel aimed at a target audience.

network a broadcast process that links, through special phone lines or satellite transmissions, groups of radio or TV stations, which share programming produced at a central location.

news the process of gathering information and making narrative reports—edited by individuals in a news organization—which create selected frames of reference and help the public make sense of prominent people, important events, and unusual happenings in everyday life.

newsgroups organized computer conferences consisting of bulletin boards and individual messages, or postings, which are circulated twenty-four hours a day via the Internet and cover a range of topics.

newshole the space left over in a newspaper for news content after all the ads are placed.

newspaper chains large companies that own several papers throughout the country.

newsreels weekly ten-minute magazine-style compilations of filmed news events from around the world organized in a sequence of short reports; prominent in movie theaters between the 1920s and the 1950s.

newsworthiness the often unstated criteria that journalists use to determine which events and issues should become news reports, including timeliness, proximity, conflict, prominence, human interest, consequence, usefulness, novelty, and deviance.

nickelodeons the first small makeshift movie theaters, which were often converted cigar stores, pawnshops, or restaurants redecorated to mimic vaudeville theaters.

O & Os network-owned-and-operated TV stations.

objective journalism a modern style of journalism that distinguishes factual reports from opinion columns; reporters strive to remain neutral toward the issue or event they cover, searching out competing points of view among the sources for a story.

objectivity in social science research, eliminating bias and judgments on the part of researchers.

obscenity expression that is not protected as speech if these three legal tests are all met: (1) the average person, applying contemporary community standards, would find that the material as a whole appeals to prurient interest; (2) the material depicts or describes sexual conduct in a patently offensive way; and (3) the material, as a whole, lacks serious literary, artistic, political, or scientific value.

off-network syndication in television, the process whereby older programs, no longer running during prime time, are made available for reruns to local stations, cable operators, online services, and foreign markets.

offset lithography a technology that allowed books to be printed from photographic plates rather than metal casts, reducing the cost of color and illustrations and eventually permitting computers to perform typesetting.

oligopoly in media economics, an organizational structure in which a few firms control most of an industry's production and distribution resources.

option time now considered illegal, a procedure whereby a radio network paid an affiliate station a set fee per hour for an option to control programming and advertising on that station.

paid circulation the process of earning magazine revenue from consumers who either pay for regular subscriptions or for individual copies at newsstands or supermarkets.

papyrus one of the first substances to hold written language and symbols; obtained from plant reeds found along the Nile River.

parchment treated animal skin that replaced papyrus as an early pre-paper substance to document written language.

partisan press an early dominant style of American journalism distinguished by opinion newspapers, which generally argued one political point of view or pushed the plan of the particular party that subsidized the paper.

pass-along readership the total number of people who come into contact with a single copy of a magazine.

payola the unethical (but not always illegal) practice of record promoters paying deejays or radio programmers to favor particular songs over others.

pay-per-view (PPV) a cable television service that allows customers to select a particular movie for a one-time $3 or $4 charge, payable to the local cable company, or $25 to $40 for a special one-time event.

people meters in TV audience measurement, devices that hook up a random sample of households to determine their viewing behavior.

performance royalty the copyright fee paid to songwriters and performers whenever their music is used on radio, television, or other media channels.

plain folks pitch an advertising strategy that associates a product with simplicity and the common person.

political advertising the use of ad techniques to promote a candidate's image and persuade the public to a viewpoint.

pop music popular music that appeals either to a wide cross section of the public or to sizeable subdivisions within the larger public based on age, region, or ethnic background; the word *pop* has also been used as a label to distinguish popular music from classical music.

postmodern period a contemporary historical era usually spanning the time from the 1960s to the present; its social values include opposing hierarchy, diversifying and recycling culture, questioning scientific reasoning, and embracing paradox.

premium cable in cable programming, a tier of channels that subscribers can order at an additional monthly fee over their basic cable service; these may include movie channels and interactive services.

press agent the earliest type of public relations practitioner, who sought to advance a client's image through media exposure.

press release in public relations, an announcement—written in the style of a news report—that gives new information about an individual, company, or organization and pitches a story idea to the news media.

prime time in television programming, the hours between 8 and 11 P.M. (or 7 to 10 P.M. in the Midwest), when networks have traditionally drawn their largest audiences and charged their highest advertising rates.

Prime-Time Access Rule (PTAR) an FCC rule that in 1970 took away the 7:30 to 8 P.M. time slot (6:30 to 7 P.M. central) from the TV networks and gave it exclusively to local stations in the nation's fifty largest television markets.

prior restraint the legal definition of censorship in the United States, which prohibits courts and governments from blocking any publication or speech before it actually occurs.

production the individuals or companies in the mass media business in charge of creating movies, TV programs, music recordings, magazines, books, and other media products.

product placement the advertising tactic of buying space for a particular product so that it appears on a movie set or a program as a supporting prop.

program-length commercials controversial thirty-minute cartoon programs developed for TV syndication primarily to promote a line of toys.

propaganda in advertising and public relations, a communication strategy that tries to manipulate public opinion to gain support for a special issue, program, or policy, such as a nation's war effort.

pseudo-event in public relations, any circumstance or event created solely for the purpose of obtaining coverage in the media.

psychographics in market research, the study of audience or consumer attitudes, beliefs, interests, and motivations.

public domain not under copyright protection; older music or written materials fall in this category.

publicity in public relations, the positive and negative messages that spread controlled and uncontrolled information about a person, corporation, issue, or policy in various media.

public journalism a type of journalism, driven by citizen forums, that goes beyond telling the news to a broader mission of helping public life go well; also called *civic journalism*.

public relations   the total communication strategy conducted by a person, a government, or an organization attempting to reach and persuade its audiences to a point of view.

public-service announcements (PSAs)   reports or announcements, carried free by radio and TV stations, that promote government programs, educational projects, voluntary agencies, or social reform.

puffery   bordering on deception, advertisements that use hyperbole and exaggeration.

pulp fiction   a term used to describe many late-nineteenth-century popular paperbacks and dime novels, which were constructed of cheap machine-made pulp material.

punk rock   rock music that challenges the orthodoxy and commercialism of the recording business; it is characterized by loud unpolished qualities, a jackhammer beat, primal vocal screams, crude aggression, and defiant or comic lyrics.

rack jobbers   sales agents in the music business who contract with general retailers such as Kmart to stock their racks or shelves with the latest CDs, audiocassettes, and music videos.

random assignment   a social science research method for assigning research subjects; it ensures that every subject has an equal chance of being placed in either the experimental group or the control group.

rap music   music that combines spoken street dialect with cuts (or samples) of older records and bears the influences of social politics, male boasting, and comic lyrics carried forward from blues, R&B, soul, and rock and roll.

rating   in TV audience measurement, a statistical estimate expressed as a percentage of households tuned to a program in the local or national market being sampled.

regional editions   national magazines whose content is tailored to the interests of different geographic areas.

reliability   in social science research, getting the same answers or outcomes from a study or measure during repeated testing.

rent-a-citizen   the process whereby competing cable companies identify and hire prominent local leaders as spokespersons during franchise negotiations.

rerun syndication   in television, the process whereby programs that stay in a network's lineup long enough to build up enough episodes (usually four seasons' worth), are sold, or syndicated, to hundreds of TV markets in the United States and abroad.

responsible capitalism   an underlying value held by many U.S. journalists and citizens, it assumes that businesspeople compete with each other not primarily to maximize profits but to increase prosperity for all.

rhythm and blues (R&B)   music that merged urban blues and big band sounds.

rockabilly   music that mixed bluegrass and country influences with those of black folk music and early amplified blues.

rock and roll   music that mixed the vocal and instrumental traditions of popular music; it merged the black influences of urban blues, gospel, and R&B with the white influences of country, folk, and pop vocals.

rotation   in format radio programming, playing the most popular or best-selling songs many times throughout the day.

saturation advertising   the ad strategy of inundating a variety of print and visual media with ads aimed at target audiences.

scientific method   a widely used research method that studies phenomena in systematic stages; it includes identifying the research problem; reviewing existing research; developing working hypotheses; determining an appropriate research design; collecting information; analyzing results to see if the hypotheses have been verified; and interpreting the implications of the study.

scoop   an exclusive story obtained by a journalist, who publicly presents the story ahead of all rivals.

Section 315   part of the 1934 Communications Act, it mandates that during elections broadcast stations must provide equal opportunities and response time for qualified political candidates.

seditious libel   in law, defaming a public official's character in print.

selective exposure   the phenomenon whereby audiences seek messages and meanings that correspond to their preexisting beliefs and values.

selective retention   the phenomenon whereby audiences remember or retain messages and meanings that correspond to their preexisting beliefs and values.

serial programs   radio or TV programs that feature continuing story lines from day to day, such as soap operas.

servers   individual "host" computer centers run (or hosted) by universities, corporations, and government agencies, all interconnected by special high-speed phone lines to the Internet.

share   in TV audience measurement, a statistical estimate of the percentage of homes tuned to a program, compared to those actually using their sets at the time of a sample.

shield laws   laws protecting the confidentiality of key interview subjects and reporters' rights *not* to reveal the sources of controversial information used in news stories.

shortwave radio   a type of radio transmission, used mostly by amateur—or ham—radio operators and governments, that can bounce a radio signal off the ionosphere halfway around the world.

situation comedy (sitcom)   a type of comedy series that features a recurring cast and set as well as several narrative scenes; each episode establishes a situation, complicates it, develops increasing confusion among its characters, and then alleviates the complications.

situational ethic   the principle that in a moral society ethical decisions are arrived at on an individual or case-by-case basis.

sketch comedy   short television comedy skits that are usually segments of TV variety shows; sometimes known as *vaudeo*, the marriage of vaudeville and video.

slander   in law, spoken language that defames a person's character.

slogan   in advertising, a catchy phrase that attempts to promote or sell a product by capturing its essence in words.

small-town pastoralism   an underlying value held by many U.S. journalists and citizens, it favors the small over the large and the rural over the urban.

snob appeal   an advertising strategy that attempts to persuade consumers that using a product will enable them to maintain or elevate their social station.

social responsibility model   a model for journalism and speech, influenced by the libertarian model, that encourages the free flow of information to citizens so they can make wise decisions regarding political and social issues.

soul music   music that mixes gospel, blues, and urban and southern black styles with slower, more emotional, and melancholic lyrics.

sound bite   in TV journalism, the equivalent of a quote in print; the part of a news report in which an expert, celebrity, victim, or person on the street is being interviewed about some aspect of an event or issue.

space brokers   in the days before modern advertising, individuals who purchased space in newspapers and sold it to various merchants.

spin doctors   political consultants who manage campaigns and attempt to favorably shape the news media's image of a candidate.

stereo   the recording of two separate channels or tracks of sound.

stereotyping   the process of assigning individuals to groups, whose members are falsely assumed to act as a single entity and to display certain characteristics, which are usually negative.

storyboard   in advertising, a sort of blueprint or roughly drawn comic-strip version of a proposed advertisement.

stripping   in TV syndication, showing a program—either older network reruns or programs made for syndication—five days a week.

studio system   an early film production system that constituted a sort of assembly-line process for moviemaking; major film studios controlled not only actors but directors, editors, writers, and other employees, all of whom worked under exclusive contracts.

subliminal advertising   a 1950s term referring to hidden or disguised print and visual messages that allegedly register on the unconscious, creating false needs and fooling people into buying products.

subsidiary rights   in the book industry, selling the rights to a book for use in other media forms, such as a mass-market paperback, a CD-ROM, or the basis for a movie screenplay.

superstations   local independent TV stations, such as WTBS in Atlanta or WGN in Chicago, that have uplinked their signals onto a communication satellite to make themselves available nationwide.

superstore   a large retail business that sells books, recordings, and new media; this contemporary trend in bookselling adapts the large retail-store concept to the publishing industry.

survey research   in social science research, a method of collecting and measuring data taken from a group of respondents.

sweeps   in TV ratings, month-long measurement periods—conducted four times a year (six times in larger markets) that determine both local and national ad rates.

syndicated exclusivity (syndex)   FCC rules that gave local stations exclusive rights in their area to syndicate TV programs, such as off-network reruns, which they had purchased.

synergy   in media economics, the promotion and sale of a product (and all its versions) throughout the various subsidiaries of a media conglomerate.

textual analysis   in media research, a method for closely and critically examining and interpreting the meanings of culture, including architecture, fashion, books, movies, and TV programs.

time shifting   the process whereby television viewers tape shows and watch them later, when it is convenient for them.

Top-40 format   the first radio format, in which stations played the forty most popular hits in a given week as measured by record sales.

transistor   invented by Bell Laboratories in 1947, this tiny technology, which receives and amplifies radio signals, made portable radios possible.

transponders   the relay points on a communication satellite that receive and transmit telephone and TV signals.

UHF   ultrahigh frequency; in broadcasting, the band in the electromagnetic spectrum that the FCC allocated for TV channels 14 through 69.

underground press   radical newspapers, run on shoe-string budgets, that question mainstream political policies and conventional values; usually refers to a journalism movement of the 1960s.

uses and gratifications model   a mass communication research model, usually employing in-depth interviews and survey questionnaires, that argues that people use the media to satisfy various emotional desires or intellectual needs.

validity   in social science research, demonstrating that a study actually measures what it claims to measure.

VALS   short for values and lifestyles, a market research strategy that divides consumers into types and measures psychological factors, including how consumers think and feel about products and how they achieve (or do not achieve) the lifestyles to which they aspire.

vertical integration in media economics, controlling a mass media industry at its three essential levels: production, distribution, and exhibition; the term is used most often in reference to the film industry.

VHF very high frequency; in broadcasting, the band in the electromagnetic spectrum that the FCC allocated for TV channels 2 through 13.

videocassette recorders (VCRs) recorders using a half-inch video format known as VHS (video home system), which allows viewers to record and play back programs from television or to watch movies rented from video stores.

video news release (VNR) in public relations, the visual counterpart to a press release; it pitches a story idea to the TV news media by mimicking the style of a broadcast news report.

virtual communities groups of computer users who are separated geographically but connected nationally and globally by their shared interests or business and their access to an online service or the Internet.

weighting in TV audience measurement, assigning more weight to a particular respondent in an attempt to correct the underrepresented group in the original sample.

wireless telegraphy the forerunner of radio, a form of voiceless point-to-point communication; it preceded the voice and sound transmissions of one-to-many mass communication that became known as broadcasting.

wireless telephony early experiments in wireless voice and music transmissions, which later developed into modern radio.

wire services commercial organizations like the Associated Press that share news stories and information by relaying them around the country and the world, originally via telegraph and now via satellite transmission.

world music sometimes called international or ethnic songs, this category includes the many different styles of popular regional and folk music from cultures throughout the world; it usually excludes classical music and the most popular forms of American or European music.

World Wide Web a free and open data-linking system for organizing and standardizing information on the Internet; the WWW allows computer-accessed information to associate with—or link to—other information no matter where it is on the Internet.

yellow journalism a newspaper style or era that peaked in the 1890s, it emphasized high-interest stories, sensational crime news, large headlines, and serious reports that exposed corruption, particularly in business and government.

zapping using a VCR to edit out commercials during the videotaping process.

zines self-published magazines produced on personal computer programs or the Internet.

zipping using a VCR to fast-forward a videotaped program through the ads during the recorded viewing.

credits

Text Credits

15, "Talk TV's Top 10" from *Broadcasting & Cable*, 12/2/96. ©1996 by Cahners Publishing Reed Elsevier, Inc. Source: Neilson Media Research. Reprinted by permission; **22,** Madonna CD covers: Courtesy of Warner Bros. Records; **37, 39,** Figures 2.1, 2.2: Eric Gagnon, from pp. 7 and 21 in *What's on the Internet*, 3e. ©1996 Internet Media Corporation. Reprinted by permission of Addison-Wesley Longman, Inc.; **44–45,** "The Word and the Web" by Eric Mendelson, from *The New York Times*, 6/2/96. ©1996 by The New York Times Company. Reprinted by permission; **61,** Table 3.1: chart of Annual Record, Tape, and CD Sales from *The New Book of Rock Lists* by David Marsh and James Bernard. ©1994 by Duck & Duchess Ventures, Inc. Reprinted with the permission of Simon & Schuster; **79,** Figure 3.2: "The Major Labels in the Sound Recording Industry" adapted from "Sony's Role in American Pop Culture" *The New York Times* (12/6/95). ©1995 by The New York Times Co. Reprinted by permission; **91,** Figure 4.1: "The Electronic Spectrum" from page 202 in The World Book Encyclopedia, Volume 6. ©1997 World Book, Inc. By permission of the publisher; **108 & 110,** Figures 4.3 & Table 4.1: "Radio Program Log for an Oldies Station" and "The Twelve Most Popular Radio Formats" from The Center for Radio Information, 19 Market Street, Cold Spring, NY 10516. Reprinted by permission; **123,** "The Consumer Electronics Industry Says: . . . " and "The Computer Industry Says: . . . " adapted from "Building Your Next TV" by Joel Brinkley. ©1997 by The New York Times Co. Reprinted by permission; **131,** Table 5.1: "Selected Situation and Domestic Comedies Rated in the Top 10." Specified excerpts from *The Complete Directory of Prime Time Network TV Shows* by Tim Brooks and Earl Marsh. ©1979, 1981, 1985 by Tim Brooks and Earl Marsh. Reprinted by permission of Ballantine Books, a division of Random House, Inc. Also adapted from *Prime-Time Hits*. ©1993 by Susan Sackett by arrangement with Billboard Books, an imprint of Watson-Gutpill Publications, a division of BPI Communications, Inc.; *The World Almanac and Book of Facts 1997* and *World Almanac Books 1996* published by K-III Reference Corporation and A.C. Nielsen Media Research. Reprinted by permission; **146,** Table 5.2: "The Top 10-Highest Rated TV Series, Individual Programs." From *TV Facts* by Corbett Steinberg. Copyright©1985. Reprinted with permission from Facts on File, Inc., K-III Reference Corporation, and A.C. Nielsen Media Research; **149,** "TV Erodes Sense of Community" from *The New York Times*, 12/21/95. ©1995 by The New York Times Co. Reprinted by permission; **158,** Figure 6.2: "The Rise of Cable Systems 1970–95." © Warren Publishing, Inc. Washington, D.C.; **164 & 175,** Figure 6.3 & Table 6.2: "The Top 20 Cable Networks" and "Top 20 U.S. Cable Operators." Reprinted by permission of National Cable Television Association; **168–169,** CNN® logo, courtesy of Cable News Network, One CNN Center, Atlanta, GA 30348; **182,** Table 7.1: "The Top-10 American Box-Office Champions" from "The 50 All Time Highest Grossing Movies" ©1997 MOVIEWEB. Based on information from Exhibitor Relations Co. Reprinted by permission. All rights reserved; **199,** Table 7.3: "The Top 10 Foreign-Language Films." ©1994 Little, Brown. ©1996 by The New York Times Co. Reprinted by permission; **221,** Table 8.1: "The Nation's Largest Daily Newspaper" adapted from *The New York Times*, 4/30/96. ©1996 by The New York Times Co. Reprinted by permission; **237,**

"Media Convergence and the *Tribune* Empire" by Christopher Harper. *American Journalism Review*, 12/96, p. 29. Reprinted with permission of American Journalism Review; **258–259,** "Alternative Magazines and the *Utne Reader*." *Utne Reader* ©1991, ©1997, ©1987, ©1993, ©1995, and ©1996 Utne Reader and Family Communications, Inc. (cover with Mr. Rogers). Reprinted by permission; **267,** *Factsheet5*, ©1996 *Stay Free!*, *Cool Beans!*, *Thrift SCORE*, and *MAXIMUMROCKNROLL*. Reprinted by permission; **270–271,** "Sex Lies & Advertising" by Gloria Steinem. *Ms.* (July/August 1990), pp. 18–28. Reprinted by permission of the author. *Ms.* Magazine 1st issue cover with first pages from four inside articles, Spring 1972. ©1972. Reprinted by permission of Ms. Magazine. "I Want a Wife" by Judy Syfers Brady. ©1970 by Judy Brady. Reprinted by permission of the author; **279,** Table 10.1: "Annual Numbers of New Book Titles Published—Selected Years." R.R. Bowker, a division of Reed Elsevier. Reprinted by permission; **286–287,** Superman, Death, and all related elements and indicia are trademarks of DC Comics ©1987. All rights reserved. Used with permission. Spiderman TM & © Marvel Characters, Inc. All rights reserved. Used with permission. TEENAGE MUTANT NINJA TURTLES™ is a trademark owned and licensed by Mirage Studios. Used with permission; **288,** "PW's 1996 Longest-Running Paperback Bestsellers." *Publishers Weekly*, January 6, 1997. Copyright ©1997 by Publishers Weekly. Reprinted by permission; **289,** Table 10.2: "Mass-Market Paperback Best-Sellers: The First Twenty-Five Years." Houghton-Mifflin, 1984. Reprinted by permission; **296,** Table 10.3: "Bookstores in the United States and Canada 1993." R.R. Bowker Reed Elsevier, New Providence, NJ. Reprinted by permission; **313,** Table 11.1: "Top 20 National Advertisers." P. 297 from *The World Almanac and Book of Facts 1977*, published by K-III Reference Corporation; Competitive Media Reporting and Publishers Information Bureau, New York. ©1996. Reprinted by permission. Table 11.2: "World's Largest Advertising Organizations." *Advertising Age*, April 21, 1997. Copyright, Crain Communications Inc. Reprinted with permission. **329,** "The 900-Number Industry." From *Marketing Madness* by Michael F. Jacobson et al. p. 131. Copyright ©1995 by Westview Press. Reprinted by permission of Westview Press; **348,** Table 12.1: "The Top 15 Public Relations Firms—1995." From *Jack O'Dwyer's Newsletter*, March 29, 1995. Reprinted with permission of Jack O'Dwyer's Directory of PR Firms, New York; **357,** Table 12.2: "PRSA Ethics Code." Reprinted by permission of K-III Reference Corporation and Public Relations Society of America; **392,** "Why Those Hidden Cameras Hurt Journalism" by Paul Starobin. *The New York Times* OP-ED, Tuesday, January 29, 1997. Copyright ©1997 by The New York Times Co. Reprinted by permission; **395,** "Atlanta Journal" logo. Reprinted with permission of Atlanta Journal Constitution; **411,** "The Wichita Eagle" logo. Reprinted with permission of The Wichita Eagle-Beacon Publishing Co., Inc.; "The Virginian-Pilot" logo. Reprinted with permission of The Virginian-Pilot and The Ledger Star, Landmark Communications, Inc. "The Wichita Eagle" logo. Reprinted with permission of The Wichita Eagle-Beacon Publishing Co., Inc. "The Charlotte Observer" logo. Courtesy of Knight Publishing Co., division of Knight Rider. "Star

Tribune" logo. Courtesy of Womack Publishing Company, Inc.; **418**, Figure 15.1: "Should the Children Watch?" *The New York Times*, December 20, 1996, p. A12. Copyright ©1996 by The New York Times Company. Reprinted by permission; **434–435**, "Violence Study Shows Television's Mental Block" by Ellen Goodman. Reprinted in *Ann Arbor News*, February 16, 1996, p. A9. ©1996 The Washington Post Writers Group. Reprinted by permission.

Picture Credits
Key: APh = Archive Photos; AP/WW = Associated Press/Wide World Photos; C-BA = Corbis-Bettmann Archive; IW = Image Works; PF = Photofest

2, Pat West/Sygma; **6**, J. Pierpont Morgan Library/Art Resource; **9**, Sygma; **11**, FPG; **14–15**, J. Kowalsky/Sygma; **16** (left), Courtesy, General Mills, Inc.; (right), PF; **19, 22**, APh; **23**, Courtesy, Warner Bros. Records; **24**, PF; **28**, Sally Weiner Grotta/The Stock Market; **29**, Richard Ellis/Sygma; **32**, *Against All Odds* Productions, © 1996, "24 Hours in Cyberspace," Photo: Guglielmo de'Micheli; **36**, Image Shop/Phototake; **38**, Will & Deni McIntyre/Photo Researchers; **41**, Superstock; **42**, Lara Jo Regan/Saba; **43**, Science Photo Library/Photo Researchers; **44**, C-BA; **45**, © 1996, courtesy, The Monastery of Christ in the Desert; **50**, © Aug. 8, 1994, *U.S. News & World Report*, Art: Dave Black; **53**, Michael Greenlar/IW; **56**, AP/WW; **60**, The Lundoff Collection; **63**, Phillipe Gontier/IW; **66**, Courtesy, Legacy Records, Div. Of Sony Music Corp.; **67**, APh; **69**, C-BA; **72**, PF; **75**, Jeff Mayer/Starfile; **76**, Courtesy, Ron Rainey Management; **77**, Courtesy of Capital-EMI Music, Inc.; **78**, PF; **80** (top), Globe Photos; **80** (bottom), AP/WW; **88**, AP/WW; **92**, Roger Violett/Gamma-Liaison; **95**, APh; **99**, PF; **102, 104**, C-BA; **107**, James Levin/FPG; **112**, C-BA; **113**, Lawrence Schwartzwald/Sygma; **118**, PF; **121**, Dane Penland; **123**, APh; **125, 129, 130, 134, 139, 141**, PF; **143**, AP/WW; **147** (top), FPG; (bottom), AP/WW; **152–153**, Gary Gershoff/Retna; **165**, Frank Rosotto/The Stock Market; **166**, © 1996, CNN; **168** (top), AP/WW; (bottom), C-BA; **169**, (top, bottom), C-BA; **170**, Provided by Nickelodeon. Used with permission; **173**, © 1996, Thomson Consumer Electronics, Inc.; **176**, James M. Kelley/Globe Photos; **180**, PF; **183**, Steve Goldberg/Monkmeyer; **184**, Edison National Historic Site, National Park Service; **187**, PF; **190** (top left, top right), **191**, (top right), PF/Kisch; **191** (top left), APh; **192, 196, 197**, PF; **198**, APh; **200**, PF; **204**, Andrea Renault/Globe Photo; **205** (top), C-BA; (center, bottom), Jose L. Palaez/The Stock Market; **212**, C-BA; **216**, Massachusetts Historical Society; **217**, Staten Island Historical Society; **219** (left), Library of Congress (LC-USZC4-3800); (right), Dept. of Special Collections, Syracuse Univ. Library; **224** (left) Walt Handelsman, © Tribune Media Services Inc. All rights reserved. Reprinted with permission; (right), Library of Congress/The Lundoff Collection; **226**, courtesy, *USA Today*, Gannett Newspapers, Inc.; **229**, Sydpix/FPG; **231**, AP/WW; **232** (left), C-BA; (right), AP/WW; **237**, courtesy *Chicago Tribune*; **239**, © Michigan Live Inc. All rights reserved; **242**, Courtesy, *Swing* Magazine, © 1997; **247**, N.Y. Public Library/The Picture Collection; **250**, C-BA; **252**, Margaret Bourke-White/*Life* Magazine, © Time, Inc.; **258–259**, © *Utne Reader*, 1991, © 1997, 1987, 1993, 1995, and 1996 *Utne Reader* and Family Communications, Inc.; **261**, Chris Johns/National Geographic Image Collection; **263**, drawing by Edward Sorel, © 1996, *The New Yorker Magazine*, Inc. All rights reserved; **264**, Courtesy, The Reader's Digest Assn. Inc.; **267**, Courtesy of *Factsheet 5*; © 1996 *Stay Free!*; Courtesy of *Cool Beans!*; Courtesy of Thrift *Score*; Courtesy of *Maximumrocknroll*; **270–271**, Reprinted by permission of *Ms. Magazine*, © 1972; **273**, Courtesy, Metro East Publications; **276** (top), PF; (bottom), © Used by permission of Doubleday Books, a division of Bantam Doubleday Dell Publ. Group, Inc. Art by Whitney Cookman; **278**, Myrleen Ferguson Cate/PhotoEdit; **282**, Library of Congress; **290**, From *Cezanne* CD-ROM, © Corbis, Inc.; **293**, © 1995 by William H. Gates III. Used by permission of Viking Penguin, a division of Penguin Books USA, Inc.; **295**, Ted Hardin; **299** (top), Irish Historical Society; (bottom), AP/WW; **300**, Illustration by Susan Rose, © Used by permission of Bantam Books, a division of Bantam Doubleday Dell Publ. Group, Inc.; **303**, Sygma; **306**, Bob Daemmrich/IW; **309**, Reprinted by permission of NIKE, Inc.; **311**, National Museum of American History/Smithsonian Institution; **317**, Andrew Christman; **318**, Courtesy, Weiden & Kennedy; Hank Perlman, Copywriter; Rick McQuiston, Art Director; Will Van Overbeek, Photographer; **321**, Courtesy Volkswagen of America; **323**, Courtesy, Bayer Corp.; Foote, Cone & Belding; **325**, George Goodwin/Monkmeyer; **326** (left), N.Y. Public Library/The Picture Collection; (right), Courtesy, WestPoint Stevens, Inc.; **331**, © 1996, Natl. Fluid Milk Processor Promotion Board; Courtesy, Bozell Worldwide, Inc.; **338–339**, courtesy, Levi Strauss & Co.; **342**, Culver; **344**, AP/WW; **346**, C-BA; **351**, Courtesy, Greater Milwaukee Convention & Visitors Bureau; **352**, AP/WW; **353**, Rob Crandall/IW; **359**, AP/WW; **360**, Courtesy, Levi Strauss & Co.; **361** (top), APh; (bottom), AP/WW; **364**, Duncan Rabani/Retna; (insert), N.Y. Public Library/The Picture Collection; **370**, Philippe Gontier/IW; **372**, Globe Photos; **374, 377**, AP/WW; **379**, Walt Handelsman, © Tribune Media Services, Inc. All rights reserved. Reprinted with permission; **381**, AP/WW; **384**, *Sunday Independent*, Dublin; (insert), AP/WW; **387**, Uniphoto; **389**, R. Mims/Sygma; **395** (left), AP/WW; (right) Courtesy, *The Atlanta Journal* and *The Atlanta Constitution*; **397**, Bob Strong/IW; **398**, Courtesy, CBS-TV; **402**, C-BA; **405**, Chris Smith/APh; **407**, W. Marc Bernsau/IW; **409**, Courtesy, *The Virginian Pilot*, Norfolk, VA; *The Wichita Eagle*, Wichita, KS; *Charlotte Observer*, Charlotte, NC; *Star-Tribune*, Minneapolis, MN; **410**, Library of Congress (LC-USF33-31326); **414**, © Sept. 11, 1995, *U.S. News & World Report*; Photo, Jeffrey MacMillan; **417**, The Lundoff Collection; **422**, NEWIST/CESA, Univ. Of Wisconsin, Green Bay; **424**, Remi Benali/Gamma-Liaison; **427**, Keystone/Sygma; **429**, APh; **430**, Ed Andrieski/AP/WW; **433–435, 438, 441, 444**, AP/WW; **446**, Jeanette Beckman/Retna; **448**, Reprint from the *N.Y. Times*, Mar. 29, 1960, Committee to Save M. L. King; **449, 450, 454**, AP/WW; **459**, Courtesy, Tamiment Library, N.Y. Univ.; **426**, AP/WW; **465**, Courtesy, IFEX, Canadian Committee to Protect Journalists, Toronto; **466**, © 1995, Time, Inc. Reprinted by permission.

INDEX

491

ABOUT THE AUTHOR

Richard Campbell is director of the School of Journalism at Middle Tennessee State University. He is author of *60 Minutes and the News: A Mythology for Middle America* (University of Illinois Press, 1991) and co-author of *Cracked Coverage: Television News, the Anti-Cocaine Crusade, and the Reagan Legacy* (Duke University Press, 1994).

He has written articles and essays on mass media for numerous publications, including *Columbia Journalism Review, Television Quarterly, Critical Studies in Mass Communication,* and *Media Studies Journal.* As an author and media critic, he has also been a frequent public speaker and has made guest appearances on NPR, Wisconsin Public Radio, WJR radio, and Detroit public television.

Campbell earned a Ph.D. in Radio-TV-Film from Northwestern University, where he was a National Danforth Fellow. For more than twenty-five years he has taught journalism and media courses to a wide variety of students, from high school teenagers in Milwaukee to Ford autoworkers in Michigan. Besides teaching in the College of Mass Communication at MTSU, he has also taught at Marquette University, the University of Wisconsin-Milwaukee, Mount Mary College, and the University of Michigan, where he won several awards for both his teaching and scholarship. He has also worked as a print reporter and a broadcast news writer.